# The Eurospy Guide

# SECRET AGENT FIREBALL

STARRING

RICHARD HARRISON · DOMINIQUE BOSCHERO
WANDISA GUIDA · DIRECTED BY MARTIN DONAN

AN AMERICAN INTERNATIONAL PICTURE
IN WIDESCOPE AND COLOR

# The Eurospy Guide

by
Matt Blake
and
David Deal

Luminary Press
Baltimore, Maryland

Cover Design/Layout Design: Susan Svehla



ISBN 1-887664-52-1
Library of Congress Catalog Card Number 2004109545
Manufactured in the United States of America
First Printing by Luminary Press an imprint of Midnight Marquee, Press, Inc.,
July 2004

This book is dedicated to the great
unsung Eurospy heroes, villains and ladies
who provided the hundreds of hours of amusement
that resulted in the book you now hold in your hands.

CRISTOPHER LOGAN
GERALDINE PEARSALL
LUCRETIA LOVE
YURI MC FEE · PAUL MUELLER
LUPE SAGARRA
DA ISTANBUL
ORDINE DI UCCIDERE
THE DEVIL'S EXECUTOR
SIGMA
SELECTA FILM
REGIA ALEX BUTLER
EASTMANCOLOR
SCHERMO PANORAMICO

# CONTENTS

# INTRODUCTION

### I Spy

For a brief period in the mid-1960s, the whole world went spy crazy. From Sri Lanka to Poland, from the US to India, cinemas were filled with the exploits of suave secret agents, glamorous femmes fatales and increasingly demented villains. The symbols and images of the genre permeated advertisements, pulp novels and television series as well. No suburban dinner party was complete without a discussion of the latest escapades of a Bond, a Bulldog Drummond or a Harry Palmer.

While the intention of this book is to examine the more obscure cinematic manifestations of sixties spy mania, it does no harm to bear this larger context in mind. Though they may be almost entirely forgotten today, these films were literally *everywhere* at the time. The closest contemporary comparison would be the sudden outbreak of crime and gangster movies following Quentin Tarantino's *Reservoir Dogs*, a work that inspired a huge round of impersonations, rip-offs and blatant copies. Beyond this, however, *Dogs* also ushered in not only an immediately recognizable style (we all started feeling cool when wearing a dark suit and shades), but also a shift in the language of filmmaking itself. Fragmented timelines and snappy, pop culture-littered dialogue may have been in existence in films before Tarantino's, but they sure weren't as popular or pervasive.

In the same way, spy films reached beyond their exploitation origins into the full view of mainstream cultural interest. It became commonplace to incorporate aspects of the genre into other works. Art and comedy films were among the most direct pilferers of spy conventions (as witnessed by Jean Luc Godard's *Alphaville* and Ted Flicker's *The President's Analyst*, respectively). Certain trademarks that became identified with the genre—gadgets, cocktail-sipping in exclusive bars, exotic location-hopping—filtered through into all types of film, from serious dramas to spaghetti westerns.

At the time, these films were hugely successful. Many of the films discussed in this work were international co-productions, financed by a range of European (and sometimes non-European) countries. The budgets may not have been huge, but even the most obscure and inexpensive of films found viewers somewhere. It's hard to believe today, but it was possible for a comparatively tiny Italian film to be shown in London, Paris, Madrid and Munich, not to mention Hong Kong, San Paolo and New York. At the time, distribution networks were less established. There was more of a need for "low grade" filler material and the big studios simply weren't creating it. This meant that any enterprising producer with a few thousand dollars in his pocket could be onto a winner.

### Beyond Bond

Of course, one figure looms large above the entire genre, that of James Bond. It is not our intention to examine the Bond films here—they have been covered at great length and in extensive detail elsewhere—but it would be negligent not to make some mention of their significance to the genre. Quite simply, without Bond the spy genre would not have existed as we know it. The Bond films formed the template from which other spy films could model their work. Their look and attitude infused nearly all of the titles examined within these pages, and many more besides.

The film industry has always thrived on making "carbon copies" and this was particularly true in Italy and Spain. Seeing a success at the box office, the common practice has traditionally been to make films that are so similar as to be virtually prosecutable. This had happened in the early sixties, first with sword and sandal movies inspired by Pietro Francisci's *Hercules* and then horror films drawn from Terence Fisher's *The Curse of Frankenstein* or Mario Bava's *Black Sunday*. It happened with westerns after Sergio Leone's *A Fistful of Dollars* and sex films after Just Jaeckin's *Emmanuelle*.

Interestingly, the film that triggered this specific avalanche of facsimiles was neither of the first two entries in the Bond series, *Dr. No* and *From Russia with Love*. Despite their eminence, it was *Goldfinger* that seemed to strike a chord with filmmakers across Europe. From this film they drew their markers, pitting their debonair heroes against demented criminal masterminds, complete with unlikely schemes for world domination and outrageously equipped henchmen. The plots vary in the detail, but at the bottom line they all follow the same narrative route.

So why are these films of any worth? If they are simply Bond simulacra, why even bother watching them? Well, the answer to this is that the devil (and pleasure) does lie in the details. Let's be frank: We're not talking about great art here. At best, these films are fast-moving entertainment, perhaps with some idiosyncrasies that give them a degree of distinction. At worst, they're simply terrible, completely lacking any originality and ideas whatsoever. However, the sheer volume of genre film production, not to mention their pervasiveness at the time, makes them more than worthy of consideration.

### The Historical Genre

It's naïve to consider the popularity of the Bond series as the only reason for the bumper harvest of spy productions that followed. Bond was only a step in the evolution of the espionage film, a genre that had been in existence since the early 1900s. As with all evolutionary steps, they are inspired not so much by a one-off incident of chance as by an assortment of circumstances.

Spy films "proper" had initially kicked off during the First World War, with productions like *Our Secret Wires* (14) and *As In A Looking Glass* (15). These films generally featured heroic American characters foiling German invasion plans and had an inevitable propagandizing element. The same basic plot continued even after the cessation of the war with the likes of *The Love Light* (21), in which Mary Pickford marries a German spy, and *Dishonored* (31), with Marlene Dietrich as a vampish double agent in Vienna. Despite a few more idiosyncratic productions (Hitchcock's *The Thirty-Nine Steps* (35), with Robert Donat foiling a gang intent upon smuggling government secrets), things remained pretty much the same into the forties and the Second World War.

It wasn't until the fifties, and a different type of hostility—the cold war—that the genre began to develop into the form that would hold sway during the period under consideration here. While a number of productions from this time (*I Was A Communist For the FBI* [51]) stuck firmly to the McCarthyist "nasty Communist" paradigm, certain other films were also beginning to show the way. *My Favorite Spy* (51), for instance, has Bob Hope getting mixed up in international espionage after being mistaken for a notorious secret agent (a plot device recycled in *Slalom* (65), *Our Man in Marrakesh* (66) and others).

The secret agent film had always been a staple of British cinema, but during this time the first European co-productions began to creep out of the woodwork. Jean Sacha's *Dangerous Agent* (52) was a very early Eddie Constantine vehicle, not dissimilar to the numerous films he'd star in during the early sixties. Jean Stelli's

*Operation Abduction* (57) features a gang kidnapping the inventor of a new and powerful type of fuel. Even agent Hubert Bonisseur, aka OSS 117—later to become one of the most prolific characters of the spy boom—appeared as early as 1956 in *OSS 117 n'est pas mort*.

So as the sixties approached, the spy film was already well established, and even prior to the advent of *Dr. No* the foundations of the genre—in its most familiar mold—were dropping into place. In France, the Eddie Constantine films, in which he regularly played a tough secret agent battling assorted bad guys with fists and guile, were appearing at an alarming pace. In Germany, the "krimi" genre, films based on the detective novels of Edgar Wallace and his son Bryan, was proving extraordinarily popular. While not strictly containing an espionage element, they explored a similar domain and, more important, mutated into another series of films inspired by a production that was to prove a huge influence: Fritz Lang's *The Thousand Eyes of Dr. Mabuse* (60).

*Mabuse* was the film that was to give the genre a number of its key building blocks, elements that would be picked up and extended by the Bond films. Here you have a villain forged in the world of the 1930s serials, a proto-Blofeld with a coterie of accomplices and an intimate knowledge of even the most secret of intelligence information. The film's title contains the villain's name rather than that of the hero's, emphasizing the priority given to the character of the agent's antagonist. The menace had shifted from foreign powers to rootless individuals, eccentric (if not downright demented) characters whose lack of scruples matched only their desire for power and riches. *Mabuse* and his progeny acted as a personification of the rogue states that were to become increasingly worrisome, and interestingly this seems to anticipate fears that were to develop after the heyday of the genre. One of the key themes running through these films is that the East and the West, despite their ideological differences, are at least playing by the same rulebook, and therefore not the most elusive of enemies. The real concern is the people and organizations that have nothing but contempt for the way that things *should* be done.

Here too, you also find the increasing fascination with technology. The post-war years saw a huge number of technical breakthroughs and, significantly, their availability to the general population. The television in the corner was a gadget, a little slice of wonder that could sit in your own living room. *Mabuse* took this further by having an entire hotel riddled with surveillance devices, and the use of such equipment is featured in virtually every subsequent genre film. Rather than being simply a matter of industry, technology was accumulating a veneer of glamour; nothing could be more exciting than being in the playpen of a laboratory full of gadgets. And these were no longer in the domain of science fiction, but of scientific potentiality. One amusement to be found in watching a sixties spy film today is in spotting the "futuristic" gadgets that *have* come to pass into everyday acceptance.

What the Bond films did bequeath to their followers were the character of the hero and the style of the film itself. While it's possible to trace the origins of the spy genre back to the 1910s, the actual spy—sixties vintage—is traceable to just one source, secret agent 007. Before this, the protagonists had tended to be either earnest idealists or dour descendents of noir detectives. After *Goldfinger*, they developed into a new breed: irresistible, flippant, sadistic lady-killers, always ready with a sarcastic quip or smarmy aside. These characters were indomitable, indestructible and cut from a far superior cloth to their oft-fallible predecessors. These were the true Neitzschean *ubermensch*: always on top however dire the circumstances; effortlessly able to blend into any situation; never subject to everyday human frailties such as fear or impatience. All of which makes these spies totally unrealistic, of course, but that's not the point. With these films the spies had—much like their megalomaniac antagonists—metamorphosed into comic strip characters.

And just like comic strip characters, they had become something for every red-blooded schoolboy to aspire to. These secret agents were not just brave, intelligent and strong; much more than this, they were actually *cool*. These guys wore the best clothes, drank in the best bars and were effortlessly able to charm the best-looking girls into their embrace. They traveled around the world—and this was at a time when the package holiday was only in its infancy—journeying to far-flung places, sampling (and, if need be, conquering) exotic cultures. In the real world the old empires may have been crumbling, but in the universe of the spy genre the European alpha male was still king.

Furthering this modish appeal, the style of the films became more contemporary, the colors gaudier, the soundtracks full of groovy beats and the moral outlook libertarian. The cinematography appropriated an air of gonzo experimentalism, cranking up the skewed camera angles and throwing in distorting filters whenever possible. The direction became more fast-paced and threw in a steady succession of set pieces. For all of their failings, you are left with the feeling that these genre films were often a product of youthfulness: Filmmakers, often holding a healthy disregard for their scripts, were willing to play with the process of filmmaking itself. Despite their apparent cynicism, the best genre films exhibit a singular joyous exuberance. The ultimate challenge was not to create a masterpiece, but to have as much fun as possible.

**The Sixties Spy Film**

As with many types of genre cinema, the sixties spy film can be broken down into several sub-strata, each of which became dominant as the decade progressed. As previously mentioned, the earliest examples tended to originate from France, and often featured Eddie Constantine. Constantine was an American actor who became a household name in French noirs throughout the fifties, most famously as FBI agent Lemmy Caution. His early sixties outings—appearing as characters such as Jeff Gordon, Nick Carter and simply Eddie—follow pretty much the same course: unspectacular, low-key affairs that trade upon the charisma of their star. These continued throughout the first half of the decade without changing much, despite the addition of a few Bondian plot elements and an infusion of Italian money.

French spy films, however, were flourishing quite apart from the ruffled Constantine. Jacques Nahum's *The Dance of Death* (60) featured Felix Marten as Simon Templar, aka The Saint, a character later reanimated as a television equivalent to Bond (and played by future 007 Roger Moore). Robert Vernay's *The Versailles Affair* (60) has Jean Thielmont as an agent attempting to retrieve some vital documents before an important conference. Georges Lautner's hugely entertaining "Monocle" films (*The Black Monocle* (61), *Eye of the Monocle* (62) and *The Monocle* [64]) featured Paul Meurisse as a foppish spy investigating a number of comically criminal incidents. Although the stories weren't going to change a great deal as the decade progressed, these all look very much like "early period" spy films—intimate and professional—and often have a slight feel of the Sherlock Holmes about them.

Meanwhile, the British were making a number of cheap fillers that trod the thin dividing line between spy and crime genres. Typical examples would include John Paddy Carstairs' *The Devil's Agent* (61), in which Peter Van Eyck plays a lovelorn double agent, and Lawrence Huntington's *Fur Collar* (62), with John Bentley as a reporter smashing an espionage ring. Such films tended to be under 80 minutes in length, had a serious tone and were shot in black and white. Designed as support features, these somewhat unappealing productions have long been consigned to the graveyard of early morning showings on terrestrial UK television.

At around the same time as *Dr. No* hit the screens, the Germans entered the field, often in co-production with Italian or French companies. These films (*Hong Kong Hot Harbor* (62), *Operation Hong Kong* (64), etc.) are immediately identifiable. Filmed in East Asia, they mix secret agent shenanigans with more mundane crime elements and star any combination of Brad Harris, Horst Frank, Dominique Boschero and Klaus Kinski.

After 1964, however, the spy film found its form. Whether in France, Spain, Italy or West Germany, filmmakers tended to follow the Bond template as laid down in *Goldfinger*. This was when the series films came into their own. Kommissar X, OSS 117, Agent 077 and many others all wowed the box office. Actors like Roger Hanin, Ken Clark, Tony Kendall and Giorgio Ardisson became stars, albeit for a fleeting moment. This was the period during which a number of the most identifiable "sixties spy films" were made and is, as such, the time from which many of the films examined within this book come.

During the same time the spy movie was flourishing, another type of film was coming into its own, the spaghetti western. Although seemingly poles apart, it's interesting to briefly look at the links between the two genres. The spaghetti western protagonist, as most famously essayed by Clint Eastwood in the films of Sergio Leone, can be seen as a spy in sagebrush clothing. He too is a comic strip hero who survives inhospitable circumstances through wit and skill, albeit clad in stubble and poncho rather than tuxedo and Brylcreem. The two genres both have their trademark elements (the bar-room brawl as opposed to the nightclub sequence, the gunfight as opposed to the cable car fight). They both also have a distinct style (guitar-based western music versus easy-listening spy tunes, close-up shots of eyes versus discordant "hallucination" sequences), and both are obsessed with gadgetry (guns are hidden in banjos, sowing machines and even bread). The spaghetti westerns were as much the children of James Bond as the spy films, albeit blessed with a slightly different visage.

In the second half of the sixties, however, the spy film began to fragment. While still going strong in the UK, where a number of relatively big budget, big name productions were still being made (Alvin Rakoff's *Crossplot* (69), starring Roger Moore), in the rest of Europe the genre was in terminal decline from 1966 onward. In Italy, the spy film mutated into the bizarre superhero genre. Based on Italian comic books (or *fumetti*), these films featured masked musclemen fighting evil Bond-style villains. Comparable to the Mexican Santo films, or even television's idiosyncratic Batman series, these incorporated much of the spy film formula, but without the spy himself (although in some cases the outrageously attired hero was inducted into the Secret Services). Examples included Nick Nostro's *Superargo vs. Diabolicus* (66), Umberto Lenzi's *Kriminal* (66) and Gianfranco Parolini's jaw-dropping *Three Fantastic Supermen* (67).

Also enjoying a brief period of popularity was the caper movie. These drew their inspiration from Jules Dassin's *Rififi* (55), fleshing out the central heist narrative with psychedelic spy stylings. Typical examples would include Guido Malatesta's *Mission Phantom* (67), with Fernando Sancho leading a group of thieves intent upon breaking into the Moscow state bank, and Jose Antonio De La Loma's *The Magnificent Tony Carrara* (68), with adventurer Thomas Hunter being duped into stealing the plans for a nuclear weapon. Complicating matters further, it wasn't an uncommon plot device for the leader of the gang to be revealed as a secret agent, working to entrap his ostensible associates (Umberto Lenzi's *Last Man to Kill* (66), Piero Pierotti's *Assalto al tesoro di stato* [67]).

By the 1970s, the glory days of the genre were over. A new feeling was in the air; the "anything goes" philosophy of the sixties was replaced by a grittier sentiment. The exotic, fantastical spy film seemed out of place in these increasingly skeptical times, and audiences turned toward urban crime thrillers and violent horror movies. The Bond series did limp on, and new espionage movies were produced, but they didn't have the same *feel*. The spy film, as defined within these pages, was something that existed solely in, and of, the sixties.

### The Spy Film Today

So then, why is the Eurospy genre worthy of consideration today? Well, partly because we live in times of growing disquiet. The genre flourished after the Cuban Missile Crisis and the Kennedy assassination, when the world situation seemed to be increasingly perilous. Today, we are faced with the unsettling prospect of widespread terrorism, and the global terrorist networks are probably closer to the villainous organizations featured in spy films than the enemies ever were.

Beyond this, there's the profound feeling that individuals and organizations over which we have little or no authority are dictating global events. An American president is elected under dubious circumstances, Britain goes to war despite it being unpopular among the electorate, and international companies seem to act independent of all rules in their chase for shareholder satisfaction. The individual is becoming secondary to the machinations of the powerful; it's a game, driven by rules that are intangible to the people. The criminal megalomaniac of the spy film can easily be seen as the metaphor for a puppet president, an international terrorist leader, or even the director of a multinational corporation. The underground or island headquarters from which they plan their schemes becomes the military base, secret hideout or impenetrable boardroom.

Combined with this, we have recently experienced a period of extremely visible technological progress. Whereas the fifties and sixties had ushered in the household availability of the television and assorted labor-saving devices, the late nineties saw the rapid uptake of the Internet and wireless technologies. This is the next stage in communications and is of immediate consequence to almost everyone. Science is always progressing, but only when that progress results in things that have an impact on everyday life do people notice it. And of course, it brings its problems: Information overload is now widespread; we're drowning in facts, figures, potentialities and possibilities. How do we filter that which is relevant? How do we make sense of it all?

What better time to be a super-slick secret agent? Someone who *understands* the games that nations are playing, someone who can process incoming information and control—rather than be controlled by—situations. Someone who is backed up by the might of military hardware and brainpower. Someone who can charm the chicks and beat up the bad guys. This is the import of the secret agent: In a world of profound flux, we need the anchor of a hero who is able to do something about the things that we, frankly, have no power over.

That, of course, and the fact that the films are bloody good fun.

### Criteria for Inclusion

When compiling this survey of the sixties Eurospy genre, two things quickly became clear. First, just how hard it is to track down copies of the films we wanted to talk about. While some of them are relatively easy to come across (*Deadlier Than the Male* and *Modesty Blaise* have both recently appeared on DVD), others are almost willfully obscure. In many cases, the only copies available have no English track or are in severely abridged versions. Even taking these (far from ideal) sources into account, some "key" films (Paolo Bianchini's *Our Men in Baghdad*, Michael Pflegher's *Serenade For Two Spies*) have remained stubbornly unavailable. With time, many of these will appear (hopefully), but at present this remains a far from complete listing since we only included titles available as of this writing. Instead, please treat it as an introduction, a taster, but still the most complete examination of such films to have appeared in print.

The second problem is that, unlike the spaghetti western, the spy film is not a self-contained genre. Caper, superhero and art—not to mention war and crime—films, all include elements more readily identified as belonging to the secret agent movie. It was our original intention to cover all productions "influenced" by the spy film made between 1960 and 1969, but it soon became clear that this was not feasible—it would involve examining up to a third of all films made during that decade. For this reason, we have decided to stick strictly to productions that specifically involve an element of espionage. Sometimes the borders are blurred—does insurance investigator Bulldog Drummond count as a spy? To us, he does, because the character is so clearly born of the Bond prototype. We have also included some fringe productions that may help to give an indication as to how the "spy film" was filtering through into other genres.

As for the temporal and geographical boundaries, we have stuck rigidly to the 1960-1969 period. There were European spy films made before and after this time, but they generally don't have the distinctive *feel* of the productions considered here. The 1972 spy film is a very different animal from its 1965 equivalent, and doesn't fall within the scope of this book.

Spy films were made around the world, and for the purposes of this work we have restrained ourselves to the most commonly accepted interpretation of "Euro productions," namely those financed or shot in the UK, France, Italy, West Germany and Spain (or a combination of any of these). We do touch on films from elsewhere: Greece (*Assignment Skybolt*) and Switzerland (*Bonditis*), for instance. However, there are many films—most particularly from Turkey and Eastern Europe—that could (and possibly should) have come into consideration here. To justify their exclusion, we have to plead a mixture of ignorance (in that we simply don't feel qualified to write about them) and obscurity (in that they're even more difficult to see than the already remote films under discussion). Again, our aim here is not for absolute comprehensiveness, but to act as a detailed initial examination of the genre.

So settle back, put on some conducive tunes, fix yourself a fine martini—shaken not stirred, of course—and enjoy this glimpse into the fabulous world of 1960s spydom.

**A Note on Video Quality**

We do not make a point to detail the image quality of the videos under review. Nearly all the films reviewed are only available on the "gray market," not having an official video release in English-speaking countries. Therefore, the visual quality of the presentations varies between bad and worse but it is currently the only way to see many of these films. We believe that all of these films, regardless of their artistic merit, deserve respect and are certainly worthy of high quality re-releases.

**Review Structure**

Film title of the review copy
Literal English translation of foreign title (if applicable)
Alternate release titles
Review body (and writer initials)
Technical credits
Country and year of release
Cast listing

**Country Abbreviations**

Belgium (Be); Czechoslovakia (Cz); France (Fr); Greece (Gr); International (Int); Italy (It); Spain (Sp); United Kingdom (UK); United States (US); Venezuela (Vz); West Germany (WG)

# ACKNOWLEDGMENTS

Many thanks to all those who have helped by providing materials, facts or just plain good conversation during the gestation and prolonged birth of this book. Special kudos to Robert Monell, Larry Anderson, Kevin Grant, Robert Mark, Rodd Dana, JC Eagle, Bertrand Von Wonterghem and most particularly Julian Grainger. Also, everybody on the Eurospy Guide Web Board and Spaghetti Western Web Board, both of which have proved invaluable sources of information. Finally, thumbs up to Sarah, who has managed to tolerate the continual tapping on my laptop over the past few years. If I've forgotten anyone; you know who you are.—Matt Blake

First, I would like to thank my good friend Chris Morrison for his undying enthusiasm and assistance throughout this project. Many thanks also to Bruno de Cock and all the eBay sellers for the wonderful Eurospy posters they sell, Craig Ledbetter at European Trash Cinema for having so many Eurospy movies available and my mailman Dave for unfailingly delivering hundreds of very important packages. Thanks as well to Julie Miller for her efforts in the final days of editing. My deepest gratitude, however, goes to the lovely Annett for her endless patience and understanding.—David Deal

# The Films A-Z

002 AGENTI SEGRETISSIMI
"the 002 secret agents"
aka Wir, die Trottel vom Geheimdienst (WG)

Before making the series of films that were to confer honorary auteur status upon him, Lucio Fulci had a rather successful career as a craftsman director, most particularly in the comedy genre. Working with stars such as Lando Buzzanca, Mario Carotenuto and, as here, Franco and Ciccio, most of these films are now entirely forgotten or ignored, judged as early jobs for hire, allowing the budding genius to learn his trade and master his obsessions. This is rather a simplistic viewpoint, forged—it has to be suspected—from the fact that these films are much more difficult to track down nowadays. In domestic terms, Fulci's comedies were probably his most successful films of all. *002 agenti segretissimi*, for instance, made twice as much money within Italy as *Zombie*, quite an astonishing fact once inflation is also taken into account.

**Italian poster for *002 agenti segetissimi***

This starts as it means to go on, with a succession of curvaceous young ladies squeezing themselves into skimpy bikinis and having a quick jive beside the beach. All of which, of course, has absolutely nothing to do with the rest of the film. The story finally commences with Franco and Ciccio breaking into a supposedly deserted villa, in hope of thieving any valuables that the careless owners have left unprotected. Unfortunately, it appears as though their information has been faulty. Rather than being empty, the villa is home to a whole swarm of spies. These guys follow the orders of a goofy robot with a fondness for staring at women's bottoms, which comes up with a ludicrous scheme to use the intruders as a tool in the game of espionage. A "false formula" is hidden inside one of Franco's fillings, thereby making him a target for assorted enemy agents (all of whom will therefore waste their time pointlessly pursuing him).

Franco and Ciccio, however, are completely unaware of all this, and simply think that they've been given a free luxury holiday. After mucking around with the high-tech controls for their hotel room, they start causing chaos on the beach (groping unfortunate women, suffering severe sunburn, etc.). At this point you start to realize something. Here you have a couple of pasty, oddly shaped people in bad swimsuits turning crimson on a beach while surrounded by picturesque, bronzed Mediterranean types. Although they may not realize it—gadzooks!—Franco and Ciccio must be British.

Anyway, things become even more confused when the agents discover that Franco has accidentally been implanted with the real formula. They try to make contact with him through the novel means of writing messages on assorted pieces of lingerie, but our heroes seem rather distracted by the ladies contained within said lingerie. Meanwhile, a whole score of Russian, Chinese and American secret agents are closing in on them.

If the mere prospect of a Franco and Ciccio film doesn't break you out into a cold sweat, *segretissimi* is a neatly made, hugely enjoyable film. It's not, perhaps, as well constructed as some of their other vehicles (*Due mafioso contro Goldginger*, for instance), but it certainly speeds along at a rate of knots and has a few good gags. There's plenty of mileage made of genre clichés, most particularly the multitude of hopeless spies managing to kill each other with idiotic gadgetry. Another good running joke has jealous husband Aroldo Tieri suspecting his wife (Ingrid Schoeller) of adultery, these suspicions multiplied by having the dopey duo appear in incriminating places at the most inconvenient moments.

As with the majority of their films, Ciccio plays the straightman to Franco, who suffers one form of humiliation after another. It seems to be something of a theme that he should experience some form of medical indignity, and here—rather than being injected in the butt or having a sex change—he undergoes a refreshing dose of electric shock treatment. He also gets tortured by having a goat lick his feet (it faints), and there's a protracted sequence wherein he tries unsuccessfully to pull out his painful (and obstinate) tooth by tying it to assorted objects (such as a big rock chucked off a cliff, and a boat). Nothing new, but most of the slapstick translates much better than could be expected. Okay, so it's hardly Oscar Wilde, but if Adam Sandler can become a box office draw I don't think the English-speaking world has any right whatsoever to be condescending toward *002 agenti segretissimi*.—MB

CREDITS: Production: Mega Film; Director: Lucio Fulci; Story: Vittorio Metz; Screenplay: Vittorio Metz, Lucio Fulci, Amedeo Sollazzo; Cinematography: Adalberto Albertini {Eastmancolor}; Music: Piero Umiliani; Editor: Ornella Micheli; Original running length: 90 mins; Filming location: Cinecitta Studios, Rome; Country: Italy; Year: 1964

CAST: Franco Franchi (*Franco*), Ciccio Ingrassia (*Ciccio*), Ingrid Schoeller (*the wife*), Carla Calo (*the Russian agent*), Aroldo Tieri (*the husband*), Annie Gorassini (*the maid*), Nino Terzo (*a Russian agent*), Poldo Bendandi (*a Russian agent*), Luca Sportelli, Enzo Andronico, Nando Angelini, Mary Arden, Puccio Ceccarelli (*a Chinese torturer*), Anna Maria Checchi, Ralf Colangelo, Mario Del Vago, Rita Forzano, Francesco Torrisi, Anita Todesco, Alessandro Tedeschi, Seyna Seyn (*a Chinese agent*), Maria Luisa Rispoli, Piero Morgia (*an American agent*)

### 002 OPERAZIONE LUNA
"002 operation moon"
aka Dos cosmonautas a la fuerza (Sp)

This is really a fringe spy film at best, and is included here only because of my well-documented obsession with Franco and Ciccio movies. Well, okay—it is actually included because a) it was the immediate sequel to the 1964 genre entry *002 agenti segretissimi* and b) it does feature secret agents, albeit in the most peripheral of senses.

A Russian spacecraft piloted by Frankovic and Cicciorna (Franco and Ciccio in deadpan mode) loses all contact with base. The Soviet authorities, anxious to avoid the embarrassment of having to admit that it may have disintegrated, come up with the cunning—not to say idiotic—ruse of launching an identical spaceship manned by look-alikes of the astronauts.

Unfortunately, the only suitable candidates they can track down who fit the bill are Franco and Ciccio (Franco and Ciccio in mugging mode), a pair of barely sentient Italian petty thieves. Handily enough, the Russian Secret Service, in the form of a gaggle of body-stockinged babes, are able to liberate them from prison. Despite their pleasure at their proximity to so many curvaceous lovelies, they are distinctly less impressed when they learn of the plan to blast them into space (maybe a certain degree of wishful thinking on the part of the scriptwriters was at play here). After much running around attempting to escape, they are recaptured, drugged and sent into orbit around the moon.

Somehow or other they make it back to earth, but are in for a surprise. The two cosmonauts they have replaced were both married to attractive young wives, and they are forced (without too much resistance) to continue with the identities they have assumed. However, Frankovic and Cicciorna unexpectedly arrive back as well—and they're none too happy with what they find.

An extremely silly film, *Luna* isn't quite as enjoyable as *Due mafioso contro Goldginger*—probably the best of the Franco and Ciccio spy spoofs. It follows pretty much the same course (they wear wigs, pratfall, chase

**talian poster for *002 operazione Luna***

each other around, are repeatedly injected in the butt with large needles, etc.), but has rather lower production values (and less amusing guest stars). It's still harmless fun (certainly no worse than a Norman Wisdom film)—and again goes to show that these films have an undeservedly bad reputation on the whole.

No Franco and Ciccio would be complete without a couple of totally bizarre moments that are less funny (ha-ha) than funny (huh?). We are treated to the spectacle of Franco turning into a woman, which is actually extremely disturbing, and a really odd sequence in which the demented duo take a spacewalk, only to be attacked by a human skull—which just happens to be floating around! While some may argue that this is early evidence of director Fulci's love of the macabre, I'll stick with the view that it's more the result of being willing to try anything for a gag (in the wholly nonregurgitational sense).—MB

CREDITS: Production: Ima Film, Agata Film; Director: Lucio Fulci; Story: Vittorio Metz; Screenplay: Amedeo Sollazzo, Jose Luis Dibildos (Spanish version); Cinematography: Tino Santoni {B&W}; Music: Carlo Gori; Editor: Pedro Del Rey; Original running length: 90 mins; Filming location: Cinecitta Studios, Rome; Country Italy/Spain; Year: 1965

CAST: Franco Franchi (*Franco/Frankovic*), Ciccio Ingrassia (*Ciccio/Cicciorna*), Monica Randall (*Ana, Cicciorna's wife*), Maria Silva (*Nadia, Frankovic's wife*), Linda Sini (*the head of the Russian training center*), Emilio Rodriguez (*Skordiakoff, a Russian Colonel*), Chiro Bermejo, Helene Sedlak [Helene Chanel], Ignazio Leone (*a Russian heavy*), Franco Morici, Enzo Andronico, Piero Morgia, Pasquale Zagaria [aka Lino Banfi] Uncredited: Francesca Romana Coluzzi

13 DAYS TO DIE
aka Agente S3S Operazione Uranio (It);
Espionage a Bangkok pour U-92 (Fr);
Der Fluch des schwarzen Rubin (WG)

This qualifies as a spy flick by the thinnest of margins. It was marketed to some countries as an Agent S3S espionage thriller, a clever attempt—by reversing the letters and numbers—to pass as one of the short series of Agent 3S3 films that starred George Ardisson. However, it is really based on the adventures of German pulp hero Rolf Torring, played here by Thomas Alder (who, by the way, committed suicide three years after this film's release).

Tracy (Torring's name is changed to Ralph Tracy—even in the groovy Gert Wilden title song—for the English language print) is called to Bangkok when a famous necklace belonging to a prince is stolen from a local museum. It turns out that the necklace holds the key to a fortune in uranium; the stones of the necklace spell out a code that when translated describe a map to the uranium field. The story takes many turns and there is more than one villain but the one with the screen time is Horst Frank, playing his usual delicious, nasty self.

Tracy is accompanied by two buddies, Warren (Peter Carsten) and Pongo (Serge Nubret). Carsten will be recognizable to fans of genre cinema and even had roles in the occasional high-profile picture like *The Quiller Memorandum*. Nubret was a famous body builder who has plenty of chances to show off his physique in the jungles of Thailand. So what we have here is a men's adventure film straight out of the magazines, featuring three jolly he-men who go around beating up the natives, trying hard to convince us they're not gay. I'm not buying it.

This embarrassingly bad C-grade film, directed and written by Manfred R. Kohler, features a pet monkey, lots of native celebration rituals, pedestrian dialogue, weak torture, lame fights, cheesy gadgets, misogyny, and racism.

**German poster for the Rolf Torring adventure, *13 Days to Die***

Stating the obvious seems to be a regular pastime with these guys ("Let me see if I've got this right…") and poor Horst is not only stuck with unusually incompetent henchmen but he has to say things like "A geologist shouldn't leave any stone unturned." There's even one character that can identify a poison by glancing at it, a talent that rivals that of Sherlock Holmes.

The best part of the movie is the soundtrack by Gert Wilden. It's a fine example of big band jazz that far outclasses the action on the screen. Luckily, slices of it are available on CD so you don't have to sit through this just to hear it.—DD

CREDITS: Production: Metheus Film, Rapid Film, Societe Nouvelle De Cinematographie, Thai Tri Mitr Films; Director: Manfred A Kohler (Alberto Cardone credited on Italian version); Story and Screenplay: Manfred A Kohler; Cinematography: Klaus Von Rautenfeld; Music: Gert Wilden; Original running length: 101 mins; Filming location: Thailand; Country: Germany/Italy/France/Thailand; Year: 1965

CAST: Horst Frank (*Perkins*), Thomas Alder (*Torring/Tracy*), Serge Nubret (*Pongo*), Peter Carsten (*Warren*), Yu Sam (*Prinz Gulab*), Chitra Ratana (*Chitra*), Jacques Bezard (*Francis*), Carlo Tamberlani (*Barrington*), Ma Suphin (*Dienerin*)

## 3-2-1 COUNTDOWN FOR MANHATTAN
aka Um Null Uhr schnappt die Falle zu (WG)

*321CFM*, the third Jerry Cotton film, boasts the coolest title sequence of the series. The montage of unrelated images looks like the opening of an early television spy show. This fun, surreal film is one of the series' best, thanks in no small part to the presence of Horst Frank. Frank seemed to be everywhere in international cinema in the sixties and seventies and here he gives his trademark eccentric performance as gang boss Larry Link. But more on him later.

When a stolen truck is discovered to be loaded with nitroglycerin, the thieves become the target of the FBI and the underworld. Jerry (George Nader) battles time and the twisted ambitions of Larry Link for control of the increasingly volatile substance.

There are two great set pieces in *321CFM*. The first occurs early in the film when Jerry and his partner Phil (Heinz Weiss) go to the high-rise apartment of the girlfriend of one of the truck thieves and find her trapped by Link's henchmen. Jerry uses a window washer's platform to lower himself to her window from the roof of the building in order to catch the thugs off guard. In the process of the rescue Jerry is knocked off the platform but manages to grab a rope, only to be left hanging 17 stories up! Meanwhile, Phil bursts in through the door to be met with a severe beating by the waiting gang. Jerry climbs back up the rope and into the apartment but the bad guys beat a hasty retreat. Be sure to catch Jerry's Clint Eastwood squint as he watches his prey escape. Everything comes together in this sequence: Rear projection and indoor sets are seamlessly matched with creative camera work, tight editing of the action maintains suspense and the stunt work is clever. This is quintessential Jerry Cotton.

The other notable sequence is an homage to film noir that is unique in the series' run. Larry Link and his men have captured Jerry and Lou, one of the truck thieves, and taken them to a subway station construction site where the nitro has been hidden. Here we step into a dark world of brutality. An atmosphere of

**German poster captures the film noir mood of the third Jerry Cotton adventure, *3-2-1 Countdown to Manhattan***

hopelessness is created by dramatic lighting and unusual camera angles. Jerry takes a beating in the Venetian shadows and Lou is tortured to death as Link stands calmly by. Even sound design comes into play as the constant subway noise adds another level of tension. Later when Jerry stumbles out of the site and into the glare of headlights, he holds his hand to his face to hide his weary eyes. The scene ends without a word, the noir tradition held high.

There's a timer installed in the FBI office that ticks off the hours before the nitro becomes completely unstable and blows a sizable chunk of Manhattan to kingdom come. Jerry's boss, Mr. High (Richard Munch), is taunted by this "digilog" clock; its rolling numbers are his personal torment. He is driven to distraction by the thing, chain smoking throughout the movie and looking more and more disheveled as the time passes. It becomes comical as he unravels in the face of disaster.

Horst Frank vests the dapper villain Larry Link with a sleazy charisma much needed to carry the slight story along. Link likes to sit in his easy chair in the middle of a wading pool in his apartment. He has his phone and liquor handy and even plays with a remote control boat. His henchmen are forced to hang around shoeless, with their pant legs rolled up so they can cater to his needs! Link has ambitions of trading the nitro to the FBI for a million dollars and calmly accepts the unsightly necessities like torture and death that one must endure on one's path to power.

Dominique Wilms as the ice queen Maureen, a partner in the original robbery, also gives a standout performance. She's tough and conniving, always sure of herself whether dealing with the FBI or the unstable Link. She has no attachments and uses her wits (and her body) to get what she wants.

You are guaranteed in a film like this to see a scene where the hero defuses an exploding device. Suspense can never be built in these situations because the hero will not be killed and the audience knows it. Yes, Jerry must stop a container of nitro from blowing up a bridge in this film. But the fun part is the visually awkward method used by the filmmakers. The odd angles of the bridge set blended with the rear projection of the Manhattan skyline create a surreal, if not entirely convincing, event.

The surreal becomes the absurd at the end of the film, however. The final scenes involving a train loaded with nitro border on the bizarre. There is very little attempt to place the action in reality, and odd scenes of slow motion rear projection, model trains used for no good reason and our hero climbing around train sets in the dark, pulling switches and levers, enforce a dreamlike quality on the viewer. It's one crazy ride and another reason why *321CFM* should not be missed.—DD

CREDITS: Production: Allianz Filmproduktion, Constantin Film Produktion GmbH, Prodex; Director: Harald Philipp; Story and Screenplay: Fred Denger, Kurt Nachmann; Cinematography: Helmuyt Meewes {B&W}; Music: Peter Thomas; Editor: Alfred Srp; Original running length: 89 mins; Filming location: New York; Country: West Germany; Year: 1966

CAST: George Nader (*Jerry Cotton*), Horst Frank (*Larry Link*), Heinz Weiss (*Phil Decker*), Dominique Wilms (*Maureen*), Allen Pinson (*Harry*), Alexander Allerson (*Husky*), Monika Grimm (*Ruth Warren*), Helga Schlack (*Helen Culver*), Ricky Cooper (*Pal*), Werner Abrolat (*Krot*), Nadie Ragoo, Gert Günther Hoffmann (*Lew Hatton*), Ingrid Capelle (*Alice*), Sigfrit Steiner (*Dr. Smeat*), Georg Lehn (*Bud Sculler*), Friedrich G. Beckhaus (*Fat Krusky*), Harald Dietl (*Lieutenant Howard*), Richard Münch (*Mr. High*)

### 7 CINESI D'ORO
"7 golden Chinese"

Filmed at approximately the same time as its partner piece, *7 Golden Women Against Two 07*, this was—for some reason—released a year later. It is technically a far superior film, yet it lacks the demented curiosity value of its bedfellow. It's still pretty screwy, for sure, but generally less "out there," and not too far removed from the greater mass of second string, zany spy and caper films. Not as trashy, maybe, but not as much down and dirty fun.

Barbikian (Vincenzo Cashino), a scientist, has managed to cultivate a terrifying virus. His ambition is to use it to blackmail the governments of the world to cease their continual, pointless warfare. Unfortunately, assorted foreign intelligence organizations have found out about his unwholesome creation, and they all want it for themselves. Their methods are devious indeed. They use their fists (with a complete lack of success) and their feminine charms (British spy Gloria Paul—who appears to be disguised as a Gypsy—strips down to a bikini and hides behind his chair).

Barbikian is a stronger man than they suppose, however, and manages to resist all of these approaches. He's helped to no end by the fact that all of these assorted secret agents seem far busier with fighting among themselves than chasing after him. In fact, everybody soon bands together to try to fend off the nasty Chinese contingent (several bald dudes and Seyna Seyn, hence the "seven golden Chinamen" title).

As far as I was able to make out, this wasn't a direct sequel to *7 Golden Women.* Although Vincenzo Cashino plays a character called Barbikian in both films, there does not appear to be any other connection between them (here he is a scientist as opposed to an art thief). That said, Cashino's performance doesn't exactly play up the differences. He wears similarly dapper threads and again smokes a pipe continually, Sherlock Holmes style (there's a good in-joke made of this when he is mugged and his briefcase spills open to reveal...a selection of pipes, in one of which the formulae is hidden). In fact, Cashino here resembles a less handsome, even hammier John Saxon.

As with its predecessor, the plot of *7 cinesi d'oro* is simplicity itself, and uses the assorted-people-chasing-after-treasure-map/secret-formula/neighbor's-dog device. There are an awful lot of (poorly choreographed) fistfights, endless scantily clad ladies and multiple double-crosses. There are other connections: Donkey riding features in both films (not exactly riveting, perhaps, but certainly unique), and there's a horror film pastiche when somebody dresses up as a mummy to frighten off some pursuers. At the climax, the vial containing the horrific bacteria is crushed, revealing that rather than causing everybody to die horribly it makes them want to party.

Possibly the best thing about the film is a great soundtrack from the excellent Gianni Ferrio, which must have had the audience shaking their booties in the cinema aisles. Realizing just how good it is, Cashino is kind enough to throw in several song and dance routines throughout the running time. These generally feature a backing band that is horribly out of time—even by the "dubtastic" standards of Eurotrash cinema—and plays entirely the wrong instruments for the song.

He was also fortunate enough to cast the English actress Gloria Paul (who was very nearly "Domino" in *Thunderball*, and also appeared in *The Three Fantastic Supermen*). She wears some truly horrible flamenco-style costumes (although not for long, they're normally shed within five minutes to reveal a much more appreciated bikini) and is actually rather good, displaying some impressive footwork in a couple of dance sequences.

All in all, then, it's not bad. Or rather, all in all it's not quite bad enough.—MB

CREDITS: Production: Accadia Film; Director: Vincent Cashino [Vincenzo Cascino] (not credited on Italian print); Story: V. Cashino [Vincenzo Cascino]; Screenplay: Giuseppe Pellegrini, Vincenzo Cascino; Cinematography: Antonio Piazza {Cinemascope - Eastmancolor}; Music: Gianni Ferrio; Original running length: 85 mins; Filming location: Cinecitta Studios, Rome; Country: Italy; Year: 1967

CAST: Gloria Paul (*a British agent*), Antonella Steni (*a French agent*), Seyna Seyn (*a Chinese agent*), Moha Tahi, Efhi Hati, Andrey Andersen, Gilbert Cina, John Loodmere (*a British agent*), Sergio Calais, Gordon Steven, Jim Scheller, Nestor Cavaricci, and with Yoko Tani (*a Chinese agent*) Not credited on Italian print: Vincenzo Cascino (*Barbikian*), Saro Patane, Salvatore Siciliano, Vincent Miguel Cascino, Jr.

### 7 GOLDEN WOMEN AGAINST TWO 07 (TREASURE HUNT)
### aka 7 donne d'oro contro 2-07 (It)

To the accompaniment of some seriously swinging incidental music, Barbikian (Vincent Cascino), a weird dude with a goatee and big trilby, runs through the back streets of Rome carrying a painting. Two thugs try to steal it from him—but they're stopped by Mark Day (Mickey Hargitay), who proceeds to beat the crap out of them in an exhibition of astoundingly poor choreography. Mark and Barbikian meet up with a blonde dame, Maria (Maria Vincent), who sings at them. They all appear to be art collectors, and the mysterious painting is allegedly a long lost work by Goya.

The next day, the self-same painting appears at an auction. How did it get there? Don't ask me. Is it the same painting? Don't ask me. I don't think the scriptwriters knew what was happening at this stage, so I sure as heck don't know why I should. Anyway, Barbikian isn't very happy about this, and several minutes of fistfighting ensue. After quizzing the auctioneer about the painting, they discover that hidden within the canvas is a secret formula (for God knows what).

Somebody mentions Africa, which happily introduces some stock footage of said continent (there seems to be no other reason for this). Seven ladies (and a couple of gents) from around the world suddenly get taxis (to Rome, apparently), and all of them buy copies of the Goya from the same auctioneer, which means that there are (at least) eight copies of the damn thing floating around. Barbikian, who is after the formula, manages steal every single one of them—leading to a large number of angry people, all determined to reclaim their appropriated possessions.

Everybody heads off to a mountain village, where the ladies remove their clothes and squirt paint at each other. Allegedly looking for the paintings (hold on, I thought Barbikian had them?) they visit a haunted castle, where they're attacked by "ghosts," which kidnap all of the girls. Who then reappear. And disrobe again. The treasure hunt continues in a similar fashion for another 40 minutes.

At certain points in the writing of this book I have seriously thought that I've been coming dangerously close to brain damage. And never more so than the hour and a half I spent watching this quite astonishingly demented piece of nonsense. It belongs alongside *Un Tango dalla Russia*, *Agente segreto 070 Thunderbay—missione Grasshopper* and (perhaps) the superior *Operation Atlantis*, as films that are so beyond the realm of normality that they form a kind of cinematic paradigm.

About as trashy as is possible to get in a single film, *7 Golden Women* has the lackadaisical atmosphere of a drug fugue. The pacing is frankly shot to hell, with the same things happening again and again and the narrative diverting into entirely extraneous avenues (normally involving a punch-up or clothes being shed) every 10 minutes. This isn't helped by the fact that for half the time people babble at each other incoherently (and often in four-second loops). God knows what the budget was for all of this, but it plays like a glorified home movie concocted by the type of person who should never, ever have been allowed near a camera. In other words, it's either some kind of intertextual masterpiece or simply out and out crap.

Nonetheless, for the first hour or so it's all hugely enjoyable. After that it does lose some of its novelty value, but you can rest assured that some example of robust silliness will crop up before too long. Just when I was beginning to drift off, it throws in an extraordinary dramatic twist, with one of the main characters revealing his true identity to be…notorious Nazi Martin Bormann! And then things carry on as normal.

To a certain extent, this *was* a glorified home movie. Director, writer and star Vincent Cascino was an Italo-Argentinian industrialist, who owned Accadia Film—under whose auspices this was made—and produced a couple of Renato Polselli films: *Le sette vipere* and *Lo sceriffo che non spara*. He was obviously a more effective businessman than filmmaker—and his performance is possibly the most amateurish of a particularly unprofessional bunch. Nonetheless, for making this and *7 cinesi d'oro* (in the following year), he deserves some kind of cockeyed recognition. Allegedly, he was hounded out of Italy a few years after this because of debts (not to mention talk of shadowy connections with the Mafia), so perhaps he wasn't such a hot-shot businessman after all.

Ex-Mr. Jayne Mansfield (Mickey Hargitay), who came to become something of a fixture in this kind of low-grade lunacy (*Bloody Pit of Horror*, *Delirium*), is surprisingly animated in the lead role. He even wrote the title tune, proving himself to be a true Renaissance man. Unfortunately, the real identity of his character is never explained. There are several references to his being a spy, but this is not enlarged upon and he seems more like a simple treasure hunter (thus making the film's inclusion in this volume a matter for some debate). Maria Vincent is dubbed with one of the most annoying accents imaginable. Her character is credited as "the voice" in the title cards, which I'd hope is some kind of ironic in-joke. Then again, Barbikan's girlfriend is dubbed with a Cockney accent that would be considered broad even at a Dick Van Dyke convention—so it's a case of anything goes, I guess.

As for the bizarre title, well it comes down to a large amount of gold dust, some handily wielded bellows and the (rather good) quote: "You're just two 007s without the 7s!" Essential stuff.—MB

CREDITS: Production: Accadia Films; Director: Vincent Cashino [Vincenzo Cascino]; Story: Vincenzo Cascino; Screenplay: Giuseppe Pellegrini; Cinematography: Antonio Piazza; Music: Italo Fischetti, Felice De Stefano; Original running length: 90 mins; Filming locations: Cinecitta Studios, Rome, with externals in Rome, Terni, Albano, Belsorano, Mazzano Romano, and Taormina; Country: Italy; Year: 1966

CAST: Mickey Hargitay (*the American, Mark Day*), Maria Vincent (*the French lady, Maria*), Luciano Paoli (*the Italian*), Vincent Cascino (*the Armenian, Barbikian*), Patrizia Mendez, Paola Mariani, Marushka Rossetti, Rossella Bergamonti, Corinne Fontaine, John Loodmere (*the Englishman*), Geoffrey Coppleston (*the auctioneer, Martin Bormann*), Eric Domain, Giovanni De Benedettis [Gianni Di Benedetto], Guido Marinelli, Nestor Cavaricci

A 008 OPERATION EXTERMINATE
aka 008 Operation Exterminate
(US, unconfirmed),
Heisse Grüsse vom C.I.A. (WG),
Operacio Exterminio (Sp),
Suspense au Caire pour 008 (Fr)

Oh boy, this one was painful to sit through. Director Umberto Lenzi, whose name will be familiar to fans of genre cinema, made several spy flicks in the sixties. His contributions, however, are relatively minor efforts and *A 008* is the exception only in that it's probably the worst. This has the economic resources and intelligence level of a network television show for kids.

Ingrid Schoeller (*Mission Phantom*) is American intelligence agent 008, masquerading as Piper Astor, a chanteuse in a casino in Cairo. For this assignment she's given the opportunity to work with Alberto Lupo (best known as the mad shape-shifting scientist in *Atom Age Vampire*), British agent 606, who takes the clever name Frank Smith here. The deadly duo must track down an anti-radar device stolen by Kemp (Ivano Staccioli) and secure the plans for same.

Schoeller was a looker all right, but as a spy she's laughable, worse than one of Charlie's Angels, a "Mata Barbie" if you will. The script seems written for the blind; most of the action onscreen is described by Piper as she skates blithely through the film stating the obvious. Frank's not much better, spending most of *his* time making sexist remarks and generally trying to score with his partner. In fact, it gets so bad at one point that Piper has to drug him so he won't jump her bones!

I'll admit to one funny line. When our two heroes are (unconvincingly) making out because they are being spied upon, Piper says "Whoever said that the English were cold?" and Frank responds, "It was the French, they're jealous." Other than that pickings are mighty slim in the positive column. There's a glove that shoots knives and Piper's lipstick shoots tear gas. The Cairo scenery is nice to look at and there's a bit of what is supposed to be Switzerland too. There's a poolside scene where Frank has a copy of Ian Fleming's "Live and Let Die," but I don't think he read very much of it. Sadly, A.F. Lavagnino's soundtrack is as uninspired as the rest of the production.

Spoiler ahead! After the two intrepid agents retrieve the plans for the device, Frank reveals that he's really agent 344 of the Soviet Secret Service and he wants those plans. Piper knew this already of course—can't fool her—so she's thought ahead and set him up for capture. Later, as Piper relaxes in a bowling alley, who should show up but Frank. It turns out he really did work for the Brits after all, so they're ready for their next mission! Thank God that didn't happen.

And lastly, here's a bit of trivia. Schoeller had a cameo in an episode of the *I Spy* television series ("Bridge of Spies," 11/19/66), the same show that featured Barbara Steele.—DD

CREDITS: Production: Romana Film, Copro Film; Director: Umberto Lenzi; Story and Screenplay: Humphrey Humbert [Umberto Lenzi], Wallace Mackentzy; Cinematography: Augusto Tiezzi; Music: Angelo Francisco Lavagnino; Original running length: 95 mins; Filming location: Incir-De Paolis Studios, Cairo; Country: Italy/Egypt; Year: 1965

CAST: Ingrid Schoeller (*Agent 008*), Alberto Lupo (*Frank, Agent 606*), Dina De Santis (*the institute director*), John Heston [Ivano Staccioli] (*Kemp*), Mark Trevor (*the monk*), Omar El Hariri (*the police captain*), George Wang (*Tanaka*), Edoardo Toniolo (*Mister X*), Nando Angelini (*the lieutenant*), Domenico Ravenna (*Heinz*), Fortunato Arena (*the scarred man*), Amed Luxor, Kuky Arena, Johnny Ravenna

## A DANDY IN ASPIC
aka Sentencia para un dany (Sp)

Oh, the trials and tribulations of being a spy. Alexander Eberlin (Laurence Harvey) is in a bad way. You see, he's a Russian spy within the British Secret Service, and has been one for 18 long years. He wants out—to go back to Russia—but is forbidden to do so by his superiors. Things have just gotten worse for comrade Eberlin too. He's been busy killing British agents on the sly and now suddenly he's been assigned to eliminate the person responsible—himself! As if that wasn't enough, the Brits think the assassin is a Russian agent, Pavel (Per Osscarson), who happens to be Eberlin's contact in London and an old friend. When Pavel turns up dead but is declared not to be the assassin after all, things get really complicated for Ebcrlin.

This is credited as an Anthony Mann production, but Mann died before filming was completed and star Harvey took over. Given the interesting premise, it's a shame the film is so disappointing. It drifts aimlessly, never creating the tension you'd expect and in the end poor Eberlin is killed after being made a monkey of by the Brits and Russians alike. Yes it was cynical, but so coldly so that the film leaves virtually no impression and that's the real crime.

Harvey's most famous role is probably that of the brainwashed soldier in *The Manchurian Candidate,* but for me he will always be the guy who got an earwig in his ear in an episode of *Night Gallery*. Here he's an angst-ridden pawn in the spy game and says things, in his stoic way, like "I'd give it all up for an identity, just to belong somewhere," and "I feel like a whore on a creaking bed."

The other major role is that of Paul Gatiss, a no-nonsense kind of spy played by Tom Courtenay. He has a gun in his little portable chair (I don't know what you call those things) and a very short temper. He thinks Eberlin is the assassin but can't prove it and his hair trigger is always about to go off. Mia Farrow is the waif-like Caroline, who mysteriously turns up in all the same places where Eberlin happens to be. Caroline turns out to be a red herring. She really is the innocent whom Eberlin loves for her innocence.

Minor roles are assayed by Harry Andrews in his typical guise as the cold-hearted bureaucrat, a very young Peter Cook as a girl-crazy agent, and Lionel Stander as a Russian agent sent to clear things up for Eberlin by providing a dead mock assassin.

There is a marionette title sequence that is nicely done and symbolic as all get-out, and

**American poster for *A Dandy in Aspic***

Quincy Jones' vague and formless score fits this meandering film but adds no weight to the proceedings. There are some nice widescreen compositions and deep focus photography to amuse your eyes, but all in all this was a doomed production from the beginning and never did find its footing.—DD

CREDITS: Production: Columbia; Director: Anthony Mann (died before completion), Laurence Harvey; Story based on the novel by Derek Marlowe; Screenplay: Derek Marlowe; Cinematography: Christopher Challis; Music: Quincy Jones; Original running length: 107 mins; Filming location: Berlin; Country: UK; Year: 1968

CAST: Laurence Harvey (*Eberlin*), Tom Courtenay (*Gatiss*), Mia Farrow (*Caroline*), Lionel Stander (*Sobakevich*), Harry Andrews (*Fraser*), Peter Cook (*Prentiss*), Per Oscarsson (*Pavel*), Barbara Murray (*Heather Vogler*), Norman Bird (*Copperfield*), John Bird (*Henderson*), Michael Trubshawe (*Flowers*), Richard O'Sullivan (*Nevil*), Geoffrey Denton (*Pond*), Geoffrey Lumsden (*Ridley*), James Cossins (*Heston-Stevas*), Calvin Lockhart (*Brogue*), Geoffrey Bayldon (*Lake*), Michael Pratt (*Greff*), Monika Dietrich (*Hedwig*), Lockwood West (*Quince*), Arthur Hewlett (*Moon*), Vernon Dobtcheff (*Stein*), Pauline Stone (*'red bird'*)

A GHENTAR SI MUORE FACILE
"in Ghentar death is easy"
aka A Ghentar le Mort Est Facile (Fr),
En Ghentar se muere facil (Sp)

During the late sixties, the war film became a popular genre among European filmmakers. In the main, these were influenced by the likes of *The Dirty Dozen* or *The Guns Of Navarone*. Often, however, they incorporated aspects of the espionage or heist movie. *A Ghentar si muore facile* probably does this more so than any other. At its heart it has a basic "revolution against a crooked dictator" scenario, but it frames this within a treasure hunt scenario that makes it worthy of examination here.

Wisecracking adventurer Teddy Jason (George Hilton) is hired by rebels from the Republic of Ghentar to retrieve a case full of documents from a plane that has crashed into the sea. He immediately has problems with the secret police, who seem to know his plans, and is forced to enlist the help of a fisherman called Botul (Vanancio Muro). After a few more scrapes he is successful in his task, but surprised to find that the case is actually full of diamonds. Intending to keep them for himself, he hides them secretly on the hull of Botul's boat.

Unfortunately, he is promptly captured by the pesky police and, refusing to talk under torture, is sentenced to imprisonment in The Mines of Paradise—a glorified prison camp in the desert. As well as suffering from the heat, exhaustive work and a period of solitary confinement, Teddy is also encouraged to talk by being tempted with a nice cool beer. This is frankly too much for a red-blooded male to take, so he organizes a daring escape with some fellow prisoners.

Escaping, however, is only the beginning of their problems since there is still a desert to cross on foot. After his companions have all died of thirst, Teddy is fortunate to be found by the men of Kim (Thomas Moore), a captain in the secret police who is in reality the head of the rebels. He agrees to help them out with their revolution, hoping that this will give him the chance to get his hands firmly back on the diamonds. An attack on the cliffside headquarters of the Dictator Lorme (Alfonso Rojas) is planned.

*A ghentar* is fortunate to benefit from an absolutely top-notch soundtrack, courtesy of Carlo Savina, which mixes a western-type title theme with some Arabian-influenced tracks to great effect. Unfortunately, the same can't really be said of much else about the film, which is generally mediocre. There is some decent underwater cinematography, but beyond that it doesn't really amount to much. Possibly the most interesting part of the film is the middle, "trekking through the desert" section. Such scenarios weren't uncommon in Euro-war films (*War Devils*, *Desert Battle*), but it appears rather idiosyncratic—and therefore memorable—within this context.

Which is a shame, as this is one of the few spy films to boast George Hilton in a lead role. A Uruguayan actor, Hilton became a big star in spaghetti westerns (*Massacre Time*, *They Call Me Hallelujah*) and giallos (*Next*, *The Sweet*

*Body of Deborah*). His lanky frame and handsome, slightly rakish visage would seem to have made him a perfect protagonist in these films but for some reason it was never to be.

Leon Klimovsky was notorious for putting his name on films that weren't actually directed by him. This enabled producers to claim tax breaks from the Spanish government, which was great for them but a severe headache for film historians trying to work out just who made the damn things. The presence of veteran Italian director Marino Girolami in a generic supervisory role could be an indication that he was the responsible party.—MB

CREDITS: Production: Marco Film, R.M. Film; Director: Leon Klimovsky; Story: Manuel M. Remis; Screenplay: Manuel M. Remis, Roberto Natale, Gino De Santis; Cinematography: Mario Fioretti {Techniscope – Technicolor}; Music: Carlo Savina; Original running length: 117 mins; Filming locations: Spain, Morocco; Country: Italy/Spain; Year: 1967

CAST: George Hilton (*Teddy Jason*), Thomas Moore [Ennio Girolami] (*Kim*), Marta Padovan (*Mary*), Venancio Muro (*Botul*), Alfonso Rojas (*Lorme*), Luis Marin (*Sirdar*), Attilio Severini, Alfonso De La Vega (*the blonde prisoner*), Jose Luis Lluch (*the swarthy prisoner*), Anne Rosas, Rafael Rosas, Gan Squir

## A MAN COULD GET KILLED
aka Welcome, Mr. Beddoes
(UK, unconfirmed)

William Beddoes (James Garner) has no sooner arrived in Lisbon than his car is destroyed in an explosion and he is whisked off to a funeral by a British embassy official—where the grieving widow, Aurora (Melina Mercouri), openly makes eyes at him. In fact, everybody is paying him an awful lot of attention, which is rather unnerving to say the least. They all seem to believe that he has something to do with a shipment of diamonds that has gone missing, but they couldn't be more wrong. He is a banker researching a hydroelectric project in the area.

It appears that the aforementioned funeral was that of a spy who knew the whereabouts of the missing diamonds (as well as the identity of a traitor within the intelligence setup). A very reluctant Beddoes teams up with Aurora, Steve Gardner (an ex-GI who is now living in Lisbon under the assumed identity of a local smuggler), and Steve's girlfriend Amy (Sandra Dee). They all decamp to the coast, where they believe the jewels may be smuggled into the country. Unfortunately, they are followed by a whole swarm of assorted spies, killers and fortune hunters, all of whom have exactly the same idea and aren't afraid of resorting to murder.

*AMCGK* is an entertaining comic romp, and not overly concerned with the ins and outs of the espionage trade—it's the type of nonsense that seemed to pop up on Sunday afternoons all the time 10 years back. The sweeping Burt Kaempfert soundtrack—including Frank Sinatra's Golden Globe-nominated version of "Strangers in the Night"—emphasizes this feeling.

It's all extremely lightweight but full of exotic sets, attractive girls, high-powered action and a healthy measure of humor. Particularly funny are the digs at the expense of the phlegmatic "Britishness" of the men from the foreign office, which are generally affectionate rather than sneering. It's also played by a variety of top-class comic performers including Roland Culver, Cecil Parker and—most particularly—Robert Coote. You've got to smile at lines such as: "He's a good chap. Got a mad wife." or (as their car explodes) "Oh dear, by the look of things we'll need a taxi…barbaric show."

Even the non-British cast members put in a good effort. James Garner is particularly effective in this type of thing, where he isn't expected to actually act as much as simply project a kind of befuddled amiability. Melina Mercouri is fabulous as a nutty, predatory femme fatale. When asked to undress, she immediately removes her false eyelashes and hair extensions. Italian spy film regulars Nello Pazzafini and Daniele Vargas turn up briefly as a pair of unfortunate assassins, as—fleetingly—does an extremely young Jenny Agutter. In fact, the only sour point is Tony Franciosa, who adopts some very strange accents and doesn't really have the comic touch needed for the role.

With high production values ensuring that it is never less than a pleasure to look at, there's really not much to dislike about this film. The main fault that could be leveled at it is a degree of repetitiveness, but such a problem is—on the whole—endemic to the genre. I was also very taken with the fact that the main villain blames his general caddishness on his wife ("You have no idea what it's like being married to you for 25 years."), and seems more concerned with his cups of tea than committing acts of insidious evil.—MB

CREDITS: Production: Univeral Pictures, Cherokee Productions; Director: Ronald Neame, Cliff Owen; Story based on the novel "Diamonds for Danger" by David Esdaile Walker; Screenplay: Richard Breen, T.E.B. Clarke; Cinematography: Gabor Pogany {Technicolor - Panavision}; Music: Bert Kaempfert; Original running length: 99 mins; Filming locations: Rome, Lisbon; Country: US/UK; Year: 1966

CAST: James Garner (*William Beddoes*), Melina Mercouri (*Aurora Celeste de Costa*), Sandra Dee (*Amy Franklin*), Tony Franciosa (*Steve Gardner/Antonio*), Robert Coote (*Hatton-Jones*), Roland Culver (*Dr. Mathieson*), Gregoire Aslan (*Florian*), Cecil Parker (*Sir Huntley Frazier*), Dulcie Grey, Martin Benson (*Politanu*), Peter Illing (*Zarick*), Niall McGinnis (*the ship's captain*), Virgilio Teixeira (*Inspector Rodriguez*), Isabel Dean (*Miss Bannister*), Daniele Vargas (*Osman*), Nello Pazzafini (*Abdul*), George Pastell (*Lazlo*), Arnold Diamond (*Milo*), Conrad Anderson (*Hienrich*), Eric Demain (*Max*), Pasquale Fasciano (*Carmo*), Ann Firbank (*Miss Nolan*), Brenda De Banzie (*Mrs Mathieson*), Nora Swinburne (*Lady Frazier*), Jenny Agutter (*Linda Frazier*), Giuliano Raffaelli (*Herman Reis, aka Ludmar*), Yamili Humar (*Rosa*). With: Pontifex, Jonas Braimer, D.A. Segurd, E. Cianfanelli, M. Bevilacqua, M.R. Caldas, O. Acursio, J. Paixio, A. Costa, L. Pinhao, G. Dusmatas, C. DiMaggio, Carlo Calisti (hotel attendent), C. Perone, Paolo Solvay, M. Tempesta, S. Minoi, R. Castelli, R. Alessandri, G. Maculani, G. Lipari, K. Goncalves

## A TOUCH OF TREASON

aka Los enemigos (Sp), Les ennemis (Fr)

This is part of the minor cycle of intimate espionage adventures the French cranked out in the era before Bond changed the face of spy movies forever. Here, the thin plot—documents stolen from the Russian embassy—is secondary to the series of small, complex moves that focus more on character than action. This is life-size drama and one of the better examples of the sub-genre.

Roger Hanin is Jean de Lursac, a French Secret Service agent called in when a Russian embassy safe is plundered of documents that could prove most valuable to other countries. The poor fellow responsible for the documents' safekeeping, a cultural attaché (Michel Vitold), is shortly thereafter kidnapped by the same thieves as insurance. What follows are the machinations of the Russians, French and Americans to retrieve the property.

The relationships within and between the various factions on the trail bring the characters to life, blurring the lines between good and bad, exploring the themes of respect, loyalty and betrayal. By the time we reach the conclusion, we know the players in this game quite well and the ending, unusually downbeat for the time, becomes that much more devastating.

If you're game to try one of Roger Hanin's many spy thrillers, this would be the one I'd recommend. It's well-written and has an excellent free jazz score by one of the greats in the business, Martial Solal.—DD

CREDITS: Production: Belles Rives, Sirius; Director: Edoardo Molinaro; Story: Based on the story "Un Certain Code" by Fred Noro; Screenplay: Andre Tabet, Eduardo Molinaro and Francois Nourrissier; Cinematography: Louis Miaille {B&W}; Music: Martial Solal; Original running length: 92 mins; Country: France/Italy; Year: 1961

CAST: Roger Hanin (*Jean De Lursac*), Pascale Audret (*Christine*), Claude Brasseur (*Vigo*), Michel Vitold (*Andrei Smoloff*), Dany Carrel (*Lilia*), Charles Millot (*Borghine*), Jeanne Aubert (*Mme De Lorsac*), Jacques Monod (*Gerlier*), Daniel Cauchy (*Patrick*), Bill Kearns (*Mike Slatter*), Nicole Mirel (*Claudie*), Georges Cusin (*the commandant*), Jean LeFebvre (*the doctor*), Michel Ardan (*Bobby*), Michel Jourdan (*Maurice*), Jacques Esterel (*the fashion designer*), Claude Chabrol (*the man in the restaurant*), Nelly Benedetti, Arlette Redon,

Jacques Pierre, Max Montavon, Alain Nobis, Monique Boiville, Raoul Saint-Yves

AGENT FOR PANIC
aka Pate Oddeleni (Cz)?

Here's an interesting little number. This is a well-made, small intrigue film with no gadgets or special effects. It's played completely straight, stars no one you or I have ever heard of and to top it off, it's an unusual look at the spy game. All the credits on this print from Sinister Cinema appear to be anglicized fakes but for one: The score was done by Evzen Illin, whose only other recognizable credit is for Milos Forman's *The Loves of a Blonde*.

Our supposed hero is American agent Joseph Kilian, played by Vlad Newmann (as billed, anyway). What begins as a standard spy flick soon shifts focus to the other side and the bulk of the film is spent with the Secret Police as they track down the spy ring that Kilian and the Western powers have built up in Prague.

This is an unusually bleak look at Cold War games for a film of this vintage (Sinister dates this as 1964 but other sources claim 1960, which seems more accurate). When Kilian approaches his old friend Jan now living in Prague, it's clear the fellow does not want to get involved in spying for the West. His wife has just entered the hospital to give birth, which means that she, and consequently he, is under the thumb of the State.

Kilian leaves Prague after convincing Jan to transmit shipment information to the West, and here's where the film takes its unexpected turn. In the offices of the Secret Police, where Jan's transmissions are soon detected, Lt. Jonas confides to his boss (of all people) that he hates this Secret Police work and longs for the old days when he was a pilot after the war. His boss gently reminds him that "no one resigns" and that he will forget the remarks... this time. Signs of humanity in the opposition are relatively rare in serious spy films until late in the cycle, when cynicism or comedy were to become the only two approaches to the genre.

It doesn't take long for the Secret Police to triangulate the source of the transmissions and when they do, just as Jan had feared, the wife and kid's "health" is threatened. There is no resistance from Jan, who immediately tells Jonas and company everything. From here on we follow the Secret Police and their plans to capture all the players in the plot to leak information to the West.

Politics is not really the main issue with the film. The situation could easily have been reversed with our side doing the same legwork to oust the "Commies." The Western powers would have been just as intimidating to their citizens as the Secret Police are here. By reversing the focus, the filmmakers are not taking sides with the State as it were, but merely holding up a mirror for the viewer, and it works.

The film has its lighter moments as well. Jonas sets up a camera in Jan's locker room at the plant where coded shipment information is dropped. When viewing the film, the men are treated to the sight of one of the female workers straightening her hose. Jonas remarks in what is likely the mildest sexy situation of the genre, "This Secret Police work has its compensation!" That's the extent of the leering.

Kilian is tricked into returning to Prague to check the links in his spy chain when his information is tinkered with. While there he has a rendezvous with one of his female cohorts. Kilian lies back on the sofa and lights a smoke and answers her question of whether he had eaten recently with "a man's appetite needs more than food." The looks between the two leading up to their (offscreen) lovemaking are worth the price of admission.

The hard reality of the situations involved in spying is never far from the center of the film, however. Kilian remarks to his lover that he'd like to get her out of Prague. She explains that the State has her son in a camp somewhere so she can't leave. Kilian says "Someday we must get you both out." When she asks if he could really do that he replies "No." Later, however, he makes a promise to try.

She takes a beating (offscreen, of course) for her complicit behavior with Kilian and the spy ring is ultimately broken, giving the East the victory this time. Kilian barely makes it back across the border on his belly but leaves us with one of the great final moments of the genre. His boss asks Kilian if he intends to return to Prague and Kilian turns to the camera and says "I made a promise to a lady," and the frame freezes.

A great amount of care is taken by the filmmakers in all departments. The black and white photography is superb, with interesting but low-key visuals and creative editing. This may be low budget but it's not low talent for either cast or crew.—DD

**Lang Jeffries has his name misspelled on the suggestive Belgian poster for *Agent X17***

CREDITS (unconfirmed): Director: Henrik Polak [Jindrich Polák]; Story and Screenplay: Jindrich Polak, Vaclav Sklenar, Ludek Stanek; Cinematography: Jan Curik {B&W}; Music: Evzen Illín; Original running length: 96 mins; Country: Czechoslovakia; Year: 1960

CAST (unconfirmed): Vlad Newmann [Juri Vrstala?] (*Killian*?), Radovan Lukavsky, Jaroslav Rozsival, Jaroslav Mares (*Lt. Jonas*?), Nadezda Gajerova, Josef Beyvl, Jaroslav Cmiral, Sylva Danickova, Vldimir Hruby, Josef Koza, Lubomir Lipsky, Frantisek Loring, Eva Senkova, Robert Vrchota, Oldrich Vykypel, Milos Willig

AGENT X-17
aka Agente X1-7 operacion Oceano (Sp),
Agente X1-7: operazione Oceano (It),
X1-7 Top Secret (Fr)

A man is murdered in an industrial estate. A distinguished-looking gent is shot by a phony security guard. What's going on? Well, it all has something to do with a certain professor Calvert, who has invented a fabulous formula that does something bizarre to the world's oceans. As is always the case with such groundbreaking scientists, there are a bunch of bad guys who want to use his work for their own evil ends.

For protection, the FBI send the professor—accompanied by his attractive daughter—on a holiday in Southern Europe (which saves on budget if nothing else). Special agent George Collins (Lang Jeffries) tags along to make sure that nothing untoward befalls them (and to check out the Mediterranean babes). Seeing as how George has managed to get involved in about six fights before even being assigned his mission, you could view this as frankly looking for trouble. Sure enough, the professor is promptly kidnapped (while our hero is busy trying to seduce a pretty stranger, no less).

Fortunately the FBI man finally manages to extract himself from the assorted females, and sets about trying to rescue his charge, who has been taken to a heavily fortified castle in the mountains. This doesn't prove to be too difficult, although he does have to burn his way out of a steel chamber by that old schoolboy standby of reflecting the sun through his shades! Unfortunately, the villains have escaped and plan to use the formula to wreak havoc upon the world...or something like that.

The only genre entry from the unfortunately named Tanio Boccia (better known for his peplums, westerns and the relative obscurity of most of his films), *Agent X-17* is a thoroughly mediocre film. There are lots of fistfights, the best of which takes place in a joinery chock full of buzz saws, but nothing to really draw the viewer into the proceedings. This is mostly the fault of the script, which is lazy at best and incomprehensible for much of the running time. The ending, for instance, is probably the most pathetic to be found within the entire genre. At one moment doomsday is fast approaching, the next our hero is happily playing around with a toy submarine and the final credits appear. Say what?

There's also a complete lack of a charismatic villain, a problem shared by many of the less effective of these films, and nothing really in the way of plot development. There's some pretty shoddy filmmaking as well; not the least is when an escape is made by parachuting from some castle battlements—only for an overhead shot of a parachute above the castle. Whew, there must have been some pretty powerful thermals around on that day.

All of the genre staples are in place. There are plentiful gadgets (exploding cigarettes, a lighter that dispenses tranquilizing drugs, and a gun-vest that makes the wearer appear to be shooting from his nipples). There's an extremely civilized bar scene, in which everybody waltzes to an easy-listening tune called "A Man Like You" and watches half-naked ladies waving multicolored feathers around. Okay, so there's not a cable car fight, but just to make us feel at home the filmmakers do include a scrap on a funicular. In all, though, there's nothing distinctive or idiosyncratic enough to give it a degree of edge.

On the plus side, Lang Jeffries is as good as ever. He's in a lighter mood than usual, and gets to hang around with beach chicks while Hawaiian-style music plays on the soundtrack. Lang being Lang, however, he's soon back to being grumpy. He punches an unfortunate waiter in the stomach for no reason whatsoever and slaps around the habitually slapped-around Moha Tahi (*The Black Box Affair*, *Nazi SS*). Beyond that, however, it's really nothing special.—MB

CREDITS: Production: Tellus Cin.ca, Coper Film; Director: Amerigo Anton [Tanio Boccia]; Story: Alberto De Rossi, Fernando Vitali, Amerigo Anton, Mario Moroni, HS Valdes; Screenplay: H.S. De Rossi, Alberto Moroni, Mario Vitali, Fernando Valdes; Cinematography: Ricardo Torres {Technicolor - Techniscope}; Music: Piero Umiliani; Original running length: 90 mins; Country: Spain/Italy; Year: 1965

CAST: Lang Jeffries (*George Collins*), Aurora De Alba, Rafael Bardem, Eleanora Bianchi (*Catherine Calvert*), Gloria Osuna, Wladimiro Tuicovic, Angel Jordan, Moa Thai, Joe Kamel, Nando Angelini, Gianni Solari, Aldo Bonamano, Andrea Scandurri

## AGENTE SEGRETO 070 THUNDERBAY—MISSIONE GRASSHOPPER
"secret agent 070 thunderbay—mission grasshopper"

This obscurity was apparently the sequel to Cesare Canevari's *Un Tango dalla Russia*, which also starred the little-known Dan Christian and was seen by approximately six people throughout the entire world. It's not a particularly great film, but it is at times decidedly odd, which actually makes for rather entertaining viewing. The fact that it was filmed in black and white also distances it from its colorful contemporaries, giving it a similar feel to an early, less witty episode of *The Avengers*.

It kicks off with a freaky sequence in which, to the accompaniment of a meandering bongo beat, the lead male and female characters address the camera against a black background. Cool, daddy-o! This fugues into a man running through some woods, obviously frightened for his life. He attempts to catch his breath beside a tree, but is garrotted by someone from behind.

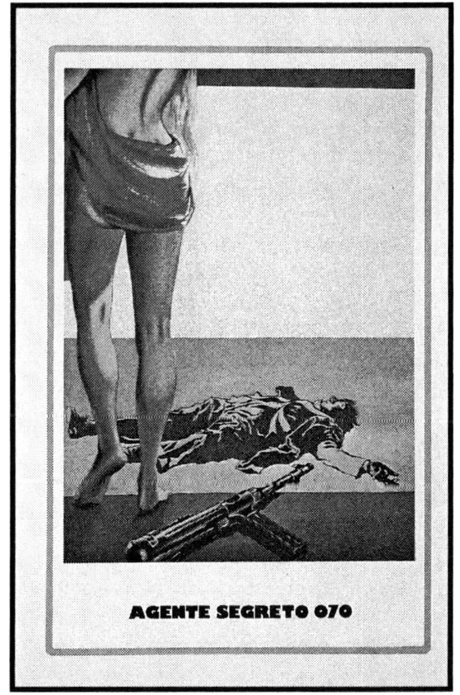


**Promo card for *Agente segreto 070 thunderbay--missione Grasshopper***

Secret Service agent Dan Cooper (Christian) is dispatched to Paris (as signified by a still shot of the Eiffel Tower) to investigate. He soon meets up with assorted petty criminals, a Scotland Yard Inspector (Roberto Messina), and a young lady who insists upon walking around the hotel in her nightie (Vasna Welsh). He spends a lot of time sitting around in cafes while accordion music plays in the background.

After being harassed by a scary posse of brunette babes in bikinis, he decides that he really ought to do more than just idle around drinking wine, and discovers that everything revolves around an illicit diamond smuggling ring, the starting point of which is a tribe of African Amazon women! Virtually all of the characters end up on a yacht bound for the Dark Continent, where everyone enjoys a big shoot-out while lots of young ladies in leopard skin lingerie run around neurotically.

This was obviously one of the less lavishly budgeted of sixties spy films, and indeed most of it looks as though it was shot in a succession of hotel rooms and staff canteens. The direction is mediocre at best, the fight choreography is absolutely terrible and the music, despite a great opening track, soon descends into the harrowing desperation of having "It's a Long Way to Tipperary" play over the end credits. And yet it's all strangely gratifying. Any film that manages to mix kung fu fighting, mad French butchers, Amazon women and "up skirt" dancing girl footage has to be on to something.

You also have the feeling that the wardrobe director must have undergone a temporary period of insanity. Apart from Roberto Messina, who seems to change his costume every five minutes, there is also a very funny minor villain who wears a different hat (porkpie, boater, etc.) in every scene. Even more amusingly, when he turns up in a sombrero (to chat with a friend in a pith helmet, no less), flamenco music plays markedly on the soundtrack.

Not that much is known about *missione Grasshopper*, even its country of origin (at a guess, it looks to have been an Italian/German co-production). The identity of director Burton Von Hooven, which would appear to be a pseudonym, remains unclear—although it has been suggested that it could have been the work of the aforementioned Cesare Canevari, a filmmaker whose work often veered into the bizarre (see his psychedelic spaghetti western, *Matolo*).

The cast is full of unknowns and second-string players. Roberto Messina, who actually has more to do than the ostensible hero, was another former stuntman who graduated into becoming a second-string thespian within the genre (as did his brother, Emilio), appearing in a variety of small-scale productions (including Angelo Dorigo's *Un colpo da re* and Renzo Cerrato's *OSS 117 Double Agent*). And he's about the most familiar performer of the bunch.—MB

CREDITS: Production: Saul Birkenbaum; Director: Burton Van Hooven [Cesare Canevari?]; Story: John Griffith; Screenplay: John Griffith, Edgar Arkoff, Hilde Weisse; Cinematography: Ernest John Mercury {B&W}; Music: Italo Fischetti; Country: Italy/West Germany (?); Year: 1965 (?)

CAST: Dan Christian (*Agente 070, Dan Cooper*), Vasna Welsh (*a secret agent*), Bob Messanger [Roberto Messina] (*Sergeant Bear of Scotland Yard*), Mills Mason (*Paco*), Ursula Rank (*Rossabella*), Lolita Ritz (*Regina*), Attilio Dottesio (*Driker*), Fred Coplan (*Brown*), Robert Fisherman (*a journalist*), Mary Anthony (*Brown's secretary*), Roy Raphaels (*Sutherland*), Liv Ferrer (*Warren*), Mike Di Maggio (*Trumbo*), Marioline Dundee, Vera Larsen, Connie Hall, Nancy Bencini, Thornton Steiger, Philippe De Nanteuil, The Hill Sisters

## AGENTE SEGRETO 777: OPERAZIONE MISTERO

"secret agent 777: operation mystery"

A car is ambushed while driving along a mountain road and its driver is killed. The killers extract a microfilm from the false heel of the dead man's shoe. So begins the first of two films made by Enrico Bomba, a prolific producer who had notably less success—if this and *Ticket to Die* are anything to go by—when he tried his hand at directing.

So what does this microfilm reveal? Well, that a certain professor Keller is conducting some very interesting experiments. He has discovered nothing less than a way to reanimate the (recently) dead. This, surprisingly enough, doesn't seem to be of that much interest to the authorities—who seem far more concerned with the fact that he's discovered a way to produce extremely cheap nuclear energy as a handy by-product.

That this top-secret research has found its way into microfilm format seems to indicate that somebody on the good professor's team is selling information to the foreign intelligence services. The FBI is alarmed at this prospect, and assigns Dr. Bardin (Mark Damon), an ex-student of Keller's now working for the Bureau, to worm out the identity of the mole.

This has a pretty cranky central conceit, but anybody hoping to find it chock full of maniacal, sharp-suited zombies will be severely disappointed. In fact, the extremely jaundiced looking Richard (Aldo Bufi Landi) provides the only evidence of the undead coming back to life. After suffering, well—death, this poor dude gets wired up to a primitive-looking machine before going AWOL, only to pop up looking rather dazed at occasional moments throughout the running time. This is a shame, as I'm sure there's some mileage in the idea of a secret agent who just happens to be...deceased. Just think, there'd be no end to the amount of sitting around in hotel bars and drinking cocktails that could be accomplished.

In fact, the most terrifying thing to be found here is the selection of horrendous interiors on display. If you ever thought that the sixties were the decade of high style, watching this will shove a heavy-soled boot through your preconceptions. Not only is the wallpaper on show absolutely vile, it actually matches the bedspreads. Fortunately the exteriors, ostensibly shot in Beirut, are rather fetching in comparison. In fact, they would be even if they were shot in that unfortunate city today.

As it is, *Agente segretto 777* is a dreary, lifeless film. There's an awful lot of sitting around and talking, a tendency that reaches its apogee with a sequence in which everybody sits around discussing just what has previously happened. This is bad enough, but that it lasts for about 20 minutes merely adds insult to injury. Especially for an audience already anaesthetized by the dull-as-ditchwater production values. I guess the film is attempting to foster a claustrophobic air of mystery in an Agatha Christie, drawing room style. Given the

**Mark Damon is menaced by Stelio Candelli in *Agente segreto 777: operazione Mistero***

participation of Seyna Seyn and Stelio Candelli, however, who both always play reprobates and act in an extremely dubious fashion, it isn't that much of a surprise when the identity of the villains is revealed.

Despite spicing up a bit toward the end, this has to count as one of the poorest genre efforts. It looks like Bomba tried to expand this into a series with the release of *Ticket to Die*, another Agente segreto 777 film, which starred "Lewis Jordan"—who here plays a secondary FBI agent—in the main role. Unfortunately, it wasn't any better, and the series drew to an unceremonious close.

This was the sole spy film for Mark Damon, an American actor who had achieved moderate success as the romantic lead in Roger Corman's *Fall of the House of Usher*. After relocating to Europe, he appeared in a number of Italian and Spanish films throughout the sixties and seventies, ranging from peplums (*Il figli di Cleopatra*) to sleazy horror (*The Devil's Wedding Night*) and a caper movie (*Colpo doppio del camaleonte d'oro*). He later reappeared as a prolific Hollywood producer, giving us such artistic masterpieces as *9 1/2 Weeks* and *Bat*21*, possibly the most commonly shown film on UK terrestrial television.—MB

CREDITS: Production: Protor Film; Director: Henry Bay [Enrico Bomba]; Story and Screenplay: Arpad De Riso, Nino Scolaro, based on a book by Dean Marton; Cinematography: Adalberto Albertini {Eastmancolor}; Music: Marcello De Martino; Original running length: 87 mins; Filming location: Bruno Ceria Studios (Trieste), Beirut; Country: Italy; Year: 1965

CAST: Mark Damon (*Dr Bardin*), Mary Young (*the professor's daughter*), Seyna Seyn (*Dr Serens*), Stanley Kent [Stelio Candelli] (*Dr Dexter*), Aldo Bufi Landi (*Richard, the "dead man"*), Lewis Jordan (*Bardin's associate*), Isarco Ravaioli (*the professor's assistant*), Walter Neng, Marie Badmayev, Franca Duccio

AGENTE SIGMA 3—
MISSIONE GOLDWATHER
"agent sigma 3—mission goldwather"
aka Mercancia humana (Sp),
Sigma Trois, agent special (Fr)

This poverty-stricken entry doesn't have much going for it. Jack Taylor is Charles Butler, agent Sigma 3 of the Secret Service. Taylor is a creepy, unconvincing hero better known as a Jess Franco sleaze regular. Here, Butler must find a kidnapped scientist who has invented an unexplained ray, which is trumpeted as a "guarantee against all air attack."

The paper-thin plot leads our spy guy to Morocco (not really) and Barcelona (really) in order to outsmart the international espionage network that plans to sell the professor to the highest bidder. They've put the poor guy into hibernation at 0 degrees Centigrade for some reason. The better to smuggle him, I guess.

**Busy Turkish poster for the unexciting *Agent Sigma 3-missione Goldwather***

The leader of the ring is an actor unknown to this reviewer but his right-hand person is none other than Silvia Solar, who did her time in genre cinema including several spy movies and Jerry Cotton films. She does all the work here, managing the entire operation from start to finish while the big man sits around getting her messages.

There are plenty of moments of unintentional humor and enough plot absurdities to make one viewing palatable. When Butler is told that the professor has been kidnapped, he responds with "The scientist?" At one point Butler is driving his nifty little sports car down the road and realizes he's being tailed. So he takes out his gun and, using the rear view mirror for reference, shoots backwards over his shoulder, hitting the tire of the car following him!

After one fight, a bad guy's toupee comes off in Butler's hand and a tattoo of a series of numbers on the top of his head is unveiled. Butler's partner asks him what it means and once again the lightning logic of our hero comes into play: "I have no idea but it's obviously a code." There are many such instances of Butler stating the obvious.

The best bits of gadgetry the writers could come with are the old microfilm-in-the-dentures trick and a tea bag that reveals a message when it gets wet. There are a few unconvincing fights, some genuine Barcelona locations, and a cable car climax. The film does boast a fairly swinging big band jazz score by Manuel Carra and there's a cheesy rock and roll band that breaks the monotony for a few minutes. Overall, this one is strictly for genre completionists or fans of Silvia Solar.—DD

CREDITS: Production: Imexcine, Estela Film; Director: Albert L Whiteman [Giampaolo Callegari]; Story: Albert King; Screenplay: Robert Christmas [Roberto Natale], Roman McLiorin [Romano Migliorini], Albert King; Cinematography: Romolo Garroni {Imexscope-Eastmancolor}; Music: Manuel Parra; Original running length: 91 mins; Country: Italy/Spain; Year: 1967

CAST: Jack Taylor (*Sigma 3*), Silvia Solar (*Catherine*), Armando Calvo (*Karamensis*),

Walter Neng, Diana Martin, Remo De Angelis, Mia Genberg, Lilian Saxon, Frank Harris, Mario Lanfranchi, Giovanna Lenzi, Aldo Rendine

ASSALTO AL TESORO DI STATO
"onslaught to the state treasure"
aka Criminal party di mezzanotte (subtitle)

The government of the isolated Arabian State of Goggiam declares its intention to nationalize the oil industry. Unfortunately, they had previously signed away the rights to mine the oilfields to an association of Western companies. In order to buy back the rights, they arrange for a shipment of $20 million to be driven to an adjacent country by van, from which it will be used to pay off the Westerners.

The oil companies, of course, aren't all that happy at seeing their investments going out the window, and one of their directors—Kaufman (Daniele Vargas)—comes up with a cunning plan to foil the intentions of the Arabs. He hires a quartet of top-notch international criminals to stage a hold-up of the van, with the understanding that they will be able to keep the booty if successful. The criminals are Johnny Quick (Roger Browne), who is to mastermind the project; Linnemann (Sandro Dori), a somewhat chubby playboy who can twist women around his little finger; Elias (Franco Ressell), an expert in drugs; and Shanda (Anita Sanders), a notorious swindler.

It doesn't take too long for the four of them to start trying to double-cross each other, and Elias also begins to behave erratically (perhaps because of his pill-popping habit). Despite this, they make their way to Goggiam and manage to complete their mission. Unfortunately, things go haywire when Kaufman, who is looking after the money while they make their way out of the country, is killed by an unidentified assassin.

This is the only spy film of Piero Pierotti, a director who dabbled in a number of genres with varying levels of success. He's best known for his peplums (*A Queen For Caesar*, *Hercules and the Masked Rider*), but also made the spaghetti western *Heads or Tails*—and would undoubtedly have made more had he not died in 1970. *Assalto* is an obscure film, which seems never to have had an English-language release.

**Anita Sanders in *Assalto al tesoro di stato***

This isn't entirely surprising, as it's frankly not that good. In fact, it stands as one of the more disappointing films to be found in the genre. It has a great cast, looks good, has a decent plot and yet it never comes together in a convincing whole, mainly because the pacing verges on the narcoleptic. Nothing much happens until halfway through the running time, and even then it's all skewed. There's an awful lot of talking and sitting around in hotel rooms, but very little in the way of action—which for an ostensible action film is a bit of a drawback. In fact, with its "giallo-esque" subplot, it resembles more an exotic Agatha Christie mystery—even ending with all the suspects gathered in a "drawing room" to see the killer unveiled. Unfortunately, as this—the most interesting aspect of the film—only really kicks off 20 minutes from the end, it all adds up to too little, too late.

In addition, some of the photography is of a substandard quality (with far too much panning and zooming), and the music tends to veer into easy-listening blandness. The cheap nature of the production is also displayed by some ridiculous continuity errors (people relocate from a desert to woodland at the drop of a hat). And if you're wondering just what the spy film connection is, well, it's not giving to much away to say that Johnny Quick is revealed to be working for American Intelligence (it all comes down to oil, you see).

As to the cast, they all stand up as well as can be expected. Roger Browne doesn't really get to do much, but looks good in a selection of safari suits and khaki shorts. Franco Ressel is good value as a livewire red herring, and Sandro Dori makes possibly the most unconvincing womanizer ever essayed on screen (he spends half his time eating, or passed out after doing so).—MB

CREDITS: Production: Romana Film; Director: Piero Pierotti; Story and Screenplay: Piero Pierotti, Gianfranco Clerici; Cinematography: Augusto Tiezzi {Eastmancolor – Widescreen}; Music: Angelo Francesco Lavagnino; Original running length: 90 mins; Filming location: Incir-De-Paolis Studios; Country: Italy; Year: 1967

CAST: Roger Browne (*Johnny Quick*), Anita Sanders (*Shanda*), Franco Ressel (*Elias*), Sandro Dori (*Linnemann*), Gino De Santis, Tullio Altamura (*Lodz, Kaufman's henchman*), Olga Sobelli (*Madame Angot*), Antonietta Fiorito, Angela De Leo, Lucio Casoria, Silvio Laurenzi, Renato Montalbano, Valentino Macchi, Rosy De Leo, Giovanni Baghino, Lina Franchi, Zuccolo di Spilimbergo, with Daniele Vargas (*Kaufmann*)

ASSASSINATION
aka La peur aux tripes (Fr)

I'll admit to being a Henry Silva fan and I'm probably guilty of cutting this film too much slack because of it. The plot is very convoluted and to be truthful, not much excitement is generated over the course of its unfolding. But if you like Silva there's something to be said for a film where his character is interesting and he's onscreen almost the entire time. This is one of those films that should be watched late at night when sleep is pressing in because it's the cinematic ambience that matters more here than the nuts and bolts of plot.

Director Emilio Miraglia (*The Night Evelyn Came Out of the Grave*), billed here as Hal Brady, has his hands full with all the

**Belgian poster for the moody *Assassination***

machinations of the story. This makes for what seems like a long film, but it really isn't any longer than most of its genre kin. Part of the problem is that the motivations of most of the main characters aren't made clear until near the end, if at all. I'm not going to step through all the twists and turns of the plot, but you should know that Silva (as John Chandler) is "killed" but is really living under his brother's name and is out for revenge because he was set up for murder. But is he now working for the good guys or the bad guys? His "widow" Barbara (Ida Galli) is totally lost and ends up marrying Bob (Fred Beir), who is working for either the good guys or the bad guys too. Needless to say, neither of these characters is given the chance to gel. The leaders of both sides are nebulous in their dealings with superiors and subordinates and the missions of each are equally cloudy. I'm willing to say that the whole thing is a cynical commentary, but that doesn't help the feeling of freefall one has during the course of watching the darn thing.

There are a few good things to say about the film. The bulk of the action takes place in European winter settings, which I consider a plus. It has a good score by Robby Poitevin that reflects the general melancholia. We also get a glimpse of a Times Square theater marquee boasting a *Tomb of Torture/Cave of the Living Dead* double feature. There are some good lines, like when Barbara asks Chandler "Can we ever live like ordinary people?" and he replies, "People like us, yeah." There's also a downbeat ending before such things were the height of cinematic fashion. So if I keep my copy of this movie it's because late one night I want to throw in a video that features Henry Silva buttoning his overcoat against the chill German wind.

Silva fans will definitely want to catch him in a nifty little crime film called *Hail Mafia!* Ida Galli, billed quite often as Evelyn Stewart, was a spy film regular who made her debut in Fellini's *La dolce vita* and went on to a solid genre career in general. Fred Beir, who did more American television than movies, is the main spy in the tepid *M.M.M. 83*.—DD

CREDITS: Production: Cinegay, Jolly Film; Director: Hal Brady [Emilio Miraglia]; Story: Emyl Bridge; Screenplay: Lou Strateman, Andy Colbert, Max Hatired; Cinematography: Eric Menczer {Techniscope - Technicolor}; Music: Robby Poitevin; Original running length: 100 mins; Filming locations: Cinecitta Studios, Rome; US; Country: Italy; Year: 1967

CAST: Henry Silva (*John/Philip Chandler*), Fred Beir (*Bob*), Evelyn Stewart [Ida Galli] (*Barbara*), Peter Dane (*Lang*), Bill Vanders (*Thomas*), Fred Farrell [Alfredo Varelli] (*Morrison*), Bob Molden (*Otto*), Karl Menzinger (*Hans*), Gunther Schultz (*the senator*), Gert von Zitzewitz (*the baron*), Valentino Macchi

## ASSIGNMENT SKYBOLT

aka Kataskopoi sto Saroniko (Gr), Operation Skybolt (Int)

What can you say about a Greek spy movie? This one has quite the pedigree. The director worked with Fritz Lang (as an editor) on *The Testament of Dr. Mabuse* and also edited the Marx Brothers classic *One Night in Casablanca*. The cinematographer, Walter Lassally, worked with director Tony Richardson on *The Loneliness of the Long Distance Runner* and *Tom Jones* and won an Oscar for his work on *Zorba the Greek*. And the composer won a Best Song Oscar for *Never on Sunday*. Elements that look good (to us) on paper include several strip acts, overt sadomasochism, and gratuitous torture.

However (you knew that was coming), what these geniuses have cranked out is a boring third-tier, no-budget spy movie with a lamentable script, television-quality sets, and badly choreographed fights. Sure, our hopes are raised when the movie opens with a stripper doing the bump and grind to a nice Greek folk song, and again 10 minutes later when we are treated to *another* strip act, this time with balloons and audience participation! But could they keep up the pace? In a word, no.

Nicolas Kirk (whose real name is Nikos Kourkoulos) is agent Don Holland, a spy who vaguely resembles Sean Connery except that he's much shorter in stature and charisma. Holland is after an H-bomb that was stolen from a NATO base in Turkey. It seems his long-lost brother Jack is somehow mixed up in this terrorist plot, but Holland says he's just going to "do his job" anyway. It turns out that Jack, who is blind and has the code name Achilles (!), is being blackmailed for no good reason, so Holland is able to "do his job" without the necessity of icing his own flesh and blood.

Holland is the kind of spy who reads Playboy in the tub (ahem), can hotwire a car with a hairpin, do long traditional Greek dances and can fit through a porthole when the going gets tough. When trapped in a dark alley with cars barreling down on him from both sides, Holland has the presence of mind to wait until the last possible second, until just before the cars collide to crush him in between, and jump up on their bumpers to escape. What a guy!

The villainess who thought up the whole idea of stealing the bomb is probably played by Anna Brazzou (the no-name cast doesn't ring any bells so your guess is as good as mine). Brazzou is the surprise evil person who has been playing an innocent and not very talented club singer for most of the film until it's time to reveal the brains behind the dastardly plot. Holland and Brazzou have a very interesting relationship. Early in the film he romances her, but when he is attacked in his room he figures her for the one who set him up. So he takes his belt off and whips her until their passion can be held back no longer and they jump into the sack.

Curious yes, but late in the film, when he's been captured and she has him tied to a bed on her yacht, she turns the tables and belt-whips *him*! Again they are both so turned on by this that she does his nether regions a favor but leaves him tied up so he still has to work to make his escape later.

I mentioned torture, didn't I? Holland goes through a rigorous session of electrical torture to his gonads that will have the males in the audience squirming in their chairs. Other than that the film is relatively tame. There's one great line when a stripper enters the dressing room, takes off her dress and asks her friend, "Don't you think I'm stacked?"

You'll get to enjoy a few of the colorful tourist sights of the Athens area of course, and there's a "humorous" nod to better films when our hero sees a headstone marked "Jimmy Bond." You may also notice an unimpressive car chase and a ring that shoots poison darts. At least the film was shot in English but nearly everyone—including a girl who is supposed to be from Manhattan—has a very thick accent. The score is an untenable mixture of traditional folk songs and discordant minor-key histrionics. No Oscar here, Mr. Hadjidakis.

Oh, and don't think about the fact that the bad guys set the H-bomb to explode in 15 minutes and still expect to get away. It's a good thing our hero turns off the detonator with—that's right—one second left.—DD

CREDITS: Director: Gregg Tallas; Cinematography: Walter Lassally; Music: Manos Hadjidakis; Original running length: 95 mins; Country: Greece; Year: 1968

CAST: Elena Nathanael, Anna Brazzou, Paris Alexander, Nicholas Kirk [Nikos Kourkoulos] (*Don Holland*)

ATTACK OF THE ROBOTS
aka Cartas boca arriba (Sp),
Cartes sur table (Fr)

I'm here to tell you this is a mediocre film but it does have a few things going for it. Primary among these is the presence of Eddie Constantine as Interpol agent Al Peterson (in the English-dubbed print). He belts the bad guys and charms the ladies as per usual but here he doesn't drink, which is quite a departure from his steady stream of whisky-drenched spy roles. Constantine was a very popular actor in Europe at the time and he made many films that fall into the espionage mold, as you will see.

Second among the film's merits would be Francoise Brion, who plays the scheming wife of mad doctor Fernando Rey. The beautiful Brion had better roles in other Constantine films, but here she gets the chance to model a few fetish outfits.

Next we have what may be the best thing about the movie after all, the photography. Much of the film is drenched in noir lighting that makes for visual interest even if one loses mental interest in the plot. Speaking of which, Rey has found a way to turn people with blood type Rhesus 0 into robots. Well they're not really robots, more like zombies. He uses these black-clad zombies to assassinate important folk, but to what end we are never quite clear. Needless to say, Eddie infiltrates and destroys. Sorry to spoil it for you.

**Belgian poster for Jess Franco's *Attack of the Robots***

Eddie is constantly followed by Sophie Hardy, who turns out to be an Interpol agent as well, and the Chinese are the foreign power interested in Rey's technique. The film follows the lines of a detective story (the cinematography works in this regard) rather than a traditional spy movie. However, Eddie is furnished with several gadgets—an exploding umbrella, electric gloves, an exploding cigar and a gas-filled pen—all of which are phony except one! I won't spoil *that* for you.

Striptease acts show up in many films of this type from the period but at least here one of the acts unfolds, so to speak, to the strains of classical music! The soundtrack is good jazzy stuff by Paul Misraki, the last good reason to take the time to watch.—DD

CREDITS: Production: Hesperia Films, Spéva Film, Ciné Alliance; Director: Jesus [aka Jess] Franco; Story: Jesus Franco; Screenplay: Jean-Claude Carriere; Cinematography: Antonio Macasoli {B&W}; Music: Paul Misraki; Original running length: 92 mins; Filming locations: Costa Blanca, Madrid, Alicante; Country: Spain/France; Year: 1966

CAST: Eddie Constantine (*Al Peterson*), Francoise Brion, Fernando Rey, Alfredo Mayo, Sophie Hardy, Marcelo Arroita-Jauregui, Mara Lasso, Antonio J. Escribano, Vicente Roca, Aida Powers, Angel Menendez, Ricardo Palacios, Dina Loy, Ramon Centenero, Antonio Padilla, Lorenzo Robledo

THE BALEARIC CAPER
aka Balaeri operazione Oro (It), Barbouze cherie (Fr), La Muerte viaja en baul (Production), Zarabanda Bing Bing (Sp)

A diver, working just off the coastline of Ibiza, recovers a metal box from a crashed airplane. Before he can return to his dinghy, however, another diver shoots him with a harpoon and takes the box. This diver, in turn, is promptly gunned down as he arrives back on land. The gunman attempts to drive off, but his path is blocked by a broken truck. He is killed by a blow-dart as he tries to have it moved. The box ends up in the hands of a gaggle of screaming girlies, who open it to reveal a scepter encrusted in precious stones. It is handed over to the director of a nearby museum (Harold Sakata—Oddjob from *Goldfinger*) for safekeeping.

Bumbling secret agent Fernando (Jose Luis Lopez Vasquez), meanwhile, has been ordered to make sure that the treasure is kept secure. He seems to spend most of his time—understandably—conducting surveillance upon the activities of Mercedes (Daniele Bianchi), a wealthy young lady with a penchant for expensive jewels. He's not the only oddball about. Polly (Mireille Darc) seems to have an unhealthy interest in the museum's latest exhibit—when she's not busy romancing local inventor Pierre (Jacques Sernas), that is. Bizarrely dressed tourists Giuliano (Venantino Venantini) and Sofia (Marilu Tolo) are also behaving suspiciously—and not just with his habit of wearing golfing clothes to the beach.

Unsurprisingly, they're all out to steal the treasure for themselves. After a number of comical incidents, it becomes clear that there are three different scepters floating around, only one of which is authentic. More sinisterly, someone is bumping off the assorted cast members. And just what has all this to do with a mysterious wooden box marked "Coopers of London," that keeps popping up in unexpected places?

*The Balearic Caper* is almost entirely frivolous, but immensely good fun. It looks like a million dollars, with crisp, colorful cinematography that shows off the Mediterranean settings to the fullest. The script, what there is of it, never gets bogged down with any of those unnecessary extravagances such as, well, plot or character development—but it's packed full of gags and comic set pieces, so it doesn't matter too much. It's interesting to see that Duccio Tessari, one of the great Italian action directors (*Kiss Kiss Bang Bang*, *Secret of the Sphinx*), contributed to the screenplay—it doesn't look or play entirely unlike one of his more lighthearted projects.

Indeed, the second half of the film is basically an extended comedy of errors, as all of the characters attempt to swap their forged scepters for what they believe to be the real one. By this stage, inevitably, everything has become so mixed up that nobody actually knows which the real one is anymore. You even get some speeded up, Keystone Cops-style car chases for your money.

As is the way with these things, there are several bizarre touches. This is not a film that is afraid to wear its influences upon its sleeves, and there is a car that's taken straight from *Chitty Chitty Bang Bang*—although this one is really rather cruddy, being able solely to drive around on its own and occasionally lift its bonnet. Stranger still, the aforementioned mysterious wooden box is not only able to shoot blow-darts, but can glide across land, sail underwater and even has a protective force field! The sight of a *Chitty Chitty Bang Bang* clone doing battle with a hovering casket is one of the more peculiar things I've seen in recent years.

Adding considerably to the entertainment value is a good cast. Regular genre stars Darc, Tolo and Bianchi are joined by Vasquez, a popular Spanish comedian, and Venantino Venantini—an Italian actor who regularly turned up in sidekick roles at the time (and often walked away with the film). It's strange to think that he's best known for being the guy who drills John Morghen's head in Lucio Fulci's *City of the Living Dead*. The only duff note is Sernas, who's likeable enough, but doesn't really have that much in the way of charisma (as opposed to, say, George Hilton). I guess that it would have been difficult not to cast him; he also gets a credit for supplying the original idea for the story.

Jose Maria Forque is an interesting Spanish director whose work is well deserving of rediscovery. Most of his films are similarly vibrant and stylish, ranging from horror (*Tarots*) to giallo (*The Eye of the Hurricane*). He also made a couple of truly demented titles: *Dame un poco de amoor* (a Spanish retread of *Head*) and *Beyond Erotica*, which features David Hemmings as a nutter who imprisons women at his isolated hacienda. Hopefully some of his oeuvre will be released on DVD someday—it's definitely more deserving than some of the bilge that turns up at the moment.—MB

CREDITS: Production: Ultra Film, Tecisa Film, Telestar Transatlantic; Director: Jose Maria Forque; Story: Jacques Sernas, based on an idea by Antonio Liberati; Screenplay: Jose Maria Forque, Giovanni Simonelli, Jaime De Arminian; Cinematography: Ceclio Paniagua {Eastmancolor – Widescreen}; Music: Benedetto Ghiglia; Original running length: 97 mins; Filming location: C.D.S. Studios, Ibiza; Country: Spain/Italy/France; Year: 1966

CAST: Jacques Sernas (*Pierre*), Mireille Darc (*Polly*), Venantino Venantini (*Giuliano*), Marilu Tolo (*Sofia*), Jose Luis Lopez Vasquez (*Fernando*), Daniela Bianchi (*Mercedes*), Harold Sakata (*the museum director*)

**Sylva Koscina is the center of attention on the Italian poster for *Baraka X 77***

BARAKA X 77

aka Agent X-77 Orders to Kill (UK unconfirmed), Agente X 77: ordine di uccidere (It), Baraka, Agent X 13 (WG), Baraka for Secret Service (unconfirmed), Baraka sur X-13 (Fr), Operacion Silencio (Sp)

The opening shot of *Baraka X 77* is of a plane flying along with obvious trouble since one of the engines is smoking like crazy. We then cut to inside the plane where Jose Suarez (as Frank) puts all the passengers to sleep with gas and steals some papers before jumping to safety as the plane crashes. However, the smoking engine is not mentioned by anyone, never becoming an issue in the scene. Perhaps the explanation was lost in translation. Apparently the distributors of the film in America played fast and loose with other details as well. In the English-language version, the title appears to be derived from a) Charles Vadile's (Gerard Barray) designation as agent X 77 and b) the mysterious words murmured by a gravely injured scientist, "Baraka 126," that are some sort of clue to the coded documents on his new invention.

The invention is another super fuel that will "advance the exploration of space by 10 years" and the plot devolves to stopping the bad guys from blowing up a factory where the invention is being worked on. This is where another glaring instance of monkeying with the plot becomes apparent. Late in the film Vadile's boss calls and tells him about this factory and where it is located. Vadile then goes through an elaborate scheme to obtain this very same information! You figure it out.

Barray is actually quite good in the role of a secret agent. He has the qualities required to seamlessly blend humor and determination, and his dark good looks are softened by an impish gleam in his eye. His love interest is Manya, played by the lovely Sylva Koscina, who graced several spy pictures. Here she plays a nurse who falls for Vadile and joins him in not only in bed but also on several adventurous episodes. The more we see of her, the better. Agnes Spaak (*Dr. Orloff's Monster*) plays a fellow agent with a weakness for men that results in her death.

Vadile drives like a maniac in his little red sports car, has a gadget that detects listening devices, and gets whipped by a muscle-bound henchman in the line of duty. Other gadgets are a gun loaded with cyanide and a cigarette that shoots gas (there are lots of gasses in this movie). The fights are okay, but there wasn't much effort put into making them appear spontaneous. In fact, the best fight Vadile has is with a woman who nearly bests him with her judo moves. The bulk of the Georges Garvarentz score consists of an annoying zither theme, but there is one nice jazz tune played on a radio.—DD

CREDITS: Production: Capitol Film, C.C.M., Prod. Cinematograficas Bacazar; Director: Edgar Lawson [Silvio Siano], Maurice Cloche (French version); Story: Odette Cloche, based on the novel "Silence Clinique" by Eddy Ghilain; Screenplay: Giovanni Simonelli, Eddy Ghilain; Cinematography: Franco Vitrotti, Juan Gelpi (French version) {Eastmancolor – Techniscope}; Music: Georges Garvarentz; Original running length: 97 mins; Country: France/Italy/Spain; Year: 1965

CAST: Gerard Barray (*Charles Vadile*), Sylva Koscina (*Manya*), Agnes Spaak (*Ingrid*), Jose Suarez (*Frank*), Renato Baldini, Yvette Lebon (*Elvire*), Aldo Bufi Landi, Gemma Cuervo (*Solange*), Gerard Tichy, Nadia Brivio, Giacomo Furia, Alberto Ceverini, Oscar Pellicer, Luis Induni

## THE BECKETT AFFAIR
aka L'Affare Beckett (It),
La Jungle des tueurs (Fr)

Here's a good, serious political thriller with a great soundtrack and a solid (if relatively minor) cast. Lang Jeffries, a spy flick stalwart, is agent OS 27, Rod Cooper, who tackles his assignment to impersonate a hit man with his usual no-nonsense approach. Starting in sword and sandal pictures, as did many of his cronies, Jeffries mined the espionage lode. Jeffries fits the bill as a rather dour but confident espionage agent, and his films are worth seeking out though few seem to be available in English on the gray market.

After a couple of (offscreen) murders, we are treated to a cool but short credit sequence with those nifty sixties graphics and a swinging tune. The Nora Orlandi soundtrack is quintessential spy pop worth the price of admission. The film spends the bulk of its running time in northern European winter settings, a favorite milieu of the spy genre and its fans, and the switch to Nicaraguan locations is handled with ease.

**Unmistakable symbolism on the French poster for *The Beckett Affair***

There are plenty of good lines to keep the viewer amused. Visiting an art gallery in Paris, Cooper is asked if a particular painting speaks to him. He replies, "Yes, mainly that this painter can't paint." When applying for the coveted job of hit man, Cooper is asked how much he hates Fidel Castro. His cynical response is, "Well, that depends on how much money you offer me." After bedding a beautiful babe, Cooper reassures her that he does indeed love her. She coos that he is perfect. Cooper then admits, "No, no, I have one little defect—I'm a liar."

Two of the most recognizable cast members are Ivan Desny and Massimo Righi. Desny played many unsavory characters in the fifties and sixties, but his spy flicks were very few. Righi was a favorite of Mario Bava, appearing in many of his films, usually playing the same type of weak-willed loser.

One interesting facet of the production is the number of times that bare breasts come this close to being exposed, but when we see a strip act in a nightclub, the stripper keeps her clothes on! There is a moment with lesbian overtones too when an older woman, one of the gang bent on overthrowing the Nicaraguan government, unzips the dress of one of her dance hall girls saying, "Any man who has you for a woman can't be too anxious to lose his life."

The plot seems a bit complex as it unravels, but as Coopers says, "Politics are full of mysteries," and director Osvaldo Civirani keeps us guessing right along with the good guys. No gadgets or raving madmen, but this one's a winner.—DD

CREDITS: Production: Wonder Film, Fono Roma, Compagnia Europea di Cinematografia; Director: Osvaldo Civirani; Story and Screenplay: Roberto Gianviti; Cinematography: Osvaldo Civirani; Music: Nora Orlandi; Original running length: 95 mins; Country: Italy/France; Year: 1966

CAST: Lang Jeffries (*Rod Cooper*), Ivan Desny (*Colonel Segura*), Krista Nell (*Paulette*), Andrew Scott [Andrea Scotti] (*Steve*), John Writing, Nathalie Nort (*Helen*), Bob Messenger [Roberto Messina] (*Aumont*), Lilia Nejung, Aldo Bonamano, Ivan Scratuglia, Max Dean [Massimo Righi], Carol Brown [Carla Calo] (*Nadia*)

## THE BIG BLACKOUT

aka New York dans les tenebres (Fr),
Perry Grant, agente di ferro (It)

This is an oddly winning film for one so hilariously inept. Star Peter Holden (as agent Perry Grant) looks the part of a suave spy and the plot is your typical far-fetched world domination type. The down side is the minuscule budget, which results not only in a bare-bones underground lair for the villain but humorous props along the way, the most funny of which we'll cover later.

The script is unnecessarily demeaning to women and that's saying a lot compared to its brethren. For instance, early in the film Grant visits the wife of a dead traitor to break the terrible news of his death to her. Before telling her however, Grant baits her into making out with him! It's scenes like this that give spy movies a bad name.

Our villain is played by Giulio Donnini, who looks very much like Peter Sellers in the role of Dr. Strangelove. He's an ex-Nazi, of all things, with the unlikely name of Anton Yosipovich, and he's invented a device that interrupts electrical power, causing panic among the populace. Actually he's invented two devices. Grant discovers one on his first trip into the underground lair. It's about the size of a book and can shut out the lights in the general area. Near the end of the film, Yosipovich unveils his more powerful model that can cloak the entire East Coast of America in darkness. It looks just like the other model, only it's huge! The sight of the mad doctor toting this contraption the size of a steamer trunk around is one of the genre's funniest images. It looks like a model built for a shrinking-people movie.

The script also contains many dialogue gems to be enjoyed. Upon capturing Grant, our villain offers to show him the whole setup of course, and he actually says, "Then I shall have to have you killed—you've seen too much." Early in the film Grant is assigned a partner to check out Yosipovitch's fashion house front. Grant will be the fashion journalist and his buddy will be his photographer. Upon arriving, Grant tells his guy in all seriousness to "look as professional as you can." His stone-faced partner replies "Okay."

Marilu Tolo plays the innocent employed by Yosipovich's right-hand man Giacomo Rossi-Stuart. When Grant finally explains to Tolo about the evil Yosipovitch, he describes him thusly: "In addition to science and espionage, he's always been interested in stock speculations." Now that's bad. Tolo gets her own silly lines to speak. When she's captured by Yosipovitch, she has faith that her spy guy will come to the rescue: "Grant will gladly risk his life if he can help others."

Rossi-Stuart has a girlfriend too, played by Seyna Seyn. She's in cahoots with the dark side naturally, but when she fails the mad doctor, he orders Rossi-Stuart to kill her then and there—which he does. It's a nice touch of poignant brutality that only fails to register much emotion because the relationship between the two lovers is never fleshed out, if you will. For some reason, Seyn is dubbed with a southern American accent here.

Other good things include an appearance by third-rate rock band The Planets (which features a drum solo), a fashion show with the usual hideous outfits including a bridal gown segment, a good soundtrack by Berto Pisano, and lots of enthusiastic fistfights. In the end things blow up only *fairly* good (another budgetary consideration) and you'll find yourself shaking your head not only at the cheapness of it all but more so at why you didn't hate it.—DD

CREDITS: Production: G.V. Fonorama; Director: Lewis King [Luigi Capuano]; Story: Ottavio Poggi; Screenplay: Remigio Del Grosso; Cinematography: Memmo [Guglielmo] Mancori {Cinemascope - Eastmancolor}; Music: Pisano-Vasco-Mancuso; Original running length: 100 mins; Country: Italy; Year: 1966

CAST: Peter Holden (*Perry Grant*), Jack Stuart [Giacomo Rossi Stuart] (*Roland*), Marilu Tolo (*Paola*), Seyna Seyn (*Sonia*), Giulio Donnini (*Anton Yosipovitch*), Antonella Murgia, Emilio Messina, Valentino Macchi, Umberto D'Orsi, Franco Balducci, Geoffrey Copleston, Mario Lanfranchi

THE BLACK BOX AFFAIR
aka Amenaza Black Box (Sp),
Black box affair: il mondo trema (It),
Le monde tremble (Fr)

**Turkish poster for the excellent *The Black Box Affair***

American-born actor Craig Hill is best known for his spaghetti westerns, but he makes an excellent secret agent and one wishes he had made more films in the genre. His steel-gray eyes and no-nonsense manner are perfectly suited for this type of thriller. Here he plays John Grant, an ex-agent coerced back into action by the promise of taking his revenge on the Russian agent Fabian (Rolf Tansa) who (mistakenly) shot his wife years earlier.

A plane bearing nuclear weapons is destroyed and the black box that verifies the authenticity and origin of attack orders is not found in the wreckage. Needless to say, if this box fell into the wrong hands, it could be decoded and false orders sent to begin another world war. When the Russians are revealed to be at a loss for its whereabouts, Grant must agree to a temporary truce with Fabian to prevent the "bamboo boys" (the Chinese) from using the box. But make no mistake, Grant will have his chance to settle his old score with the cad Fabian.

This film comes as a pleasant surprise. It strikes a perfect tone of lighthearted brutality and will please the aficionado and the casual viewer alike. Grant is teamed up with his old partner Pablo (Luis Marin), a part-Apache nicknamed Sitting Bull, naturally. The guy's also a ventriloquist (!) and has a mean streak a mile wide, so settle in for a buddy movie as these two make mincemeat of the opposing spies.

There are plenty of good fights to enjoy here. At one point Grant is holding three guys at gunpoint when he decides to toss away his gun and practice his hand-to-hand! A little later after Grant and Pablo rough up another three of Fabian's men, Pablo leaves his own mark by carving the foreheads of the thugs with FA, BI and AN with his trusty knife. Fabian fights back by blowing up a commercial airliner when he thinks Grant is on it. These guys are serious.

Grant's main squeeze here is Teresa Gimpera (*The Exquisite Cadaver*), who gets a little more entwined in the plot than usual, and Georges Rigaud has a cameo as a flustered general. Gianni Ferrio contributes a good spy score and a swinging title song.

Director Marcello Ciorciolini, billed here as James Harris and who directed several of the Franco and Ciccio comedies, makes good use of the colorful locations and keeps things moving at a good clip for most of the film. There's a bit too much amusement park footage in Vienna—except for a peek inside a spook house—and things degenerate into a shoot-'em-up in the end, but don't let that deter you. This one's above average in all departments.—DD

CREDITS: Production: Kinesis Film, Surgo Film, Alexander Film, Kalender Film International; Director: James Harris [Marcello Ciorciolini]; Story and Screenplay: Marcello Ciorciolini, Nino Cuevedo; Cinematography: Francisco Sanchez Munoz {Eastmancolor}; Music: Gianni Ferrio; Original running length: 96 mins; Country: Italy; Year: 1966

CAST: Craig Hill (*John Grant*), Teresa Gimpera (*Floriane*), Luis Marin (*Pablo*), Rolf Tasna (*Fabian*), Patricia Carr (*Miriam*), George Wang, Moha Tahi (*Ambra*), Georges Rigaud, Herbert Montureano, Ferdy Unger, Tony Francis, Mark Paskin

BLUEPRINT FOR A MASSACRE
aka Tecnica para un sabotaje (Sp),
Tecnica per un massacro (It)

Holy cow, someone's blowing up toy planes! Or, as a comatose newsreader would have it, the "...aroused (sic) public is in a state of alarm over continued air disasters that have struck at our military bases in the Mediterranean." Not to worry, more interesting things are afoot, most especially crotch-level shots of a beatnik babe shimmying about to the truly drugged-out Piero Umiliani title tune (performed by a certain Angel and The Brains!). Now that's what I call an opening.

After managing to avoid the clutches of the aforementioned boogying lassie, Danny O'Connor (German Cobos) travels to Beirut to see if he can put a stop to this sabotage (not to mention take in a cheesy nightclub act or two). The Secret Service suspect it's all the work of an ex-soldier called The Renegade, who heads an underground organization based in Istanbul.

He soon meets his contact, Steve Brand (Franco Ressel, resplendent in a white flat cap and cravat), who tells him that the planes are destroyed by having nitric acid added to their fuel—which means that someone must have infiltrated the military bases that house them. After a minor fracas while trying to find out some information, he trails a minor hoodlum to a yacht owned by anheiress named Ava (Maria Mahor).

After another plane explodes, the man who guards the fuel tanks is killed in a gunfight with the military police. He had been drugged with ATP, a substance that eliminates the individual's will and makes him susceptible to brainwashing with hypnosis. This means, of course, that it's not long before O'Connor is being subjected to the old mind-bending treatment and sent off to cause yet more damage.

*Blueprint For A Massacre* is a sequel to director Montero's *Desperate Mission*, which was filmed in the same year. In both of them, German Cobos plays Agent Z55, although for some reason the character name here is Danny O'Connor rather than Robert Manning. In many ways—despite looking cheaper and having an even flimsier plot—it is a distinct improvement upon its (rather gloomy) predecessor. Although it doesn't maintain the high kitsch level of its astonishing first five minutes, that doesn't mean that there aren't plentiful opportunities for mucho grooving to the superlative beat soundtrack (someone, please, release this on CD).

Cobos also seems to have settled more into the role. Whereas in the previous film he came across as a moribund Sean Connery, here he demonstrates an athletic touch and seems more at home with the lighter material. It is absolutely no surprise when Franco Ressel is revealed to be the mysterious Renegade (who seems to have absolutely no motive for his skullduggery apart from sheer cussedness). With his ever-present smug smile, twinkling eyes and ice cream suit, Ressel was a habitual villain in B movies from the sixties and seventies, and could always be relied upon to give a good show. Bald ex-stuntman Pietro Ceccarelli also has a bigger role than normal as a villain with a deadly lead (rather than left) hand.—MB

CREDITS: Production: Cineproduzioni Associate, Cesareo Gonzales; Director: Robert M. White [Roberto Bianchi Montero]; Story and Screenplay: Jesus Maria De Arozamena; Cinematography: Giuseppe La Torre {Techniscope – Technicolor}; Music: Piero Umiliani; Original running length: 104 mins; Country: Italy/Spain; Year: 1966

CAST: German Cobos (*Danny O'Connor*), Maria Mahor (*Asia*), Frank [Franco] Ressel (*Steve Brand*), Gaby B. Andrews [Gabriella Andreini], Mary P. Count [Maria Pia Conte], Erik Schippers, Irving G. Mayer, Charles Jerwis. Uncredited: Pietro Ceccarelli (*Max*)

BODY IN CENTRAL PARK
aka El club de los asesinos de Brooklyn (Sp),
Der Morderclub von Brooklyn (WG),
Murders Club of Brooklyn (unconfirmed)

New life is given the Jerry Cotton series by the introduction of color in the fifth installment. Director Werner Jacobs previously helmed the German language version of *Psycho-Circus* and co-directed *Horror Hotel*, and his enthusiasm for this material shows. Even the now-familiar themes by Peter Thomas are sassier and brassier, complimenting the new look.

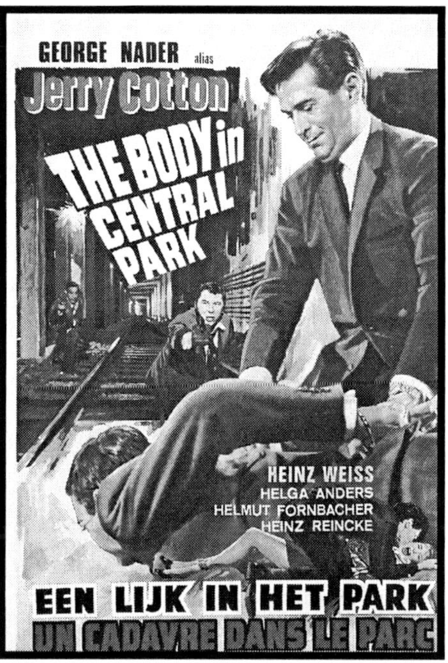

**Belgian poster for the first color Jerry Cotton film, *Body in Central Park***

A group of wealthy businessmen are threatened with the death of their children unless they pay one million dollars each. Jerry (George Nader) and his partner Phil (Heinz Weiss) are called in to ferret out the perpetrators. After a case of mistaken identity results in the death of an unrelated girl, Jerry suggests a payoff with newspaper instead of money and a stakeout to catch the killers. When the plan fails, the businessman's daughter is killed. Then a second and third businessman are extorted as Jerry and Phil scramble to end the deadly game.

Right off the bat we're treated to some derring-do by our heroes. Upon returning late one night to Jerry's apartment, he and Phil notice something wrong. Using a handy construction crane, Phil lifts Jerry to the window of his high-rise bachelor pad where he bursts in and beats up the waiting bad guys. This episode, unrelated to the rest of the following story, is deftly handled by the filmmakers and is fun to watch unfold. Jerry's apartment is decorated in particularly bad taste and includes an HO racing track with a tiny Jaguar car that Jerry must play with during his off hours.

The story seems like a swipe against the wealthy elite, and Jerry makes it clear that he holds the businessmen in low regard. For the most part, the men are depicted as callous, only concerned with the expense of extortion. No one would consider Jerry Cotton a liberal, but his disdain for the moneyed classes is an interesting facet of the character.

The crooks run circles around our boys for most of the movie. The first drop, where Jerry convinces the victim to substitute newspaper for cash, has Jerry and Phil standing around in front of footage of JFK airport not realizing that the suitcase was retrieved hours ago, resulting in the death of the man's daughter. The second drop is no more successful, as the money is swiped right from under Jerry's nose. The third attempt salvages the money but the daughter and her guardian Phil are both kidnapped. Jerry can't win for losing!

This third attempt had Jerry drop the money from a bridge onto a moving train. Jerry makes the jump onto the train as well and subdues the know-nothing thugs who were supposed to retrieve it. The sequence is a textbook example of action editing. Using three elements—Nader on a real moving train, Nader on a studio train set and stunt men on the real train—the sequence is one of the more successful blends of studio and exterior action in the series.

Phil's kidnapping prompts an unusual tender moment for Jerry as he goes through Phil's desk late one night and stumbles onto photos of the two of them on a fishing trip. Camaraderie in the extreme, wouldn't you say? There's also a strange and pointless plot twist when Jerry fakes his own death to confuse the kidnappers. This extravagance goes nowhere, but Jerry's full of ideas!

It's not much of a surprise when the "insider" culprit is revealed during the denouement, which plays like an old murder mystery story, but the final chase is a hoot as more studio antics try to pass as outdoor adventure.

Karel Stepanek (*The Frozen Dead*) plays one of the businessmen, and his son is played by Helmut Fornbacher, who was the gang member Percy in the first Cotton flick, *Operation Hurricane: Friday Noon.* Stepanek's daughter will be recognized by genre fans too: Dagmar Lassander shows up in Mario Bava's *Hatchet for the Honeymoon*, *Forbidden Photos of A Lady Above Suspicion*, *Legend of the Wolf Woman*, Lucio Fulci's *The Black Cat* and *House by the Cemetery.*—DD

CREDITS: Production: Allianz Filmproduktion, Constantin Film Produktion GmbH; Director: Werner Jacobs; Story: Alex Berg [Herbert Reinecker]; Cinematography: Franz X. Lederle; Music: Peter Thomas; Original running length: 96 mins; Filming location: New York; Country: West Germany; Year: 1967

CAST: George Nader (*Jerry Cotton*), Heinz Weiss (*Phil Decker*), Helmut Fornbacher (*Bryan Dyers*), Karel Stepanek (*Dyers*), Helga Anders (*Edna Cormick*), Helmut Kircher (*Bernie Johnson*), Heinz Reincke (*Sam*), Helmuth Rudolph (*Mr. Johnson*), Dagmar Lassander (*Jean Dyers*), Wolfgang Weiser (*Harry Long*), Daniel Dimitri [Slobodan Dimitrijevic] (*Malbran*), Franziska Bronnen (*Susan, a secretary*), Wolfgang Spier (*Randolph Warner*), Paul Muller (*Blees*), Rudi Schmitt (*Mr. Cormick*), Ira Hagen (*Sally Chester*), Horst Michael Neutze (*Richard Nash*), Reiner Brönneke (*Allan Byrnes*), Peter Lehmbrock, Richard Münch (*Mr. High*)

## BONDITIS

Suave, tuxedo-clad secret agent Frank Born (Gerd Baltus) manages to steal a secret formula hidden deep inside a subterranean base, pausing only to nonchalantly beat up a chubby Oliver Hardy look-alike. Or does he? Well, no. In reality Frank is a rather drab little nobody, plagued by dreams in which he is James Bond. Unfortunately, these dreams always turn into nightmares and he always dies horribly at the end of them.

**American poster for *Bonditis***

Things are getting desperate. He tries to kiss his doctor while daydreaming about a sexual escapade, calls his boss "Goldfinger" ("It went right to his head!"), and generally suffers from the nervous trauma of having to save the world every night. Finally, his psychologist diagnoses the problem: Bonditis, a disease ("like chicken pox") that is best cured by having a few weeks out of town.

Sensibly enough, Frank figures that the best way to get over his problem is to have a holiday in Switzerland, "the most innocuous country in the world." Unfortunately, just about every criminal organization and intelligence agency has figured the same thing. Russians, Americans, karate-fighting babes, nymphomaniac maids, men from UNCLE—they're all lurking about somewhere. And they all seem to think that Frank is in fact a hotshot secret agent.

The main villains in the piece are led by an evil, harp-playing old lady, with a bunch of "nephews" as henchmen. Their persistent attempts to capture our hero only help to persuade him that his hallucinations are becoming all the more powerful. Then he meets a female agent, Hata Sari (Marian Jacob), who forces him into helping her fulfill her mission by recovering a microchip hidden inside an egg and returning it to the American authorities.

Well, you don't get to see many Swiss films, but this is one of them (albeit with some input from Germany). As you'll undoubtedly have realized from the above synopsis, *Bonditis* is hardly the most serious of films. An amiable parody, it takes swipes at all the conventions and clichés of the genre by contrasting the "illusion" (the spies) with the "reality" (hapless Frank). It has useless gadgets (ice-pick submarine guns, a transistor hidden inside a Swiss music box), glamorous girls, and a plot that manages to be simultaneously simple and completely incomprehensible.

In fact, Gerd Baltus' Frank—a cross between Derek Nimmo and British Chancellor Gordon Brown—seriously reminded me of Austin Powers in the way that he bumbles through all manner of escapades, singularly unaffected by it all. Speaking of which, although this isn't as effective as Luciano Salce's *Slalom* (or another reference point, *The President's Analyst*), it is far better than Mike Myers' somewhat tiresome Powers films. The parody is less broad and scatological, relying on a charming sense of whimsy to carry things through. It certainly looks like it must have been a ball to make, the Swiss locations giving rise to assorted Alpine nonsense (including yodeling and gratuitous lederhosen-wearing) and some gorgeous landscapes.

It all ends up with Born tied atop a burning pyre at a festival while hidden in a "dummy" costume, like nothing so much as an irie *Wicker Man.* And any film that has wah-wah'ed trumpets impersonating chicken clucks on the soundtrack simply can't be faulted.—MB

CREDITS: Production: Turnus; Director: Karl Suter; Story and Screenplay: Karl Suter; Cinematography: Renato Faccinetto, Freddy Knubel {Technicolor}; Music: Werner Kruse; Country: Switzerland/West Germany; Year: 1968

CAST: Gerd Baltus (*Frank Born*), Marion Jacob (*Hata Sari*), Christiane Rücker (*the blonde*), Herbert Weicker ("*Der Asket*"), Bella Neri (*Heidi*), Gert Westphal ("*Der Brandmeier*"), Albert Mol ("*Der Weiche*"), Max Werner Lenz (*the hotel manager*), Henning Schlüter ("*Der Ringer*"), Peter Capra ("*Agentlehrbub*"), Sidney Arnold [Sydney Arnold] (*chief to Hata Sari*), Zarli Carigiet ("*Huttenwart*"), Moses LaMarr (*Prince von Tsulutsim*), Rosana (*the princess*), Paula Li Shiu (*head Chinese agent*), Phao Yan Tiong (*1st Chinese agent*), Michael Chen Ming Li (*2nd Chinese agent*), I Kan Wan (*3rd Chinese agent*), Kurt Bigger ("*Pfandfinderfuhrer*"), Elmar Schulte (*chief Russian agent*), Giovanni Früh (*Russian agent*), René Mathis (*the Italian*), MacGregor (*the weapons specialist*), Jerry Braward (*the blonde in the dream*), Marion Garai (*the train passenger in the dream*), Peter Oehme (*the Arab in the dream*), Julio Pinheiro (*the Indian*)

CARRE DE DAMES POUR UN AS

"square ladies for an ace"

aka Carre de dames pour Layton (orig title), Demasiadas mujeres para Layton (Sp), Layton...bambole e karate (It), Pokerspiel um vier Damen (WG)

The Intelligence Services are after a criminal mastermind called Gregory (Francois Maistre), and pull in a number of his known

**Spy imagery in the classic style on the Turkish poster for *Carre de dames pour un as***

acquaintances for questioning. Unfortunately, before they can find out anything interesting, a group of villains burst in and slaughter everybody. Gregory, it seems, is not a very nice man and he seems determined to wipe out every intelligence-operative his men can lay their hands on.

Only one man can find him, secret agent Layton (Roger Hanin), who keeps his true occupation so secret that not even his firecracker girlfriend, Marion (Catherine Allegret), knows what he does for a living. This makes things rather complicated when she discovers him *in flagrante*, as part of an undercover operation, with a female agent. Like any sensible man, he decides the best thing to do is hide from all of these women, get a hotel room of his own and enjoy an old-fashioned, boys-only game of poker.

Anyway, after all of this nonsense he finally knuckles down to his mission, which is made more difficult by the fact that Gregory has undergone extensive plastic surgery, so nobody knows what he looks like. Soon, however, he manages to obtain a rather obscure clue as to the villain's whereabouts: a pair of false teeth. Quite what these symbolize is a whole different matter, but if anyone can crack the mystery, our man Layton can.

*Carre de dames* is a lesser-known film from popular French star Roger Hanin. Which is a bit of a shame, as it's pretty darned entertaining. It's not really concerned with building up a great deal of tension, being happy to trot along in a suitably blithe fashion—and it's none the worse for that. This is from the breed of spy film that could be described as lighthearted as opposed to comic (in the Lando Buzzanca/Franco and Ciccio sense), and as such is slightly more palatable to the jaded palate of your average contemporary consumer.

Hanin understands all of this perfectly, and keeps his tongue firmly in cheek throughout, bringing an easygoing charm (more restrained than in most of his other genre performances) to the fore. He makes a good double act with a particularly pesky Chihuahua, eats lots of nice-looking food and sleeps with virtually every woman who moves (it must have been a hard life acting in these films). At one point a passerby exclaims, "He looks just like Belmondo," which may not be true but does sum up the mood perfectly. There's also a commendable running joke involving a group of elderly American tourists, led by tour-guide Marion, who appear just about every time he gets frisky with another woman. As an interesting trivia point, Hanin also happens to be the brother-in-law of former French president Francois Mitterand.

Also of note is a slightly odd, very good soundtrack from French sex-dwarf Serge Gainsbourg, and a truly effective climax set in a bullring. Strangely enough, the central premise of the film—that of the secret agent whose significant other is unaware of his true vocation—is distinctly similar to that of James Cameron's *True Lies*.—MB

CREDITS: Production: Societe francaise de Cinematographie, Agata Films, Leone Films, Ci Ti Cinematografica; Director: Jacques Poitrenaud; Story based on the story by Michael Loggan; Screenplay: Georges Bardawil, Gerard Carlier, Jacques Poitrenaud; Cinematography: Jean-Loup Debadie, Manuel Merino {Eastmancolor – Cinemascope}; Music: Serge Gainsbourg; Original running length: 90 mins; Country: France/Spain/Italy; Year: 1966

CAST: Roger Hanin (*Layton*), Sylvia Koscina (*Dolores*), Francois Maistre (*Gregory*), Catherine Allegret (*Marion*), Dominique Wilms (*Petula*), Guy Delorme, Laura Valanzuela (*Rosario*), Luis Pena, Francisco Piquer, Jose Jaspe (*Layton's partner*)

CAVE OF DIAMONDS

aka Die Diamantenhölle am Mekong (WG), Infierno de Mekong (Sp), Mission to Hell (US), La sfida vien de Bangkok (It)

This is probably best taken as a precursor to the far-superior Kommissar X series. In many ways it is a traditional adventure film, recalling the Gordon Scott Tarzan movies that had passed their zenith some years before. It's also not dissimilar to the "women in prison" films—like Eduardo Mulargia's *Escape From Hell*—that were to come more than 10 years later. However, there are aspects that give it away as spy film proper: exotic locations, international espionage, babes and an entertainingly insane villain.

Yakiris (Gianni Rizzo) is the nutter in this case, commandant of an illicit diamond mine hidden in the heart of the Thai jungle. The gems he unearths are then sold through a complex system that manages to keep the whereabouts of their origins secret. Unfortunately, this chain is being threatened by the interference of a known criminal, The Yellow Tiger (Philip Lemaire), who is already under the watch of the authorities.

Meanwhile, suave (i.e., repulsive) journalist Walter Compton (Paul Hubschmid) is carrying out his own investigations. He follows Van Meeren (Horst Frank), a representative of The Syndicate who has been assigned the task of tracking down the titular location. Somehow, they both contrive to go on safari into the Mekong, along with guide Joe Mullen (Brad Harris), a ditzy aristocrat broad and her prissy butler. Not, however, before everyone takes time out to visit a sleazy bar, where a dark-haired dame dressed like a chocolate box dances in an alarmingly similar fashion to my dad when he's drunk. Anyway, when they finally start their trek, they find that The Yellow Tiger is determined to make life difficult for them...and that's before they come face to face with the increasingly demented Yakaris.

There are some glaring problems with this mediocre production, not least of which is the lack of a sympathetic figure at the center. Brad Harris is fine as, well, Brad Harris really, but he always works best when he has a suitable sparring partner, and Paul Hubschmid falls woefully short in this department. There is also the use of some highly discordant stock footage. In one sequence it looks like a van is being chased by an elephant that is speeding through a *Star Trek*-style wormhole. The screenplay could have used some tightening—all too often we are led down irrelevant trails that act as more of a distraction than an embellishment—and the photography and music are reasonable at best.

However, there are compensations. Gianni Rizzo, a chubby actor who obviously impressed director Parolini (he went on to have major roles in several of his westerns), is delightful as the camp (in more than one sense) villain. It's also nice to see Horst Frank in a rare good(ish) guy role, although he still manages to wear his Panama in a cheekily lopsided manner and continually balance a smoke from his lower lip.

*Cave of Diamonds* can be safely filed as an adequate filler. It's painless, even momentarily enjoyable, and as such it does all that it set out to accomplish—while remaining simultaneously rather anonymous. The sole spy connection is

**Gianni Rizzo wields his whip in this German lobby card for *Cave of Diamonds***

that an unexpected character is revealed to be working for Interpol at the climax.—MB

CREDITS: Production: Matheus Film, Rapid Film, S.N.C.; Director: Gianfranco Parolini; Story and Screenplay: Johannes Kai, Gianfranco Parolini; Cinematography: Rolf Kästel, Francesco Izzarelli {Eastmancolor}; Music: Martin Böttcher; Original running length: 87 mins; Country: Italy/West Germany; Year: 1964

CAST: Paul Hubschmid (*Walter/Werner Hornfield*), Marianne Hold (*Vivian Lancaster*), Horst Frank (*Van Meeren/Jack McLean*), Brad Harris (*Jo Warren*), Dorothee Parker (*Gloria Pickerstone*), Chris Howland (*Smokey*), Philippe Lemaire (*Richard*), Gianni Rizzo (*Yakiris/Dr Sartori*), Michèle Mahaut (*Jeanette May-Wong*), Adriana Ambesi (*Tanzerin*), Richard Glemnitz (*a journalist*)

### CERO SIETE CON EL DOS DELANTE (AGENTE JAIME BONET)
"zero seven with the two ahead (agent Jamie Bonet)"

MI5 is in trouble. All of its agents are being relentlessly pursued by the enemy, which makes the day-to-day business of international intrigue extremely difficult. But what are they to do? Devise ever more subtle methods of espionage? Employ the most able individuals to outwit the Soviet threat? Heck no. They decide that what they need is a total goon of a spy, one who by his very unwitting actions is liable to throw anyone attempting to follow him—or even understand just what he's actually doing—into a complete state of confusion.

Conveniently enough, there happens to be just such a goon within easy access: Jaime (Cassan), a waiter at MI5 headquarters. Not only is this guy entirely accident prone, he also has a disconcerting habit of breaking into "pop-tastic" song whenever a backing band appears on the scene. He's soon put through a rapid training program, which sees him trained in judo and shooting (he's proves to be a natural at both, despite encountering slapstick problems while trying to show off).

Deciding that he's just about ready for his first mission, they send him on a trip to Barcelona, where his task is to track down a football—inside of which is hidden a top-secret microfilm. He soon attracts the attention of a number of dubious characters, all of whom are also after the microfilm (and all of whom appear to be even more hopeless than our hero). Thankfully, he is being assisted by a quartet of young ladies, who do their best to keep him out of any serious trouble.

Well, you don't get many musical/comedy/spy hybrids, but this is one of them. If you think the idea of merging such disparate—if not incompatible—genres is slightly wild, what makes it even harder to get a handle on is the fact that the hero is hardly a lithe, jiving youth (in the Frankie Avalon, Cliff Richard mold). He's actually a slightly portly, middle-aged chappie who looks alarmingly like your best mate's annoying dad. At one point he performs a particularly "hysterical" routine, involving prattling around on a stage with a whistle, which the crowd seems to enjoy but literally had me scrambling for the front door in an effort to escape.

There is a lot of physical humor, but not quite the same level of pratfalling nonsense as there is to be found in the Franco and Ciccio films, which stand as the hallmark for this type of thing. Unfortunately, it also doesn't approach the level of frank bizarreness of those films—which is what makes them most worth watching in the first place. There's plenty of speeded-up footage, as well as the quacking trumpet noises so beloved of low humor. One of the more idiosyncratic moments finds a villain poking his finger into Jaime's ear—only for its tip to emerge from the opposite side of his head. And that's one of the more sophisticated jokes.

This is also one of those films where all of the ladies are shot in such a way that they look deeply unattractive—even the ones who are rather gorgeous when they appear elsewhere. The female lead (Encarnita Polo), who also gets to perform a couple of song and dance routines, resembles nothing so much as one of those noxious tweenies that children were into a couple of years back. And speaking of children, I'm sad to report that rather a lot of them feature in this production—always the sign of a film to be viewed with utmost caution.

Even though *Agente Jaime Bonet* may appear naïve (if not downright stupid) to our cynical, contemporary palates, it should be noted that it was extremely successful domestically at the time of release—making far more money than such insignificant items as *The Ipcress File*. It should also be noted that however dumb it may be, this shows far more vim and vigor than many of director Igancio Iquino's "straight" films, which tend to be true no-budget trash of the lowest order.—MB

CREDITS: Production: IFI España; Director: Ignacio Iquino; Story: Ignacio Iquino, Armando F. Matias Guiu; Screenplay: Paquita Vilanova; Cinematography: Julio Perez de Rozas {Eastmancolor - Panoramica}; Music: Enrique Escobar; Original running length: 101 mins; Filming locations: Sitges, Barcelona, IFI Studios; Country: Spain; Year: 1966

CAST: Cassen (*Jaime Bonet*), Encarnita Polo, Gustavo Re, Joaquin Soler Serrano, Salvador Escamilla, Fernando Rubio, Luis Oar, Pajarito, Tunet Vila, Luis del Pueblo, Javier Conde, Alberto Gadea, Juan Manuel Simon, Ramon Hernandez, Telesforo Sanchez, Carmen Gallen, Juan Aymerich, Eduardo Lizarza

THE COBRA
aka Die Cobra (WG), El Cobra (Sp),
Il Cobra (It), Le Cobra (Fr)

The movie starts off well enough with a cheesy rock score by Anton Garcia Abril that leads into a cool psychedelic credit sequence, but it's all downhill from there. Peter Martell, who made a lot of spaghetti westerns, is a less-than-likeable lead. He's a swarthy brute with John Wayne delivery who is always getting the gun knocked out of his hand. Martell is Mike Rand, an ex-Treasury agent who, we are told, was discharged from a high security post "for the good of the nation." He must be a bad boy, all right. Rand says "man" a lot and muscles his way into bed with the high-class likes of Anita Ekberg. Her name's Lou and she runs a women's spa when she's not shooting up drugs. Ekberg looks pretty darn good for a strung-out junkie, but she's not given nearly enough to do here. The other big star, the one who is given way too much to do, is Dana Andrews. Andrews is Kelly, Rand's boss, and he's in on

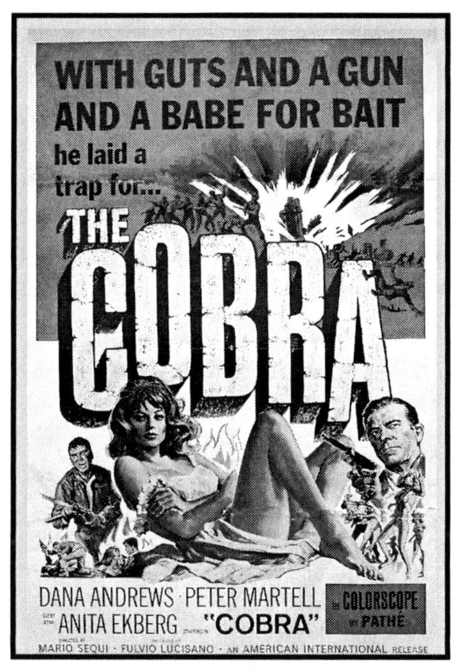

**American poster for *The Cobra***

a surprising amount of the action in the film. One wonders why, exactly. Andrews seems pretty deep into the sauce and his boot-blacked hair doesn't melt away the years the way they thought it would.

Kelly draws the picture for us of the diabolical plan of the Red Chinese to flood the country with opium. He feels that we'll all become raving junkies with no will of our own because he says, "The future of our country and the whole free world is at stake," therefore we need Mike Rand, a loser drunkard, to save us. By the way, Martell didn't make any more spy flicks, thank goodness.

Kelly's boss is Hullinger (Peter Dane), who plays around with Ekberg and acts so damn suspicious that you're sure he's in on the drug plot. He disappears toward the end of the film, his previous actions unexplained. The real bad guy, The Cobra, wears a black nylon mask to hide his true identity and his character is so well thought out that when his mask is torn off at the end of the film, you say to yourself, "who?" I'm going to reveal his identity but it won't spoil it for you because you'll never watch this if you know what's good for you. The villain of the piece is Stiarkos, a nightclub owner. He's played by Jesus Puente, who is not given enough screen time to register with the audience, so when Kelly removes the mask at the end he has to say "Stiarkos!" to remind us.

It's at Stiarkos' nightclub where we get to watch too much pseudo-native dancing before the booth that Kelly and Rand are sitting in revolves and they end up in a hidden office in a back room. This is where we first see the masked villain. He hands over the floor to a crazy Chinese guy who does a dog-and-pony show for our two heroes. He has a light board where he superimposes the "black chrysanthemum chart" over a map of the US that details the cities where the opium will be spread. This Chinese starts getting all excited, talking about his plans to "bring about the collapse of an already decaying society" and starts shaking and nearly foaming at the mouth. Everybody just looks at each other and then, embarrassed, The Cobra interrupts him. You know it's pretty bad when the villain, who wears a black mask and has the nickname of The Cobra, thinks you're crazy.

The poorly staged third act is the climactic attack on the oil refinery where the opium is loaded onto tanker ships. A special commando team is called in to help and these guys are unbelievable. They all have matching blue jackets and golf clubs! They actually take these golf clubs on the mission too, but they never use them. Are they supposed be incognito as a hopelessly lost foursome? We didn't notice a golf course next to the refinery, but maybe they know something we don't. The whole thing is truly bizarre but it sounds funnier than it really is, believe me.

There are some normal funny bits in the film. At one point Rand has to steal the bad guy's car to escape. As he's fighting with a thug, Rand suddenly slams the guy's hand in the car door. This is shocking because you don't expect it and the rubber hand gag is actually done well enough to evoke a scream of pain in the viewer. There's another weird moment when Rand, walking around a hotel, bumps pretty hard into a passing woman. He offers his apology and she says "No, I liked it!" and we never see her again.

To sum up, aside from a couple of bright spots, this is not really a good or fun film. You would have to be in a pretty tight spot to want to spend your time with Mike Rand, man.—DD

CREDITS: Production: Italian International Film, Dollar Film, Productores Exibidores; Director: Mario Sequi; Story: Adriano Bolzoni; Screenplay: Cumersindo Mollo; Cinematography: Enrique Toson, Claudio Racca {Techniscope – Technicolor}; Music: Anton Garcia Abril; Original running length: 98 mins; Filming location: Cinecitta Studios, Rome; Country: Italy/Spain; Year: 1967

CAST: Dana Andrews (*Captain Kelly*), Anita Ekberg (*Lou*), Peter Martell [Pietro Martellanz] (*Mike Rand*), Elisa Montes (*Corinne*), Jesus Puente (*Stiarkos*), Peter Dane (*Hullinger*), Luciana Vincenzi (*Ulla*), George Histman [Luigi Montefiore] (*Crane*), Omar Zoulfikar (*Sadek*), Giovanni Petrucci (*King*), Eshane Sadek Karter (*Gamal*), Chang'E (*Li Fang*), Conrado Sanmartin, Guido Lollobrigida (*the killer*), Jacques Stany (*employee of the journalism agency*), Lidia Biondi, Aldo Cecconi, Franco De Rosa

## CODE NAME: JAGUAR

aka Corrida pour un espion (Fr),
Persecución a un espía (Sp),
Spion, der in die Hölle ging, Der (WG)

This is the most serious of the contributions Ray Danton made to the genre of Eurospy movies. While still being light-hearted in nature, this film at least acknowledges the deaths of human beings in the line of duty. Danton is Jeff Larson, who his boss says can be trusted "with anything except, of course, my own daughter." Larson is shown to be rather cold-hearted about the deaths he causes, but in the end he is touched by the passing of his old friend and fellow agent Bob Stuart.

Stuart is played by Roger Hanin, who was secret agent Tiger in several movies. Stuart, injured some years before, was brainwashed but manages to overcome this handicap and free Larson from his Russian captors; he is shot to death for his trouble.

The film opens with a startling scene. A small boat is adrift when suddenly a huge submarine surfaces just behind it. The image catches us off guard and reminds us that unseen danger lurks just below the surface of everyday life. The event is caught on film by a nifty little button camera and transmitted to the Russians, kicking off the adventure. Other gadgets in the film include a device that unlatches doors, a brainwashing machine that flashes pretty colors on one's eyes (though it seems to do nothing when used on Larson), and a set of communicator rings that come in handy several times. The music, by Michel Legrand, is an unobtrusive and enjoyable Latin spy mixture.

The cast is world-class too. We have Horst Frank playing his usual bad guy who is shot, tortured and finally poisoned to death. Joining the fun is Wolfgang Preiss, Conrado San Martin (*The Awful Dr. Orloff*), and Carl Lange. The ladies include Pascale Petit as Pilar Perez, Larson's alliterative co-agent in Spain, Helga Sommerfeld (*Phantom of Soho*), and Grit Bottcher (*The College Girl Murders*) as the one pretty girl on a Russian trawler who ends up with Larson in her bedroom (of course).

One scene in particular is worth mentioning. Larson's disarming of a Russian mine that is protecting a surveillance camera is amusing for a couple of reasons. First of all, they have an audio recording of a previous—unsuccessful—attempt to disarm a similar mine which Larson listens to as he works. All he has to do is follow what they did and...uh, stop before the part where they blew up. And secondly, it's another instance of the filmmaker's old saw of generating "suspense" by having our hero defuse a bomb. Yawn.

If you're in the mood for a fast-moving, enjoyable adventure with a good cast, check this out. You won't be disappointed in these Bondian antics. Larson is...well, as he would put it, "Don't strain yourself, baby. No one's come up with the right word yet!"—DD

CREDITS: Production: Transatlantic Productions, Midega Films, Hans Oppenheimer; Director: Maurice Labro; Story: Claude Rank; Screenplay: Jean Meckert, Maurice Labro; Cinematography: Roger Fellous {Eastmancolor - Scope}; Music: Michel Legrand; Original running length: 103 mins; Country: France/Italy; Year: 1965

CAST: Ray Danton (*Jeff Larson*), Pascale Petit (*Pilar*), Helga Sommerfield (*Line*), Horst Frank (*Pedro*), Wolfgang Preiss (*Captain Parker*), Carl Lange (*Goloch*), Charles Regnier (*Rios*), Corrado Sanmartin (*Luis Moreno*), Manuel

**A gun blocks Ray Danton's face on the French poster for *Code Name: Jaguar***

Gil, Grit Bottcher, Roger Hanin (*Bob Stuart*), Alfonso Roas, Mario De Barros, Helga Lehner, Jose Bastida, Hector Quiroga, Pilar Gomez Ferrer, Antonio Pica, Rafael Vaquero, Lorenzo Robledo, Trio de Ases, Roberto Rey

Il CORAGGIOSO, LO SPIETATO, IL TRADITORE

"the brave one, the pitiless one, the traitor"

aka Acción en Caracas (Vz),

Le courageux, le traître et le sans pitié (Fr),

El hombre de Caracas (Sp),

Dem teufel ins gesicht gespuckt (WG)

Venezuela: a country in the throes of civil unrest. Revolutionaries, urged on by a seedy-looking chap in a brown leather jacket, hijack a train and murder everybody on board. Meanwhile, a man named Juan Sevilla (Espartaco Santoni) manages to escape from a hard-labor camp, despite being chased by a large number of soldiers and tracker dogs. Stealing a motorboat, he makes his way to Caracas where, attempting to avoid the police, he takes refuge in a bar. Conveniently enough, the gang who hijacked the train (including a bunch of pointy-bra-wearing lasses and led by someone who looks a college lecturer) are hanging out and go-go dancing in the very same place.

Impressed with his fighting (and fleeing) skills, they promptly equip him with an ice cream suit and a cravat (sounds like my kind of revolution). Inveigled into helping steal a truckload of explosives from an army depot, he is able to blow it up when some of his companions try—for some reason or other—to kill him. None too concerned, our man hangs around on the beach for a bit, taking the opportunity to chat up one of the more attractive female gang members.

It's all a cunning ruse, of course. Juan is actually an undercover agent whose mission has been to infiltrate the gang and bring about its capture. Unfortunately, things don't always work out quite as planned, and they discover his true intentions.

*Il Coraggioso* is generally credited to Juan Xiol Marchal, a little-known filmmaker who handled a couple of other, nongenre films (including *Seven Dollars For A Gringo*). However, certain sources name Eduardo Mulargia, a prolific director of better than average (if low-budget) B movies, as the real director. This isn't implausible: A similar thing happened with the western *Why Go On Killing*, which had Jose Antonio De La Loma as the named director. If so, this stands as Mulargia's only spy film, which is both surprising and a shame—it seems like a genre he could (and does) have some fun with.

If he was the director, it would certainly explain why this has a definite spaghetti western feel to it, as he was making rather a lot of them at the time (*Go With God Gringo*, *Cjamango*.). There are plenty of sweaty bandito types, much use of the close-up and a number of gunfight scenes. In fact, the whole thing is very much like a contemporary version of Leopoldo Savona's great western, *Killer Kid*—in which Anthony Steffen infiltrates a band of Mexican rebels—that was made the same year.

It also brings to mind a later, more exploitative Mulargia film, *Orinoco*, which again sets the action in South America (albeit with lots of bare-breasted ladies indulging in lesbian shenanigans). All of which adds up to make *Il Coraggioso* one of those strange films that, although very definitely belonging to a particular genre, seems to point up the similarities that underlie many of them. When it all boils down to it, the subtextual difference is that in spy films the bad guys wear sunglasses.

As for the film itself, it stands as better than average. The beginning quarter of an hour is fast paced and with virtually no dialogue whatsoever, the plotting is tight, there are some groovy sets and it's all filmed immaculately. As well as the inevitable scrap on a cable car (which leads to a hilarious bit of overacting as a minor villain plummets to his doom), there's a nice cat and mouse chase in a steelworks. Espartaco Santoni makes for rather a charmless, moody hero—which actually works surprisingly well (he was married to Mexican actress and co-star Tere Velasquez). He was also the lead in *Goldface*—which was also partly shot in Venezuela under the auspices of production companies Cineproduzioni Associate and Cin.cas Balcazar at around the same time. The climax does go on for way too long, but apart from that you couldn't really ask for more.

Unfortunately, this proved a particularly difficult film to track down. The only version I was able to find was an old print from Spanish television that flickered around like a flapper on coke. Another one to add to the "please release a letterboxed, English- language DVD" list.—MB

CREDITS: Production: Cineproduzioni Associate, Prod Cin.cas Balcazar; Director: Juan Xiol Marchal, Edward Muller [Eduardo Mulargia] (supervising director); Story and Screenplay: Conrad A. Roberts, Edward Muller [Eduardo Mulargia]; Cinematography: Mario Bistagne {Techniscope – Technicolor}; Music: Felice Di Stefano; Original running length: 90 mins; Filming location: Caracas; Country: Italy/ Spain; Year: 1967

CAST: Robert Anthony [Espartaco Santoni] (*Juan Sevilla*), Albert Alvarez (*Pedro*), Helene Chanel, Tere[sa] Velasquez, Ivy Holzer, Steffi Palmer [Stefania Possamari], Manuel Monroy, Ugo Pimental, Franco Beltramme, Belen Diaz, Jesus Maella

CRIME STORY

aka Colpo sensazionale al servizio del Sifar (It), S.I.D. contra Kocesky (Sp)

When an agent is killed in the line of duty, his buddy Robert Roller (Stan Cooper)—who also happens to be a wealthy playboy—is asked by the Secret Service to find out exactly who was responsible. At first he is reluctant, but soon becomes curious about the case. The only clue: a piece of paper in the dead man's pocket with the name of a respected scientist, professor Antinori (Livio Lorenzon), scribbled on it.

The professor, it seems, has invented a serum that enables human beings to become immune to the effects of radiation poisoning. The enemy (unstated, but with extravagantly Russian-esque names) want to lay their hands on it, with the intention of vaccinating their own population before commencing an all-out nuclear attack. Aware that Roller could be a danger to their plans, they attempt to entrap him through the use of beautiful, deadly women. This is deservedly unsuccessful.

Things become decidedly more complicated when Roller is framed for a murder. He manages to avoid arrest by citing diplomatic protection, but the police are far from happy. Knowing that time is not on his side, he sets a trap, with the professor acting as bait to catch the villains. It seems, however, that one of his colleagues is a traitor.

*Crime Story* is hardly the most exciting of spy films. It's bogged down by a really quite terrible script, one completely lacking in originality, disjointed and full of characters who appear for five minutes before vanishing into the ether. It certainly looks as though the version under review has suffered from some serious scissors-work, as several highly credited performers (Raho, Righi, Rossi Stuart) only have walk-on parts at most.

Having a certain level of narrative leeway is practically the prerogative of the genre, but this takes it to ridiculous extremes. Just how the unstated enemy agents fit in with all this (apart from padding out an extra minute) is completely beyond me, as the rest of the malefactors are either jealous associates of the professor or members of the local criminal underground. In fact, these guys don't even turn up in the Italian version. Plot strands are introduced and then forgotten about with willful abandon—which matches up with the fact that characters appear wearing different clothes in the same scene but is simply frustrating for the viewer.

Adding to this problem is the fact that, for the most part, this is played far straighter than is usual—perhaps reflecting its status as a late entry in the spy cycle. For sure, all of the genre trappings are present: hidden island bases, death by harpoon gun, babes tied to surgical tables and tortured. But it's all treated as though we're meant to take this nonsense seriously—which, of course, makes it impossible to do so.

The other major problem is the presence of Stan Cooper in the lead role. A familiar performer from the late sixties and early seventies, most of his films are terrible—and the ones that are any good seem to work despite, rather than because of, him. Here, he's simply far to wet to play a deadly secret agent, and seems far too preoccupied with keeping his suit clean and hair tidy. At one priceless point he falls down some stairs for no reason whatsoever. He isn't pushed, there isn't a tripwire—he's simply a klutz.

Director Merino, who also worked with Cooper on *Hell Commandos*, *More Dollars for the McGregores* and *Return of the Zombies*, is not at his best here. He attempts to throw in as many bizarre lighting effects as possible, but no amount of trickery could have much of an effect. Fortunately, things are buoyed up somewhat by an extraordinarily hysterical climax, which throws in catfights, colored gas, more harpoon guns and some terrible choreography. It's just a shame that it all ends with someone chucking a gun at the villain's head!

Apart from that, only a characteristically bellicose performance from Livio Lorenzon—and the sight of habitual spaghetti western villain and Sergio Leone favorite Aldo Sanbrell wearing a cheeky false wig and moustache—stands out as being anything more than thoroughly so-so.—MB

CREDITS: Production: Ikon Film, Hispamer Film; Director: Jose Luis Merino; Story: Gaetano Quarteraro; Screenplay: Gaetano Quarteraro, Lorenzo Artale; Cinematography: Emanuele Di Cola {Eastmancolor}; Original running length: 89 mins; Country: Italy/Spain; Year: 1967

CAST: Stan Cooper [Stelvio Rosi] (*Lt. Robert Rava*), Helga Liné (*Elizabeth, Antinori's daughter*), Humi Raho [Umberto Raho] (*police commissioner*), Max Dean [Massimo Righi] (*The Prince, "Princey Boy," an informer*), Gaetano Quartararo (*the colonel*), Aldo Sambrel (*Scarabesca*), Paco Sanz (*Professor Cociste*), Charles Sterling, Helena Sammarina [Yelena Samarina] (*Barbara*), Ivan Scratuglia (*El Moro, boat owner*), Ingles Rufino [Rufino Inglés]

(*the general*), Jack Stuart [not visible], Isarco Ravaioli (*Special Agent George Hansen*), and with Aurora De Alba, Livio Lorenzon (*Professor Antinori*).
Uncredited: Fulvio Mingozzi (*Rulos, 1st assistant*).

DANGER!! DEATH RAY
aka Mike Morris jagt Agenten in die Hölle (WG), Nido de espias (Sp), Il raggio infernale (It), Le rayon infernal (Fr)

Professor Carmicheal is a scientist who seems to take an unwholesome degree of pleasure in demonstrating his new, spanking Death Ray to all and sundry, on a top-secret basis of course. It arouses the interest of NATO, which realizes its potential as a defensive weapon to help ensure world peace. Which is useful, as the only way you can harm someone with the darned thing is to get within five meters and point it at them. Nonetheless, it also arouses the attention of Frank (Nello Pazzafini), a big dude in unlikely spectacles, who promptly kidnaps the inventor intending to force him to make one for his own personal use. Well, it's better than a fiber-optic lamp, I guess.

Special agent Bart Fargo (Gordon Scott), who seems more accustomed to lolling around in bed displaying his manly torso, is assigned the mission to locate and retrieve Carmichael. He promptly recognizes Frank from CCTV footage, and jets off to Rome and then Barcelona in his search for the missing scientist. Along the way he is shot at by a guy with a silly false beard, has a fight in a trendy bar, and flirts with an "artist" (Maureen Denphy) who likes painting nudes and painting in the nude. Just to make sure we understand the proper scheme of things, it's only a matter of minutes before our man Bart has her doing his ironing—what a guy!

Frank, naturally, is revealed to be working for someone else, someone who happens to be very close to the professor and who is determined that no one should foil their insane plot. Which, unsurprisingly, Bart does.

So is *Danger!! Death Ray* an allegory about the way in which single-minded scientists create weapons of mass destruction for altruistic reasons, only to see their creations misused by assorted power brokers? Frankly, no. It's a middling spy film that never really seems to go anywhere apart from yet another fistfight, meandering along to its own aimless rhythm—one that leaves the audience adrift after about 30 minutes. It's not a terrible film, despite the best efforts of a special effects team that seem determined to film the worst "toy submarine in a bathtub" shots ever. There are some half-good sequences, most notably the one in which Fargo has to make his way through a heavily booby-trapped villa. It just fails to become anything other than dedicatedly average—which is probably all it ever had ambitions to be.

Gordon Scott was a former Tarzan star and one of the best of the peplum stars, appearing in great films such as *Goliath and the Vampires* and *Duel of the Titans*. As well as being well-muscled and actually looking pretty good (as opposed to just looking big), he could actually act a bit. He made a couple of reasonable westerns: *The Tramplers* and *Buffalo Bill, Hero of the Far West*. He's perhaps a bit too baby-faced to be believable as the rather clinical Bart Fargo, but he does look good in shades and a suit. Chunky Nello Pazzafini, a stuntman turned actor who must have appeared in well over a hundred films throughout the sixties and early seventies, has a good role and does well with it. Perhaps the most interesting performance comes from Massimo Righi, another great Italian character actor, as the weak-willed gangster who becomes one of Fargo's strongest allies.

**Belgian poster for *Danger!! Death Ray***

There's also a very odd final scene. As our hero and his annoying lady friend get down to what you'd expect your average secret agent and lady friend to do at the end of a spy movie, they are interrupted by his radio watch, which is promptly chucked out the window and lands in the swimming pool. Only to reappear in someone's (perhaps that pesky SFX technician's) hand, who chucks it—again—into the swimming pool. A continuity gaffe that merely confirms the general sloppiness of the film-making and paucity of the production values on show.—MB

**Belgian poster for *Danger Route* features a slinky Barbara Bouchet**

CREDITS: Production: Meteor Film, Leda Film; Director: Frank G Carrol [Gianfranco Baldanello]; Story: Dick Arthur, Al Christian [Aldo Cristiani]; Screenplay: Paul Fleming [Domenico Paolella], Jaime Comas, Juan Cabezas; Cinematography: Manuel Hernandez San Juan {Eastmancolor - Panoramica}; Music: James Anderson [Gianni Ferrio]; Original running length: 89 mins; Filming locations: Interstudio, Modena, Capri; Country: Italy/Spain; Year: 1967

CAST: Gordon Scott (*Bart Fargo*), Maureen Delphy (*Lucy*), Ted Carter [Nello Pazzafini] (*Frank*), Albert Dalbes (*Dr. Carver*), Silvia Solar (*Carver's girlfriend*), Max Dean [Massimo Righi] (*Al*), Tor Altmayer [Tullio Altamura] (*Professor Carmichael*), Rossella Bergamonti (*Roberta, Raymond's secretary*), Valentino Macchi (*cctv camera operator*), Tina Di Pietro, Ignazio Balsamo, Carlos Hurtado, Juan Sant [St.] Cruz (*Raymond, the head of intelligence*), Julian MacMillan [Giulio Maculani] (*Gary, Frank's accomplice*), Fernando Rubio, Jane Peters, Larry Sheffield, Edwin Moore

DANGER ROUTE
aka Ruta peligrosa (Sp)

Based on the novel "The Eliminator" by Andrew York, this deeply cynical look at the spy game is one of the unsung gems of the genre. It was the only spy film in director Seth Holt's short career, although he had previously worked on the *Danger Man* and *Espionage* television series. Holt started one more film, *The Curse of the Mummy's Tomb*, but didn't finish it due to his untimely death.

This is one of those movies where everyone's motives are suspect and should be for good reasons. Hardly anyone is who they seem to be and if indeed they are genuine, they end up as dead as the straw men in the end. There are many levels to *Danger Route*, all working to subvert our expectations as well as those of Jonas Wilde (Richard Johnson), the agent caught in the middle of the power plays going on around him. Johnson is well cast, as his sour demeanor and world-weary looks perfectly embody the frustrated, suspicious Wilde.

Take his latest assignment for example. Wilde is told to kill a defector who is coming over to our side, and who, it is thought, could do significant damage to the Brits if he were to reach the shores of America. The Americans have the defector and the Brits are willing to let them chalk it up to their own inefficiency if he meets with an "accident." This little setup, with its own cynical ambiguities, encapsulates the attitude of the film. No one is to be trusted, everyone is suspect.

To accomplish the task, Wilde ingratiates himself with one of the staff, Rhoda (Diana Dors), where the defector is to be taken before leaving for America. Wilde affects a working-class accent and charms the unsuspecting, needy woman into taking him into her bed. The themes of alienation run solid in every direction of the film. Wilde previously had made an unexpected visit to his superior, Canning (Harry Andrews), at his home and notes to the man how Canning's wife doesn't think Wilde fits into their upper-class world. Not only is Wilde an outsider in Canning's world, he's an outsider in Rhoda's world as well. His life is a lie. From the false identity set up for him when he's not working to the false identities he assumes when he goes to work, it's a vicious cycle that Wilde admits is wearing him down.

Wilde's girlfriend, Jocelyn (Carol Lynley), also leads a double life. She supposedly has a job in market research, which of course isn't true. Appearances are so jaded in the film that even her false identity is a cynical one. Disenchantment with the powers that be is expressed by Wilde's closest friend, Stern (Gordon Jackson), when he says, "It doesn't matter what country you work for. If you're not a member of the ruling class, you're a sheep. In England you have to be born a shepherd, I'm afraid." Even Stern turns the tide on Wilde in the end, an event that barely registers on the psyche of Wilde by this time.

At one point, the supposed niece (it goes on and on!) of an associate of Wilde's asks if Jonas is his real name. Wilde's answer is, "I've caused an awful lot of trouble for a lot of people." This niece, Mari (Barbara Bouchet), is supposed to be from California but turns out to be from Hungary. The deceptive atmosphere also pervades the traditional hierarchy in Whitehall. But to say more about that would be saying too much. Trust no one when you watch this film.

In Wilde's world, even the bad guys are good guys. Temporarily captured during his assignment, his captors are from the CIA—supposedly on the same side as the British. His interrogator, Lucinda (Sam Wanamaker), remarks during their little chat that "You British…you still trust each other." But nothing could be further from the truth. Lucinda arranges for Wilde to escape so he can be followed. Wilde discovers the transmitter and symbolically sends Lucinda on a wild goose chase.

Understandably, Wilde would like to escape the game and hands in his resignation during the course of the film. Naturally we know this is impossible. Even Whitehall is not above using a little blackmail to get their way. The freeze-frame of Wilde at the end of the film tells us that his predicament is as unchanging as that of the Cold War politics surrounding him.—DD

CREDITS: Production: Amicus Productions; Director: Seth Holt; Story based on the novel "The Eliminator" by Andrew York; Screenplay: Meade Roberts; Cinematography: Harry Waxman; Music: John Mayer; Original running length: 95 mins; Country: UK; Year: 1968

CAST: Richard Johnson (*Jonas Wilde*), Carol Lynley (*Jocelyn*), Barbara Bouchet (*Mari*), Sylvia Syms (*Barbara Canning*), Diana Dors (*Rhoda*), Harry Andrews (*Canning*), Gordon Jackson (*Stern*), Maurice Denham (*Ravenspur*), Sam Wanamaker (*Lucinda*), David Bauer (*Bennett*), Julian Chagrin (*Matsys*), Reg Lye (*Balin*)

## DANIELLA BY NIGHT

aka Capricci borghesi (It), Daniela (Sp),
De quoi tu te meles, Daniela (Fr),
Zarte haut in schwarzer seide (WG)

This is a pre-Bond spy adventure centered around stolen microfilm, a small and common plot for the time before the genre took to more aspiring heights. Elke Sommer plays Daniella Neumann, who is hired to replace a murdered model for Count Castellani's (Ivan Desny) fashion house in Rome. Castellani is a spy you see, who is using the business as a cover for his trafficking in stolen microfilm. These efforts become complicated when Castellani's romantic liaisons begin encroaching on his nefarious activities and Daniella is drawn in merely as a result of her proximity. Castellani convinces her of his good intentions, passes the film to her and the chase is on.

I can honestly say this is the first 1960s Eurospy flick I've seen that features full frontal nudity—and by the star herself, no less. Apparently the film was somewhat scandalous at the time, which no doubt helped ensure profits where they were not necessarily deserved. The offending scene takes place in a strip club appropriately enough, shortly after a poorly choreographed segment where five strippers remove their tops somewhat in unison. Daniella has just stolen the microfilm back from the thief who stole it from Castellani, and she is chased onstage where two thugs remove her clothing in an effort to find it. The crowd is led to believe

**A poor likeness of Elke Sommer on the Belgian poster for *Daniella by Night***

this is all part of the show of course, as Daniella is rather politely stripped and modestly reveals her every charm to the cheering mob. At least she didn't give up the microfilm. But where is it? I won't spoil it for you but it's not where you think it is.

Daniella knows no more about the various spies on her tail than we do, but it is hard for us to believe that Desny is playing a good guy when he's played such a splendid villain in so many other genre offerings. The bulk of the film is spent with Daniella avoiding capture by all the factions chasing her. When it finally comes down to brass tacks at the end, the real good guy is revealed to be journalist-cum-spy Karl (Helmut Schmid, *The Head*), which isn't particularly surprising to us because he's a rather strong-jawed fellow who hasn't done any nasty things as the picture has unfolded.

Charles Aznavour and Georges Garvarentz, two big names in the field, contribute an excellent jazz score that is practically wall-to-wall. The bottom line, so to speak, is that this slight tale is entertaining enough once but undoubtedly its notoriety is the real reason it has survived at all.

First Run Features has released this on DVD but the dark, scratchy print and low-grade authoring result in a viewing experience that is little better than a VHS tape would provide. It is presented full frame, which appears correct, and in French language with English subtitles.—DD

CREDITS: Production: Contact Organisation, P.I.P., Pandora Film, Branoner; Director: Max Pecas; Story based on a novel by Walter Ebert; Screenplay: Wolgang Steinhardt; Cinematography: Andre Germain; Music: Charles Aznavour, Georges Garvarentz; Original running length: 85 mins; Country: France/West Germany; Year: 1961

CAST: Elke Sommer (*Daniella*), Ivan Desny (*Count Luigi Castellani*), Helmut Schmid (*Karl Bauer*), Kathe Haack (*Daniela's mother*), Romana Rombach (*the director*), Danik Patisson (*Claudine*), Claire Maurier (*Esmerelda*), Rene Dary (*Rene Lanzac*), Sandrine (*Nicole*), Brigitte Banz (*the mannequin*), Andre Dumas, Robert Blome, Francoise Alban, Ruddy Lenoir, Robert Darame

THE DAY THE HOTLINE GOT HOT
aka Hotline (US, alt), Le Rouble à deux faces (Fr), El Rublo de las dos caras (Sp)

Once upon a time in Stockholm, there was a man who always told the truth—he was otherwise normal…

Poor old Eric Ericson (George Chakiris): He simply can't tell lies, which means that he isn't a particularly good computer salesman. It also creates some social difficulties ("I just…don't want to come to dinner").

Meanwhile, a bunch of old biddies attack a Stockholm telegraph office and force the young operator, Natascha (Marie Dubois), to send a series of messages that seem intended to start a quarrel between the Kremlin and the White House. Even more bizarrely, poor Natascha is then chloroformed by the sinister spinsters and bundled into a trunk. They seem to be following instructions from a dodgy character called Truman (the excellent Gerard Tichy)—who also happens to be the "top contact in Europe" for both the Russian and American intelligence services.

**George Chakiris and IBM product placement in *The Day the Hot Line Got Hot***

okay, but you can't help but feel that Jean Seberg would have made much more of the role. Fortunately, old pros Robert Taylor and Charles Boyer are on hand to provide some suitable thespian class.

This is another one of those films (see also *Hot Enough For June*) in which the West and East are shown as being almost exactly the same. The Boyer and Taylor characters are mirror images of each other, and most of their agents are so used to working for both sides that they can't even remember who's who. One of the most attractive things about these films is the way that they have absolutely no respect for the authority figures—and even a concept—of the Cold War. Considering that Senator Joe McCarthy was still embarking on his anti-Communist crusade a little more than 10 years beforehand, this was actually quite groundbreaking (although it was only a matter of time until people began to realize quite how patently ridiculous the whole thing was). Perhaps this refreshing cynicism had something to do with the fact that *Hot Line*'s American co-writer Paul Jarrico had been blacklisted in the early fifties.—MB

Eric becomes mixed up in all of this nonsense through the oldest plot device in the book. Upon arrival in Barcelona for a new job, he picks up the wrong trunk. Yes, rather than containing his luggage, it actually contains the unfortunate Natascha. Moreover, the biddies—as well as an assortment of secret agents—are all too aware of this, and want their prisoner back. They also seem to believe that Eric is working for someone (other than IBM, that is).

Amongst all the merry frolicking, there is actually something resembling a plot buried way down here somewhere. Truman is planning to kidnap the heads of both the American and Russian Secret Services (Robert Taylor and Charles Boyer, respectively) for a decidedly unique reason (that I will resist elaborating upon). He's planning to use Natascha—who has been blamed for the inflammatory telegraphs—as bait to attract them to Barcelona.

The tone for *Hot Line* is set by the incredibly cheesy title sequence, which ushers in yet another slice of entertainingly trivial Euro-fluff. Snazzily directed and amiably scripted, it has all the depth of a puddle, but there are far worse ways of spending 90 minutes. The idea of "evil" old ladies carrying out acts of international espionage is a good one, and as much mileage as possible is made out of it.

On the other hand, I can't say that I was hugely taken with the two leads. Oscar- winner George Chakiris (for *West Side Story* in 1961) looks suitably preppy, but is hardly the most charismatic of performers. Marie Dubois is

CREDITS: Production: Balcazar P.C, Intercontinental Productions; Director: Etienne Perier; Story: Gordon Trueblood, Dominique Fabre; Screenplay: Paul Jarrico; Cinematography: Manuel Berenger {Eastmancolor - Panoramica}; Music: Paul Misraki; Original running length: 100 mins; Country: Spain/France; Year: 1968

CAST: Charles Boyer (*Vostov*), Robert Taylor (*Nicholson*), George Chakiris (*Eric Ericson*), Marie Dubois (*Natascha*), Gerard Tichy (*Truman, aka Vasili Smirnoff*), Marta Grau (*old lady*), Irene D'Astrea (*old lady 2*), Josefina Tapias (*old lady 3*), Maurice de Canonge (*the hotel manager*), Gustavo Re (*the Spanish inspector*), Oscar Pellicer, Frank Oliveras, Jack Rocha, Mel Welles (*General Bukov*). Uncredited: Al Mulock (*prospective IBM customer*)

DEAD BODY ON BROADWAY
aka Broadway sangriento (Sp),
Deadly Shots on Broadway (Int),
Todesschusse am Broadway (WG)

The Jerry Cotton series goes out on a sleazy note as the filmmakers add nudity, profanity and more brutality in a vain effort to keep the series afloat. Even Peter Thomas lets us down with a signature song that will have you grinding your teeth.

Undercover FBI man Johnny Peters (Dean Heyde) dumps a load of gold bars off a pier just before being killed by the gang he had infiltrated. The gang is captured but the leader, Costello (Miha Baloh), is liberated by a rival gang who thinks he knows where the gold is—which he doesn't. Jerry (George Nader) tracks down Johnny's girlfriend, Cindy (Heidy Bohlen), thinking she might have a clue—which she doesn't. Cindy agrees to help but soon finds Costello (who has changed his face) and the rival gang both after her and the gold while Jerry tries to sort out the mess.

Jerry is plainly in a bad mood for much of the film and I don't blame him. Perhaps Nader was supposed to play Jerry a bit tougher this time, but he just comes across as a jerk, making snide remarks and bickering with partner Phil (Heinze Weiss) like they were an old married couple. Jerry gets chained up and beaten in the course of this adventure but it's nothing compared to what the character of Cindy has to put up with.

Cindy is constantly the object of suffering throughout the film. She's sprayed in the face with chemicals, forcibly abducted twice, tortured, and then a transmitter the size of a cigarette is injected under her skin. She spends much of the time in the line of fire—always where the action is—but she still manages to sing that lousy song at the club where she works not once but twice. What a trouper. The club where she sings has a wild ultra-modern design, but that song she sings is so terrible that you have to wonder if it's a really a Peter Thomas composition. Other locations don't come off as well. Early in the film as Jerry begins his search for Cindy, he visits a dance studio that is supposed to be just off Broadway, but clearly this place is some warehouse on the outskirts of Berlin, time zones away from The Great White

**Belgian poster for the final Jerry Cotton film, *Dead Body on Broadway***

Way. It's here we go where no Cotton film has gone before: blatant sexploitation, timid though it may seem. Witness the spectacle of a skinny dancer taking her top off in a manner as far from erotica as the studio is from New York.

Jerry continues his search, stopping in at the "Flamingo" casino in Las Vegas. You won't believe what is supposed to pass as this big-name gambling den. A few slot machines and a couple of tables is not the image the real Flamingo would like to have presented, I'm sure. It's so hopelessly and depressingly low-rent you think you're watching an American film! Jerry eventually ends up at Boulder Dam (!) where Cindy has gone to escape the glamour (and danger) of Vegas.

Once Jerry returns Cindy to NYC, he and Phil install a surveillance camera in her apartment. At one point the boys gleefully watch her take her clothes off. I guess they forgot to mention the camera to her. This ill-conceived racy moment is so completely out of character for our straight-arrow heroes that you know something has gone horribly wrong. The hidden camera does lead to one truly classic JC moment however. Jerry notices two thugs going through Cindy's place and he naturally races up to beat the dickens out of them. When Phil sees what's going on, he too tears up to the apartment to help Jerry. When Phil bursts into the room—gun in hand—Jerry, disheveled from the fight, just looks at him and says "Well Phil, that's no way to come into a lady's bedroom."

Another curious dialogue line occurs when Costello is broken out of the police van that was taking him to prison. Tear gas is shot into the van through the air vent. The dim bulbs passing as cops are suddenly surrounded by the gas and when one cop asks his partner what's going on, his brighter half responds "I dunno. Lousy New York fog, eh?"

There is one strange stunt in the film when Costello, during one of his escapes, kidnaps a kid and makes his getaway in a milk truck. Jerry manages to jump onto the truck and get to the back of it without being noticed. He then takes out his trusty Swiss Army knife, loosens one of the metal bars on the floor, and uses it to propel himself through the wall and into the cab of the truck! Jerry's mind works in mysterious ways. Costello has fled the truck by this time, but not before giving the kid a toy to play with: a live hand grenade! You gotta like this guy.

In the end, Costello figures out the location of the gold bars and is dredging the water in an effort to bring up the gold when Jerry arrives to save the day. Their fight results in the poignant but extremely unlikely death of Costello by accidental gold bar bludgeoning! The finale has Cindy returning to the club to sing that damn song again, but there's a surprise waiting: Dieter Eppler makes an unbilled appearance as her agent! His familiar face makes one remember the simpler times when women were exploited with their shirts on. So goes the saga of Jerry Cotton. Like most film series, the final fade is not on the brightest note, but this note still has a certain ring.—DD

CREDITS: Production: Allianz Filmproduktion, Terra Filmkunst; Director: Harald Reinl; Story and Screenplay: Rolf Schulz, Christa Stern; Cinematography: Heinz Hölscher {Eastmancolor}; Music: Peter Thomas; Original running length: 89 mins; Filming locations: Las Vegas, New York, Hamburg; Country: West Germany; Year: 1969

CAST: George Nader (*Jerry Cotton*), Heinz Weiss (*Phil Decker*), Heidy Bohlen (*Cindy Holden*), Miha Baloh (*Joe Costello*), Michaela May (*Alice Davis*), Horst Naumann (*Woody Davis*), Konrad Georg (*Mr. Ross*), Herbert Fuchs (*Butler Robin*), Manfred Reddemann (*Hairy*), Karl-Heinz Thomas (*Dick*), Ulli Kinalzik (*Freddy*), Arthur Brauss (*Hank*), Rudolf Fernau (*Nasen-Charly*), Dean Heyde (*Johnny Peters*), Gerd Frickhöffer (*Bob Hiller*), Klaus Hagen Latwesen (*Tonio*), Belarminou Gomis (*Jim the butler*), Albert Venohr (*Mr. Truman*), Dieter Eppler (*Cindy's agent*)

## DEAD RUN

aka Chauds les secrets, Qui veut tuer Carlos (orig Fr), Deux billets pour Mexico (Fr), Geheimnisse in goldenen Nylons (WG), Segreti che scottano (It)

Berlin in winter. The days are wet and dark, the deeds darker. Thus the scene is set for one of the genre's most enjoyable serious entries. Yes, it's a simple story—there are no madmen with visions of world domination, no fancy gadgets to distract—but it's a story told with flair and the swift pace is that of the petty thief on the run, drawn into a high-stakes game of espionage.

Director Christian-Jaque pulls all the elements together this time—a first-rate score by Gerard Calvi, a great and varied cast, an excellent script and appealing locations—resulting in a minor gem. Dutch camera angles abound as we chase the European winter in Berlin, Lucerne, Paris and Vienna. The look of the film manages to stay just this side of drab. The natural light is weak, but the feeling isn't one of hopelessness; rather it's a sort of dignified gloom.

Peter Lawford, in a restrained performance, is Stephen Daine, a CIA man sent after stolen secret documents. He describes himself as "...a frogman, parachutist. I can do the supersonic war cry that kills at 63 feet. I know 10 languages, 12 dialects. I'm a walking computer..." Dain's interplay with lovely innocent Suzanne Belmont (Ira von Furstenberg) maintains a humorous mood but never swerves into camp.

The rest of the cast is filled with names familiar to the Eurotrasher: Werner Peters, Horst Frank, Luciano Pigozzi, Herbert Fuchs

**Another busy Turkish poster this time for the spy/crime hybrid *Dead Run***

and Wolfgang Priess, to name a few. Each of these gentlemen has earned their place with their journeyman efforts in many films made in the sixties and seventies. It's most enjoyable every time a familiar face shows up.

Peters (with hairpiece) plays Bardieff, a higher-up in the "international organization" also on the tail of the secret papers. Frank plays Manganne, his sadistic ally, naturally. Manganne's specialty is torture and when he inadvertently kills the man who originally carried the papers, Bardieff remarks to him "Many of your patients seem to die on you these days." To which Manganne replies, "Since when is death not a normal, rational outcome of torture?" He's got a point.

Georges Geret (*They Came to Rob Las Vegas*) is Carlos, the small-time crook who steals the wrong thing when he grabs a briefcase dropped by a henchman in the line of duty. Carlos spends the rest of the film trying to sell the documents that were inside it, touching off a bidding war of sorts within the ranks of spies from all sides. At one point, Carlos tries to unload the papers on an unbelieving attaché from the American embassy. He humors Carlos by telling him that they are simply overrun with secrets at the moment and that unless they are Red Chinese in origin, they just can't be bothered to purchase them. Carlos gets the last word, however, by stealing the man's wallet on the way out.

If you're looking for a well-crafted piece of espionage drama that treads the fine line between humor and bleakness, and features a stellar cast at their best, you just found it. As Carlos remarks halfway through the film "Spying is no job, it's a profession," and this is a very professional look at it indeed.—DD

CREDITS: Production: S.N.C. Intermondia Films, T.C. Productions, C.G.F. Metheus, C.C.C. Films; Director: Christian-Jaque; Story based on the novel by Robert Sheckley; Adaptation: Michel Levine, Christian-Jaque; Cinematography: Pierre Petit; Music: Gerard Calvi; Original running length: 95 mins; Country: France/West Germany; Year: 1967

CAST: Georges Geret (*Carlos*), Peter Lawford (*Stephen Daine*), Ira de Furstenberg (*Suzanne Belmont*), Jean Tissier (*Adelgate*), Horst Frank (*Manganne*), Maria-Grazia Buccella (*Anna*), Werner Peters (*Bardieff*), Stephan Wischnewski (*Dr Klaus*), Eva Pflug (*Lili Manchingen*), Wolfgang Kieling (*Wolfgang*), Alan Collins [Luciano Pigozzi] (*Van Joost*), Bernard Tiphaine (*Julian*), Roger Treville (*the American general*), Maurice Magalon (*Pierre*), Pierre Rousseau (*friend of the American diplomat*), Wolfgang Preiss (*Noland*), Herbert Fuchs (*Herbert*), Christian Brocard (*a drink seller*), Henri Guegan, Michel Charrel, Guy Delorme, Jean Minisini, Jack Jourdan (*henchmen of Manganne*), Maurice Garrel, Dean Heyde

## DEADLIER THAN THE MALE
aka Mas peligrosa que los hombres (Sp)

Despite not being a strict spy film—hero Bulldog Drummond is an insurance investigator rather than a secret agent—*Deadlier than the Male* is possibly the most "Bond-esque" of productions examined here (albeit with a generous measure of *The Avengers* to keep things fresh). It isn't so much the plot itself, despite several scenes being borrowed almost wholesale from the better-known series, but more in the general look and style of filming.

**Nigel Green attacks an unarmed (but not outwitted) Richard Johnson in *Deadlier Than the Male***

This is partly because it's stylistically similar and partly because it obviously had a decent budget. Also, however, it's because the underlying themes—the British class system, the decline of the empire, the inherent corruption of business (and by extension, successful businessmen)—are almost identical.

Picture the scene: You're a tip-top agent, just recording details of your latest assignment on the beach, when two gorgeous babes emerge from the surf. What are you going to do? Well, chirpily hail them, hoping to insinuate your way into their affections, of course. Unfortunately, in this case the two babes are the downright dangerous Irma Eckman (Elke Sommer) and Penelope (Sylva Koscina). Result: one distinctly dead agent. And one cleverly twisted Bond reference (Ursula Andress in *Dr. No*).

It turns out that this assassination has something to do with some dirty goings-on at the Keller Corporation, an oil company in the middle of a huge merger with some anonymous Arabians. The merger had been opposed by their eponymous founder, who has conveniently just died in a plane explosion. It seems that the assorted directors of the Keller Corporation had been impatient with the owner's intransigence and had contracted a company to "intervene," a company that happens to be represented by Irma Eckman.

Only one man can possibly be assigned the investigation: Bulldog Drummond (Richard Johnson), the smoothest chap this side of Chelsea. Drummond manages to discover that Irma's organization is involved in another job, trying to secure some vital oil rights in the unwilling country of Achman. In order to do this, they are planning to assassinate the young King of the country, King Fedra (Zia Mohyeddin).

*Deadlier than the Male* is a hugely entertaining film, enjoyable for both genre fans and those of more mainstream tastes. It plays up the parody elements, but not to an irksome degree, and features enough action and intrigue to keep the attention gripped. Direction and cinematography are capably handled, and there's a superb soundtrack—including a Scott Walker title tune (that was later covered by popsters SPACE)—which somehow manages to even out-Barry John Barry. There's also a rather bizarre climax involving a giant, malfunctioning chess set and an exploding hairpiece.

Possibly the greatest factor in its favor is the excellent cast. Anything that features Leonard Rossiter getting paralyzed with a poisonous ring and then chucked out of a hotel window can't be bad. Richard Johnson is one of the most effective of sixties spy performers. Like Sean Connery, he is able to switch from charm to ruthlessness (as witnessed when he threatens to break an attacker's legs) at the drop of a hat. He's one of the breed, the upper-middle-class foot soldiers who propelled the empire toward "greatness." He's equally at home discussing fine wine, speaking Japanese, wooing the ladies or kicking the crap out of a black-belt karate expert. He also wears a mean cardigan.

His nemesis is Petersen, played by Nigel Green (who had also portrayed the villain in *The Ipcress File*, and remains one of the most underappreciated of British performers). Petersen bears some similarity to Dirk Bogarde's Gabriel in *Modesty Blaise*, a far less effective—albeit better-known—film. He is also an upper-class oddball, firmly ensconced on a remote island with a selection of beautiful, deadly women, and always looking for a good conversation…if only his plans for world domination didn't necessitate him killing all of his confidants.

Even with these two, the show belongs to Elke Sommer and Sylva Koscina. As a pair of bickering, bitchy assassins with a selection of increasing ridiculous murder weapons, they anticipate Mr. Kidd and Mr. Wint (Putter Smith and Bruce Glover) from the later Bond film *Diamonds Are Forever*. Except that they're rather more attractive. There's an absolutely hilarious sequence in which the somewhat ditzy Koscina sizes up ingenue Virginia North, and conveys her condescension in a look that speaks simply volumes (and is thoroughly deserved; Ms. North is a *terrible* actress).

*Deadlier than the Male* was something of a success, not least because most of the marketing featured the female leads wearing bathing costumes and gripping harpoon guns. Nonetheless, advertising alone cannot guarantee success, and this is a quality production. Trivia fans may also be interested to note that Kitty Swan, who had appeared in a number of spy films (*Nazi SS*, *The Big Blackout*), pops up in an uncredited role.

CREDITS: Production: Greater Films Ltd, Universal Pictures; Director: Ralph Thomas; Story: Jimmy Sangster; Screenplay: Jimmy Sangster, Liz Charles-Williams, David D. Osborn; Cinematography: Ernest Steward; Music: Malcolm Lockyer; Original running length: 98 mins; Country: UK; Year: 1967

CAST: Richard Johnson (*Bulldog Drummond*), Elke Sommer (*Irma Eckman*), Sylva Koscina (*Penelope*), Nigel Green (*Carl Petersen*), Suzanna Leigh (*Grace*), Steve Carlsen (*Robert Drummond*), Virginia North (*Brenda*), Justine Lord (*Miss Ashenden*), Zia Mohyeddin (*King Fedra*), Lee Montague (*Boxer*), Yasuko Nagazumi (*Mitsouko*), Laurence Naismith (*Sir John Bledlow*), George Pastell (*Carloggio*), Milton Reid (*Chang*), Leonard Rossiter (*Bridgenorth*), Didi Sydow (*Anna*), Dervis Ward (*Keller*), John Stone (*Wyngarde*), William Mervyn, Jill Banner. Uncredited: Kitty Swan (*Fourth assassin*)

## THE DEADLY AFFAIR

This much-touted mainstream entry is recommended to serious spy buffs as a well-crafted, bleak treatise on perceived realities. Deeper than the bulk of the other films included here, the pleasure is derived from sifting

**American poster for *The Deadly Affair***

through the strata of meaning in John Le Carre's story and reveling in the fine performances and top-notch filmmaking.

James Mason is Charles Dobbs, a desk-bound member of MI5 drawn into active espionage when, after routinely confronting an associate about a letter alleging his Communist sympathies, the fellow commits "suicide." Dobbs has his own problems as well, however. His wife, Ann (Harriet Andersson) is notoriously unfaithful and he permits her infidelities but it is destroying him, a metaphor for the Cold War that eats away at our "civilized" society.

Her latest fling involves an old friend, Dieter Freey (Maximilian Schell) who, it turns out, was using her as a ruse to track Dobbs. Dobbs' private world proceeds to crumble and mesh uncomfortably with the case he's investigating.

This is one of those movies where you'll recognize all the actors: Harry Andrews, Roy Kinnear, Robert Flemyng, Lynn Redgrave, David Warner, etc. One standout is Simone Signoret as Elsa, a woman without a country, who scorns Dobbs and his attempts at clearing up the death of her husband. A concentration camp survivor, Elsa has no illusions about patriotism or allegiances in that regard, remarking to Dobbs, "I am a battlefield for you…toy soldiers."

The masks the characters wear are systematically torn away, including the not-so-closeted homosexuality of Dobbs' superior, whose nickname around the offices is "Marlene Dietrich." The climactic revelation of Freey as the contact for the other side occurs at the theater during the court intrigue of Marlowe's "Edward II," reflecting the machinations of the players in the film.

Quincy Jones plays some fun cinematic tricks with the soundtrack (Astrud Gilberto sings the theme song) and it is appropriately melancholy for the material. Director Sidney Lumet is in fine form here and through the half-light of Freddie Young's cinematography is revealed the gray world beneath our intricately constructed lives.—DD

CREDITS: Production: Sidney Lumet Film Productions Ltd.; Director: Sidney Lumet; Story based on the novel "Call for the Dead" by John Le Carre; Screenplay: Paul Dehn; Cinematography: Freddie Young {Technicolor}; Music: Quincy Jones; Original running length: 107 mins; Country: UK; Year: 1966

CAST: James Mason (*Charles Dobbs*), Simone Signoret (*Elsa Fennen*), Maximilian Schell (*Dieter Freey*), Harriet Andersson (*Anna Dobbs*), Harry Andrews (*Inspector Mendel*), Kenneth Haigh (*Bill Appleby*), Roy Kinnear (*Adam Scarr*), Max Adrian (*the adviser*), Lynn Redgrave (*Virgin*), Robert Flemyng (*Samuel Fennan*), Corin Redgrave (*the director*), Les White (*Herek*), June Murphy, Frank Williams, Rosemary Lord (*the witches*), Kenneth Ivew (*the stagehand*), John Dimech (*the waiter*), Julian Sherrier (*the head waiter*), Petra Markham (*the daughter at the theater*), Denis Shaw (*the landlord*), Maria Charles (*the blonde*), Amanda Walker (*the brunette*), Sheraton Blount (*Eunice Scarr*), Janet Hargreaves (*the ticket clerk*), Michael Brennan (*the barman*), Richard Steele, Gertan Klauber (*the businessman*), Margaret Lacey (*Mrs. Bird*), Judy Keirn (*the stewardess*), The Royal Shakespeare Company in scenes from Marlowe's "Edward II": David Warner (*Edward*), Michael Bryant (*Gaveston*), Stanley Lebor (*Lancaster*), Paul Hardwick (*the young Mortimer*), Charles Kay (*Lightborn*), Timothy West (*Matrevis*), Jonathan Wales (*Gurney*)

**Turkish poster for the Jerry Cotton film *Death and Diamonds***

DEATH AND DIAMONDS
aka Dynamit In Gruner Seide (WG),
Dynamite in Green Silk (US, unconfirmed),
Los Angeles: hora 1430 (Sp),
Piu grande colpo della malavita (It)

Some memorable things happen in the sixth Jerry Cotton film as the series begins to wind down. Veteran genre director Harald Reinl takes over the trio of films that bring our hero's adventures to a close and with him casting and content evolve. By this time Reinl was a mainstay in German cinema with Edgar Wallace krimis, Dr. Mabuse thrillers and Winnetou westerns already under his belt, and this same year he would make the memorable *Blood Demon.*

But first, this modest entry is notable for its colorful cast and Jerry's (George Nader) hopeless accent as he impersonates a British criminal. A dying crook tips the FBI about a British ex-con soon to join an LA-based gang with plans for a major heist. The Brit is intercepted and Jerry infiltrates the gang as Rick Trevor, alarm specialist. The gang is run by a mysterious man who gives orders to his second in command, Bloom (Carl Mohner), over a radio. Jerry immediately causes friction by coming between Bloom and the object of his affection, Lana (Silvia Solar), the owner of the club where the gang hides out. Jerry is subsequently framed for murder to keep him in line. The big heist is a diamond robbery, and Jerry soon realizes he will have to disable an alarm he is not familiar with.

Mohner was the muscle in *Rififi* and genre fans will recognize him from *Cave of the Living Dead* and Radley Metzger's *Carmen, Baby*. Solar is back with a meatier role this time as Lana, who will suffer under the lash for Jerry. You will no doubt spot Dieter Eppler as a gang member. Eppler worked with Reinl on many of the director's films, not to mention his role as the main bloodsucker in *Slaughter of the Vampires*. Perennial servant Albert Bessler has a small role as…a butler. Bessler was a regular in the Edgar Wallace thrillers cranked out in Germany in the 1960s, but his most appropriate cameo to mention is in Bryan Edgar Wallace's *Secret of the Black Trunk* as an American FBI man.

Jerry as the Brit Rick Trevor is Nader's most annoying character. Not only is his accent laughable, but the guy is such a nosy whiner that soon we're empathizing with the gang as they tire of his antics. Near the end of the film the gang tries to get rid of Jerry by putting him in an industrial furnace and turning up the heat. For some reason Jerry must bone up on his piano playing skills for his impersonation, and we meet his tutor, who happens to be his mom! Thankfully this talent is never needed in the film.

For the first time the setting is not New York but southern California, so we get to see lots of footage of mid-sixties LA, enjoyable in itself. Reinl has a bit of fun the first time we enter the Green Silk bar—a German building older than LA itself by the way. Go-go girls are dancing away to the tunes of Peter Thomas, and Reinl cuts from a pair of white billiard balls to the jiggling white bikini top of one of the dancers. Groovy!

The diamond heist itself is accomplished with the awkward and highly unlikely method of a remote-control vacuum cleaner. The tube of the machine is snaked through an air-conditioning duct into a room of unconscious diamond dealers and maneuvered around via a tiny camera to suck up the booty. There's a lot of technical hooey used to gloss over the details of the operation and it is staged well enough to obscure what would most likely be a complete failure.

The twists and turns of the final act do afford us a few amusing moments. At one point, the unfortunate Lana is whipped by the girlfriend of the boss until Jerry gives up the location of the diamonds he stole from under Bloom's nose. It's a minor exploitation element of the type relied upon more frequently in the later series entries. Also, Jerry performs the improbable stunt of jumping through the windshield of an oncoming car and—after arriving in the front seat—knocking the driver unconscious with a well-placed punch to the face! He also manages a 100-foot leap from a bridge onto a speeding boat. Danger is Jerry's middle name.—DD

CREDITS: Production: Allianz Filmproduktion, Cineproduzioni Associati, Constantin Film Produktion GmbH; Director: Harald Reinl; Story based on "G-Man Jerry Cotton" by Rolf Schulz, Christa Stern; Screenplay: Renate Willeg; Cinematography: Franz X. Lederle; Music: Peter Thomas; Original running length: 91 mins; Country: West Germany; Year: 1967

CAST: George Nader (*Jerry Cotton*), Heinz Weiss (*Phil Decker*), Silvia Solar (*Lana*), Carl Möhner (*Bloom*), Claus Holm (*Lancaster*), Marlies Draeger (*Mabel*), Günther Schramm (*Tackley*), Karlheinz Fiege (*Santon*), Dieter Eppler (*Tomasio*), Käthe Haack (*Mrs. Cotton*), Horst Niendorf (*FBI chief*), Rainer Basedow, Hans Waldherr, Richard Haller, Claus Tinney, Günther Mack, Udo Kaemper, Maria von Holten, Rolf Eden, Albert Bessler, Giorgio Benito Bogino, Pietro Ceccarelli, Andrzej Zaorski, Claudio de Renzi (*FBI agents*)

## DEATH IN A RED JAGUAR

aka L'homme à la jaguar rouge (Fr), El Jaguar rojo (Sp), Morte in Jaguar rossa (Fr), Der Tod in roten Jaguar (WG)

When I think of *DIARJ*, the seventh Jerry Cotton film, I think of the baby-faced killer whose small role here manages to dominate my memories of this movie. The unevenness of the production, however, is certainly due more

**Outstanding French poster for *Death in a Red Jaguar*, one of the best Jerry Cotton films**

to heights achieved than depths plumbed. The film succeeds on levels no other Cotton entry even attempted to reach, but as a result the more mundane aspects suffer in comparison. Other Cotton films have invested their criminal characters with personalities, but here director Harald Reinl creates a genuinely fascinating, albeit repulsive, professional killer.

We first meet the psycho killer Arthur Davis (a disturbingly effective performance by Gert Hauke) at what is supposed to be a Rockettes performance at Radio City Music Hall as he gazes longingly at the dancers (curiously enough, Jerry is at the same show). We follow Davis on his next hit and this first murder is easily the strangest set piece in all the Cotton films. Davis rings the doorbell of his victim, but the door is answered by a little girl. The presence of this innocent girl confuses Davis, who goes to a nearby pub to call his contractor. Told to go ahead with the hit, Davis bolsters himself by zoning out to a record playing on the jukebox. Peter Thomas's eerie, distorted music in this scene is perfect for observing the sickness within the killer. Returning to fulfill his obligation, Davis kills both the girl and her mother—obviously achieving a sort of sexual satisfaction in the act.

A second murder reveals more of the nature of Davis. Forcing his victim to drive, Davis sits in the front seat of the car waxing poetic about conversing with someone he's about to kill. "This is the first time I've had a chance to talk to anyone before I..." He trails off a moment. "It's very odd. I'm sure I've missed something very exciting in life. The sensation is rather unusual." This is creepy stuff for an unpretentious crime thriller. Unfortunately, this interesting character is extinguished a third of the way into the film.

As you may have guessed, Jerry is up against a murder-for-hire organization. A special silencer is being used in murders across the country, and Jerry travels to San Francisco to work with an old friend on the case. It isn't long before Jerry orders a contract on himself in a desperate attempt to expose the brains of the outfit.

*DIARJ* is the only Cotton film to feature an American special guest star. Robert Fuller (*The Brain From Planet Arous*), as Charlie, makes the most of his pre-title cameo, shooting his way into a theater and taking a bevy of beauties hostage. Jerry takes Charlie by surprise with another one of his death-defying stunts, swinging on a well-placed rope through the window of the room where Charlie is keeping the law at bay with a machine-gun. Once Charlie is subdued we never see him again.

Speaking of stunts, Jerry pulls one off in the film that will leave you slack-jawed. Tied to the end of a railroad spur, with a train bearing down on him, Jerry manages to pick up a stray piece of metal with his feet and kick it perfectly down the rail so that it lodges under the wheel of the locomotive, stopping it inches from his chest. Even Jerry is amazed at the miracle that has saved his life.

One unusual aspect of *DIARJ* as compared to the other Cottons is the emergence of a strong female character on the right side of the law. The lovely Daniela Surina (*The Dead Are Alive*) gives an earnest performance as Ria Payne, the smart and tough secretary to Jerry's old pal Sam Parker (Herbert Stass). Ria relies on her wits and her karate skills to help Jerry, and it's too bad she wasn't a regular in the series.

The (obviously) evil psychiatrist in the film, Dr. Saunders, is a bit of typecasting for Carl Lange. Lange was another Edgar Wallace regular and he also had a sizable part in Reinl's *Blood Demon.* What cracks me up is the extraordinarily creepy painting and medieval weapons that grace his office. I'm sure these create a comforting environment for his mentally ill patients.

I won't spoil the surprise ending, but I will tell you that Jerry convinces his own killer to use blanks when it comes time to put Jerry away for good. The edge Reinl gives this entry puts it near the top of the series, but even this success couldn't keep the show going past one more adventure, *Dead Body on Broadway.*—DD

CREDITS: Production: Allianz Filmproduktion, Constantin Film, Cineproduzioni Associate; Director: Harald Reinl; Story and Screenplay: Alex Berg [Herbert Reinecker]; Cinematography: Franz X. Lederle {Eastmancolor. - Panoramico}; Music: Peter Thomas; Original running length: 91 mins; Filming locations: San Francisco, Hamburg; Country: West Germany; Year: 1968

**Turkish poster for *Death is Nimble, Death is Quick***

CAST: George Nader (*Jerry Cotton*), Heinz Weiss (*Phil Decker*), Herbert Stass (*Sam Parker*), Grit Böttcher (*Linda Carp*), Kurt Jaggberg (*Peter Carp*), Gert Haucke (*the assassin, Kit Davis*), Daniela Surina (*Ria Payne*), Giuliano Raffaelli (*Francis Gordon*), Friedrich Schütter (*Mr. Carp*), Karin Schröder (*Ann Gordon*), Carl Lange (*Dr. Saunders*), Frank Nossack, Britt Lindberg (*Eve Cunnings*), Giorgio Benito Bogino (*Bruce Baxter*), Harry Riebauer (*Steve Dilaggio*), Susanne Hsiao (*Saunders' Assistant*), Hans Epskamp (*Henry Jackson*), Rinaldo Zamperla, Doris Steinmueller, Hubert Mittendorf, Ilse Steppat (*Mrs. Cunnings*), Manuela Schmitz (*Jane Gordon*), Robert Fuller (*Charlie*)

DEATH IS NIMBLE, DEATH IS QUICK
aka Karate en Ceylon (Sp),
Kommissar X—Drei Gelb Katzen (WG)

In Ceylon, a couple of thugs try to abduct a beautiful heiress. They are unsuccessful, but during events an embassy official is killed by a kung-fu blow. He is not the first to die in such a manner, and the authorities call in help—martial arts expert Captain Tom Rowland (Brad Harris). The family of the girl, meanwhile, hires Joe Walker (Tony Kendall) to put an end to the successive extortion demands.

So we are reintroduced to the excellent Kommissar X series, this being the fourth entry into the continuing saga. Previously our heroes had found themselves battling LSD smugglers and robotized women. Here it is the turn of a mysterious Eastern sect, The Three Cats, originally formed in response to English colonialism and now resurrected for more nefarious purposes.

It soon becomes clear that the cult is being used by a mysterious leader to silence his enemies. Joe and Tom survive several assassination attempts before discovering that it is in fact Dr. Flynn, a notorious scientific maverick. To continue his immoral experiments he has had to adopt a different identity and finance himself through criminal activities, hence the kidnapping efforts.

This is a wonderfully entertaining film with enough idiosyncratic moments to make it stick in the mind. The villain's hideout is a lovely place known as Death Lake, an extremely odd location full of warped and long-dead trees protruding from unhealthily still water. In a nod to *Dr. No*, it is also prowled by a fire-breathing "dragon," but if anything, this sequence is even more effective than the lavishly budgeted one that inspired it.

The stunt work in this is also outstanding. An early rooftop chase is literally staggering, and all the more so for being obviously performed by the actors rather than body doubles. The credit for this must go to Brad Harris and big, bald Dan Vadis, a veteran from the peplums, who coordinated all their action choreography themselves. There is also a stirring climactic kung-fu fight between them that actually feels painful to watch.

At this stage, all the familiar Kommissar X conventions were pretty much in place: the two leads continually sparring, the gorgeous babes, the criminal group, the eventual revelation of the top villain. The gadgets are confined to a shower that spouts lethal liquid and some shirts that are so loud they act as radar-blockers. Above all, there is a fine thread of hokey dialogue, mainly centering around saucy innuendo that wouldn't be out of place in a *Carry On* film. Boy, this film is so good-natured that you even laugh at the exploding-cigarette joke, which would generally leave you depositing your video in the blender.

Best line: "You're even more repulsive than your bacteria..." and never has a truer word been said.—MB

CREDITS: Production: Danny Film, Danubia Film, Filmedis, Films J. Willemetz, Parnass Film; Director: Rudolf Zehetgruber; Story and Screenplay: Rudolf Zehetgruber; Cinematography: Klaus von Rautenfeld; Music: Gino Marinuzzi, Jr.; Original running length: 90 mins; Filming location: Ceylon (Sri Lanka); Country: West Germany; Year: 1966

Cast: Tony Kendall [Luciano Stella] (*Joe Walker*), Brad Harris (*Tom Rowland*), Ann Smyrner, Dan Vadis, Siegfried Rauch, H.D. Kalatunga, Michele Mahaut, Philippe Lemaire, Erno Crisa, A. Jayaratna, Rolf Zehett, Paul Eeckmann, Werner Hauff, Joe Abey, Chandrika Lyanegi.

## DEATH ON A RAINY DAY

aka Chinos y minifaldas (Sp), Morte in un giorno di pioggia (It), Der sarg bleibt heute zu (WG)

This opens very strongly: A coffin is carried into a bleak churchyard, while mournful organ music plays on the soundtrack. Slowly, it is lowered into an open grave—only for it to burst open and the man within, secret agent Paul Riviera (Adrian Hoven), to start shooting at everybody in the immediate vicinity with a machine gun. As some funky music kicks in, a helicopter appears and tows the sarcophagus—and its containee—straight to the office of his boss! Okay, so it may be a left-field crib from *You Only Live Twice*, but it's an effective crib nonetheless.

We soon cut to another spy, Bruno (Barth Warren), who is stuck in a quarry having a whole load of trouble with a gang of incompetent Chinamen. These buffoons—who make up in numbers what they lack in proficiency—are under orders from a certain Dr. Kung (George Wang), who has a devious, not to say incomprehensible, plan. This has something to do with The Red Scorpion, whatever that may be. Fearing the consequences if he should succeed, the intelligence services determine to locate it first.

To this end, Bruno and Paul are sent to Hong Kong. Their mission doesn't start auspiciously: The plane they are traveling on is hijacked, and they are only able to escape thanks to a dart-shooting brogue. Upon arrival, their mission seems to involve rescuing a large number of giggling damsels from Dr. Kung's basement, gate-crashing casinos, and causing all kinds of havoc in a local brothel.

*Death* is rather an odd film. Hardly a genre classic, it's entertaining in a harmlessly kitsch way. The production values are acceptable, the script entirely irrelevant and it benefits from an above-average Jerry Van Rooyen (*Vampyros Lesbos*) soundtrack. In fact, it resembles one of Jesus Franco's better films of the period, what with all its crazy set pieces, numerous nightclub scenes, and countless women chained up and shot through red and blue filters. Interestingly, the hero of this piece, Adrian Hoven, went on to play a villain in Franco's similarly jazzy *Sadisterotica*, *Kiss Me Monster* and *Succubus*, with which this also shares a production company, Aquila Film.

It doesn't really strive for thrills, being more content as a laid-back, eccentric comedy (anticipating shows like *The Persuaders*). Hoven and Warren make an enjoyable double act, and are even shown as down-and-outs in the closing moments, a touch that could have come straight from a Franco and Ciccio movie. Gerard Landry also has an amusing support role as an intelligence chief who seems far more concerned with inspecting his nubile, female cadets than any stuffy nonsense such as overseeing espionage operations or anything like that. Mostly, however, there is an awful lot of fistfighting, and even more semi-naked girls—most of whom our heroes attempt to grope at one point or another.

**Brad Harris takes a flying leap from Tony Kendall's motorcycle in *Death Trip***

Director Ramon Comas (who scripted *Password: Kill Agent Gordon* and *Rififi in Amsterdam*) has also managed to create one of the most extreme of "exotic East" films. The Orient is portrayed as a land of mystery and danger, as passionate as it is dangerous—and yet also rigidly bound by social (and antisocial) hierarchies. The spy is one of the few Westerners who can understand, and even manipulate, this alien environment. Of course, it all has absolutely nothing to do with the fact that dubbing Chinese performers with a silly accent is always a good opportunity for a cheap laugh. No, that has nothing to do with it. Nothing at all. No sirree.—MB

CREDITS: Production: Procensa Films, D.A.G.A. Cinematografica/Aquila Film; Director: Ramon Comas; Story and Screenplay: Chris Chatterley, Ramón Comas, Keith Luger, José Luis Madrid; Cinematography: Eloy Mella {Eastmancolor}; Music: Piero Umiliani, Jerry Van Rooyen (German version); Original running length: 99 mins; Filming location: Hong Kong; Country: Spain/Italy/West Germany; Year: 1967

CAST: Adrian Hoven (*Paul Riviera*), Barth Warren (*Bruno Nussak*), Gérard Landry (*Commander Fernion*), Teresa del Río (*Sonia Bellford*), Lilia Neyung (*Leila Wong*), Karin Feddersen (*Francoise*), Wolfgang Preiss (*Dr. Cronwell*), Josyane Gibert (*Pamela*), George Wang (*Dr. Kung*), Claudia Gravy (*Dr. Kung's assistant*), Manuel Escalera, Roberto Llamas

DEATH TRIP

aka Comisario X los tres perros verde (Sp), Le Commissaire X traque les chiens verts (Fr), Kill Me Gently (US), Kommissar X—Drei Grune Hunde (WG)

This, the third of the Kommissar X films, is often credited to Gianfranco Parolini. That might be erroneous. Certainly, the print that I saw had Rudolf Zehetgruber—who would also go on to helm *Death is Nimble, Death is Quick* in the same series—as the named director. However, it's always difficult to tell exactly who was actually doing what in these productions. It's certainly difficult to highlight any huge differences in style from a Parolini film.

Turkey is in the grip of an international syndicate of drug smugglers. Bearing this in mind, it seems a rather strange tactic for Interpol to send one of its agents, Capt. Rowland (Brad Harris), into Istanbul with a £1,000,000 stash of liquid LSD. Inevitably, it has soon been stolen by a mysterious organization headed by an anonymous master criminal, The Green Hound. What they don't know is that the narcotic has already been swapped for a canister of harmless sugar.

Meanwhile, Joe Walker (Tony Kendall) is carrying on in his normal incorrigible fashion: going into a bar, starting a fight, kissing any poor female who happens to be in the area. Deciding that enough is enough, The Green Hound's right-hand men—Kimow (Samson Burke) and Shapiro (Herbert Fuchs in ridiculous hat)—decide to spike his drink. This has the bizarre effect of actually turning him into a normal human being. The cheesy grin disappears, as do the excruciating asides and self-satisfied posturing. Of course, without his superhuman powers of smarm he's pretty helpless and is soon captured, as are Capt. Rowland, tour guide Leyla (Olga Schoberova), and a fellow American Allan Hood (Dietmar Schonherr). Knowing that the drugs have been swapped, the villains determine to find out their true hiding place whatever it costs.

I have to admit that I was rather disappointed by all this. It wasn't really because of any actual fault in the film, but more because, considering that it is a Kommissar X film dealing with LSD, I was expecting something completely outrageous. As it is, *Death Trip* features absolutely no wacko visuals and trippy camera angles, which is a great opportunity that was missed. Instead it plays, as with *Kill Panther Kill*, more like a straight gangster story with some batty touches (such as the donkey that can project its thoughts—don't ask).

On the other hand, it's fast paced and enjoyable, with some fabulous scenery and enough foolishness to guarantee any serious film critic a coronary. Weaselly Herbert Fuchs is always worth a look, and ex-wrestler turned peplum star Sammy Berg (Luigi Capuano's *The Mighty Warrior* and *The Three Stooges Meet Hercules*) looks reasonable in a suit.

I just wanted the camera to circle round while everyone laughs maniacally, the music gets frantic and voices slow down to half speed in pure "triptastic" style.—MB

CREDITS: Production: Parnass Film, Cinesecolo, Comptoir Francais Du Film, Hungar Film; Director: Rudolf Zehetgruber; Story based on a novel by Bert F. Island; Screenplay: Giovanni Simonelli, Rudolf Zehetgruber; Cinematography: Baldi Schwarze, Angelo Lotti {Eastmancolor}; Music: Francesco De Masi; Original running length: 90 mins; Filming location: Istanbul; Country: West Germany/Italy; Year: 1967

CAST: Tony Kendall (*Jo Walker*), Olga Schoberová (*Leyla*), Brad Harris (*Capt. Rowland*), Sabine Sun (*Joyce Hilton*), Andrea Aureli, Rossella Bergamonti (*Jenny*), Samson Burke (*Kemal*), Emilio Carrer (*Inspector Rebat*), Herbert Fuchs (*Ed Shapiro*), Christa Linder (*Gisela*), Dietmar Schönherr (*Allan Hood*), Carlo Tamberlani (*Konsul Snyder*), Rolf Zehett (*Alman*)

THE DEFECTOR

aka L'Affare Goshenko (It), El Desertor (Sp), L'Espion (Fr), Lautlose Waffen (WG)

A melancholy air permeates *The Defector*. Perhaps the knowledge that this was Montgomery Clift's last role taints the viewer's experience somewhat, but there certainly is very little else memorable about the film. Clift looks gaunt and nervous and even the actors around him seem to sense his imminent demise. Raoul Levy (who also died the same year) directs with a listless hand and never draws any emotion from what could have been a much more resonant movie. Levy had just come off a terrific little road movie about hit men called

**Belgian poster for Montgomery Clift's last film *The Defector***

*Hail Mafia!*, and in that light we are doubly disappointed with this lackluster effort.

Cynicism is the main theme here, and although the film tries to take on the larger issues of patriotism, loyalty and betrayal it pulls up short, relying instead on cliché and a surface resemblance to better examples in the genre. Clift is a professor who is threatened (by Roddy McDowall in a small role) with the denial of government grants unless he will try to secure information while on a trip to East Germany. The man assigned to stop Clift in Leipzig (Hardy Kruger) is also a scientist and at one point he too is a victim of his government's underhanded methods of persuasion. This parallel is intriguing, but one has the feeling the issue was a casualty of adapting a novel ("The Spy" by Paul Thomas) to the screen, and we are left to connect the character's dots. Kruger is excellent by the way, and manages to be the heart and soul of the film.

Serge Gainsbourg's score is as sparse and forgettable as the film itself, relying on the occasional militaristic theme to bolster the sagging visuals. Genre fans may recognize Clift's love interest, Macha Meril, from Dario Argento's *Deep Red*. Never very good or very bad, consider *The Defector* an ambience picture; it has a certain feel to it, but one that slips too easily through your fingers.—DD

CREDITS: Production: PECF, Rhein Main Films; Director: Raoul Levy; Story based on the novel "The Spy" by Paul Thomas; Screenplay: Raoul Levy; Cinematography: Raoul Coutard; Music: Serge Gainsbourg; Original running length: 100 mins; Filming location: Munich; Country: France/West Germany; Year: 1966

CAST: Montgomery Clift (*Professor James Bower*), Hardy Krüger (*Counselor Peter Heinzman*), Roddy McDowall (*Agent Adam*), Macha Méril (*Frieda Hoffman*), David Opatoshu (*Orlovsky*), Christine Delaroche (*Ingrid*), Hannes Messemer (*Dr. Saltzer*), Karl Lieffen (*the Major*), Uta Levka, with Curd Jürgens. Uncredited: Jean-Luc Godard (*a double agent*)

**German lobby card for *Desperate Mission* features Yoko Tani and the incredible hulk of Milton Reid**

DESPERATE MISSION

aka Agent Z55 mission desperee (Fr), Agente Z55, misión Hong-Kong (Sp), Agente Z55: missione disperata (It), Die Chance ist gleich Null (WG), Z55 mision desperada (Sp)

After a rather dull first hour, this evolves into something much grittier than your normal spy film. With an onus on nighttime photography (which often makes things rather difficult to make out), a preponderance of hard-hitting fistfights and a particularly nasty face-burning scene, it all leaves one with the (ultimately misguided) feeling of being a rather somber affair. It definitely seems to lack the glamorous ambience that pervades the majority of its peers. However, this all doesn't mean *Desperate Mission* is ultimately any better than average, and at several points this hapless reviewer found himself in need of a swift Raspberry Collins to offset the dangerous onset of sleep.

Professor Larsen (Paco Sanz), a prominent nuclear scientist, is freed from a Chinese prison camp by a group of Japanese judo experts. They take him to Hong Kong, where he can wait in hiding while transportation to America is arranged. However, his main contact, Agent Z51, is killed before anything can be finalized. Knowing the delicacy of matters, the US Secret Service send in their best agent, Robert Manning, aka Z55 (German Cobos). His mission is to both relocate the AWOL academic and avenge his murdered associate.

It's not long before Manning discovers that a disparate group of individuals are taking a close interest in his activities. There's a suspicious pair of "bodyguards" (Milton Reid and Yoko Tani) who persist in trying to pay him to work for them, not to mention an annoying blonde, Sally (Susan Baker), and her camp chum, The Baron (Gianni Rizzo). Now every good camp villain should have a pet—in Bond films, these ranged from piranhas to sharks to, err, a cat. Unfortunately, the Baron was dealt a rather duff card in the vicious fauna stakes. His particular mammalian sidekick is...an armadillo ("an animal that's quite affectionate, despite its rude exterior")! Now there's nothing that quite so diminishes the tension of a scene as much as having a goddamned armadillo wandering around in the background. Sometimes I'd swear that these Italian filmmakers threw in such outrageously absurd elements just to completely confuse the unsuspecting viewer, stumbling across their long-forgotten works after 35 years of total obscurity.

Anyway, Mr. Z55 is soon wandering around an assortment of judo clubs, hoping to locate the one-handed black-belt who had been working with his predecessor. He also manages to visit an assortment of swanky drinking establishments, hoping to find a long-stemmed glass full of a well-mixed martini (and who wouldn't). It doesn't take him too long to locate the professor, but that's only the beginning of his troubles.

*Desperate Mission* has a few things in its favor. There's a great title sequence, faultlessly blending animation, lounge vibes and shooting silhouettes, which conjures up memories of *The Avengers*. Francesco De Masi's soundtrack is enjoyable, and there's a nice supporting cast, including a couple of unexpected performers. Milton Reid was a familiar face in British films, often appearing as a mute butler or bodyguard (see *Adventures of a Private Eye*, *Au Pair Girls*, *Dr. Phibes Rises Again* and *Dr. No* among others). He's not a great actor, for sure, but has a formidable presence and a bad complexion. Yoko Tani was a French actress who appeared in many Euro productions as a token Oriental (i.e., giggling regularly, looking demure, trying to kill people) before her death in 1999.

Apart from that, though, it's pretty much a motley assortment of the usual clichés: stupid passwords, hat-wearing villains and stilted "suave" dialogue ("What kind of chicken are you, Mr. Manning?"). Unfortunately, things aren't helped along too much by rather stodgy direction, with the exception of a good shoot-out in a cinema, from the usually reliable Roberto Montero. Lead actor German Cobos certainly looks like Sean Connery, and acts in a much more vicious way than is expected, but fails to really engage.—MB

CREDITS: Production: Cineproduzioni Associate, C. Balcazar, Les Films Copernic; Director: Robert B. White [Roberto B. Montero]; Story and Screenplay: R.B. White [Roberto B. Montero], Ray Calloway [Mario Colucci]; Cinematography: Ken Foster; Music: Francesco De Masi; Original running length: 90 mins; Filming location: Hong Kong; Country: Italy/Spain/France; Year: 1965

CAST: German Cobos (*Robert Manning*), Susan Baker (*Sally*), Yoko Tani (*Su Ling*), Gianni Rizzo (*"the Baron"*), Milton Reid (*Cheng*), Paco Sanz (*Professor Larsen*), Leontine May, Anthony Blade, Florence Simpson, George Chow, Audrey Rosales, Alfred Ngo Uncredited: Giovanni Cianfriglia (*the Baron's henchman with woollen hat*), Romano Puppo (?*Thug in cinema*?)

THE DEVIL'S AGENT
aka El Agente del diablo (Sp),
Im Namen des Teufels (WG)

*The Devil's Agent* is a serious, character-driven espionage drama with the cast to pull it off. Aside from several high-profile players, there are many recognizable character actors that pop up throughout the film—not the least of which is the celebrated Billie Whitelaw in a small but memorable role as a nightclub hostess. The main themes explored here are ones of alienation, misplaced loyalty, suspicion and futility. Rather bleak, yes, but carried off so well as to be if not entertaining, at least thought-provoking.

An accidental meeting with an old friend, Baron von Staub (Christopher Lee), puts Droste (Peter Van Eyck) under suspicion by the Americans as a spy. When Droste is duped into bringing a package back from his

**Belgian poster for *The Devil's Agent*, an exploitive title for a serious spy film**

visit to von Staub's estate in East Germany, he is arrested and pressed into service for the American intelligence community under threat of imprisonment. Droste must carry out missions that place him in jeopardy as a spy for the East as well as the West. The course of the film takes us through the career of the reluctant spy as his fragile world begins to crumble and he is finally worth nothing to either side—a fugitive with nowhere to run, a dead man walking.

The film is a fine example of the Cold War pre-Bond era of spy films that espoused a deep cynicism not seen again until much later in the cycle, after the jaunty spoofs had run their course near the end of the decade. The filmmakers impress upon us that ultimately there is very little difference between "us" and "them" in the spy game, and neither side is taken here. The downbeat ending is a foregone conclusion, and while this is no classic, it is not without its redeeming qualities.

Peter Van Eyck made quite a few spy films and his main love interest is played by the lovely Marianne Koch, who gives a good performance as a woman who takes a chance on a man only to find out he was lying to her by no choice of his own. Most of the characters in the film experience a similar catharsis somewhere along the line and the attentive viewer will not come away unscathed.—DD

CREDITS: Production: British Lion, Emmet Dalton, Bavaria; Director: John Paddy Carstairs; Story based on the novel "Im namen des Teufels" by Hans Habe; Screenplay: Robert Westerby; Cinematography: Gerald Gibs {B&W}; Music: Philip Green; Original running length: 77 mins; Country: West Germany/UK; Year: 1961

CAST: Peter van Eyck (*Droste*), Marianne Koch (*Nora*), Macdonald Carey (*Mr. Smith*), Christopher Lee (*Baron von Staub*), Albert Lieven, Billie Whitelaw (*Piroska*), David Knight (*Father Zambory*), Marius Goring (*Gen. Greenhahn*), Helen Cherry (*Countess Cosimano*), Colin Gordon (*Count Dezsepalvy*), Niall MacGinnis (*Paul Vass*), Eric Pohlmann (*Bloch*), Peter Vaughan (*Chief of Hungarian Police*), Michael Brennan (*Horvat*), Jeremy Bulloch (*Johnny Droste*), Walter Gotell (*Dr. Ritter*), John Cowley (*Funnel-Shaped Man*), Peter Lamb (*Muller*), Christopher Casson (*the headmaster*), Bart Bastable (*the cattle truck driver*), Charles Byrne (*Vazlan*), Vincent Dowling (*Father Farcosc*), Adrian Cronin (*the young priest*), Robert Lepler (*the head waiter*)

THE DEVIL'S MAN
aka Devilman le diabolique (Fr),
Devilmann Story (It)

If you are like me, you can appreciate the special merits of a bad movie on their own terms. I suppose many of the films that fall into our beloved genre of Eurospy would be tagged as "bad" by most viewers, but I'm not talking about just your everyday run-of-the-mill bad movie here. There are some films so nonsensical that they reach a certain nadir of "bad." In fact, they take on the quality of a fever dream. *The Devil's Man* is such a film.

Guy Madison is Mike. I didn't catch his last name after two viewings and it may indeed be possible that it is never given. I'm apt to believe this, because I don't think the villain's name was ever given either! But anyway, Mike must be some sort of secret agent. He gives his profession as newspaperman and also as editor of a science magazine during the course of this adventure, but he's way too efficient at fisticuffs, gunplay, horseback riding and bringing down super villains for a journalist, in my opinion. Mike's true occupation is never revealed—he just shows up and takes over. He also has a mysterious partner who follows him around, but apparently that's not important either.

Madison was known primarily as a star of western films and television, but he made his share of adventure films in Europe as well, including *The Executioner of Venice* and the intentionally silly *Superargo*. Luisa Baratto, who plays Christine, the missing professor's daughter, was also in *Superargo* with Guy. She didn't make any other spy movies during her short career, but she did manage an appearance in the cult favorite *Bloody Pit of Horror*. We're in much more familiar territory with Luciano Pigozzi, aka Allan Collins, who plays the evil one's right hand henchman-scientist. Pigozzi has a cult following to this day and is known as the "the Peter Lorre of Italy."

So Mike and Christine track her missing scientist father to somewhere in Africa where they roam the markets looking for information. These scenes are amusing because the location footage does not even come close to matching the scenes with the actors. Scenes like this are not unusual in B-grade flicks, as we all know, but it's the vast difference in quality—the cheap and easy ethic of the filmmakers—that make them special here.

The same thing occurs as the two—after finding their man—are making their way through the desert to a place no one will go because evil spirits live there (this kind of spooky rhetoric is thrown into the film for no good reason, but that's par for the course). As they are resting, a screaming horde of armed horsemen attacks. Well, at least moving pictures of the horsemen attack. This is inadequate filmmaking at its finest.

Mike is shot and left for dead in the attack, and Christine is captured by the bad guys. Mike is rescued by a local nomadic tribe, whose chieftain happens to have a daughter who has also been kidnapped by the villain. She does make an appearance later in the film when she's offered to Mike for his pleasure, but then she disappears again never to be seen (or rescued). The chieftain fixes Mike up and tells him that "this ointment will heal your wounds in a matter of hours." I love this cheesy way of explaining away a gunshot wound so our hero doesn't have to be bogged down by it for the rest of the film.

**Bizarre imagery on the Belgian poster for the equally bizarre *The Devil's Man***

Mike uses the old impersonate-a-guard trick to gain entrance to the madman's compound, a vast complex that consists of one hallway everyone runs down many times and an experimentation theater. There's a weird-looking ray-gun type of machine in there that looks like the one in *The Invisible Ray* with Karloff and Lugosi. We first see this machine used to make a corpse very strong for a short period of time, after which the villain says, "That proves our experiment." The evil genius in the film wears a silver mask and looks like a Mexican wrestler—which he may be because I didn't recognize the actor once the mask came off to reveal a fellow with some sort of skin problem. After the corpse experiment, Mr. Mask wants to do the same with a live body. When Pigozzi makes the mistake of saying "You must be joking," our villain says "I never joke."

More weird dialogue: Pigozzi visits Mike (who has been captured) in his cell and tells him of their experiments with "certain primates, studying their psychological reactions to captivity underground." Mike responds to this benign description with, "You people are just maniacs!"

And talk about vague scientific mumbo jumbo, this film is full of it. There's a weird wall of lights in the room with the ray gun that registers something or other. It's too incomprehensible for small minds like mine, because I could not make any sense of what was going on when Mike was hooked up to the machine. It loses something in the dubbing I guess. The villain claims that "the genius embodied in this entire complex" (!) will be transplanted into a brain they have sitting around, which will be put into his head! Now I may not be up on the latest scientific transplant data, but I can see some problems with this plan. And they call him mad.

Mike escapes and returns with a screaming horde just in time to save Christine from having her brain pulled out for some reason by her zombie dad. This is when the evil compound is destroyed and I mean destroyed. The model of this fortress blows up and blows up and blows up. They must have been making nitro on the side in this place.

Really about the only halfway decent thing to mention about the movie is the sometimes okay score. It has its mock modern jazz moments. Other than that, all I can say is *The Devil's Man* should be watched late at night in some sort of inebriated state. You won't believe it in the morning either way.—DD

CREDITS: Production: Lion International; Director: Paul Maxwell [Paolo Bianchini]; Story and Screenplay: Paul Maxwell [Paolo Bianchini], Max Caret; Cinematography: Alan Jones [Aldo Greci] {Techniscope – Technicolor}; Music: Patrick Leguy; Original running length: 87 mins; Country: Italy; Year: 1967

CAST: Guy Madison (*Mike*), Liz Barrett [Luisa Baratto] (*Christine Becker*), Diana Lorys (*Yasmin*), Alan Collins [Luciano Pigozzi] (*Professor Becker*), Bill Vanders, Ken Wood [Giovanni Cianfriglia]

## DICK SMART 2.007

Someone has stolen some vital components from an American nuclear laboratory, which means that whoever has taken them will be able to create an atom bomb of their own. Only one man can possibly track down the thieves: Dick Smart, a no-good playboy who occasionally keeps himself solvent by carrying out work for the Secret Service, at a cost of $1,000,000 a job. Dick could certainly do with the money, since he's just lost his house on a bad bet.

For some reason or other, he heads down to Rio—for all the plot tells you it could easily be because he just wants to look at some young Brazilian ladies in skimpy bikinis. He's on the right track, though. It all has something to do with a dodgy dame called Lady Lister (Margaret Lee), who has created something called a "reducer." This is able, when allied with great heat (such as a nuclear explosion, hence the thefts), to create diamonds from carbon instantaneously. What's a chap to do? Well, why not just head to the beach and chat up a few gorgeous girls.

Despite these distractions, Dick's soon on her trail (not to mention in her bed). There is, however, a fly in the ointment: Lady Lister's partner, Black Diamond (Ambrosio Fregolente), who plans to steal the device and keep all of the spoils for himself.

Franco Prosperi is best known as the co-director of the hugely popular *Mondo Cane*, although this can't really have involved much more than rummaging through the film archives and gluing the best bits together. Away from Mondo movies—and he was involved in a number of other, equally popular ones—he also directed a couple of really very good, stylish thrillers: *The Professional Killer* and *Every Man Is My Enemy*, both of which starred the excellent Robert Webber. In between these, however, he churned out this cheap, obscure spy film that, while being unquestionably entertaining, resembles an explosion in an ideas factory.

There's simply so much going on that it's impossible to keep up with the—already-threadbare—narrative. This is especially true of the first half-hour, which is all but incomprehensible. After that it does settle down a bit, but the filmmakers are still happy to wander off in whichever direction happens to take their fancy. Undoubtedly, the fault for this lies firmly with Prosperi, who should have kept a much tighter control on things. Maybe it was the fact that he was making a comedy that allowed him to become so self-indulgent, or maybe because he was allegedly hitting Bolivian marching powder rather heavily at the time. Whatever, it does end up as something of a disappointment if you are expecting a taut, well-composed spy film.

**Soundtrack for *Dick Smart 2.007***

But hey, a little bit of self-indulgence can be a good thing, and *Dick Smart* is nothing if not entertaining. In fact, it's probably one of the 10 most enjoyable examples of the genre. The dialogue is rapier sharp ("I love young ladies like you. You don't say much, and when you do you say 'Aaaiiiieeee'") and it moves faster than a commuter with diarrhea.

Best of all, there's a veritable menagerie of ridiculous gadgets, ranging from the "BGR" (Beautiful Girl Radar) to a rather cool little motorbike/gyrocopter/submersible, that looks as though it would fall apart if someone were to hiccup nearby. There's also a bed with built-in handcuffs, which sounds like a must for bondage freaks, and a particularly irritating chess computer that insists upon laughing at its opponents. I was also taken with the unique twist upon the habitual cable car scene: This time the hero escapes by making use of a handbag to surf down the wires.

It also benefits from a couple of likeable leads. Richard Wyler is actually much better than I expected. He tends to come over as rather dour, which wouldn't be suitable for a spy film at all, but here he displays a deft sense of the ridiculous. Margaret Lee is frankly gorgeous, and gets to sport a series of absolutely outrageous haircuts (as well as a particularly snazzy trouser suit). Special mention must also go to Ambrosio Fregolente, who is good value as the voicebox-using, dastardly villain.—MB

CREDITS: Production: Filmstudio; Director: Frank Shannon [Franco Prosperi]; Story: Giorgio Moser; Screenplay: Ottavio Alessi, Giovanni Simonelli, Duccio Tessari, Giorgio Moser; Cinematography: Roberto Gerardi {Eastmancolor}; Music: Mario Nascimbene; Original running length: 100 mins; Filming locations: Incir-De Paolis Studios, Rio de Janeiro; Country: Italy; Year: 1967

CAST: Richard Wyler (*Dick Smart*), Margaret Lee (*Lady Lorraine Lister*), Rosana Tabajos (*Jeanine Stafford*), Flavia Baldi (*Patricia*), Helio Guerriero (*Scioloff*), Ambrosio Fregolente (*"Black Diamond"*), Valentino Macchi, Max Turilli (*one of Lady Lister's scientists*), Tullio Altamura (*Mr Conterill, one of Lady Lister's scientists*), Bernadette Kell, Giuseppe Schettino, Assunta De Paoli, Amedeo Riva, Guido Lanzi, Paolo Guerrino Conti. Uncredited: Romano Puppo (*thug stealing device from bedroom*)

## THE DIRTY GAME

aka Guerra secreta (Sp),
La guerra segreta (It), La guerre secrète (Fr),
Spione unter sich (WG)

Three quickies for the price of one and you get what you pay for. The plots of the individual segments are necessarily simple, but each short film is better than the last. Robert Ryan is peripherally involved in each and his cynical narration seems appropriate only for the last story, where even the good guys are bad. Italian, French and British filmmakers each take their turn in presenting the trio of tales.

Part One. Vittorio Gassman is the ladies' man secret agent Perego, who assumes the identity of a professional kidnapper in order to infiltrate the other side, which wants a professor and his formula for a new jet fuel. It is said that "with a cupful a jet could fly around the world," so it's no wonder that both sides are curious. It's interesting that the leader of the kidnappers, Italian dissidents working for the Red Chinese, makes clear that the professor is just as disenchanted with the US as with the Communists after the US tried to strong-arm him into giving them the formula. Perego is sent in to set up the kidnappers for failure, making the US look good when they save him, and it works, eventually. Fairly cynical yes, but this is child's play.

Director Carlo Lizzani shows very little flair for this sort of thing: It's by-the-numbers all the way. The climax takes place at Pompeii, so the last few minutes at least have some visual interest. Other than that, one must look to the other segments for inventiveness. By the way, at the end of the film, Ryan's narration mentions that the US military got the formula for the super fuel. I wonder what ever happened to it.

Part Two. Here we have a two-and-one-half-hour James Bond movie stripped down to about 20 minutes or so. The budget is even less than that. The plot may be Bond but the secret agent is definitely not, even though the bottom line—success—is the same. Lalande (played by Andre Bourvil) makes no bones about his everyman appearance, remarking to the femme fatale at one point "Take it easy. I'm not James Bond and you're no Pussy Galore either."

Lalande has 36 hours to put an enemy underwater installation out of business. This type of story seems exceedingly slapdash for such a short running time. Things must happen so quickly that it seems clearly impossible. This isn't to say that the segment isn't enjoyable, because it is. Part of the fun is watching a balding, ordinary guy do all the stuff that usually only pretty boys get to do: discover dead bodies, climb around buildings at night, challenge lady spies and even have spear-gun fights while scuba diving.

One amusing turn happens when Lalande has his briefcase stolen. He immediately calls his contact and tells him to get to the hospital because very soon a man will be brought in with third degree burns on his hands and face. Sure enough, that's what happens; the briefcase was booby-trapped. When Lalande gets to the hospital he is told that the victim was carrying an Egyptian passport. Looking at the bandaged man, Leleande remarks, "Well, he certainly looks Egyptian."

A good middle segment, Lelande's adventure (directed by Christian-Jaque, *Dead Run*) leads nicely into Part Three, Terence Young's completely bleak look at the spy game. Young, who by this time had made two Bond films, *Dr. No* and *From Russia With Love* and would go

**Belgian poster for the spy anthology *The Dirty Game* features French actor Andre Bourvil**

on to make *Thunderball*, takes top honors for the best segment of the three.

Henry Fonda, an agent in deep, deep cover, crashes through the border from East Berlin only to discover his nightmare just beginning. This tale of a spy coming in from the cold is told with a visual and thematic style very much akin to the films noir of the forties and fifties. The steady rain, mysterious figures huddling in the shadows, the complete absence of the sun and the fatalistic trajectory of the helpless protagonist are all symbolic of the grim internal landscapes explored within the noir cycle. They work beautifully here to represent a paranoid's fantasy that turns out to be all too real.

This segment is by far the most cynical of the three and stands as one of the genre's best examples of the senselessness of the Cold War. Fonda plays a spy who was planted in the East when merely a child, just in case a need for him should arise. In other words, his soul was never his own. Upon arriving at the Berlin border station, his troubles continue unabated, as his trip to the military barracks is so confusing that the soldiers escorting him get lost! Not a good sign.

Refused asylum at the barracks, Fonda is put up in a hotel for the night that is crawling with enemy agents who want to kill him. He isn't in the room for five minutes before snipers wound him. A short time later, he has to beat an encroaching killer off the windowsill with a towel rack he tore off the wall. Even the help that arrives is not what it seems.

Peter Van Eyck is one of the players on the US team. Here he is typecast as a double agent, but this shouldn't deter you from watching the pawns at play in this particularly dirty game.—DD

**Very nice Belgian poster for the tame *Double Man***

CREDITS: Production: Fair Film, Euro International Film, Franco London Film, Eichberg Filmproduktion, Landau-Unger Production; Director: Terence Young, Christian-Jaque, Carlo Lizzani; Story: Jacques Laborie, Jacques Remy; Screenplay: Jacques Remy, Ennio De Concini, Christian-Jaque, Philippe Bouvard; Cinematography: Enrico Menczer, Pierre Petit, Richard Angst; Music: Robert Mellin, Gian Piero Reverberi; Original running length: 118 mins; Filming location: A.T.C. (Grottaferrata) Studios, Berlin; Country: Italy/France/US; Year: 1965

CAST: Robert Ryan (*General Bruce*), Henry Fonda (*Colonel Kourlof*), Vittorio Gassman (*Perego*), Annie Girardot (*Monique*), Peter Van Eyck (*Pete Hatkin*), Mario Adorf (*Callahan*), Robert Hossein (*Dupont*), Andre Bourvil (*Julien Lalande*), Georges Marchal (*Serge*), Maria Grazia Buccella (*Nathalia*), Jacques Sernas (*Glazou*), Gabriella Giorgelli, Klaus Kinski (*the Russian agent*), Wolfgang Lukschy (*the Russian general*), Nino Crisman, Oreste Palella, Louis Arbessier (*Ivanov*), Violette Marceau (*Lisa*), Helmut Wildt (*Perry*), Gabriel Gobin (*O'Hara*), Jacky Blanchot (*Joe*), Renato Terra Caizzi

## THE DOUBLE MAN
aka Mi doble en los Alpes (Sp)

What we have here is another one of those old-fashioned, competent and ultimately boring espionage cash-in flicks. Filled with B-movie stars and journeyman character actors, these films are like comfort food for the movie buff: They're only satisfying on a superficial level and thus forgettable in the long run.

This one happens to be a ski holiday for all involved. The son of CIA agent Dan Slater (Yul Brynner) is killed while skiing in the Austrian Alps. Slater travels to the resort town, suspicious that his son's death was murder. Two bloody holes (made by ski poles) in the kid's clothes confirm his worst fears. His son was pushed from the cliff, killed so that Slater would indeed show up. It turns out that resident baddie, Berthold (Anton Diffring), wants to substitute a double for Slater so the doppelganger can return to Washington and undercut Western security.

There's lots of talk and some nice snow photography but little action to speak of during the course of this overlong melodrama. Plenty of rear projection (we can't have the stars on the slopes) keeps the reality in check, and the score sounds like it was a made-for-television hack job. There's a night race featured near the end that makes for some nice visuals, and a modern art gallery with plenty of abstract paintings and Calder-like sculpture to look at, but these are fleeting pleasures.

Britt Ekland plays the innocent who gets slapped around by Slater's double (also played by Brynner) and quickly forgives him even though she doesn't yet know he's an evil agent. The usual pop cynicism about paranoia in the espionage world is on display, but it seems only half-hearted and is betrayed by good triumphing over evil in the end. The best line is Slater confronting his double with the words "You're a bastard" and the double responding, "I'm you."

The big confrontation in the end is settled by an old friend of Slater's, who knows that Slater "never loved a damn thing in his life." It's pretty bad when you can pick the fake Slater because he's capable of love. This is a by-the-numbers time filler for the completionist only. We're talking blandsville, baby.—DD

**Vincent Price (center) as the amusing Dr. Goldfoot in *Dr. Goldfoot and the Girl Bombs***

CREDITS: Production: Albion Film Corp; Director: Franklin J. Schaffner; Story based on the novel "Legacy of a Spy" by Henry S. Maxfield; Screenplay: Alfred Hayes, Frank Tarloff; Cinematography: Denys N. Coop {Technicolor}; Music: Ernest Freeman; Original running length: 105 mins; Country: UK; Year: 1966

CAST: Yul Brynner (*Dan Slate /Kalmar*), Britt Ekland (*Gina*), Clive Revill (*Frank Wheatly*), Anton Diffring (*Berthold*), Moira Lister (*Mrs. Carrington*), Lloyd Nolan (*Edwards*), George Mikell (*Max*), Brandon Brady (*Gregori*), Julia Arnall (*Anna*), David Bauer (*Miller*), Ronald Radd (*the general*), Kenneth J Warren (*the police chief*), David Healy (*Halstead*), Carl Jaffe (*the police surgeon*), Frederick Schiller (*the ticket seller*), Douglas Muir (*Wilfred*), Ernst Walder (*Frischauer*), Bee Duffell (*the woman on the train*), John G. Heller (*the bartender*)

DR. GOLDFOOT AND THE GIRL BOMBS
aka Dr. Goldfoot and the Love Bomb (Int);
Dr. Goldfoot and the 'S' Bombs (Int);
Dr. Goldfoot and the Sex Bombs (Int);
Spie vengono dal semifreddo (It),
Spies Come from Half-Cold (Int)

Mario Bava finally managed to get his hands on Vincent Price for this one. However, the evil bastard who also managed to saddle him with Franco, Ciccio *and* Fabian deserves to be flayed alive.

Dr. Goldfoot (Price) attempts to gain riches by creating female explosive robots that are detonated while in the clasp of important politicians and military men, but the idiotic trio appear and ruin the fun.

I know that this film has a lot of detractors—I seem to remember it appearing in a "Worst Films Ever Made"-type book some years back—but I actually found it hugely enjoyable. There's something about these manic Italian comedies that plugs directly into the province of surrealism, especially if they are as well handled and vivacious as this one. Like the best of the *Carry On* films, it abandons any vestiges of reality at the first possible moment and adopts an "anything goes" attitude.

The general weirdness is exaggerated by some extremely and deliberately crude acting. Franco and Ciccio mug in their usual relentless fashion, and when they don't play a joke for too long it can be very funny. There is one nice moment when they attempt to hide among the legion of robo-women in a predictable but gratifyingly stupid way.

The head honcho in the ham stakes here, though, is Vincent Price. My God, the guy looks as though he was having fun! This was the one of the first in a trail of films that took him away from the Gothic tragedy of Corman's Poe adaptations into an area which I personally find much more appetizing: the self-consciously hokey horror film. Anyone surprised to find an actor of Price's caliber in a Franco and Ciccio movie should bear in mind that a) they were hugely popular at the time and b) Buster Keaton appeared in their *Due Marines e un generale*, made the year before.

In no way is this one of Bava's best but, like *Five Dolls For An August Moon* (which I am unashamed to admit that I actually enjoy watching more than any of his other works), his basic lack of interest in the plot has a beneficial effect. It allows him to indulge in his eccentricities at the complete expense of narrative.

Taken on its own merits, then, *Dr. Goldfoot and the Girl Bombs* is a riotous mess, and there's nothing wrong with that. Just don't watch it expecting a wry and witty comedy. If you do it'll probably appear on your "Worst Films Ever Made" list.—MB

CREDITS: Production: Italian International Film; Director: Mario Bava; Story: Fulvio Lucisano; Screenplay: Franco Castellano, Pippo [Giuseppe Moccia], Franco Dal Cer; Cinematography: Antonio Rinaldi {Technicolor}; Music: Lallo [Coriolano] Gori; Original running length: 100 mins; Filming location: Cinecitta Studios, Rome; Country: Italy/US; Year: 1967

CAST: Franco Franchi (*Franco*), Ciccio Ingrassia (*Ciccio*), Fabian [Forte] (*Bill Dexter*), Vincent Price (*Dr. Goldfoot/Willis*), Francesco Mule (*Colonel Benson*), Laura Antonelli (*Rossana, Benson's secretary*), George Wang (*Fong*), Moana Tahi, Mario Bava (*the angel*)

**Italian locandina for *Due mafioso contro Goldginger***

DUE MAFIOSO CONTRO GOLDGINGER
"two of the mafia against Goldginger"
aka The Amazing Doctor G (US, unconfirmed), Operacion Relampago (Sp), Two Mafiosi Against Goldfinger (US, unconfirmed), Zwei Trottel gegen Goldfinger (WG)

Franco and Ciccio were an extremely popular Italian comic duo who appeared in a huge number of productions throughout the sixties and early seventies. They specialized in parodies of genres that were fashionable at the time, including spaghetti westerns (*Two Sons of Ringo*), epics (*I figli del Leopardo*), and gangster movies (*Due mafioso contro Al Capone*). If something proved popular in the cinemas, you could guarantee that the duo would be appearing in a slapstick take-off a few months later.

Their films are all pretty similar. They tend to involve a large amount of pratfalls, mugging and shouting at each other. They are, to say the least, an acquired taste—and even more so because most of their material is unavailable in anything but its original Italian-language version. The one film in which they have starred that is widely available in English, *Dr. Goldfoot and the Girl Bombs*, just goes to show how much their particular brand of comedy also loses in translation.

Here they play a couple of petty criminals who have been paid to take a photograph of a renowned military strategist, Colonel White (John Karlsen). When they attempt to do so, however, they are appalled to find that someone has replaced their camera with one that shoots bullets! Seeing their target has died, they sensibly decide to skedaddle. A mysterious mute, Molok (Dakar), collects the lifeless body.

Meanwhile, the head of the Secret Service, Herman (Andrea Bosic), is becoming concerned at the way in which several prominent politicians and powerbrokers are becoming traitors. They all seem to have a bizarre microchip implanted behind their left ear, which he surmises is some kind of controlling device. He assigns his top agent, 007 (an early appearance by giallo star George Hilton, strangely hiding behind a "George Hamilton" pseudonym) to investigate. He doesn't get very far, being shot by the apparently reanimated White (who wears one of the strange chips).

Franco and Ciccio somehow witness this, are caught by Molok and taken to the headquarters of a wealthy, megalomaniac scientist: Goldginger (Fernando Rey). They are subjected to a short bout of circular saw torture before Goldginger discovers a couple of chess pieces in their pockets. Assuming that Franco is a master at the sport, he challenges him to a game—which inevitably ends in chaos. After much running around and shouting they do eventually manage to escape.

Herman, however, thinks that he can use the hapless pair, and decides that they should infiltrate the madman's lair (in blackface, natch). Firstly, they have to be trained in the techniques of the sixties spy: camouflage (Franco disguises himself as a sofa), riding bicycles, avoiding the temptation of a femme fatale, rugby and anything else the scriptwriters can dream up.

The starting point for this outing was obviously the phenomenally successful Bond film *Goldfinger*. Among the lampoons are the Oddjob-lite Molok (complete with exploding shoe to throw at his victims) and Franco, painted Shirley Eaton-style, in gold. There's also all the normal tomfoolery involving booby-trapped cars and secret weapons disguised as everyday objects. I particularly enjoyed the sequence in which the titular tit-heads accidentally have their set of deadly, special-issue toiletries swapped by accident, and are left to disarm Molok with a tube of toothpaste. It's all pretty crude, and the humor never approaches anything resembling wit, but is quite enjoyable if you're willing to enter into the puerile spirit of things.

One thing that is always surprising about the Franco and Ciccio films is that they are generally very well made. This has a great Umiliani soundtrack, superb cinematography and more than adequate direction. It was obviously cheap, but the production values are reasonably high. It's hard to imagine their British equivalent, the *Carry On* films, attracting an actor with the caliber of Fernando Rey.—MB

CREDITS: Production: Fida Cin.ca, Epoca Film; Director: Giorgio Simonelli; Story and Screenplay: Alessandro Continenza, Dino Verde, Amedeo Sollazzo; Cinematography: Isidoro Goldberger {Techniscope – Technicolor}; Music: Piero Umiliani; Original running length: 85 mins; Filming locations: Cinecitta Studios, Rome and Roma Film; Country: Italy/Spain; Year: 1965

CAST: Franco Franchi (*Franco*), Ciccio Ingrassia (*Ciccio*), Gloria Paul (*Marlene*), Fernando Rey (*Goldginger*), Andrea Bosic (*Colonel Herman, head of the Secret Service*), Rosalba Neri (*the secretary*), Dakar (*Molok*), Giampiero Littera (*Dupont*), Barbara Nelli (*Mrs. Dupont*), John Karlsen (*White*), George Hamilton [George Hilton] (*Agent 007*), Mario Pennisi, Luis Pena (*an associate of Goldginger*), Alfredo Mayo, Les Gingers Girls, Enzo Andronico, Mario Frera, Alfredo Adami, Guglielmo Spolettini [Guglielmo Spoletini], Elisa Montes (*Mary*), Nino Milano, Mario Boninos, John Karby, Nino Terzo (*a policeman*), Lino Banfi (*an agent*), Adolfo Belletti (*the hotel concierge*)

## ELEKTRA 1

aka Con la morte alle spalle (It),
Con la muerte a la esplada (Sp),
Typhon sur Hambourg (Fr),
With Death on Your Back (Int, unconfirmed)

A nutty megalomaniac called Elektra (Daniele Vargas) has created a hideous new drug. It sends anyone who takes it into a paranoid delusion, and makes them determined to lash out at whosoever they see as a threat. As a warning, his men test it on an American colonel, who promptly almost launches a nuclear strike on Russia. Seeing how successful it is, they attempt to sell it to the Chinese, who are very interested indeed.

Understandably concerned, the US and Russian authorities try to discover an antidote. A German professor makes good with the task, but is murdered before he can pass it on to the intelligence services—which serves them right for planning to meet him in a Hamburg fashion house (always a hotbed of dubious activities). Fortunately his assistant, Monica (Vivi Bach), manages to escape with the formula in a briefcase. She is helped in this by Gary (George Martin), a suave cat burglar known as The Lynx, who is under the misguided belief that her briefcase is chock full of jewels. When he discovers exactly what she is carrying, he steals it from her and tries to sell it to Elektra. Despite a couple of hitches (like their attempt to double-cross him), his plan succeeds.

However, he also has a deeper intention. He manages to convince the Chinese that Monica wasn't just the professor's assistant, but his partner, and is thus equally able to formulate the antidote. This, of course, kick-starts the whole cat and mouse chase all over again, as she is kidnapped by the villains and transported to their secret Alpine headquarters. Can Gary

**George Martin means business as the star of *Elektra 1***

rescue her and thereby save the world? It's no contest.

*Elektra 1* is really a rather mediocre genre entry. It's an extraordinarily addle-brained story embellished by a huge amount of totally unnecessary incidentals. Much of the running time is taken up by the comic interplay between KGB agent Ignazio Leone and his FBI counterpart, Michael Monfort. Capable though both these performers are, it does hugely distract from the central momentum of the narrative. Exactly why these organizations are actually involved in the first place is never adequately resolved, and why they're so absolutely incompetent soon becomes the overbearing question.

It's a shame, as the scriptwriters were obviously trying to do something different with their hero character. Gary is not a secret agent, he's a rather seedy little thief (albeit with a cool sports car and a penchant for white dinner jackets). You keep on expecting him to be revealed as an undercover operator, but his prime motivation until the very end remains his own wallet. George Martin does reasonably well with the role, and is certainly acrobatic, but doesn't really have the raffish charm to pull it off as effectively as, say, George Hilton or Giuliano Gemma. He does get to run around a lot in a wetsuit, and at one point is fed a narcotic that has the curious effect of making Rosalba Neri repeatedly change color.

This was the only spy film of Alfonso Balcazar, although his brother Jaime Jesus helmed the caper movie *Fistful of Diamonds*. One of the major figures of Spanish cinema, his family owned the Balcazar Studios, in which an awful lot of films were shot, and his name can be found as the producer or writer of a number of genre entries. Although hardly stylish, he does manage to include a couple of very impressive car chases (one of which lasts about five minutes) and a fun barroom brawl. There's also an effective climax in which Martin and Bach have to escape from a cable car while being shot at by a dive-bombing plane. He was responsible for much more impressive work in other genres (spaghetti westerns *Sonora* and *Clint the Stranger*, and the well-respected horror film *La Casa de las muertas vivientes*).—MB

CREDITS: Production: West Film, Comptoir Francais du Film, P.C. Balcazar; Director: Alfonso Balcazar; Story and Screenplay: Jose Antonio De La Loma, Alfonso Balcazar, Giovanni Simonelli; Cinematography: Victor Monreal {Stereovision 70 – Eastmancolor}; Music: Klaus [Claude] Bolling; Original running length: 86 mins; Country: Spain/Italy/France; Year: 1967

CAST: George Martin (*Gary*), Vivi Bach (*Monica*), Rosalba Neri (*Silvana*), Michael Monfort (*Bill*), Klaus Jurgen Wuschov [Wuchlow] (*Klaus*), Ignazio Leone (*Ivan*), Daniele Vargas (*"Elektra"*), Maria Badmayev (*Mrs. Van Hallen*), Robert Party (*Colonel Randolph*), Georges Chamarat (*Professor Roland*), Antonio Ho De Lima, Paola Natale (*csc*), Juan Llusa and with Gerard Landry (*the commissioner*). Uncredited: Lorenzo Robledo (*ambusher of army truck*)

ESPIONAGE IN LISBON

aka 077 intrigue à Lisbonne (Fr), Da 077: intrigo a Lisbona (It), Mision Lisboa (Sp)

This is one where the missing scientist—who's been hiding out and is killed early in the film—leaves very complicated instructions for finding his hidden formula. Here's how it goes: Buried inside two different books of Italian folk songs are underlined musical notes, but they don't mean anything unless you have a key. The key happens to be F-A-D-E or fa-la-re-mi, which will help decipher the notes into an old song about a ruin outside Lisbon where the formula is hidden inside a bell. No wonder it takes a good 100 minutes to find the darn thing!

Brett Halsey is George Farrell, agent 077. We know this because someone writes "0-7-7" on a piece of paper during a casino scene. Farrell is literally dragged out of bed, where he was entertaining a lady, and sent to Lisbon to find the missing scientist. He never does find him, but it's a lot of fun anyway as he and fellow agent Terry Brown (Marilu Tolo) put the pieces of the puzzle together.

Fernando Rey is our main villain, but has surprisingly little screen time to build much of a character. We do, however, get to see him communicate twice with a never-revealed superior via a hidden radio in the nether regions of a mannequin. The other villain—or villainess—is Moira Johnson (Jeanne Valerie), who gets more screen time and is more effective at (temporarily) thwarting the good guys, but who simply gives up three-quarters of the way through the movie.

There's a mysterious man in the film who monitors the action on an omniscient camera in a briefcase (much like a laptop computer), when he's not spying on semi-nude ladies with the device, that is. And he turns out to be a good guy! The man is Alfredo Mayo and he will be familiar to those who watch spy movies.

The score by Daniel White is pretty bland Big Band jazz stuff and is sometimes grossly inappropriate to the action. A good score is one thing this film certainly lacks.

There are a few gadgets used by both sides, some more successfully pulled off than others. The aforementioned briefcase is one, and there's a pencil gun and a purse gun too. There's a flashlight with dual bulbs, one infrared to reveal hidden messages, but the kicker is a little number used by Farrell to eavesdrop. It's a listening device disguised as a bug! Really. It's a remote-control fly about the size of a peach pit. While the idea is funny, the execution is poor as Farrell is obviously following this bug on a string with his little control unit. It's a crack-up.

We also have yet another scene where a kid shoots his toy gun at the secret agent. The twist

**Italian poster for Espionage in Lisbon**

this time is that the agent buys the boy's little dart gun and actually uses it! But not to shoot anyone. He shoots the dart at a window and cuts the glass around it to break into a house.

There's a musical number in the film too. Marilu Tolo uses her cover as a nightclub singer to purr a samba-inflected jazz number. It's okay in that overly dramatic way that these supposed performers use when they only sing one song per night. Other than that, we get to watch some bad jazz dancing, a fashion show with some atrocious hats, and we get a couple of glances at a few old jazz album covers.

There's a fun sequence when Terry Brown finds a dead double agent in her hotel room and Farrell helps her get rid of him by taking him through the raucous party next door. There are some genuine laughs here. We never see the party, only hear it, but an extra treat is the unbilled cameo by George Nader as a drunk who stumbles into the bathroom and mistakes the corpse as a fellow inebriate.

The film runs a bit long, like this review, and culminates in a gun battle with really bad sound effects for the guns used by heroes. Anyway, I recommend this film by director Tulio Demicheli (*Assignment Terror*) as a good teaming of Halsey and Tolo despite its shortcomings.—DD

CREDITS: Production: Hesperia, Speva, Terra Film; Director: Tulio Demicheli; Story: David Khune [Jesus Franco]; Screenplay: Marcel Felt, Juan Cobos, Jose De La Bayonas; Cinematography: Angelo Lotti {Techniscope – Technicolor}; Music: Daniel White; Original running length: 90 mins; Filming locations: Vallehermosa (Madrid), Incir-De Paolis Studios, Rome, Lisbon; Country: Spain/Italy/France; Year: 1965

CAST: Brett Halsey (*George Farrell*), Marilu Tolo (*Terry Brown*), Fernando Rey (*Von Keister*), Jean Valerie (*Moira*), Daniel Ceccaldi (*Robert Scott*), Alfredo Mayo (*Losky*), Irah Eory (*Olga*), Barbara Nelli (*Pamela*), Erica Bianchi (*the girl in bikini*), Francesca Rosano, Angel Terron, Rafael Bardem, Miguel Paenzuela, Barbara Nelli, Maria Rivas, Vicente Roca

**Spanish poster that touts *Espionage in Tangiers* as an unofficial entry in the 077 series**

ESPIONAGE IN TANGIERS
aka Marc Mato, agente S.077 (Sp),
S077 spionaggio a Tangeri (It)

This short film—the review print only runs about an hour—is by-the-numbers spy stuff but it is never boring. It doesn't have time to be. Luis Davila is agent Mike Murphy (for us English speakers) and he's after a ray gun that completely disintegrates whatever gets in the way of its blue beam.

The pre-credit sequence shows us what this terrible weapon can do. The first test the scientists perform on the gun is to shoot it out of the window of the laboratory at a car in the parking lot. The owner is probably still wondering happened to it. Later after the inventor has gone mad with power, he demonstrates the gun against…a fireplace. This guy could use some imagination.

The main villain here is Rigo (Alberto Dalbes), but he doesn't have much screen time. Who does? In a film with barely enough time to get off the ground we have not one but two femmes fatales. Genre regular Jose Greci is Lea, who works for Rigo and likes being slapped around. Perla Cristal is Magda, who owns a local club and is working against Rigo for the ray gun.

At the climax of the film all the principals are gathered for the sale of the gun to an unnamed foreign power when the scientist decides to take his gun and escape on a boat. After a minor tussle with Murphy, the guy falls overboard. End of movie. And just when you were settling down for some more fun.

The ratio of action per minute is way up there. Four people are killed in the first five minutes. The last of these is unfortunate enough to have his head caught in a car window and is then dragged down the street. There are plenty of well-staged fights, car chases, gun battles, torture and people getting slapped around.

Murphy drives a big ol' white Cadillac convertible and says things like "It's nothing serious, somebody shot me." At one point Murphy is trapped in a room that begins to flood with water. Then multi-colored lights begin to flash for no reason other than they look cool—you gotta like that. Rigo has a nifty little video communicator that he uses on a commercial flight. When it beeps, he looks at the guy sitting next to him as if to say "Don't pay any attention, I'm just talking to myself."

The score by Benedetto Ghiglia is an unobtrusive mixture of jazz and easy-listening. The credits run over action stills from the movie—another nice touch. There's even a credit for an actor named Joe Camel. You could actually do a lot worse than this little adventure, believe me. Director Gregg Tallas, who also co-wrote this, has made a pretty fun no-budget thriller that falls into the so-bad-it's-good category.—DD

CREDITS: Production: Atlantida C.C., Dorica Film; Director: Gregg Tallas; Story: Heriberto A Curiel; Screenplay: Gregg Tallas, Jose Luis Jerez; Cinematography: Alvaro Mancori, Rafael Pacheco {Eastmancolor – Panormaica}; Music: Benedetto Ghiglia; Original running length: 92 mins; Country: Italy/Spain; Year: 1965

CAST: Luis Davila (*Mike Murphy*), Jose Greci (*Lea*), Alberto Dalbes (*Rigo*), Perla Cristal (*Magda*), Ana Castor, Tomas Blanco, Remigio Del Grosso, Alfonso Rojas, Barta Barry, Joe Camel

FANTABULOUS INC
aka Il Donna, il sesso, il superuomo (It)

Here's a rather obscure item that could do with some serious restoration work and a high-quality DVD re-release. It's not a perfect film—far from it—but it oozes "cult" from every entertaining minute of its running time. Born partly from the late-sixties craze for comic strip superhero movies (Diabolik, Kriminal, et al.), it also leeches into the vibrant counter-cultural values of the time to create something far more anti-authoritarian and anarchistic (both in terms of narrative and context) than most of its forebears.

Amiable Richard Vernon (Richard Harrison) is returning home one night when he finds that his car has broken down. Something weird is evidently going on, as everybody he meets is wearing sunglasses, and there's a very odd dude wandering about with steel claws instead of hands. Has he stumbled across a bizarre cult of beatniks? No, he is in fact the target of a kidnap plot and, despite his protests, is drugged and spirited away.

When he wakes up, he is in a hospital and the nurse insists upon addressing him as "Mr. Mayer." Even more mysteriously, a look-alike corpse—dressed in his clothes, no less—has turned up at the local morgue, although this isn't enough to fool his fiancée, Deborah (Judy West), into believing him dead. He is being held captive by a top-secret scientific organization, Fantabulous Inc., which is seemingly run by a bunch of complete lunatics. These whackos reprogram him, wiping his memory and connecting his brain to a giant computer, not to mention transforming him into a super-strong, super-intelligent super...man.

**Adolfo Celi starred in *Fantabulous Inc***

Why are they doing this? Well, to sell him to the highest bidder. They reckon that the governments around the world will be more than happy to pay for a "hero" who can uphold law and order (and keep any rebellious varmints in their place—jail, of course). They're right. After demonstrating his power by having him steal vital atomic plasma from a military base, the offers come pouring in. But their superman happens to catch a glimpse of Deborah, and his memory begins to return.

This is an archetypal sixties film, chucking in all kinds of ideas, styles and obsessions to come out with something gloriously messy and endlessly watchable. There's a crazy-baby mix of psychedelic comedy, cool cinematographic tricks and just plain weirdness, as well as your habitual fashion models, beat music, sci-fi style costumes and pointless grooving. What's not to like? Plotwise, it obviously anticipates *Robocop*, but stylistically it's closer to Corrado Farina's popular (and over-rated) *Baba Yaga*—not least because of the use of comic strip panels to intersperse the narrative, but also because of the emphasis upon fashion photographers, models and great pop-art designs and costumes.

This willingness to meander gives rise to some gloriously odd moments: Vernon attempts to escape from his confines by the holding onto a bunch of balloons (which just happen to be lying around) and floating out of a window. Upon discovering that the one weakness with their superman is his uncontrollable love of sex, one of the scientist's questions: "Maybe there's money to be made in porno films?" This also gives rise to a funny sequence in which they attempt to stimulate him by having a succession of young ladies undress for him ("The intellectual woman, reading a newspaper").

There's also an interesting post-modern spin given to it all by the fact that Deborah is an actress, appearing in a crappy commercial featuring a masked superhero called, you got it, Fantabulous. This turns out to be an advertisement for the forthcoming superman ("With Fantabulous, danger goes away"), luring the slothful population into a desire for some kind of hero figure. Of course, the fact that this hero figure stands for upholding the status quo doesn't really matter, it's the packaging that counts. As the sales pitch puts it: "Liberty…secured by order, an order based on discipline. Discipline insured by authority." This superman isn't going to be on the side of the good, he's going to be on the side of authority—a Fascistic implication that is emphasized by the villains' Neitzschean obsession with creation of a Nazi-style *ubermensch*. Unfortunately, this attempt to critique the comic strip adaptations of the time is rather undermined by the fact that most of them feature the superhero as an anarchistic, anti-authoritarian figure anyway.

If you're wondering what any of this has to do with spies, well, the main secondary hero, McFitzroy (Nino Fuscagni) is a secret agent trying to uncover what's going on in the Fantabulous headquarters.—MB

CREDITS: Production: Summa Cin.ca, Procinex; Director: Sergio Spina; Story and Screenplay: Furio Colombo, Ottavio Jemma, Sergio Spina; Cinematography: Claudio Ragona {Eastmancolor}; Music: Sandro Brugnolini; Original running length: 95 mins; Filming location: Incir-De Paolis Studios; Country: Italy/Spain; Year: 1967.

CAST: Richard Harrison (*Richard Vernon, aka Kar Mayer*), Adolfo Celi (*"Beethoven"*), Judy West (*Deborah Sands*), Nino Fuscagni (*Leonard McFitzroy*), Fabienne Fabre (*Alice*), Enzo Fiermonte (*General Van Pelt*), Gustavo D'Arpe (*Professor Cronin*), Silvio Bagolini (*Uncle Mac*), Sandro Moretti (*an official*), Arturo Dominici (*Captain Fenninger*), Nino Vingelli (*Lawrence*), Giacomo Furia (*Ogilvy*), Aldo Bonamano (*Soviet official*), Ghislaine Barbot, Anita Cartinovis (*Krone's two officials*), Manlio De Angelis, Virginio Gazzolo, Mickey Knox, Renzo Marignano, Giulio Maculani, Federico Valli, Giancarlo Sisti, Gino Turrini. Uncredited: Claudio Ruffini (*Frank, a guard*)

FBI OPERAZIONE VIPERA GIALLA

"FBI operation yellow snake"

aka FBI operacion vibora amarilla (Sp),

Im nest der gelben Viper—

Das FBI schlagt zu (WG)

A pipe-smoking man is ambushed and gunned down while leaving his country house. In the ensuing tussle, the killers manage to get away, but not before the man's son has managed to seriously bite one of them on the wrist.

Fifteen years later the boy has grown into Van Dongen (Helmut Lange), an FBI agent. He is sent to Cape Town—which also happens to be where his father was killed—to investigate a gang of criminals, apparently led by Allun (Gerard Landry, uncredited on some prints), who have stolen some cases of uranium. They are known as The Golden Viper because anyone who betrays them, or tries to pry too far into their activities, is killed by a poisoned blow-dart.

Van Dongen is fortunate to arrive at the same time as a couple of new members of the gang, and seizes the opportunity to take one of their places. Allun, however, has his suspicions and sets a test in a cable car to reveal which of his men is the infiltrator. Van Dongen keeps his cool, so that the wrong man is suspected and killed.

It soon becomes clear that the gang actually has a secret leader and that Allun is really only the second in command. Furthermore, Van Dongen is able to discover that this man sports an identical scar to the one that would now be carried by

**Belgian poster for *FBI operazione vipera gialla***

the man who had killed his father. He suspects that this may in reality be Sanders (Massimo Serato), a police commissioner who seems worryingly reluctant to display his wrist.

*Vipera gialla* is a decidedly mediocre effort that suffers from a slow pace and a notable lack of action. More of a slow burner, the film does have some interestingly composed set pieces, not least of which is the arrival of a bunch of divers at the gang's secret hideout. It's similar in feel, storyline and atmosphere to earlier German/Italian co-productions such as *Cave of Diamonds* and *Operation Hong Kong*, with a load of double-crossing villains engaged in small-scale shady activities being foiled by an upright leading chap. You almost expect Brad Harris to pop up at any moment.

Probably the most memorable thing about it is Moira Orfei as Allun's sidekick. She has something of Betty Page about her, not least because she spends most of the film parading around in basque, heels and stockings. It also helps that she appears to be wearing less a wonder than a miracle bra, which does truly frightening things with her bosom. Helmut Lange makes a more interesting hero than usual, less cocksure and with a hint of melancholy about him.

Fortunately he gets to hook up with a drunken colonialist in a pith helmet, which seems to breathe some life into him. Massimo Serato contributes his token smooth villain performance.

Alfredo Medori only directed five films: *Rhythm of India*, *Sfida nella citta dell'oro*, the mediocre spaghetti western *Death on the High Mountain*, a documentary called *Inferno nel Pacifico*, and this. None of them exactly set the box office alight. At a guess, story supplier Ralph Anders could be a pseudonym for Raoul Andre, director of *Jeff Gordon, Secret Agent* and *Mission to Caracas*.—MB

CREDITS: Production: Labor Film, Imperial Film, Castello Film; Director: Alfredo Medori; Story: Ralph Andres [Raoul Andre]; Screenplay: Alfredo Medori, Joachim Bartsch; Cinematography: Hank Kuhle {Agfacolor}; Music: Francesco De Masi; Original running length: 86 mins; Filming location: South Africa; Country: Italy/West Germany/Spain; Year: 1964

CAST: Helmut Lange (*Tom Van Dongen*), Moira Orfei (*Lolanda*), Massimo Serato (*Sanders*), Peer Schmidt, Sam Garter, Michael Kirner, Adeline Wagner, Nikki Bester, Harris Parloff, Harry Victor, Edward Canterbury, Danielle Margold, Brian Lowerthal, Joe Masicano, Allan Prior, Harald Lake. Uncredited: Gerard Landry (*Allun*)

## FORMULA C-12 BEIRUT

aka Agent 505—Death Trap Beirut (unconfirmed),
Agent 505 todesfelle Beirut (WG),
Agente 505 muerte en Beirut (Sp),
Baroud à Beyrouth pour F.B.I. 505 (Fr),
From Beirut with Love (UK, unconfirmed),
La trappola scatta a Beyrut (It)

A couple of beautiful girls are murdered while sunbathing at a luxury hotel. The killer too is murdered, but able to reveal—before dying—that they were disposed of because they "knew too much." Something bad is being planned in Beirut, and it has something to do with a man called The Sheikh, who has only four fingers. It seems this isn't a lone incident. The Sheikh is also thought to be behind the assassination of several prominent scientists.

Interpol agent Richard Blake (Frederick Stafford) is sent to investigate. He promptly eludes some villains by duping them into kidnapping the wrong person, an unfortunate, bumbling traveling salesman (Harold Leipnitz). In fact, Beirut is stuffed full of villains, most of whom are revealed to have recently been released from prison, and who have taken part in a charitable "rehabilitation" program. The same guys who run this program also finance a scientific institution that is looking to reclaim infertile desert land for farming.

One of their experiments involves the seeding of clouds with mercury, which (somehow or other) is supposed to make it rain. The one problem with this is that a criminal organization has infiltrated the institute, irradiated their supply of mercury and is now threatening to launch it at Beirut in a rocket (doesn't that just always happen).

This is another snappy spy film from director Manfred Kohler, which looks like a million

**Beautiful German poster for *Formula C-12 Beirut***

dollars. The high production values result from a reasonable budget and a good measure of talent. Ennio Morricone supplies a rare spy film soundtrack, adding another element of class to the proceedings, and the location filming is handled with style. There is also some good stunt work, including a fabulous "hitching a ride on the back of a helicopter" sequence.

As with *Target For Killing*, the script includes a good mixture of humor and action, although in this case it is perhaps a little more unfocused. Things are rather confused for large swathes of the running time, and the nature (and intention) of the villains is often annoyingly obscure. But these are minor complaints and in no way hinder the enjoyment of the film as a whole. Among the gadgets on display are a deadly telephone, a floating car and a gun that shoots bullets made of ice (see also *The Killer Likes Candy* and *Ring Around the World*).

Frederick Stafford is likeable in the lead role, coming across as a distinctly smooth chap who spends a large amount of his time fending off the amorous advances of a coterie of femmes fatales. He's also able to spot the bad guys by the shoddy workmanship of their tailoring, which simply adds to his sophisticated air. Harold Leipnitz, who played a pipe-smoking agent in *Inferno a Caracas*, steals the show as a crackpot criminal "mastermind." Winningly, he reserves the right to evil cackling for himself and blames his lunacy on his wife ("I've even forgiven you for your nagging and your stupidity and your ridiculous attempts to outsmart me!").

Other points of interest include a brief shot of a cinema playing *Last Plane to Baalbeck* and a funny scene in which a bad guy goons around with some radioactive rods before coming down with a severe bout of radiation poisoning. It looks to have been predominantly German-made but, apart from Morricone, there are a few Italian names in the crew list (most particularly producer/scriptwriter Mario Siciliano, who ran Metheus Film and was later to become an interesting director in his own right [*Cowards Don't Pray*, *Malacchio*]). Good stuff.—MB

CREDITS: Production: Exportfilm Bichoff, Co. GMBH, Lyonnaise Films; Director: Manfred Kohler; Story and Screenplay: Mario Siciliano, Manfred R Kohler; Cinematography: Ralph Castell {Eastmancolor}; Music: Ennio Morricone; Filming location: Beirut; Country: West Germany/Italy/France; Year: 1966

CAST: Frederick Stafford (*Richard Blake*), Genevieve Kluny, Chris Howland (*Bob O'Toole*), Harold Leipnitz (*Fred Köhlin*), Giselle Arden (*Monique*), Will Berger [Willy Birgel?] (*Omar Abdullah*), Pierre Richard, Patrick Bernard. Uncredited: Renato Ewert, Willy Birdel, Carla Calo (*villainess at "the Red Cockatoo"*)

FROM ISTANBUL, ORDERS TO KILL
aka Da Istambu ordine di uccidere (It),
Istamboul, carrefour de la drogue (Fr)

Occasionally a low-budget film achieves a sort of quaint lyricism, a quality arrived at not by intention but by necessity. You may count *From Istanbul, Orders to Kill* among those few films. Take the pre-credit sequence for example: A woman on the run is pursued in an empty building by several gunmen. She gets the best of two of them but is killed by a third, a calm and rail-thin man who steps over her body to answer a ringing phone. Standing in the oblique shadows, the man informs the caller that he has reached a wrong number.

Later another man enters, finds the dead woman and bemoans her passing. In the heel of her shoe, he discovers a roll of microfilm and then the phone rings. Another wrong number. The minimalist approach to photographing the death scene coupled with the absurdity of errant connections is disorienting. Even though we are comfortable recognizing the thriller film conventions, there is an esoteric element that eludes and amuses us.

Christopher Logan (a pseudonym for Mauro Parenti, who played the Diabolik knock-off Phenomenal) is offered twenty grand by CIA agent Williams to impersonate someone named Felix, who smuggles drugs for an international crime syndicate. The plot becomes convoluted concerning who is betraying whom, but the story is not the primary reason for watching. We are unfamiliar with most of the actors in this somewhat-obscure offering, but it certainly appears to be genre film stalwart Janine Reynaud who gets killed in the opening scene.

The scene in which Williams shows Logan slides of Felix, the man he is supposed impersonate, is a no-budget masterpiece. On a completely black set, the two actors hover over the slide projector, the only source of light in the room. Again the stark minimalism serves the scene perfectly. We understand exactly what's going on without the trappings of an actual office, which would only emphasize the economic shortcomings of the filmmakers. Unfortunately, this slide show appears to be the only preparation that Logan undergoes before jumping into the role of Felix. Hence, there are too many scenes of Logan staring blankly into the distance when he's confronted with situations that require him to actually be this person called Felix. Can't win'em all.

Logan must go to Istanbul to pick up a load of drugs, which he must later sell back in Italy. Once more economics come into play as there are lots of (actually interesting) travelogue shots of Logan walking around the real Istanbul, killing time to the jazzy beats on the soundtrack. Speaking of which, the score is a set of terrific combo jazz pieces by an unknown composer. It could easily stand on its own and is another one of the elements that lift this film above its lowly brethren.

The icy hit man (who has his own musical motif here) is a convention that we are used

**Classic imagery of the beautiful French poster for *From Istanbul, Orders to Kill***

to seeing in the genre. At the end of this film, as in many others, the killer goes over the top after shooting two of Logan's lovers, laughing maniacally as he corners our hero. Yes, the killer is undone by the almost-dead, wayward-yet-repentant woman, but his downfall does not result in his death. Logan, disgusted with the man's ilk, leaves him alive and walks away, past the bodies of the women left in the wake of this adventure. The ending is one of those classic freeze frames, a nice, final low-key touch to an unusual gem in the rough.—DD

CREDITS: Production: Sigma Cin.ca; Director: Alex Butler [Carlo Ferrero]; Story based on the story "The Devil Executor" by Robert Nislen; Screenplay: Alex Butler [Carlo Ferrero], Frank Mirror; Cinematography: Hugh Hamilton {Ferraniacolor}; Music: Sandro Brugnolini; Original running length: 88 mins; Country: Italy; Year: 1965

CAST: Christopher Logan [Mauro Parenti], Juri McFee [Nino Fuscagni], Geraldine Pearsall, Lucretia Love, Paul Muller, Lupe Sagarra, Calibe Serel, Frank Vidaris, Sam Tinkham, Margie Ladford, Art Tinkham

FULLER REPORT
aka Dejemos pasar manana (Sp),
Rapporto Fuller, base Stoccolma (It),
Svetlana uccidera il 28 settembre (It, alt),
Trahison a Stockholm (Fr)

Ken Clark is such a lug. All he wants out of his visit to Stockholm is a Swedish girl, but luckily for us he gets much more. I say luckily because this is a heck of a fun movie. Clark plays Dick Worth, an American racecar driver in Stockholm to put on an exhibition that his boss Bennet (Jess Hahn) hopes will result in orders for cars. At least that's what Worth believes. Worth gets drawn into CIA business when he is mistaken for a spy and takes on the job of recovering the Fuller Report, CIA information about an assassination plot.

Clark was a major player in spy films in the sixties. His hunky blond good looks kept him in the spy biz as agent 077 in several films, but *Fuller Report* is one of his best and probably the best spy film that Sergio Grieco—who worked with Clark several times—managed to crank out, despite the preposterous plot.

**Ken Clark with a gun to his head on the Belgian poster for *Fuller Report***

The above-mentioned Jess Hahn got around in the spy world too. Here he plays a bad guy who's in cahoots with some highly placed officials in the US and British governments who want to assassinate the President. You see, they all believe the US should dominate the world and think the President is going to compromise that goal by making some sort of deal with Red China. They want to use a double of a defecting ballerina, Svetlana Golyadkin (Beba Loncar), to kill the Prez and put the Russians in a bad spot. I told you it was preposterous, but despite the complexity everything actually falls together pretty well and makes for an enjoyable adventure.

The entire production is visually impressive, especially an interrogation and gunfight sequence that takes place in a lumber yard. At the end of this sequence, after Worth and Golyadkin have temporarily escaped the clutches of the bad guys, she says to him, "I was afraid they would kill you," and he responds, "Yeah, me too."

The racing car milieu makes for some fun, but the hands-down winner here is the killer score by Armando Trovajoli. It's practically nonstop jazzy spy pop that will have you humming long after the VCR has rewound. Look for this one, it's recommended.—DD

CREDITS: Production: Fida Cin.ca, Les Productions Jacques Roitfeld; Director: Terence Hathaway [Sergio Grieco]; Story: Sandro Continenza, Roberto Gianviti; Screenplay: Sandro Continenza, Roberto Gianviti, Alberto Silvestri, Franco Verucci; Cinematography: Stelvio Massi {Technicolor – Techniscope}; Music: Armando Trovajoli; Original running length: 100 mins; Filming locations: London, Stockholm, Zurich; Country: Italy/France; Year: 1967

CAST: Ken Clark (*Dick Worth*), Beba Loncar (*Svetlana Golyjadkin*), Lincoln Tate (*Pearson, a CIA agent*), Jess Hahn (*Ed Bennett*), Paolo Gozlino (*Max*), Serge Marquand (*Borjansky, a Russian agent*), Mirko Ellis (*Jimmy, a mechanic*), Sara Ross, Nicole Tessier, Claudio Biava (*Vasili, a Russian agent*), Gianni Brezza (*Clay, a CIA agent*). Uncredited: Lars Passgård (*Knut, Greta's partner*), Sten Ardenstam (*CIA agent*)

FURIA A MARRAKESH
"fury to Marrakesh"
aka Joe Fleming rechnet ab (WG),
La mort paye en dollars (Fr)

This was the unofficial third in the series begun with *Secret Agent Fireball* in 1965 (also directed by "J. Lee Donen") and continued with Antonio Margheriti's *Killers Are Challenged* the following year. By all accounts, the central character was originally called Dixon, but on some prints was renamed "Bob Fleming" to cash in on the popular aforementioned films. Stephen Forsyth, a young American actor, also stepped in to replace Richard Harrison. Unfortunately, he is one of the main problems with the film. He's simply too baby-faced to be a convincing secret agent, looking more like a pop star than a highly trained killer. He was extremely effective in Mario Bava's *Hatchet For A Honeymoon*, in which he played a psychotic mommy's boy, but simply isn't the right person for the role here.

A criminal organization called Losca manages to discover a secret bunker, in which are hidden a huge amount of US and Sterling banknotes, forged by the Third Reich during the Second World War in order to flood the economies of their allied enemy. The members of Losca, inevitably, want the loot for themselves, but their plans are jeopardized when one of their members steals a small amount of the notes for his own use. He is discovered and killed, but has already passed some of the counterfeit currency onto his accomplices. Greta (Cristina Gajoni, in an astounding wig) is sent to retrieve the cash.

The forgeries, however, are already in circulation. The CIA has traced a large amount of them being used by a young lady, Dora (Dominique Boschero), at the New York Trade Fair. Vodka-drinking agent Bob Fleming ("eugh, you drink vodka!") is sent to find out what's going on. After questioning her, he discovers that the organization is based in Marrakesh, and persuades her to act as a mole. After traveling to Beirut, several attempts to assassinate him follow (car bomb, encasing him in concrete, etc.), none of which succeed.

Eventually things relocate to Europe, as Fleming attempts to track down the secret bunker somewhere in the Swiss Alps (this is not a film that skimps on the locations). It also becomes increasingly clear that someone in the CIA is working for Losca, someone who is very close to Fleming.

It's a crying shame that *Marrakesh* isn't more widely available than it is (the version under review was recorded from German television). For despite the miscasting of the central role, this is one of the very best of the genre. There are some cool stunts (most notably a fun beachside car chase and some good aerial work), great sets, lots of gadgets (X-ray glasses that are used to undress female agents, flame-throwing cigarette lighters), and as much belly dancing as one could possibly wish for in a film.

Mino Loy was an underrated director, best known for his documentaries and Mondo films, who seemed most capable at working in "extreme" locations. Here, things are particularly effective once the action has settled amidst the snow-capped mountains. His best work probably remains *Desert Battle*. Interestingly, future cult director Sergio Martino had some input into this production, as did scriptwriter Ernesto Gastaldi, a duo who would go on to make some of the very best gialli during the 1970s.—MB

**Antonella Murgia and Stephen Forsyth having a bad day in *Furia a Marrakech***

CREDITS: Production: Zenith Cin.ca, Radius Productions; Director: J. Lee Donen [Mino Loy and Luciano Martino]; Story and Screenplay: Jualian Berry [Ernesto Gastaldi]; Cinematography: Florian(o) Trenker {Eastmancolor}; Music: Carlo Savina; Original running length: 96 mins; Filming locations: Titanus Studios, Switzerland, Morocco; Country: Italy/France; Year: 1966

CAST: Stephen Forsyth (*Bob Fleming/Dixon*), Dominique Boschero (*Dora*), Jacques Ary (*Alexander King, aka "Charley Clark"*), Cristina Gajoni (*Greta*), Terry (*Ulla*), Anthony Scott, Antonella Murgia, Gianni Di Benedetto, Conrad Nail, Kirk Zinnemann, Silvio Bagolini (*Lester, the CIA armorer*), John Hawkwood, Anatole Fryd, Louis Creinz, Mary Perren, Mitsouko (*Louise*)

**Plenty of action surrounds Ken Clark on the French poster for *Fury On the Bosphorus***

FURY ON THE BOSPHORUS
aka Agente 077: dall'Oriente con furore (It),
From the Orient with Fury (UK),
Fureur sur le Bosphore (Fr),
París-Estambul, sin regreso (Sp),
Vollmacht für Jack Clifton (WG)

Professor Kurtz (Ennio Balbo), the inventor of (ho-hum) a disintegrating gun, is kidnapped by a bunch of blue-suited cats (who hide him in a double bass case). The Secret Service receive a phone call from some chap claiming to have important information, and agent Dick Malloy (Ken Clark) is sent to try to meet him in a local gambling den. Unfortunately, a poisoned dart kills this contact before he can reveal anything (apart from cryptically referring to Beethoven's Fifth Symphony).

In fact, this refers to a record upon which is a vital clue. The trail leads to a ridiculously French bar where everybody wears berets and red T-shirts. Understandably, Malloy proceeds to get involved in a huge rumpus with several heavies and they smash the place to pieces. Such is the fate that should be suffered by all such theme pubs. Many more fistfights, chases and similar shenanigans follow.

It turns out that the villain is (yawn) trying to force the professor to construct his super weapon so it can be used as some part of a terrible scheme (such as, he can run around laughing madly while vaporizing everything in his sight). Everyone decamps to Istanbul so they can watch some belly dancing and eat some Turkish food, which is fair enough I suppose. Everything drifts toward a predictable climax.

Maybe after watching 100-odd spy films on the trot I have become somewhat jaded, but this counts as a huge disappointment. It obviously had a decent budget, and the same team was also responsible for a brace of rather good genre entries (*Fuller Report*, *Mission Bloody Mary*). *Fury*, however, never manages to become anything more than lackluster. This is particularly due to a plot that is less simple than retarded. It seems to have been the case that they simply jotted down a few holiday destinations they'd like to visit before even thinking about a script. This is also one of those films wherein a) someone "sings" with a voice that appears to have passed through seven amplifiers and a series of reverb pedals and b) absolutely nobody can shoot straight.

Even the cast is somewhat wasted. Ken Clark makes a rather odd secret agent, looking like a tennis star kitted out in a bow tie and bowler hat. Fortunately, his athletic performance enables him to overcome this initial incongruousness. Unfortunately, he is also saddled with some truly appalling dubbing ("tell me the truth, baby!") and is referred to by the villains as "big boy" once too often for comfort. Margaret Lee only shows up for a few minutes, doing a patentable ditzy Monroe impersonation, and Fernando Sancho appears for even less (taking off on his Mexican bandito persona—this is the best bit of the film).

At the climax, the hero explains his presence to the villain by exclaiming "I'm here to prevent you from committing other stupid crimes!" Which just about sums it up, really.—MB

CREDITS: Production: Fida Cin.ca, Les Productions Jacques Roitfeld, Epoca Film; Director: Terence Hathaway [Sergio Grieco]; Story and Screenplay: Arpad De Riso, Nino Scolaro, Alessandro Continenza, Leonard Martin; Cinematography: Juan Julio Baena {Techniscope – Technicolor}; Music: Piero Piccioni; Original running length: 95 mins; Filming locations: Cineccita Studios, Rome, Paris, Madrid, Istanbul; Country: Italy/France/Spain; Year: 1965

CAST: Ken Clark (*Dick Malloy*), Margaret Lee (*Evelyn Stone, Counter-Espionage Service*), Fabienne Dalì (*Simone Coblenz*), Evi Marandi (*Romy Kurtz, the professor's daughter*), Philippe Hersent (*Commissioner Heston, Malloy's boss*), Michaela [Mikaela, aka Michaela Wood] (*Doña Dolores López*), Fernando Sancho (*loud dinner customer in Paris restaurant*), Vittorio Sanipoli (*Vardar, bomb maker and deserter from the Czechoslovakian army*), Loris Barton, Ennio Balbo (*Professor Franz Kurtz*), Frank Ressel [Franco Ressel] (*Goldwyn, "the chief"*), Claudio Ruffini (*Werner, also called Pierre, Sarkis thug in trench coat*), Pat Basil [Pasquale Basile] (*Sarkis thug with drooping moustache*), Norman Preston, Joseph Powers, Mark Selmon, Alan Collins [Luciano Pigozzi] (*Karsa, man with eye patch*), Tomás Blanco, John Hamilton [Gianni Medici] (*Captain Ali ven Locum, Turkish secret police*), Richard Levin, Jean Lyonel, Dean De Grassi [Dario De Grassi] (*Boris Molotov, Romy's boyfriend*). Uncredited: Lorenzo Robledo (*Agent Mike*), Calisto Calisti (*Hassan, Turkish informant*), Gabriella Giorgelli (*girl at roulette table in casino*), Feridun Cölgecen (*maitre d', Turkish nightclub*).

FX-18

aka Coplan, agent secret FX18 (Fr), Orden: FX 18 debe morir (Sp), Uccidete agente segreto 777—stop (It)

The first is the worst, as the old saying goes, and it certainly holds true here. This was Ken Clark's first foray in the spy genre and it's easily the weakest of his half-dozen adventures. *FX-18* is a juvenile take on one of Paul Kenny's Coplan novels, although I suspect it's been "dumbed down" beyond recognition. Ken's name in the English-dubbed print is Francis Cabtree or something like that, and he's given the voice usually reserved for thugs.

Second-billed Jany Clair, who plays Patricia, is a pouty beauty given little to do but get slapped around and tortured. Yes, this is a world where the men are brutes and the women like it.

A cigarette blowgun is the only gadget worth mentioning and the fights are sloppy and poorly staged. They do blow up a model yacht and a real plane for excitement.

The script is the weakest link in this simple story. Aside from the smarmy sexual innuendoes, there was only one funny line I could remember. Francis and Patricia pose as newlyweds for some reason, and when they order drinks in the hotel bar she asks for lemonade with cream while Francis has tomato juice with milk. One of the bad guys who happen to sit at the next table mumbles under

**Dramatic Belgian poster for Ken Clark's first spy film, *FX-18***

his breath "Anybody who drinks something like that couldn't be anything else other than Americans."

Director Maurice Cloche takes the blame this time around because it seems all the departments of filmmaking are second rate. Even the score by Eddie Barclay and Michel Colombier, which has its jazzy moments, is largely forgettable. There's some nice scenery off the coast of Spain to look at, but that isn't enough to salvage this wreck. Unless you're a Ken Clark completionist, skip this one and watch any of his other spy flicks.—DD

CREDITS: Production: C.F.P.P., Producciones Cinematograficas Centro, Rotor Film; Director: Maurice Cloche; Story based on "Coplan Tente Sa Chance" by Paul Kenny; Screenplay: O.C.M. and Christian Plume; Cinematography: Baina {Eastmancolor -Techniscope}; Music: Eddie Barclay, Michel Colombier; Original running length: 97 mins; Country: France/Spain/Italy; Year: 1964

CAST: Ken Clark (*Coplan*), Jany Clair (*Patricia*), Amedee Domenech (*Fondane*), Jacques Dacqmine (*Le Vieux*), Cristina Gajoni (*Arlette*), Daniel Ceccaldi (*Noreau*), Margit Kocsis (*Lila Sari*), Claude Cerval (*Barter*), Ramon Centenaro (*Legay*), Lorenzo Robledo (*Alfonso*), Anselmo Cid (*Rodriguez*), Guy Delorme (*Lattina*), Astrid Caron (*Carla*), Henri Guegan (*Alderner*), Jean-Pierre Laverne (*Morvil*), Pierre Parel (*Mairesse*), Beni Deus (*Gunsson*), Robert Favart (*the Italian colonel*), Jose Noguero (*the Spanish colonel*), Roberto Camardiel (*Mazekia*), Andre Cagnard (*the killer*), Antoine Baud (*Barter's henchman*), Aida Power, Lucia Anram, Sabine Sun, Robert Verbecke

FX 18 SUPERSPY

aka Agente 777: missione Summergame (It),
Coplan FX18 casse tout (Fr),
The Exterminators (Int), Geheimauftrag
CIA—Istanbul 777 (WG),
Objetivo Matar (Sp)

Given the time period, this should be counted among the most brutal, cynical and paranoid of spy thrillers. Director Riccardo Freda dealt with the underbelly of the human soul in many of his works and here he pulls no punches, so to speak. Inspired by the novels of Paul Kenny, Freda turns spy guy Coplan into a steely-eyed killer—an anti-hero in a universe composed of the bad, the ugly and the worse. And women don't escape Freda's gaze: They are portrayed as either criminal or dead.

Our film opens with a striptease, a promising start for many spy films of the era, but very few minutes go by before Richard Wyler, as Coplan, guns down a waiter in cold blood. The poor guy wasn't even threatening, he was just opening a bottle of champagne! It turns out the waiter was a spy, of course, but in this film nearly every human being is a spy, thug, whore or dead and many times a combination of these.

The very next sequence is a perfect example of the elements of adventure in the film being repeatedly subverted by unrelenting violence. Coplan is using an airplane to chase down a truck and finally lands the plane on top of the moving vehicle. It's an amazing stunt, comparable to Bond, but when Coplan manages to overpower the driver and open the trunk being carried, he finds that the man inside is dead from the long bloody spikes driven into the top of the trunk as if it were a modern iron maiden. It's a bizarre nod to Freda's reputation as a director of horror films and a calculated shock for the viewer. This film is anything but light-hearted.

Besides appearing in several spy films, Richard Wyler was the eponymous *Man From Interpol* in the UK television series. Here he has a partner from the Israeli Secret Service, Shaimoun, played by Gil Delamare—who is also credited with "special effects." Delamare was a stuntman by trade and probably choreographed the many fights in the film. He died the year after this film came out at age 42 while in the midst of another movie.

At one point, Coplan and Shaimoun duke it out with several bad guys and Coplan ends up pinning one of them to the wall with a chair. After a short interrogation, Coplan, still holding the man to the wall, tells Shaimoun to kill him and Shaimoun dutifully puts a gun to the man's head and pulls the trigger. This being 1965, the man's brains do not splatter all over our heroes, but the scene is done with such ferocity as to be disconcerting just the same.

Coplan is a suave killer who thrives on violence and expects the same from all he meets. His expectations are invariably met. Coplan burns the hand of a nosy bellhop with a cigarette, slaps around a female working for the other side, and in another ferocious scene drowns an enemy agent in a sink full of water. The discovery of the body of a female Israeli agent who was tortured and murdered (offscreen) is met with nonchalance by Coplan, but at least Shaimoun is visibly upset.

The sassy beauty Jany Clair shows up 45 minutes into the film as a traitorous whore (what else), but her high billing turns out to be not much more than a cameo, unfortunately. Clair was in many sword and sandal movies. usually playing traitorous whores.

This is a generally exciting film that moves at breakneck speed and has plenty of credible action. It is, however, marred by one really phony scene of Coplan doing a wheelie on a motorcycle with one hand as he shoots the driver of the car he's chasing with the other. No way.

The final act is played out in an amazing location in Turkey. These unusual rock formations and caves have appeared in films before and after, but they never cease to be visually stunning. This is where the villain, played by an actor whose name we are not familiar with, has his underground lair (housing a nuclear rocket, of course), and we can't fault his choice of location. There is some bad continuity in the final car chase as scenes alternate between dirt road and asphalt, but they wrap it up with a car jump onto a ferry—accomplished by Delamare. Throughout the film we are treated to an excellent jazz score by Michel Magne that punctuates the sour world Coplan inhabits.—DD

CREDITS: Production: A C.F.F.P., Camera Films, Cinerad production; Director: Riccardo Freda; Story based on the novel "Stop Coplan" by Paul Kenny; Screenplay: Claude Marcel Richard; Cinematography: Henri Persin {Eastmancolor}; Music: Michel Magne; Original running length: 95 mins; Country: France/Italy; Year: 1965

CAST: Richard Wyler (*Francis Coplan*), Gil Delmaire (*Shaimoun*), Jany Clair (*Helen*

**Large format German poster for Riccardo Freda's *FX-18 Superspy***

*Jordan*), Robert Manuel (*Hartung*), Jacques Dacqmine (*the old man*), Guy Marly (*Said*), Valeria Ciangottini (*Gelda*), Huong Ham-Chan (*the Chinese engineer*), Christian Kerville (*Argaz*), Andre Cagnard (*John*), Maria-Rosa Rodriguez (*Shiela*), Jean-Pierre Jamic (*a henchman*), Jacky Balnchot (*a henchman*), Bernard Lajarrige (*Bruno Schwartz*), Yvan Chiffre (*a henchman*), Robert Favart, Tony Moreno, Fernand Bercher

GOLDSNAKE

aka Goldsnake Anonima Killers (It), Mission suicide à Singapour (Goldsnake) (Fr), Operazione Goldsnake (It, alt), Singapur, hora cero (Sp), Suicide Mission to Singapore (US, unconfirmed)

When the US government finds out that a Chinese scientist, Chang, has discovered a means of creating astonishingly small atomic weapons, they are concerned. A device the size of a Ping-Pong ball could wipe out a large city. Fortunately, the scientist has escaped to Singapore with his son, albeit with the downside that no one actually knows where he is.

**Another classic Italian poster, this time for *Goldsnake***

Secret agent Kurt Jackson (Stelio Candelli) is dispatched to the city, with orders to track him down and bring him back to America or, at the very least, prevent the Chinese from being able get him (or his work) back.

After meeting his local contact, Jean (Juan Cortes), who seems to live in a villa populated entirely with Asian babes, Jackson bumps into a dodgy blonde called Evelyn. After following her, he discovers that her home is a huge modernist construction, has a moat and is protected by a network of tin-pot security devices—which would appear to vindicate his suspicions.

She is, in fact, a prominent member of a criminal gang that covets the scientist for themselves. They hope to track him down and auction him off to the highest bidder, whether this be the American government, the Chinese or someone else altogether. Unfortunately, they're not the only ones with this idea. Several other underworld organizations are also hoping to lay their hands on the elusive Mr. Chang.

This was the only spy film directed by Ferndinando Baldi, a better-than-average filmmaker who lent his talents to a number of genres, peplums (*David and Goliath*), westerns (*Texas addio, Get the Coffin Ready*) and even a giallo (*Nove ospiti per un delitto*). Although not as convincing as his most effective work, or as strange as his best- known film, *Blindman*, *Goldsnake* is a reasonably pleasing production.

The film makes superb use of the Singapore locations—smoky opium dens, rickety harbors and tropical vegetation (this was, of course, before it became a pristine city of skyscrapers and banks). There are some most impressive scenes. One that particularly sticks in the mind is simply composed around a couple of the actors sitting in a villa while piano music plays in the background, a strangely compulsive moment of tranquility (before the gunplay starts again). You do have the feeling that there's quite a lot of filler material to make up the running time. But this isn't always unpleasant if handled well, especially if it's accompanied by a good soundtrack. This one is particularly effective, ranging from manic high-hat thrills to lugubrious torch songs.

The script is, of course, complete piffle, but there are a few distinctions to capture the attention. As well as the essential booby-trapped matches, which must have been standard issue for sixties spies, there's also a gun disguised as a mandolin—a precursor to the more famous "gun inside a banjo" as wielded by William Berger in *Sabata*. It's also quite interesting that this is one of very few Euro-films of the period to feature a number of Asian actors in more than minor fodder roles. There really are only about four western performers to appear throughout the entire running time, which somehow lends the proceedings a slight feeling of (entirely misplaced) authenticity.

As well as Yoko Tani, playing her normal duplicitous Oriental character, giallo favorite Annabella Incontrera (*Black Belly of the Tarantula*, *Crimes of the Black Cat*) provides the female interest. Appearing regularly in westerns, this was a very rare spy role for her. Stelio Candelli, more regularly to be found as a grizzled villain in films such as *Last of the Mohicans* (the 1964 version) and *Death in Haiti*, may seem a rather peculiar choice to play the hero, but he's actually rather good, looking much more boyish than was to be expected. In the same year, he appeared in a forgotten BBC series called *Vendetta*, playing an ex-Mafia member turned crime investigator.—MB

CREDITS: Production: Seven Film, Alexandra Prod.ni Cin.che, Paris Cannes Productions, Hispamer Film; Director: Ferdinando Baldi; Story: Maria Del Carmin Martinez; Screenplay: Ferdinando Baldi, Maria Del Carmin Martinez; Cinematography: Emilio Foriscot {Techniscope - Technicolor}; Music: Carlo Savina; Original running length: 97 mins; Filming location: Hong Kong; Country: Italy/France/Spain; Year: 1966

CAST: Stanley Kent [Stelio Candelli] (*Kurt Jackson*), Annabella Incontrera (*Helen*), Yoko Tani (*Annie Wong*), Juan Cortes (*Jean*), Sellah Melan

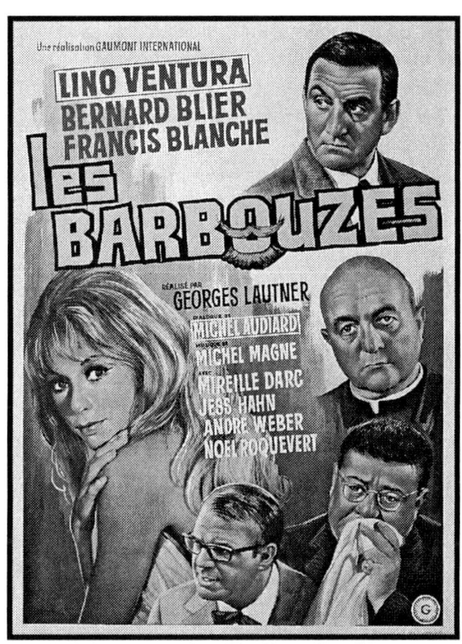


**Belgian poster for *The Great Spy Chase***

### THE GREAT SPY CHASE
aka Les Barbouzes (Fr);
Quattro spie sotto il letto (It)

This film kicks off with a multiple homicide on a train—which manages to be both effective and idiosyncratic—as a whole menagerie of assassins bump each other off (by poison gas, gunshot, strangulation, etc.). It seems that in the midst of all this, the plans for an innovative thermonuclear device have gone missing. The best secret agents in the world—including the French Francis Lagneau (Lino Ventura), the Russian Boris Vassiliev (Francis Blanche) and the Swiss Eusebio Cafarelli (Bernard Blier)—are assigned to recover them by their respective countries.

Lagneau's inquiries begin with the scientist who had invented the device. And who, unfortunately, happens to have just died. So he turns his attention instead toward the dead man's widow (Mireille Darc), hoping that she knows something of his contraption. She seems rather more concerned with what type of dress she should wear to the funeral, and Lagneau's plans are further upset by having all of the other spies appear at the wake, each adopting a suitably ridiculous persona. There follows an intricate game of intrigue as they all attempt to outwit each other. What none of them realize is that somebody is making fools of them all. Or maybe not.

With this and *The Monocle*, Georges Lautner proved himself to be the master of the delightfully inconsequential spy film. Both films are almost determinedly lightweight; they're more concerned with raising a smile than engaging the brain. And there's certainly nothing wrong with that. In fact, Lautner is one of the great unheralded French filmmakers of the 1960s, and despite his unrepentantly populist approach, he even had some contemporary admirers in France. It's a crying shame that his films have fallen into obscurity, and they're certainly deserving of some kind of revival today.

*The Great Spy Chase* was actually a vague follow-up to his earlier film, *Les Tontons flingueurs,* aka *Crooks In Clover*. This had also featured Ventura, Blier and Blanche, albeit playing hopeless gangsters rather than spies. Both are affectionate parodies, though of different genres, and feature clever screenplays from Michel Audiard (who would script many memorable crime films through the sixties and seventies).

With its snappy dialogue and effective direction, *Spy Chase* is, quite simply, funny. There's a decent mix of slapstick and wit, and the performances from all concerned are far better than could possibly have been expected. Lino Ventura carries the film in his normal understated way, and even amusingly manages to beat up a couple of kung-fu fighters. Bernard Blier is good value too, and one particularly tasteful moment finds him using the body of a hanging man to swing out of the way from a gang of pursuers.

Most of the action takes place in a baroque chateau, which finds the high-tech gadgetry of the assorted agents repositioned within decidedly more aristocratic environs. On their first night at the chateau, the agents discover their rooms to be full of deadly boobytraps: acid coming out of the shower; scorpions in the bed; an exploding toilet. Not too dissimilar to your average British hotel, then. There are listening devices planted just about everywhere, not to mention an impressively increasing number of corpses littering the grounds (most of these are servants, bizarrely dressed in Alpine farmer costumes for some reason or other). Just adding to the homey feel of the place are assorted portraits with eyes that move, and a dead body in the piano. It's all rather like an affectionate dig at the Hotel Luxor from Fritz Lang's *The Thousand Eyes of Dr. Mabuse*.

The standout sequence finds a veritable army of Chinese villains attempting to capture the castle and becoming involved in a huge battle with the spies...all of this while Ms. Darc carries on with her normal womanly duties (brushing her hair, eating supper and so on). This could well have been lifted from the famous sequence from *Carry On Up the Khyber*, wherein a group of phlegmatic Brits continue with a dinner party while their colonial headquarters is being besieged by mad natives.

Also of note is a typically Francophile dig at American crassness in the persona of Jess Hahn's cigar-chomping, dollar-obsessed arms dealer, O'Brien. Among other indignities, he is repeatedly thrown out of windows—a running joke that packs a good punch line when Ventura once again attempts to defenestrate him from a hotel, only to discover that the window has been painted on!

*The Great Spy Chase* is one of the best films to be covered in these pages, and certainly one of the best spy/comedy hybrids. It is up there with *Slalom*, and well worth the effort to seek out. The beginning 10 minutes are a bit confusing (especially if watched in an unfamiliar language), but your patience will be well rewarded.—MB

CREDITS: Production: Corona, S.N. Gaumon, Sicilia Cinematografica, Ultra Film; Director: Georges Lautner; Story and Screenplay: Michel Audiard, Albert Simonin; Cinematography: Maurice Fellous {B&W}; Music: Michel Magne; Original running length: 109 min; Filming location: Portugal; Country: France/Italy; Year: 1964

CAST: Lino Ventura (*Francis Lagneau*), Francis Blanche (*Boris Vassiliev*), Bernard Blier (*Eusebio Cafarelli*), Mireille Darc (*Amaranthe*), Jess Hahn (*O'Brien*), André Weber (*Rossini*), Louis Arbessier (*the Swiss colonel*), Françoise Giret (*Madame Pauline*), Violette Marceau (*Rosalinde*), Anne-Marie Blot, Yves Elliot, Jean-Pierre Moutier, Jean-François Régnier, Michel Dupleix (*the spy with Fiduc*), Gérard Darrieu (*Fiduc*), Luce Bonifassy, Lutz Gabor (*the German colonel*), Yuzuru Shoji, Raoul Saint-Yves (*the railway employee*), Philippe Castelli (*the porter*), Robert Secq (*Benarshah*), Yochka, Charles Millot (*Hans Muller*), Noël Roquevert (*Colonel Lanoix*), Dominique Valensi (*Madame Pauline's daughter*), Monique Melinand (*Madame Lagneau*), You-You Shogi, Luce Bonifassy, Robert Dalban (*the truck driver*), Hubert Deschamps (*the customs officer*), Michel Dacquin (*the spy on the train*), Marius Gaidon (*the spy with the knife*), Georges Gueret (*the American in Lisbon*), Huong Ham Chan (*the Chinese man on the train*), Jacques Balutin

## HAMMERHEAD

Now, there are many ways to start a film with a resounding bang—a murder, an action set piece, hell, even just an enigmatic event. However, I'm hard pressed to think of anything that starts quite as explosively as *Hammerhead*, which manages to cram in just about all of my favorite sixties clichés before the credits have finished rolling. You want naked (bad) tuba players? You got it. You want semi-clad females being covered by the contents of a giant tomato ketchup bottle? You got it. You want a ludicrous performance artist shooting dummies in the head? You got it. You want a full-fledged hippie riot…? Well, I guess you can probably see where I'm coming from.

Quite what this has to do with anything in the plot is a thoroughly moot point, but among the audience is secret agent Charles Hood (Vince Edwards). When the police start putting a downer on things, he makes off in his Jag, only to find chiffon-clad babe Sue Trenton (Judy Geeson) hiding in his back seat. After admonishing him for his tea bags ("A nasty American invention"), she immediately tries to seduce him (unsuccessfully—our man generally has a taste for more sophisticated ladies).

Hood is posing as an art dealer shipping a couple of crates full of goods (pornography, to be quite specific) to a mysterious criminal called Hammerhead (Peter Vaughan) in Lisbon. His mission is to find out what the man is up to, as the Secret Service has indications that he's plotting something big (although they're not sure exactly what).

In no time at all, our man is firmly ensconced on Hammerhead's rather magnificent yacht, not to mention attracting the attention of his host's concubine, Ivory (Beverley Adams). It all has something to do with a mysterious package that has been posted by a small-time criminal. Once Hood has managed to recover it—not an easy task—the extent of Hammerhead's scheme becomes clear: He plans to have one of his men impersonate an important diplomat, thereby gaining access to a top-secret report about a missile defense system.

*Hammerhead* is a thoroughly entertaining piece of kitsch bunkum, easily as amusing as the better-known Bulldog Drummond films *Some Girls Do* and *Deadlier Than the Male*. Although it doesn't manage to uphold the momentum (or the cheesiness) of the first five minutes, it comes close, featuring a large amount of pointless grooving, fake hippies and pseudo-psychedelic embellishment. Indeed, if it were essential to find some kind of theme, it would have to be the relationship between the establishment and the new, energizing youth culture of the time. This is most emphatically demonstrated in the juxtaposition of a hokey psych-out and a stuffy classical music performance.

But who cares? Far more important, this film has a couple of great comic sequences. Most notable is one scene in which Geeson and Edwards manage to escape their captors by attracting the attention of an unfortunate

**American poster for *Hammerhead***

passing motorcyclist (Kenneth Cope, of *Randall and Hopkirk [Deceased]*). There's nothing extraordinary in that, apart from the fact that they're trapped in a coffin on the back of a hearse at the time. There's also a very bizarre ending ("See that crazy Valentine!"), which sees youth coming through with flying, albeit body-painted, colors.

Technically, *Hammerhead* is more than adequate. Director Miller had been making (generally forgotten) films since the 1930s—including a Joan Crawford vehicle, *The Story of Esther Costello*, in 1957—and he obviously knew his stuff. Here he keeps things vaguely grounded, which is fine, but it would have been interesting to see how it would have turned out if someone more in touch with the much-depicted counterculture had been involved (Miller was 59 years old when this was made). The photography is easy on the eyes, with great use made of the narrow, cobbled Lisbon backstreets. Probably the largest problem is the lack of focus in the first half. It's never made clear exactly why British intelligence has such an interest in Hammerhead (or the mysterious package).

Vince Edwards makes a decent fist of the lead role, but it is difficult to see quite why he is so attractive to the assorted females on display. He's rather charmless and with a receding hairline, not unlike seventies Italian star Antonio Sabato. As for the villain, I'll quite happily watch anything with Peter Vaughan in it—heck, if he appeared in a bank advertisement I'd pay attention—and it's a shame that he's less well represented within the spy genre. Way down the cast list, you can find familiar names such as Windsor Davies (*L'oro di Londra*, *It Ain't Half Hot Ma'am*) and David (Darth Vader) Prowse, merely adding a diversity of flavor to the fun on hand.—MB

CREDITS: Production: Columbia; Director: David Miller; Story based on the novel by James Mayo; Screenplay: Herbert Baker, William Bast; Cinematography: Wilkie Cooper, Kenneth Talbot {Technicolor}; Music: David Whitaker; Original running length: 100 mins; Country: UK; Year: 1968

CAST: Vince Edwards (*Charles Hood*), Judy Geeson (*Sue Trenton*), Peter Vaughan (*Hammerhead*), Beverly Adams (*Ivory*), Michael Bates (*Andreas/Sir Richard*), Penny Brahms (*Frieda*), Kathleen Byron (*Lady Calvert*), Patrick Cargill (*Condor*), Veronica Carlson (*Ulla*), Jose de Carvallo, Tomas de Macedo, Diana Dors (*Kit*), Joseph Furst (*Count Ortega*), Romo Garrara (*Marcel*), Patrick Holt (*Huntzinger*), William Mervyn (*Perrin*), David Prowse (*George*), Tracy Reed (*Miss Hull*), Douglas Wilmer (*Vendriani*), Jack Woolgar (*Tookey Tate*), Maggie Wright (*Roselle*), Earl Younger (*Brian*).

## HANDLE WITH CARE
aka La Hora Del Asesino (Sp),
Silenzio: Si uccide (It)

Here's a relatively obscure entry in the genre. It's another of Robert Mark's Italian spy flicks and here his character's name is Mark Roberts! Mark made at least three low-budget spy thrillers (once billed as Rodd Dana), but he is one of the least-known and underappreciated spy guys. He is a likeable, athletic actor with good comic timing, but doesn't really have the level of charisma that demands he be taken seriously. He fares fine though as the ladies' man with more luck than skill in the espionage game. His character in this film is constantly in trouble with his boss and ends up in jail twice in the first 20 minutes.

**Turkish poster for *Handle With Care***

Roberts is assigned to halt arms traffic to Africa and after a few quick stops in London, Barcelona and Paris, the bulk the film is spent in Tunisia, a rather unusual locale for films of this ilk. This is one of those movies where a simple plot becomes complicated for no reason and the bottom line is that very little really happens. And what does happen is either predictable or handled with only a minimum of imagination.

Paul Muller doesn't have much a chance to fill out his villain role, since most of the screen time is taken up with the two females. Luisa Rivelli is the knockout who has more up her sleeve than she lets on, and Sheyla Rosin is the enemy agent who runs up against Roberts' good luck more times than is good for her.

Just about the only unusual thing to report is a strip club, supposedly in Paris, that has an Old West motif with little cowgirls serving the drinks. There are no gadgets to speak of and Gino Peguri's score is adequate and forgettable. Fans of Rivelli or Mark will find this watchable, but unless you're a genre completionist, spend your time elsewhere.

Note: The Italian-language version of this includes a lot of extra footage, including a hilarious sequence in which Robert Mark takes a protracted near-naked jog through the crowded streets of Sidi Busaid. Quite why this should be cut out is confusing, but apparently there is *another* English print of the film in existence, so maybe the scene can be found in that one if it should ever resurface.—DD

CREDITS: Production: Com Mo Do Ro; Director: Guido Zurli; Story and Screenplay: Lorenzo Gicca Palli; Cinematography: Giuseppe Aquari; Music: Gino Peguri; Original running length: 88 mins; Filming locations: London, Paris, Tunis, Sidi Busaid; Country: Italy; Year: 1967

**Peter van Eyck, Leticia Roman and Antonio Vilar on a German lobby card for *High Season For Spies***

CAST: Robert Mark (*Mark Roberts*), Luisa Rivelli (*Diana*), Sheyla Rosin, Paul Muller (*Thetokis*), Rita Klein (*Thetokis' henchwoman*), Lea Lander (*assassin with killer spider*), Vincent Thomas, Mimmo Maggio (*a ship captain and smuggler*), Pino Sciaqua, Marco Pasquini, Claudio Trionfo, Domenico Ravenna and with Mia Genberg, Gianni Santuccio (*Mark's boss*)

HIGH SEASON FOR SPIES
aka Comando de asesinos (Sp),
Sechs pistolen jagen Professor Z (WG)

When an eminent scientist is kidnapped from his laboratory by a bunch of goons in sunglasses, Jack Haskins (Antonio Vilar) is sent to try to find him. The search starts with the professor's pretty blonde assistant, but things are immediately confused when someone attempts to shoot Haskins at an airport car park. Fortunately, another agent working for a different organization, Genet (Peter Van Eyck), has been shadowing him—and is able to dispose of the attempted assassins.

They soon meet up with one of the professor's old colleagues, a certain Zandor (Jose Cardoso). The fact that this guy seems overly self-confident marks him as being suitably suspicious for anyone who has seen any spy films. The agents, meanwhile, are busy doing what agents do: strip-searching attractive young ladies, visiting trendy bars, scrapping with each other and so on. It comes as a shock when, after all of this hard work, Zandor turns up with a bullet in his temple.

Things aren't helped at all by the fact that assorted other questionable individuals—not to mention the police—are poking around. It would appear that just about everybody is after the professor's invention, and they're willing to go to any lengths to retrieve it for themselves.

*High Season For Spies* has a groovy soundtrack, lovely cinematography and looks like a million dollars. The direction is better than average, it swoops along at a swift pace and has more than enough double-crosses and narrative twists to maintain the interest. It's just a crying shame that the whole damn thing is so difficult to follow if you're watching it in an unfamiliar language. For native English speakers, that's the only way you are going to watch it. That's not to say that it's incredibly complicated; it's actually very simple, but there are very few catches to hook onto—making it difficult to keep up with what's going on.

There are a few points of interest. This is another film to feature a masked ball (see also *Secret Agent Superdragon*), which seems to be a suitable metaphor for espionage as a whole: a game for members of the leisure classes with a taste for the unknown. There's also a certain whodunit feel to the proceedings, including the habitual drawing-room sequence as an inspector attempts (unsuccessfully) to unravel the truth, Agatha Christie-style.

Also notable is the central rapport between the two spies, a relationship that's actually very well done. You're never entirely sure how they view each other (except with a degree of uneasy, mutual respect)—especially as it seems to change subtly according to how the plot is developing. Again, this is nothing particularly new, but it seems to work here partly because of the good playing of the two leads, both of whom are more mature than is usually found in the genre.

Peter Van Eyck, in particular, seems to be enjoying himself, continually grinning and yet occasionally displaying a degree of harshness that's most effective. This is a very rare contemporary role for Portuguese actor Antonio Vilar, who had some success in the 1950s with films such as Jose Luis Saenz de Heredia's *Don Juan* and Jose Forque's *Embajadores en el infierno*.

Further down the cast list can be found such familiar Hispanic character actors as spaghetti western habitué Frank Brana and Riccardo Valle, best known for playing the deranged Morpho in Jesus Franco's *The Awful Dr. Orloff.* Italian actress Leticia Roman was in several films during the early sixties, most notably Mario Bava's *The Girl Who Knew Too Much*, and this was the last time she appeared onscreen. Julio Coll was one of the most respected Spanish directors at the time, although little of his work made it into the English language. It's a shame, as this one shows a lot of promise.—MB

CREDITS: Production: Hispamer Films P.C., International Germania Film, Producciones A.V.; Director: Julio Coll; Story based on a novel by Dick Haskins [A. Andrade]; Screenplay: Jose Huici, Julio Coll; Cinematography: Mario Pacheco {Eastmancolor - Panavision}; Music: Jose Luis Navarro; Original running length: 86 mins; Filming locations: Lisbon, Costa del Sol; Country: Spain/Portugal/West Germany; Year: 1966

CAST: Peter Van Eyck (*Pierre Genet*), Antonio Vilar (*Jack Haskins*), Mikaela (*Professor Zandor's wife*), Letitia Roman (*Ellen Green, the professor's assistant*), Klaus Juergen [Wussow] (*Johansson*), Americo Coimbra, Antonio Pica (*a scientist*), Ricardo Rubinstein, Jose Cardoso (*Professor David Zandor*), Artur Smedo [Artur Semedo], Frank Brana (*Johanssen's henchman*), Ricardo Valle (*the police inspector*?), Mario De Barros, German Grech, Juan Cortes (*head of intelligence services*), Carlos J. [Jose] Teixeira, Issa Marinas, Carina Monti, J. Mario. Uncredited: Corny Collins (Jenny Renoir)

## HONG KONG HOT HARBOR

aka Heißer Hafen Hong Kong (WG),
Secrets of Buddha (UK),
Il segreto di Budda (It)

Tokyo. A gang of criminals steal a top-secret microfilm, within which is contained the formula for a new, valuable chemical. They plan to pass it on to a contact in Hong Kong, but unfortunately a bunch of local hoodlums find out about their plan and decide to appropriate the formula for themselves. It doesn't prove too difficult for them to dispose of the Japanese villains, but the formula itself falls into the hands of a journalist, Peter Holberg (Klausjurgen Wussow).

Holberg is investigating the activities of the assorted underground cartels, but the number of rapidly accumulating corpses soon attracts the attention of local police inspector MacLean (Brad Harris). MacLean's hardly the subtlest of characters, so the bad guys aren't slow to notice his scrutiny. After luring him to a sleazy nightclub, they trick him into smoking a dodgy cigarette. While he's passed out in the gutter—hey, we've all been there—they search his hotel room, but are unable to find a thing.

This does allow Holberg to work out that the leader of the gang is named Malik (Horst Frank). Working with a lady friend, Joan Kent (Marianne Koch)—whose brother had been murdered by the same guys earlier—he's soon on their trail.

*Hong Kong Hot Harbor* is yet another of the early, primarily West German spy films—see also *Operation Hong Kong*, *Cave of Diamonds*—made a couple of years before the genre proper kicked off. They usually feature a hero who is a journalist (or of a similar civilian bent) falling afoul of a local Mafia-type organization (often with a secret leader and a predilection for using exotic trimmings in their dastardly deeds). It also shares with them an Asian setting, complete with exaggerated performances from Asian supporting actors who seem to think they're in a 1930s gangster movie, and several cast members (Harris, Frank, Parker, etc.).

As such, the films were often not strictly secret agent films—but they follow such a similar narrative path that it would be frankly churlish to exclude them from consideration here. In fact, they act as a useful bridge between the Edgar Wallace krimis and the later, more extravagant Bond-style productions. So although you don't get much in the way of gadgetry (and you do get way too much talking), many genre fixtures are present: an exotic location, cool babes and a neat nightclub scene complete with belly dancer (they're just two-a-penny in Hong Kong).

**Dominique Boschero and giant rodent in this British lobby card for *Hong Kong Hot Harbor***

It's all pretty well done, and is probably better than either of the aforementioned films, mainly because it has a far more interesting hero. While Dietmar Schonherr and Paul Hubschmid were rather bland, Wussow has an odd, slightly puckish feel about him (he also has the ability to look about 10 years older from one scene to the next). It's not surprising that he turned up as a villain in films like *Commando des asesinos*. His only problem is that he's outdone by both Horst Frank—at his most malevolent—and Dominique Boschero (who performs possibly the most ludicrous exhibitions of beat dancing committed to celluloid).

As well as the occasional fistfight and a relatively bloody cutaway of someone being shot in the forehead—unusual for the time—this film also features a great chase through a highly kitsch "Chinese" theme park. An unholy cross between Disneyworld and Lao Tzu, I'm almost certain it is the same place that popped up a few years later in *La Judoka dans l'enfer*.—MB

CREDITS: Production: Rapid Film, Cineproduzioni Associate; Director: Jurgen Roland; Story and Screenplay: Gerd Christoph, Giorgio Simonelli; Cinematography: Klaus von Rautenfeld {Eastmancolor}; Music: Gert Wilden; Original running length: 102 mins; Country: West Germany/Italy; Year: 1962

CAST: Marianne Koch (*Joan Kent*), Klausjürgen Wussow (*Peter Holberg*), Dominique Boschero (*Colette Maybonne*), Brad Harris (*Inspector MacLean*), Carlo Tamberlani, Dorothee Parker, Chu Mu, Richard Liu, and Horst Frank (*Malik*)

## HOT ENOUGH FOR JUNE
aka Agent 008 3/4 (US), Agent 8 3/4 (US)

With *Deadlier Than the Male* and *Some Girls Do*, Ralph Thomas took the parodist's sword to the James Bond phenomenon. With *Hot Enough For June* he stayed firmly within the spy genre, but focused his attention on the thrillers as popularized by John Le Carre (the tagline read: "He's a special kind of spy…he doesn't know enough to come in from the cold!"). Although not quite as effective as his other genre entries, this is nonetheless a diverting, feel-good film—which eventually becomes a suitably compelling romantic comedy.

When secret agent 007 is killed (all you see of this are his gadgets and gun being put into storage), a replacement is needed to carry out a top-secret mission. In a recruitment drive that wouldn't be out of place for the contemporary intelligence services, they decide to find their new man by placing an advertisement in the local job center!

Aspiring novelist Whistler (Dirk Bogarde), whose laziness is matched only by the poverty of his writing skills, is devastated when given no option by the benefits clerk but to apply for and his opposite number (Robert Morley) points out a truism that is common to many genre films: The cultural disparities between the East and West are mainly ones of vocabulary and lifestyle. When it comes down to it, everyone is basically the same (see also *The Day the Hotline Got Hot*).

**Dirk Bogarde and the lovely Sylva Koscina in *Hot Enough For June***

As well as a likeable script and capable direction, this is also fortunate to boast a fabulous cast. Dirk Bogarde is great as the hapless hero, and interacts well with the delightful Sylva Koscina (who has simply fabulous eyebrows—none of those over-plucked arches for Sylva, she has splendid, full-bodied brows). And anything that features both Robert Morley and John Le Mesurier simply can't be bad.—MB

the job. Unfortunately, he is kept in the dark about the nature of his potential employers, who claim to be an international glass manufacturing company. Despite being possibly the worst interviewee ever ("Where did you go to school?" "Oh, here and there."), he is taken on (mainly because he can speak Czech).

On his first day, he is told that he is to visit a glass factory in Prague. Unfortunately, he's so naïve that he doesn't suspect anything, even when told that a vital part of his assignment is to pick up a secret formula from a character who will respond to a memorized password ("Hot enough for June?"). At first all seems to go well. Not only does he succeed in meeting his contact, he's also fortunate enough to be chauffeured by the rather attractive Vlasta (Sylva Koscina). The two of them soon become close, but unfortunately the authorities (who happen to be headed by Vlasta's dad [Leo McKern]) know far more about his mission than he does.

With the entire Czech police force on his tail, Whistler slowly becomes aware of his situation and is forced to rely upon his (generally underdeveloped) wits to try to make his way to the safety of the British Embassy. His only ally in this plight is Vlasta, who has fallen in love with him.

The majority of *Hot Enough* is taken up with Whistler's adventures behind the Iron Curtain, and with drawing a jolly contrast between the Western and the Soviet ways of life. The similarity between the Leo McKern character

CREDITS: Production: Rank Film; Director: Ralph Thomas; Story based on the novel "Night of Wenceslas" by Lionel Davidson; Screenplay: Lukas Heller; Cinematography: Ernest Steward {Eastmancolor}; Music: Angelo Francisco Lavagnino, Muir Mathieson; Original running length: 98 mins; Country: UK; Year: 1964

CAST: Dirk Bogarde (*Nicholas Whistler*), Sylva Koscina (*Vlasta Simoneva*), Robert Morley (*Cunliffe*), Leo McKern (*Simoneva*), Roger Delgado (*Josef*), John Le Mesurier (*Allsop*), Richard Vernon (*Roddinghead*), Amanda Grinling (*Cunliffe's secretary*), Noel Harrison (*Johnnie*), Derek Nimmo (*Fred*), Jill Melford (*Lorna*), Norman Bird (*employment exchange clerk*), Andre Charisse, Frank Finlay (*British embassy porter*), Derek Fowlds (*sun-bathing man*), Sandra Hampton, Philo Hauser, John Junkin (*clerk in opening scene*), Gertan Klauber (*technician in Czech glass factory*), Igo Meggido, William Mervyn (*passenger on plane*), Richard Pasco (*Plakov*), Eric Pohlmann (*Galushka*), John Standing (*men's room attendant*), Alan Tivern, Brook Williams

HUNTER OF THE UNKNOWN
aka 3S3 agente especial (Sp),
Agent 3S3, massacre au soleil (Fr),
Agent 3S3 pokert mit Moskau (WG),
Agente 3S3: massacro al sole (It)

Despite a good cast, this Caribbean adventure is...bad. There's no other way to put it. George Ardisson kicked butt in his previous outing as agent 3S3 Walter Ross in *Passport to Hell*, but this time the yawns will win out. Director Sergio Sollima (credited as Simon Sterling), who also had the helm of the previous film, loses the reins early and this ill-defined effort wanders aimlessly as various things blow up.

Part of the problem here is the lack of a good villain. We have a criminal organization that isn't very organized; a scientist who's doing something with poison gas; Russian, American and British secret agents; a crazy general and local rebels who've built gliders to aid in their cause for something or other. You see what I mean.

**George Ardisson looking serious on the German poster for *Hunter of the Unknown***

The cast did have potential, however. Ardisson is always fun to watch. His boy-next-door good looks and feline manner make for a good secret agent. Frank Wolff, a Roger Corman alumnus, isn't given enough to do in the role of Russian agent Mahlinkov, who impersonates Ross' contact in San Felipe. The British agent Melissa is played by the lovely Evi Mirandi (*Planet of the Vampires*), but her situation is similar to Wolff's. The bad guys had potential too. Given the chance, Michel Lemoine, whose startling looks graced many genre films in the sixties and seventies, could've been the villain this picture needed, but no. His Radik, head of the elite guard, is sadistic and a touch effeminate but is never allowed to flower. Fernando Sancho plays his usual gregarious role as General Siqueiros, the figurehead set up to rule the little island, but he's not up to much except whoring in his elaborate brothel that features theme rooms and "authentic eunuchs."

Good things about the movie include the aforementioned brothel, a fun score by Piero Umiliani, and a few fights to show off Ardisson's prowess. Probably the funniest theme running through the picture is the total disregard for human life displayed by the opposition. Early in the film an airplane having engine trouble needs to lighten the load, so men are thrown out because they "cost less than the guns" the flight is carrying. Later a new shipment of bazookas is tried out on moving targets—you guessed it, their own men suffice for this exercise too. Life is cheap on San Felipe. But that's about all I can salvage out of this dreary flick that only Ardisson fans will find even remotely entertaining.—DD

CREDITS: Production: Cineproduzioni Associate, Cesareo Gonzales, Les Films Copernic; Director: Simon Sterling [Sergio Sollima]; Story: Simon Sterling [Sergio Sollima]; Screenplay: Simon Sterling [Sergio Sollima], Simon O'Neil [Giovanni Simonelli], Jesus Maria De Arozamena; Cinematography: Carlo Carlini {Techniscope – Technicolor}; Music: Piero Umiliani; Original running length: 120 mins; Filming locations: Barcelona, Ibiza, Toledo, Madrid, Berlin, Rome; Country: Italy/France/Spain; Year: 1966

CAST: George [Giorgio] Ardisson (*Ross, Agent 3S3*), Frank Wolff (*Mahlinkov*), Evi Marandi (*Melissa*), Fernando Sancho (*General*

*Siqueiros*), Eduardo Fajardo, Leontine May (*Josefa*), Luz Marquez (*Senora Barrientos*), Michel Lemoine (*Radik*), Claudio Ruffini, Salvatore Borgese, Maria Granado, Porfiria Sanchez, John Karlsen, Kitty Swan, Beni Deus, Luis Induni, Dina Loy, Ursula Rank, Frank Castle, Jose Riesgo

HUNTING THE UNKNOWN
aka Dodici donne d'oro (It),
Comisario X (Sp),
Kiss Kiss Kill Kill (US, alt),
Kommissar X—Jagt auf Unbekannt (WG)

I'm pretty sure that when God created man, He had no idea that man would come up with anything quite this daft. Then again, He could also be indirectly blamed for the creation of Robin Williams, so I suppose we shouldn't hold it against the Old Fellow.

Smooth dick (as in private eye) Joe Walker (Tony Kendall) is picked up by an attractive lassie, Joan Carroll (Maria Perschy), who offers him a substantial fee to find her nuclear scientist brother Bob. After accepting, he returns to his hotel, where he pauses to comment "The shorter the skirts, the lovelier the guests..."

**Compelling artwork of the Finnish poster for *Hunting the Unknown***

In his hotel room he finds another attractive lassie, Bobo (wearing a lavender wig). After a quick snog he dons a tasty suit—proudly displayed on a mannequin in the wardrobe—and heads off to a nearby nightclub. Unfortunately, his harmless evening of cocktail drinking and ogling the females is interrupted when a performer (who also wears a lavender wig) is killed by a poison dart. Immediately becoming the prime suspect, he is interviewed by his old friend Captain Rowland (Brad Harris), who happens to be in the location investigating the murders of some prominent businessmen.

It turns out that the two cases are connected. A local multimillionaire, Oberon (Jacques Bezard), is bumping off all of his partners. Not content with just being incredibly rich, he also plans to hold the economies of the world to ransom with his huge stockpile of irradiated gold. It goes without saying that he also has a desert island hideaway and an army of "robotized" women—hence the wigs—to do his dirty work.

This is unadulterated fun all the way through. It doesn't make sense, of course, but you don't watch sixties spy films with any expectation that they will. There are silly haircuts, devious devices and smart suits aplenty. The villain is suitably insane, the chauvinist innuendo suitably regular and—best of all—the robotized women all go on the rampage at the end like a bizarre high-fashion girl gang.

Gianfranco Parolini's direction is unassailable throughout. As well as keeping everything at a breakneck pace, he throws in a couple of nice stylistic touches that linger in the mind. The great sets and costumes indicate that the budget was reasonably high and the score is just on the right side of being irritatingly catchy.

There's also a nice, relatively substantial role for Pino Mattei, the ex-fencing master who appeared (momentarily) in a number of Parolini's early productions. His balding, bearded features can also be spotted in Antonio Margheriti's entirely preposterous *L'Inafferrabile invincibile Mr. Invisibile* and F.J. Gottlieb's *Spy Today, Die Tomorrow*.

The original inspiration for this, by all accounts, wasn't so much the mega-successful Bond films as the rather less renowned Jerry Cotton series, that owed quite a debt to the earlier krimi genre.—MB

CREDITS: Production: Metheus Film, Parnass Film; Director: Frank Kramer [Gianfranco Parolini]; Story based on a novel by Bert F. Island; Screenplay: Giovanni Simonelli, Gianfranco Parolini, Werner Hauff; Cinematography: Francesco Izzarelli {Eastmancolor – Ultrascope}; Music: Bobby Gutesha; Original running length: 93 mins; Country: Italy/Germany; Year: 1965

CAST: Tony Kendall [Luciano Stella] (*Joe Walker*), Brad Harris (*Tom Rowland*), Maria Perschy (*Joan Smith*), Christa Linder (*Pamela*), Nikola Popovic (*Oberon*), Joseph Matthews [Pino Mattei] (*Kan, Oberon's man*), Ingrid Lotarius, Simon O'Neil [Giovanni Simonelli], Jacques Bezard (*Captain Olsen*), Danielle Godet (*Pat*), Liliane Dulovic (*Nancy*)

## HYPNOS—FOLLIA DI UN MASSACRO

"Hypnos—folly of a slaughter"

aka Hypnose ou la folie du massacro (Fr)

As the tail end of the spy genre approached, things became increasingly curious. Acknowledging that the straight Bond formula was coming to the end of its natural lifespan, filmmakers began looking elsewhere for ingredients to spice up the cinematic mix. Some turned toward the emergent crime thrillers and giallos (*Assassination*, *The Last Chance*), creating a new subgenre that slowed down the pace and added existential trappings. Others looked to *Rififi*, veering into the extravagant (and not so extravagant) heist movie. And then you have films like *Hypnos*, which chuck in as many disparate frames of reference as possible, with the result that they end up being, well…odd.

This film borrows its central premise, that of an evil organization brainwashing unsuspecting individuals into committing ghastly acts, from *The Manchurian Candidate*. It's a familiar premise: Both *Blueprint for a Massacre* and *Spies Strike Silently* feature hypnotized lackeys doing the dirty work for demented megalomaniacs. Here, though, the unfortunate victim Natalie (Rada Rassimov), who has been kidnapped and reprogrammed, is sent into a homicidal fit by a subliminal message inserted into a cheesy film on her television. It could potentially be argued that this is some kind of critical comment upon the psychological effects of the creeping ubiquity of television itself, but I think that would belabor the point somewhat. This is not a film that is overly preoccupied with philosophical matters.

In form, though, *Hypnos* belongs firmly to the late-period spy/thriller model. The hero, Doctor Henry Spengler (Robert Wood), suspects that something funny is going on when Natalie—his girlfriend—seems to have no recollection of her murderous turn. His investigations lead him to a film library, where he is able to steal a copy of the print in question. Unfortunately, this brings him to the attention of a gang of villains, who promptly make an unsuccessful attempt to kill him. He soon discovers that everything originates from the mind control experiments of a now-disillusioned scientist, professor Kennitz (Fernando Sancho), experiments that have been commandeered by a shadowy criminal cartel. Just to add another cross-genre touch, the leader of this lot is a weird dude who wears an iron mask over his face.

As you can probably tell from the above synopsis, *Hypnos* is not your average spy flick. Veering from international espionage to police procedural, from conspiracy thriller to superhero film, it ends up being a wholly eccentric slice of sci-fi freakiness. Tonally, the very contrast between the slow, moody opening half and the outlandish conclusion—complete with wobbly "futuristic" sets and analogue bleeps and whooshes on the score—merely accentuates the ridiculousness of the production as a whole. And, hey, I'm not complaining. After watching a huge amount of well-nigh interchangeable films, it makes a refreshing change to find something that's—if entirely cockeyed—at least unique.

There's actually a lot to like here, apart from the general level of dementia on display, that is. The photography is fun, with oddly placed shots and angled camerawork accentuating the disorientating nature of the plot; the soundtrack is fabulous; and the direction sturdy (not to mention surprisingly restrained, for the first hour at least). Although it seems to have had a low-ish budget, with a large amount of the running time featuring a small number of characters and restrained to a clinic setting, the production values are kept at least *relatively* high. There are also some decently filmed sequences, the most effective of which is when Woods examines the film in a deserted warehouse while sinister footsteps echo in the background.

The more I see of his work, the more I become convinced that Paolo Bianchini is a very peculiar filmmaker. This isn't entirely dissimilar to *The Devil's Man*, which he made the same year and also features sci-fi elements and an inexplicably masked villain (and which happens to be a bit of a favorite of mine, despite David's less-than-convinced review elsewhere). His other work includes the apparently straight spy film *Our Men in Baghdad*, a bunch of good westerns (including the essential *I Want Him Dead*), the weird superhero film *Superargo and the Faceless Giants* and *SuperAndy*, a jaw-dropping pastiche of *Superman* featuring Italian-American comedian Andy Luotto.

*Hypnos* is also notable for being a lone spy role for spaghetti western star Robert Woods (*Seven Pistols for the MacGregors*, *My Name is Pecos*). He's not at all bad, entering into the spirit of things with some aplomb and never playing it for laughs (as could quite easily have been done). He gets good support from Giovanni Cianfriglia, as a nattily sports-jacketed policeman, who started off as a double for Steve Reeves in peplums before becoming a notable secondary performer throughout the sixties (*Killer Kid*, *Two Pistols for a Coward*). He also played the titular, be-masked role in Bianchini's aforementioned *Superargo and the Faceless Giants*, which gives a little intertextual twist to things.—MB

CREDITS: Production: Cinecris; Director: Paul Maxwell [Paolo Bianchini]; Story and Screenplay: Max Carot, Paul Maxwell [Paolo Bianchini]; Cinematography: Henry Marchall [Erico Menczer] {Cromoscope – Eastmancolor}; Music: Carlo Savina; Original running length: 90 mins; Country: Italy; Year: 1967

CAST: Robert Wood (*Henry Spengler*), Rada Rassimov (*Nicole Bouvier*), Ken Wood [Gianfranco Cianfriglia] (*Inspector Griffith*), Fernando Sancho (*Professor Kennitz*), Piero Gerlini (*Commissioner Cazale*), Lino Coletta (*Maurice, the false policeman*), Nino Vingelli

## INFERNO A CARACAS

"hell to Caracas"

aka Cita con la muerte en Caracas (Sp), Fünf vor zwolf in Caracas (WG)

Blonde nymphet, Helen Remington (Christa Linder), is kidnapped by two guys with goofy haircuts (one of who is habitual Euro-villain Sal Borgese). Her dad, an oil magnate, is convinced that blackmail lies behind this, and hires private detective Jeff Milton (George Ardisson, with peroxided hair) to find out a) who has taken her and b) where she is hidden.

Inevitably, the trail begins in a sleazy striptease club—where Milton has to fight off the attentions of an assortment of feisty females. Conveniently, it appears that the kidnappers are working for the club owner, who carries out a bit of international drug trading on the side. Milton is captured, taken to an island hideout and tortured, but soon manages to use his superior fighting skills and quick wits to escape. That's not the worst of it, though. While questioning a suspect, he is shot with a poison dart. When he wakes, she is naked and dead, and he is the prime suspect.

On the run, his only allies are Interpol agents Alan Shepperton (Harald Lepnitz) and Florence (Pascale Audret), who seem to spend most of their time bickering, smoking a pipe (in his case) and cooking (hers). With their undisclosed help, the police are soon able to arrest the nightclub owner, who has been smuggling the drugs by stitching them into the bikinis of her strippers!

None of this helps with finding out what has happened to young Ms. Remington, who has been strapped, along with a bomb, to the girders of an oil rig. This is all part of a devious plot to destroy the Venezuelan oil fields. Meanwhile, the fact that Horst Frank is hanging about in the background (as the police doctor) should be enough to reveal the identity of the true villain of the piece.

*Inferno a Caracas* is a reasonably effective spy film, if nothing particularly special. The production values are quite high, with one particularly effective machine gun battle between the army and the villains. Unfortunately, the effect of this is somewhat foiled by an absolutely terrible superimposed explosion effect toward the climax. The script is nothing new, although one idiosyncrasy is that the hero seems rather peripheral to the majority of the action. During the major gunfight, he is buried beneath a truckload of sand, and it's often up to Shepperton to work out just what's going on (much to his own misfortune).

George Ardisson was often referred to as "the Italian James Bond," and it's true that he's pretty good in the lead role. Particularly effective when he's in more subtle mode (as when dodging out of sight or carrying out a bit of undercover reconnoitering), he's definitely no slouch in the scrapping department either. He also has a rather devilish grin, which gives his character an appropriately sinister undertone. For those of you so inclined, he spends a significant amount of the running time scampering around in some rather skimpy swimming trunks.

This was director Marcello Baldi's only genre entry (although his Gina Lollobrigida vehicle *The Stuntman* (68) could possibly be considered a caper film). He worked on a number of peplums (*Saul and David*, *Jacob the Man Who Fought with God*) before drifting into television movies during the late seventies. He acquits himself adequately, although it would have nice if he could have introduced a touch of the bizarre to make things stand out a bit.—MB

CREDITS: Production: Rapid Film, G.M.B.H., P.E.A., S.N.C.; Director: Billy Marshall [Marcello Baldi]; Story: K.H.Vogelmann; Screenplay: K.H.Vogelmann, Giovanni Simonelli, Lionello De Felice, Marcello Baldi; Cinematography: Rolf Kastel {Eastmancolor – Ultrascope}; Music: Piero Umiliani; Original running length: 90 mins; Country: Italy/France; Year: 1966

CAST: George [Giorgio] Ardisson (*Jeff Milton*), Luciana Angiolillo (*Violet Watson*), Pascale Audret (*Florence*), Christa Linder (*Helen Remington*), Patric Bernard, Sal Borgese (*the killers*), Maria Julia Diaz (*Dolores*), Mario Grant (*the president*), Jose Castillo Escalona (*Inspector Sabana*), Andres Pascual Valeriano (*Remington*), Harald Leipnitz (*Alan Shepperton*), Horst Frank (*Nelson*). Uncredited: Giuseppe Castellano?

**German poster for *Inferno a Caracas***

INTRIGO A LOS ANGELES
"intrigue to Los Angeles"
aka Agent 707: intrigo a Los Angeles (It, re-release), FBI enquete a Los Angeles (Fr)

A dancer is found dead; beside her is a copy of a trashy pulp novel, "The Striptease of Death." The murder has something to do with the disappearance of a professor Weiss (Stefano Pfau), who had been working on a top-secret atomic formula. The concerned FBI sends two of its top agents, David Blair (Luciano Marin) and Thelma Avery (Mary Luger), to find out what's happened to him.

Their attention soon becomes focused on a down-at-the-heels nightclub run by George (Gaetano Quarteraro, something of a regular in these early sixties cheapies). This place seems to have rather a lot of deceased ex-workers, many of whom seem to have been killed by poison darts (always the sign of a distinguished drinking hole). George, along with his "proto-goth" sister Jean (Carol Walker), has kidnapped the professor, and they intend to sell his formula to the highest bidder.

*Intrigo a Los Angeles* is an obscure, low-budget affair that looks as though it was filmed a lot earlier than it actually was. There are no big (or even middle-range) stars, no exotic loca-

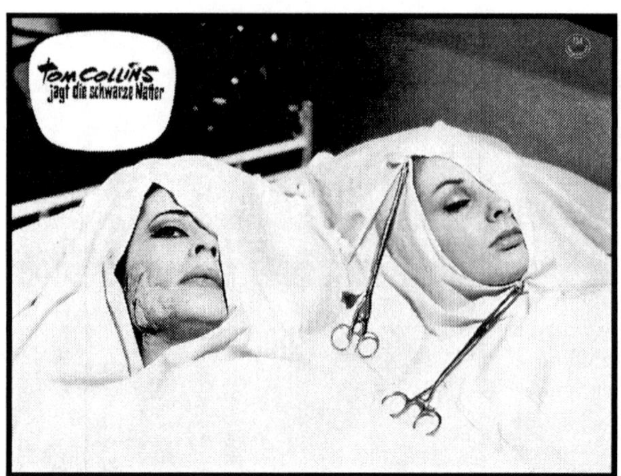


**Carol Walker, Mary Lugar and surgical horror, spy-style on a German lobby card for *Intrigo a Los Angeles***

tions, and the cast could be easily counted on the fingers of both hands. The jazzy score—an early effort from Piero Umiliani—and rather staid direction (from Romano Ferrara, who would later helm *Gungala*) both give this a feel similar to the Eddie Constantine films wowing the box-office in France at the time. The rather stagy art direction also helps make this an internally focused film, completely lacking the exotic sets and storylines that distinguish later genre efforts.

The two leads, who both seem to have stepped straight out of the 1950s, further accentuate this old-fashioned ambience. Luciano Marin makes a rather baby-faced hero, and doesn't exhibit any of the lounge sensibilities that you'd expect from your average cinematic secret agent. Mary Luger spends most of her time being harried, and her plaid skirts and blouses are rather dowdy in comparison to some of the fashion excesses sported by her contemporaries.

A substantial amount of the running time is also taken up with a variety of burlesque acts featuring well-rounded ladies in stockings. In fact, it's hard not to feel that these were one of the main motivations for making the film—pulling in the punters with the promise of a quick flash of thigh. One of these acts, with a girl emerging from a coffin before doing a dance-and-disrobe turn, could have come from a Jesus Franco movie. This is overshadowed, however, by a strip routine featuring a clown costume. It keeps the audience (of one person) understandably attentive, being one of the most disturbing things I have seen in a good few years.

Also notable is the way in which the film veers totally off into a "medical horror" narrative, filched wholeheartedly from the popular films *Eyes Without a Face, The Awful Dr. Orloff*, et al. Jean has been horribly scarred on the left side of her face, and she forces the professor (who just happens to be an expert at this kind of thing) to carry out a "face transplant." And Thelma could prove to be the perfect donor. Amusingly, after the operation is carried out, she impatiently rips off her bandages after just a few minutes to reveal absolutely no scarring whatsoever—but it turns out that she's been duped by the judicious use of makeup. Duh!—MB

CREDITS: Production: Cinelions, Publi Italia; Director: Roy Freemount [Romano Ferrara]; Story: Lucio Marcuzzo; Screenplay: Adriano Baracco; Cinematography: Adalberto Adalberti {Eastmancolor}; Music: Piero Umiliani; Original running length: 85 mins; Country: Italy; Year: 1964

CAST: Carol Walker (*Jean Lovering*), Mary Luger (*Thelma Avery*), Luciano Marin (*David Blair*), Gaetano Quarteraro (*George*), Renato Terra Caizza (*Elston*), Stefano Pfau (*Professor Weiss*), P. Cruciani

INTRIGUE AT SUEZ
aka Un colpo da mille miliardi (It),
Frauen als Köder für CD 7 (WG),
Un golpe de mil millones (Sp), Intrigue à Suez (Fr), Turkish Connections (Int)

An accident at a nuclear plant causes the exposure of several workers to radiation. An ambulance transporting two of the survivors to hospital is carjacked. Special agent Ted Frazer (Rick Van Nutter) is assigned to investigate.

He travels to Istanbul, where he tries to track down a man called Shelby (Massimo Pietrobon), who is believed to be involved with events somehow. After visiting a sleazy

Turkish drinking establishment—and watching some belly dancers—he ends up in a brothel and meets Prinzi (Marilu Tolo), a young lady who would appear to have been hitting the hash rather heavily. She happens to be the lover of a rich shipping magnate and oil dealer called Theopolous (Eduardo Fajardo).

After watching some more belly dancing (by a particularly unattractive performer who looks like Sonja from the British television show *Eastenders*), Frazer tracks down some minor blackguards to a supposed medical center. Unfortunately, he is captured and subjected to some cheesy death ray torture before coming face to face with the main villain: Theopolous, whose guilt is perfectly apparent to all by the way in which he is attended to by a veritable army of identically be-(mini)skirted dollybirds and insists on stroking a cute puppy (which must have been sedated), Blofeld-style.

He's the mastermind behind a dastardly plot to detonate the nuclear reactor of a cruise ship (which had been designed by the two abductees from the beginning, remember them?) that is traveling up the Suez. The intention is to cut off the canal and therefore artificially inflate the price of oil.

This is a well-made but rather unexceptional film with a deadly serious attitude that totally belies its absolutely preposterous plot. It suffers badly from lackadaisical pacing and from being overly talky. Obviously it acted as a warning to the governments of the time, as surprisingly enough the idea of nuclear-powered cruise ships never really took off.

Its mediocrity is a shame, because Paolo Heusch, who demonstrates a distinct knack at using off-kilter framing shots and exotic locations, actually directs it very well. Particularly good use is made of the climactic passenger liner setting. With the characters running around in the flashing lights of the steamy engine rooms, it resembles nothing so much as the inhospitable spaceship backdrop to Ridley Scott's fabulous *Alien*. There's also a great soundtrack from the ever-reliable Piero Umiliani.

The splendidly named Californian actor Rick Van Nutter is best known for being married to Anita Ekberg from 1963 to 1975, as well for his performance as Felix Leiter in *Thunderball*. He actually appeared in several Euro-productions, the most interesting of which are probably *Seven Hours of Gunfire* and two films by Antonio Margheriti: *Dynamite Joe* and the odd sci-fi outing *Assignment Outer Space*. He's actually rather effective, looking like an older Clint Eastwood, and he brings a harder edge to the role than could have been expected.—MB

CREDITS: Production: Pacific Cin.ca, Oceana P.I.C., Les Films Corona, Atlantida Film; Director: Paolo Heusch; Story: Fulvio Gicca; Screenplay: Fulvio Gicca, Pierre Levy, Luis Jerez; Cinematography: Rafael Pacheco {Techniscope – Technicolor}; Music: Piero Umiliani; Original running length: 90 mins; Filming locations: Clinica Moscati (Rome), Istanbul; Country: Italy/France/Spain; Year: 1966

CAST: Rick Van Nutter (*Ted Fraser*), Marilu Tolo (*Prinzi*), Eduardo Fajardo (*Telly Theopulos*), Philippe Hersent (*Gottlieb*), Massimo Pietrobon (*Shelby*), Jose Jaspe (*Fraser's Turkish contact*), Alberto Dalbes, Jacques Stany, Giancarlo Cappelli, Carlos Dunaway, Gino Marturano (*Fraser's boss*), Dick McNamara, Mirella Pamphili. Uncredited: Rita Berger (*Liane*), Senta Rothenberg (*Michaela*)

## IT MEANS THAT TO ME
aka Me faire ca a moi (Fr)

You either like Eddie Constantine or you don't. If you do, you'll watch him in almost anything, and this little film qualifies as "almost anything." Eddie just doesn't seem his jocular self here, as if sensing the director's meandering method and flat humor.

Eddie plays a newspaperman who was framed for a jewel robbery in Marseilles a couple of years before this adventure. When he is offered his reputation back, Eddie agrees to deliver some microfilm to—you guessed it—Marseilles. The bulk of the film is taken up with his journey to the city and his attempts to avoid capture before his oft-delayed appointment. After hiding in the Spanish Quarter, Eddie finds his contact dead and his girlfriend a spy for the other side.

At one point Eddie is captured by a cadre of international spies, all of whom sport sunglasses all the time, a gag that wears rather thin. Another group of suspicious characters call themselves The Negotiants, a group of (what else) negotiators but who, what, where, when, and why, no one reveals. The film feels like an attempt at political parody that may have played well to a 1960 French audience but the message is lost on the 21st-century viewer. The results are dull and uninspired for the most part.

There are some nice locations in the Spanish Quarter and an interesting short scene inside of a church that uses a black background and lit candles to create an evocative atmosphere, but these few highlights are outweighed by scenes like a boring boat chase and drawn-out set pieces that go nowhere. Michel Legrand's eclectic score fits this odd film, but is rarely bold enough to make an impression. All in all, this is one of the lesser Constantines and there are quite a few others to choose from for a better evening's entertainment.—DD

CREDITS: Production: Ares, Paris Overseas Films; Director: Pierre Grimblat; Story based on a story by Jean-Michel Sorel; Screenplay: Claude de Givray, Pierre Grimblat, Francois Truffaut (uncredited); Cinematography: Michel Kelber {B&W}; Music: Michel Legrand; Country: France; Year: 1960

CAST: Rita Cadillac, Henri Cogan, Eddie Constantine, Pierre Grasset, Bernadette LaFont, Gracieux Lamparti, Jean-Louis Richard

ITALIAN SECRET SERVICE
aka Il Nostro agente Natalino Tartufato
(It, re-release)

Industrial espionage: It's a nasty business, all right. With millions of dollars in the balance it's no wonder that corporations, even governments, will do anything to obtain—or prevent others from obtaining—a secret formula.

Just ask Natalino Tartufato (Nino Manfredi). Years after the war, the unskilled, Italian ex-resistance fighter is pressed into government service to spy on the members of a neo-Nazi organization, The Black Crab. They want the bomb, he is told, and Natalino rises to the patriotic occasion. Given the order to kill the young man he's been spying on, Edward Stevens (Jean Sobieski), Natalino thinks twice and his espionage career takes an unexpected turn...with hilarious results. You see, Stevens is not a neo-Nazi at all but the keeper of the formula for Coca Cola (here called Cola Cola for obvious reasons) and he wants to give the secret to the Russians, the bastard.

This is one of a handful of sixties spy comedies that actually succeeds in being funny. It manages to skewer the spy genre and corporate America (among others) with its double-edged sword of clever situational comedy and a wry script. Nino Manfredi is perfect as the nonplussed hero, taken advantage of, but who finally manages to turn the tables on his tormentors. The fine supporting cast, including Clive Revill, Giampiero Albertini and Gastone Moschin, is kept focused by director Luigi Comencini, and the twists and turns of the plot lead to a satisfying conclusion.

The humor comes fast and furious but this rarely verges on vaudeville or degenerates into pop wackiness like many of its self-conscious brethren. Natalino receives a briefcase full of gadgets, of course, but this one has useful items like a meat hook and an exploding suppository. Some of the jokes were well-worn before they appeared here ("This car is a hazard." "No, it's a Fiat."), but they're delivered straight rather than shamelessly digging for a laugh.

The main gag that brings the principals together is when Natalino is told he'll make $100,000 if he does away with the "neo-Nazi" Stevens. Natalino is no killer, so he farms the job out to a local ruffian for half the loot. The ruffian then offers half of his half to his shady lawyer to do the dirty work. Naturally, the lawyer offers the job to yet another incompetent, and so on. Finally, Natalino himself is approached by a stranger and offered $1,000 if he'll knock off a certain neo-Nazi! The circular nature of the gag is worked with great ease and feeds into the irony that is at the center of the film.

"Half the world with Cola Cola, half the world without." It's a dangerous situation and not one this group of Italians can resolve, but it sure is fun watching them try.—DD

CREDITS: Production: Rizzoli Film; Director: Luigi Comencini; Story: Leonardo Benvenuti, Piero De Bernardi, Massimo Patrizi, Luigi Comencini; Screenplay: Leonardo Benvenuti, Piero De Bernardi; Cinematography: Armando Nannuzzi {Eastmancolor}; Music: Fiorenza

Carpi; Original running length: 105 mins; Filming locations: London, Rome; Country: Italy; Year: 1967

CAST: Nino Manfredi (*Natalino Tartufato*), Francoise Prevost (*Elvira*), Clive Revill (*Charles*), Jean Sobieski (*Edward Stevens*), Giampiero Albertini (*Ottone*), Alvaro Piccardi (*Ciro*), Enzo Andronico (*Femore*), Loris Bazzocchi (*agent*), Attilio Dottesio (*Russian commander*), Anastasia Stevens (*Russian interpreter*), Gianni Pulone, with Giorgia Moll (*secret agent*), Gastone Moschin (*advocate*)

JAMES TONT OPERAZIONE DUE
"James Tont operation two"
aka The Wacky World of James Tont
(US, unconfirmed)

In this sequel to the successful *James Tont Operazione UNO* (see entry), Lando Buzzanca once again plays the hapless titular agent. This time he starts off in his usual incompetent fashion: Tripped up by a small girl while at a conference, he breaks his leg and has to take some rest and recuperation at a health spa. There he meets the sinister Joe Street (Loris Gizzi), a wealthy industrialist with a sideline as a criminal mastermind. The two buffoons immediately become embroiled in a fracas over a pretty nurse, a to-do that ends up with Street subjected to a premature aging drug. Not overly happy with this, the villain mucks around with the controls of a bath, freezing Tont into a block of ice. Well, it's better than flushing yourself down the toilet, as he did in the previous escapade.

Fortunately, the Intelligence Agency is able to defrost him and, with criminals around the world believing that he is dead, he is easily able to slip into another identity. Unfortunately, this identity happens to be "Bingo Kowalski," a jiving beatnik who looks frighteningly similar to Jimmy Saville. His mission is to infiltrate "the scene" and discover the whereabouts of a missing lump of uranium. This situation obviously gives him the opportunity to ingest far too much LSD, and he immediately starts seeing his boss speaking to him from the artwork of a cigarette packet.

Tont soon discovers the uranium hidden inside a guitar owned by Helene (Claudie

**Italian poster for *James Tont operazione DUE***

Lange), a pretty lass with a sweet hat. She is working for—surprise, surprise—the increasingly demented Street, who has a dastardly scheme: turn the spire of St. Peters into a giant rocket, in which he will be able to escape after looting the Vatican. Quite what all this has to do with the radioactive material is frankly by the by. Having a coherent narrative is the least of the filmmaker's concerns.

Once again, this is a totally foolish, rather enjoyable way to spend 90 minutes. Although it's possibly not quite as effective as *UNO*, Buzzanca is very likeable in the role, and Loris Gizzi—as in the previous film—is on hand to portray the bad guy. There are some great groovy tunes, often played by guitarists holding their instruments as if they were ukuleles, and the jokes come thick and fast. Gadget lovers get a number of examples here: false teeth that allow the hero to eat his way through jail bars, and a device that dehydrates people (thereby allowing them to be carried around in a paper bag before being reconstituted through the addition of water), being the most notable.

Interestingly, although a lot of this seems to have been "inspired" by *Thunderball* (screwy, sci-fi plotline; underwater sequences; monocle- (as opposed to eye-patch)-wearing villain); certain bits could almost have been copied by later Bond films. The rescue of the "dead" hero after a burial at sea predicts the start of *You Only Live Twice*, while the health spa settings anticipate those of *Never Say Never Again.*—MB

CREDITS: Production: Panda Cin.ca, Cineurope; Director: Bruno Corbucci; Story: Ermanno Donati, Luigi Carpentieri; Screenplay: Bruno Corbucci, Vittorio Vighi, Mario Guerra, Antoinette Pellevant, Ermanno Donati, Luigi Carpentieri, Ugo Liberatore; Cinematography: Alessandro D'Eva {Eastmancolor}; Music: Bruno Canfora; Original running length: 91 mins; Filming locations: Incir-De Paolis Studios, London; Country: Italy/France; Year: 1965

CAST: Lando Buzzanca (*James Tont*), France Anglade (*Helene*), Loris Gizzi (*Joe Street*), Claudie Lange (*Clarissa*), Antonella Murgia (*Samantha*), Jacques Dufilho (*"Y"*), Geoffrey Coppleston (*head of intelligence agency*), Furio Meniconi (*Korkus*), Aldo Bonamano, Mirko Valentin (*Street henchman*), Franco Ressel (*astronaut Jeff Clifford*), Enzo Consoli (*street henchman*), Francesco Sormano, Sara Tonini, Renato Montalbano (*street henchman*), Franco Gula (*street advisor*), Mario De Simone, Fiorella Ferrero, Bruno Scipioni

JAMES TONT OPERAZIONE UNO
"James Tont operation one"
aka James Tont operacion Uno (Sp)

Of all the Bond films, it was *Goldfinger* that really kick-started the whole spy genre into prodigious action. While *Dr. No* and *From Russia with Love* had been fairly low-key (for Bond films, at any rate), the mix of eccentric villains, goofy gadgets and screwball plotlines that made up the third entry in the series proved particularly popular. And not just with the audiences—filmmakers around the world took their cues, creating a number of spoofs, copies and critiques. *James Tont Operazione UNO* was reasonably quick off the mark and, like Franco and Ciccio's *Due mafioso contro Goldginger*, sought to parody not only *Goldfinger* in particular but also the whole Bond phenomenon.

As such, the film doesn't really have anything by way of a plot, being more a succession of gags, comic turns and singularly peculiar conceits. Inept secret agent James Tont (Lando Buzzanca) is sent to investigate a conspiracy, the exact nature of which is unknown, being planned by a certain Goldsinger (Loris Gizzi). His mission does not start promisingly: After being drugged by a blonde, he wakes up to find himself entirely covered in gold paint. Fortunately, this has a decidedly less fatal effect than it did on Shirley Eaton, and he's soon up and on the case again.

It turns out that Goldsinger is a music industry magnate (think of a corpulent Phil Spector), with a handy sideline in carrying out work for the Chinese government. More specifically, he has manufactured a golden disc that, when played at a commemorative United Nations assembly, will cause the entire building in which it is being held to blow up. James has to use all of his wiles to prevent this from happening, although more often than not he succeeds despite his incompetence or thanks to the help of his partner, Barbara (Evi Marandi).

As well as the aforementioned body-painting scene, the most obvious nods to *Goldfinger* are in the characters of Kayo and Goldginger, played by George Wang and Loris Gizzi, respectively. The former is based on Harold Sakata's Oddjob, albeit equipped with deadly fingernails rather than bowler hat. The latter is a potty tycoon and megalomaniac, surrounded by a variety of lethal females. Gizzi even looks suspiciously similar to Gert Frobe. There's also an entertaining pastiche of the Bond laboratory sequences, featuring a variety of rather crappy gadgets and a particularly crazed "Q" (anticipating the spin that John Cleese would bring to the role in a good 30 years).

As with many of its type, *Uno* is at its most effective when taking its model to absurd ex-

**Italian poster for *James Tont operazione UNO***

tremes. A particularly Italianate twist is given to the secret agent's inevitable "customized" car: rather than an Aston Martin, it's a Fiat Uno. Possibly the most off-the-wall moment comes when the hero escapes from a bunch of villains by…flushing himself down the toilet! That's not the kind of thing you'd find Sean Connery getting up to.

Overall, this is a likeably goofy enterprise that manages to succeed within its own terms. It's certainly better than some of its type (such as the later Buzzanca/Corbucci collaboration, *Spia spione*), and was successful enough to spawn a sequel, the imaginatively titled *James Tont Operazione DUE*. Buzzanca is pretty good in the role, far better than he can be, and there's some great stunt work on display (most particularly during a car chase, when one brave chap surfs a car while it's driving along on two wheels).

It's not recommended to everyone, but for those who don't start hyperventilating at the mere thought of a comedy spy film, there is some worth to be found if you stick with it. Just don't ask me what on earth that talking mouse is supposed to signify.—MB

CREDITS: Production: Panda Cin.ca; Director: Bruno Corbucci; Story and Screenplay: Bruno Corbucci, Giovanni Grimaldi; Cinematography: Alessandro D'Eva, Raffaele Masciocchi; Music: Marcello Giombini; Original running length: 88 mins; Country: Italy; Year: 1965

CAST: Lando Buzzanca (*James Tont*), Evi Marandi (*Barbara*), Gina Rovere (*Narda*), Loris Gizzi (*Goldsinger*), Evi Rigano (*Joyce Patterson*), George Wang (*Kayo*), Walter Maestosi (*Reider*), Alighiero Noschese (*Noskes*), Licia Lombardi, Susanne Clem, Lilia Neyung, Bruno Scipioni, Claudio Guarino, Franco Ressel (*Las Vegas hotel clerk*), Mario De Simone, Mario De Grad, Mario Mariani, Corinne Fontaine

JEFF GORDON, SECRET AGENT

aka Des frissons partout (Fr), Eddie wieder Colt-richtig (WG), Jeff Gordon ataca (Sp), Jeff Gordon il diabolico detective (It)

Eddie Constantine plays FBI agent Jeff Gordon, a hotshot dude who makes an entrance by breaking up a (somewhat inept) jewelry heist. One of the robbers, Gregori (Victor Beaumont), manages to make an escape and Gordon is rapidly on his trail (to the accompaniment of a totally cheesy piece of music that could have been reused by Woody Allen in *Sleeper*). This leads him to a gang of hoods—as elusive as they are dangerous—who are busily carrying out a series of robberies, cat burglaries and your simple smash-and-grabs.

**Eddie Constantine engages in full-contact billiards on the Belgian poster for *Jeff Gordon, Secret Agent***

After a quick scrap in a Turkish bath (don't ask), Jeff's investigations take him to a clinic/health spa, run by Dr. Mercier (Nando Gazzolo), situated in the middle of the French countryside. He promptly hits on a variety of local ladies—all in the name of intelligence gathering, of course—and meets up with Liza (Perrette Pradier), a suspicious blonde who turns out to be private eye (and who is not to happy to discover that the Feds are after the same prey).

They join forces and both enroll as patients at the clinic, allegedly in need of urgent rest and relaxation. They find the guests to be a bizarre bunch. Not least is Yanakos (habitual weirdo Daniel Emilfork), who insists on prancing around clutching a tennis racket, and a mysterious individual who is walking around with bandages all over his face. Things prove not to be particularly peaceful either: An attempt is made on Liza's life when a poisonous snake is released into her room (she escapes by screaming at it). Shockingly enough, it turns out that Dr. Mercier has a nifty sideline as a plastic surgeon, and has specialized in literally rearranging the faces of any underground figures on the police "most wanted" list. Our man Gordon sets about trying to break up this unsavory operation by any means possible.

*Jeff Gordon, Secret Agent* was made during the height of Eddie Constantine's popularity, and saw him adopting a new character, Jeff Gordon, who proved to be not entirely different to his earlier Lemmy Caution—and not too far removed from his later Nick Carter. There was a sequel in the following year, *Ces dames s'en mèlent*, and Giacomo Rossi Stuart played a character of the same name in the Miguel Iglesias film *Occhio per occhio, dente per dente* (which was actually an entry in the entirely separate Agent Z-55 series).

It's not hard to see why these films have gained something of a cult reputation over the years. This one features plenty of silly comedy moments (men standing on rakes and knocking themselves unconscious, to name but one), and some absolutely dreadful choreography, but the whole thing is bizarrely enjoyable. There's a charismatic leading man, a plot that's simpler than a Roman road, lots of attractive girls (often scrapping with each other), and plenty of meandering fight sequences.

It's all slightly old fashioned, as emphasized by the jazzy soundtrack—which occasionally veers into the type of thing which was used to accompany the "comedy animal" sequences in Tarzan films. And if you're looking for something high-tech, well, as advanced as the gadgets in this film get is a rusty old tractor pulling a hay wagon. Some of the supporting performers are…shall we say, theatrical. Not Eddie, though, who's as cool as a diced cucumber in an igloo. In fact, a large amount of the running time is spent watching him either chatting up or fending off the ladies, which is a relatively pleasant way to spend an hour and a half. He also seems to have a predilection for tormenting a poor guy in a wheelchair, who gets slapped every time he appears onscreen.

As for production values: Although obviously filmed on a low budget, this does sport some lovely black and white cinematography, courtesy of Henri Persin. The direction by Raoul Andre is capable enough (and far better than his work on *Mission to Caracas*), and the script doesn't strive for any nonsense such as originality or significance. A trifle then, but a winning one.—MB

CREDITS: Production: Jacques Roitfeld, Fida Cinematografica, Films J. Manzon; Director: Raoul Andre; Story and Screenplay: Michel Lebrun; Cinematography: Henri Persin {B&W}; Music: Henri Persin; Original running length: 89 mins; Country: France/Italy; Year: 1963

CAST: Eddie Constantine (*Jeff Gordon*), Janine Vila (*Liliane*), Perrette Pradier (*Liza*), Clement Harari (*Lorenz, aka Dr. Mercier*), Victor Beaumont (*Gregori*), Sophie Hardy (*Claudine*), Andre Bernard (*Bertin*), Nando Gazzolo (*Dr. Mercier*), Daphne Dayle (*Barbara*), Jean-Jacques Steen (*Sam*), Paul Bonifas (*the notary*), Gisele Robert (*Dodo*), Sonia Silver (*Martine*), Henri Lambert (*Jojo*), Willy Black (*Emile*), Patricia Viterbo (*a nurse*), Dominique Zardi (*Lucien*), Bernard Musson (*a paralytic*), Daniel Emilfork (*Yanakos*), Mirielle Gallot, Corinne Bloch, Josy Andrieu, Jean Galland, Albert Dinan

## LE JUDOKA DANS L'ENFER

"the Judoka in hell"

aka Casse-tete chinois pour le judoka! (Fr, alt), Die 7 Masken des Judoka (WG), Ore Violente (It), Rompecabezas Chino (Sp)

Marc St. Clair, aka Judoka (Marc Briand), travels to Tokyo with his chums Jennifer (Marilu Tolo) and Clyde (Paolo Tiller). Clyde is on a special mission. As a pilot, he is to fly over China taking unauthorized aerial photographs. The others, meanwhile, lay around getting drunk on saki and eating sushi—which seems a rather unfair division of labor.

Clyde, however, never returns from his task. The American authorities appear to know nothing, and they assume that he has been shot down at sea. They are wrong. A young Chinese girl finds Judoka (despite several attempts upon her life) and reveals that his friend has been captured by The Black Dragon, a notorious and deadly secret society. Unfortunately, she is kidnapped before she can reveal where he is being held.

After plenty more exposition, it becomes clear that The Black Dragon are trying to brainwash Clyde into dropping a bomb on New York, thereby triggering a new world war. Fortunately, Jennifer and Judoka soon determine that the organization is based on a secret island, and determine to rescue their friend (and thus foil the evil scheme).

**Maria Minh shows courage in a German lobby card for *Judoka dans l'enfer***

This average actioner was the sequel to Pierre Zimmer's *Judoka Secret Agent*, (see entry) although all that they really have in common is the Judoka character (played by different actors) and the presence of Marilu Tolo in the cast (albeit in different roles). Of course, they both also act as a bridge between the Hong Kong martial arts movies that were to become so popular in the early seventies, and the traditional spy film.

The Judoka is a role that could almost have been written for Brad Harris. A karate-chopping, fist-throwing, kung fu expert, he spends most of his time running around and beating the crap out of people. Although Marc Briand isn't bad, he doesn't have the self-deprecating charisma that Harris brought to the Kommissar X films (and most particularly the superior *Death Is Nimble, Death Is Quick*, to which this bears the most similarity).

That said, the stunt work and choreography is convincing (especially a great rumble in a somewhat kitsch Buddhist temple garden); minor instances of sadism are on display (some poor Asian gets a syringe in the back of his skull). There's also use of speeded-up and reverse photography, which brings to mind the comedy spaghetti westerns that would proliferate in the subsequent decade. Maurice Labro's direction is perfectly adequate, and the locations are well used (this isn't one of those films that has a couple of exotic exterior shots and then the rest is filmed in a car park).

One of the most distinctive aspects of this Judoka film is the relationship between the two main characters. Cheeky Marilu Tolo (a brunette Barbara Windsor with sensibly sized breasts) is perpetually trying to seduce Judoka, with absolutely no success. His resistance to her female charms acts to prove that he's hardly your typical philandering secret agent, although he does get to sneak off and play with some giggling geishas.—MB

CREDITS: Production: G.R.K., Films Corona, Discobolo; Director: Maurice Labro; Story based on the novel "Judoka en Enfer" by Ernie Clark; Adaptation: Jean Meckert, Maurice Labro; Cinematography: Didier Tarot; Music: Van Tyenen, Antoine Duhamel; Original running length: 100 mins; Country: France/Italy; Year: 1968

CAST: Marilu Tolo (*Jennifer*), Marc Bryan [Marc Briand] (*Marc St. Clair*), Heinz Drache (*Finn/Von Sturm*), Paolo Tiller (*Clyde Garland*), Maria Minh (*Su Tchuen*), Jean Ferre (*the giant*), Francois Maistre (*Chang-Lee*), Adaly Bell (*Alize*)

JUDOKA SECRET AGENT
aka Carnet per un morto (It),
Le Judoka agent secret (Fr)

Once upon an age, I guess, judo must have been cool. By the time I reached school, it was the preserve of those weird kids who were also disturbingly attentive during chemistry lessons. The thought of grappling with a fellow spotty adolescent never really appealed to me. Smoking, drinking, walking around in an angst-fueled daze, these were the things that true men did. As such, the idea of a Judo-kicking hero—as we have here—was rather out of date by the mid-seventies (soon to be followed by roller-skating heroes and disco-dancing heroes).

A man is gunned down on the Paris streets. Before he dies, he is able to pass a small booklet to Catherine (Patricia Viterbo). Hoping to uncover the identity of the killer, she takes it to secret agent/judo expert Judoka (Jean-Claude Bercq), who leaves it with his boss to examine. He, of course, has more important things on his mind, namely wining and dining his new lady friend.

At a cabaret show, Judoka watches a really strange performance in which a young lady disrobes before embracing a giant snowman (hey, it was the sixties). He also meets Vanessa (Marilu Tolo), a sultry dame who seems to know more than she lets on, and witnesses a dodgy bunch of guys up to no good in the basement. After a bit of a scrap, he's knocked unconscious and imprisoned upon a barge—but manages to escape without too much trouble.

The whole plot seems to have something to do with a record producer called Dominique (Perrette Pradier) and a spooky old dude who wears a pair of glasses with one lens blacked out (a fashion tip later taken up by Sheila Keith in Pete Walker's classic *House of Whipcord*). It all ends up with a big speedboat chase down the Seine, during which all of the bad guys meet their inevitable doom.

As you can probably tell from the above synopsis, this is a rather episodic film. There's nothing in the way of narrative drive, and the plot is minimal in the extreme. None of the supporting characters are developed at all (indeed, they frequently drop out of the story for vast swatches of time). Even the villain, such as there is one, is rather a dullard. It's all a bit of a mess, lacking anything in the way of sparkle or genuine quality.

In its favor, there is a good soundtrack (the "oompah"-type cue that accompanies the above-mentioned cabaret performance is particularly effective, believe it or not). Director Pierre Zimmer may have no idea about pacing, but he stages some pretty decent choreography (especially one sequence in which a fight is shown by the use of shadows cast on a wall by a street lamp). Better known as an actor (*Every Man Is My Enemy*, *XXL*), he also made a documentary (*Camino de Santiago de los Franceses*) and the little- known drama *Donnez-moi dix hommes desperes*. There's one particularly amusing moment in which some poor unfortunate suffers a karate punch across the face. His expression is worth the price of admission alone.

Despite prominent billing, Michel Lonsdale (Hugo Drax in *Moonraker*) only appears during the last quarter. Patricia Viterbo drowned during the filming, which at least explains why her character virtually disappears after about 20 minutes. The best performer is Jacques Garcin as Judoka's sidekick, who gets to look particularly goofy in a terrible beatnik-style wig.

This film must have been reasonably successful; a sequel, the marginally more effective *Judoka dans l'enfer*, appeared the following year (albeit with a different star and director).—MB

CREDITS: Production: France Cinema Productions, Tigielle 33; Director: Pierre Zimmer; Story based on "The Judoka Dans La Ville" by Ernie Clark; Adaptation: Jacques Guymont, Pierre Zimmer; Cinematography: Gilbert Sarthre {Eastmancolor}; Music: Armand Zeggian, Roland Vincent; Original running length: 95 mins; Country: France/Italy; Year: 1966

CAST: Jean-Claude Bercq (*the Judoka*), Marilu Tolo (*Vanessa*), Perrette Pradier (*Dominique*), Patricia Viterbo (*Catherine*), Henri Garcin (*Jacques*), Yves Brainville (*the patron*), Michel Lonsdale (*Perkins*), Fernand Berset (*the commissioner*), Mick Besson (*the sound technician*), David Tonelli

### KILL PANTHER KILL

aka Gangsters per un massacro (It),
Kommissar X—Drei Blaue Panther (WG),
Tres panteras azules (Sp)

Uber-theif Arthur Tracy (Franco Fantasia) manages to escape from prison with the help of his old accomplice Anthony (Siegfried Rauch). Four years before, they had stolen a set of extremely valuable diamonds, which have been reluctantly looked after by Tracy's brother, Robert (also Fantasia) and his wife, Elizabeth (Erika Blanc). Inevitably, Robert is soon murdered so that Arthur can take his place and try to discover where the booty has been hidden. Elizabeth becomes suspicious of her "husband" (maybe it's the way that he insists on slapping her around with alarming regularity while shouting "Where are the diamonds?" that's the giveaway).

Thankfully, both Joe Walker (Tony Kendall) and Captain Tom Rowland (Brad Harris) happen to be in the area.

**Erika Blanc and Siegfried Rauch in Kill Panther Kill**

There is no such thing as a dull Kommissar X film, but this is a bit less outrageous than some and, maybe, a little less riotously enjoyable. Unlike the previous entries in the series, there are no mad scientists, no subterranean hideouts and no preposterous machines to duplicate/sterilize/turn women's hair lavender. In fact, it's almost more like a straight gangster story, a feeling accentuated by the proliferation of characters wearing bad trilbies. Good god, there aren't even any ray guns!

On the other hand, it's all told in a very accomplished fashion. There are some impressive sequences set in what must have been the Canadian World Expo, full of geodesic domes and cable cars. Tony Kendall gets to steal a young lady's clothes while she's swimming and then play peeping tom—but he's wearing an attractive cardigan, so that's alright. Brad Harris gets to fall in love and act all soppy before beating the crap out of everyone. Best of all, everyone gets to dress up in cowboy drag that's more *High Chaparral* than *Django*, making things even campier than normal.

Secondary villain Siegfried Rauch, a staple in these Eurospy films, resurfaced in the seventies as a "token German" in a variety of Second World War films—most notably John Sturges' enjoyable *The Eagle Has Landed* and Sam Fuller's superb *The Big Red One*. Interestingly, regular Parolini scriptwriter Werner Hauff (*Sartana*, *The Tall Women*, *Hunting the Unknown*) has a fleeting role in this as a policeman. Director Parolini, who often had cameos in his own films, also appears as a pork-pie hat-wearing minor gangster.—MB

CREDITS: Production: P.E.A. Cin.ca, Parnass Film, I.P.S.; Director: Frank Kramer [Gianfranco Parolini]; Story based on the Kommissar X books by Robert F. Atkinson; Screenplay: Gianfranco Parolini, Giovanni Simonelli, Gunter Rudorf; Cinematography: Francesco Izzarelli {Eastmancolor}; Music: Marcello Giombini; Original running length: 93 mins; Filming location: Montreal; Country: Italy/West Germany; Year: 1968

CAST: Tony Kendall [Luciano Stella] (*Joe Walker*), Brad Harris (*Captain Tom Rowland*), Erika Blanc (*Liz Hillary*), Franco Fantasia (*Robert and Arthur Hillary*), Corny Collins (*Emily*), Hannelore Auer (*Betty*), Siegfried Reich (*Anthony*), John Francis Littlewood [Gianfranco Parolini] (*Smokey*), Erwin Strahl (*Inspector Lefevre*), Frank Valentin, Carlos De Castro (*William Rogers*), Laci von Ronay (*Inspector Barry*), Werner Hauff (*Inspector Jackson*), Pino Mattei (*the killer*), Jens Herold (*the doctor*)

THE KILLER LIKES CANDY

aka Un asesino para su majestad (Sp), Un Killer per sua maesta (It), Le Tueur aime les bonbons (Fr), Zucker für den Mörder (WG)

*The Killer Likes Candy* could just as easily have been a cop thriller, but for the element of Mark Stone (Kerwin Mathews) being a US government agent. Locations in Venice and

**Another dramatic Belgian poster this time with a poor likeness of Kerwin Mathews in *The Killer Likes Candy***

Rome keep things visually interesting, the cast is filled with recognizable faces, and the score by Gianni Marchetti is appropriately jazzy.

In the pre-credit sequence, we witness the first assassination attempt on the king of Kifiristan—the case that Stone will be assigned. Interestingly enough, the killer Oscar Schnell (Bruno Cremer) is disguised as a priest. Schnell climbs the stairs of a church steeple to take aim at the king with his high-powered rifle, then loads the gun with an ice bullet, a trick used two years earlier in *Ring Around the World*, also scripted by Ernesto Gastaldi. Schnell fails in his mission this time, but kills an American agent posing as a bodyguard for the king.

When we first meet Mark Stone—whose nickname is Angel Face—he is doing a rather poor impersonation of a fashion photographer and we therefore have the pleasure of watching a slew of bikini-clad lasses posing atop an ornate fountain. Once given his new assignment to guard the king, Stone is told to keep his cover as the photographer as long as possible, but he immediately abandons the ruse and we don't blame him.

Stone's sidekick, Costa, is played by Venantino Venantini (*Gates of Hell*, *Cannibal Apocalypse*), and his talent for comic relief is balanced nicely by his fighting abilities. Marilu Tolo is the love interest, Sylva, who sneaks around the royal quarters claiming to be physician to the king's harem.

The main bad guys are played by Werner Peters and Gordon Mitchell. Peters—with ever-present cigarette—is the president of a meat-packing company who hires assassins on the side. A mainstay of the German Edgar Wallace krimis and Dr. Mabuse films of the early sixties, Peters does his usual great job here, alternately commandeering and sniveling. When Peters spills the beans to Stone about the identity and location of Schnell, the killer returns to douse Peters with gasoline and set him afire! In reality, Peters only lived three more years, a great loss for European cinema lovers. Gordon Mitchell is equally well known. Amid countless appearances in sword and sandal, western and adventure films in the sixties and seventies, Mitchell made a career out of getting his ass kicked by better-looking heroes, but managed to live to the ripe old age of 80.

But back to the film. A second attempt is made on the king's life when Schnell waltzes right into the basement of the hotel where the king is staying to plant a bomb on the elevator. So much for Stone's improved security measures. Using his sixth sense, Stone has the king use the service elevator instead and the bomb plot fails. We don't get to see the explosion—for budgetary reasons—and upon hearing it, one of the king's aides starts to panic, but Stone reassures him that, "We'll put out a story to cover the explosion." One wonders just how that would be accomplished.

Attempts are made on Stone's life too, as if guarding the king wasn't enough. One such attempt occurs in the Orsini Gardens at Bomarzo. Filled with giant, bizarre statuary, the gardens are a terrific place to stage a chase and shoot-out. As it happens, Stone is shot in the arm before escaping this nightmarish place. But before he can have the wound attended to, Stone changes clothes and travels out of the city with the king to the secluded clinic where the king has his heart checked (bad news), goes with the king to a soccer game, returns to the hotel where political fanatics try to kill the king, stays with the king while his heart is checked again, and travels back out to the clinic where the king will have an operation. Then after checking

**Terrific artwork of the Finnish poster for Antonio Margheriti's *Killers Are Challenged***

all the security at the clinic, Stone finally says, "I'd like to have a little time off to get this arm fixed up." The guy is superhuman.

The film features lots of fistfights, one of which occurs at the meat-packing plant, naturally. At the end of the prolonged fight, Costa dumps a handy bucket of blood over the head of one of the henchmen and proclaims he will become a vegetarian!

When searching Schnell's room, Stone and Costa find a copy of *Guns and Ammo* and a suitcase full of guns. Ah, the good old days before airport security. Meanwhile, the killer plans to coerce Sylva to kill the king during his operation. He kidnaps Sylva's mom, kills her dad and even kills her dog. The king survives the operation, but for a moment it's touch and go. It's during that moment that Stone finds out who really is behind the assassination attempts. I won't spoil it for you.

The catacombs of the monastery make for a creepy place to stage part of the climactic gun battle between Schnell and Stone—lots of skeletons and such. Stone even uses a skeleton's hand to hold a flashlight. The monastery apparently opens up to a marble quarry and this provides the filmmakers with the opportunity to have the villain of the piece fall from a great height to his death. The plot may be simple, but Mathews makes for a good hero, and *The Killer Likes Candy* has enough going for it to make it worth seeking out.—DD

CREDITS: Production: Franca Film, Eichberg, Criterion Film; Director: Richard Owens [Federico Chentrens]; Story based on the novel "A coeur ouvert pour face d'Ange" by Adam Saint-Moore; Screenplay: Maurice Cloche, Giovanni Simonelli, Charels Dorat, H. Inattilger; Cinematography: Fausto Zuccoli {Techniscope – Technicolor}; Music: Gianni Marchetti; Original running length: 99 mins; Filming location: Istanbul; Country: Italy/West Germany/Paris; Year: 1968

CAST: Kerwin Mathews (*Mark Stone*), Marilu Tolo (*Sylva*), Venantino Venantini (*Costa*), Bruno Cremer (*Oscar Schnell*), Ann Smyrner (*Veronica*), Werner Peters (*Guardino*), Gordon Mitchell (*Tony Govic*), Lukas Amman (*Re Faud*), Sieghardt Rupp (*Ali*), Riccardo Garrone (*Nicolo*), Fabienne Dali (*Guardino's lover*), Alain Saury (*General Habal*), Giuseppe Addobbati (*the Count*), Elisa Cegani (*Signora Boldani*), Valentino Macchi (*thug at abbattoir*), Gianni Gori, Rod Carter, Charlotte Falchin, Elisabeth Thompson

KILLERS ARE CHALLENGED
aka A 077: sfida ai killers (It),
Bob Fleming...mission Casablanca (Fr),
Bob Fleming: mission Casablanca (WG),
Reto a los asesinos (Sp)

This is one of only two spy flicks that prolific genre director Antonio Margheriti made in the sixties. His other one was *Lightning Bolt*, made the same year, and that one is easily is the lesser of the two. At least there are some actual locations used in *Killers* and Richard Harrison is a more appealing leading man than Anthony Eisley. The female quotient is upped here as well, with Susy Anderson and Janine Reynaud among the ladies in action.

Richard Harrison, the rather dull-looking American southpaw, is one of those stars who has had an inexplicably long career. Not really much of an actor, he does have an appealing quality about him that carried him through dozens of lead roles in sword and sandal, adventure and western pictures. I like Harrison, but his performances always seem to disappoint.

Harrison plays Bob Fleming, an all-American CIA agent impersonating a scientist, Coleman, who's developed a new form of energy that would make all other types of fuel obsolete. I always wonder at these plots because usually the secret formula is saved by the good guys, but the world is never changed by the outcome. I guess all the secret formulas for new fuels and such are being kept secret by the government for the same reasons the bad guys wanted them. Super-efficient new fuels would collapse worldwide markets, crushing economies everywhere, and we'd all be doomed anyway.

There's a female agent who keeps saving Fleming's butt in this film. She's Velka, a Russian no less, played by Susy Anderson. It's kind of funny the way she keeps chasing after Fleming, saving his life time after time and he's sort of oblivious to the whole thing. She's after the formula too, but is a gracious loser in the end. Anderson didn't make any other spy flicks, but you may recognize her from Mario Bava's *Black Sabbath*.

The real evil lady here is Wandisa Guida, who plays Terry Coleman, the wife of the scientist that Fleming is impersonating. Guida has an untrustworthy look, so it comes as no surprise that her character is actually running the whole show and wants her husband and his formula to disappear.

Janine Reynaud and Mitsouko are two of Terry Coleman's…henchpersons, I guess we'd call them now, and both were in their share of spy flicks. Here, Reynaud gets a chance to whip the tender flesh of Mitsouko, who's dressed in a black slip for the occasion. Later, however, Mitsouko betrays the other women and dies for it. Reynaud has an equally unspectacular demise.

*Killers* has a good, fun score by Carlo Savina with lots of jazzy sounds to its credit. In one scene after Fleming asks a cab driver to take him somewhere with local charm, the belly dancing sequence we see next suddenly turns into a go-go fest with lots of hip dancers! It's at this same bar where Fleming puts in ear plugs to listen to the bug he just planted on Mitsouko, and we watch all the wild dancing but hear only what he's hearing. It's a fun sight gag that actually works. Another funny bit is when Fleming has to steal a car from some poor soul for a chase and then, so she can chase after Fleming, Velka steals the car of the next guy who comes along and stops to help.

There's one good fight with Fleming where the thug puts on some brass knuckles with nasty-looking spikes and ends up with them stuck in his own throat. Fleming then mails the dead thug back to the bad guys! The downside to the good fight is one of those silly bar fights (including dwarf gags) that go on forever near the end of the film. It's a huge mistake by Margheriti that just kills the momentum.

There are a few gadgets used in the film too, like a ring that detects poison and little transmitters about the size of a button. Hands down, the best use of a gadget occurs early in the film when a thug drops a little lighter bomb into Fleming's coat pocket. Fleming turns around and gives it right back, unbeknownst to the thug. This bad guy then walks back to the car with his cronies and counts down the seconds until they all blow up.

Here you have a middle-of-the-road espionage flick (written by Ernesto Gastaldi) with a few more ups than downs—just enough to keep things interesting. Beware the silly bar fight, however.—DD

CREDITS: Production: Zenith Cin.ca, Flora Film, Regina Film; Director: Anthony Dawson [Antonio Margheriti]; Story and Screenplay: Julian Berry [Ernesto Gastaldi]; Cinematography: Richard Thierry [Riccardo Pallotini] {Eastmancolor – Widescope}; Music: Carlo Savina; Original running length: 90 mins; Filming locations: Titanus Studios, Geneva, Morocco; Country: Italy/France; Year: 1966

CAST: Richard Harrison (*Bob Fleming*), Susy Andersen (*Velka*), Wandisa Guida (*Terry Coleman*), Marcel Charvey (*Coleman*), Jeanini Reynaud (*Halima*), Jim Clay [Aldo Cecconi] (*Tommy Sturgeon*), John Hawkwood, Frank Dillon [Fredlyn Frank], Freddy [Goffredo] Unger (*Mark, a killer*), Gianni Di Benedetto (*CIA chief*), Claudio Biava (*a villain*), and with Mitsouka (*Moira*)

This is a decidedly unfunny spoof done in that carefree, late-sixties style that is by turns boring and irritating. It also has the nerve to clock in at 100 minutes, adding insult to injury. There are plenty of Bondian asides including the credit sequence, which unsuccessfully apes the designer look of the 007 films. The Bruno Nicolai score has its moments, but that doesn't qualify as the savior of this tedious time waster.

Giuliano Gemma, better known for his string of spaghetti westerns, is Kirk Warren, an agent being sent to the gallows at the beginning of the film. Called back into service four seconds before his death, Warren is assigned to steal a secret formula before the mysterious Mr. X can get his hands on it. Warren accepts the assignment, naturally, but he intends to sell the formula to Mr. X himself. After all, patriotism was so passé in 1967.

Warren enlists the aide of three compatriots: a professor with the nickname "Radar Blip," who uses his nose to detect things like death rays and such; an accident-prone safe cracker whose tools include a corkscrew, a can opener, etc.; and an acrobat. Does it get any wackier than that? Well, yes.

This film is chock full of nonstop gags and the hit rate is extremely low. We are treated to exploding golf balls, a wise-cracking parrot, secret agents in trash cans (a la *Get Smart*), a pistol that shoots laughing gas, the old dead-body-in-the-closet routine, the collapsing bed gag, a talking pigeon, a one-man submarine, an amphibious car and more, much more. We also have a non-Asian Asian character who dresses like a harlequin and rides roller skates on his yacht, amusement park humor—with roller-coaster rides, funny mirrors, etc.—bad guys who shoot each other by mistake, speeded-up chases and a cake in the face. There's more, of course, but you get the idea. Anything and everything that seemed remotely funny (and the chances were indeed remote) is thrown into this movie.

Georges Rigaud is Wilcox, who heads the Secret Service but does double duty as the villain of the piece, Mr. X. Mr. X is the chief of a commercial espionage organization that plans to sell the formula to the highest bidder.

**Rare Turkish poster for *Kiss Kiss Bang Bang* trades on Giuliano Gemma's Ringo persona**

It's all very silly, but that doesn't translate as funny. Director Duccio Tessari, who made lots of sword and sandal adventures and spaghetti westerns, includes plenty of "op art" sight gags that come across as simply self-conscious eyesores—except the cartoons by Bruno Bozzetto, whose paycheck must have been large indeed.

I will admit to chuckling a couple of times—like when the guy tears apart the phone in frustration as he talks on it (you have to be there)—but don't bother tracking this one down, you'll only be disappointed.—DD

CREDITS: Production: Prod. Cin.che Mediterranee, Rizzoli Film, Prod. Cin.cas Balcazar; Director: Duccio Tessari; Story and Screenplay: Bruno Corbucci, Fernando Di Leo, Duccio Tessari; Cinematography: Francisco Marin {Techniscope – Technicolor}; Music: Bruno Nicolai; Original running length: 112 mins; Filming locations: Rome, London; Country: Italy/Spain; Year: 1966

CAST: Giuliano Gemma (*Kirk Warren*), George Martin (*Chico Perez*), Lorella De Luca (*Frida Kadar*), Nieves Navarro (*Alina Shakespeare*), Danielle Vargas (*Tol Lim*), Cesarina Riccarda Guazzelli (*Frida's aunt*), Antonio Casas (*Pro-*

*fessor Padereski*), Pajarito (*Dupont*), Georges Rigaud (*Sir Sebastian Wilcox*), Carlo Gentili Del Carrasco, Franco Morici, Amparo Diez, Nick Anderson [Nazzareno Zamperla], Juan Torres

KISS ME MONSTER
aka Besame Monstruo (Sp), Castle of the Doomed (Int), Küß mich, Monster (WG)

*Kiss Me Monster* was shot at about the same time as *Sadisterotica*, and once again features Rosanna Yanni and Janine Reynaud as the statuesque "Red Lips" girls, a detective duo with undefined links to Interpol. Jesus Franco is again the director, and this is very much a film that is drawn from his idiosyncratic brain. In other words, it's quite unlike anything else in the genre. It's a phantasmagoric mixture of ultra-camp and virtually incomprehensible hi-jinks. Apart from the central characters, this also features a number of minor characters who happen to be—or happen to be posing as—secret agents, but the plot is the stuff of pure fantasy. As one of the characters states: "There's some kind of madman who's developing humans out of tin cans, or something like that…"

Most of the narrative comes in the form of a flashback, commencing when the girls are disturbed in the middle of the night by a musician,

**DVD cover art for *Kiss Me Monster***

who hands a mysterious score to them before unceremoniously dying. Using an astonishing leap of logic, they connect him to a secret sect called The Abilenes, which includes a number of scientists among its membership. These guys also dress up in red robes and black Ku Klux Klan hoods. Anyway, they are anxious to find out who has murdered one of their most prominent members, professor Bertrand, and contract Regina and Diana to do so on their behalf.

Bertrand, it turns out, was an interesting character: He had been working on a secret formula that had enabled him to create…artificial humans. The only problem with these homunculi is that they lack any intelligence whatsoever, and furthermore their creation also involves—for some reason or other—the regular kidnapping of beautiful women. This was something of a preoccupation for Franco, who featured beautiful women being kidnapped by half-witted hominids throughout his career, from *The Awful Dr. Orloff* to *Faceless* and beyond.

The girls take the logical step of furthering their inquiries by taking a striptease job on the island of—inevitably—Abilene. This brings them into contact with a motley bunch of lounge lizards, an island full of pseudo-Amazons with a dislike of men and copious sub-humans dressed in big red underpants. It becomes clear, of course, that the murder of the professor is of rather less interest to all of these fruitcakes than the whereabouts of his formula.

This is another entirely bonkers, hugely enjoyable film, which just goes to show what Franco was capable of when the mood took him. It's just a shame that the mood only took him for about 20 of his numerous films. As in *Sadisterotica*, the plot is born of horror film motifs, but merged with swinging sixties style and espionage trimmings to create a wholly phantasmagoric mess. For some reason, it reminded me of Gordon Hessler's likeable *Scream and Scream Again* (if merged with *Absolutely Fabulous*).

Jazzy and frantic, it treads a fine line between the amusing and the tiresome. It's at its best when glorifying in the absurdity of the plot, throwing in increasingly surreal conceits in a desperate need to keep the audience's attention. It's at its worst when trying to be self-consciously funny (the whole shebang is quite weird enough in itself, thank you very much). That said, it looks fantastic, there's a great score, and Franco keeps things as tasty and light as a fine soufflé (albeit while still displaying his usual ineptness when it comes to action sequences).

The script makes absolutely no sense, but that's not really the point. *Kiss Me Monster* is more like a sixties "head" film, and with its prominent use of music it plays like an extended pop video. The narrative merely serves as a means of taking us from one performance—whether it is a song or a striptease—to another. This link between the soundtrack and the images is further accentuated by the regular inclusion of "Greek chorus" figures, who appear regularly to sing some clues and strum guitars.

This throws the pacing into freefall, a problem not exactly helped by the fact that several sequences appear to have been thrown in at complete random. One particularly protracted nightclub sequence, which seems to last for about five minutes, has no bearing upon the plot whatsoever. But, heck, it also features a random babe gyrating semi-naked on a red carpet and quite obviously edited in from another Franco film, so just who gives a damn?

The dialogue, which gives nonsequitors a new life of their own, is part hilarious and part infuriating. Prime samples would have to include: "I was taken prisoner by a group of queer virgins and was put in a cage. One of them worked me over with a whip, then they let me out again, and they gave me a funny kind of whistle as a farewell present!" This is actually one of the more sensible extracts. Most of it is spoken by Yanni and Reynaud, who both give good performances, and Adrian Hoven pops up toward the end as another Interpol agent (or is he?), who's ordered around by an entirely unexplained girl on a sofa.

Not a great film, by any means. Not even a particularly good film, when it comes down to it, but most certainly one of the most idiosyncratic and memorable genre entries that you're likely to come across. This one will stick in your head like Super Glue.—MB

CREDITS: Production: Aquila Film, Films Montana; Director: Jesus Franco; Story and Screenplay: Jesus Franco, Karl Heinz Mannchen, Luis Revenga; Cinematography: Jorge Herrero, Franz Hofer {Eastmancolor}; Music: Fernando Garcia Morcillo, Jerry van Rooyen, Daniel White; Original running length: 87 mins; Filming locations: Spain, West Germany; Country: Spain/West Germany; Year: 1969

CAST: Janine Reynaud (*Diana*), Rosanna Yanni (*Regina*), Chris Howland (*Francis McClune, an Interpol Agent*), Michel Lemoine (*Jacques Maurier*), Manuel Velasco (*Andy, sometimes called "Anthony"*), Manuel Otero (*Dmitri*), Ana Cesares (*Linda*) and Adrian Hoven (*Eric Vicas*) Uncredited: Carlos Mendy, Barta Barri (*Professor Bertrand, aka "Inspector Kramer"*), Marta Reves (*Irina*), Nelida Quiroga, Fernando de Rojas, Maria Antonia Rodonda (*Balumba*), Gregorio de Mora (*Andros*), Maria Dom (*Anita*), Jesus Franco (*Abilene contact*)

## KISS THE GIRLS AND MAKE THEM DIE

aka Besame y no me mates (Sp),
Operazione paradiso (It, alt),
Se tutte le donne del mondo (It)

It's amazing what a decent budget will do for a film. Most of the Eurospy flicks made in the sixties were shot on minuscule budgets, so it's a pleasant experience to watch one with a modicum of financial class. *KTGAMTD* is a tongue-in-cheek Bondian adventure that rivals the official product in all departments. Mike Connors, as Kelly, CIA agent 409, has what it takes to be a spy. He's good on his feet, has excellent comic timing and looks good in a tuxedo. Too bad he didn't make more of this type of film. Raf Vallone makes a good villain too. Suave and dangerous by turns, his Ardonian is clever, resourceful, and has a great pad. There are plenty of gadgets and humor and some (but not enough) beautiful women. And it's shot in English, too.

The film opens with a brief, humorous jungle scene and then jumps into an exciting chase sequence around Rio's famous Corcovado. Kelly pieces together a plot to sterilize America (and zen zee vorld!) while working with a British agent, Susan Fleming (Dorothy Provine), and her chauffeur/partner, James. Both agents have plenty of gadgets

**German poster for Mike Conners' only foray into Eurospy, *Kiss the Girls and Make Them Die***

to get them out of the many scrapes they find themselves in. Kelly sports a nifty-looking watch communicator, a knife in his belt buckle, a flashlight gun and a dart gun in his shoe. Susan rivals these with a poison-tipped ring, a pen that shoots darts and a mascara pencil that shoots bubbles of sleeping gas. Terry-Thomas—in a nice low-key though still humorous performance—is a super chauffeur and fussy Renaissance man who knows karate and speaks obscure Peruvian dialects, among other qualities. The Rolls Royce he's most proud of has so many amenities and gadgets that it has a personality all its own.

Susan parades around in a hideous collection of hats and gowns with an affected upper-class accent in her disguise as a bon vivant. Ardonian, meanwhile, has a great house and an even better underground lair that holds the rocket that will carry his deadly satellite into orbit. His villainy is demonstrated when he cold-heartedly kills the Red Chinese benefactors who supplied him with a much-needed part for his device. In a bold sexual statement for the times, it is revealed that he is impotent and it's this malady that is driving his twisted desire to render the rest of the world sterile. But never fear. He meets his end in an ironic way befitting his kind.

Among the other treats that await you are the old scorpions-in-the-orchids trick, the old exploding-puppet trick, an amphibious vehicle, the old boa constrictor-in-the-feather-boa gag and a fall-apart car. Since the action takes place in Rio, we are once again privileged to watch the usual Carnival footage, an endlessly fascinating time-waster for filmmakers but one that wears thin on the viewer. It seems that all spy adventures in Rio take place during Carnival time. And since Kelly is always eating bananas, you know there will be a banana peel gag in there somewhere.

The bevy of beauties features Margaret Lee and Marilu Tolo, both spy film regulars, but neither is given much screen time, unfortunately. There is one henchman you will recognize: Oliver MacGreevy, always the baldheaded heavy. The soundtrack by Mario Nascimbene is a purposeful mix of Latin-inflected tunes and action motifs that works well but isn't particularly memorable. All this pleasing nonsense is presented in a matter-of-fact way without the grandiose posturing of Bond or the mugging comedy of other spoofs. Enjoy.—DD

CREDITS: Production: Dino De Laurentiis Cin. ca; Director: Dino Maiuri, Henry Levin; Story and Screenplay: Dino Maiuri, Jack Pulman (US version); Cinematography: Aldo Tonti {Technicolor}; Music: Mario Nascimbene; Original running length: 106 mins; Filming location: Brazil; Country: Italy; Year: 1966

CAST: Dorothy Provine (*Susan*), Michael Connors (*Kelly*), Raf Vallone (*Ardonian*), Margaret Lee (*Grace*), Nicoletta Machiavelli (*Sylvia*), Sandro Dori (*Omar*), Marilu Tolo (*Gioia*), Seyna Seyn (*Wilma Soong*), Oliver McGreevy (*Ringo*), Beverley Adams (*Karin*), Jack Gwillim (*the British Ambassador*), Edith Peters (*Maria*), Andy Ho (*Ling*), Renato Terra, Hans Thorner (*Kruger*), Nerio Bernardi (the *papal envoy*), Roland Bartrop, Michael Audley (*Major Davis*), Terry-Thomas (*James/Lord Aldric*), Esmeralda Barros, Dorival Carper, Paulo Copacabana, Cosme dos Santos, Eliezer Gomes Guidarino Guidi, Milton Leal, Waldir Maia, Adriano Reys, Rosana Tapajós

KOROSHI
aka Danger Man: Koroshi

This film is actually two episodes of the British television series *Danger Man* slapped together to make a feature. The episodes, *Koroshi* and *Shinda Shima*, were the last two episodes made of the series (and coincidentally, the only two shot in color) before Patrick McGoohan left to begin work on his labor of love, *The Prisoner*. According to some sources, "Koroshi" translates as "film noir," but in that episode the word is associated with a Kabuki "murder scene," the poetry of death, as it were. The phrase "Shinda Shima" supposedly translates as "murdered island."

Patrick McGoohan plays John Drake, the droll and deadly agent who, in *Koroshi*, tracks down a recently revived cell of an ancient organization of assassins led by Ronald Howard. The operation is ridiculously easy and seems even shorter than the original hour-long time slot it was made to fill. Agent Yoko Tani is killed off in the first two minutes of this episode, but shows up in the second as her own sister! This episode features a few bland gadgets like a flower pot transmitter that also emits poison gas, a cufflink explosive, and a watch that detect bombs. Other than the typical (for the time) practice of using Caucasian actors to portray Asians, there is very little noteworthy about the segment.

Just when you thought the world was safe from ancient assassination organizations, the bridge sequence informs us that there is another cell of these evildoers who have taken over an island in the South Pacific. In *Shinda Shima*, McGoohan impersonates an electronics expert to infiltrate the gang and this episode fares better than the previous one—but barely. After he attempts to kill the leader (George Coulouris), McGoohan escapes and rounds up the exiled inhabitants of the island to return and take possession of what was once theirs. This episode features the most tedious of conceits: the underwater knife fight. There's a little more action here but you know things are bad when local villagers (nonactors) are used as a fighting band in the grand finale.

The episodes necessarily move fast but they're still boring, flaunting lots of talk and a little action every once in a while to keep the audience from dozing off. And talk about cheap: The cardboard sets look terribly flat and unconvincing, while rear projection and stock footage stand in for actual locations. You can forget about being carried away to exotic locales with this film.

**Patrick McGoohan as John Drake in *Danger Man***

*Koroshi* director Michael Truman worked on *The Saint* television series, as did *Shinda Shima* director Peter Yates, but Yates will always be remembered for making *Bullitt*. There is no credit for the uninspired score.—DD

CREDITS: Production: Incorporated Television Company; Director: Michael Truman, Peter Yates; Screenplay: Norman Hudis, Ralph Smart; Original running length: 104 mins; Country: UK; Year: 1966

CAST: Patrick McGoohan (*John Drake*), Maxine Audley (*Pauline*), Amanda Barrie (*Rosemary*), Christopher Benjamin (*Potter*), Mona Chong (*first girl islander*), George Coulouris (*controller*), John Garrie (*old Japanese man*), Kenneth Griffith (*Richards*), Ronald Howard (*Sanders*), Kristopher Kum (*passport official*), Burt Kwouk (*Tanaka*), Robert Lee (*manager of Two-Tailed Dragon*), Paula Li Shui (*second girl islander*), Jeremy Longhurst (*Fortune*), Anna

Mai (*airline clerk*), Edward Ogdon (*Edward Sharp*), Yoko Tani (*Ako Nakamura/Miho*), David Toguri (*Commander Yamada*), Tommy Yapp (*contact man*), Lilani Young (*Japanese granddaughter*), Barbara Yu Ling (*hostess*)

LADIES' MAN
aka Lemmy pour les dames (Fr),
Lemmy y las aspias (Sp)

More a murder mystery than a spy flick, *Ladies' Man* qualifies under a vague espionage angle. Four beautiful women (naturally), who happen to be married to powerful men in politics and industry, are blackmailed into revealing government secrets. Neither the information they pass nor the government receiving the secrets are ever disclosed. The women are susceptible to extortion because in their younger, wilder days they smoked some opium and inadvertently killed a friend they thought had died from the experience. When one of the ladies decides to tell all to Lemmy Caution (Eddie Constantine), she is killed and his investigation exposes the spy ring.

Constantine reprises his role as the hard-drinking FBI agent Lemmy Caution, with his usual winning sarcasm, whose fame is such that when we first see him he is being mobbed by female admirers. Such is the life. There are plenty of humorous moments, nice cars and beautiful women to keep the viewer amused, but this film, like many in the series, tends to slide by without making much of an impact. Paul Misraki's score is as undistinguished as the rest of the film. *Ladies' Man* is a pleasant diversion and the popularity of Constantine at the time is easily understood as he chides the bad guys, woos the women and relies on brains and brawn to get the job done.

**Cartoonish Belgian poster for the Eddie Constantine vehicle *Ladies' Man***

As mentioned, all of the actresses are striking beauties. The girl whose murder kicks off the plot, Yvonne Monlaur (*Brides of Dracula*), is not even billed for her small but pivotal role on the American print of *Ladies' Man*. Francoise Brion, Claudine Coster and Eliane D'Almeida round out the female troupe. Of the males, Jacques Berthier and Guy Delorme are the most recognizable.—DD

CREDITS: Production: C.I.C.C. Films, Films Borderie; Director: Bernard Borderie; Story based on the novel by Peter Cheyney; Screenplay: Marc-Gilbert Sauvajon, Bernard Borderie; Cinematography: Armand Thirard {B&W}; Music: Paul Misraki; Original running length: 97 mins; Country: France; Year: 1962

CAST: Eddie Constantine (*Lemmy Caution*), Françoise Brion (*Marie-Christine*), Claudine Coster (*Françoise*), Eliane D'Almeida (*Sophie*), Yvonne Monlaur (*Claudia*), Jacques Berthier (*Dr. Nollet*), Robert Berri (*Dombie*), Guy Delorme (*Mirko*), Lionel Roc (*Hugo*), Paul Mercey (*Commissioner Boumègue*), Jacques Hilling (*hotel manager*), Jean-Marc Allègre, Annie Valentin, Anne-Marie Dance

THE LAST CHANCE
aka Jaque mate internacional (Sp),
Scacco Internazionale (It)

This was Tab Hunter's only spy movie, thank goodness. He's a lousy actor—even flubs his lines at one point—so it's fortunate for us that this aging beach bum didn't find more work in the genre. The film is convoluted and doesn't make much sense in the end, so it's hard to give a damn about Tab anyway. Tab's a journalist, Patrick Harris, who prints a story that neither the good guys nor the bad

**Something Weird video tape of *The Last Chance***

guys like very much. Hence, he's marked for death by bad spies and framed for murder by the good spies. He can't win.

There are a few good things about this general failure of a film. Daniela Bianchi is a big plus. She plays Tab's jealous wife, Helen, who turns out to be…never mind.

Two more actors help to ease the pain of watching too much Tab. Umberto Raho and Franco Ressel aren't given enough to do here, but their presence will help keep you awake. Both are good guys in this film—a rare treat in itself. At one point Raho plays the piano for a stripper in a classy club. What's funny in this scene is that he answers the phone next to his piano during the performance. Ressel plays a cop, but with all the spies around he doesn't get very much screen time.

Michael Rennie, who plays a diplomat, gets killed at a party. Luisa Barrato (*Bloody Pit of Horror*), billed here as Liz Barrett, plays Rennie's wife (and Patrick's former lover). She gets killed too.

The score by Carlo Rustichelli (conducted by Bruno Nicolai) is one of the best things about the film. There's an eccentric hit man as well, perennial bad guy Luciano Rossi (billed here as Edward Ross). He uses an eye patch instead of just closing one eye when he aims his rifle. It may sound okay, but frankly speaking, you won't be missing much if you don't take a chance on this time-waster.—DD

CREDITS: Production: Cinematografica Italiana; Director: Niny Rosati [Giuseppe Rosati]; Story and Screenplay: Niny Rosati [Giuseppe Rosati]; Cinematography: Gabor Pogany {Eastmancolor - Cromoscope}; Music: Carlo Rustichelli; Original running length: 90 mins; Country: Italy; Year: 1969

CAST: Tab Hunter (*Patrick Harris*), Daniela Bianchi (*Helen Harris*), Liz Barrett [Luisa Barratto] (*Stefanie MacConnell*), Edward G. Ross [Luciano Rossi] (*Besive, the Killer*), Michael Rennie (*George MacConnell*), Bill Vanders (*Clark*), Franco Ressel (*Inspector*), Umberto Raho (*Carlo*), Leonardo Bruno, Carlo Delle Piane, Bill Cross, Claudio Guarino, Vladimiro Tuicovich, Mirella Panphili

## LAST MAN TO KILL

aka 1.000.000 de dollars pour 7 assassinats (Fr), King hetzt 7 Killer (WG), Un Milione di dollari per sette assassini (It), Un millon de dolares por siete asesinos (Sp)

This was director Umberto Lenzi's last spy flick and it shows a marked improvement over his first, *A 008 Operation Exterminate*, despite the fact there's only a year between them. *LMTK* qualifies as a spy flick by the skin of its teeth, since you don't know until the very end that Michael King (Roger Browne) is a secret agent, but it is an entertaining and capable example from a director who did better with cops and cannibals. Of course, you get an inkling that things may turn "spy" when a missing formula for a new carburant comes into play about an hour or so into the picture.

King masquerades as a thief and killer (his trademark is the king of diamonds, which he leaves on his victims' bodies) in order to track down said formula. He is hired by a wealthy man, Simpson (Carlo Hinterman), to find his kidnapped son. When the son turns up dead, Simpson hires King again to kill his son's murderers. Of course all this is a plot by Simpson's wife, Anna (Erika Blanc) to gain possession of the formula, which the mastermind of the kidnapping happens to have. It's

**Umberto Lenzi's *Last Man to Kill* is marketed as a crime film on the Belgian poster**

all very complicated but gets straightened out by the end.

Other than Blanc, the cast is unexceptional, filled with the usual familiar faces of supporting players. Our pseudo-villain, Pavlos (Antonio Gradoli, billed here as Anthony Gradwell) wears black gloves and has drops put into his eyes on a regular basis. We later find out that he has the formula microfilmed onto his contact lenses, hence the need for eye drops. That still doesn't explain how he could see anything at all or why he wears black gloves. All villains should have a cultivated eccentricity, I guess.

The film features pretty good fight choreography (and there are a lot of fights), some brutality (a woman is burned with a cigarette before being slapped around), a Victorian strip act and a bathing suit fashion show. Angelo Francesco Lavagnino managed to come up with a fairly swinging soundtrack this time, another improvement over his meandering, lifeless sounds for *A 008*. As a matter fact, the composer did the soundtracks for all of Lenzi's spy flicks.

Amusements include the scene where King meets with Simpson to break the news about his dead son. Simpson says "Go ahead tell me, I'm ready for the worst," and when King tells him the worst, Simpson faints. When Anna surprises King in his hotel room to ostensibly get more information about her murdered son, she puts the moves on him. King puts her down quick with, "Did anybody ever tell you you're a bitch?" and then sleeps with her anyway. There's a scene in a nightclub where a gal belts out the same song that Ingrid Schoeller sang in *A 008*. They couldn't come up with another song?

They drink a lot of Johnny Walker in this movie too, bottles of it. Gadgets include binoculars that take photos onto the lens caps (huh?), an exploding apple, and the old cigarette pack communicator. And last, it's worth noting that King plays the violin but he uses the case to carry a machine gun. There's plenty here to enjoy for fans of the genre, so settle back with that bottle of JW and make like a spy.—DD

CREDITS: Production: Romana Film; Director: Umberto Lenzi; Story: Gianfranco Clerici; Screenplay: Gianfranco Clerici, Umberto Lenzi; Cinematography: Augusto Tiezzi {Eastmancolor}; Music: Angelo Francesco Lavagnino; Original running length: 93 mins; Country: Italy; Year: 1966

CAST: Roger Browne (*Michael King*), Jose Greci (*Ellen*), Anthony Gradwell [Antonio Gradoli] (*Paulus*), Monica Pardo (*Lilli*), Tor Altmayer [Tullio Altamura] (*Figuerez*), Dina De Santis (*Betty*), Marc Trevor [Sal Borgese], Valentino Macchi (*police sergeant*), Red Carter (*Bruto*), Dakar (*Also*), Wilbert Bradley (*Doney*), Renato Montalbano, Francesco De Leone, Ivan Basta, with Carlo Hintermann (*Simpson*) and Erika Blanc (*Anna*)

## LAST PLANE TO BAALBECK

aka Un Aero per Baalbeck (production title),
FBI operazione Baalbeck (It),
La Moneda Rota (Sp),
La Moneta spezzata (production title)

Normally I make clear the identities of the agents and villains in these reviews, but part of the fun of watching *Last Plane* is discovering for yourself just who is who. Is Nick Mann (Jacques Sernas) the agent sent to stop the illicit arms sales to the Middle East? Is Isabel Moore (Rossana Podesta) the drug-

**Excellent likenesses of George Sanders and Yoko Tani on the Belgian poster for the fun *Last Plane to Baalbeck***

addicted stewardess out to make a big score? Is Makowski (George Sanders) running the show behind his archaeologist day job? Or is it Asia (Yoko Tani), his assistant, who is the real brains behind the operation?

I'll tell you one thing, it ain't Folco Lulli. Here Lulli's a jolly fellow in the company of Mann, but just whose side is he on? Lulli does things in this movie like shoot seagulls from Mann's yacht. Not only that, his gunfire turns out to be Morse code! It's a good thing ammunition is cheap when you have to send long messages.

Mann looks good in his tailored suit, driving around in his nice Thunderbird convertible, but his motives are always in question…except when it comes to Isabel. When he says things to her like, "If we base our friendship on mutual mistrust it will last a lot longer," you know where he's coming from. Isabel doesn't really look like the morphine addict she's supposed to be, but you never know.

Now George Sanders *looks* like a blind archaeologist prince who seems to be the head of the gun-running operation. No question, or is there? Good old Yoko Tani has the quality as an actress to be good or evil at the drop of a hat. She's another one you can't be sure of, except when she urges the captured Makowski to take the cyanide pill hidden in his seeing-eye dog's collar. What a pal.

The true identity of the secret agent isn't revealed until well over an hour into the picture, so in the meantime you can enjoy the groovy jazz score by Marcello De Martino, the nice black and white photography of some exotic and ancient Beirut-area locations, and the fun gangster-era lingo of the bad guys like "go fly a kite," "you heels," and the ever-popular "you dirty low-down rats." And don't laugh when a cop tells his men to go over the classifieds in the newspaper for the last two years and see if there's a secret code. They find one. This is an enjoyable little thriller with a good cast that's worth catching when you have the chance.—DD

CREDITS: Production: F.I.C.I.T, Coliseum Film, Telestar, A.G. Film; Director: Marcello Giannini, Hugo Fregonese (supervising director); Story based on "Una Moneta Spezzata" by Romolo Marcellini; Screenplay: Marcello Giannini, John Melson; Cinematography: Aldo Giordani, Alfio Contini {B&W}; Music: Marcello De Martino; Original running length: 95 mins; Country: Italy/France/Lebanon; Year: 1964

CAST: Jacques Sernas (*Nick Mann*), Rosanna Podesta (*Isabel*), George Sanders (*Makowski*), Yoko Tani (*Asia*), Folco Lulli, Alfredo Varelli, Leopoldo Trieste, Miranda Martino, Milena Bettina, Isarco Ravaioli, Cinzia Abbenante, Mounir Maasri

LICENSE TO KILL
aka Las aventuras de Nick Carter (Sp),
Nick Carter non perdona (It),
Nick Carter va tout casser (Fr)

Eddie Constantine's most famous character is that of FBI agent Lemmy Caution, but he also made several films as private eye Nick Carter. *License to Kill* is one of these. This time, Nick uncovers a plot by an international spy ring led by the Chinese to steal a new invention and sell it to the highest-bidding nation. The first half of the film plays out as a murder mystery when an old family friend of Nick's, the inventing scientist, is killed by the scheming

**Eddie Constantine does a violent dance on the Belgian poster for *License to Kill***

organization. Once the plot is revealed, Nick spends the rest of the film in a cat and mouse game with the spy ring, including faking his own death to draw out the villains.

This really does seem like a holdover from the Nick Carter films of the 1930s and 1940s with its pulp plotting and yellow peril elements. There's even a dame in distress (Daphne Dayle) who's held over a giant pot of boiling oil. The upper hand changes so often in the last half hour that you'd swear this was a condensed serial.

The invention is a small flying saucer-type unit that can bean birds by remote control and is used once to knock a plane out of the sky. It doesn't seem that special to us, and the primitive special effects don't improve that impression one bit. But we liked how the scientist described the little UFO: "An infant might work it, it's so simple to operate. I've tried to consider the military intellect."

Nick carries a suitcase full of gadgets with him and uses several during the course of the adventure including a portable gas mask with matching gas dispenser and a wristwatch with a heating element on the face that's darn handy for burning the ropes tying one's hands. The nastiest gadget, however, isn't one of Nick's. It's a pistol that injects a poison needle into the hand of the shooter—very effective. But Nick relies more on his fists than his gadgets, taking on three or four guys several times, and it's even fairly convincing on occasion. So, if you like old serials or pulp magazines, you won't be disappointed in this Eddie vehicle.—DD

CREDITS: Production: Chaumiane Production, Florida Films, Filmstudio; Director: Henri Decoin; Story: Jean Marcillac; Screenplay: Andre Haguet, Andre Legrand; Cinematography: Lucien Joulin; Music: Pierick Houdy; Original running length: 94 mins; Country: France/Italy; Year: 1964

CAST: Eddie Constantine (*Nick Carter*), Daphne Dayle (*Catherine*), Paul Frankeur (*Antonio*), Valery Inkijinoff (*Li-Hang*), Barbara Sommer (*Gladys*), Andre Valmy (*Daumale*), Charles Belmont (*Bruno*), Margo Lion (*Marie-Jeanne*), Yves Rousselin (*Colibri*), Jean-Paul Moulinot (*Fromentin*), Mitsouko (*the Chinese girl*), Yvonne Monlaur (*Mirielle*), Gil Delamare, Yvan Chiffre, Antoine Baud, Jean-Pierre Janic, Andre Cagnard, Eric Vasberg (*Li-Hang's men*)

## LIGHTNING BOLT

aka Deathbeam (Dutch video), Operacion Goldman (Sp), Operazione Goldman (It)

This is one cheesy movie and a lot has been written about it (mostly bad), since it is widely available on the gray market. But there are things (mostly bad, again) worth mentioning and it is easier to write about a bad movie than a good one.

Director Antonio Margheriti is well known by B-movie buffs. He didn't feel the need to specialize and cranked out many low-budget copies of whatever genre happened to be popular at the moment in the sixties and seventies. You can find his name on science fiction, adventure, sword and sandal, horror, exploitation, western, giallo and even cannibal movies.

Anthony Eisley (*Wasp Woman*) plays our hero, Harry Sennett, and had his hair dyed red for the occasion. Sennett is your typical ladies' man agent who has the enviable assignment of posing as a millionaire playboy with a checkbook backed up by Fort Knox. This checkbook and matching unlimited expense account come in handy several times. When we first meet him,

Sennett is buying an airplane—what a rogue. Later, when he is being held at gunpoint by a sweaty underling, Sennett offers to write the man a check for 10 million dollars if the he will let him go—and the guy accepts! Good help is hard to find these days. Near the end of the picture, Sennett meets up with the not-so-super villain in his lair and offers to buy the guy's entire operation! It doesn't work this time of course, but you have to wonder what Sennett was thinking, if you bother to wonder about anything in this movie.

Sennett works for the Federal Security Investigation Commission—Section S to be exact—and his boss and cohort in this adventure is Capt. Pat Flanagan (Diana Lorys), otherwise known as Agent 36-22-36. As one would expect by Flanagan's nickname, there is much leering and sweating by her male bosses when she is introduced as beautiful... and lethal! She spends a fair amount of the first half of the movie sopping wet when she and Sennett are trapped in a disguised grain silo on the Florida coast (yeah, right). Our chubby villain is Rehte (Folco Lulli), who owns a brewery with the ugliest beer trucks around as a cover operation. However, those beer trucks have laser rocket interrupters as standard equipment, so one shouldn't complain.

*Lightning Bolt* features smart-ass, hard-boiled narration by Sennett and many moments of unintentionally laughable dialogue—the kind that would make Ed Wood proud. By the way, Sennett stays at the Hotel Florida while in Cape Canaveral, and in the full-frame video version of the movie the name reads Hotel Florid, which seems appropriate. Nonsensical situations and actions abound in this movie. When, as mentioned earlier, Sennett and Flanagan are trapped in the silo and it is filling with water, Sennett dives to the bottom several times to try to open the door. Rehte is watching of course and says, "If he goes down there again, open the door." When Sennett does indeed try it again, the door is opened and he's washed away by the torrent of water. Sennett returns to get Flanagan (helpless female syndrome) and they leave. At this point we hear Rehte yelling, "They are escaping!" Good villains are also hard to find these days.

The special effects are as to be expected—not very special. One example is when Sennett

**A favorite Freudian Eurospy image on the German poster for *Lightning Bolt***

is high-tailing it in his Jaguar to try to stop a rocket launch that he knows will be sabotaged. I can live with the poorly blended stock footage and rear projection that looks off-kilter, but the model Jaguar speeding up to the model launching pad is too much. It's Margheriti time! Truth be told, there is some not-bad miniature work during the climax of the movie when the undersea lair is destroyed.

We also have the old red-yarn-as-the-laser-beam trick made famous in Italy, and the Bauhaus-inspired architecture near Rehte's brewery that tips us off yet again that we're not in Florida. On the other side of the coin—and I'm glad there is another side—is the cool hibernation machine that Rehte uses to store people who have betrayed him. At the touch of a button, he can deactivate a chamber and the occupant turns into a skeleton. Creepy. When Sennett is sentenced to hibernation, he turns off the controls with his feet, which the henchmen forgot to tie down. Rehte should pay for better henchmen.

Rehte wants to put a laser (or as he says "lahser") cannon on the moon, so naturally he didn't want NASA to get there first. His undersea lair uses lava for an energy source, so at the end we have lots of steaming red liquid to destroy the models as our hero escapes. Though the movie has a few charms, they are outweighed by too much silliness, a weak villain, and the sense that the time spent watching it is worth more than the budget spent making it.—DD

CREDITS: Production: Seven Film B.G.A., Prod. Cin.cas Balcazar; Director: Anthony Dawson [Antonio Margheriti]; Story: Alfonso Balcazar; Screenplay: Alfonso Balcazar, Jose Antonio De La Loma; Cinematography: Riccardo Pallottini {Techniscope – Technicolor}; Music: Riz Ortolani; Original running length: 90 mins; Country: Spain/Italy; Year: 1966

CAST: Anthony Eisley (*Harry Sennett*), Diana Lorys (*Pat Flanagan*), Wandisa Leigh [Wandisa Guida], Folco Lulli (*Rehte*), Ursula Parker (*Sylvia*), Paco Sanz (*Dr. Rooney*), Jose Maria Caffarel (*Archie White*), Renato Montalbano, Oreste Palella, Luciana Petri, Tito Garcia

**A tense moment on this lobby card for *The Limbo Line***

THE LIMBO LINE

This obscure British spy film centers on an international organization that exists to kidnap Soviet defectors, sending them back to Russia—a passage known as "the Limbo Line"—for repatriation and "re-education." Their latest target is Irina (Kate O'Mara), a talented ballerina currently performing in London. Agent Richard Manston (Craig Stevens), who had been investigating the abductions, it told to quit the case because the Cold War is, apparently, thawing. He refuses, and rapidly inveigles himself into Irina's affections.

Despite some concerns from the upper echelons of the Communist party, villain Oleg (Vladek Sheybal) continues with his plan, and has his henchmen snatch Irina. Manston, of course, is watching and swiftly follows the trail. This leads him to a tour operator called Hardwick (Robert Urquhart), who smuggles the kidnap victims out of Britain under the cover of running a coach trip. Somewhere along the way, however, he manages to get captured, and finds himself being taken to Germany alongside his "beloved."

Despite obviously having a limited budget, *Limbo Line* is a bit of a grower, drawing you into its low-key shenanigans almost despite yourself. Based on a novel by popular author Victor Canning (his works were also adapted into the Burt Reynolds vehicle *Shark!* and Basil Dearden's *Masquerade*), the scriptwriters wisely decided to ape the John Le Carre—as opposed to Ian Fleming—genus of spy film, concentrating upon dialogue and character rather than action and extravagance. This brings about a slight kitchen-sink feel to proceedings, with plenty of soap opera bickering between the members of Manston's team and subplots involving the bureaucracies of both the Russian and British Secret Services.

The dour ambience is further accentuated by a terribly downbeat ending, and the fact that the hero is decidedly unsympathetic, happy enough to endanger others in the desire to track down his targets. In fact, all of the characters are painted with a realistic brush: The heroine looks shell-shocked through most of the running time and the baddies are entirely self-serving. Even lovely old Norman Bird—as one of the good guys—extracts information from Hardwick by threatening to drown his unfortunate girlfriend in the bath.

Director Sidney Gallu—who had worked regularly on *The Avengers*—does attempt to inject some style into things through the use of frequent close-ups and off-kilter camera angles. Unfortunately the photography is rather understated, giving it all a rather subdued look, and the only prints that seem to exist nowadays really don't do it any favors. Don't get fooled by the story line into believing this features a selection of exotic exteriors. The nearest this gets to mainland Europe is a couple of obvious back-projections and a selection of wet-looking chrysanthemum bushes in the home counties.

This was one of a handful of titles made by Trio Film, a British company that specialized in low-budget productions. Others included a spy film—*The Man Outside*, also directed by Gallu—and a couple of Euro-thrillers: *Amsterdam Affair* and *Why Would Anyone Want to Kill a Nice Girl Like You?*, featuring genre regulars Peter Vaughan and Paul Hubschmid.

There's an interesting cast, including Ferdy Mayne (*The Fearless Vampire Killers*) and Jean Marsh (the British television series *Upstairs, Downstairs*). Kate O'Mara doesn't really have that much do except look like a rabbit in the headlights, but she went on to achieve some fame in *Dynasty*. Craig Stevens was an American star who had been appearing in B movies since the 1940s, the best known of which is probably *The Deadly Mantis*. He became a star with his Emmy-nominated performance in the television series *Peter Gunn*, but never had much success in films, and drifted further into television acting as the seventies progressed.

One final point of note is that this really sees the relationship between the spy-guy hero and his immediate superior taken to its logical conclusion. Not only are they wary of each other (as in the normal "M"/Bond model), they actively *loathe* each other. It's not a particularly fun picture, then, but not one without its (albeit morose) virtues.

CREDITS: Production: Group W Films, Trio Film; Director: Samuel Gallu; Story based on the novel by Victor Canning; Screenplay: Donald James; Cinematography: John Wilcox {Eastmancolor}; Music: Johnnie Spence; Original running length: 99 mins; Country: UK; Year: 1968

CAST: Craig Stevens (*Richard Manston*), Kate O'Mara (*Irina Doskaya*), Moira Redmond (*Ludmilla*), Vladek Sheybal (*Oleg*), Norman Bird (*Chivers*), Robert Urquhart (*Ted Hardwick*), Ferdy [Ferdinand] Mayne (*Sutcliffe*), Yolande Turner (*Pauline*), Eugene Deckers (*Cadillet*), Frederick Jaeger (*Alex*), Alan Barry (*Williams*), John Horsley (*Richards*), Eric Mason (*Castle*), Aubrey Richards (*Dr. Hollis*), James Thornhill (*Pieter*), Jean Marsh (*Dilys*), Joan Benham (*Lady Faraday*), Rosemary Rogers (*Joan Halst*), Hugo de Vernier (*Halst*), James Donnelly (*Richie*), Bernard Davies (*Allen*), Denys Peek (*Jan*), Anna Willoughby (*the dancer*)

**Bob Peak's famous artwork on the American poster for *The Liquidator***

THE LIQUIDATOR
aka El liquidador (Sp)

This is one of those high-profile spy spoofs that's lighter than air and unrewarding in all departments. It made money, no doubt, but time has not improved this tired exercise in predictability. The humor is flat, the situations lack suspense and it is only redeemed by a cast of familiar faces, none of which is given much of a chance to shine.

At the end of World War II, Sgt. Brian "Boysie" Oakes (Rod Taylor) accidentally saves the life of British agent Mostyn (Trevor Howard). Years later, Mostyn's mistaken impression of Oakes as a potent killer leads him to recruit the fumbler as a private executioner. Oakes' job is to get rid of potential spies, as the establishment has been embarrassed by a series of spy scandals. Oakes, who doesn't have the gumption to actually kill anyone himself, hires out his assignments to another professional killer. All goes well until Oakes disobeys orders and secrets Mostyn's secretary (Jill St. John) away for a weekend in Monte Carlo. Once there, Oakes is captured by the enemy and falls into a plot to assassinate the Duke of Windsor and steal a top-secret military airplane.

All plot and no substance, this viewer's scant enjoyment of the film consisted almost entirely of spotting the familiar cast of supporting players. Wilfred Hyde-White is the quintessential bureaucrat and Akim Tamiroff is once again the ambitious but inadequate enemy agent. Daniel Emilfork and Henri Cogan, veterans of many French spy flicks, are his right-hand men, and there's a cameo by genre favorite Suzy Kendall at the end of the film.

There are many more recognizable actors here of course, but that probably won't be enough to satisfy a spy film buff. Not for one moment do we believe any of the precarious situations in which Oakes finds himself, nor do we care. Jack Cardiff's breezy direction matches Lalo Schifrin's inconsequential score, guaranteeing a less-than-memorable experience. It's simply a matter of there not being any "there" there.—DD

CREDITS: Production: Metro-Goldwyn-Mayer; Director: Jack Cardiff; Story based on the novel "The Liquidator" by John Gardner; Screenplay: Peter Yeldham; Cinematography: Ted Scaife {Metrocolor}; Music: Lalo Schifrin; Original running length: 105 mins; Filming location: Elstree; Country: UK; Year: 1965

CAST: Rod Taylor (*Boysie Oakes*), Trevor Howard (*Colonel Mostyn*), Jill St. John (*Iris*), Wilfrid Hyde-White (*Chief*), David Tomlinson (*Quadrant*), Akim Tamiroff (*Sheriek*), Eric Sykes (*Griffen*), Gabriella Licudi (*Corale*), John Le Mesurier (*Chekhov*), Derek Nimmo (*Fly*), Jeremy Lloyd (*Young Man*), Jennifer Jayne (*Janice Benedict*), Heller Toren (*Assistant*), Betty McDowall (*Frances Anne*), Jo Rowbottom (*Betty*), Colin Gordon (*Vicar*), Louise Dunn (*Jessie*), Henri Cogan (*Yakov*), Daniel Emilfork (*Gregory*), Scott Finch (*operation officer*), Ronald Leigh-Hunt (*Mac*), Richard Wattis (*flying instructor*), David Langton (*station Commander*), Tony Wright (*flying control*), Suzy Kendall (*Judith*)

**Italian poster *LSD: Hell for a Few Dollars More***

LSD: HELL FOR A FEW DOLLARS MORE

aka LSD—una "Atomica" nel cervello (It), LSD il piacere mortale/LSD inferno per pochi dollari/LSD—la droga del secolo (It, alt), LSD Inferno For a Few/LSD Flesh of Devil (US, unconfirmed), Prisonniers du plaisir (Fr)

This film opens with a nasty scene: A young boy uses his toy car to blow up two men and a blowgun to murder a third. This killer kid is none other than Rex Miller, who professes to want to grow up to become a secret agent. And indeed he grows up to be Guy Madison, a spaghetti western star who has the distinction of being in two of the strangest spy flicks of the era, this one and *The Devil's Man*. Rex is a secret agent working for an undisclosed country when a bizarre plot is uncovered to take over the world by dosing important "nerve centers" with potent LSD. Rex, impersonating one of the drug carriers, infiltrates the organization that thought up this deranged plan, exposes Mister X (Adriano Micantoni) and saves the world.

The film postures itself as being anti-drug, of course. We are presented with "documentary" footage of an army platoon that was secretly given LSD in their morning coffee. Like a dance team, the group of soldiers suddenly stop their maneuvers and freak out on cue. Not only do they all peak at the exact same moment, but each has a different, wildly exaggerated reaction to the drug—all bad of course. We are told that taking LSD leads to madness and death. Later, the bad guys test out their stuff on one of their women and sure enough, a short while after ingesting the LSD the poor gal jumps out a window. That's one less female to get in the way.

The LSD trips represented are only somewhat hallucinatory, using minor tricks of lighting or superimposition to portray the wild effects of the drug. There isn't much imagination (or money) spent on convincing us of the horrors of LSD, so these sequences are unfortunately rather dull and repetitive, which in turn makes the drug seem like a boring way to amuse oneself. The anti-drug stance is undermined considerably when at the end of the film, Rex and fellow agent Virginia (Franca Polesella) accidentally ingest LSD and have a great time! They dance around laughing and mugging as their boss stands approvingly by, smiling in the parental manner of benevolent authority.

Virginia turns out to be another secret agent only at the end of the film. Up until that time she has been the evil gang's chemist and love interest for Rex. And what woman wouldn't fall for a suave man who says things like "So you're a chemist. I'm surprised you don't have short hair and glasses." and "For an intelligent girl I find you most attractive."

This low-budget film has lots of low-budget gadgets and such. Rex talks into a book and—rather unconvincingly—a mantel clock like he's actually sending messages. In one scene he plugs an earphone into a lamp and, amazingly, can hear everything going on in the next room. Virginia uses only a lipstick communicator, but Rex's snorkel tube converts to a blowgun. Wow. One of the bad guys has electrified bars that enclose his living room when required and a statue that breathes fire in one of the better sequences. There's also a briefcase that shoots something deadly and makes a funny noise.

Rex has a transmitter implanted in his neck before he infiltrates the gang. The scene of the operation to accomplish this uses fairly graphic surgery footage in a startling moment that looks more like a Filipino horror movie. The best line in the film is spoken by Mister X as he describes his international crime syndicate: "We're a secret organization with a strange name: ECHO." Finally, the film boasts an excellent sound track by Egisto Macchi. There are plenty of catchy tunes and thrilling motifs for spy music fans that easily outclass the visuals.—DD

CREDITS: Production: Bema Film; Director: Mike Middleton [Massimo Mida]; Story: Tiziano Cortini, Vittorio Orano; Screenplay: Bruno Baratti, Odoardo Fiory; Cinematography: Silvano Ippoliti {Eastmancolor}; Music: Egisto Macchi; Original running length: 90 mins; Country: Italy; Year: 1967

CAST: Guy Madison (*Rex Miller*), Franca Polesello (*Virginia*), Mario Valgoi (*Korba*), Lucio De Santis (*Jimmy*), Adriano Micantoni (*Mr. X*), Lucia Modugno (*the drugged girl*), Luciano Rossi (*Stanis*), Pier Annibale Danovi, Isarco Ravaioli (*Alex Corey*), Virginio Gazzolo, Enrico Ribulsi, Emilio Marchesini, Mariella Zanetti, Karin Skarreso

## LUCKY THE INSCRUTABLE

aka Agente speciale LK (It), Lucky, el intrépido (Sp), Lucky M. füllt alle Särge (WG), Unternehmen Midas (WG working title)

This is a very silly movie. It's an *Airplane*-style, comic book-type secret agent adventure with Ray Danton as Lucky the Inscrutable, a master of disguise, among his many other amazing qualities. He's not only prepared for every situation, he's an expert in every situation. The gags fly fast and furious and with so many jokes thrown our way, some are sure to stick. And some do.

I'll admit that I'm not a big fan of director Jess Franco, and I had serious misgivings about this flick, but after half an hour it had won me over. It has a terrific Bruno Nicolai score and boundless enthusiasm for the material. Danton turns out to be a good comedian in his last spy flick.

Our villain is Goldglasses (Franco favorite Marcelo Arroita-Jauregui), who specializes in counterfeiting, and he takes an enormous amount of pride in his various triumphs in

**Soundtrack for *Agente speciale LK***

making fake money. Dante Posani is Lucky's partner Michael, who turns on Lucky in the end, sort of. Films like this are supposed to have a twist, yes?

Lucky is hired by Archangel, the secret society of financiers, to squash the counterfeiter. When sent to Rome he goes to the Market of Spies, where sellers of secrets call out their wares like hot dog vendors. "Russian secrets!" "French microfilm! Filthy French microfilm!" When a woman tries to kill Lucky, she's hit by a car during her escape. Before she dies, she rattles off a series of numbers to Lucky, who asks her what they mean. She says, "It's the license number of the idiot who ran over me." Ba-doom. Lucky is given a case of weapons by Archangel that includes exploding pills. The bottle reads: dosage—one for every 27 adults. You get the idea.

Rosalba Neri has a charming but small role as a sexually frustrated Albanian police commissioner. After capturing Lucky, there's quite the funny interrogation scene as she whips her subordinates in her rage at his remarks about her femininity. Despite her sex kitten image, Neri was one of the better actresses in genre cinema, but her talents were mostly wasted. Here she shows an affinity for comic timing that outshines every other actress in the film. Lucky wins her over, of course, so we get to view the sexy Rosalba before she disappears from the screen for good.

There's plenty to laugh at—and groan at—during this chase-heavy comedy that should ultimately tickle your funny bone. If you're feeling Lucky, it's not a bad way to waste 90 minutes. By the way, is that an uncredited Dieter Eppler as Hans the assassin?—DD

CREDITS: Production: Atlantida Film, Dauro Films, Fono Roma, Explorer Film '58; Director: Jesus Franco; Story and Screenplay: Jose Martinez Molla, Julio Luis Buchs; Cinematography: Fulvio Testi {Technicolor - Techniscope}; Music: Bruno Nicolai; Original running length: 91 mins; Country: Spain/Italy; Year: 1966

CAST: Ray Danton (*Lucky*), Rosalba Neri (*Yaka*), Dante Posani (*Michael*), Hector Quiroga, Marcelo Arroita-Jauregui (*"Goldglasses"*), Barbara Bold, Teresa Gimpera

## MADIGAN'S MILLIONS

aka L'agente quasi speciale Frank Putzu (It, alt), Un Dollaro per 7 vigliacchi (It), El millon de Madigan (Sp), Zwei Nummern zu gross (WG)

Ex-gangster Mike Madigan (Cesar Romero) is making a living as an insurance salesman in Rome after his deportation—on charges of racketeering—from America. Until he is murdered, that is. The local police launch an investigation, but they appear unwilling to listen to FBI claims that the dead man had over a million dollars worth of cash—made from his previous illicit activities—stashed away. They have some good reason for this doubt: He had apparently been leading a drab, frugal life in a ramshackle apartment. Given this lack of cooperation, the FBI is forced to send in an undercover agent to investigate. The only person they can think of is Jason Fister (Dustin Hoffman), a clumsy treasury agent with an uncanny sense for financial irregularity (and a habit for getting up the nose of his boss).

After playing the klutz for a while (by locking himself in a toilet, driving on the wrong side of the road, etc.), Fister's mission doesn't start well: Upon searching the dead man's office, he becomes prime suspect when the building superintendent is murdered. After extricating himself from jail, he becomes interested in Madigan's girlfriend, Vicky Shaw (Elsa Martinelli), who claims to know nothing. Despite Fister's doubts, they start to become close. Things are complicated further when the gangster's old partner, Turini (Riccardo Garrone), also turns up and wants the money for himself.

It's always good to see a young actor taking his first steps in the profession, and with *Madigan's Millions* you have the chance to see Dustin Hoffman before *Midnight Cowboy*, *Kramer vs. Kramer*, or *Rain Man*. Before, in fact, his cupboard started filling up with assorted awards, plaudits and handsome paychecks. Producer Sid Pink hired him after seeing him perform in an off-Broadway show, in what was hoped to be the first of a multipicture deal. Unfortunately, during filming, Hoffman received a call to audition for *The Graduate*. This counts as one of the great shames of all time. Just imagine: Dustin Hoffman in...*Candidate for a Killing*! Dustin Hoffman in...*Witch Without a Broom*! Oh, what could have been...?

Unfortunately, Dustin is actually rather annoying here, coming across as something of a low-rent Woody Allen—a diminutive boob who is propelled by events into becoming something of an unlikely hero. At least he seems to be having fun, although by all accounts he managed to irritate just about everybody involved in the production. His performance pales when compared to that of, say, Dirk Bogarde in the not entirely dissimilar *Hot Enough For June*. Then again, he's not helped by a script that—although it keeps things lighthearted throughout—never actually manages to be remotely funny. The level of humor is easily gauged by the running gag in which our hero has to continually correct people's mispronunciation of his name as Foster. Crazy stuff, huh?

In fact, *MM* is something of a disappointment all round. The story is pure fluff, the direction is less than inspired, and it all adds up to as much as a dot com's savings account. There are a few failed attempts at style, the most notable of which is a bizarre editing effect between certain scenes, which looks as though the film is being chewed up. Purely on a single-minded level, the whole film also comes across as a spoof of the gangster as much as the spy genre. On the positive side, there is a good title tune, a reasonable car chase and some nice performances from underappreciated Euro character actors such as Fernando Hilbeck (as an embattled embassy official) and Gerard

**Video cover art for *Madigan's Millions***

Tichy (as Fister's irascible boss). But that's about it, really.

As with many of the enigmatic Mr. Pink's films, this is undone by its very insubstantiality: It feels like a film made by a bunch of mates and an overconfident (although not huge) budget. It also has the usual confusion over the identity of the actual director. Giorgio Gentili is credited in some sources, but it was actually Stanley Prager—an American stage comedian—who filled that role (and whose inexperience shows through). Coincidentally, Prager only just beat out Mike Nichols for the job—and it was Nichols who would go on to make...*The Graduate*.—MB

CREDITS: Production: Hercules Cin.ca, L.M.; Director: Stanley Prager, Dan Ash [Giorgio Gentili] (credited on Italian prints); Story and Screenplay: James Heneghan, Jose Luis De La Bayonas; Cinematography: Manuel Rojas {Eastmancolor – Stereorama}; Music: [Gregorio] Garcia Segura; Original running length: 95 mins; Country: Italy/Spain; Year: 1968

CAST: Dustin Hoffman (*Jason Fister*), Elsa Martinelli (*Vicky Shaw*), Cesar Romero (*Mike Madigan*), Gustavo Rojo (*Lieutenant Arco*), Fernando Hilbeck (*Mr. Burk*), Riccardo Garrone (*Matteo Turini*), Franco Fabrizi (*Condon*), Gerard Tichy (*Ogilvy, Fister's boss*), Jon De Milte, Daniele Vargas (*Gianni Lo Cascio*), Jose Maria Caffarel (*police commissioner*), Pino Polidori (*Pretty, Turini's man*), Ennio Antonelli (*Basilio, Turini's man*), Fortunato Arena (*Pastore, Turini's man*), Remo De Angeli [Remo De Angelis], Vittorio Bonos, Gigi Bonos, Isabel Hidalgo, Maria Pilar Porro. According to some sources: Rina Mascetti, Hector Quiroga, Umberto Raho

**Soundtrack for *El Magnifico Tony Carrera* (*The Magnificent Tony Carrera*)**

THE MAGNIFICENT TONY CARRERA
aka Carrera—Das Geheimnis der blonden Katze (WG), Carrera: The Secret of the Blonde Cat (unconfirmed), El Magnífico Tony Carrera (Sp), Il Magnifico Tony Carrera (It), Ramdam à Amsterdam (Fr), Samtpföchen deht sein letztes Ding (WG)

Racecar driver (now was there ever a more archetypal glamorous sixties occupation?) Tony Carrera (Thomas Hunter) has a guilty secret. He used to be an international jewel thief, notorious for writing "I'm sorry" wherever he struck. This past soon catches up with him in the form of Ursula (Gila Von Weitershausen), the daughter of an old partner of his. She blackmails him into going to Holland and stealing an attaché case from a safe there, claiming it contains some documents that are of vital importance to national security.

Despite making several attempts to escape, he finally agrees to go along with her—partly because his curiosity is piqued by the idea of opening an ostensibly unbreakable safe. His master plan: Rather than breaking in. he decides to pack himself up in a box, get it placed into the vault and then, after nabbing the briefcase, breaking out. However, he still has his doubts about his new partner and her friends, not least of whom is a dodgy bloke called Rick (Albert Farnese).

The plan works well enough, despite a couple of minor hitches, but it turns out that Tony was right in his suspicions. It soon becomes clear that the suitcase contains the prototype for a nuclear device, which means that Tony—who has already been double- crossed by Rick and co.—becomes the subject of a massive manhunt. He decides that the only thing to do is to steal the prototype back from his original employers.

*MTC* is a lightweight concoction that's pretty easy to sit through. You get pervy Dutch soldiers spying on girls throwing beach balls around (what is it about naked girls and beach balls?), hotels full of nighty-clad nymphos and—best of all—a fun scene in which the hero tries to steal the uniform from a policeman being serviced by a prostitute. Gianni Marchetti's score reflects all this amiable nonsense, fluctuating wildly between psychedelic beats and comic interludes. Overall, it comes across as a blithe partner piece to Sergio Grieco's similarly themed *Fuller Report*.

However, Jose Antonio De La Loma is one of the most infuriating of European directors. His work veers wildly between the excellent and the appalling, even in the same film. This is one of his better efforts, with a cracking pace and some memorable moments. The central heist is very well done, with a pop-art feel to the proceedings (and lots of polystyrene thrown in for good measure), as is a tense chase up some cooling towers. Just when you're really enjoying things, though, he decides to throw in a hideous little brat for absolutely no reason (apart from satiating the sentimental streak within small-town Mediterranean audiences).

American Thomas Hunter, never the most animated of actors, doesn't really convince as a wisecracking charmer. Far better are the supporting performers. Ex-American football star Walter Barnes appeared in several Euro-productions, most notably Sergio Sollima's classic western *The Big Gundown* and, although he only appears in the last third of this, he lights up the screen whenever he does. German actress Gila Von Weitershausen is cute as a button, a cut-price Jean Seberg—she went on to appear in a huge number of international productions such as Claude Chabrol's *Death Rites* and Jesus Franco's *X312—Flight to Hell*. Loveable, greasy lard-ass Fernando Sancho is also entertaining as "Einstein" ("We all had to choose (a name), I chose Eisnstein…he was a hippie like myself.") and poor old Erika Blanc has a rather thankless role as Carrera's ditzy fiancée (complete with miniature dog and a succession of outrageous clothing).—MB

CREDITS: Production: Moncayo Film, Cineproduzioni Associate, Hape Filmproduktion; Director: Jose Antonio De La Loma; Story: Jose Antonio De La Loma; Screenplay: Jose Antonio De La Loma, Carlo Fadda, Milo G. Cuccia; Cinematography: Victor Monreal Sarto {Eastmancolor}; Music: Gianni Marchetti; Original running length: 101 mins; Filming location: Amsterdam; Country: Spain/Italy/West Germany; Year: 1968

CAST: Thomas Hunter (*Carrera*), Gila Von Weitershausen (*Ursula*), Walter Barnes (*Senator W.T. Barnes*), Erika Blanc (*Antonella Amaldini*), Antonio Casas (*Van Huysen, a Dutch commissioner*), Alberto Farnese (*Rick*), Gérard Tichy (*Serge*), Dieter Augustin, Enzo Fiermonte (*Arnaldo*), Frank Oliveras (*Cornelius, a private investigator*), Óscar Pellicer, Gaby Go (*Sonia*), Michael Münzer (*Gordon*), Hans Waldherr (*Peppino*), Wim de Meyer (*Gaston*), Corrado Guarducci, Ini Assmann (*Sammy*) and with Fernando Sancho (*Einstein*). Uncredited: Barbara Behrendt, Anders Roemer, Willy Vierhaus, Franco Ressel [not visible], Piet Hendriks

MAKE YOUR BETS, LADIES

aka Faites vos jours, mesdames (Fr), Feu a volonte (Fr, alt), Fire at Will (Int, unconfirmed), Hagan juego, señoras (Sp)

A good cast does not a good movie make. Director Marcel Ophuls (*The Sorrow and the Pity*) doesn't seem to care about the material at

**German poster for *Make Your Bets Ladies* starring the ubiquitous Eddie Constantine**

hand, and this film will pass before your eyes without making much of an impression. Eddie Constantine, he of the slew of spy flicks, is his usual winning self, but even he doesn't invest much in his role as FBI (CIA?) agent Mike Warner. Warner's on the trail of a kidnapped scientist and uncovers the gang of high-class dames responsible, led by the gypsy Soledad (Nelly Benedetti). These gals want a ransom of 20 million dollars worth of uncut diamonds and fur coats. Women.

Luis Davila seems like the only actor even trying here. He plays the dapper Russian agent Boris (naturally) who's also after the inventor of a ring that paralyzes those who have the misfortune of being slugged by someone wearing it. Davila displays real charisma here and is the only standout, even allowing for the many beautiful women gathered together as the gang of supposed man-haters. The real villain, played by Georges Rigaud, is another two-dimensional character who shows up near the end only to be knocked off a tall building in short order. But by that time you won't care anyway.

This uninspired (and overlong) exercise substitutes lethargic fights and boring comic antics for the action it desperately needs. The bland big band jazz score by Ward Swingle doesn't do much to improve the goings on either.

About the only memorable event is when Warner and company become trapped in a locked room. The lights go out and gasoline begins to flood in around them. Drowning in gasoline in complete darkness seems a particularly nasty way to go, if you ask me.

Only for Constantine completionists, this one can be skipped by the casual genre explorer. When Warner says at one point "Those bad old spies hurtcha, baby?" the answer is definitely yes.—DD

CREDITS: Production: Spéva Films, Ciné Alliance, Hesperia Films; Director: Marcel Ophuls; Story: Jacques Robert; Screenplay: Jacques Robert, Marcel Ophuls; Cinematography: Jean Tournier {B&W - Panoramica}; Music: Ward Swingle; Original running length: 86 mins; Country: France/Spain; Year: 1964

CAST: Eddie Constantine (*Mike Warner*), Laura Valenzuela (*Isabelle*), Alfredo Mayo, Nelly Benedetti (*Soledad*), Luis Davila (*Boris*), Enriqueta Carballeira, Daniel Ceccaldi, Dieter Kollesch, Georges Rigaud

MAN ON THE SPYING TRAPEZE

aka Anonima de asesinos, Jerry Land: cazador de espias (Sp), Jerry Land cacciatore di spie (It), Jerry Land chasseur d'espions (Fr), Warteliste zur Hölle (WG)

American Wayde Preston is better known as a star of spaghetti westerns, but like many of his Euro-comrades he had to try his hand at the spy game. This would be his only foray into the genre, but based on the results he could have made a career of it. Preston's easy-going personality works well toward defining the unruffled spy archetype. The plot here is unnecessarily complicated, but the predictable twists, unexplained turns and dropped balls are forgivable since the picture has enough redeeming qualities to recommend it.

You know you're in for a good time when a film opens with a car chase, especially when a Piero Umiliani soundtrack wails on as a car goes over a cliff and explodes. The camera surveys the wreckage and then zooms

**Belgian poster for the cleverly-named *Man On the Spying Trapeze***

in on some false teeth uppers, the grisly but humorous detritus of death. Turns out those teeth house a hidden camera. Cool. This film isn't gadget-heavy, but there is a spray that reveals footprints when the user wears special glasses, and a receiver that fills an entire suitcase (must be a Russian model) and the cigarette case transmitter that goes with it.

Preston is agent Jerry Land, who travels from Madrid to Rome to New York to Beirut and back again several times in his quest to bed as many women as possible and, oh yes, to solve the case. His boss always seems to be hanging around with him in these exotic locales, so suspicion lies heavy. Jerry's micro-managing boss is played by Reinhard Kolldehoff, a fellow who looks as guilty as sin anyway. You'll probably recognize him from his turn in *The Thousand Eyes of Dr. Mabuse* as the club-footed menace. Jerry's main love interest (and he has a few here) is played by Helga Sommerfeld, but her part is limited as the victim of an unexploited blackmail subplot that seems tossed in as an afterthought.

The film has its share of violence and torture too. The fights are choreographed well and feature lots of judo and karate-type action. Jerry gets the best of the multiple (and recognizable) henchmen he frequently takes on. Violence against women gets a leg up when a nosy maid who succumbed to Jerry's charms is thrown over a balcony when her weakness is discovered by the bad guys who hired her. But don't worry, it was just a dummy. The torture scenes are stretched out long enough to be uncomfortable. There's the head-squeezing electroshock therapy—a high-tech solution—and its simple but effective counterpart, the burning of the fingers. After this last method, Jerry says wryly "You can have the microfilm. I'm not Joan of Arc."

Throw in some good location shooting in Beirut and that cookin' Umiliani soundtrack and you have an above-average actioner worth investigating.—DD

CREDITS: Production: Juan de Orduña P.C., Produzioni Europee Associate, Filmproduktion Ernst V. Theumer; Director: Juan De Orduna; Story: Nino Stresa; Screenplay: Nino Stresa, Juan de Orduna, Fortunato Bernal; Cinematography: Aldo Ricci {Eastmancolor - Techniscope}; Music: Piero Umiliani; Original running length: 92 mins; Filming locations: Rome, New York, Lebanon; Country: Spain/Italy/Germany; Year: 1966

CAST: Wayde Preston (*Jerry Land*), Helga Sommerfeld (*Solange Dubonnet*), Gianni Rizzo (*Stephanopoulos*), Pamela Tudor (*Yasmine*), Kai Fischer (*Fauzia*), Sergio Mendizábal (*Jose*), Lisa Halvorsen (*Lyda*), Reinhard Kolldehoff (*Dick Collins*), Antonio Duran (*John Parker*), Noe Murayama (*Mr. Wong*), Franco Fantasia (*Boris*), Robert Johnson, Jr. (*Major Larighy*), Javier Loyola, Joaquín Bergía, Judit Kepler, Joaquin Bergia, Antonio Pica, Francisco Villar, Juan de Haro

## MAN OUTSIDE

aka De Espladas a Scotland Yard (Sp),
...Und Scotland Yard schweigt (WG)

This is one of those old-timer spy flicks like *Where the Spies Are* with David Niven and *The Deadly Affair* with James Mason that sport an aging marquee name trying to cash in on the espionage craze. This one is neither as embarrassing as the former nor as capable as the latter. Van Heflin is the world-weary

**Simple but effective artwork on the Italian locandina for *Man Outside***

agent wrongly accused, who negotiates the dark underworld of spies from all nations in order to clear his name.

Heflin is surrounded by familiar character actors that give this B picture more resonance, players like Ronnie Barker, Peter Vaughn and the serpentine Charles Grey. Director Samuel Gallu plays this one by the numbers, but in the case of a film whose story is just a degree short of cliché, his approach should have perhaps been abandoned for one of greater experimentation. Photographically more chances are taken and cinematographer Gilbert Taylor (who shot the original *Star Wars*) keeps the drab color palatte's visual interest up by using odd angles and a probing camera. Unfortunately, the video suffers immensely from a full-frame presentation that renders action scenes nearly incomprehensible.

The main female here, a dead spy's sister, is played by Heidelinde Weis, and it's a relief that the story doesn't call for her to sleep with Heflin. There isn't much remarkable about the picture, so I would call it an ambience film in that it's a comfortable, unchallenging relic from a bygone age of filmmaking.—DD

CREDITS: Production: London Independent Producers; Director: Samuel Gallu; Story based on the novel "Double Agent" by Gene Stackelborg; Screenplay: Samuel Gallu; Cinematography: Gilbert Taylor {Technicolor}; Music: Richard Arnell; Original running length: 97 mins; Country: UK; Year: 1967

CAST: Van Heflin (*Bill MacLean*), Heidelinde Weis (*Kay Sebastian*), Pinkas Braun (*Rafe Machek*), Peter Vaughan (*Nikolai Volkov*), Charles Grey (*Charles Griddon*), Paul Maxwell (*Judson Murphy*), Ronnie Barker (*George Venaxas*), Linda Marlowe (*Dorothy*), Gary Cockrell (*Brune Parry*), Larry Cross (*Austen*), Bill Nagy (*Morehouse*), Paul Armstrong (*Gerod*), Derek Baker (*Gerod's assistant*), Frank Crawshaw (*drunken hick*), Christopher Denham (*detective sergeant*), Gabrielle Drake (*B.E.A. girl*), Archie Duncan (*superintendent Barnes*), Hugh Elton (*Vadim*), Carole Ann Ford (*Cindy*), Willoughby Grey (*the detective inspector*), Harry Hutchinson (*the caretaker*), Carol Kingsley (*the barmaid*), Alex Marchevsky (*Mikhail*), Carmel McSharry (*Olga*), Suzanne Owens (*the attendant*), John Sterland (*Spencer*), Roy Stone (*Albert*), Martin Terry (*the gambling club barman*), Rita Webb (*the landlady*), Anna Willoughby (*the boutique attendant*)

MANHATTAN NIGHT OF MURDER
aka Asesinato en Manhattan (Sp),
Mordnacht in Manhattan (WG)

Let's face it, the second Jerry Cotton film is a decidedly lackluster affair and probably the weakest in the series. What's surprising is that director Harald Phillip also made the next installment in the series, *3-2-1 Countdown for Manhattan*, which turned out to be one of the best. Here, though, the story is banal, the crooks have no charisma, and the low-rent appearance gives the film a hang-dog feel.

**German poster for Jerry Cotton's sophomore slump *Manhattan Night of Murder***

In *MNOM* Jerry (George Nader) battles the "Hundred Dollar Boys," racketeers who offer businesses insurance against ruin for $100 a month. When a young boy witnesses a killing during one of the gang's shakedowns, the FBI is called in. Jerry tracks down members of the gang before discovering the leading citizen who secretly heads the operation.

The protection racket story probably seemed like a relic even in 1965 and was no doubt the impetus to focus much of the screen time on the mechanics of criminal detection. We are treated to seemingly endless footage of scientific activity and computer technology as the FBI narrows down the suspects. Gadgets actually play a part in our heroes' efforts as well, but hidden cameras and radar transmitters are the extent of the toys they get to play with.

The idea that we're supposed to be in America gets lost when Jerry's partner Phil (Heinz Weiss) takes over a local business to experience a shakedown firsthand. A gas station we're told is located in Brooklyn is nestled on a hill surrounded by wayward cobblestone streets—Brooklyn via the Balkans. The owner of the quaint business gets a lesson in citizenship when Phil's refusal to pay for protection results in the gas station's complete destruction.

One gang member is played by one of genre cinema's most familiar faces, Paul Muller. He too becomes uniquely aware of the concept of criminal justice. It seems the gang wants to get rid of Muller, so they rig him up to a bomb in an old warehouse that will explode when someone opens the door to the room where he's tied up. When Jerry arrives to save the day, Muller tells him to come in the through the window. Good idea, except that when Jerry makes his way to the second-story room and opens the window, the draft causes the door to nudge the bomb and Muller is blown to smithereens.

The appearance of Silvia Solar holds out hope of a notable femme fatale, but it comes to naught. Solar, who looks like a Vegas version of Emma Peel in her sequin jumpsuit, is given nothing to do but stand on the sidelines looking worried. A lost opportunity if ever there was one. Luckily, this was just a sophomore slump and the series picks up considerably with the next entry.—DD

CREDITS: Production: A Constantin Films, Allianz production; Director: Harald Phillip; Story: Alex Berg; Cinematography: Walter Tuch {B&W}; Music: Peter Thomas; Country: West Germany; Year: 1965

CAST: George Nader (*Jerry Cotton*), Heinz Weiss (*Phil*), Monika Grimm, Elke Neidhardt, Kurd Pieritz, Silvia Solar, Daniel Dimitri, Paul Muller

MARIE-CHANTAL VS. DR. KHA
aka María Chantal contra el doctor Kha (Sp),
Marie-Chantal contre docteur Kha (Fr),
Marie Chantal contro il Dr. Kha (It)

Marie-Chantal is a rather annoying young French lady who is used to fine food, civil company and fashionable clothes. Then, in the dining car of a train, she bumps into Bruno Kerien (Roger Hanin)—a spy and killer. While sharing a glass of wine, he passes an unusual broach to her.

Letting this strange experience wash by without too much thought, she continues with her ski holiday. The resort, however, seems to

**The comic stylings of the Belgian poster for *Marie-Chantal vs Dr. Kha***

be filling up with increasingly odd characters: Johnson (Charles Denner), a weedy (Rowan Atkinson look-alike) spy with a camp voice; Russian agent, Ivanov (Serge Reggiani); and his creepy *JOE 90*-style son. These numbskulls busy themselves by searching each other's rooms, poisoning a barman (played by Chabrol himself), and basically being rather a pain. While they're trying to kill each other with their explosive cigarettes, Kerien is murdered by another assassin, who works for criminal mastermind Dr. Kha (Akim Tamiroff).

With this, Marie starts to notice that something very bizarre may be going on. It's a realization that becomes even clearer when Kerien's "widow," Olga (Stephane Audran) appears—and promptly tries to steal the aforementioned broach. Fortunately, our heroine's strength has been built up by the many years she has spent on the piste (ski run); she manages to escape and makes her way to Morocco (it's a hard life).

Unfortunately, Dr. Kha's ruffians (and all the other goons) are still after her. After a near-fatal encounter with them, she finds a suitable ally in Paco Castillo (Francisco Rabal), a mysterious chap given to hanging around in Turkish baths. He tells her that he works for an organization formed by a Professor Lombardi, which is dedicated to the struggle for world peace. By this time, of course, everyone has completely lost track of what these characters are actually looking for, or even why the broach is so important (don't ask me, I haven't a clue!).

This is a very nice-looking, immensely entertaining film. The direction and cinematography are top-notch, representing a huge leap from Chabrol's previous work (such as *The Tiger Likes Fresh Meat*). In fact, *Marie-Chantal* has all of the ingredients you could possibly ask for from a good spy film: fun characters, self-awareness, good music, loads of color and some beautiful babes in minimal amounts of clothing. In essence, it has a certain sense of vitality that's common to most of the best cinema to emerge from the sixties—a celebration of the art and possibilities of filmmaking. Hey, these guys were going to exotic places, surrounded by beautiful people and wearing fashionable threads. They were having damned good fun, and that can be infectious if combined with talent.

It also features some hilariously slapdash choreography. I'm willing to give the benefit of the doubt and assume that this was deliberate, because it sure is funny. The sequence where Rabal fights Antonio Passalia by slapping him around the face (ooh, get you!) literally had me doubled up. The whole film has the feel of a light parody, which is balanced just right so as not to tip into the annoyingly slapstick or, even worse, the po-faced.

Indeed, only two possible downsides come to mind. First, during the last third the cast whittles down to Rabal, Laforet and Tamiroff, which excludes several of the (even) more agreeably left-field characters. Second, I haven't been able to track down an English-language version—someone release this on DVD, please.—MB

CREDITS: Production: Rome-Paris Films, DIA Films, Dia P.C., Mega Films, Maghreb Uni-Films; Director: Claude Chabrol; Story based on an idea by Jacques Chazot; Screenplay: Christian Yves, Claude Chabrol; Cinematography: Jean Rabier {Eastmancolor}; Music: Pierre Jansen, Gregorio Garcia Segura; Original running length: 114 mins; Country: Spain/France/Italy/Morocco; Year: 1965

CAST: Serge Reggiani (*Ivanov*), Roger Hanin (*Bruno Kerrien*), Marie Laforet (*Marie-Chantal*), Francisco Rabal (*Paco Castillo*), Charles Denner (*Johnson*), Akim Tamiroff (*Dr. Kha*), Stephane Audran (*Olga*), Pierre Moro (*Hubert*), Gilles Chusseau (*Gregor*), Antonio Passalia (*Sparafucile*), Robert Burnier (*the killer*), Gerard Tichy (*the hotel manager*), Claude Chabrol (*the barman*), Bernard Papineau, Caffarel (*the man killed on the train*), Eugenio Da Pietro, Henri Attal, Onofrio Ancoleo, Serge Bento, Lahcen Boukis, Pierre-Francois Moreau

## MARK DONEN AGENTE Z7

aka Agente Z-7, operación Rembrandt (Sp),
Karate a Tanger pour agent 27 (Fr),
Rembrandt 7 antwortet nicht… (WG), Z7
Operation Rembrandt (US, unconfirmed)

A texbook example of the Eurospy genre, this film is chock full of double-crosses, exotic locations (they seem to shift settings every five minutes), fistfights and beautiful babes. It's not a great film, but it moves along nicely with just the right mix between action and whimsy. There are cheesy gadgets (including a hilarious cardboard submarine), minor doses of sadism, and an ultra-cool hero (who gets to zoom around in a jetpack during the climax). Unfortunately, there doesn't seem—at present—to be an English-language version available anywhere.

Professor Leibrich has invented something terrible: a contraption formed of rickety-looking metal tubes that concentrate sun rays into a deadly matter-destroying laser beam. The machine also has the side effect of burning out the eyes of anyone in the vicinity not fortunate enough to be wearing protective sun goggles. Unfortunately, a loony colleague named Kosky (Carlo Hintermann), planning to sell the device to the highest bidder, betrays him. Secret agent Mark Donen (Lang Jeffries) is sent to try to rescue the professor (as well as to ensure that his deadly work is destroyed). Donen makes his way to Brazil, where he soon joins forces with Seyna (Mitsouka), a Chinese agent, who is also looking for the professor.

The villains, however, have a plan. They substitute the scientist for one of their own men (who has been given an artificial aging drug) and arrange for him to be "rescued." Mark realizes that something is a bit dodgy, but keeps it secret from Seyna, which is smart, since she promptly betrays him and skedaddles back to China with the false professor. Some of Mark's fellow agents—unaware of the substitution—promptly launch an attack on the Chinese base where they believe their quarry to be held.

Our hero, meanwhile, is busying himself with tracking down Kosky's secret hideout. And what exactly does all of this have to do with a Rembrandt that everyone seems to be searching for? God only knows.

**Lang Jeffries shows off his jet pack skills in this German lobby card for *Mark Donen Agent Z7***

This was Giancarlo Romitelli's first spy film. He also made the far less effective *Si muore solo una volta* the following year. Here he manages to craft a solid genre entry, with exactly the right mix of thrills and silliness. He's greatly helped by a useful screenplay (which throws just about every genre cliché into the mix) and great cinematography from the prolific Guglielmo Mancori (most particularly a bizarre sequence set in the professor's house, which is littered with crooked, empty picture frames).

Adding greatly to the entertainment value is a nice cast. Lang Jeffries is at his best and proves to be a rather nifty flamenco dancer to boot. Carlo (*Operation Atlantis*) Hintermann—equipped with a particularly manic fright wig—looks like a deranged Andy Warhol, but doesn't really have too much to do. Spanish character actor Miguel Del Castillo has a reasonably meaty role (for a change), and habitual chrome-domed villains Alvaro De Luna and Luciano Catenacci (hiding behind the Max Lawrence pseudonym he also used in Mario Bava's *Kill, Baby, Kill*) turn up as villains.—MB

CREDITS: Production: Ca. Pi. Film, Agata Film, Planet Film; Director: Giancarlo Romitelli; Story: Giancarlo Romitelli; Screenplay: Giancarlo Romitelli, Ennio De Concini, Robert Veller; Cinematography: Guglielmo Macori {Technicolor – Techniscope}; Music: Aldo Piga; Original running length: 100 mins; Filming location: Incir-De Paolis Studios; Country: Italy/Spain/West Germany; Year: 1965

CAST: Lang Jeffries (*Mark Donen*), Carlo Hintermann (*Kosky*), Mitsouko (*Seyna*), Laura Valenzuela (*Irene*), [Lore] Dana Nusciak (*Jane*), Alvaro De Luna (*Kosky's man*), Joachin Hansen (*Peter/Pierre*), Lorenzo Robledo (*the colonel*), Luis Pe[g]na, Christiane Maybach, Miguel Del Castillo (*Oropeza*), John Matthews [Giuseppe Mattei] (*Juan, Kosky's man*), Max Lavrence [Luciano Catenacci] (*Seyna's bald accomplice*), Romano Giomini Possibly: Claudio Ruffini (*Kosky's man*)

MASTER STROKE

aka Colpo maestro al servizio di Sua Maestà Britannica (It), Die Doppelgänger (WG), Gran golpe al servicio de S. M. Británica (Sp), The Great Diamond Robbery (Int)

The opening sequence of this film sets the tone for all that follows. We are plunged into the climactic scene in a spaghetti western. Richard Harrison, bearded and dressed in black, is called out for his final gunfight by the serape-wearing hero with no name, portrayed by George Eastman. The anticipation is played out in typical Italian style, all meaningful glances and the cocking of guns. When the tension reaches the boiling point, Harrison's gun fails and the camera pulls back as he complains to the film's director about it! We've been suckered.

**Adolfo Celi features prominently on the Italian poster for Michele Lupo's *Master Stroke***

Harrison is Arthur Lang, a mediocre actor with a shady past who is offered the part of a lifetime: impersonate the security chief (also played by Harrison) of a major diamond concern, assist in a robbery and make a cool 250 grand. Bernard (Adolfo Celi) is the mastermind behind the plot, and the first half-hour of the film details the preparation and execution of the daring heist. Once the job is over, Bernard is revealed as a member of the Secret Service; the whole thing was a plan to prove that the security chief was guilty of systematic diamond thefts. But wait. Is Bernard who he says he is? And what about the security chief and his so-called girlfriend, Eve (Margaret Lee)? I'm not telling.

The myriad twists and turns, complications and unveilings, are part of what make this film so enjoyable. To preserve the surprises for the first-time viewer, it wouldn't be fair to go into the plot machinations. Suffice it to say that this is one hell of a fun ride that won't disappoint fans of spy/action/heist thrillers. From the cool animated title sequence to the great soundtrack by Franceso De Masi to the solid Euro-cast of genre veterans (most of whom get killed), this is pure enjoyment from start to finish.

There are lots of quotable lines in the film too. For instance, when Bernard's heist plan is revealed to Lang, he says, "I'm an actor, not a thief." To which Bernard replies, "Your acting is worse than stealing." There are more in-jokes and special appearances than this reviewer could recognize, but this movie has the feel of an insider's paradise. This is not an out and out comedy by any means. The complexities of the plot are taken seriously enough by director Michele Lupo to keep the action compelling, and good locations and top-notch photography are the icing on the cake. It would be nice to see a widescreen version of this sleeper, but the full-frame video presentation won't spoil the fun of this highly recommended adventure.—DD

CREDITS: Production: Fida Cin.ca, Atlantida Film; Director: Michele Lupo; Story and Screenplay: Sandro Continenza, Roberto Gianviti, Jose Luis Martinez Molla; Cinematography: Francisco Sanchez {Techniscope – Technicolor}; Music: Francesco De Masi; Original running length: 100 mins; Country: Italy/Spain; Year: 1967

CAST: Richard Harrison (*Arthur Lang*), Adolfo Celi (*Mr. Bernard*), Margaret Lee (*Eve, the blonde*), Antonio Casas (*Colonel Jenkins*), Gerard Tichy (*Max*), Livio Lorenzon (*Miguel*), Ennio Balbo (*the surgeon*), Alan Collins [Luciano Pigozzi] (*Billy*), Eduardo Fajardo (*Mr. Ferrick*), Andrea Bosic (*Mr. Van Doren*), Mary Arden (*Dorothy*), Jacques Herlin (*Goldsmith*), George Eastman [Luigi Montefiore], Tom Felleghy, Dan Moor, Robert Stevenson [Roberto Dell'Acqua]

## MATCHLESS
aka Mission Top Secret (Fr)

Comedy is hard, the old saying goes, and apparently it was too hard for the writers of this film and for director Alberto Lattuada, whose leaden hand prevents any actual humor from seeping through. The film has a good cast, at least in the major roles, which keeps the proceedings from becoming downright unbearable, but we can't think of any other reason to watch this dog.

Patrick O'Neal is Perry Liston, a journalist who writes a column under the pseudonym "Matchless." At the beginning of the movie, he's being tortured in a Chinese prison as a spy. He's not a spy, but they think he is. In his cell that he shares with true spy Hank Norris (Henry Silva), Liston's given a ring by a dying man containing a liquid that will make the wearer invisible for 20 minutes at a time. After his escape, the knowledge of this nifty power makes Liston a hot commodity to the US as an agent. They recruit him to steal a briefcase from villain Gregori Andreanu (Donald Pleasence) that contains vials of a never-explained nature.

There's a gag early in the film that borders on funny—the idea is funny if not the execution. While in China, Liston is tortured with a centrifugal device that spins him around at great speeds. After his escape to the West, Liston is again tortured by the US as a spy using the exact same device. It turns out they bought it from a Chinese salesman. That's about as funny as it gets, folks. Most of the humor is very poorly paced, with lines like "Call me sometime, I'm in the code book," and performances that smack of a distinct lack of direction. There's the usual invisibility sight gags and pedestrian humor such as Norris watching "The Man from AUNTIE" on the television. Speaking of Silva, one feels kind of sorry for him here, hung out there to be funny. He's a great talent and it's painful to watch him flailing about trying to find the right tone.

The major bright spot in this drab show is Ira von Furstenberg (in her film debut), who plays O'Neal's contact in London, Arabella. She has great comic timing and looks terrific in this film. And Donald Pleasence is good as the eccentric Andreanu, with his continental accent and flights of fury. Between the two of them you almost have a movie.

For the rest of the time, however, you have to sit through tired gags like the invisible Liston getting involved in a boxing match in order to flummox Andreanu's fighter. And let's not forget the old red-yarn-as-laser-beams trick. That's how you know this is an Italian flick. There are the occasional moments of competency in Morricone's soundtrack but mostly it's as boring and disconnected as the onscreen antics.

Action scenes fare no better. During the climactic chase, they drive cars onto the top of a moving train, but it's edited so poorly (maybe on purpose) that one can't tell if they really pulled it off or not. There's also an amphibious car, and any time you see one of those in a movie you know it's going in the water. On the whole, the film is rather tedious and only recommended for fans of Ira.—DD

CREDITS: Production: Dino De Laurentiis Cin.ca; Director: Alberto Lattuada; Story: Ermanno Donati; Screenplay: Dean Craig [Piero Regnoli], Luigi Malerba, Alberto Lattuada, Jack Pulman; Cinematography: Alessandro D'Eva {Technicolor}; Music: Gino Marinuzzi, Ennio Morricone; Original running length: 104 mins; Country: Italy; Year: 1967

CAST: Patrick O'Neil (*Perry "Matchless" Liston*), Ira Furstenberg (*Arabella*), Donald Pleasence (*Andreanu*), Nicoletta Machiavelli

**Sought-after Belgian poster for *Matchless* featuring Ira von Furstenberg**

(*Betsy*), Henry Silva (*Hank Norris*), Elizabeth Wu (*O-Lan*), M. Mishiku (*Li-Huang*), Handy Ho (*O-Chin*), Jacques Herlin (*O-Chin's doctor*), Valerij Inkijinoff (*the hypnotist*), Giulio Donnini (*the professor*), Howard St. John (*General Shapiro*), Sorrell Brooke (*Colonel Coolpepper*), Tiziani Cortini (*Hogdon*), Lewis Jordan, Ennio Antonelli, Alfredo Martinelli, Gianluigi Crescenzi, Geoffrey Copplestone, Cesare Castelbarco, Emilia Di Santangelo, Ugo Attanasio

MEXICAN SLAY RIDE

aka Coplan III (It, orig), Coplan ouvre la feu à Mexico (Fr), Entre las redes (Sp), Frank Collins 999—Mit Chloroform geht's besser (WG), Moresque: obiettivo allucinante (It)

Note: The only English-language print of *Entre las redes* extant, the print used for this review, is missing at least 30 minutes of footage, all from the central part of the film. While this certainly hinders the reviewer, we felt it was worth covering what is left of this pedigreed example of the genre for the monolingual English speakers among us.

**Photo montage version German poster for Riccardo Freda's *Mexican Slay Ride***

Riccardo Freda is now sometimes dismissed as a director unworthy of the adulation he has received in the past. This is not the place to debate Freda's position in the pantheon of film directors, but it is worth noting that his two entries in the Eurospy genre are fairly highly regarded. They are both adventures based on Paul Kenny's secret agent Coplan and both are filled with action, cold-eyed brutality and touches of outright horror. Freda's other spy film is *FX 18 Superspy*, starring the stone-faced Richard Wyler in the role of Coplan, and it is recommended.

Here, stalwart Lang Jeffries plays Coplan. When valuable paintings stolen by the Nazis in World War II begin to resurface, he is assigned to find out their origin. Freda's leanings toward horror reveal themselves early when Coplan receives a phone call from a desperate female who has information for him. When he visits the girl's room he finds that her blood has soaked through the floor from upstairs; the dripping of it into a sink below tips Coplan to her whereabouts. It is her microfilm of the missing paintings that kicks off the adventure.

Coplan finds his way to Mexico and meets his contact in an amusement park. In one of the most bizarre scenes of this type in the genre, the contact decides to impart his information to Lang while riding a rollercoaster. Not only is it rather conspicuous having two guys in suits and ties riding a rollercoaster, but it must be one of the world's hardest place to speak, hear and concentrate. This certainly makes the audience uneasy and the actors appear quite uncomfortable doing it as well. Not knowing if this scene is taken directly from the book, one has to wonder if this is a mark of Freda's genius or caprice.

Action is order of the day, and in one breathtaking and unbroken sequence, Coplan is caught in a dogfight while flying a small plane, jumps from the damaged plane into a moving car, and commandeers the vehicle to Acapulco where he's meeting up with his contact again (who happens to be cliff-diving there). The contact is shot during his dive and Coplan pursues the car of the fleeing assassin while parasailing (!) with one hand and shooting the fellow dead with the other.

The miniature work in the film, however, is of the most primitive form. We have model car and plane crashes that Roger Corman would turn down as too childishly conceived. Gadgetry is kept to a minimum, with only an exploding pen and a flame-throwing cane on display. Violence and brutality, on the other hand, are commonplace. Coplan chloroforms Sabine Sun while he's in bed with her, hits a guy in the face with a corkscrew, and sets a couple of other guys on fire as he makes the requisite casual remark. There's also a gun battle at a funeral with bullets flying from the back of the hearse.

We're only 40 minutes into the film and just as we're introduced to the apparently paranoid Silvia Solar, there is an abrupt cut and we're now with Coplan in what appears to be the underground lair of the villain. Coplan is wearing coveralls and listening to the ultimate plan of the villain, which is to replace President Johnson with an enemy agent who will force World War III. I think we missed something here. Coplan has been captured along with Solar, and they proceed to escape and destroy the fortress as she screams counterproductive things such as, "It's no use. Let's give ourselves up!"

When Coplan and Solar meet up with the supposed villain, Coplan dispatches the evil fellow by crushing his skull with a vice the guy conveniently had in his apartment. There's still time for the last-minute double-cross by Solar but Coplan, suspecting as much, has planned ahead and comes out on top by using the old backfiring pistol trick. It will be a pleasure to watch the unexpurgated version of this film someday. With this much happening in 55 minutes, I look forward to the seeing the other 30 or so.—DD

CREDITS: Production: P.C. Balcázar, Fida Cinematografica di Amati Edmondo; Director: Riccardo Freda; Story based on the novel "Coplan fait peau neuve" by Paul Kenny; Adaptation: Bertrand Tavernier, Christian Plume; Cinematography: Paul Solignac, Juan Gelpi {Eastmancolor - Techniscope}; Music: Jacques Lacome; Original running length: 93 mins; Filming locations: Barcelona, Mexico, Paris; Country: France/Italy/Spain; Year: 1967

CAST: Lang Jeffries (*Coplan*), Silvia Solar, Sabine Sun, Jose Maria Caffarel, Luciana Gilli, Guido Lollobrigida, Robert Party, Francisco Cebrian, Frank Oliveras [Franco Pesce], Osvaldo Genazzani, Antonio Orengo, Tomas Torres, Maria Dolores Rubio

**German video cover art for *Million Dollar Man***

MILLION DOLLAR MAN
aka Der Goldene Schlüssel (WG),
L'Homme qui valait des milliards (Fr),
Der Milliarden dollar mann (WG),
L'uomo che valeva miliardi (It)

No, no, not THAT one. This "Million Dollar Man" is Jean Sarton (Frederick Stafford), a thief with a taste for elaborate plans, who has ended up in jail. He doesn't know his luck: His cellmate is Andre Novak (Raymond Pellegrin), a former Nazi collaborator who happens to know the whereabouts of a million dollars worth of counterfeit money (which had been manufactured during the war with the intention of flooding the American economy). There's only one thing to do: The two of them make a daring escape. They're helped in this by Muller (Peter Van Eyck), a smooth criminal with a past as a former Nazi officer. Muller, unsurprisingly, wants the money for himself, and promptly tries unsuccessfully to betray the two fugitives.

Novak, however, makes a rather stupid attempt to contact his daughter, Barbara (Ann Duperey), who is being watched by the Muller's men. He is recaptured, bundled into a plane and flown to Morocco (where the money is hidden). This proves to be a problem for Jean, who still doesn't know the actual location of the forged currency. After some discussion with Barbara, he is able to work out where they may have been headed, and they follow the trail to Africa.

Jean also has an ulterior motive. He's an FBI agent, who had been planted in the prison with the goals of winning Novak's confidence and tracking down the counterfeit cash. If he can also round up some fascist criminals while doing so, all the better.

This is a borderline spy entry that splits neatly into three acts. This first is centered around prison life and the jail break, the second has a more noir-ish feel as the criminals attempt to elude each other in the Parisian streets, and finally the action decamps from Europe and it becomes more like a standard espionage scenario. It's almost as though there are three films, each of a different type, which have been shoehorned together into one finished product. It also goes some way toward demonstrating just how important the globetrotting settings were in creating the unique ambience of the genre.

The story itself is nothing new. The "Nazi gold" narrative can also be found in *Furia a Marrakesh*, and having an apparent gang member revealed as an agent occurs in several genre entries (*Rififi in Amsterdam*, for instance). What makes this different is that, for the first two-thirds at least, *Million* completely avoids the playful, lighthearted approach common to the genre. It plays more like an early seventies Alain Delon or Jean Paul Belmondo movie, and is none the worse for it. The violence feels real; when people die you actually *believe* in their death. There are no gadgets, no flashy stylistic quirks. Just down and dirty crime intrigue played out against a grimy urban backdrop of hotels, cafes and department stores.

Also of note are the ways in which the two leads use skills acquired in prison (such as communicating by tapping water pipes) for their advantage in the outside world. Your average sixties agent would always be on the lookout for new abilities that could give the upper hand in otherwise hopeless situations, wherever such abilities are acquired.

Technically, the film is competent enough. The direction and cinematography are capable, if rather unspectacular. It's certainly well-enough made, but isn't one that you'd watch for its cinematic dexterity, and the music is rather underwhelming, further accentuating the low-key feel to proceedings. Fortunately, there's a high-quality cast including such reliable faces as Frederick Stafford (who also featured in director Michel Boisrond's *OSS 117 From Tokyo with Love* the previous year), Jesse Hahn, and the particularly slimy Peter Van Eyck (in a refreshingly unpleasant role). Ann Duperey also adds a certain amount of glamour as the damsel in distress.

Spaghetti western fans may be interested to note that at one point Stafford and Duperey meet in a flea-pit cinema, which appears to be playing *The Hills Run Red* (Dan Duryea's name is prominently displayed on the bill-boards).—MB

CREDITS: Production: France Cineam Productions, S.N.E.G., C.M.V., Produzione Cinematografica; Director: Michel Boisrond; Story based on the novel by Jean Stuart; Screenplay: Michel Lebrun, Michel Boisrond; Cinematography: Raymond Lemoigne, Marcel Grignon {Franscope}; Music: Georges Garvarentz; Original running length: 90 mins; Country: France/Italy; Year: 1967

CAST: Frederick Stafford (*Sarton*), Raymond Pellegrin (*Andre Novak*), Ann Duperey (*Barbara*), Peter Van Eyck (*Muller*), Bernadette Robert (*Juliette*), Jean Franval (*Larneaux*), Sylvain Levignac (*Georges*), Sarah Stephane (*Monique, an Agent*), Henri Czarniak (*Mario*), Christian Barbier (*Carl*), Jess Hahn (*Henry, Sarton's contact*), Henri Lambert (*the prison guard*), Jacques Dynam (*Loulou*), Nicole Debonne, Andre Badin

## THE MILLION EYES OF SUMURU
aka The 1000 Eyes of Su-Muru (Int),
El Millon de ojos de Sumuru (Sp),
The Slaves of Sumuru (Int)

"In the war against mankind, to achieve our aim, a world of peace and beauty ruled by women, we have but one weakness which must be rooted out and destroyed, love." That is the awkwardly worded objective of the evil and mad female villain Sumuru. It's a tall order and one that she has no chance of achieving, of course. The small order that was assigned to director Lindsay Shonteff was to make an enjoyable film. He too falls short of that goal—way short.

Top-billed Frankie Avalon is millionaire playboy Tommy Carter, but thankfully he is not the star of the show (and we are also thankful that he didn't make any more spy flicks). Actually, George Nader, as CIA agent Nick West, gets the bulk of this duo's screen time and while Nader is no Marlon Brando, at least he's a step up from Avalon. Shirley Eaton is Sumuru, head of an evil organization (composed of women, naturally) who want to rid the world of men. Eaton plays it straight, while Nader and Avalon are saddled with delivering the worst lines ever given to would-be spies during the 1960s.

Nader was near the end of his eight-film run of German Jerry Cotton adventures by this time, a series for which he was much better suited. Eaton can also be seen in the uncalled-for sequel to this time-waster, *The Seven Secrets of Sumuru*, aka *Future Women*, aka *Rio 70*, one of the 500 or so films of Jess Franco. One seriously doubts that it was an improvement.

**Popular George Nader features prominently on the German poster for *The Million Eyes of Sumuru***

Sax Rohmer, who wrote the Sumuru stories, probably rolled over in his grave when this was released. It is unabashedly terrible. It contains all the lame humor and tactless dialogue of Shonteff's other spy spoof, *The Second Best Secret Agent in the Whole Wide World*, but lacks even that film's cohesiveness.

However, there is one classic scene near the beginning of the film. The camera prowls around a circle of sitting women, all watching with various degrees of pleasure a bound man whose neck is shortly broken between the legs of a black-clad female killer. It is definitely the best sequence in the film, which isn't saying much. The rest of the way is a grueling filmic journey that seems much longer than its 95-minute running time.

We have the expected lesbian overtones, but what's bad is watching Nader handle the multitude of women who throw themselves at him while Avalon spouts lines like, "I wonder if this is where I'm supposed to sing." It's downright embarrassing.

The best performance in a drive-by role is given by Klaus Kinski. Sure, it's his trademark eccentric character, but he has natural comic timing and the genuinely funny moments he generates are a breath of fresh air. The other two cast members worth mentioning are Maria Rohm and Wilfred Hyde-White. Rohm was a future Jess Franco regular, poor thing, but curiously enough, she's credited as Senta Berger's stunt double in *Our Man in Marrakesh*, which coincidentally features Hyde-White.

At the end of the film, Eaton escapes the assault on her compound unscathed, something we can't claim for the audience. Do yourself a favor and skip this stinker.—DD

CREDITS: Production: American International Pictures, Sumuru Films; Director: Lindsay Schonteff; Story based on the books by Sax Rohmer; Screenplay: Kevin Kavanagh; Cinematography: John von Kotze {Technicolor}; Music: John Scott; Original running length: 95 mins; Country: UK; Year: 1967

CAST: Frankie Avalon (*Tommy Carter*), George Nader (*Nick West*), Shirley Eaton (*Sumuru*), Wilfrid Hyde-White (*Colonel Baisbrook*), Klaus Kinski (*President Boong*), Patti Chandler (*Louise*), Salli Sachse (*Mikki*), Ursula Rank (*Erno*), Krista Nell (*Zoe*), Maria Rohm (*Helga*), Paul Chang (*Inspector Koo*), Essie Huang (*Kitty*), Jon Fong (*Colonel Medika*), Denise Davreux (*Sumuru guard*), Mary Cheng (*Sumuru guard*), Jill Hamilton (*Sumuru guard*), Lisa Grey (*Sumuru guard*), Christine Luk (*Sumuru guard*), Margaret Cheung (*Sumuru guard*), Louise Lee (*Sumuru guard*)

MISSION BLOODY MARY
aka Agente 077: missione Bloody Mary (It),
F.B.I. contre Lotus Bleu (Be),
Jack Clifton: Mission Bloody Mary (WG),
La muerte espera en Atenas (Sp),
Operation Lotus Bleu (Fr)

This was the first of the popular Agent 077 films starring Ken Clark, all of which but one were directed by the experienced Sergio Grieco. Here, CIA chap Dick Malloy (Clark) is given the task of finding a "Bloody Mary," an extremely powerful new kind of atom bomb. The bomb has been stolen by The Black Lilly, a master criminal whose true identity is unknown. He soon traces it to a beauty clinic (conveniently enough) presided over by a sinister plastic surgeon, Dr. Batti (Umberto Raho). Also working there is an undercover agent, Elsa Freeman (Helga Line), to whom our hero immediately takes an understandable shine.

The villains, meanwhile, are trying to ship their haul to Greece, where it is to be collected by some envoys from China who are willing to pay handsomely for such a powerful device. Malloy manages to smuggle himself on board the freight vessel being used for transport, and soon he manages to get mixed up in all manner of trouble.

Add to this a gang of incompetent Russians, a number of double-crosses, and an assortment of unbelievable gadgetry and you have a highly entertaining example of the genre. There are a few action highlights, such as a well-handled rooftop chase and shootout, and the plot is interesting enough to keep you involved.

This film is quite serious-minded and as such, lacks the cheese factor of, say, the Kommissar X series. However, Sergio Grieco knows his directorial stuff and there's a nice supporting cast.—MB

CREDITS: Production: Fida Cin.ca, Les Productions Jacques Roitfeld, Epoca Film; Director: Terence Hathaway [Sergio Grieco]; Story and Screenplay: Alessandro Continenza, Marcello Coscia, Leonardo Martin; Cinematography: Juan Julio Baena {Technicolor - Techniscope}; Music: Angelo Francesco Lavagnino; Original running length: 95 mins; Country: Italy/Spain/France; Year: 1965

Cast: Ken Clark (*Dick Malloy*), Helga Line (*Dr. Elsa Freeman*), Philippe Hersent (*Heston, the CIA chief*), Mitsouko (*Fuong*), Susan Terry (*the blonde*), Mirko Ellis (*Dr. Betz*), Andrea Scotti, Dario Michaelis, Umi [Umberto] Raho (*Dr. Batti*), Erika Bianchi, Franca Polesello, John Jordan, Peter Blades (*the tiger*), Brand Lyonel, Alfredo Mayo, Tomas Blanco, Peter Bosch, Ignazio Leone, Anthony Gradwell [Antonio Gradoli] (*MacGreen*), "Sranoli" (*Lester*)

**Helga Line gives one of her trademark sideways glances to Ken Clark in *Mission Bloody Mary***

MISSION TO CARACAS
aka Missión especial en Caracas (Sp), Mission speciale a Caracas (Fr), Missione Caracas (It)

**Belgian poster for *Mission to Caracas* plays down the cruise ship mileu of the film**

This should be named *Mission FROM Caracas*, because the bulk of the film takes place on a cruise ship that leaves Caracas on the way to France. There's no doubt that this is indeed a real cruise ship on a real cruise. Talk about saving money on sets. Rod Carter (*Giants of Thessaly*) is special agent Becker, who's after a briefcase that rather cleverly disguises some secret documents. The documents are being smuggled aboard a cruise ship but, as luck would have it, Becker gets into a minor car chase on his way to the dock and smashes his car up. When he wakes up in the hospital, he discards his head bandage and dresses to leave. When his nurse tells him he has a fractured skull, he says "Oh, so what? I only stay in bed for a reason," and kisses her. He misses the boat, so he makes a dramatic entrance by dropping from a helicopter onto the deck. Nothing like keeping a low profile. From here on in it's all about tracking down that darn briefcase.

Rod Carter isn't a very charismatic actor and in fact, the entire male cast is forgettable with the exception of Michel Lemoine, who gets killed off too early. It's the female cast that is worth noting for a change. This film features sizable roles for three genre regulars and real beauties at that: Jany Clair, Janine Reynaud and Yvonne Monlaur. It's a casting coup and the novelty that keeps this picture from floundering entirely.

Well, there is one other facet of the film worth mentioning: the curious dialogue. The first villain (he doesn't last long) says to his right-hand man, "I'm a monster. I was born for evil," and the reply is, "If good had been as profitable to you as evil, you would have been one of the great benefactors of humanity." That guy knows the right thing to say to the boss. When Jany Clair gets her hands on that briefcase (which contains diamonds as well as the documents) halfway through the film, she hides a few diamonds in her bra: "I want to smuggle out a couple of samples. We'll have them expertized." When Becker is scolded by his boss for not getting his hands on the briefcase fast enough, his boss says, "This is inadmissible!" Another bad guy brags, "When I don't kill for business reasons, I kill for my pleasure." And there are many more examples of inept writing and translating, believe me.

Other strange things include frogmen in the desert, a swimsuit fashion show, a seven-woman catfight and a movie camera that shoots poison darts. The fights are pretty bad, sometimes comical, and there's a running gag about a maid who's always finding the dead bodies. Michel Magne's score is odd, post-bop jazz, as if he recognized that this film needed all the help it could get.

We mentioned about the documents being cleverly disguised in the briefcase. We'll let Becker explain: "The documents are designed in the leather by means of a radioactive isotope, I'd say probably Iridium 192 with a period of 60 days. After that time the drawings simply disappear." Pretty cool.—DD

CREDITS: Production: C.F.F.P., Cine Italia Film, Urfesa Film production; Director: Raoul Andre; Story based on the novel by Claude Rank; Screenplay: Gianfranco Parolini (Italian credits), Jean Curtelin; Cinematography: Pierre Petit {Eastmancolor}; Music: Michel Magne; Original running length: 87 mins; Filming locations: Caracas, Guadeloupe; Country: France/Italy/Spain; Year: 1965

CAST: Rod Carter (*Gil Becker*), Jany Clair (*Dominique*), Louise Carletti (*Martine*), Alain

Gotvalles (*Boris*), Saro Urzi (*H.C.D. Vasson*), Yvonne Monlaur (*Muriel*), Dominique Page (*Ariel*), Michel Lemoine (*Lois De Quemenec*), Dominique Saint-Pierre (*Veronique*), Mireille Granelli (*Caroline*), Josy Andrieu (*the singer*), Alain Bouvette, Paul Demange, Christa Lang, Henri Lambert, Manuel Zarzo, Sonia Bruno, Angel Del Pozo, Liana Orfei, Claude Salez

MISSION TO VENICE
aka Agent special a Venice (Fr),
Mission to Die (Int),
Mord am Canale Grande (WG),
La Spia che venne dall'ovest (It), Trampa secreta (Sp),
Voir Venise et crever (Fr, alt)

This is a pre-Bond spy story that plays more like a mystery for the first hour. It is an exceedingly conventional *Boy's Life*-type adventure starring fresh-faced, preppy Sean Flynn as Michael Newman, water polo player and Izod-wearing rich kid. The wife of his dead dad's best friend approaches him and asks his help in locating her husband, who has disappeared somewhere in Venice. It turns out that her glass dealer hubby is a spy who has been marked for a traitor. Newman, ever the naïve boy, doesn't believe this traitor business for a second and he turns out to be right, of course. The spy is being held by the bad guys, who want him to give up the secret document he has hidden.

What goes on as the plot unfolds is not very interesting, really. There's lots of off-season Venice to look at and it's quite photogenic as far as that goes. Speaking of photogenic, the love interest/femme fatale is played by the gorgeous Karin Baal. She didn't make any other spy flicks and besides being in a couple of the German Edgar Wallace mysteries, it is curious to note that she played Fabio Testi's bitch of a wife in the famous giallo *What Have You Done to Solange?* in 1972. You would not believe it was the same person.

The rest of the cast sports a few recognizable faces, most notably Daniel Emilfork, who spends most of the movie looking ominous. As is typical of his appearances in several small French spy flicks of the early sixties, Emilfork doesn't have enough to do here, his bird-like features being what filmmakers focus upon. The soundtrack by Alain Goraguer is one of this film's finest assets, however. It is swinging jazz combo stuff that outclasses the pedestrian antics it supports. As a curio this is watchable, but it can only be recommended to the completionist.—DD

**Something Weird videotape of *Mission to Venice***

CREDITS: Production: Films Metzger et Woog, Le Films Marceau-Cocinor, Adelphia Compania Cinematografica, Eichberg Films; Director: Andre Versini; Story based on the story by James Hadley Chase; Cinematography: Andre Germain {Dyaliscope}; Music: Alain Goraguer; Original running length: 100 mins; Country: France/Italy/West Germany; Year: 1964

CAST: Sean Flynn (*Michael Newman*), Karin Baal (*Maria Natzke*), Madeline Robinson (*Mme. Tregard*), Pierre Mondy (*Paul*), Ettore Manni (*Giuseppe*), Hannes Messemer (*Carl Natzke*), Jacques Dufilho (*Cesar*), Jacques Monod (*Colonel Vallin*), Daniel Emilfork, Margaret Hunt

MISTRESS OF THE WORLD
aka Herrin der Welt 1. Teil Herrin der Welt (first part) (WG), Herrin der Welt 2. Teil Angkor-Vat (second part) (WG), Formel des Todes 1. Teil (first part) (WG televison), Formel des Todes 2. Teil (second part) (WG television), Il mistero dei tre continenti (It), Les mystères d'Angkor (Fr), La signora del mondo West (It, production)

A rather confusing item, this international co-production was cobbled together from a two-part movie, *Herrin der welt—Teil 1* and *Herrin der welt—Teil 2*. It appears that there were two different versions of the single film released: in France as *Les mysteres d'Angkor* (clocking in at 151 minutes), and in Italy as a seriously truncated 113-minute version called *Il Mistero dei tre continenti*. The version under review, an international print entitled *Mistress of the World*, also has a running time of just under two hours, indicating that it could be a re-dubbed release of the Italian version. Although some sources give the date as 1959, filming actually finished at the very beginning of 1960, meaning that it does (just barely) classify as a fully fledged sixties spy film.

Nobel prize-winning professor Johansson (Gino Cervi) is carrying out some of his experiments when something goes dreadfully wrong: A bizarre magnetic field paralyzes all of the hydroelectric installations in Europe. He has created a formula that transforms light rays into a deadly form of energy. Unfortunately, before Interpol can bring Johansson under their protection he is kidnapped, and an investigator who manages to discover something about the abductors is murdered.

To find Johansson, a group of top European agents are ordered to work in collaboration. Chief among them are Swede Peter Lundström (Carlos Thompson) and Italian Biamonte (Lino Ventura). They soon discover that Johansson was snatched by a woman, Madame Latour (Micheline Presle), and has been transported to China. Unfortunately, their task isn't made any easier by the fact that they also have to protect the professor's uppity daughter, Karin (Martha Hyer).

*MOTW* is a quite stupendously dull film. This is partly because it suffers from some of the worst editing imaginable, but also because

**Italian artwork for *Mistress of the World***

the script is incredibly slight for such a long running time. It's hard to imagine just what it's like in its full, unabridged, three-hour glory. Basically a remake of an old twenties serial, it certainly has the feel of something that would be a lot more compulsive if split into 30-minute segments. Viewed in one sitting, it comes across as simply so much repetition.

It doesn't help that the first half is extremely confusing: Characters drop in and out with nary a mention, and sequences end abruptly without proper conclusion. An attempt to explain just what the hell's going on is made by the inclusion of a voiceover, but unfortunately this doesn't shed much light on anything (and is dubbed by someone with such a peculiar voice, it just ends up being distracting). Admittedly, most of these problems are in some part because this version is missing well over an hour's worth of footage, but unfortunately it has proved difficult to track down the original German film(s) for comparison.

Things do perk up toward the last third, when it develops into your basic, old-fashioned "exotic" adventure (in much the same way as Gianfranco Parolini's much better *Cave of Diamonds*). This gives rise to a whole menagerie of stock footage wildlife, rubber snake wrestling and near-quicksand death experiences, which is actually all rather jolly under the circumstances. There's also a decent climax, with the main protagonists battling it out in a Buddhist temple while monks go—seemingly undisturbed—about their daily worship in the background.

As for performances, Argentinean Carlos Thompson—who was better known for being married to Lilli Palmer—is a vacuum. He was also the lead actor in the English television series *The Sentimental Agent*, some episodes of which were edited together into a film version called *Our Man in the Caribbean* (also featuring Diana Rigg and Shirley Eaton). Interestingly, that was a spin-off from another series, *Man of the World*, starring Craig Stevens. Serendipity, don't you love it!

Martha Hyer does her best with a rather uninteresting role. Sabu, better known as Mowgli in *The Jungle Book*, is pretty good as the professor's assistant, and Lino Ventura steals the whole show despite disappearing (without explanation) halfway through. Director William Dieterle was one of many ex-pat Germans to flourish in the early days of Hollywood, picking up plaudits for work such as *The Life of Emil Zola* and *Portrait of Jennie*. He returned to Europe in the late fifties, where his career rather fizzled out.—MB

CREDITS: Production: CCC Filmproduktion GmbH, Franco-London Film, Continental Produzione; Director: William Dieterle (completed by Richard Angst after Dieterle had a disagreement with the producer); Story based on "Herrin Der Welt"; Screenplay: Jo Eisinger, H.G. Petersson [Harald G. Petersson]; Music: Roman Vlad; Original running time: 98 mins; Filming locations: Thailand, Cambodia, Germany, Hong Kong, China, Tibet, France, Sweden; Country: West Germany/France/Italy; Date: 1960

CAST: Martha Hyer (*Karin Johanson*), Carlos Thompson (*Peter Lundström*), Micheline Presle (*Madame Latour*), Wolfgang Preiss (*Brandes*), Sabu (*Dr. Lin-Chor*), Carl Lange (*Berakov*), Leon Askin (*Fernando*), Valerij Inkijinoff (*the priest*), Gino Cervi (*Professor Johanson*), Lino Ventura (*Biamonte*), Hans Nielsen (*Colonel Dagget*), Charles Régnier (*Norvald*), Jean-Claude Michel (*Ballard*), Carlo Giustini (*John, a sailor*), Georges Rivière (*Logan*), Jochen Blume (*Bertrand*), Rolf von Nauckhoff (*Dalkin*), Jur Arten, Ali Benmussa, Hans-Jürgen Bodinus, Edgar Faiss, Kunibert Gensichen, Peter Hippler, Bob Iller, Wolfgang Kühne, Bruno W. Pantel, Reginald Pasch, Peter Purand, Oskar Sabo, Jr., Eleonore Tappert, Harro Tenbrook, Egon Vogel

**Bad guy Gerard Blain has the upper hand on hero Fred Beir on the French poster for *M.M.M. 83***

M.M.M. 83
aka Missione morte Molo 83 (It),
Objectif Hambourg mission 083 (Fr)

This by-the-numbers spy thriller is so low-key as to lull the even the most avid fan to sleep. Director Sergio Bergonzelli has no flair for the hackneyed material, making it seem as if the principlals just want to get the whole thing over with. The viewer will sympathize.

Fred Beir is Jack Morrow, the Interpol agent who must find a scientist's stolen documents. Assigned to work with the scientist's colleague, Robert Gibson (Gerard Blain), Beir must contend with rival spy factions before discovering that—oh my God!—Gibson masterminded the entire plan. The weak-chinned Beir is a recognizable actor not so much from his spy films, but from his many appearances on American television in the sixties and seventies.

The film has very, very little to recommend it despite a decent cast. Sure, you get to watch Pier Angeli, but she pretty much has the Karin Dor role of deer in the headlights. Another enticement would be Silvia Solar, who at least gets to make out with Morrow before disappearing altogether. Even Alberto Dalbes is relegated to bad guy #3, whose double gets to fall off a crane.

Speaking of which, the climactic gun battle at Pier 83 (hence the title) consists of lots of aimless shooting and many falls from great heights into water. When the only highlights are a couple of car chases and the same number of fistfights (one at a circus), you know you just paid a visit to dullsville, baby. In fact, a visit to a taxidermist's shop is the most memorable scene in the whole damn thing and that is saying very little. Even the Piccioni score is uninspired, with only one or two interesting moments. Do yourself a favor, pass this one by and watch the grass grow instead.—DD

CREDITS: Production: Film D'Equipe, Olympic Prod. Cinematograficas, France Cinema Productions; Director: Sergio Bergonzelli; Story and Screenplay: Victor A Catena, Adalberto Albertini, Sergio Bergonzelli, Carlo Musso, L. Marchand; Cinematography: Eloy Mella; Music: Piero Piccioni; Original running length: 90 mins; Country: France/Italy/Spain; Year: 1965

CAST: Fred Beir (*Jack Morrow*), Gerard Blain (*Robert Gibson*), Albert Dalbes (*Ben Youssef*), Silvia Solar (*Janette*), Anna Maria Pierangeli (*Helene*), Gianni Solaro (*the excellency*), Mario Lanfranchi, Andre Lorugues, Ignazio Dolce, Mario Magnolia, Gigetto [Luis] Chavarro, Mario Frei, Bruno Arie, Franco Daddi and members of the Circus Togni

## MODESTY BLAISE

*Modesty Blaise* is, barring the James Bond and Harry Palmer films, probably the best known of the sixties spy oeuvre. This isn't just because it obviously benefited from a substantial budget and enjoyed a degree of notoriety at the time. It's also because—thanks to repeated broadcasts on television—it has become something of kitsch favorite to a generation of impressionable youths blown away by its camp sensibilities, astonishing visual excesses and, well, the fact that it's chock full of gorgeous females. And I'm proud to say that I count myself among these impressionable youths. It had been some time, however, since I last saw it—so when it was released in an immaculate print on DVD, it seemed like a temptation too delicious to resist. Unfortunately, the years have passed, and turned me into a cynical old goat: *Modesty*'s charms left me distinctly unimpressed.

British Intelligence's best man is the unfortunate victim of a booby-trapped doorbell, and all that remains of him is a rather battered bowler hat. Needing someone whose cunning is matched only by his valor, the men in pinstripe suits turn to Modesty Blaise (Monica Vitti), a notorious thief-cum-mercenary, whom they hire to take on the dead man's mission: Accompany a shipment of diamonds that is being used as payment for the rights to a bunch of Arabian oil fields. She immediately calls in her chuffin' Cockney sparra' partner, Willie Garvin (Terence Stamp), despite some reluctance on the part of MI5 (mainly because he's lower class, but also because of his sordid reputation ["We've checked out your Willie…"]).

They both head to Amsterdam, where a number of sinister-looking fellows are wandering about, trying to blow up barges and the like. It seems that someone is determined to sabotage their mission, and that someone looks increasingly like Gabriel (Dirk Bogarde), a master criminal who had been thought long dead. He isn't, of course, but quite what he's up to doesn't seem of much concern to the scriptwriters. Suffice to say that he's a bad guy, he's very alive and he's totally nuts.

If you're looking for tight plotting, slow-burning tension and moody ambience, you've come to the wrong place. This was adapted from a successful comic strip (first published in the Evening Standard in 1963) and—like Mario Bava's *Diabolik*—it is less interested in drama than in being a cinematic pop artwork. It's dripping with crazy designs, beat music and extravagant art direction. The men wear snappy suits, the women wear astonishing dresses (dif-

***Modesty Blaise* lobby card featuring Monica Vitti**

refers to his mother, I'd like to think that his dialogue was improvised, since it is far funnier than anything else in the script.

And therein comes the first of *Modesty Blaise*'s big problems. The villain is simply so entertaining that he completely overshadows the ostensible heroes.

Modesty herself is, when all's said and done, rather bloody hopeless—always needing to be rescued by somebody or other. Monica Vitti is a good actress, but she doesn't quite have the vim to pull it off—despite the selection of eye-catching frocks that she gets to wear. Terence Stamp, it has to be said, is frankly annoying in this. With his estuary accent and tousled hair, he resembles nothing so much as a dreary footballer or one of the less pleasant members of a terrible boy-band.

ferent in every scene, of course), and if there were any dogs, they would be ridiculously coiffeured poodles or, possibly, huskies. It's just that kind of film. It's never mentioned, but the shortened version of Modesty would be Mod, and that says it all, really.

So, what else do you get? Well, there's plenty of fun to be had. There's some pointless pigeon abuse (never to be frowned upon), some torture by modern art (as opposed to tortuous modern art) and, on a couple of occasions, Modesty and Willie even break into song, *Chitty Chitty Bang Bang*-style. There's also some high-quality mime mishandling (the face-painted cretin gets strangled between a pair of thighs—in mid-mime—and thrown off a cliff).

There are entertaining performances from such classy stalwarts as Harry Andrews, Clive Revill, Micheal Craig and, er, John Karlsen. Best of all, though, is the uncontrollable Dirk Bogarde. It's hard to believe this is the same guy who was in *Hot Enough for June*. No longer playing the matinee idol, he's transformed into...well, the campiest villain this side of Alan Rickman. Sporting an astonishing pair of spectacles, he is the apotheosis of desert island megalomaniacs: He has his own organ-playing friar, a mad dominatrix assistant (the hilarious Rossella Falk, owner of the aforementioned thighs), shockingly dyed silver hair and astonishing wall decorations. As he continually mourns his victims ("two children, split-level house in Woking, rubber plant in lounge") and

Then again, neither of them is helped by the extraordinarily messy script. Although credited to Evan Jones (a frequent Joseph Losey collaborator [*These Are the Damned*]) who went on to write *Funeral in Berlin*), there were earlier treatments from Sidney (*Endless Night*) Gilliat and Suso Checci D'Amico (*Rocco and His Brothers*). Somewhere along the line, the idea of narrative thread was simply thrown out the window. We're expected to know who Modesty is, why MI5 would call her in, and exactly what the nature of her relationship with Gabriel is. Even assuming that we do have this completely absent background knowledge, the central story is left to flounder about helplessly at the whim of whatever conceit has attracted the attention of the filmmakers in the moment. As for a climax, who needs it? We get loads of idiots in Arab costumes running around for no reason whatsoever.

Joseph Losey was a director who aroused strong feelings. To some he was one of the greatest filmmakers of his time, and certainly some of his work would seem to confirm this reputation. After initial success in the US (*The Boy With Green Hair*, *The Prowler*), he fell afoul of the fifties witch hunts and, refusing to testify, emigrated to the UK. There he made a series of gripping films throughout the early sixties (including *The Criminal*, *These Are the Damned* and *The Servant*). Unfortunately, he could also direct a real stinker, and while his best work is relatively small scale and claustrophobic, his aptitude for the large scale would appear to be questionable from the results on evidence here.

And on to the third problem: It's entertaining, it's easy to watch but...it's not half as clever or funny as it seems to think it is. At times, the constant stream of irony—and costume changes—becomes entirely tiresome. The central characters spend an awful lot of time pratting around with each other—almost as though we're supposed to be so blown away by their wonderfulness that we can damn well just watch them do whatever they want. The filmmakers are obviously attempting to parody the spy-film genre, and fair enough, but they don't have the wit to realize that the whole genre is frankly a self-parody. And this has the effect of making *Modesty Blaise* more similar to the much-reviled *Casino Royale* than the innocent, charming *Diabolik*. It's like watching a film with a self-satisfied smile on its face. And there's nothing that you want to do more when confronted with a self-satisfied smile than dislike its owner.—MB

CREDITS: Production: 20th Century Fox; Director: Joseph Losey; Story based on the comic by Peter O'Donnell, Jim Holdaway; Screenplay: Evan Jones; Cinematography: Jack Hildyard; Music: John Dankworth; Original running length: 119 mins; Filming locations: Amsterdam; Country: UK; Year: 1966

CAST: Monica Vitti (*Modesty Blaise*), Terence Stamp (*Willie Garvin*), Dirk Bogarde (*Gabriel*), Harry Andrews (*Sir Gerald Tarrant*), Michael Craig (*Paul Hagan*), Scilla Gabel (*Melina*), Tina Marquand (*Nicole*), Clive Revill (*McWhirter/the sheikh*), Rosella Falk (*Mrs. Fothergill*), Joe Melia (*Crevier*), Lex Schoorel (*Walter*), Silvan (*the great Paco*), Jon Bluming (*Hans*), Roberto Bisacco (*Enrico*), Saro Urzi (*Basilio*), Giuseppe Pagnelli (*Friar*), Alexander Knox (*Minister*), Michael Chow (*Wang*), Marcello Turilli (*Strauss*), John Karlsen (*Oleg*), Robin Fox (*doorbell ringer*)

**French DVD cover art for *The Monocle***

THE MONOCLE
aka L'Ispettore spara a vista (It), Le Monocle rit jaune (Fr), El Monoculo (Sp)

The French have a way with the spy film, and this must be among the most eccentric spy films of the 1960s. Paul Meurisse plays Major Theobald Dromar, aka The Monocle, a fey secret agent who wears a monocle (hence the nickname) and cultivates an array of other odd mannerisms. Dromar is exceptionally successful in his work while putting up with the vulgar heathens on both sides of the law that surround him.

This adventure of The Monocle matches the strange character of Dromar to a T. There is some nice high-contrast black and white photography and a great cool jazz score by Michel Magne, who also scored the Fantomas films. But the highlights of the film revolve around the curiosities tossed at the viewer with nonchalance. Director Georges Lautner had charge of the previous Monocle films as well, so his feel for the character is ingrained.

The plot is simple enough, but has little to do with one's enjoyment of the film. Dromar investigates acts of sabotage where nuclear research is being conducted. Locations in Hong Kong and Macao are used to great effect. Hong Kong never looked so densely crowded nor

Macao so spare and haunting. There is lots of street footage in both places, some typical, but most not so.

Dromar has a great blue collar-type sidekick, Poussin, played by Robert Dalban (also in the Monocle's previous adventures and the Fantomas films). Poussin plays straight man to Dromar, with a pragmatic, though long-suffering, air and gets some of the best lines in the film. Once in Hong Kong, Dromar is assigned a young associate, Frederic (Olivier Despax), to facilitate his way around, who learns from the ever-so-aloof master the ways of the secret agent. Certainly of note is the presence of Barbara Steele in her early prime. However, it must be said that she looks far from her best here. Perhaps it's the makeup or lighting, but her otherworldly visual appeal is lost, replaced by a gaunt and homely look. Her acting is fine of course, but this isn't her movie. She does receive what is probably her most bizarre screen kisses from Dromar.

This being a French film, we get to enjoy various jabs at the inferiority of things that are not French. When young Frederic mentions that they might consult with the British authorities, he is met with grumblings from Poussin and immediately responds with, "I do not believe we are at war with the English!" Dromar then quips "True, young man, however, no one is entirely at peace with them." Time is also taken to belittle the local cuisine of the Orient, and Poussin even goes so far as to prepare coque au vin in their room rather than eat Chinese.

Things begin to get strange about 20 minutes into the film when our hero smokes opium with an informant in a literally laid-back scene exquisitely played by the cast. When Poussin bursts in on the smokers with the news that they are surrounded by bad guys, Dromar lazily replies that, "If we must die, we must die" as he takes another hit off the pipe. Later Dromar remarks on the pleasurable experience, saying that it reminded him of his college days. This gentleman is not your typical super-spy.

One of the leads in the case is a beautiful girl (naturally) who arranges a meeting with Dromar to give him information. When Dromar and Frederic show up at the appointed place by the seashore in Macao, they find the woman dead in a fishing net. This scene is handled quite delicately compared to the rest of the goings on and is followed by a reflective sequence as we follow the men walking back to the city accompanied by more of that cool jazz.

The silliness resumes shortly thereafter as the two are attacked by at least a dozen henchmen and Dromar remarks, "Unless I'm mistaken, we're starting a fight sequence." He then gives instruction on the proper shooting of a firearm to the young Frederic. Apparently, if one steadies one's gun barrel on the left hand just so, the aim becomes not only perfect but supernatural in its ability to massacre the minions. Dromar manages to kill two men with one bullet not once but twice.

There's a curiously reverent scene in a shrine when Dromar meets with the Celestial King to discuss the group of his followers who are committing the acts of sabotage so annoying to the West. Amidst the candlelight, the two men trade nuggets of gracious wisdom back and forth like it was a meeting of the Buddhas. Dromar manages to discover the next target of the terrorists, but not who is responsible. The old man firmly believes that his follower, misguided though he may seem, could be "the hand of God."

There are no gadgets in this movie whatsoever, but Dromar carries cigarettes that require no matches. One simply lights them by striking one end against the pack. I guess those never caught on. Another notable event is a cameo appearance by Lino Ventura. You can't miss him.

The kidnapping attempt of Dromar and company in the floating restaurant is the *piece de resistance* of the film. Our heroes' dinner is drugged before the bad guys make their play, which goes a little way toward explaining the bizarre action that takes place. When the gang members make their appearance, they dance across the floor with snapping fingers and attitude a la *West Side Story*. It's a surreal tableau of tumbling acrobats and slow-motion kung fu fighting guaranteed to drop the viewer's jaw.

One of the most unusual spy film experiences, *The Monocle* grows on you if you give it a chance. As Dromar says at one point, "The more I see of the Chinese, it's amazing how like the French they are."—DD

CREDITS: Production: Laetitia Films; Director: Georges Lautner; Story: Colonel

Remy, Jacques Robert, Albert Kantof; Screenplay: Jacques Robert, Albert Kantof, Georges Lautner; Cinematography: Maurice Fellous {B&W}; Music: Michel Magne; Original running length: 100 mins; Country: France/Italy; Year: 1964

CAST: Paul Meurisse (*Theobold Dromard, aka The Monocle*), Robert Dalban (*Poussin*), Barbara Steele (*Valerie*), Marcel Dalio (*Elie Mayerfitsky*), Olivier Despax (*Frederic*), Renee Saint-Cyr (*Mme Hui*), Edward Meeks (*Major Sidney*), Pierre Richard (*Bergonian*), Holley Wong (*Oscar Hui*), Lily Hong-Hong (*Cora*), Kwan Chin-Liang (*Ye*), Henri Nassiet (*the Colonel*), Michel Dupleix (*the Colonel's assistant*), Raymond Meunier (*the interviewer*), Lino Ventura (*Elie's client*), Marcel Bernier (*the Colonel's man*), Guy Henry

**Italian poster for Sergio Corbucci's violent *Moving Target***

MOVING TARGET
aka Bersaglio mobile (It),
Fluchtpunkt Akropolis (WG)

Sergio Corbucci directed several excellent and influential spaghetti westerns in the sixties and seventies. Here he successfully applies his violent style to a crime film turned spy flick, resulting in one of the grittiest examples of the genre. Ty Hardin is Jason, a master thief who escapes the law in Greece and is blackmailed into stealing a tooth from a corpse in a prison morgue. It's a grisly piece of business that sets the tone for things to come. Jason isn't about to give up this tooth once he knows its worth, so he spends the bulk of the film trying to keep it away from people he doesn't like until he can figure out who will buy it without killing him. The tooth turns out to contain a microfilmed list of agents all over the world, so it's no wonder that everyone wants to get their hands on it.

Hardin, who unfortunately didn't make any other spy flicks, leads a fine cast of genre regulars including Michael Rennie and Gordon Mitchell in one of his nastiest roles. Rennie plays Major Clark, an agent in the British Secret Service who harbors dark secrets, and Mitchell is The Albanian, an absolutely ruthless killer who'll stop at nothing to get his grubby paws on that film, including killing innocent children.

Mitchell is featured in one memorable scene worthy of rewinding the tape to catch again. It's a small scene in the museum at the Acropolis where The Albanian is holding Jason and a female guide. When The Albanian threatens the girl, Jason gives in and tells him that the film is in his car. While a heavy goes out to check the car, The Albanian kills a few minutes by wandering around the museum shop and nonchalantly knocks the penis off a "priceless" statue with the barrel of his gun. It's worth the price of admission.

Jason is constantly on the run from agents, thugs and cops and Corbucci keeps things moving with plenty of action. With almost nonstop car chases (including a nice open- bridge jump), fistfights and gun battles, this film seems a natural precursor to the Italian cop thrillers of the 1970s. There are even strip acts and machine guns pulled from violin cases. The twists and turns are really packed into the last few minutes, proving it ain't over till it's over.

The stylish opening credit sequence, which has Jason running for his life as he escapes the cops, is good enough to be repeated when we hit the full-circle ending. You won't mind. Ivan Vander's big band jazz score is serviceable, but the general air of brutality could have used music a bit more dramatic. This is an excellent hybrid film, a bridge to the next decade of violent thrills that any fan of Italian cinema will enjoy.—DD

CREDITS: Production: Rizzoli Film; Director: Sergio Corbucci; Story: Massimo Patrizi; Screenplay: Massimo Patrizi, Franco Rossetti, Sergio Corbucci; Cinematography: Ajace Parolin {Eastmancolor}; Music: Ivan Vander; Original running length: 92 mins; Country: Italy; Year: 1967

CAST: Ty Hardin (*Jason*), Michael Rennie (*Major Clark*), Paola Pitagora (*Greta*), Vittorio Caprioli (*Billy*), Gordon Mitchell (*The Albanian*), Vissili Karamensinis, Giulio Coltellacci, Nando Poggi, Hunt Silvers, Eric Shippers, Valentino Macchi, James Clay [Aldo Cecconi], with Graziella Granata (*Rumba*)

NAZI SS

aka Borman (It), Le retour des loups (Fr)

This came three years after *Piege pour un espions*, director Bruno Paolinelli's other genre outing. Sandro Moretti starred in both films, using his "Robert Kent" alias, as a character called, ahem, "Robert Kent." In Italian prints, however, he is referred to as "Bob Gordon," so whether this is a sequel or there were some extremely unimaginative dubbers working on both productions, could be a matter of some debate. Suffice it to say that they share many of the same traits: a vaguely interesting central premise, extremely low production values, excessive length and a strangely subdued, almost somnolent atmosphere.

In Rome, a protracted car chase ends when a man is gunned down. Before he dies, he mumbles incoherently about Martin Bormann, Hitler's notorious sidekick, being alive and in hiding. Agent Robert Kent is assigned the case, with early indications being that the nasty Nazi has had plastic surgery and is now living somewhere in South America—Paraguay, to be precise. There he's planning to initiate a new master plan, thus erasing the painful memories of being vanquished at the end of the Second World War. Said "master plan" commences with the theft of a Chinese U-boat armed with two atomic missiles, which understandably arouses the interest of officials in Peking.

Agent Kent, meanwhile, is mucking around in Italy, where he impersonates the dead man at the beginning (who was also an agent and had managed to infiltrate the villain's camp). This involves him wandering off to a ski resort, where he handily bumps into a feisty Nazi-hunter, Erika (Liana Orfei). He soon tracks down the (penny-pinchingly small) gaggle of Fascists, who are hoping to use the purloined sub in order to kick off a third world war—from which they can emerge as the leaders of a new world order.

*Nazi SS* is about as cheap as they come—without being made in Turkey, that is—and is frankly a pretty terrible movie. It exhibits many of the trademarks of low-budget spy films: excessive amounts of the running time filmed in hotel rooms, an overly complex plot, and the regular mention of several exotic locales—but with filming restricted to that resort just down the road. In fact, the nearest this gets to globetrotting is having shots of a revolving toy globe, which is somehow supposed to convey how international the whole thing is.

Worst of all, it is one of those productions that suffer from having an excessive amount of badly inserted stock footage. This starts off harmlessly enough, with a rather amusing example of how not to land a plane on an aircraft carrier (in black and white, natch). However, after being shown about seven minutes of World War II newsreels—and then a few additional minutes of Chinese military processions—you start to have the feeling that the entire plot was molded around the contents of the nearest film archive. I'm surprised they weren't just a little bit more cheeky, actually crediting Hitler, Mussolini, Mao, et. al.—who certainly have more screen time than most of the actual performers.

Adding to the problems is the performance of Sandro Moretti who, adequate though he may be as a supporting actor in peplums such as *Goliath and the Dragon* and *The Corsican Brothers*, simply doesn't have the charisma to carry the role. He seems much too boyish, and the fact that he persistently gets beaten up doesn't really help matters. Liana Orfei is fine as Erika, but Dominique Boschero really doesn't have much to do and Adriano Micantoni's villain is hardly featured at all.

It's a pity really, as there's the germ of a good idea in there somewhere, and certain aspects (a procession of villains clad in full KKK get-up, a chase involving the inevitable ski-lift, the link between the neo-Nazis and the American extremists) aren't half bad. There's also a commendable Biamonte and Grisanti animated title sequence and a particularly surreal bit in which—for no reason at all—the hero is seen playing with a giant Scalectrix set. Unfortunately, it's also the kind of film wherein the main villain—Herr Bormann excepted—is called Barry, which just about says it all.—MB

CREDITS: Production: Italspettacolo, Saba Cin.ca, Radius Productions; Director: John Huxley [Bruno Paolinelli]; Story: John Huxley [Bruno Paolinelli]; Screenplay: Jack Souryan [Giovanna Soria]; Cinematography: Bob Presley [Vitaliano Natalucci] {Techniscope - Technicolor}; Music: Teo Usuelli; Original running length: 88 mins; Country: Italy/France; Year: 1966

CAST: Robert Kent [Sandro Moretti] (*Colonel Robert Kent*), Liana Orfei (*Erika*), Dominique Boschero (*Carson's henchwoman*), Moha Tahi (*the Chinese colonel*), Kitty Swan (*Bob's water-skiing girlfriend*), Serge Nadaud, Adrian Mikel [Adriano Micantoni] (*Barry Carson*), Dany Crawfordow, Ray Moore, with Paul Muller (*the General, head of American Intelligence*)

NOBODY RUNS FOREVER
aka The High Commissioner (US),
Nadie huye eternamente (Sp)

This is the least well known of director Ralph Thomas's sixties spy films, and deservedly so. Whereas *Hot Enough for June*, *Deadlier than the Male* and *Some Girls Do* are light, colorful concoctions, *Nobody Runs Forever* is a rather stodgy, histrionic affair. There is also some justifiable debate as to whether it actually belongs to the genre—seeing as how it doesn't feature any honest-to-God spies—but its pedigree and espionage plot qualify it as deserving of some discussion.

**DVD cover art for *Nobody Runs Forever***

Brash Aussie copper Scobie Malone (Rod Taylor) spends most of his time dealing with outback drunkards and purse snatchers, which means that he's more surprised than anyone when summoned to Sydney and assigned a red-hot case. Several years earlier, a man named Corliss had apparently murdered his wife and disappeared before any charges could be leveled. Now he has been tracked down. After assuming a new identity, he entered politics and is now no less than the High Commissioner, Jack Quentin (Christopher Plummer), himself.

Quentin is based in London, where he's currently chairing a high-fallutin' conference, and Malone is dispatched to bring him back quietly. Malone, however, has his doubts about the man's guilt, so isn't disagreeable when it's suggested that he should delay his mission for a few days. There's time enough to end the conference and bring about world harmony, peace and free school lunches for all. As long, that is, as Quentin doesn't mind him acting as an unobtrusive bodyguard during that time.

This soon proves to be rather convenient, as all manner of shenanigans are going on: assassination attempts are made; a hip CIA agent (Calvin Lockhart) is nosing around; somebody seems intent upon ruining the conference. Could it be party girl Maria (Daliah Lavi), of whom one smartass reasonably asks: "Does she look like the kind of girl who spends every night crying into her pillow over the state of the world?"

Considering that the story for this film is so patently ridiculous, the fact that it is tackled with an entirely straight face has to be admired, if not exactly commended. Beyond the preposterous central conceit of a wanted man becoming a respected (world- famous) diplomat, this also features some astoundingly dumb moments. At one point, Malone identifies someone as being a potential Communist because they...drive a red mini! Possibly the apogee of ludicrousness comes at the climax. When someone discovers that a large bomb has been hidden in a clock and has only 20 minutes until detonation, it is driven—by taxi—across London and dumped in the villain's lounge. Have these people ever tried to get from Hammersmith to Oxford Street in the rush hour?

All of this would be tolerable if the main thriller elements—did Quentin murder his wife? Who wants to disrupt the conference?—didn't feel so insubstantial. While the former question is explained in an outbreak of searing melodrama (thanks mainly to Lilli Palmer's over-the-top performance), the latter appears almost as an afterthought. No adequate explanation is given at all (beyond the fact that Miss Lavi is patently foreign and brunette).

While the production values are high enough, they have no chance in patching over these plot fissures. At least Rod Taylor is entertaining to watch, spending most of his time antagonizing the stuffy Brits and craving a cold beer. You also get some cool clips of late sixties-era tennis tournament Wimbledon, which all looks very genteel—almost as though the players are about to stop for a nice tea break at any moment.—MB

CREDITS: Production: Rank Film Organization, Selmur Productions, Rodlor Inc.; Director: Ralph Thomas; Story based on the novel by John Cleary; Screenplay: Wilfred Greatorex; Cinematography: Ernest Steward {Eastmancolor}; Music: Georges Delerue; Filming locations: London, Sydney; Country: USA/UK; Year: 1968

CAST: Rod Taylor (*Scobie Malone*), Christopher Plummer (*Sir James Quentin*), Lilli Palmer (*Sheila Quentin*), Camilla Sparv (*Lisa Pretorius*), Daliah Lavi (*Maria Cholon*), Clive Revill (*Joseph*), Lee Montague (*Donzil*), Calvin Lockhart (*Jamaica*), Derren Nesbitt (*Pallain*), Edric Connor (*Julius*), Burt Kwouk (*Pham Chimh*), Russell Napier (*Leeds*), Ken Wayne (*Ferguson*), Charles "Bud" Tingwell (*Jacko*), Franchot Tone (*Ambassador Townsend*)

## NONE BUT THE LONELY SPY
aka Ballade pour un voyou (Fr)

This film doesn't have much to offer the viewer in either quality or quantity. It is both too short (the English-dubbed print runs a mere 80 minutes or so) and too weak in storyline to amount to anything.

Vincent Vivant (Laurent Terzieff) is the hooligan of the original French title, who is hired to deliver a suitcase. We know the case belongs to a rogue spy, that it contains secrets to be sold, and that it is rigged to explode if forced open. When Vivant figures out that he will be killed upon completing his mission, he takes the case to a friend to see if they can get it open—which is where things start to go wrong.

Unfortunately, we couldn't care less by this point. We never get a sense of who Vivant is or how the relationships around him and with him have developed. We are left with two-dimensional characters in a one-dimensional story.

Hildegarde Neff, as Vivant's girlfriend Martha, is not given enough to do here, but she does have a couple of good scenes with the great (and very young-looking) character actor Philippe Noiret as the cop, Mathieu, who busted Vivant once upon a time. Supposedly there is something going on between Martha and Mathieu, but the script dances so lightly around their relationship that it doesn't ever take shape.

The only other genuine asset to the film is the presence of Daniel Emilfork as a very odd gangster assigned to tail Vivant. Emilfork, whose stark, birdlike appearance and strange manner make him the most memorable actor in the film, is apparently trying to learn the language by repeatedly listening to an educational record album, and can only repeat what he's heard no matter the situation. Emilfork was

**tFrench poster for *None But the Lonely Spy***

in a surprising number of spy movies—any of which are probably better than this one.

The score by Samson Francois is a sparse affair and although it is somewhat angular at times, it is generally conventional in nature.—DD

CREDITS: Production: Les Editions Cinegraphiques, Camera; Director: Claude-Jean Bonnardot; Music: Samson Francois; Country: France; Year: 1963

CAST: Laurent Terzieff (*Vincent Vivant*), Hildegard Knef (*Martha*), Michel Vitold (*Stephane Donnacil*), Daniel Emilfork (*Donacil*), Etienne Bierry (*Max*), Philippe Noiret (*L'inspecteur Mathieu*), Marc Duchamp (*Philippe La Roche*), Jacques Bertrand (*Martial*), Jean Martin (*Le chef de la P.J.*), Robert Bousquet (*Robi*), Andre Weber (*L'homme de surplus*), Nancy Holloway (*La modele noire*), Gisele Grimm (*La coiffeuse pour hommes*), Simone Rieutur, Yves Arcanel (*Un inspecteur*), Bruno Balp, Leo Baron, Jean Blancheur (*Sebastien*), Danile Crohem, Gilber Denoyan, Marc Eyraud (*Le radiologue*), Maurice Garrel (*Un inspecteur*), Olivier Mathot, Michel de Re (*Paul Verini*), Philippe Auber

OCCHIO PER OCCHIO,
DENTE PER DENTE
"eye for an eye, tooth for a tooth"
aka Agente Z-55, mision Coleman (It),
Destino: Estambul 68 (Sp)

Despite having a journalist—as opposed to a secret agent—as its hero, *Occhio per occhio, dente per dente* is worthy of inclusion in a listing of spy films. This is because it plays almost exactly like one and because it was marketed, in Spain at least, as the third and final entry in the Agent Z55 series. How true this was is debatable. Roberto Montero and German Cobos, director and star of both *Desperate Mission* and *Blueprint for a Massacre*, had jumped ship, their places filled by Miguel Iglesias and Giacomo Rossi Stuart. The name of the lead character had also changed (although, in fairness, it was inconsistent in the previous films) and, confusing matters even further, was now shared with that of the Eddie Constantine character in *Ces dames s'en mèlent* and *Jeff Gordon, Secret Agent*.

As for the plot: Jeff Gordon is a journalist who is about to poke his nose into a whole bunch of trouble. While carrying out an investigation into a counterfeiting ring, he runs into a particularly nasty bunch of bandits who, not keen on having their activities revealed in print, administer a severe beating to him. These guys are also about to step up their activities. Failing in their ambition to create perfectly forged banknotes, they kidnap the celebrated scientist Professor Norton, with the express intention that he should show them just how it can be done.

Gordon isn't about to give up, and joins forces with Mary, the Professor's daughter. Things are made more difficult because every time he comes close to uncovering the whereabouts of the gang, the person he's talking to happens to be murdered by some guy with a blow-dart cigarette holder (which does make you wonder why this dude doesn't just murder him). Fortunately, he does have some help: One of the gang is in reality an undercover Interpol agent, and together they set about calling a halt to these unsavory activities.

A decidedly minor film, this came rather late in the cycle and has remained resolutely obscure. It's not bad, but there's very little to recommend it as one to seek out. The plot is uninspiring, the direction and cinematography—despite having their moments—are no better than average. The first half feels very jittery, with scenes lacking any sense of cohesion, and it suffers as a whole from not having a truly notable villain. The pacing is also afflicted by the filmmaker's apparent need to insert a fight scene every three minutes. Admittedly, some of these are quite well done, but there is a fine line between action and overkill.

That said, some of the location work is decent enough, with some good chases through Turkish mosques, and there's a fun scene, stolen almost wholesale from *North by Northwest*, in which the hero is force-fed a bottle of whisky and coerced into driving down a dangerously winding road. There's also an entertaining moment set in the box at a baseball game, the amusement deriving from the fact that it's decked out in the most absurd 1940s wallpaper (did they really have this at sporting venues?). Giacomo Rossi Stuart is also rather good in the lead role. He has something of the arrogance that is demanded of the part, and it's a shame that he didn't have the starring role more often.

There are possibly two good reasons to look up *Occhio per occhio* (as well as simply for the sake of being a completionist). First, this has a rare substantial genre role for Pietro Ceccarelli, the bald Italian actor who played a henchman in a huge amount of these films (*Special Cypher*, *A Fistful of Diamonds* and many more). Like many actors of the time (Nello Pazzafini, Freddy Unger, Giovanni Cianfriglia, etc.), he started off as a stuntman before gaining larger and larger roles toward the end of the sixties. Here he effectively plays the main baddie (along with the strangely understated Giuliano Raffaelli [*Operation White Shark*]) and, although he's not exactly a great actor, he certainly has an undeniable presence—and looks as though he throws a mean punch.

Second, just when you can feel your eyelids begin to droop and over three-quarters of the running time has passed, you get an absolutely classic uncredited Victor Israel cameo. Spanish character actor Israel is something of a cult hero. His unprepossessing features have graced a huge number of Spanish films or co-productions, from westerns (*Companeros*) to horror films (*Night of the Howling Beast*)—though not, I trust, romantic comedies. Here he plays a drooling, eye-popping pervert with wild hair—just the type of guy your average heroine wants to avoid being locked up with. Especially as he has a strange predilection for covering people with creosote and feeding them to his rats.—MB

CREDITS: Production: Prod. Cin.cas Balcazar, Cineproduzioni; Director: Miguel Iglesias; Story: Simon O'Neill [Giovanni Simonelli]; Screenplay: Ray C. Calloway [Mario Colucci], Jose Antonio De La Loma, Alfredo Medori (Italian version); Cinematography: Jospeh L. Tower [Giuseppe La Torre] {Techniscope – Technicolor}; Music: Franco Pisano; Original running length: 107 mins; Country: Spain/Italy; Year: 1967

CAST: Jack Stuart [Giacomo Rossi Stuart] (*Jeff Gordon*), Lea Nicholls, Peter Barclay [Pietro Ceccarelli] (*Capo's henchman*), Monica Randall (*Nicole Sheldon*), Julian Rafferty [Giuliano Raffaelli] (*"Capo"*), Gilda Geoffrey, Luis Tejeda, Erik Shippers, Tomas Torres. Uncredited: Victor Isreal (*geek with rats*), Jack Rocha (*bald villain*)

## ONE-EYED SOLDIERS
aka Il Segreto dei soldati d'argilla (It)

In Nassam, a totalitarian (Eastern bloc) country, a man falls from the bell tower after being pursued through an old church. Before he dies, he is able to whisper the phrase "July 18th …one-eyed soldiers," but just what does he mean? Could it have anything to do with his job as a UN representative?

A short time later, reporter Richard Owens (Dale Robertson) arrives in the country, hoping to discover the secret behind the "one-eyed soldiers." He soon bumps into some curious traveling companions: Harold Zavor (Guy Deghy), a rotund, bizarrely accented fellow and Gheva Berens (Luciana Paluzzi), a feisty babe who's as adept with a gun as she is determined to cross the border. He also manages to antagonize the military authorities, who have an inherent dislike of Americans in the first place.

After absconding with Gheva (hey, who could blame a hot-blooded male?), he discovers that she is actually the dead man's daughter. Just about everyone is after her, because they believe that she may have some idea as to what her father's dying words meant. Unfortunately, she doesn't know a thing.

Zavor, however, does. He tells Owens it's all to do with Caporelli (Mile Avramovic), a notorious gangster who had started out as the commandant of a concentration camp. While carrying out this unsavory occupation, he had secreted a huge amount of money in a Swiss bank account, and had been using Berens as a money mule to ship it back across the border into Nassam. Unfortunately, the diplomat had taken it for himself, hiding it in an unknown location to which his last phrase must have been alluding.

*One-Eyed Soldiers* is an extraordinarily uneven film, even despite the fact that the version under review clocks in at a measly 70 minutes. The mood veers from that of zany parody to po-faced thriller at a moment's notice, almost as if two entirely different films have been cut together by a drunken editor (which may not actually have been far from the truth). The first half—all 35 minutes of it—is ridiculously confused, with absolutely no scene setting at all. We are introduced to Nassam as being ruled by a Soviet-style government/military police, but this interesting setting is then completely abandoned. By the end of the film, it seems as though the makers have forgotten about it all as well—but at least it gives a good reason for most of the cast to wear breeches at one point or other.

Despite this haywire quality, it's not by any means unenjoyable. Well, it doesn't really have the chance to be, but there are also some extremely odd things going on as well. There's a kind of Gothic, freak-show element to the proceedings, the kind of thing that David Lynch could easily have come up with. The villain not only has a very murky past, he also happen to be...a dwarf ("The dwarf, twisted shape of death!"). One with an extremely peculiar accent as well. I almost expected him to start dancing backwards at any moment. The diminutive despot has a suitable nemesis in Zavor's assistant, The Mute, a former victim who had had his ears and tongue cut off while he was a prisoner of war (and who drives around in a Mario Bava-style horse and carriage.

Completing the bizarre triumvirate of players is Guy Deghy, a portly British actor, who is immensely enjoyable and comes across as a cu-price—yet somehow even campier—Robert Morley. His girth gives rise to some terrible dialogue ("Has something upset you, such as a fat man...who interests me!") and some extremely poor attempts at humor. Not least is one sequence in which patrol guards attempting to apprehend him carry out their task by hauling in all the chubby people they can find. This includes a chambermaid, who is only revealed to be a "real" woman when her blouse is ripped off to reveal a gargantuan brassiere. She also happens to be played by Deghy, a very Morley-esque touch.—MB

CREDITS: Production: Debora Film; Director: Roy Ferguson [John Ainsworth], Jean-Christophe [John Ainsworth]; Story: Roy Ferguson [John Ainsworth]; Screenplay: Richard Aubrey; Cinematography: Enzo Serafin {Ultrascope - Eastmancolor}; Filming location: Yugoslavia; Country: Italy/Yugoslavia; Year: 1965

CAST: Dale Robertson (*Richard Owen*). Luciana Paluzzi (*Gava Berens*), Guy Deghy (*Harold Zabò/fat woman on bicycle*), Andrew Faulds (*Colonel Ferrer*), Mile Avramovic (*Antonio Caporelli, the dwarf*), Mirko Boman (*the mute*), Boza Drnic [Bozidar Drnic] (*Dr. Charles Berens*), Dusan Tadic (*Günther, Cap henchman*), Milan Bosiljcic, Dragan Nikolic (*1st Bernes pursuer*), Zvonko Jovcic (*Caporelli's overweight henchman*), Slavo Plavsic [Slavoljub Plavsic-Zvonce], Predrag Milinkovic (*police sergeant*), Milutin Mirkovic. Uncredited: Calisto Calisti (*taxi driver*), Piero Gerlini (*customs clerk*), Mario Lanfranchi, Tullio Altamura (*customs official*), Mirko Valentin (*Caporelli henchman in white jacket*).

## ONLY THE COOL

aka Children of Mata Hari (Int), Dossier 212 destinazione morte (It), Mision torpedo (Sp), La Peau de Torpedo (Fr), Pill of Death (UK)

This, one of the premier ambience films of the genre, appears at the end of the sixties cycle of spy films, a fitting coda to the genre. It is a serious, even dour film that focuses

**Soundtrack for *La Peau de Torpedo* (*Only the Cool*)**

equally on both sides of the espionage fence with sympathies for neither. Here, spying is a business but it is not without its emotions—emotions suppressed and discarded as required—and death is almost always a matter of honor. When death is unexpected, however, it is also unfair, a matter of happenstance that triggers far-reaching consequences.

Dominique (Stephane Adraun) is married to a spy, Nicolas (Frederic de Pascuale), but she doesn't know it. She thinks he deals in antiques and that his long trips are centered around lectures and acquisitions. But he's really a spy for the other side. His latest disappearance is actually an assignment to photograph some important documents. Upon his return to Paris, he is ordered to hole up with his contact (without telling the wife), which adds fuel to Dominique's long-burning fire of marital disillusionment. When a friend mentions that she saw him, Dominique tracks Nicolas down and in a moment of passion, kills him and the girl he was staying with. This event triggers movement by the French government in the person of Coster (Michel Constantine) and by his counterpart, Nicolas' boss, Helen (Lilli Palmer). Dominique goes on the lam without any idea of the repercussions of her actions, and hides out in a derelict freighter on the Normandy coast with its free spirit of a caretaker, Jean (Angelo Infanti). The rest of the film focuses on the machinations by both sides that inevitably lead to Dominique.

The complexities of the film extend beyond plotting. The good guys in the film are hardly more than ciphers: They play the espionage odds—sometimes winning, sometimes losing—without developing traits one would associate with human character. The bad guys on the other hand, are well-rounded people who suffer and consider but do their jobs anyway. There's a nice sequence involving an operative of Helen's who is obviously in love with her. She assigns him to search the apartment where Dominique killed her husband for the missing microfilm that is now, unbeknownst to Helen, in the hands of the government. The game of cat and mouse with Coster's agents following the fruitless search takes on the ironic qualities of a suicide mission. When Helen reads in the paper about her agent's death, her reaction is fleeting but deeply felt.

Helen is sent two hit men, "torpedoes." One is sent to eliminate Dominique while the other is there to tidy up any loose ends left dangling in case something goes wrong. Dominique's would-be killer is Pavel (Klaus Kinski, a man of many movies). Pavel is eccentric, of course, but restrained and business-like as well, and uses a harpoon-type pistol in the line of duty. Pavel's failure in his mission is spectacularly unspectacular: He breaks his back after taking a fall on the ship where Dominique has been hiding. In a brilliant bit of scripting, a helpless Pavel accepts the cyanide pill offered by Coster after Helen is apprehended because her capture wiped out any negotiating power that Pavel had. And Helen calmly and expectedly meets her maker in one of those terrific downbeat endings that would flourish in the films of the next decade.

Suicide—the controlled death—plays a large part in the film. It is a means of conquering enemies, expressing love, admitting defeat. It's those who live on in their confusion and misery that we must pity. The last shot of Dominique is one of despair as she gazes upon the calm, dead face of Helen, who accepted her death without hesitation.

This fine mood piece is complimented by a melancholy score by Francois de Roubaix that captures the ennui without bringing too much attention to itself.—DD

CREDITS: Production: Comacico, Films Copernic, Orion, Mars Film; Director: Jean Delannoy; Story based on the novel by Francis Ryck; Adaptation: Jean Cau, Jean Delannoy; Cinematography: Edmond Sechan, Didier Tarot; Music: Francois de Roubaix; Original running length: 110 mins; Country: France/Germany/Italy; Year: 1969

**A serious John Ericson wonders how he ended up in *Operation Atlantis***

CAST: Klaus Kinski (*Pavel*), Stephane Audran (*Dominique*), Michel Constantin (*Coster*), Lili Palmer (*Helen*), Jean Claudio (*Fedor*), Frederic de Pasquale (*Nicolas*), Georges Lycan (*Torpedo 2*), Angelo Infanti (*Jean*), Noelle Adam (*Laurence*), Pierre Koulack (*an inspector*), Michel Charrel (*an inspector*), Jacques Harden (*an inspector*), Christine Fabrega (*Sylviane*), Catherine Jacobsen (*Francoise*), Aime de March (*the salesman*), Bernard Musson (*the inspector at Fecamp*), Micheline Luccioni (*the post mistress*), Roger Favart (*the chief inspector*), Roger Lumont, Marie-Pierre Casey (*the woman at the morgue*), Rita Maiden, Paul Pavel, Yves Massard, Philippine Pascal, Christian Brocard (*man at the morgue*), Roland Malet (*police agent*), Gerard Dauzat

OPERATION ATLANTIS
aka 003 Agent secret (Fr),
Agente 003, operacion Atlantida (Sp),
Agente S03 operazione Atlantide (It)

This is one of those free-wheeling, stream-of-consciousness films that, while it may not actually be much good, remains hugely enjoyable, especially if tackled with the assistance of a large supply of margaritas. There's a definite feel of early-thirties programmer about it, a bizarre mixture of assorted thrills-and-spills with "futuristic" technology and silly costumes. It's all absolute hokum, of course, but since when has that been something to hold against a film?

Secret agent George Steel (John Ericson) is told a fantastic tale. Apparently a gaggle of survivors from Atlantis have made their new home in the wilds of North Africa, which by chance also happens to be on top of a huge hoard of uranium. Nobody seems to question this as being even remotely unusual. His job is to find out where it is and whether the Atlanteans can be negotiated with. However, there is a problem. A gang of international criminals, headed by a certain Ben Ulla (Beni Deus), is already on the trail—and they have a serious head start.

After his main contact is found dead, Steel takes the logical investigative step of going to a local nightclub (where a great song is being played in the background). Here he is knocked out with a drugged soda dispenser, packed into a suitcase and dumped into the cargo hold of a plane heading toward Arabia—apparently bound for Ben Ulla's desert camp. Fortunately, he has been assigned the help of Fatma (tiny munchkin Maria Granada)—who could well be a double agent—and she manages to arrange for his escape.

Then things start getting really strange. Using protective costumes (which look like funky diving suits), Fatma and Steel manage to get through the "magnetic force field" that protects the "new Atlantis." They find the inhabitants to be an amenable bunch—until, that is, their Princess (Berna Rock) falls for the American. It is soon revealed that the "Atlanteans" are, in fact, Chinese! They have discovered a new metal, rubidium, which originates from an ancient meteorite and gives off a deadly form of radiation (it has the somewhat unique effect of turning people into blocks of ice). God knows why they feel the need to adopt silly moustaches and the identity of a mythical civilization, but there you go.

Enormous fun, *Operation Atlantis* is undoubtedly one of those films that's best approached once the critical faculties have been somewhat disengaged. Casting a wide net, the scriptwriters try to borrow from just about every genre going: costumes from Flash Gordon, hero from Bond and desert sequences from *Lawrence of Arabia*. It all ends up playing like one of the late, fantastical peplums—most particularly those of the left field producer/director Emimmo Salvi (*Vulcan Son of Jupiter*, *The Giant of Metropolis* [directed by Umberto Scarpelli]).

One of the most enjoyable things about the whole nonsense is that, while there are many pleasurable incidentals to keep the viewer amused, the central plot just keeps getting wilder and wilder. It's hugely complicated, and virtually impossible to follow exactly what's going on, but that doesn't really matter when the events portrayed are becoming ever more eccentric with each minute. But I mentioned incidentals, and these include a goon equipped with a huge pair of deadly pincers, an X-ray scene in which the ribcage being viewed is about three times the size of the chest ostensibly housing it, a radio transmitter embedded in the hero's elbow and many more.

Technically, *Atlantis* isn't bad. Domenico Paolella was a better-than-average Italian director who had made several decent peplums and would later make a couple of good westerns (*Hate for Hate*, *Execution*) and crime films (*Stunt Squad*, *Gardenia*). This is probably his wackiest film, and is handled in a sturdy, unextravagant style. He seems particularly enamored of the aforementioned pincers, which he places in the foreground of several camera shots. There's also a great soundtrack.

German-born actor John Ericson (real name: Joseph Meibes) is, it has to be said, hardly the most animated of performers. In fact, he couldn't be more wooden if you were to paint him brown and put drinks on him. That said, he grows into the role and even demonstrates a certain flair for humor as the story gets ever more outrageous. Aside from appearing as guest star in a huge number of television series (*Murder, She Wrote; The A-Team*; *The Invaders*), he also cropped up in a number of films from the US (*Seven Faces of Dr. Lao, Bedknobs and Broomsticks*) and Europe (*Slave Queen of Babylon, Heads or Tails*).—MB

CREDITS: Production: Splendor Film, Fisa; Director: Paul Fleming [Domenico Paolella]; Story and Screenplay: Vinicio Marinucci, Victor Auz, Jose Lopez Moreno, Domenico Paolella; Cinematography: Raffaele Masciocchi, Francisco Sanchez Munoz {Techinscope – Technicolor}; Music: Teo Usuelli; Original running length: 95 mins; Filming location: Almeria; Country: Italy/Spain; Year: 1965

CAST: John Ericson (*George Steele*), Berna Rock [Bernardina Sarrocca] (*Albia, the chief's daughter*), María Granada (*Fatma, the sheikh's daughter and fake Balaban*), Carlo Hinterman (*Professor Günther Reich, a scientist*), Beni Deus (*chief of R.I.U./Benula*), José Manuel Martín (*Nailavi*), Erika Blanc (*Malavita, Nailavi's girlfriend*), Tullio Altamura (*adviser to Chief Solus*), Dario De Grassi [c.s.c.] (*Yussef, Nailavi's brother*), Mino Doro (*Chief Solus*), and with Cristina Gaioni [Cristina Gajoni] (*Rosie*). Uncredited: Luigi Tosi, Franco Ressel (*Fritz, lab worker*), Tina Conte (*nightclub singer*), Renato Terra Caizzi

## OPERATION COUNTERSPY

aka Agent Pik As—Zeitbombe Orient (WG), As de pic, operacion controespionaje (Sp), Asso di picche operazione controspionaggio (It)

Here's another recommended George Ardisson spy flick. If you're not a fan of Ardisson by now, you should be. He didn't make that many spy films and of those only a couple are truly enjoyable (*Passport to Hell* is a must-see), but Ardisson fits the spy guy bill to T. He's got the looks and the athletic skills and it's too bad he didn't have a long run in the genre like Ken Clark or Roger Browne. For a non-spy Ardisson fix, check out *Date for A Murder*.

What we have here is pretty standard spy stuff, but the cast holds some pleasures, it's colorful and well photographed, has lots of action, moves quickly and it's just nutty enough to be entertaining. Ardisson is Lord

George Moriston, a jetsetter who leads a double life as a spy. Moriston is called on to impersonate the Velvet Claw (Umberto Raho) and open the safe of a Russian spy. The safe contains photos of six cities, mysterious clues to…what? I'll tell you. They would eventually lead the curious to the underground lair of a lunatic villain, what else?

This is definitely a grade-B villain we're talking about here (as of this writing, we haven't been able to determine the actor's name). This fellow's "plan" is to ignite a worldwide nuclear war—creating devastation and havoc—and then take over what is left. It's not the best plan a super-villain ever came up with. In fact, when his evil female companion (Helen Chanel) gets wind of this, she calls him crazy and tries to kill him! When she fails at this, the villain slaps her around and chains her up onto his spider wall and whips her. The sight of Helen Chanel, garments rent, pinned to a wall with a giant spider pattern behind her should be enough to convince you of this film's merits.

Ardisson has plenty of opportunity to shine here. His Lord Moriston is too much of a rogue (he hits on every woman he meets and succeeds without fail), but he's got a smart wardrobe and gets in plenty of scrappy fights. The tight spots he finds himself in—and these are almost constant—are resolved in logical ways for a change. In fact, the script in general is very logically and methodically plotted, it's just that the payoff is silly.

Speaking of wardrobes, near the end of the film we join our villain in his underground lair and everyone—including the fat villain himself, who should know better—is wearing these silly silver jumpsuits with spiders on the chests (that unexplained spider motif again). When Chanel shows up without her suit on, she is scolded by her evil one, but she just laughs at him. "Did you really think I was going to wear one?" It's a great moment of reality. Another wardrobe eccentricity is the fact that all the bad guy's thugs wear blue turtlenecks so they can tell whose team they're on.

There are some cool cars in this movie—big ones with fins—which are always welcome. Chanel does a wicked belly dance and gets a long death scene. Moriston uses

**Unusual brooding artwork on the German poster for *Operation Counterspy***

an exploding bullet (loaded very carefully into his gun) and gets mildly tortured with electricity. And there's a nifty animation scene at the end when the villain is electrocuted and his body disintegrates into a pile a bones. Franco Pisano's score is forgettable. It would be nice to see a wide, clean print of this, since it appears to be quite accomplished in the areas of cinematography and art direction.—DD

CREDITS: Production: Cineproduzioni Associate, Prod Cin.cas Balcazar, Les Films Copernic, Herman Film; Director: Nick Nostro; Story and Screenplay: Sim O' Neill [Giovanni Simonelli], Nick Nostro; Music: Franco Pisano; Original running length: 107 mins; Filming locations: Barcelona, Paris, Turkey; Country: Italy/France/Spain/Turkey; Year: 1965

CAST: George [Giorgio] Ardisson (*Lord Moriston*), Lena Von Martens (*Alina*), Helene Chanel (*Pat*), Joaquin Diaz (*Oakis*), Corinne Fontaine (*Claudie*), Emilio Messina (*Peter*), Ricardo Rodriguez (*Gussie*), Umberto Raho, Angel Grey, Tom Felleghi, Thea Fleming, Leontine May [Leontina Mariotta] (*Alice*)

**American half-sheet for *Operation Double 007***

tOPERATION DOUBLE 007
aka O.K. Connery (Int), Operation Kid Brother (US), Operation frere cadet (Fr), Todos los hermanos eran agentes (Sp)

Another touchstone of the Eurospy subgenre, *Operation Double 007*, better known as *Operation Kid Brother*, is a fair Bond copy—albeit on a slightly smaller scale—and is as entertaining as any of the legitimate Bond films. This was the first time out for Neil Connery (brother of Sean) and it was the only spy movie in his movie mini-career. He manages just fine as the super-surgeon cum super-spy, although his distinct lack of charisma makes for a rather bland lead performance.

Fortunately, director Alberto De Martino keeps this colorful, active film moving at a good clip so we don't have too much time to mull over Connery comparisons. The use of Connery's real name for his character is a strange stroke, due no doubt to the forbidden use of the name Bond. It sort of screws up the (weak) attempts at Bond humor when you can't even say the word.

Thank goodness Connery is surrounded by exotic locations, beautiful women and villains as good as Adolfo Celi. Celi plays it to the hilt as Thair, the number-two villain of Thanatos who wants to be number one. Celi is deservedly one of the most famous Italian character actors, but perhaps the film's finest asset is the presence of the lovely Daniela Bianchi as Maya, a bad girl turned good.

Other actual actors holding this film up include a slew of Bond players such as Bernard Lee, whose Bond character "M" is called Cunningham for this outing. Familiar face Anthony Dawson plays the evil, soon-to-be-toppled Alpha, and Lois "Miss Moneypenny" Maxwell gets out of the office and into the action this time as the machine- gun-wielding Max.

Thair is one serious gadget-happy babe magnet. He does stuff like watch movies on the bare back of one of his multitude of women, and his yacht must be magical because it's easily twice as big on the inside as on the outside. He has a remote-control bomb car and gun barrels that descend from the ceiling of his office. He can wear a huge gold caftan when everyone else is in black tie—and pull it off. You gotta love this guy.

The first time we meet Connery he's giving a demonstration of a Tibetan hypnotherapy technique called "hypnosis of total recall" at a plastic surgeon's convention. Yeah, it's lame mumbo jumbo, but the funny bit happens when a kidnap attempt is made on his hypnosis subject. Suddenly a brawl breaks out and these mild-mannered plastic surgeons turn into fierce, fighting stuntmen who manage to defeat the bad guys.

This is an entirely gadget-driven flick. We have knives with shooting blades, elaborate (and time-consuming) mechanical methods of sneaking patients out of hospital rooms, the old flower-camera-in-the-lapel trick and feather boa dart guns. We even have a colored-light torture scene. This is where a little slice of overt lesbianism is displayed in a takeoff on the Rosa Klebb character from *From Russia with Love*. Drooling over the sobbing torturee, "Klebb" begs the girl to talk, making the attractive offer of "you'll live with me like a princess" as she fondles the girl. Creepy.

Other strange things happen in this movie as well. When Connery arrives in Malaga, Spain, there's a really crummy rock band playing at the airport for no reason. After Maya's troupe of Can-Can dancers waylay some troops, they change clothes and become members of The Wild Pussy Club! And for some reason, Thair has submarines docked next to his yacht. A lackey says to him, "Don't you think they look suspicious?" to which Thair basically says no.

The whole sequence where Connery semi-rescues a crew of blind workers from Thair's factory is bizarre. Thair hires blind people to make radioactive rugs. When Connery walks up to one of the blind rug makers and mentions that working with radioactive materials will kill him, the man suddenly yells to his buddies, "They're trying to murder us. That is why we have the sores. We must go!" The revolt is quelled, but the bitter taste of stupid plotting sticks with you.

Nonsense ranks high on this film's list. One of things that old Tibetan hypnotic technique is good for is leaving a bunch of information in the head of an unknowing subject. Connery says it makes the person a sort of "human electronic brain." Just think about that for a moment. We also have the logic of modifying a statue, valued at $900,000 for its perfection of beauty, so that it will shoot a sword blade into a bad guy. But hey, evilness makes weird things happen, I guess.

You could do worse than this Bondian escapade. There's plenty to look at and laugh at and there's a Morricone/Nicolai score to boot. We should be used to checking our brains at the door by now.—DD

CREDITS: Production: D.S. Cin.ca; Director: Alberto De Martino; Story: Paolo Levi; Screenplay: Paolo Levi, Frank Walker, Stanley Wright, Stefano Canzio; Cinematography: Alejandro Ulloa {Techniscope – Technicolor}; Music: Ennio Morricone, Bruno Nicolai; Original running length: 105 mins; Filming locations: Monaco, Marrakesh, Spain; Country: Italy; Year: 1967

CAST: Neil Connery (*Dr. Neil Connery*), Daniela Bianchi (*Maya*), Adolfo Celi (*Thair*), Agata Flory (*Mildred*), Yachuko Yama (*Miss Yashuko*), Bernard Lee (*Mr. Cunningham*), Lois Maxwell (*Max*), Franco Giacobini (*Juan*), Anna Maria Noe (*Lennie*), Anthony Dawson (*Alpha*), Guido Lollobrigida, Leonardo Scavino, Francesco Tensi, Vittorio Consoli, Mirella Pamphili, Nando Angelini, Franco Ceccarelli, Margareta Horowitz, Antonio Gradoli, Mario Soria

OPERATION HONG KONG
aka Da 077: criminali ad Hong Kong (It),
Mystère de la jongue rouge (Fr),
Mystery of the Red Jungle (US, alt),
Weisse Fracht fur Hong Kong (WG)

A large drug transaction being conducted off the Hong Kong coast goes badly wrong when a masked man on a powerboat makes off with the stash. It turns out that this is Robert Perkins (Horst Frank), ostensibly a happily married businessman but in reality a member of the gang which he has just duped.

Two agents working for "077," Larry MacLean (Brad Harris) and Ted Barnikoff (Dietmar Schoener), arrive on the scene. Their task is to expose the organization for which Perkins works, therefore stopping the illicit drug trade. Despite the fact that they're too busy chasing local skirt to get very far very quickly, they manage to meet Claire Landon (Maria Perschy), who is being used as an unknowing drug mule—she has bought a china Buddha in a local store that is stuffed full of heroin.

In the meantime, they pose as a couple of shady no-goods (without too much trouble, it must be said), and are hired as pilots by the organization. Before they find out any more they are arrested, and while they languish in jail, Ms. Landon is kidnapped. Unfortunately, an escape attempt is ruined when their accomplices—including Perkins, who has realized their true identity—betray them. Ted is captured and Larry is left for dead. Bad move, chaps.

In many ways, *Operation Hong Kong* can be seen as part of a grouping along with *Cave of Diamonds* and *The Secret of the Chinese Carnation*. They all share Oriental settings, an old-fashioned crime film structure (of the Edgar Wallace school) and a dull German star alongside the sterling Horst Frank, Brad Harris and (with the exception of *Carnation*) Philippe Lemaire (who comes across like Freddie Starr after a bottle of whisky).

This is a reasonably well-made film, but you can't help but feel that it lacks a certain something. It could be that it's all so relentlessly humorless or it could be that it never strives for any kind of eccentricity or uniqueness—but ultimately it's a disappointing experience. Giorgio Stegani, credited as director of the Italian version, went on to do much better work with *Ypotron*. Maybe it's unfair to blame him too much, as some of the trouble must certainly stem from the dual-billed Helmut Ashley—it would be interesting to discover just who was responsible for what—and the generally uninspired script.

Dietmarr Schonherr, the aforementioned dull German star, has actually had a long and estimable career. Starting off in the late forties with films such as *Junge Adler* and *Das Fraulein und der Vagabond*, his latest performance was in 2001's *Leo and Claire*. Along the way he was in several television productions, the most notable of which was *Raumpatrouille Orion*, an equivalent of *Star Trek*. Apart from being married to actress Vivi Bach, he also hosted a very early German game show (*Wunsch dir Was*) and various talk shows. He is now mostly known for his ecological campaigning and humanitarian work in Nicaragua. Which just goes to show that some actors can be more interesting offscreen than on.

Unfortunately—much as it pains me to say it—a cheesy nightclub act and some silly giant clothespin torture alone, even if combined with characters hiding under a mound of boxes clearly marked "explosives," do not a good movie make.—MB

CREDITS: Production: Rapid Film, Terra Film, Mercury Film, Gala International Film, S.te Nouvelle de C.ie; Director: Giorgio Stegani (Italian version), Helmut Ashley; Story and Screenplay: Werner P Zibaso; Cinematography: Klaus Von Rauthenfeld, Elio Polacchi {Ultrascope – Technicolor}; Music: Willy Matthes; Original running length: 88 mins; Filming location: Hong Kong; Country: West Germany/France/Italy; Year: 1964

CAST: Brad Harris (*Larry Maclean*), Maria Perschy (*Claire Landon/Claire Laudon*), Horst Frank (*Robert Perkins*), Philippe Lemaire (*Laurent*), Lily Mantovani (*Nancy Lee*), Mario Lanfranchi (*Colonel Strong*), Dietmar Schonherr (*Ted Barnikoff/Ted Barnekow*), Dorothy Parker (*Susan Collins*), Pascale Roberts (*Margaret Perkins*), Chu Shao Chuan, Yven Shiutai

OPERATION HURRICANE:
FRIDAY NOON
aka Jerry Cotton G-man agent C.I.A. (Fr),
La Jungla de los gangsters (Sp),
Schüsse aus dem Geigenkasten (WG),
Tread Softly (UK, unconfirmed)

This one is a favorite. The first film in the Jerry Cotton series, *OHFN* is also one of the most enjoyable—despite the meaningless and awkward retitling.

A gang of thieves operating with comical precision opens a secret safe in Pasadena, then travels to Chicago to unearth a cache of hidden gold bars. These interstate robberies—both of which include the cold-blooded murder of innocents—get the attention of the FBI. The only clues are a couple of vague phone calls to FBI headquarters and a single gold ingot left behind by the gang. This gold bar is Jerry's (George Nader) ticket to infiltrating the gang as they prepare for their biggest job yet, a diamond heist.

Shortly we're introduced to Jerry's boss, Mr. High (Richard Munch), who complains of being confined "behind a wall of filing cabinets" as he watches new recruits in training. Then we meet Jerry's partner Phil (Heinz Weiss) as he boxes a brute who outweighs him by a hundred pounds. Director Fritz Umgelter isn't above using symbolism to establish the omniscience of the FBI. For example, when Jerry and Phil meet in High's office, the boss' shadow covers one end of Manhattan to the other as he walks past a free-standing map of the island.

Jerry's infiltration of the gang is priceless. The gang operates out of a bowling alley and Jerry—dressed in his tough-guy teddy boy outfit—enters the bar and starts a fight to prove his worthiness. He practically wipes out the whole gang single-handedly before whipping out the gold bar and asking for a job. Notice how the score goes into a loop during the fight like a needle stuck in the groove of a record. Actually, the Peter Thomas score is tightly incorporated with the action throughout the film. Murmurs of the phrases "don't do it" and "crime doesn't pay" can be heard during the action, breaking the "fourth wall" with music. By the way, Thomas not only provided the music for the Cottons and many Edgar Wallace thrillers (most of which is available on CD), he also scored Harald Reinl's speculative documentaries *Chariots of the Gods* and *In Search of Ancient Astronauts*.

We've all seen unsuccessful uses of rear projection in low-budget films, but one sequence in *OHFN* takes the cake. After his true identity is discovered by the gang, Jerry makes his escape by leaping onto a passing truck. There's a shot of Nader hanging onto a truck as footage of streets whizzing by is actu-

**Belgian poster for *Operation Hurricane: Friday Noon,* the film that launched the Jerry Cotton series**

ally projected onto the side of the truck itself! You'll be rewinding that tape to make sure you saw what you thought you saw.

Another classic Jerry Cotton moment occurs late in the film when Kilborne (Franz Rudnick), the leader of the gang, is holding a gun on JC. Jerry calmly admonishes Kilborne to think carefully before firing: "Nobody shoots an FBI man. That's one rule all outlaws respect." Kilborne hesitates just long enough for Jerry to draw his gun and shoot. "Because we're faster," Jerry adds matter-of-factly.

We get one last cheesy special effect in the finale. Phil takes a speedboat over to the pier where the rest of the gang meets up, and finds himself in pulp-style danger as the gang rolls flaming barrels of gasoline at him. He escapes in the melee but the boat is destroyed. Actually it's a little toy boat that explodes with all the force of a firecracker. Not exactly a James Bond budget, but it's all in good fun.

On a side note, both Heinz Weiss and Richard Munch played villains in Edgar Wallace films: Weiss in *The Green Archer* and Munch in *Inn on the River*. And in those films, each used similar means of dispatching their enemies: Weiss a bow and arrow and Munch a spear gun.—DD

CREDITS: Production: Studio Hamburg, Allianz Film, Astoria Films; Director: Fritz Umgelter; Story based on the novel "G-Man Jerry Cotton"; Screenplay: Georg Hurdalek; Cinematography: Albert Benitz {B&W}; Music: Peter Thomas; Original running length: 89 mins; Filming locations: New York, Berlin; Country: West Germany; Year: 1965

CAST: George Nader (*Jerry Cotton*), Heinz Weiss (*Phil Decker*), Richard Munch (*Mr. High*), Hans E. Schons (*Cristallo*), Franz Rudnick (*Kilborne*), Helmut Förnbacher (*Percy*), Robert Rathke (*Latschek*), Hans Waldherr (*Babe*), Philippe Guégan (*Sniff*), Sylvia Pascal (*Kitty*), Heidi Leupolt (*Mary*), Helga Schlack (*Helen*), Joachim Rake (*Camp-Leiter*), H.M. Crayon (*Everett*), Matthias Ndongé (*William*), Willy Wiesgen (*Anstreicher*), Marinda Ambrozia (*Viktoria*), Mita von Ahlefeldt (*Mrs. Baker*), Frank Strass (*Dr. Bliss*)

OPERATION POKER
aka Operación Póker: agente 05-14 (Sp), Operazione poker (It)

Yet another of Roger Browne's half-dozen spy flicks and the first one for director Osvaldo Civirani. This is a rather middle-of-the-road film, but it is unusual in that we get two adventures for the price of one. The code name "Operation Poker" refers to Glenn Forest's (Browne) assignment to observe the former assistant to a Russian professor (who likes to play poker) and try to figure out not only what the stolen invention is, but where it is. Sounds hard? It must be, since they give up the entire operation when the answers are not forthcoming. The next assignment is to safeguard a Vietnamese diplomat who is promptly kidnapped. Actually, the diplomat is working for the Red Chinese and as luck would have it, he wants the same invention the Americans want. Things tend to work out for Forest, I'd say.

There are also two main femmes fatale but neither one's talents are showcased. Top-billed Jose Greci is simply one of Forest's girlfriends, who seems to follow him around the world bitching about how he never has time for her. Last-billed Helga Line is also a paramour of Forest's, but she's really a Russian agent who is killed early in the film for supposedly blowing her cover.

The invention everyone is after is definitely of the science fiction type. It's a special tie-clip that when used with a pair of infrared

**Appropriate imagery on the Belgian poster for *Operation Poker* starring Roger Browne**

contact lenses enables the user to see through walls. The guy who stole it from the professor is putting it to good use by wearing it while playing poker—and cleaning up. He should think bigger. The first thing Forest does when he discovers this little novelty is use it to spy on his girlfriend getting dressed. That's more like it.

The poor secret agents unlucky enough to be assigned to the diplomat's case all end up meeting elaborate ends. One agent is shot by his car when he steps on the gas pedal. Another is blown up by a remote-control boat and yet another—female naturally—is gassed while taking a shower.

This film really gets around. We travel from the Riviera to Geneva to Paris to Casablanca (the Casbah no less) and to Copenhagen. We even get a tour of the Tuborg brewery—there's a prolonged gun battle amidst the giant beer tanks. Talk about product placement. We have several fights of course, but only one of them is a good, long knock-down-drag-out that leaves both participants gasping for air. And there's one funny scene where Forest is surprised by a gunman in his back seat. So what does he do? He pushes a button and the entire back half of his car ejects!

For all its advantages, this isn't really a very good film. As I mentioned, it is middle-of-the-pack stuff. You could do worse, but you could definitely do better.—DD

CREDITS: Production: Wonder Film, Alcocer; Director: Osvaldo Civirani; Story and Screenplay: Roberto Gianviti; Cinematography: Alfonso Nieva; Music: Piero Umiliani; Original running length: 120 mins; Filming locations: Incir-De Paolis, Ballesteros Studios; Country: Italy/Spain; Year: 1966

CAST: Roger Browne (*Glenn Forest*), Jose Greci (*Liz Anderson*), Sancho Gracia (*Johnny Parker*), Helga Line (*Diana*), Bob Messenger [Roberto Messina] (*Omar*), Carol Brown [Carla Calo] (*an enemy agent*), Andrea Scotti (*Frederick Anderson, an agent*), Angel Ter, Catherine Schouse, Rufino Ingles (*an intelligence chief*), Jose Riesgo, Mario Donen (*Erik Broder, an agent*), Gregorio Wu (*Yun Tao*), William Bo, Juan Cortes (*an intelligence chief*). Uncredited: Emilio Messina (*a henchman*)

OPERATION WHITE SHARK
aka AD3 operation raquin blanc (Sp),
AD3 operazione squalo bianco (It)

Welcome to the low-rent district. While *Operation White Shark* is colorful in places, it is clear that the filmmakers were working with a budget embarrassingly low even for Eurospy knockoffs. The opening scene provides the first clue: The head of Intelligence has an office that consists of a desk, a couple of props and blue curtains that suffice for walls. We're in for some third-rate spy action.

It's the old kidnapped scientist routine for this adventure, but it will take an extraordinary man to accomplish the mission since the qualifications are described thusly: "We must find a man with perfect knowledge of Italian, French and a complete understanding of nuclear science and the man must also be an expert sailor." No problem. The computer, "Jerry," recommends Mark Andrews, agent A.D.3 (Rodd Dana, aka Robert Mark). When we first meet Andrews he's in a barroom brawl in what must have been the only available set, an Old West saloon outfitted with a Pepsi machine. This is America, folks, really. When Andrews' flight to Europe arrives, he's smooching so heavily with the girl in the seat next to him that he doesn't realize the plane has landed. Now I think we have an idea what our man is like.

Andrews' contact is Terry Benson (Franca Polesello) and Andrews does his best, in true spy tradition, to demean her as an empty-headed broad. But notice when the two are attacked on the dark alley set that Terry dispatches three female assassins attired in black leotards while Andrews can only manage to subdue their supremely fat leader after she tosses him a gun.

There's no true villain in the film—only a vague criminal organization known as The Third Eye—but one of the rival gangs is headed by sexy Janine Reynaud. We're introduced to her character, Freda, in a club as she belts out a cool song with a snazzy rock combo behind her. Reynaud is excellent when it comes to providing convincing lesbian overtones. After capturing Terry, Freda caresses herself slowly as her minions threaten Terry with a blowtorch.

**Enticing artwork on the Italian locandina for the low budget *Operation White Shark***

This is one of those movies with many quotable lines. The fun begins in the first scene (the one with the curtain walls) as the mission is being discussed. When the head of Intelligence says "The first experiment is scheduled in less than a week. We must put a stop to it," the response given is, "That gives us less than a week's time, boss." After a bar fight with Andrews, one of the hoods is told, "Don't act like an idiot, well not here anyway." The secret device that everyone's after is described like this: "It's what scientists call an atomic detonator." What I thought was the funniest line is spoken by Lucia Modugno as she chats with Andrews: "One thousand plus two hundred more equals one thousand two hundred." Andrews responds with, "You sure are a whiz with figures."

Dialogue does not provide the only humorous moments. When Andrews infiltrates the underwater atomic lab he strangles one bad guy using the remote-control arms designed for handling dangerous materials. Cool. Andrews no sooner gets the kidnapped scientist out of his cell when the poor guy is shot in the back. He didn't even get three feet! However, much of the movie consists of threadbare sets, boring boat chases and even more boring underwater fights. And in the grand finale we are expected to believe that Freda can be trapped when Andrews drops a fishing net over her escaping boat. On the plus side, Robbie Poitevin provides an entertaining score that far outshines anything on the screen.

Trivia note: The Italian two-sheet poster for *Operation White Shark* is prominently displayed during an episode of television's *I Spy* called "The Bridge of Spies" (11/19/66) that takes place in Italy. The gag is that the "real life" spying done by our heroes Culp and Cosby is nothing like the grandiose adventures portrayed on the poster. Unfortunately for us, the artwork on the poster is much more exciting than the movie it advertises.—DD

CREDITS: Production: Madison Film; Director: Stanley Lewis [Walter F. Ratti]; Story: Luigi Angelo, Italo Fasan, Filippo Ratti; Screenplay: Luigi Angelo; Cinematography: Vitaliano Natalucci; Music: Robby Poitevin; Original running length: 85 mins; Filming location: Elios Studios; Country: Italy; Year: 1966

CAST: Rodd Dana [Robert Mark] (*Agent AD3*), Franca Polesello (*Terry*), Alan Banthe, Francesco Mule, Janine Reynaud (*Freda*), Lucia Modugno, Nino Vingelli, Julian Rafferty [Giuliano Raffaelli], Louis Moore, Robert Kurt, Fernand Angels, Fred Tyler, Gianni Manera, Aldo Sala, Tullio Altamura, Mary Anthony, Silvano Silvani, Nino Nini, Vittorino Mangano, Romolo Diori, Giana Matarazzo, Elio Bonadonna, Pietro Ruffini

OSS 117 DOUBLE AGENT
aka Murder for Sale (US, alt), Niente rose per OSS 117 (It), No hay flores, OSS 117 (Sp), Pas de roses pour OSS 117 (Fr)

The role of novelist Jean Bruce's hero Hubert Bonnisseur de la Bath (actually from a novel by Josette Bruce this time) is taken by John Gavin. Here Bath is using the name Jonathan Roberts, who impersonates "Killer" Chandler, who is then given the name James Mulligan to accomplish his assassination mission. Got that? We'll stick with Roberts for convenience. It's all a rather complex ruse in this so-so adaptation redeemed in part by an interesting cast and a bouncy score by Piero Piccioni.

**John Gavin hops over his designation on the Belgian poster for *OSS 177 Double Agent***

Roberts is a bland hero in a bland movie with bland ambition. The film opens nicely with Roberts and company robbing a bank—and slaughtering several cops and innocent bystanders during their getaway. The whole thing turns out to a fake, put up by Roberts to secure his plastic surgery-enhanced impersonation of "Killer" Chandler. Those shot down were in on the plan and one female "victim" remarks in the ambulance how Roberts, after his surgery, is "even better looking now." The supposed robbers switch cars later, but they change to a car that is the same model and color as the one they used in the robbery! They still escape detection by the local bumbling cops.

The ever-dependable Curd Jurgens as The Major runs The Organization, which coerces criminals into performing high-level assassinations. Jurgens, playing his villain with an effeminate touch, gets most of the good lines in the film. After rescuing Roberts from the cops, Roberts thanks The Major for saving his life, to which The Major replies "Lives are hardly worth saving." Near the end of the film when things start falling apart for The Major, he clasps his hands together, and looking skyward says, "Oh, when will my prayer for one single intelligent henchman be answered?" That's a question the audience has no doubt been asking too.

While The Major is sitting around his fancy villa listening to his thugs play classical music, others in the cast pay their dues. The delectable Rosalba Neri has a small part as Conchita, the exotic dancer who turns Roberts into the cops. Brightening the screen only for mere minutes, Neri drops out of sight too quickly but not before teasing us with some skin. Luciana Paluzzi is Maud, The Major's doctor in residence. She sleeps with Roberts but then has the dirty task of "vaccinating" him with poison. This is the premiere device of the film: Roberts must get a shot of the antidote at a precise time of the day during his assignment or he will die. You just know the filmmakers are going to milk this for all it is worth and they do try. But we know Roberts isn't going to die, so when the time comes to sweat the situation out, the whole thing seems contrived and irritating.

Robert Hossein plays the doctor who must administer the antidote to Roberts. Roberts' main squeeze is Aicha (Margaret Lee), daughter of the banker who ordered the hit that Roberts is assigned. George Eastman—whose list of acting pseudonyms is as long as his arm—plays Karas, The Major's right hand man. He's all long hair and beard and Roberts calls him Neanderthal.

The film is played with tongue firmly in cheek; fisticuffs with bullfight music in the background, silly cops, stuttering henchmen and lines like, "The truth seldom comes out and never out of the mouth of a woman." The bad guys use poorly chosen code names to communicate on the short wave radio, so when ruffian Karas picks up the microphone and says "Goofy here!" we know we're in trouble.

The convolution of names for our hero is symptomatic of the plot. Near the end of the film Roberts fakes the death of the man he was sent to kill, Van Dyck, and then narrowly escapes death himself. The result is some people think Van Dyck is dead and some people think Roberts is dead, while other people know one or the other is alive. It's all so confusing! The grand finale just peters out when Karas shoots his own boss, so the last not-so-big fight is between Karas and Roberts. The Major doesn't even have enough life in him to pull the self-destruct lever he showed us earlier. Ho hum. There are certainly better OSS 117 films and better spy flicks in general for you to waste your time on.—DD

CREDITS: Production: Da. Ma. Cin.ca, P.A.C.; Director: Jean-Pierre Desagnat, Renzo Cerrato; Story based on a novel by Jean Bruce; Screenplay: Michel Levin, J.P. Desagnat, Pierre Foucaud, Renzo Cerrato, Andre Hunebelle; Cinematography: Tonino Delli Colli {Technicolor}; Music: Piero Piccioni; Original running length: 110 mins; Filming location: Cinecitta Studios, Rome; Country: France/Italy; Year: 1966

CAST: John Gavin (*Bath/Roberts*), Curd Jurgens (*"The Major"*), Luciana Paluzzi (*Maud*), Margaret Lee (*Aisha*), George Eastman [Luigi Montefiore] (*Karas*), Guido Alberti (*Melik*), Piero Lulli (*Van Dyck*), Robert Hossein (*Dr. Saadi*), Rosalba Neri (*Conchita Esteban*), Renato Baldin [I] (*CIA agent*), Luciana Bonanni (*the policeman*), Romano Moschini, Rajan Baldwin [Raf Baldassarre], Seyna Seyn, Giovanna Pallavicino, Roberto Messina, Emilio Messina

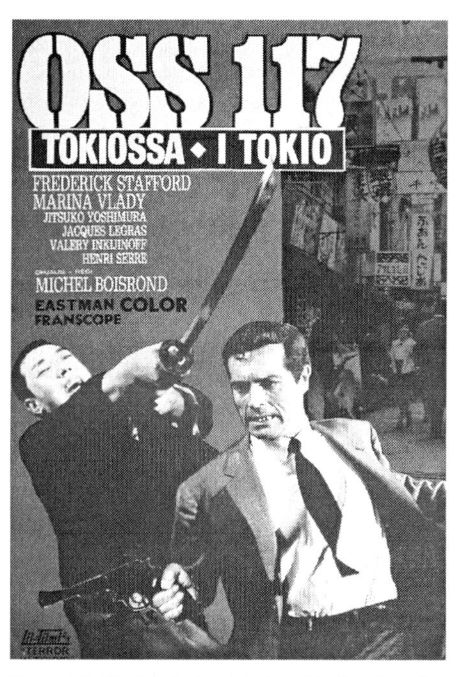


**Frederick Stafford about to lose his head on the Finnish poster for *OSS 117 From Tokyo With Love***

OSS 117 FROM TOKYO WITH LOVE
aka Atout coeur à Tokyo pour OSS 117 (Fr),
OSS 117 a Tokyo si muore (It),
OSS 117—Teufelstanz in Tokio (WG),
Terror in Tokyo (Int), Tokio hora cero (Sp)

Frederick Stafford's second and last adventure as Hubert Bonniseur de la Bath, aka OSS 117 is a well-made but ultimately disappointing feature. The film starts out with a nifty car chase, but unfortunately that level of excitement is never regained and the result is a rather dull film. The self-assured Stafford is never allowed to showcase the talents he displayed in *OSS 117 Mission for a Killer* and even the lovely Marina Vlady isn't enough to perk things up.

This time Hubert is assigned the task of derailing the plans of The Organization, whose new weapon is a missile that can't be detected or destroyed. The missiles are deployed from miniature F107 planes that are launched from a ship at sea. Vlady plays Eva Wilson, the wife of John (Henri Serre), a bigwig in The Organization. Part of the problem with the film is the lack of a good villain. John Wilson is only one of several ill-defined characters who run things, so we never get a handle on just what Hubert is up against.

Director Michel Boisrond does what he can with the material, but the lack of a good story dooms this from the start. Michel Magne's score is appropriately flavored with Asian spice but is otherwise forgettable.

There are some semi-interesting bits to keep an eye out for if you find yourself unable to resist a viewing. There's a horrendously ugly brooch that doubles as a transmitter, which comes with the standard eyeglasses used as receiver. There's a Rube Goldberg reference, too. We also have a scene in a photography parlor where the customers take pictures of strippers in action.

The dialogue is not completely without humor. At one point Eva asks Hubert, "Has anyone ever slapped your face?" To which he replies, "No. I usually kill them before they get their hand up."

And there's a pretty good fight between Hubert and a giant Japanese fellow and I mean giant. This guy is huge. Hubert even sets him on fire during the tussle! Hubert must do battle against a sword-wielding opponent at one point and manages to escape becoming a pincushion.

Jitsuko Yoshimura plays a Japanese Secret Service agent and I could swear that she was one of the eponymous *Black Tight Killers*, a terrific spy-type action thriller made the same year in Japan.

At any rate, I recommend checking out *OSS 117 Mission for a Killer* to see what Stafford is capable of when given the right material. You can skip this one as an also-ran that doesn't measure up.—DD

CREDITS: Production: P.A.C., Films Victory, Lux; Director: Michel Boisrond [Co-directors: Michel Wyn, Jean-Pierre Desagnat]; Story based on the novels by Jean Bruce; Screenplay: Marcel Mithois; Cinematography: Marcel Grignon {Eastmancolor, Franscope}; Music: Michel Magne; Original running length: 90 mins; Country: France/Italy; Year: 1966

CAST: Frederick Stafford (*Bath, OSS 117*), Henri Serre (*John Wilson*), Colin Drake (*Babcock*), Marina Vlady (*Eva Wilson*), Valery Inkijinoff (*Yekota*), Mario Pisu (*Vargas*), Jacques Legras (*Chan*), Jitsuko Yoshimura (*Tetsuko*), Billy Kearns (*Smith*), Eric Vasberg (*the chauffeur*), Hiroshi Kato, Kan Nikonyanagi, Hiroshi Minami, Del Negro, Bert Bertram, Jean Lemaitre, Jacques Francel, Eiju Kim

## OSS 117 MISSION FOR A KILLER

aka Furia à Bahia pour OSS 117 (Fr), Furia en Bahia (Sp), OSS 117: furia a Bahia (It), OSS 117—Pulverfass Bahia (WG)

This was director Andre Hunebelle's third crack at OSS 117, the hero of Jean Bruce's novels, and we consider it probably his best effort. Hunebelle made two others in the series before this and he would try once more, but it was pretty much a hollow exercise by then.

*OSS 117 Mission for a Killer* has a lot going for it, including Frederick Stafford. He's just right as the smart and tough Hubert Bonnisseur de la Bath. He has an easy air of capability about him and we were surprised to learn that this was his first film credit. Stafford, who died in a plane crash in 1979, played the same role in *OSS 117 From Tokyo with Love*. His biggest break, however, came when he played the lead in *Topaz* for Alfred Hitchcock.

After four political assassinations occur inside a month—all perpetrated by drug-induced innocents—Hubert is sent to Rio to track down the source of the narcotic. Since it's Rio, we are treated to the requisite Carnival footage, but it doesn't take up too much time. The Latin-inflected score by Michel Magne is just fine and in fact blends well with the Rio and Bahia area locations.

Our heroine this time is played by Mylene Demongeot. Her character, Anne-Maria, is a refreshing change of pace. She's a pretty tough cookie who's not afraid to get into the action. This was Demongeot's only spy flick, but she appeared in all three of the Fantomas films made in the sixties.

And speaking of action, this film has plenty. Stafford is a good fighter and the fight choreography in general is first-rate and exciting. One memorable fight involves a bad guy with a blowtorch who during the course of the fisticuffs sets his cohort on fire not once but twice, and it is very convincing. Another good fight is played out aboard a private jet, and when the pilot is accidentally shot during the melee, it's nail-biter time as Hubert and company try to subdue the thugs and gain control of the aircraft.

There's a nifty action sequence when Hubert and Anne-Maria are driving out to her ranch in Bahia. The opposition sets the road on fire in front of them and when they stop, the road behind them is also set ablaze. Well, Hubert simply drives through wall of flame but as he races down the road we see that his tires are on fire! It's a fun image to see this car driving down the road with all four tires engulfed in flames.

There's intentional humor too. Hubert, ever the ladies man, is asked if he is fond of children and responds, "Yes, when their mother's pretty." When he takes Anne-Maria out to dinner, Hubert asks for champagne. When the waiter brings it, Hubert asks what kind it is and the waiter says it's from Mexico. Hubert then asks what kind of whisky they have and the response is Portuguese scotch, so he orders two Brazilian vodkas instead.

The rest of the cast is largely unknown, at least within the spy genre. You may recognize a couple of faces among the supporters, however. One is Perrette Pradier, who impersonates Consuela Moroni, the secretary of Hubert's contact in Rio. You might say she's a phony Moroni. Sorry.

Our villain is Carlos (Francois Maistre), the leader of a small army who entertains mad visions of world domination from a compound deep in the Brazilian jungle. Once Hubert and company have been captured and brought to the compound, the film turns into your basic shoot-'em-up fare. Things blow up real good and a military air strike is called in, turning the proceedings into a jungle warfare flick. Anne-Maria is kidnapped as a last-ditch effort to shield the villain, but she overturns the boat in which they were escaping and Carlos is sent over the falls to his demise. The final stunt has Hubert jumping from a plane into the river to save Anne-Maria, and the last scene is the two of them in tight embrace amidst the beautiful raging waterfalls. To sum up, this is a superior example of the genre and well worth seeking out.—DD

**French poster for *OSS 117 Mission For a Killer***

CREDITS: Production: P.A.C., P.C.M.; Director: Andre Hunebelle; Story based on a novel by Jean Bruce; Screenplay: Jean Halain; Cinematography: Marcel Grignon {Eastmancolor}; Music: Michel Magne; Original running length: 99 mins; Country: France/Italy; Year: 1965

CAST: Frederick Stafford (*Hubert Bonnisseur de la Bath/OSS 117*), Raymond Pellegrin (*Leandro*), Mylene Demongeot (*Anne-Maria*), Francois Maistre (*Carlos*), Jacques Riberolles (*Miguel Sulza*), Yves Furet (*Clark*), Guy Delorme (*Karl*), Perrette Pradier (*Consuela Moroni*), Rico Lopez (*Ellis' killer*), Jean-Pierre Janic (*Ludwig*), Dominique Zardi (*the killer*), Yvan Chiffre (*a henchman*), Adjudo Ribiero (*Enrique Salerno*), Claude Carliez (*Tomas Ellis*), Gilbert Servien (*the hospital receptionist*), Jean Minisin (*Ellis' killer 2*), Michel Thomass, Richard Saint-Brus (*the director of the hotel*), Eric Vasberg (*a henchman*), Henri Attal (*a killer*), Gerard Moisan, Andre Cagnard, Guy Fox

**French poster for *OSS 117 Prend des vacances***

OSS 117 PREND DES VACANCES
"OSS 117 takes a holiday"
aka OSS 117 Takes a Vacation
(US, unconfirmed)

In need of some rest and recreation, OSS 117 (Luc Merenda) decides to visit his aunt, Countess de Labarthe (Edwige Fueillere) at her country estate. No sooner has he arrived than he's attacked by a couple of hoodlums in the stables, but nobody seems to pay much attention to this—they're more concerned with trying to encourage a taciturn parrot to speak. After another fracas, he decides that spending his holidays in Brazil would be a far more relaxing proposition.

His idleness doesn't last long. A killer has been hired to dispose of him, and the callous fellow shoots a cocktail shaker out of his hands. It's just hellish trying to plan a tranquil recreation when you're a dashing secret agent (although he could think of spending it in Switzerland; nothing ever happens there). Several more assassination attempts fail—including one in which a young lady, with whom Hubert is dallying, conveniently loses all of her clothes.

Behind all of these disruptions is a certain Colonel Balestri (Jess Morgane), who lives in a fantastic, inaccessible mansion on a cliff edge. He also has a predilection for bird impersonations, a personal samba band and a prima donna of a wife (Genevieve Grad), who spends most of her time shagging the servants.

This was the final OSS 117 film, and represents the bog-end of the series in much the same way as *The Tiger Gang* did for the Kommissar X films (or, perhaps, *Never Say Never Again* for the Bond franchise). It came right at the end of the spy film cycle, just squeezing in before the arrival of the seventies, and is a very tired affair indeed. It has a couple of serious problems. First, the script is absolutely terrible, there is no narrative flow and it all ends up seeming a bit pointless. Second, it really doesn't know where to position itself. Is it a comedy or a thriller? It's certainly not very tense, and the parody elements are never really developed.

As if acknowledging these ruinous deficiencies, Pierre Kalfon attempts to divert the audience's attention by throwing just about every conceivable gimmick into the mix. The editing is frankly bizarre, including irrelevant inter-cuts and freeze-frames (my favorite of which is some stock footage of wild boars foraging, shunted inconsiderately into the middle of a fight scene). The attention of the camera occasionally floats off into nowhere, allowing for some descriptive text to scroll up the screen or another monologue to echo forth from one of the lead characters. Dramatic musical cues blast from the soundtrack at entirely inappropriate moments, and there are some really strange sound effects going on (one scene has the completely inexplicable noise of a woman continuously whimpering in the background, which nobody even comments upon).

It's a bit of a shame, as it's not all bad. The Brazilian locations are effective, there are some decent action sequences, and the climactic pyrotechnics are relatively impressive. Luc Merenda is also rather good in the lead role. Handsome and acrobatic, he seems to be rehearsing for his later crime film persona that was to develop throughout the following decade. Tarcizio Meira, a prolific Brazilian television star, also puts in a good performance as a killer. Amusingly, there's a cameo for an irritating little hippie who looks suspiciously like notorious director Jesus Franco.—MB

CREDITS: Production: Films Number One, Vera Cruz Films, Inducine; Director: Pierre Kalfon; Story based on the novel "Vacances pour OSS 117" by Jean Bruce; Screenplay: Pierre Kalfon, Jean Bruce; Dialogue: Pierre Philippe; Cinematography: Etienne Becker {Eastmancolor}; Music: Andre Barly; Original running length: 90 mins; Filming location: Brazil; Country: France/Italy/Brazil; Year: 1969

CAST: Luc Merenda (*Hubert, OSS 117*), Norma Bengall (*Anne*), Edwige Feuillere (*Countess de Labarthe*), Elsa Martinelli (*Elsa*), Genevieve Grad (*Paulette Balestri*), Jess Morgane (*Colonel Balestri*), Tarcizio Meira (*the killer*), Rossana Ghessa (*Anna*), Sergio Hingst (*Santowski*), Ivan Roberto, Marie-Laure Marcombes (*Diane*), Pierre Philipe, Pierre Dourne, Yann Arthur (*Yann*), Jorge Luis Costa (*Flavio*), Almir De Freitas (*Almir*), Vittorio Rubello (*Marcello*), Bernard Lorain (*the general*)

OSS 117 SE DECHAINE
"OSS 117 breaks out"
aka OSS 117 (Sp), OSS 117 segretissimo (It)

This was the first of the OSS 117 series, based on a series of books by Jean Bruce. As such, it was one of the swiftest off the mark among the post-Bond franchises—and with its final installment coming in 1969 (*OSS 117 prend des vacances*), it was also the longest lasting. In many ways it shows its early vintage. It has more the feel of a late- fifties noir than a mid-sixties spy film. There's no criminal mastermind, no gadgets and no ribald silliness. There is, however, lots of talking.

While exploring some underwater caverns in Corsica, diver Renotte (Henri-Jacques Huet) is attacked and the man who hired the diver, Roos (Jacques Harden)—a secret agent—is killed by an unseen assailant. Womanizing playboy Hubert Bonisseur de la Bath, aka OSS 117 (Kerwin Mathews)—who thinks nothing of spontaneously shagging female strangers (and they enjoy it!)—is sent to investigate. Attacked by an ugly goon with a knife within five minutes, he seems perfectly capable of disposing of all who try to stop him.

Renotte, meanwhile, is doing his own investigating—assisted by token blonde Brigitta (Nadia Sanders). Pretty soon someone has laced their whisky with poison, and although Hubert manages to interrupt the guilty party, he is too late to save the diver's life. Even worse, he also becomes the main suspect.

It's all down to a network of spies who have infiltrated the island. They are using the underground grottos as a base from which they can monitor the activity of American nuclear submarines, and are determined to protect their secret at all costs. They also have a mole in Hubert's camp.

*OSS 117* boasts some good location work, but then again it would be pretty hard to screw up filming nice shots in Corsica. Further heightening the old-fashioned feel of things is the black and white cinematography, as well as a rather lackadaiscal attitude toward pacing (it is a good 20 minutes too long). There's also a rather odd soundtrack, not entirely dissimilar to that of *Vampyros Lesbos* with its use of deep, reverbed male vocals and jazzy orchestrations.

The presence of plentiful underwater action anticipates that of *Thunderball*, and although handled relatively well, its effectiveness is somewhat curtailed by sound effects that resemble nothing so much as someone blowing into a bucket through a straw. It would be churlish, however, to protest too much when this does allow for the presence of babes in wetsuits.

Standout amongst the cast is Daniel Emilfork, the weird-looking Chilean actor who

**Just another day in the death of a spy in *OSS 117 se dechaine***

resembles a sinister Lindsay Kemp (or possibly an even campier, balding Marc Almond).

French director Andre Hunebelle was better known for his adventure films, often starring Jean Marais (*Le Bossu*, *Le Capitan*). As well as the OSS 117 series, he was also behind the hugely popular Fantomas films. Funnily enough, this wasn't the first time that the character of Hubert Bonisseur de la Bath had appeared onscreen. Ivan Desny had played him in Jean Sacha's 1956 production *OSS 117 n'est pas mort*, which is generally not considered to be part of the series.—MB

CREDITS: Production: P.A.C., Films Borderie, Produzioni Cinematografiche Mediterranee; Director: Andre Hunebelle; Story based on the novel "OSS 117 Prend Le Maquis" by Jean Bruce; Screenplay: Andre Hunebelle, Pierre Foucauld, Raymond Borel, Richard Caron, Patrice Rondard; Cinematography: Raymond Lemoigne; Music: Michel Magne; Original running length: 110 mins; Filming location: Corsica; Country: France; Year: 1963

CAST: Kerwin Mathews (*Hubert Bonisseur de la Bath*), Nadia Sanders (*Brigitta*), Henri-Jacques Huet (*Nicolas Renotte*), Albert Dagnon (*Forestier, a French agent*), Irina Demick (*Lucia*), Daniel Emilfork (*Sacha*), Jacques Harden (*Roos*), Roger Dutoit (*Mayan*), Andre Webber, Gisele Grimm, Michel Jourdan, Jean Paul Moulinot, Yvan Chiffre, Henri Attal, Henri Guegan, Mazzacorati, John Geoffroy, Rico Lopez, Arielle Coignet, Marc Mazzacurati

## OTLEY

aka Otley sin balas y disparando (Sp)

Thanks to a good lead performance, a terrific supporting cast and a smart and witty script, this anti-establishment spy spoof succeeds where others have failed. Certainly it has its annoyances, like the lame Beatles rip-off signature tune and the obligatory modness of some of the characters and dialogue, but overall this one hits the mark.

Tom Courtenay is Gerald Arthur Otley, a general layabout and petty thief with an uncanny knowledge of antiques. After bedding his landlady—apparently a regular occurrence—she evicts him ("When you

**Belgian poster for the clever and funny *Otley* starring Tom Courtenay**

moved in here it was a furnished flat.") and Otley finds himself homeless. After a party he manages to get a couch for the night with a friend who, unbeknown to Otley, is a traitorous spy. With Otley passed out on the couch, his friend is killed, and Otley wakes up in the middle of Gatwick Airport's airfield two days later with a hangover. From here on it's a series of misadventures as the cops want him for the murder and spies from both sides of the fence think he knows something.

One of the true delights here is the solid cast of character actors doing what they do best. Freddie Jones is great as the fey and deeply mannered Proudfoot, a middleman for the other side who lives in an apartment decorated like the "Baghdad Hilton." Leonard Rossiter is the assassin Johnston, who keeps chickens and runs a tour bus on the side. There's even a minor role for Ronald Lacey, the Nazi villain of *Raiders of the Lost Ark*, as a henchman coming down with the flu.

It's refreshing to discover a film of this period that doesn't cross the line too often into camp and one that is genuinely (and intentionally) funny. There are lots of throwaway lines to keep you laughing. At a party full of pretentious people, Otley is encouraged to "discuss Antonioni," to which he replies, "I can't stand all that Spanish dancing." Johnston kidnaps Otley and puts him to work on the farm. When Johnston asks him how the work is going, Otley remarks that his "mind's too clogged up with sex and football." When one character is asked how his wife is, he replies, "Oh she's still the same sweet gin-sodden bitch she always was." When Otley finds himself at a health farm awaiting instructions, the camera casually takes in a conversation between two of the elderly residents: "I always thought colonic irrigation was something to do with agriculture."

Situational comedy has its moments as well. One involves Otley's midday rendezvous with Proudfoot at the London Playboy club: "What's this, the naked lunch?" Another is Otley trying to pass his driving test while being chased by bad guys: "Okay Mr. Otley, you've passed. See, I'm filling in the pass form now!"

Recruited to draw out a double agent (who suffers a rather nasty death), Otley discovers that the head of a secret government agency (Alan Badel) turns out to be a traitor as well, and the bugger not only gets away with it, but is knighted! That's the rub. In the end, Otley's back where he started, homeless but not loveless. Not bad for what has probably become a forgotten film by now.—DD

CREDITS: Production: Open Road Productions, Bruce Coan Curtis Film; Director: Dick Clement; Story based on the novel by Martin Waddell; Screenplay: Dick Cement, Ian Le Frenais; Cinematography: Austin Dempster {Technicolor}; Music: Stanley Myers; Original running length: 91 mins; Country: UK; Year: 1968

CAST: Tom Courtenay (*Gerald Arthur Otley*), Romy Schneider (*Imogen*), Alan Badel (*Sir Alex Hadrian*), James Villiers (*Hendrickson*), Leonard Rossiter (*Johnston*), Freddie Jones (*Philip Proudfoot*), Fiona Lewis (*Lin*), James Bolam (*Albert*), James Cossins (*Geffcock*), James Maxwell (*Rollo*), Edward Hardwicke (*Lambert*), Ronald Lacey (*Curtis*), Phyllida Law (*Jean*), Geoffrey Bayldon (*Inspector Hewett*), Frank Middlemass (*Bruce*), Damian Harris (*Miles*), Robert Brownjohn (*Paul*), Maureen Toal (*the landlady*), Barry Fantoni (*Larry*), Bernard Sharpe (*Tony*), Paul Angelis (*the police constable*), David Kernan (*the ground steward*), Sheila Steafel (*the ground stewardess*), Katherine Parr (*the newsagent*), Kathleen Helm (*the dietician*), Norman Shelley (*the businessman*), John Savident (*the second businessman*), Ken Parry (*the third businessman*), Jonathan Cecil (*the young man at party*), Georgina Simpson (*the young girl at party*), Ron Owen (*the hotel waiter*), Stella Tanner (*the traffic warden*), Robin Askwith (*the 1st kid*), Kevin Bennett (*the 2nd kid*), Kenneth Cranham (*the 3rd kid*), Robert Gillespie, Don McKillop (*the police driver*)

**Italian poster for *Our Agent in Casablanca***

OUR AGENT IN CASABLANCA
aka The Killer Lacks a Name (US, unconfirmed), Nostro agente a Casablanca (It), Nuestro agente en Casablanca (Sp), Two Boys for Murder (US, unconfirmed)

I would classify this as an ambience picture. Lang Jeffries is an appealing skinny-tie spy guy, but the story is weak and the whole thing is rather dull, I'm afraid. Picturesque locations and Giovanni Fusco's soundtrack—a nice blend of Moroccan and spy pop—help to create an atmosphere, but this is not a riveting adventure.

Jeffries is pill-popping agent Brian Kervin, doing his duty in Casablanca and environs. A top-secret dossier is stolen and is apparently incriminating enough to swing a foreign country against the US. The documents reveal a high-level official as a Nazi, but we still want him on our side.

There's not really much to report here. The main henchman (named Drakko, naturally) is equipped by the Chinese with a metal hand that can electrocute on contact. This is only exploited a couple of times and not to very good effect. Drakko dies by his own hand, so to speak, when he accidentally touches a power line. Russian spies are involved too, but only peripherally.

The women on display are generally treated poorly, but they do have a few surprises up their collective sleeve for our hero. Lines like, "Anything that involves money attracts women like flies" cement the demeaning treatment they're given. In the end, a pair of femmes fatale die in a fiery crash for their crimes, but the only other real action sequence is an ill-conceived crop duster chase on a beach. It's not very exciting despite some good stunt work.

Kervin takes pep pills because he wants to stay awake. Yeah, right. At one point he is drugged with a truth serum and the combination of this with the pills in his system must certainly cloud his thinking, because his method of overcoming the drowsiness is to burn his arm with a lighter. It's time this boy had a vacation.

The English dubbing for this print is bad enough to disorient the viewer, jumping ahead to the next scene before righting itself or repeating spoken lines so it sounds like spy rap. Unfortunately there's not enough humor or weirdness to recommend this one.—DD

CREDITS: Production: Filmes Cin.ca, Oceania Prod. Cin.che Internazionali, Prod. Cin.cas Demicheli; Director: Tulio Demicheli; Story: Tulio Demicheli; Screenplay: Vittoriano Petrilli, Fulvio Gicca Palli; Cinematography: Angelo Lotti {Techniscope – Technicolor}; Music: Giovanni Fusco; Original running length: 91 mins; Country: Spain/Italy; Year: 1966

CAST: Lang Jeffries (*Brian Kervin*), Thea Fleming, Barbara Nelli, Olga Omar, Pier Paolo Capponi, Ruben Rojo, Paco Moran, Jose M. Caffarel, Zara Guash, Maria Badmajev

**A restrained Margaret Lee on the Belgian poster for Claude Chabrol's *Our Agent Tiger***

OUR AGENT TIGER
aka An Orchid for the Tiger (US),
Der Tiger parfümiert sich mit Dynamit (WG),
La tigre profumata alla dinamite (It), Le tigre sa parfume a la dynamite (Fr),
El Tigre se perfume con dinamita (Sp)

Roger Hanin is Louis Rapiere, aka The Tiger, his recurring character in several spy flicks. He beds the babes and gets beat up regularly, but manages to overcome in the end and this adventure is no exception. This time he's up against a lunatic ex-Nazi type called Hans Wunchendorf—also known as The Orchid—who wants to rule the world with his master race (of course) via his evil organization. Initially, Tiger is supposed to recover 20 million dollars in gold bars discovered in a sunken ship, which he does, but the operation unveils The Orchid and his mad scheme, so Tiger takes after him too.

Director Claude Chabrol—he of the high-brow reputation—made several spy flicks in the sixties. Here he manages a moderately interesting adventure with some arresting images like a gathering of flashlights in the darkness, an ornate horse-drawn hearse making its way through the jungle, and the disconcerting sight of sharks nailed to several doors.

Margaret Lee plays Pamela Mitchum, a devotee of The Orchid, who is later revealed to be Patricia Johnson of the CIA. The highlight of her role here has to be the few minutes we see her dressed in a leopard skin, chained up like a pulp magazine victim. You see, The Orchid's headquarters in Guyana happens to be the zoo, so when her true identity is discovered, my only guess is that she simply had to be dressed like that to compliment her surroundings.

The zoo front is used to smuggle coded message tapes in the bellies of sharks. When Tiger finds this out he sets us up for the line, "A shark a day to the Hamburg zoo? Sounds fishy." Guyana is crawling with spies. At one garden party there are agents from the CIA, Russia, Cairo, East Berlin and China (the Peking Mata Hari), but Tiger has the most trouble with The Orchid's men. The fight coordinators on the film get a high-profile credit up front and they live up to it for the most part. The film is pretty brutal really—life is cheap in Guyana—and the fights are long and mean. Tiger is penned in and bullwhipped at one point by two Aryan musclemen in the most sadistic scene.

The Orchid's men try everything on Tiger. While he's driving down the road, they actually lasso him around the neck! Tiger then manages to remain driving while dragging the surprised henchman behind the car. This guy is tough. They also try to run him down with a car. They fail, of course, and smash into a storefront instead. Tiger then remarks, "He drives like an American."

The film sort of peters out at the end, however. No big explosions or climactic fights; instead, the bad guys are trapped (like animals) in the zoo and arrested. The end. The score by Jean Wiener is somewhat cheesy in the French music hall style, and therefore pretty much forgettable. This is a middle-of-the-road spy adventure, not entirely without interest especially if good fights are one of your enjoyments.—DD

CREDITS: Production: Progefi, Dino De Laurentis, Francisco Balcazar; Director: Claude Chabrol; Story: Antoine Flachot, Jean Curtelin; Screenplay: Jean Curtelin; Cinematography: Jean Rabier {Eastmancolor - Techniscope}; Music: Jean Wiener; Original running length: 85 mins; Country: Italy/Spain/France; Year: 1965

CAST: Roger Hanin (*Louis Rapiere*), Michel Bouquet (*Jacques Vermorel*), Margaret Lee (*Pamela Mitchum*), Roger Dumas (*Duvet*), Georges Rigaud (*Commander Damerec*), Michaela Cendali (*Sarita Sanchez*), Dodo Hassad Bahador (*Hans Von Wunchendorf*), J.M. Caffarel (*Colonel Pontarlier*), Carlos Casaravilla (*Ricardo Sanchez*), Claude Chabrol (*the drunken doctor*), Michel Etcheverry, Pepe Nieto (*Sergei, a Russian agent*?)

## OUR MAN IN JAMAICA
aka 001, operación Caribe (Sp),
A001 operazione Giamaica (It),
Scharfe Schüsse auf Jamaica (WG)

Larry Pennell. You may not know the name, but you'll sure recognize him from his many television appearances in the sixties, most

**Jose Marco is about to lose his gun to Larry Pennell in this German lobby card for *Our Man in Jamaica***

likely his recurring character of Dash Riprock in the *Beverly Hillbillies*. I figure he was a workout buddy of Brad Harris (Pennell looks buff here), and Harris used his Euro-connections to get the secret agent gig for Pennell. The result is a darn likeable little film in a sixties television kitsch sort of way, because that's the level of the production values. It's very colorful with good use of the Jamaican locations that helps to offset the cheap interiors and inadequate acting.

Pennell is Ken Stewart, agent 001, and all the chicks are crazy about him of course, even the ones twice his age who beg for one of his kisses. Pennell didn't make any more spy flicks, which is too bad because he's a likeable actor who can carry the role off pretty well. Brad Harris tags along as Mike Jefferson from Military Intelligence and has a British accent on the English-dubbed print. Harris gets to do some fun stunt work here and his character actually gets killed, something that doesn't happen that often.

The rest of the cast is pretty weak. Barbara Valentin has a medium-sized role as a bitch. She was the most…memorable girl in the sleaze classic *Horrors of Spider Island*. The very slight love interest is Margitta Scherr as Jane Peacock, the sister of the agent previously assigned to the case. She looks so skinny here that you fear for her health. The villain of the piece, played by Robert Camardiel, is Elmer Hayes, a name perfect for the *Beverly Hillbillies*. Hayes is actually an escaped criminal with a grudge against the US for sentencing him to die in the electric chair, so he's building an army.

Plusses for the film include a fun score by Marcello Giombini that runs along Bondian lines, one gadget—a transmitter/receiver unit known as a "special high frequency interception and recording apparatus" made by Sanyo—and the huge statues of Inca gods in an antique dealer's bizarre living room. The fight scenes are good and we suspect Brad Harris had something to do with that aspect. It also has one of those scenes you see occasionally in the genre where a kid threatens our hero menacingly with a toy gun.

The last 10 minutes of the film get pretty strange as Hayes straps Stewart into his homemade electric chair and spouts off about enlisting the aid of China and Russia to punish America for being mean to him. But you won't be able to take your eyes off Stewart in this scene because the wires attached to his head make him look like Cleopatra.

Director Ernest Von Theumer (billed as Richard Jackson) pulls it off despite the minuscule budget and even though the odds are against it, the film works fine as light fare. Stewart gets a good last line too: "What an impossible life; either the gangsters are after your hide or the women are!"—DD

CREDITS: Production: A P.E.A., Cin.ca, Theumer Film, Apolo Film; Director: Richard Jackson [Ernest Von Theumer]; Story and Screenplay: Kurt Vogelmann, Antonio Del Amo; Cinematography: Aldo Ricci; Music: Marcello Giombini; Original running length: 74 mins; Filming locations: Jamaica, Rome, Madrid; Country: Italy/Spain/West Germany; Year: 1965

CAST: Larry Pennell (*Ken Stewart*), Roberto Camardiel, Barbara Valentin (*Gloria*), Brad Harris (*Mike Jefferson*), Linda Sini (*Sra Cervantes*), Margaret Scherr (*Jane*), John Bartha, Ralf Baldwin [Raffaele Baldassarre], Nando Angelini, Wolfgang Kieling, Robert Camardiel (*Elmer Hayes*)

## OUR MAN IN MARRAKESH
aka Bang Bang You're Dead (US),
Intriga brutal (Sp)

"I think there's been some foul play," says Tony Randall upon discovering a dead body—with a knife in its back—stashed in the closet of his hotel room. Comedy is hard, and although this one spends too much time as a chase movie, it is still largely successful thanks to a great cast and good script.

Randall is Andrew Jessel, a land speculator for a luxury hotel chain. He lies about his intentions, which is one of the reasons he gets involved in this mistaken identity comedy. Luckily—for us and him—his cohort in the adventure is the lovely Senta Berger as Kyra Stanova, who, it is revealed, works for a branch of the CIA. The two actors work well together as they run from the bad guys until things get cleared up. Berger is good at telling the tales that keep Randall, and us, guessing and

**Germans Klaus Kinski and Senta Berger get better exposure than hero Tony Randall on the German poster for *Our Man in Marrakesh***

Randall's everyman is the perfect foil for the intrigue that surrounds him.

Supporting these two is a cast of character actors you will undoubtedly enjoy. Herbert Lom is Casimir, a powerful international fixer and the main bad guy here, and his breezy girlfriend is Margaret Lee. Lom's number-one henchman is Klaus Kinski, who was born to play bad guys and did—lots of times. Other players include Wilfred Hyde-White, John Le Mesurier and Terry-Thomas.

Director Don Sharp, in his only spy outing, has crafted an enjoyable and funny film that doesn't resort too often to slapstick or other forms of cheap laughs. It manages to tread the line between humor and danger, keeping the viewer interested enough to evoke plenty of hearty chuckles. A light and entertaining spy comedy, this is one of the best of the bunch.—DD

CREDITS: Production: Towers of London, American International; Director: Don Sharp; Story and Screenplay: Peter Yeldham; Cinematography: Michael Reed {Technicolor}; Music: Malcolm Lockyer; Filming location: Marrakesh; Country: UK; Year: 1966

CAST: Tony Randall (*Andrew Jessel*), Senta Berger (*Kyra Stanova*), Terry-Thomas (*El Caid*), Herbert Lom (*Mr. Casimir*), Wilfrid Hyde-White (*Arthur Fairbrother*), Grégoire Aslan (*Achmed*), John Le Mesurier (*George Lillywhite*), Klaus Kinski (*Jonquil*), Margaret Lee (*Samia Voss*), Emile Stemmler (*hotel clerk*), Helen Sanguinetti (*Madame Bouseny*), Francisco Sánchez (*Martinez*), William Sanguinetti (*police chief*), Hassan Essakali (*motorcycle policeman*), Keith Peacock (*Philippe*), Burt Kwouk (*export manager*)

## PASSPORT TO HELL

aka Agent 3S3 kennt kein Erbarmen (WG),
Agent spécial 3S3: passeport pour l'enfer (Fr), Agente 3S3 Operazione Inferno (Production title), Agente 3S3, pasaporte para el infierno (Sp), Agente 3S3: passaporto per l'inferno (It)

This is the first of George Ardisson's spy flicks, and it's a damn good beginning. Ardisson made his share of spaghetti westerns, was in several of Mario Bava's costume epics and even had a bit in Fellini's *Juliet of the Spirits*. Here he plays Walter Ross, agent 3S3, a designation meaning secret agent number 3 of the 3rd Special Division, and he pretty much kicks butt. Ardisson was an excellent fighter and he has plenty of chances to show off those skills, including a particularly brutal match-up against Dakar, a man twice his size.

Ross is assigned to befriend a young woman, Jasmine (Barbara Simons), to find out the whereabouts of her father (ex-agent Henry Dvorak) who purportedly runs The Organization, a private spy association. Ross is even given a special bullet with an "A" carved in it to use on Dvorak, who has been using the name Mr. A. Turns out that Mr. A was killed by Steve Dickson (Georges Riviere) and Jackie Yen (Seyna Seyn) a year earlier, and they have been perpetuating his existence until the time was right for them to take over. So much for being able to use that bullet.

Of the three principals just mentioned, this was Barbara Simons' only film credit (according the Internet Movie Database), Georges Riviere didn't make any other spy movies, and only Seyna Seyn hit the spy circuit regularly. By the way, Fernando Sancho, who usually played

**Turkish poster for *Passport to Hell* features common Eurospy themes**

Mexican generals in spaghetti westerns, has a cameo here as a Russian diplomat.

We are treated to a terrific Piero Umiliani jazzy soundtrack that kicks in with the cool credit sequence and barely lets up the rest of the way. This was also director Sergio Sollima's first spy flick, and he keeps things tight and on the move throughout.

Fun things include the winter Vienna locations, the unusual geographical and architectural locations in Lebanon, arm wrestling with a glass of beer between the combatants, litmus paper that can be used to detect poison in one's drink, a pendant transmitter with the receiver in a pair of eyeglasses and a needle-shooting compact case. The script is good without a lot of nonsense, and one line that sticks with this viewer is spoken by Jackie Yen: "I hate violence when it's used against myself." Don't we all.

The real attraction here is the tailor-made role for Ardisson. He's a snappy dresser and doesn't come across as your typical smarmy secret agent. Rather he's in control and doesn't need a lot of gadgets to get the job done. He's worth watching the film for even if it wasn't as good as it is. Recommended.—DD

CREDITS: Director: Simon Sterling [Sergio Sollima]; Story and Screenplay: Alfonso Balcazar; Cinematography: Charlie Charlies [Carlo Carlini] {Techniscope – Technicolor}; Music: Piero Umiliani; Original running length: 102 mins; Country: Italy/France/Spain; Year: 1965

CAST: George [Giorgio] Ardisson (*Ross, Agent 3S3*), Barbara Simons (*Jasmine*), Jose Marco (*Ahmed*), Georges Riviere (*Professor Steve Dickson*), Frank Andrews [Franco Andrei] (*Bellamy*), Liliane Fernani (*Karina*), Seyna Seyn (*Jackie Yen*), Charlie Kalinsky (*Salkoff*), Leontine May (*Fawzia*), Paco Sanz (*Nobell*), Henri Cogan (*Sanz*), Fernando Sancho (*Colonel Dolukin*), Tom Felleghy (*Major Taylor*), Anthony Gradwell [Antonio Gradoli] (*Captain Moran*), Steve Gordon (*Bob*), Dakar (*Gutierrez*), Sal Borgese, Jeff Cameron, Artur Gardner, Hugh Gregor, Beatrice Altariba (*Elisa Von Sloot*)

PASSWORD: KILL AGENT GORDON
aka L'agent Gordon se dechaine (Fr),
Agente Gordon operazione Mogador
(production), Operación Mogador (Sp),
Paris Estambul sin regreso (Sp),
Password uccidete agente Gordon (It)

Director Sergio Grieco again pits Roger Browne against Franco Ressel, just as he did in *Rififi in Amsterdam*. This time Ressel plays the villain Albert Kowalski in drag and in a wheelchair for the bulk of the film, a strange angle that's never fully explained. Roger Browne is agent Douglas Gordon, who has a nifty designer wardrobe and charm enough to unite superpowers in thwarting Kowalksi's plans.

Helga Line is Karin, a Russian agent who works with Gordon for this adventure. She gets strapped to an electrocution table in just her slip for her trouble, too.

Gordon uses the slight cover of talent agent for this assignment, a cover that he really doesn't use much. At the beginning of the film we hear Gordon talk about this arrangement in voiceover, "...everything from dog acts to opera singers. They've even given me a client to represent. I sure hope *she's* not a dog."

This movie has lots of fistfights, even when they have no correlation with the plot. At one point Gordon is in a salon at a casino and two thugs jump him—fists flailing—and for a couple of minutes Gordon holds his own. Then, just as quickly, the thugs are called off and a lady enters the room and claims the whole thing to be a misunderstanding! It's at this same casino where Gordon gives a cute girl some cash to gamble for him. When she loses the dough, he says, "Perhaps I'd be luckier if I played your telephone number," and she gives it to him.

The lovely Rosalba Neri has a small but sexy role as Amalia, a dancer who works with Gordon for a short time before being executed. Darn. When Gordon meets her for the first time, he says, "I'll bet you'd be just great at free-style wrestling."

Gordon uses a couple of gadgets during the course of his assignment. He has an electric razor that doubles as a microfilm projector, an exploding watch and a big ring on his finger that contains acid. He uses the ring to open a lock that has his hands secured behind his back. How he does that without melting his fingers is a mystery. Karen has a nifty gadget of her own too. It's a mascara pencil that is in reality a tiny laser weapon developed by the East Germans. When she shoots it, the laser lines are drawn onto the film itself.

Exotic locations like Paris, Tripoli and Madrid, a fun score by Piero Umiliani and put-off lines for girls that don't measure up ("You're very sweet and someday I want you to meet my twin brother.") help to keep this average actioner afloat. But when you're villain is named Kowalski, you know you're not in for a first-class ride.—DD

CREDITS: Production: Claudia Cin.ca, Procensa; Director: Terence Hathaway [Sergio Grieco]; Story and Screenplay: Gian Paolo Callegari, Lucio Battistrada, Ramon Comas De Torres; Cinematography; Juan Julio Baena {Techniscope – Technicolor}; Music: Piero Umiliani; Original running length: 95 mins; Filming locations: Incir-De Paolis, Paris, Tripoli, Madrid; Country: Italy/Spain; Year: 1965

CAST: Roger Browne (*Gordon*), Helga Line (*Karin*), Michael Rivers (*Rudy Shwartz*), Franco Ressel (*Albert Kowalski*), Rosoalba Neri (*Amalia*), Andrea Scotti (*Walter*), Susan Terry (*Aicha*), Mila Stanic (*Magda*), Giorgio

**Crude but effective artwork of the Belgian poster for *Password: Kill Agent Gordon***

Ubaldi (*the fighter*), Peter Blades, Beni Deus (*the grocery lorry driver*), Leu Lii Young (*Leo Pat*), Frank Liston [Franco Lantieri], Dario De Grassi, Enzo Andronico, Angel Menendez (*Kurt, man in helicopter*), Rossella Bergamonti (*lady gambling in the casino*), Francesca Rosano, Maria Barba, Anthony Gradwell [Antonio Gradoli] (*LaPepe*), Alfonso Rojas (*Manuel*), Cheu Yea Hong, Wally Seeber. Uncredited: Umberto Raho (*member of tour group*)

PIEGE POUR UN ESPIONS
"trap for the spies"
taka OSS 77—operazione fior di loto (It)

Unbeknownst to the United Nations, China has built an atom bomb. Professor Yen, a scientist who has worked on the project, decides to defect and reveal all. He escapes in a plane, but it is shot down over Italy (which would have been guaranteed to cause a diplomatic incident, I should have thought). Fortunately he manages to parachute free, but is badly injured in the fall.

Hearing that something is afoot through the grapevine (and undoubtedly wanting a nice holiday), assorted secret agents converge upon Rome. Among them is CIA man Robert

**The Yellow Peril looms large on the Belgian poster for *Piege pour un espions***

Kent (Sandro Moretti), whose mission is to find out the Professor's secret and pass it on to the American authorities. He immediately runs into trouble with an Oriental-type sporting an evil Roger Moore-style raised eyebrow. He also discovers that all of his contacts have been murdered (finding a handy blonde in the same room as their corpses, he doesn't hesitate to invite her back to his hotel for a little slap and tickle).

Several shenanigans follow: Kent is kidnapped and escapes, gets into fights with kung-fuing Chinamen, takes a young lady back to his room only to discover Dominique Boschero already occupying his bed (happens to me all the time). He finally traces Professor Yen to a rural hospital, but everyone is captured by the villains when he falls for the oldest trick in the book, stopping to pick up a "damsel in distress" (aka evil, leather-trousered dominatrix).

Another entry in the "Yellow Peril" subgroup of spy films, *Piege* is actually a very effective little number from Bruno Paolinelli (who went on to direct *Nazi SS* the following year). It's snappily made, with some dashing camerawork and a likeable Bacalov soundtrack. It is a little slow moving, especially the first half hour or so, but manages to stay involving even when the basic (putting it lightly) script is at its least effective.

Fortunately, there's also a feast of babes to keep the attention perky. Dominique Boschero is gorgeous, but manages to give one of the most unconvincingly lip-synced song and dance routines ever. Her paltry attempts at miming would frankly put the awful efforts to be seen on *Top of the Pops* to shame. Yoko Tani plays a female Fu Manchu with some relish. She whips her men, drives over people's heads and goes all gooey when face to face with her handsome adversary. Speaking of whom, Sandro Moretti makes a game attempt at the lead role but isn't entirely persuasive; he just seems a bit too young and lightweight. Strangely, he's credited as Robert Kent, the same name as the character he plays—a cogent display of lack of imagination if ever there was one.

The best bit? Well, I was particularly taken with the sequence in which our hero escapes some pursuers by jumping off a bridge, using a truckload of sheep to break his fall. And if you were wondering what the OSS 77 of the title referred to (apart from simply name-checking the OSS 117 films), it's the name of the hospital to which the Chinese defector is taken.—MB

CREDITS: Production: Italspettacolo, Radius; Director: John Huxley [Bruno Paolinelli]; Story: John Huxley [Bruno Paolinelli]; Screenplay: John Huxley [Bruno Paolinelli], Joseph Jacob, Claude Brown; Cinematography: James V Nathan [Vitaliano Natalucci] {Techniscope – Technicolor}; Music: Luis Enrique Bacalov; Original running length: 103 mins; Country: Italy/France; Year: 1965

CAST: Robert Kent [Sandro Moretti] (*Robert Kent/Wilson*), Dominique Boschero, Gaia Germani, Yoko Tani (*Chinese agent*), Paule Albert, Roy Moore, Jean-Louis Tristan, Don Marshall, Taso Yong Tsing, Wu Cheo Tsing Po, Wu Pak Chiu

## THE QUILLER MEMORANDUM
aka Conspiracion en Berlin (Sp)

Simply plotted yet deceptively complex, this mainstream, low-key espionage yarn has aged like fine wine over the years. My guess is that the film was dismissed unfairly upon its release, coming as it did during the year of the spy, 1966. The glut of product caused it to be given short shrift, but the years have been kind and it is almost universally appreciated now for the gem it truly is. Yes, it is somewhat dour and decidedly subversive, but it manages to be compelling entertainment due mainly, in my opinion, to the performance of George Segal.

Segal is Quiller, the third man in on a job that has taken the lives of his predecessors, to ferret out a nest of neo-Nazis in West Berlin headed by the formidable Oktober (Max Von Sydow). Quiller is briefed by the perversely calculating Pol (Alec Guinness), who sets up their first meeting in the stadium built by the Nazis in 1936 for the Olympics. What follows is a cat and mouse game between Quiller and Oktober, but who is the cat and who is the mouse?

Quiller's plan to force the hand of the organization by making unsubtle inquiries works like a charm and we're barely 30 minutes into the movie when he is captured and interrogated by Oktober in an extended sequence that is a tour de force. Set in the rococo ruins of the aristocracy, the interrogation takes on the qualities of a dream as Quiller is drugged and then cajoled by Oktober to no avail.

Quiller has also made the acquaintance of a schoolteacher named Inge, played by Senta Berger, who never looked more luminous than she does here. Their relationship is as curious and slippery as the politics between the two nations they represent. Screenwriter Harold Pinter's shadowy conversations are handled beautifully by the two actors, both playing each other like they were delicate instruments.

Director Michael Anderson isn't shy with the symbolism, which makes the film a rich experience upon multiple viewings. For instance, Quiller enters the stadium for his meeting with Pol by walking between two giant monolithic towers that at once point out his precarious position in this affair and the isolation of his profession and his person.

Segal's disingenuous personality works very well in the role of Quiller, a character who is as manipulated as he is manipulating. He's surrounded in this world of lying and spying by a cast that is equally up to the task.

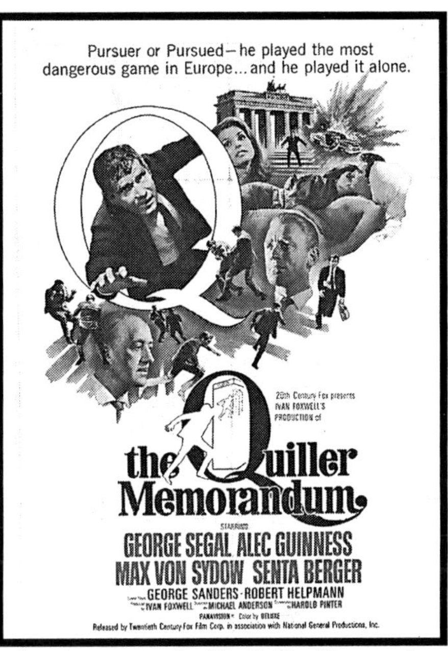


**American poster for *The Quiller Memorandum***

As mentioned, Senta Berger is not only very beautiful, but she exhibits a talent here that she was rarely able to display and certainly not in her other spy roles.

The British aristocracy is delightfully skewered by the fine pair of George Sanders and Robert Flemyng as the upper-crust manipulators of the fates of the agents in the trenches. You may also recognize Peter Carsten as Hengel, Quiller's cover in Berlin, but keep your eye out for a fleeting appearance by the ubiquitous Herbert Fuchs.

All in all, this a well-crafted film graced even further by that old-fashioned Technicolor palatte and a perfect bittersweet ending. John Barry's score is mostly the repeated motif of the melancholy hit song, "Wednesday's Child," but it remains fresh and eloquent throughout.—DD

CREDITS: Production: Cathay, Ivan Foxwell Productions, Rank Film Organisation; Director: Michael Anderson; Story based on the novel "The Berlin Memorandum" by Adam Hall; Screenplay: Harold Pinter; Cinematography: Erwin Hillier {Technicolor}; Music: John Barry; Original running length: 105 mins; Filming location: West Berlin; Country: UK; Year: 1966

CAST: George Segal (*Quiller*), Alec Guinness (*Pol*), Max Von Sydow (*Oktober*), Senta Berger (*Inge*), George Sanders (*Gibbs*), Robert Helpmann (*Weng*), Robert Flemyng (*Rushington*), Peter Carsten (*Hengel*), Edith Schneider (*the headmistress*), Günter Meisner (*Hassler*), Ernst Walder (*Grauber*), Philip Madoc (*Oktober's henchman*), John Rees (*Oktober's henchman*), Herbert Fuchs

**Anthony Perkins makes an idiot of himself for the ravishing Brigitte Bardot in *Ravishing Idiot***

RAVISHING IDIOT
aka Un Adorabile idiota (It), Agent 38-24-36 (US), Une ravissante idiote (Fr)

Brigitte Bardot is indeed ravishing, but this film is idiotic. She plays Penelope Lightfeather (oh, that's hilarious), newfound girlfriend of embittered Harry Compton (Anthony Perkins). He wants to betray England and spy for the Russians, so his Russian uncle (Gregoire Aslan) signs him up to steal a secret document. The Brits, however, want the document stolen to reveal a traitor in their midst. Many shenanigans later, Penelope turns out to be a spy and Harry sees the error of his ways.

This is one excruciatingly unfunny film. It wants to be an anti-establishment comedy yet remain patriotic. No wonder it doesn't work. There's so much speeded-up action here that it becomes dizzying. Naturally, slapstick humor abounds, including zany antics like a runaway vacuum cleaner (ha ha) and poodle chasing (stop, it's killing me). It's also filled with unsubtle sexual innuendo, not uncommon for the time but so poorly handled it must have been embarrassing even then.

There are a few good lines (the Brits discuss a security leak by saying "Terribly sorry sir, but there's a traitor in your entourage.") and Anthony Perkins is a good sport, of course. He has a natural gift for comedy, but he can't salvage this material. Director Edouard Molinaro, on the other hand, displays a distinct lack of comedic flair.

At one point Penelope is asked by a policeman to present her papers. The first thing she pulls out of her purse is a card for the "Society For the Care and Protection of Animals," a nice little in-joke about Bardot's rabid attitude concerning animal rights. The film is way too long and Michel Legrand's score is as annoying as the action onscreen, but Bardot sure is ravishing.—DD

CREDITS: Production: Belles Rives, Flora Film; Director: Eduoard Molinaro; Story based on the novel by Charles Exbrayat; Screenplay: Edouard Molinaro, G.A. Tabet; Cinematography: Andreas Winding {B&W}; Music: Michel Legrand; Original running length: 105 mins; Country: France/Italy; Year: 1964

CAST: Brigitte Bardot (*Penelope Lightfeather*), Anthony Perkins (*Harry Compton/Nicholas Maukouline*), Grégoire Aslan (*Bagda*), Denise Provence (*Lady Barbara Dumfrey*), André Luguet (*Sir Reginald Dumfrey*), Charles Millot (*Balaniev*), Hélène Dieudonné (*Mamie*), Jacques Monod (*the surgeon*), Paul Demange (*the bank director*), Jean Marc Tennberg (*Inspector Cartwright*), Martine de Breteuil (*Marjorie*), Hans Werner (*Donald Farringdon*), Robert Murzeau (*Clement*), Jacques Hilling (*the Lord Admiral*), Annick Allieres (*Eleanor, the servant*), Van Doude (*the policeman*), Jacques Dynam (*the second policeman*), Robert le Beal (*Captain Fellow*), Dominique Page (*Rosemary*), Max Desrau (*Harry's colleague*), Pierre Duncan (*Peter Walker*), Jean-Pierre Laverne (*the chef*), Martine de Breteuil (*Marjorie*), Philippe Castelli (*restaurant customer*), Michel Dupleix (*James W.C. Tapple*), Robert Saint-Yves (*the policeman in the park*), Federica Layne (*Maud Smith*), Marc Arian (*the servant*), Guy Grosso (*an interrogator*), Michel Garland (*an interrogator*), Raoul Guylad (*Barbara's horseman*), Louise Chevalier (*the interrogator*), Adrien Cayla-Legrand (*guest at the reception*), Yvon Sarray (*a policeman*), Henri Marteau (*Herbert*), Robert Blome, Nadine Tallier

RED DRAGON

aka A 009: missione Hong Kong (It), Das Geheimnis der drei Dschunken (WG), Mision en Hong Kong (Sp), Mission a Hong Kong (Fr)

Here's a rather bland spy thriller that will pass before your eyes without making much of an impact. One would think that Stewart Granger would make a fine secret agent, but he comes across as more of a jerk than anything else. The first time we see him, he's on vacation, sitting on his living room floor playing with his model train set that brings him his liquor. I guess that's appropriate somehow, the guy sitting home alone getting plastered. He certainly couldn't have many friends, since he's condescending to everyone except pretty girls.

Granger is Michael Scott, an FBI man who is out of his element (and must be out of his jurisdiction) in Hong Kong investigating the smuggling of nuclear weapons. Better known for costume epics, war, and adventure films in the 1940s and 1950s, Granger slummed in the sixties making low-rent spy flicks.

Scott is naturally assigned a beautiful woman, Carol (Rosanna Schiaffino) to work inside the evil organization. Schiaffino is certainly attractive enough, but for her to fall for the smarmy Granger, a man at least twice her age, is pushing it. They fall in "love" and we are treated to the image of a satisfied woman after he beds her. Schiaffino was a busy actress in costumers in the sixties, but you might want to check her out in *The Witch*, a dreamy horror flick that also stars Richard Johnson.

We are burdened with a comedy relief sidekick, Smoky (Harald Juhnke), whose supposed knowledge of Hong Kong and the Chinese language is, shall we say, sadly lacking. The first time we meet Smoky, he's having his hair washed at an outdoor barbershop and his hair is full of shampoo. Oh, that's funny. Smoky doesn't do much except fall in the water and get hit on the head. The German actor would make no more spy flicks, thank goodness.

**Spanish poster for *Red Dragon* captures the beautiful Rossana Schiaffino**

On the plus side, we have Horst Frank as Pereira, the resident thug, but even his talents are pretty much wasted here. It's a good hour before he's allowed to confront Scott after Scott is easily captured sneaking around the warehouse where the nuclear goods are stored. Pereira threatens but Scott gets the best of him, saying, "You must have been a beautiful child. Your mother must have loved you. Did you know her?" Pereira fumes. It isn't until very near the end of the film when the two have an unexciting fistfight.

Paul Klinger is Scott's contact, Norman, the double agent running the smuggling operation. Klinger would only make three more films, none in the spy genre, before succumbing to a heart attack. Sieghardt Rupp, who plays Pierre, Norman's right-hand man, made a lot of westerns in the sixties.

Director Ernst Hofbauer didn't make any more spy films and that's okay. This half-hearted effort has some nice locations, but there are two many negatives about it to make it worthwhile. All the physical confrontations in the film are weak, as if Hofbauer disdained violence. I mentioned the lame fistfight between Scott and Pereira toward the end. There's also an interrogation of Carol that is embarrassing in its execution. She has a cigarette pointed in her direction, but that's about the extent of it. Not that I want to see her tortured, but perhaps the scene would have been better left out. Hofbauer sure didn't know what to do with it. The worst of it comes at the end of the film where control of the situation—who has the gun, in other words—switches back and forth between Scott and the bad guys half a dozen times in the last 10 minutes. It gets rather silly.

The film boasts a Riz Ortalani score, but even that doesn't help much. If your cup of tea is to listen to Stewart Granger belittle the Chinese for using chopsticks, then by all means, have at it.—DD

CREDITS: Production: P.E.A., Arca Filmproduktion; Director: Ernst Hofbauer; Story based on the novel "La Riviere De Trois Jonques" by Georges Godefroy; Screenplay: Hans Karl Kubiak, Werner P Zibaso; Cinematography: Hans Karl Kubiak, Werner P. Zibaso; Music: Riz Ortolani; Original running length: 85 mins; Country: Italy/West Germany; Year: 1965

CAST: Stewart Granger (*Mike Scott*), Rosanna Schiaffino (*Carol*), Paul Klinger (*Norman*), Margit Saad (*Blanche Coty*), Sieghardt Rupp (*Pierre Milau*), Helga Sommerfeld (*Danny Davis*), Franco Fantasia (*Robert Grant*), Horst Frank (*Pereira*), Harald Juhnke (*Smoky*), Chitra Ratana (*Mai Tim*), Paul Dahlke (*John Harris*), Suzanne Roquette

## THE RELUCTANT SPY

aka Agente secreto (Sp), Geheimagent S. schlägt zu (WG), L'honorable Stanislas, agent secret (Fr), How To Be A Spy Without Even Trying (Int), Spionaggio senza frontiere (It)

What we have here is a delightful French romantic comedy with espionage overtones

**Energetic artwork on the Belgian poster for the romantic *The Reluctant Spy***

that even the most spy-hardened viewer will find diverting. Jean Marais is a harried businessman with the unlikely moniker of Stanislas Everest Dubois, who stumbles into true love and the danger of espionage in the same night. Dubois inadvertently picks up the wrong coat while on his first date with Ursula (Genevieve Page) and thus begins the sequence of events that leads him into a world of humorous cops, dimwitted spies, curmudgeon cab drivers and other sundry characters that cause him much frustration.

The plot, having to do with the ubiquitous secret microfilm, is not so important, as everything turns out all right and hardly anyone suffers. No, we're more concerned with the amusing situations and eccentric people who seem to appear at every turn than whether the good guys will persevere.

This is actually quite a funny film, with lots of little successful bits of business. We have police who are overly concerned with the proper serving of tea and spies who aren't very good at math. There's a funny part that involves the use of an (undoubtedly rare) car phone that still elicits a chuckle even in this day and age of cell phones. Then there's a fight in a bar, over which we hear a television lecture about a piece of classical music. When the fight spills over into an adjacent apartment, a deaf old man reading a Felix the Cat comic is oblivious to the brouhaha going on behind him. Even when the fight devolves into slapstick antics in the bedroom of an elderly couple, the humor remains. Better yet, there's a truly amusing exploding cigarette gag that's still funny after multiple viewings, but we won't spoil it with the details. This is indeed a very difficult film not to like.

There are more throwaway lines and gags here that work than can be found in many out and out comedies. When Dubois dreams of his new girl one evening, he envisions her in the garb of the famous spy, Irma Vep. When one of the spies is given torn bills as the first half of payment for services to be rendered, he remarks "This reminds me of when we were electioneering...in South America." When Dubois is coerced into spying for his country, instead of being called "bait" he is termed a "strategic intermediary."

Marais is a winning hero who deftly carries the film, and Page is cute and clever as the love interest. Gaia Germani has a small role as a double agent who meets her end in Marais' apartment.

The score by Georges Delerue is unobtrusive but also unmemorable. Co-writer and director Jean-Charles Dudrumet assumed the same roles a couple of years later for *Killer Spy*, also starring Marais as Dubois. The finale of this film charges wholeheartedly into the improbable, but all is forgiven by the viewer won over so completely from the start.—DD

CREDITS: Production: Films De La Licorne, Italgamma; Director: Jean-Claude Dudrumet; Story: Michel Cousin, Jean-Charles Dudrumet; Screenplay: Michel Cousin; Cinematography: Pierre Gueguen; Music: Georges Delarue; Original running length: 91 mins; Country: France/Italy; Year: 1963

CAST: Jean Marais (*Stanislas*), Genevieve Page (*Ursula Keller*), Gaia Germani (*Andrea*), Noel Roquevert (*Commissioner Mouton*), Maurice Teynac (*Thirios*), Jean Galland (*Derblay*), Mathilde Casadesus (*the diva*), Marcelle Arnold (*the secretary of Stanislas*), Christian Marin (*the secretary of Mouton*), Jean-Loup Reynold (*a heavy*), Germaine Dermoz (*Stanislas's mother*), Helene Dieudonne (*the grandmother*), Louis Arbessier, Jean Ozenne, Michel Seldow, Yvonne Clech, Raoul Billerey, Paul Faivre, Max Montavon, Made Siame, Christian Lude, Robert Rollis, Marcel Merovee, Jacques-Henri Duval, Robert Seller, Pierre-Jacques Moncorbier, Pierre Tornade, Jean-Henri Chambois, Andre Gilles, Paulette Noizeux, Sylvain, Jean-Pierre Zola, Jean-Pierre Vaguer, Fred Fisher, Georges Bever, Marcel Loche

## REQUIEM FOR A SECRET AGENT

aka Der Chef schickt scinem besten Mann (WG), Consignia: Tanger 68 (Sp), Requiem per un agente segreto (It)

Stewart Granger's last foray into the spy genre opens with a stripper act where a bullfight film is projected onto a girl's body as she seductively removes her clothing. I can't help but see this as a metaphor for the general attitude of the film in treating women as appliances, or worse. Of Granger's spy films made in the sixties, this is the most violent and misogynist.

This time Granger is John "Bingo" Merrill, a son of a bitch by his own boss' reckoning, and we can't disagree. When we first meet Bingo, he's playing the opportunist, arranging for a judge to be smuggled across the Berlin border and taking the family's jewelry in return. The film wants to be a morality play, but the lack of conviction for such things shows through too often to be taken seriously. By the time old Bingo makes his pseudo-repentance, it's too little too late for the viewer to believe in it.

The violence in the film is handled well enough, avoiding the area of outright cruelty, but too often the misogynist flavor of it will leave a bad taste in the average viewer's mouth. At one point, Bingo returns to his contact's female partner, bloodied and beaten after having escaped from Rubek (Peter Van Eyck). After a moment of mothering, the sight of blood becomes too much of a turn-on for the little lady and she practically attacks Bingo. You can sure tell this written by men.

Bingo's attitude toward women is reconfirmed throughout the film, with lines like "I've made it a habit never to tell women the truth.

**Stewart Grainger looking guilty on the German poster for *Requiem For a Secret Agent***

The few times I have, they didn't believe me." But the greatest offense against the viewer is a scene with the lovely Daniela Bianchi. Her character up to this point has been shown to be stupid and vindictive but not evil, yet we're supposed to believe she deserves the serious slapping around she receives from Bingo. After she takes a half-dozen slaps, she pulls a gun on him. He wrestles it behind her back and pulls the trigger, killing her. It's shock enough when this happens, but we recoil at Bingo's jaded lack of remorse when he calls her an amateur who deserved what she got.

From this point on the viewer's already-strained identification with Bingo is completely severed, and we start rooting for the bad guys. But they have their own set of problems devised by the writers. Rubek has a young protégé, a remorseless killer whom Rubek picked up when he was a kid. It's obvious that the two have more than a platonic relationship, which is certainly no crime in itself, but you get the feeling the filmmakers view homosexuality as intrinsic to being on the "wrong" side of the political spectrum.

The film itself is a pretty tight little espionage thriller, but the hidden agendas of the filmmakers make it clear we're in the hands of the less capable. What could have been a cynical look at the meaninglessness of politics at this level—and it certainly tries to be that—instead reveals itself as a showcase of redneck attitudes and poor judgment.—DD

CREDITS: Production: P.E.A. Cin.ca, Constantin Film, Prod. Cin.cas Venus; Director: Sergio Sollima; Story: Sergio Sollima; Screenplay: Sergio Sollima, Sergio Donati; Cinematography: Carlo Carlini {Techniscope – Technicolor}; Music: Antonio Perez Olea; Original running length: 108 mins; Filming locations: Incir-De Paolis, Morocco, Tangiers, Rabat, Marrakesh; Country: Italy/West Germany/Spain; Year: 1967

CAST: Stewart Granger (*John "Bingo" Merrill*), Daniela Bianchi (*Edith Bressart*), Peter Van Eyck (*Rubeck*), Giulio Bosetti (*Erick Olafsson*), Maria Granada (*Betty Lou*), Luis Induni (*Felix Bressart*), Franco Andrei (*Ned Robbins*), Wolf Hillinger (*Aleksej*), Mirella Panfili (*the stripper*), Beni Deus, Enrique Navarro, John Karlsen, with Gianni Rizzo (*Atenopoulos*), Georgia Moll (*Evelyn Bressart*)

RESIDENCE FOR SPIES
aka Ça barde chez les mignonnes (Fr),
Golden Horn (US, alt),
Residencia para espías (Sp)

The High Priest of Hackdom, Jesus Franco, was a frequent dabbler within the spy genre. Then again, he was a frequent dabbler in every genre, so it's hardly surprising. What is more unexpected is that his spy films tend to actually be quite good. OK, I have to admit here that I'm not one of the diminutive maestro's biggest fans, and find his, ahem, freeform approach to filmmaking rather soporific.

That doesn't mean I don't admire the guy. I mean, he spent the whole of the sixties and early seventies traipsing from one exotic location to another, accompanied by a gang of mates and some beautiful women—making films whenever he couldn't find a good restaurant to sit in all afternoon. You've got to give respect where it's due. And furthermore, all of *Lucky the Inscrutable*, *Sadisterotica*, *Kiss Me Monster* and *Attack of the Robots* are pretty decent, enjoyably camp productions.

So it's gratifying to come down to earth with the thoroughly mediocre (and long obscure) *Residence for Spies*.

A spy has infiltrated American Intelligence in Istanbul, and is passing top-secret documents to all and sundry. Secret agent Dan Leyton (Eddie Constantine) is dispatched to investigate. He immediately finds one of his contacts murdered, but nonetheless makes his way to their evil headquarters—a training camp for prospective spies, which seems to be entirely populated by extremely attractive, extremely randy young women. Dan makes his presence known by playing an organ accompaniment while the ladies sing a particularly tuneless rendition of "When the Saints Go Marching In," which is so dirge-like it could almost have been arranged by Leonard Cohen.

Unfortunately, Leyton seems far more interested in mucking around with the frisky females than doing any investigating. Fortune, however, favors the foolhardy. He discovers a couple of likely looking suspects (one of whom is a proto-hippie with an astonishingly bad haircut) hiding in the attic/chicken pen. It eventually turns out that the camp doctor, in allegiance with a local diplomat, is responsible for leaking the information.

Let's look at the negatives first. The script is dreadful, drifting along in no particular direction. Sequences occur that have absolutely no relevance to anything else, and are obviously included only to accommodate cameo performers (Howard Vernon getting killed, spaghetti western veteran Chris Huerta smoking a pipe and wearing a fez, etc.). The situation—a training camp for lissome ladies—is hardly used to its full cheesy potential. At one moment the plot threatens to break into full giallo mode (a la *Blood and Black Lace*, with its similar enclosed setting), but this just fizzles out.

It's also rather talky, perhaps because when there is any choreography it is so staggeringly poor that even Franco must have realized it was a good idea to keep it scarce and short. Not unexpectedly, given the director, there's also more zooming to be found than at Brands Hatch on a Grand Prix Sunday. There are also some totally pointless cutaways and point of view shots, which are so frankly irrelevant they almost fool you into thinking that they symbolize something.

**Sex, violence and a recognizable spy on the Turkish poster for *Residence For Spies***

For all of its defects, there are some positive notes to be found. The easy-listening score has its moments (definitely not including the aforementioned interpretation of "Saints..."), and it's hardly trying to watch Diana Lorys—a much underused and underappreciated actress—in assorted states of undress. Craggy Eddie Constantine is as enjoyable as ever (few actors can boast a career spanning Jean Luc Godard and Jesus Franco in successive years). The sets are also vibrant, but you'd have to be truly incompetent to make Istanbul look boring. And, if nothing else, you can at least appreciate *Residence* for its unique "death by X-ray machine."—MB

CREDITS: Production: Hesperia Films, Elysee Films; Director: Jesus Franco; Story based on a novel by Michael Loggan; Screenplay: Jesus Franco; Cinematography: Antonio Macasoli {Eastmancolor - Panoramica}; Music: Odon Alonso, Adolfo Waitzman; Original running length: 89 mins; Country: Spain/France; Year: 1966

CAST: Eddie Constantine (*Dan Leyton*), Diana Lorys (*Janet Spokane*), Otto Stern, Anita Hofer,

Tota Alba (*Commander Pendleton*), Maria Paz Pondal, Chris Huerta (*the bar manager/arms dealer*), Dina Loy, Lola Gaos, Hector Quiroga, Antonio Jiminez Escribano, Nora Romo, Pilar Vela, Gonzalo Esquiroz, Howard Vernon (*Sr. Radek*), Jesus Franco (*piano player*). Uncredited: Patty Shepard (*girl*)

RIFIFI IN AMSTERDAM
aka Du Rififi a Amsterdam (Fr),
Rififi ad Amsterdam (It),
Rififí en Amsterdam (Sp)

Some movies just don't make a lot of sense no matter how many times you watch them. This one doesn't quite achieve the fever dream status of say, *The Devil's Man*, but it is nonetheless a confusing mess that will amuse only the diehard fan.

Director Sergio Grieco made a string of spy movies in the sixties, mostly with Ken Clark as the hero. On *Rififi*, however, he seems to have dropped the proverbial ball. It's not that the film is incompetent, but the complicated plot goes nowhere until we reach a whacked-out ending.

**Bikini babe with gun gets the point across on the Turkish poster for *Rififi in Amsterdam***

Indicative of the confused plotting, Roger Browne plays Rex Monroe, but he's really (as we find out at the end) Col. Ross Morrison, super-spy. Morrison is on the trail of Max Fischer (Franco Ressel), who is supposedly dead but he's not, he's just crazy. Most of the film is spent with Morrison on a wild goose chase devised no doubt by the mad Fischer but carried out by his right-hand man, Vladek (Umberto Raho). Vladek has Morrison tramping all over Europe to deliver the stolen diamonds—actually fakes switched by Vladek—back to Vladek himself. And all this for no good reason I could discern.

But never mind that. Things get really zany in the last 15 minutes when we "discover" that Fischer is really still alive but has gone mad in his quest for world domination (really, we knew he was still kicking earlier in the film when Morrison stealthily enters his "widow's" room and finds lots of framed newspapers detailing the death of her husband and a picture of the recognizable actor who will portray him later).

Fischer's mad scheme has to do with a laser cannon that is a million times more powerful than an ordinary laser, which he has aimed at a French H-bomb plant in the Sahara. But that's not the crazy part. He thinks that because Morrison had infiltrated the gang that stole the diamonds for Fischer's laser, that the resulting destruction will be blamed on the US, plunging them into political turmoil. America will then take on Fischer as the President's counselor, which will give him the power to rule the world. And they call him mad. But enough "plot."

As I mentioned before, the film is not incompetent. The nonsense is handled quite well really, but this results in a lack of silliness to detail at length. You do have a great score by Piero Umiliani to enjoy along the way, though.—DD

CREDITS: Production: Claudia Cin.ca, Procensa; Director: Terence Hathaway [Sergio Grieco]; Story and Screenplay: Lucio Manlio Battistrada, Armando Crispino, Ramon Comas de Turnes; Cinematography: Eloy Mella {Eastmancolor}; Music: Piero Umiliani; Original running length: 90 mins; Filming locations: Amsterdam, Granada, Tenerife; Country: Italy/Spain; Year: 1967

CAST: Roger Browne (*Rex Monroe/Ross Morrison*), Aida Power (*Oriana Ray*), Umi [Umberto] Raho (*Vladek*), Franco Ressel (*Mr. Fischer*), Frank Liston [Franco Lantieri] (*embassy attache*), Tullio Altamura (*the ambassador*), Michael Rivers (*Bernard*), Julio Perez Tabernero (*Manolo*), Tito Garcia (*Ben, a Wladeck henchman*), Ivan G Scrat[uglia], Angela Alarguenzoro, Jules Benning, Evely Stewart [Ida Galli] (*Mme. Fischer*)

RING AROUND THE WORLD
aka Duel dans le monde (Fr),
Duello del mondo (It)

We open with the old ice bullet trick. Giacomo Rossi-Stuart is the cold-as-ice (and unnamed) killer who guns down a man in the middle of the street. Next is a similar killing on the beach and then one at a Bangkok tourist attraction. This last killing is unusual in that the victim films his own assassin (very unprofessional to leave such a clue, Giacomo). Gum-chewing insurance investigator Fred Lester (Richard Harrison) is assigned to find out why these men, all holders of large life insurance policies, have died and left their insurance payoffs to various banks. The trail leads Lester around the world as promised—from London to Rio, Brasilia and Hong Kong—but the truth of the matter resides much closer to home.

*RATW* falls just outside the strict definition of spy film but like its nearest kin, the Bulldog Drummond films of the sixties, it is interchangeable with the true spy flicks of the period. Harrison makes for an unconventional hero, however. He wears glasses and he's good at his job but certainly not infallible. Actually, this is one of Harrison's best performances. He sort of feels his way along and comes out on top due less to his skill than his luck.

Halfway through his investigation, Lester is assigned to drag around a "dead" client's daughter, Mary Brightford (Helen Chanel, who just drips sex appeal here), for romantic interest. Lester doesn't mind at all and neither do we. Sure, she tries to kill him during the course of events, but only because she's forced to. He forgives her and so do we.

One of the minor pleasures of watching Eurospy films is the time capsule views we get of exotic locations around the world, and

**The modern art and architecture of Brasilia are featured on the Italian poster for *Ring Around the World***

this film holds a special place in that regard. As mentioned, one of the spots we visit is Brasilia. When this was filmed, the mid-sixties, Brasilia was a brand new ultra-modern city, still somewhat underdeveloped. Lester and Rossi-Stuart have a car chase around the vast landscapes, giving us a fascinating look at the art and architecture of what is still considered an audacious triumph of style. *RATW* is unique in this respect. I know of no other Eurospy flick to give us such a treat.

The near-finale shootout also uses an interesting location. It looks like a Hong Kong amusement park and its unusual nooks and crannies play well with the gun battle. Plus the scene leads to a knock-down, drag-out fight between Lester and Rossi-Stuart. You can guess who wins.

Other fun bits include a drowning demonstration ("This is how we found him."), a fab rock band, a ring that contains a garrote wire, a phony plane explosion, poison lipstick and Chinese girls dancing around a jukebox. There's plenty of action, intentional humor, beautiful women and a terrific Piero Umiliani soundtrack. What's not to like?

By the way, those ice bullets are really made of "a chemical compound that dissolves instantly while causing heart failure and leaving absolutely no traces." Except a bullet hole, of course.

CREDITS: Production: Leone Film, Radius Productions, Zenith Cinematografica; Director: Arthur Scott [Luigi Scattini]; Story and Screenplay: Ernesto Gastaldi; Cinematography: Claudio Racca {Technicolor}; Music: Piero Umiliani; Original running length: 85 mins; Country: France/Italy; Year: 1966

CAST: Richard Harrison (*Fred Lester*), Sherrill Morgan [Helen Chanel] (*Mary Brightford*), Jack Stuart [Giacomo Rossi-Stuart], Dominique Boschero (*Yo-Yo*), Bernard Blier (*Lord Berry*), Jose Lewgoy

RING OF SPIES
aka 003 contro intelligence service (It),
Ring of Treason (US)

Based on the true-life (UK) Portland spy case, this begins in true documentary style with a short history of spies including file and newsreel footage and even a couple of snippets from our film to give it that bit of authenticity. We

**American poster for *Ring of Spies***

then follow the rather dull factual details of real life and how each of us is vulnerable to the erosion of political loyalties in the post-war era.

This is actually one of the last of this type of small-scale spy story. It is of interest primarily because its star, Bernard Lee, helped usher in a new, sensational type of spy film by playing the character "M" in *Dr. No*, released a year earlier. The two could not be further apart in style and content, not so much because this is based on fact but because Bond would put an end to this kind of kitchen-sink espionage. It would no longer be interesting to imagine that your neighbor was a spy. Fantasy had trumped reality in the spy game by then.

When a tipsy Henry Houghton (Lee) commits a faux pax at a diplomatic party, he winds up transferred to a Navy outpost where he is invited by people with thick accents to commit treason. Disenchanted with his country and himself, Henry decides to pass secret documents in exchange for modest amounts of money. He engages—or rather bluntly steers—a co-worker, Elizabeth (Margaret Tyzack), who holds the keys to the safe, to help him sneak documents out on the weekend where they can be photographed, converted to microdots and transmitted to foreign powers. Henry blows the money they receive on a new car and in the local pubs, which raises the suspicions of his superiors. From here on in it's the mechanics of surveillance until all the players can be rounded up: the swinging photographer (William Sylvester) who was Bernie's main contact and the inconspicuous old couple (David Kossoff and Nancy Nevinson) who managed the technical end.

There's little to recommend in this competent fossil of a film. The admonishment at the end to be suspicious of those around you seems quaint and a relic of another era, an era that had passed even as this film hit the theaters.—DD

CREDITS: Production: British Lion Film Corporation; Director: Robert Tronson; Story and Screenplay: Peter Barnes, Frank Launder; Cinematography: Arthur Lavis {B&W}; Original running length: 90 mins; Filming location: London; Country: UK; Year: 1963

CAST: Bernard Lee (*Henry Houghton*), William Sylvester (*Gordon Lonsdale*), Margaret Tyzack (*Elizabeth Gee*), David Kossoff (*Peter*

*Kroger*), Nancy Nevinson (*Helen Kroger*), Thorley Walters (*Commander Winters*), Gillian Lewis (*Marjorie Shaw*), Newton Blick (*P.O. Meadows*), Philip Latham (*Captain Ray*), Cyril Chamberlain (*Anderson*), Justine Lord (*Christina*), Patrick Barr (*Captain Warner*), Derek Francis (*Chief Superintendant Croft*), Edwin Apps (*Blake*), Basil Dignam (*2nd member at Lords*), Paul Eddington, Norma Foster (*Ella*), Richard Marner (*Colonel Monat*), Garry Marsh (*1st member at Lords*), Brian Nissen (*Lt Downes*), Hector Ross (*Superintendant Woods*), Margaret Ward (*Muriel*), Anita West (*Tilly*)

SADISTEROTICA

aka The Case of the Two Beauties (Int, unconfirmed), El Caso de las dos bellezas (Sp), Red Lips (Int, unconfirmed), Rote Lippen (WG), Two Undercover Angels (US), Der Wolf—Horror pervers (WG)

**DVD cover art for *Sadisterotica***

This ultra-cheesy nonsense sees Jesus Franco at his very best. It's incredibly silly, of course, but features glamorous babes, pop-art sets, terrible fashions and a complete absence of sense. It's all just about whacked-out enough to make you forget that it's put together with the director's indomitable lack of panache. It's not good, but it's good fun, which is all you can hope for, really.

Janine Reynaud and Rosanna Yanni are Diana and Regina, partners in a detective agency. Their trademark is to leave a red lipstick mark wherever they have investigated/broken into/drunk from. They are currently looking into the disappearance of Lida Regnier (Mariá Antonia Redondo), the latest in a series of fashion models to have gone missing in mysterious circumstances.

Little do they know that she has been snatched by the extremely hairy Morpho (Michel Lemoine), at the bequest of loopy artist Klaus Tiller (Adrian Hoven, decked out in goatee and eyepatch, looking like a cut-price Christopher Lee). Fortunately, the potty painter gives himself away by exhibiting a portrait of his victim in public, the stupidity of which seems perfectly natural in the scheme of things here. Tiller isn't satisfied with this, and later kidnaps a nightclub dancer, whom he photographs being molested by his hirsute assistant.

Anyway, our heroines are soon on his trail. Diana catches his eye while strutting her stuff on the dance floor, and only just manages to avoid being grabbed by Morpho ("the unshaven idiot," as she calls him—which is something of an understatement, to say the least). To recover from the stress, they decide to go on holiday (which gives them much opportunity for the wearing of frivolous bikinis).

Meanwhile, a couple of hopeless peripheral characters—Italian playboy Vittorio (Manolo Otero) and hardboiled (yet camp) detective McClune (Chris Howland), who uses the pseudonym James Bond—stumble around looking bemused. Of course, everyone ends up in the same resort, leading to much japery as they all try to avoid or abduct one another.

It eventually becomes clear that Tiller is not who he seems. He has been using the photographs of his terrified victims as the basis for his (crap) art, painting them in their death throes before encasing the corpses in plaster and disguising them as sculptures (a plot device familiar from many films, not least is the Mike Raven vehicle *Crucible of Blood*). He is now determined to make Diana his latest, and most inspirational, model.

Along with its partner piece, *Kiss Me Monster*, this counts as a borderline spy film. The central characters bestride the secret agent and *Diabolik* strands, international private eyes (a la Kommissar X) with a tendency to dress up in bodystockings and facemasks. It also exudes the untrammelled "anything goes" spirit that characterizes the best of the genre. As someone who wasn't even alive in the sixties, I'm starting to strongly worry that my perception of the most swinging of decades is being somewhat tarnished by exposure to these films, populated as they are by LSD-gobbling, clothes-shedding groovesters (with no sense of rhythm). Surely it wasn't really like this? I mean, my parents were at large back then!

*Sadisterotica* has several plus points. The easy-listening soundtrack is very nice (if not as good as that of *Vampyros Lesbos*). There's a great title sequence, albeit it is shunted—seemingly at random—in the middle of a sequence in which the unfortunate Lidia prances around in a wedding veil, basque and stockings. The dubbing of the English-language version is frankly insane, with that strange mixture of torpor and extravagance ("That means we're dealing with an insane murderer!"). Best of all, it's just the right length at 80-odd minutes.

Whatever anyone says, I remain unconvinced as to Franco's talents as a director. He has a terrible sense of pacing, no self-control (admittedly not necessarily a bad thing) and often, frankly, doesn't seem to give a damn. All of his trademarks are present and correct: risqué (hokey) nightclub acts, an odd henchman called Morpho, a Franco cameo (as a hopeless art dealer), strong female characters and a generous amount of nudity (considering that otherwise it could have been a children's movie). He obviously liked the central premise of two ditzy (but somehow effective) female detectives investigating outlandish crimes. He remade it—with diminishing returns—about 10 times (as in *Les Emmerdueses* and *Two Female Spies With Flowered Panties*). In fact, his earlier black and white film, *Labios Rojos*, was most probably the first time he tackled this particular subject.

Possibly the only film ever made to feature torture by martini, two other things really struck me while re-watching this. First, both Reynaud and Yanni—despite having undoubtedly great figures—look disconcertingly like transvestites, with their big hair, garish clothes and masculine features. Second, if the chaps from popular UK sitcom *The League of Gentlemen* were ever looking for suitable raw material, they could do a lot worse than turning their attention in this direction.—MB

CREDITS: Production: Films Montana, Aquila Film; Director: Jesus Franco; Story: Karl-Heinz Mannchen; Screenplay: Jesus Franco, Luis Revenga; Cinematography: Jorge Herrero, Franz Hofer {Eastmancolor - Panoramica}; Music: Fernando Garcia Morcillo; Original running length: 92 mins; Country: Spain/West Germany; Year: 1967

CAST: Janine Reynaud (*Diana*), Rosanna Yanni (*Regina*), Adrian Hoven (*Tiller/Mr. Radeck*), Chris Howland (*Inspector Francis McClune*), Alexander Engel (*Albert Carimbuli*), Marcelo Arroita-Jáuregui (*Inspector Tanner*), Manolo Otero (*Vittorio Freda*), Maria [Dorit] Dom (*the dancer*), Ana Casares (*Radeck's assistant*), Michel Lemoine (*Morpho*), Mariá Antonia Redondo (*Lida Regnier*), Vicente Roca (*gallery manager*), Jesus Franco (*Napoleon Bolivard*), Marta Reeves (*Isma*), Elsa Zabala, Ana Puértolas, Manuel Velasco (*the receptionist*). Uncredited: Pilar Clemes, Julio Perez Tabernero, Milo Quesada

## THE SECOND BEST SECRET AGENT IN THE WHOLE WIDE WORLD
aka Licencia para matar (Sp), Licensed to Kill (UK)

Let's be frank: This is one damp spoof. I'll go into the details of this deadly dull affair if, for some reason, you're interested. Tom Adams is Charles Vine, an inexperienced agent whose assignment is to keep an eye on a scientist (Karel Stepanek) as he prepares his formula for "Regrav," a process that reverses gravitational waves. Vine is "a double 0 number, licensed to kill" and he certainly does make use of that particular privilege. During the course of the film Vine kills more than a dozen people. It's not the number that gives one pause, it's the callous and somehow nonchalant way he goes about it that is perturbing. Vine is, by his own confession, in it for the money. but one suspects he gets a certain pleasure out of taking lives as well.

Stepanek, as the Swedish scientist, gives the best performance of the movie. but that's not saying much. The entire production is so lifeless that the actors seem to just want to get it over with—and one can hardly blame them. The film starts off with a bad-taste killing when a nanny pulls a machine gun out of her baby buggy and slaughters a man in front of her two infant charges. Then we are treated to a lame theme song by Sammy Davis, Jr. and it's all downhill from here, folks. The film suffers from poor pacing, badly choreographed gun battles and worse fight scenes and the whole thing feels much longer than its 95-minute running time.

Tired gags include the budget crunch at the Secret Service, an opposition organization that's run like a corporation, silly names, bad accents, transvestite agents (Vladimir Shee-Hee), even mock Russian is spoken—all fall flat. The filmmakers make several passing references to that "other" secret agent, as if by invoking the spirit of Bond, some of that magic might hopefully rub off on this production. No such luck. (There is one funny name that got a chuckle: Sadistikov, the assassin ordered to kill Vine.)

**American poster for *The Second Best Secret Agent...* features an unusual graphic style**

There's a Russian agent trained to impersonate Vine (Tom Adams again), what they call a "Siamese," but that idea goes nowhere as well, since he just gets killed off without accomplishing anything. We also have those annoying illogical double-crosses whose only purpose is to further the plot. And what a plot. It's so complicated that it takes a five-minute expository scene at the end to clear it up for those audience members who stuck around. I won't even bother to try to explain it.

The dragged-out ending has Sadistikov stalking Vine near the docks, but it lacks any suspense whatsoever and so turns out be just a nicely photographed location sequence. Director Lindsay Shonteff seems bored with most of the material, which translates directly to the viewer. The score by Herbert Chappell is actually okay, but tends to meander when it should be focusing our attention. This dead fish actually spawned two sequels, both starring Tom Adams; *Where the Bullets Fly* and *Somebody's Stolen Our Russian Spy* (see reviews), but do yourself a favor and avoid this one.—DD

CREDITS: Production: Alistair Films; Director: Lindsay Shonteff; Story and Screenplay: Howard Griffiths, Lindsay Shonteff; Cinematography: Terry Maher {Eastmancolor}; Music: Bertram Chappell; Country: UK; Year: 1965

CAST: Tom Adams (*Charles Vine*), Karel Stepanek (*Henrik Jacobsen*), Veronica Hurst (*Julia Lindberg*), Peter Bull (*Masterman*), John Arnatt (*Rockwell*), Francis de Wolff (*Walter Pickering*), Felix Felton (*Tetchnikov*), George Pastell (*Russian commissar*), Judy Huxtable (*computer centre girl*), Gary Hope (*army officer*), Denis Holmes (*Maltby*), Billy Milton (*Wilson*), Carole Blake (*crossword puzzle girl*), Tony Wall (*Sadistikov*), Oliver MacGreevy (*1st Russian commissar*), Stuart Saunders (*police inspector*), Paul Tann (*Vladimir Sheehee*), Shelagh Booth (*a governess*), John Evitts (*a killer*), Robert Marsden (*August Jacobsen*), Mona Chong (*a Chinese girl*), Michael Godfrey (*Roger*), Julian Strange (*the hotel clerk*), Claire Gordon (*the hospital doctor*), Sarah Maddern (*a hotel maid*), J.A.B. Dubin-Behrmann (*Slavonic official*)

SECRET AGENT FIREBALL

aka Bob Fleming hetzt Professor G. (WG), Da 077: le spie uccidono a Beirut (It, alt), Espias en Beirut (Sp), Les espions meurent a Beyrouth (Fr), Le Spie uccidono a Beirut (It), The Spy Killers (UK)

For a film that has a lot going for it—a good cast, gadgets, a good score, an Ernesto Gastaldi script, not to mention a reputation—this isn't a very exciting spy thriller. Not that it's a disaster, but it's a by-the-numbers exercise that doesn't bring anything new to a genre that was in mid-cycle at the time of filming. That a spy film should seem tired when their ilk were at their peak of popularity is beyond this reviewer.

Richard Harrison takes the role of Bob Fleming (here dubbed "Bart"), agent X117, for his first foray into the genre. His last spy flick, *Killers Are Challenged*, released the following year, is another chapter in the Bob Fleming two-picture series. Harrison is a rather dull but likeable lead who never seems quite comfortable in his roles no matter the genre—sword and sandal, spaghetti western, or action—but he sure had plenty of work in his long career.

**Swedish poster for *Secret Agent Fireball* uses a mix of titles and languages**

When we first meet Fleming here, his lovemaking is interrupted by a phone call from his boss in what must be the single most common scene in spy films. You'd think those spies would learn to take the phone off the hook. Fleming is outfitted with a pen "designed for the detection of certain microwave frequencies," another pen that is really a blowtorch, microtransmitters in aspirin tablets (that can also be taken internally for headaches), a matching watch receiver, unlimited expenses and permission to kill. Fleming chases after some microfilm stolen from the Russians, spending most of his time in Beirut environs going through the motions of fistfights, humorous chases, knife fights (cinema's most boring type of duel), boorish behavior toward women, etc. Lots of things blow up too.

Fleming's main squeeze here is Elena (Wandisa Guida), a scientist's daughter. Guida's looks are reminiscent of The Pretenders' Chrissy Hynde. She tortures well. Her torturer is the inimitable Luciano Pigozzi. He is entrusted with a nifty tobacco pipe blowgun, which he uses with effectiveness. Pigozzi is a specialist in the role of psychotic killers who are so well suited to henchman positions. The evil female role is assayed by none other than Dominique Boschero, another regular in spy films of the period. I told you it was a good cast.

Favorable things about the film—to use the term loosely—would include a nightclub that features phones at each table that one can use to contact other patrons. This novelty apparently wasn't enough to bring in the public, so the club also booked a female wrestling floor show. It's a bizarre touch early in the film that is never quite equaled, but there are other odd bits.

While in Hamburg, Fleming runs afoul of the authorities, who for some reason use amphibious vehicles in their pursuit of criminals. When Fleming boards his flight on the first leg of his adventure, he kills the time by reading the movie tie-in for the Fred MacMurray film *Bon Voyage!* While on the airplane, he coincidentally meets up with Elena and, using the subtle charms of the sixties spy, he attempts to seduce her by issuing forth a wolf whistle. Her response is, "Do you often break out into bird calls?" His debonair reply: "It's my mating call."

The funniest gag in the film is when Fleming steals a helicopter while chasing a kidnapped Elena. The helicopter runs out of gas and Fleming sets it down at a gas station to fill it up. The best part, however, is when the attendant asks if Fleming would like his windshield cleaned.

**Margaret Lee gets the drop on Ray Danton on the Belgian poster for *Secret Agent Superdragon***

Director Luciano Martino was better known as a producer, and it would seem there is good reason. At least Martino's minor effort had a pro when it came to scoring films. Carlo Savina had a long career ahead of him at this point and he does an excellent job of producing hip spy tunes for this otherwise lackluster outing.—DD

CREDITS: Production: N.C., Devon Film, Radius Productions; Director: Martini Donan [Mino Loy and Luciano Martino]; Story and Screenplay: Julian Berry [Ernesto Gastaldi]; Cinematography: Richard Thierry [Riccardo Pallottini] {Eastmancolor – Widescreen}; Music: Carlo Savina; Original running length: 98 mins; Filming locations: Paris, Hamburg, Beirut; Country: Italy/France; Year: 1965

CAST: Richard Harrison (*Agent 077*), Dominique Boschero (*Liz*), Wandisa Guida (*Elena*), Carrol Brown, Alan Collins [Luciano Pigozzi], Jim Clay [Aldo Cecconi], Franklyn Fred, Audry Fischer, Clement Harari, Jean Ozenne

SECRET AGENT SUPERDRAGON
aka Höllenjagd auf heiße Ware (WG),
New York appelle Superdragon (Fr),
New York chiama Superdrago (It),
Nueva York llama a Super Drago (Sp)

*Secret Agent Superdragon* has become a touchstone of Bondian spoofs thanks to wide availability on the gray market and the misguided shenanigans of *Mystery Science Theater 3000*. Those who actually watch this movie will find, much to their surprise, that it is a competent and fairly serious exercise compared to many of its genre kindred. Admittedly there is enough cheapness and silliness to keep the viewer from thinking too highly of it, but it won't disappoint entirely.

Ray Danton, he of the cleft chin and dark good looks, is Bryan Cooper, aka Superdragon. Danton went on to much success on television as an actor and director. He's in his prime here, playing the ladies' man super-spy in what will no doubt be considered his quintessential portrayal.

We are also treated to the lovely talents of Marisa Mell as Charity Farell, another reason for the film's relative success. The other famous female is Margaret Lee as Cynthia "Comfort" Fulton, one of Cooper's compatriots. Comfort and Charity. You caught that, I'm sure.

They say this type of film is only as good as its villain and I'm afraid that Fernand Lamas played by Carlo D'Angelo (*I Vampiri*) just doesn't cut it. In fact, the whole set-up for the film is probably its weakest element. Lamas is experimenting with a drug called Syncron, which basically just messes with people's heads, making them fight and have seizures and such. The improved version, Syncron II, unveiled near the end of the film doesn't seem to be much more impressive. Syncron's vague properties mesh well with Lamas' vague plan to take over the world. If I were one of the half-dozen industrialists who are investing in his wacky scheme, I'd be a bit worried by now.

As I mentioned earlier, the film takes itself fairly seriously in mood and tone. This isn't just a romp in Bond's pajamas. The photography is evocative of a thriller in the many night scenes, but its special charm is bringing out a full palette of colors that still impress when watching a faded print. Sure, some of the sets are cheap, but they are offset by the picturesque Amsterdam locations. The score by Benedetto Ghiglia is excellent and the acting is at least competent.

While not being entirely gadget-driven, there are enough fancy devices to keep the bad guys at bay. We have two-way communicator watches, the bullet-proof vest gun, inflatable pillows for when you're stuck in a coffin at the bottom of the river, and that flashy machine at the end: "Have you ever had a bath in electricity?"

One of my favorite scenes is when Cooper interrogates the guy who runs the refreshment stand at the bowling alley. It's a small scene, but it takes on some bizarre qualities all its own. Cooper slaps this guy around enough to make things interesting and then somehow the guy is shot by a passing car before he can talk. We never see a car nor can we figure out, based on the logistical information given us (which is none) how it was physically possible for this to happen. It's like a dream.

I also like the scene where one of the thugs throws a knife at Cooper and it bounces off. We know Cooper is wearing a bullet-proof vest, so no further explanation is necessary; the set-up implies that he would be shot and recover. That moment of confusion for the knife-thrower works for me, what can I say. Some of the other attacks on Cooper's life are perpetrated by distinctly untalented hitmen. First of all, they don't try very hard and then they immediately kill themselves. How did they get this far in the thug game anyway?

Also worth noting is the cool little fire-breathing dragon that appears when Baby Face (Jess Hahn) joins Cooper's crew on this adventure. I get the dragon reference but it seems strange to me that this thing is let loose in someone's office. I mean, that is serious fire it's breathing. And why does Cooper take everyone's cigarette away from them, take a couple of puffs and put it out? Just personality quirks, I guess. The extremely tacky explosion of the (model) plant where the Syncron is made near the end of the film is the icing on the cake. *Superdragon* is not as bad as some folks would lead you to believe nor is it a classic, but it holds a special place in the genre.—DD

CREDITS: Production: Ramo film, Fono Roma, Gloria Film, Les Films Bernard Borderie, C.I.C.C.; Director: Calvin Jackson Padget [Giorgio Ferroni]; Story and Screenplay: Mike Mitchell, Bill Coleman, Remigio Del Grosso, Roberto Amoroso, Giorgio Ferroni; Cinematography: Tony Secchi {Ramovisioncolor}; Music: Benedetto Ghiglia; Original running length: 100 mins; Filming locations: Amsterdam; Country: Italy/France/Spain; Year: 1966

CAST: Ray Danton (*Bryan Cooper, aka "Superdragon"*), Margaret Lee (*Cynthia Fulton, aka "Comfort"*), Carlo D'Angelo (*Fernand Lamas*), Jess Hahn (*"Babyface"*), Marisa Mell (*Charity Farrell, aka "Rembrandt 13"*), Adriana Ambesi, Solvi Stubing, Marco Guglielmi (*Alex*), Gerard Haerter [Herter] (*Professor Kruger*), Carlo Hintermann (*Coleman, head of the Secret Service*), Jacques Herlin (*Ross*), Benito Stefanelli (*Valiky*), Renato Romano (*the gym master*). Uncredited: Nello Pazzafini (*Knife-throwing guard at party*)

## THE SECRET OF THE SPHINX

aka La esfinge sonrie antes de morir (Sp), Du grisbe au Caire (Fr), Heiße Spur Kairo-London (WG), La Sfinge sorride prima di morire—stop—Londra (It)

Duccio Tessari is, like Sergio Sollima, a difficult director to pigeonhole. Unlike Sergio Corbucci, Mario Bava or Dario Argento—all of whom became associated with a particular genre and have amassed a significant cult following—Tessari flitted from one type of film to another without appearing uncomfortable. As a result, he has remained a less easily identifiable filmmaker. His work is often as good as that of the aforementioned directors, but less convincingly press-ganged into supporting some kind of auteur theory. He is equally happy with roustabout action pictures (*A Pistol for Ringo*, *My Son the Hero*) and more somber, elegiac pieces (*The Return of Ringo*, *The Bastards*, *The Blood-Stained Butterfly*). At the same time, however, his films retain a certain classiness that differentiates them from the work of capable, but less inspired, craftsmen such as Mario Caiano, Paolo Bianchini and Ferdinando Baldi.

Thomas (Tony Russel), a Lloyd's Investigator (a proxy secret agent a la Bulldog Drummond) based in Cairo, is assigned to look into a large amount of gold that has gone missing from the Egyptian National Bank. He immediately becomes interested in the members of a group of archaeologists working in the desert—not least because they include a feisty blonde, Helene (Maria Perschy). When she seems slightly unsettled by his attentions, he does what every sensible man would—present her with a gold ingot!

To be honest, though, Helene appears to have a few issues of her own. Especially when she decides to shoot away at some poor dude whom Thomas is about to interrogate. Nevertheless, he seems happy to overlook this, and is soon impersonating her husband, a Dr. Blomberg, in order to infiltrate the diggers. He suspects that the gold is hidden in a cargo of "treasures" that is to be shipped out of the country, and is determined to both prevent this and discover which of the group is responsible. Could it be Professor Green (Ivan Desny), the ultra laid-back pipe-smoker in charge? Or perhaps Marian (Manuela Kent), the token bookish lady who turns into top-class totty as soon as she takes off her specs and hat? Or maybe even Ahmed (Salah Zoulfikar), the typically dodgy Egyptian security agent?

Apart from being yet another film to prove the truth in the old adage that you should never trust a man in a porkpie hat, *Secret* is an absolutely astounding-looking production. It scores points because the sets are an integral part of the plotting, rather than simply looking like stock travelogue footage, and they are shot as effectively as any cinematography to be found within the genre. The editing is pretty darned good too, especially one sequence in which Russel and Perschy have a long conversation while walking through assorted background locations. Of course, the North African setting does also give rise to several broader-than-broad "Comedy Arab" performances, but that doesn't distract from the proceedings too much.

Script-wise, this really owes as much to the "desert adventure" school of films as to the Bond formula. It has comedy moments, but is in general far less amiable than Tessari's other spy film, *Kiss Kiss Bang Bang*—although it does make up for this by having an effective mystery element as well as lots of people sweating heavily in the heat. Tessari handles things as well as you'd expect, although he does seem rather caught between being deadly serious and totally flippant (e.g., having the surviving characters speak to the camera as a finale). It's also surprisingly slow moving in places—especially in the first half.

Overall, it is a slightly perplexing film. Undoubtedly of a high caliber, it still leaves you feeling that it could have been something, well, something more. Maybe if someone could be kind enough to issue it as a spanking English-language DVD, it would make it easier to appreciate its undoubted qualities more fully.—MB

CREDITS: Production: Italcine TV, Top Film Production, Copro Film; Director: Duccio Tessari; Story: Guido Zurli; Screenplay: Guido Zurli, Duccio Tessari; Cinematography: Franco Villa; Music: Mario Migliardi; Original running length: 90 mins; Filming location: Egypt; Country: Germany/Italy/Egypt; Year: 1965

CAST: Tony Russel (*Thomas*), Maria Perschy (*Helene Blomberg*), Ivan Desny (*Professor Green*), Manuela Kent (*Marta*), Salah Zoulfikar (*Ahmed*), Tor Altmayer [Tulio Altamura] (*Franz*), Evar[isto] Maran (*Alain Nol*), Joseph [Giuseppe] Fortis (*an archaeologist*), Franco Ressel (*Tchourov*), Gigi Ballista (*the forger*)

**Spanish poster for *The Secret of the Sphinx***

SFIDA NELLA CITTA DELL'ORO
"challenge in the city of gold"
aka Heisses Land (WG),
tDer teufel von kapstadt (WG)

This is another "quest for a hidden microfilm" movie. In this case, the stolen film is hidden inside a small African statue as a means of smuggling it through Customs. The plot then goes a bit haywire, with events centering upon a woman named Veronica, who watches one of the worst exhibitions of tribal dancing—performed by pain-resistant mystics with sharp weapons—ever committed to celluloid. This actually becomes rather unpleasant, with assorted children apparently attempting to shish kebab themselves with sharp skewers (one guy even attempts to flame-grill himself—no kidding). It is also frankly interminable and, believe it or not, merely the first of five or so equally lengthy—and irrelevant—dance routines.

Finally the plot kicks in again, and it becomes clear that the artwork in which the microfilm is hidden has become confused with an identical statue that belongs to Veronica. The villains are none to happy to discover what has happened, and are determined to recover the film. It doesn't take them long to work out where it is, and they make a singularly unsuccessful attempt to snatch it back.

Fortunately, Interpol inspector Jochen Wilke is on the case, and his investigations begin, surprisingly enough, in a rather empty bar (this guy seems to spend literally all of his time in one nightclub or another). He chats up a brunette "beauty," who takes him back to her hotel room and treats him to a bout of Spanish guitar-playing, which causes him to promptly pass out (well, the drugs may have had something to do with it, but...). Things meander on in a similar fashion for the rest of the running time, as it becomes clear that the microfilm reveals the whereabouts of a case full of diamonds, lost off the coast of Africa in a sunken wreck. The gangsters—led by a scarred dude in a wheelchair—manage to recover it, but Jochen is on their trail.

*Sfida nella citta d'oro* is a forgettable action film that sits squarely within the early—predominantly German—genre form. The villains are hoodlums, the hero a glorified policeman accompanied by an innocent who has stumbled into some dirty doings. The emphasis is on international crime rather than international espionage, making it play more like Edgar Wallace in shorts than anything else.

The plot, as you may have gathered, is rather inconsistent. The first two-thirds revolve around the activities of Veronica and her annoying friend, a fresh-faced amateur detective whose perky eagerness is matched only by his capacity to irritate any member of the audience over six years old. Both of these characters, however, entirely disappear in the final 30 minutes, while a whole new group of characters are introduced. The tone is equally variable, as the po-faced proceedings are overwhelmed by an out-and-out slapstick finale, a brawl that actually manages to feature not only a talking parrot and a conveniently placed gong, but also a frisky midget.

Possibly the most unique aspect of the film is the unusual South African settings. These were also featured in director Alfredo Medori's other, better genre entry, *FBI operazione vipera gialli*. In this case, however, it seems as though the film has been basically split down the middle, with the first section shot in South Africa and the last section in Italy. All of the Italian performers (Montalbano, Borromeo, even Edward Canterbury) only appear after the hour mark, despite getting high-profile billing.—MB

CREDITS: Production: Cineproduzioni Associate, Centropol Film, Lothar Lomberg; Director: Alfredo Medori, Hermann Kugelstadt (German version); Story and Screenplay: Larry Madison, Heinz Bothe Pelzer; Cinematography: Fracesco Izzarelli, Hans Kuhle {Eastmancolor – 3D system}; Music: Francesco De Masi, Hugo Strasser; Original running length: 90 mins; Filming location: South Africa; Country: Italy/France; Year: 1962

CAST: Luisella Boni [Brigitte Corey], Robert Mitchell, Michael Kirner, Silvia Simon, Corrado Annicelli, Nuccia Cardinali, Charles Borromel, Edoardo Toniolo, Renato Montalbano, Gehrard Steinbeck, Claudio Marzulli, Sandy Bichet, Mario Pirri, Millicent Tutad, Carlo Janni, Leslie Richtfield, Oliver Randall, Joan Fraser, Robin Malan, Edward Canterbury, Harry

Victor, Lonis Franks, Khadidja Sydow, Garry Harendse, Clifford Ringquesy

SHADOW OF EVIL
aka Banco a Bangkok pour OSS 117 (Fr), Heisse Hölle Bangkok (WG), OSS 117—Gamble in Bangkok (Int), OSS 117 minaccia Bangkok (It), Panico en Bangkok (Sp)

Despite the bad rap this OSS 117 adventure has taken over the years, a recent reevaluation suggests that kinder words be spoken about it. The US re-titling, *Shadow of Evil*, turns out to be quite appropriate for a low-key adventure that relies more on atmosphere than action. This is not to say that the film is a resounding success, but neither is it one of the genre entries that should be passed by entirely.

Director Andre Hunebelle made four OSS 117 movies in the sixties, of which this is the second. One might argue that Hunebelle's familiarity with the character of Hubert Bonnisseur de la Bath led to his experimenting with different approaches in filming his adventures. Hunebelle takes a noir approach, at least visually, to large sections of the film. Much of the action takes place at night with plenty of shadows in which our characters can hover. Contrary to what the film's detractors say, this is a good-looking film even if experienced as a bad VHS dupe. The score by Michel Magne uses Eastern influences to good effect in creating soundscapes rather than themes, an unusual approach for the genre.

The film opens promisingly as an agent is riddled with machine gun bullets after he drives around the night streets of Bangkok long enough for the credits to roll. OSS 117, here taking the name Robert Barton, is called in to take his place and Kerwin Mathews steps into the role for the second time. Mathews is a likeable hero. He's good looking, suave, has a silky voice and he wears his suit and skinny tie well. He doesn't come across as cynical as some of the other leading men of the genre, so even though he seems to have every possible angle figured, there is an element of innocence to the characters he plays.

Barton selects a right-hand man, Sansok (Akom Mokranond) to assist him in the investigation, and this guy always comes through. At several points in the film Sansok is at the right

**Turkish poster for the low-key OSS 117 film adventure *Shadow of Evil***

place at the right time with the right implements of destruction.

The film relies less on gadgetry than on straightforward detective work, but we do get the old receiver-in-the-Chesterfields-cigarette-pack trick. This comes in handy almost immediately when Sansok uses it to warn Barton about an intruder in Barton's room. When Barton returns, he has a good kung fu-based fight with the burglar that manages to smash every piece of balsa wood furniture in the room. When our hero comes out on top, the bad guy tries to take a cyanide pill, but Barton interferes. As soon as Barton looks away, the determined fellow takes a flying leap off the balcony to his death, an unexpected turn of events to say the least.

The main bad guy here is Dr. Sinn (love that name), played by Robert Hossein. Hossein is not a particularly charismatic villain, which ultimately hurts the picture. Dr. Sinn is introduced to us as a healer, magician and hypnotist who captivates the Westerners around him. I don't know about that, but he does manage to convey a certain amount of creepiness. However, it is hard to believe that he could build a modest company of followers devoted to his insane quest to spread the plague around the world. At one point in the film, Barton is to be subjected to a super lie detector, but Barton punches the henchman and puts him in the chair instead. The man tells Barton about Sinn's little hobby—The People Elect—an organization of the intelligentsia planning the elimination of all inferior men with a new virus of plague. In Sinn's words, "to save mankind, the greater part of mankind must die." And they call him mad.

Two of the females in the cast succumb to the charms of Robert Barton during the course of the film. One, Eva (Dominique Wilms), is a follower of Sinn working within the good guys' organization. She comes to her senses near the end of the film and helps to free an imprisoned Barton, but must die for her traitorous acts. The other is Sinn's sister, Lila (Pier Angeli), a wispy beauty first duped by her brother to drug Barton, but she always remains true to her spy guy throughout the film, naturally. Neither of these women is given enough to do, but such is the way when there's spying to be done.

The Bangkok locations seem pretty bland all in all, with Hunebelle resisting the urge to include too many travelogue scenes. The cast drives around in big American cars—which is cool—while everyone in the real world around them drives the tiny cars that actually work in such crowded conditions.

There is one humorous element in the film: the trials and tribulations of an ex-Nazi spy trying to get his hands on the same information that Barton is after. Immediately upon arriving at the airport, Barton notices this guy take his picture. When Barton "accidentally" bumps him and ruins the film, the poor fellow seems nonplused. Later, a bomb is planted in Barton's car with a timer set to go off 15 minutes after he picks it up at the hotel. After Barton drives the car around for 14 of those minutes, the unfortunate spy manages a bit of a coup and steals a surveillance tape from Barton but also makes the mistake of stealing his car to get away. Needless to say, that's the last time we're bothered with the little rogue spy.

Sinn maintains your basic villain's lair under a remote monastery where the plague virus is synthesized. This lair does provide for some nice visuals, but as with the rest of the film, it is kept low-key rather than too flashy. The climactic battle at the end of the film is in keeping with this philosophy too. A few plague-infested rats are let loose and things blow up pretty good, but it's a low-budget affair. *Shadow of Evil* is not a failure, but neither will it land at the top of most people's list. Make up your own mind.—DD

CREDITS: Production: P.A.C., C.I.C., Dama Films; Director: Andre Hunebelle; Story based on "Lila De Calcutta" by Jean Bruce; Screenplay: Raymond Borel, Pierre Foucaud, Andre Hunebelle, Michel Lebrun, Patrice Rondard; Cinematography: Raymond Lemoigne {Franscope – Eastmancolor}; Music: Michel Magne; Original running length: 118 mins; Filming location: Bangkok; Country: France/Italy; Year: 1964

Cast: Kerwin Mathews (*Robert Barton/ Hubert Bonisseur de la Bath/OSS 117*), Robert Hossein (*Dr. Sinn*), Pier Angeli (*Lila Sinn*), Sing Milintrasai (*Prasit*), Dominique Wilms (*Eva Davidson*), Henri Virlojeux (*Leacock*), Jacques Hilling (*Hogby*), Gamil Ratib (*Akhom*), Jacques Mauclair (*Mr. Smith*), Colette Teissedre (*Dr. Winter*), Henri Guegan (*Karloff*), Raoul Billerey (*Christopher*), Yabumoto Svichi (*a Tibetan*), A. Makaranond (*Sonsak*)

SI MUORE SOLO UNA VOLTA
"it died only once"
aka Man stirbt nur einmal (WG)

After a protracted car chase, agent Mike Gold (Ray Danton) is unable to prevent his contact and friend, John Malsky (Marco Guglielmi), from being killed in a gunfight. Sent on a new mission to Beirut, Gold makes his presence known by rescuing a blonde from a kidnapping attempt in the airport car park. After engaging in a bit of rumpy-pumpy, he gags her and dumps her in the bath—which seems like no way to treat a lady!

Upon giving the kidnappers a surprise (by rerouting their gas lead into the living room and causing an explosion), he further torments them by draining out their brake fluid and encouraging them to drive round a corner particularly fast. Such frolics, of course, tire a chap out, so he takes a deserved rest with the blonde (who seems to have recovered from her dunking) in a bar, where they watch a bizarre African/contemporary dance. The entertainment is interrupted when Gold is threatened by several hoodlums led by Manuel (Fernando Cebrian, who appears to be wearing a very obvious false beard).

It soon becomes apparent that our hero has stumbled across an international criminal organization led by Professor Ackerman (Julio Pena), who has a penchant for playing chess blindfolded. Also working for them is none other than John Malsky, who has been blackmailed into joining them because of his serious drug problem. God knows what they're up to, but Gold has soon infiltrated their resort hideout, where he takes time out to watch some kids frugging (the camera repeatedly focuses upon the young ladies' breasts).

More nonsense unfolds. Helicopters are blown up, people are knocked unconscious by poison gas, the villains fall out and cars are driven off cliffs. Gold is left having to save the day before Ackerman's men cause a huge explosion at a nuclear reactor.

*Si Muore* is an enjoyable, if mediocre, film. The plot is basic, but made up for by some capable (and occasionally wayward) direction from Giancarlo Romitelli, a nice soundtrack and a willingness to just get on with the necessary action. The cinematography is rather schizophrenic. It looks great, but sometimes the mood just seems to get the better of someone—and a succession of zoom shots or eccentric camera angles are chucked into the mix. This oddness is exemplified by the climax, much of which is seen from the hero's point of view as he decimates the bad guys.

What saves this from being decidedly average is the capable cast. Ray Danton has a deftness of touch that he brought to all of his spy roles, and it really suits his character here. Julio Pena makes a suitably urbane (if utterly corrupt) villain and Marco Guglielmi, who also appeared with Danton in *Secret Agent Superdragon*, is very good in a larger- than-normal role. Pamela Tudor, an actress I have never found at all attractive, receives prominent billing despite appearing in nothing more than a glorified cameo role.

One major problem with the film is a notable lack of continuity. Characters drop in and out of the action, forgotten about for long periods of time (or totally), and the villains don't receive any kind of comeuppance. In mitigation, this could well have been due to cuts in the version under review (from German television).—MB

CREDITS: Production: Asa Cin.ca, Centauro Film; Director: Don Reynolds [Giancarlo Romitelli]; Story and Screenplay: Don Reynolds [Giancarlo Romitelli], Augusto Caminito, J. Hernandez, Jose Luis Dibildos; Cinematography: Carlo Carlini, Aldo Greci, Julio Ortaz [Ortas] {Eastmancolor – Asacolor}; Music: Carlo Savina; Original running length: 80 mins; Filming location: Cinecitta Studios, Rome; Country: Italy/Spain; Year: 1967

CAST: Ray Danton (*Mike Gold*), Pamela Tudor (*Ingrid*), Marco Guglielmi (*John Malsky*), Julio Pena (*Ackerman*), Sylvia Solar (*Jane*), Dada Gallotti (*Silvia*), Fernando Cebrian (*Manuel*), Francesca Rosano (*Alina*), Mirella Pamphili (*Eve*), Rossella Bergamonti (*Gloria*), Daniele Dentice (*Winston*), Don Reynolds (*Rabat*), Gilberto Galimberti (*Rub*), Mario Landoni (*Archeopoulos*), Mario Sabatelli (*Kemal*). Uncredited: Mario Brega (*Galante*)

SICARIO 77—VIVO O MORTO
"Sicario 77—dead or alive"
aka Agente End (Sp)

An old man in a pawnshop is so engrossed in his decrepit alarm clock that he doesn't notice when a spooky blond dude wanders in, assembles the machine gun formerly hidden in his violin case, and blasts him into oblivion. After picking up a single dollar note from the cash drawer, the killer departs.

It seems that this dollar note has a highly important message written on it in that old schoolboy standby, invisible ink. Secret agent Lester (Robert Mark), who is nicknamed "End" because of his ability to see every mission through, is assigned with the task of retrieving it. He immediately suspects an underground character, Mr. King (Jose Bodalo)—and his instincts prove to have some substance when he finds that the blond guy is one of his henchmen. The two of them soon meet up (at the Mayfair "Kit Cat Club," where the waitresses wear bunny ears) and promptly have a big fight,

**Robert Mark has the biggest gun in *Sicario 77--vivo o morto***

from which the pale-haired fellow emerges decidedly the worse.

It seems that King has a dastardly plan. He has used a secret device to sabotage an American spacecraft—Mercury Five—at launching. Even worse, he is blackmailing the authorities by threatening to destroy their atomic stockpile.

This is a rather complex genre entry, with multiple double-crosses and assorted scheming characters. It's also a rather verbose film, which makes watching the German video copy rather an effort. There was an English-dubbed version made, but this seems to be lost at present. However, as it also happens to be a rather interesting, extremely stylish affair, it is not too much of a trial if you just relax and let the look of the thing wash over you. There's also a great soundtrack, which uses a jazzy baseline, flutes and Spanish guitars to extremely good effect.

Director Mino Guerrini keeps things interesting with the use of a lot of bizarre camera angles and extreme close-ups. He also seems extremely fond of panning the camera around to follow characters in the foreground, before picking up—and focusing on—a more relevant activity in the background. His other genre entry, *Date for a Murder*, was also a fascinatingly off-kilter, visual treat—which makes the fact that he spent most of his career directing obscure comedy films all the more surprising. Maybe it had something to do with the fact that the cameraman was no other than multiple-Oscar-winner Vittorio Storaro (*Apocalypse Now*, *The Last Emperor*).

You also get a few nice gadgets and set pieces. The hero shoots himself with a "radioactive" bullet, which allows him to simulate being dead, and uses a tape recorder that's hidden in his shoe. There are a couple of very good fight scenes—which have a little more realism to them than is often the case—and your obligatory tussle in a cable car. The climax finds Lester running around and blowing everything up with an enormous bazooka, which is as entertaining as it is unlikely.

Lead actor Robert Mark is pretty good. Slightly dour, he brings a seriousness to things. Certainly not a pretty boy, you actually believe him to be capable of throwing—and receiving—a punch. The pinnacle of his achievement has to be escaping from a whole gaggle of men…while strapped to a medical table. He also isn't above crushing one villain to death beneath a forklift truck for no good reason and shooting another in the back while he's unconscious. That's nothing in the gratuitous violence stakes, though. Another poor chap gets a fishhook in his eye.

Jose Bodalo is an effective villain. With his henchmen dressed in black leather uniforms, a penchant for having female associates whipped (when they fail him, of course) and a fairytale castle hideaway, he encapsulates the perversity that runs through the genre. This is especially effective, as his portrayal is rather subdued, coming across as a normal businessman, bringing to mind the banality of evil.—MB

CREDITS: Production: Adelphia Compagnia Cin.ca, Prod. Cin.cas Balcazar; Director: Mino Guerrini; Story and Screenplay: Mino Guerrini, Adriano Bolzoni, Alfonso Balcazar, Sabatino Ciuffini; Cinematography: Aldo Scavarda {Techniscope – Eastmancolor}; Music: Giorgio Zinzi, Marcello Riccio; Original running length: 90 mins; Country: Italy/Spain; Year: 1967

CAST: Robert Mark (*Ralph Lester*), Alicia Brandet (*Minnie*), John Stacy (*"number 1," Ralph's boss*), Jose Bodalo (*Mr. Rudolf King*), Monica Randall (*Barbara*), Enrico Manera (*Alfred*), Maria Badmayew (*"Madame"*), Sonia

Romanoff [aka Sarah Ross], Francoise Fioretti, Demofilo Fidani (*Mr. King's aide*), Piero Morgia (*the boxer*), Francesco Tenzi, Lino Ranieri, Ivan G Scratuglia, Nino Casale (*Ted Mulligan*), Maria Pia Zambelli. Not visible and not credited: Francisco Cebrian, Armando Calvo. Uncredited: Luciano Rossi (*Dr Gross*), Tom Felleghi (*head of British intelligence*), Moisés Augusto Rocha (*a villain*)

SIETE MINUTOS PARA MORIR
"seven minutes to die"
aka Agente Howard:
7 minuti per morire (It)

Secret agent Ray Monks (Ruben Rojo) is murdered while recovering some top-secret documents from a shadowy individual in the backstreets of Hong Kong. Bill Howard (Paolo Gozlino) is ordered to find out who is responsible, and to make sure the documents are returned to the American authorities. Bill seems to have a thing for the Asian ladies, which means that his task is an entertaining diversion from chatting up as many females as possible. And things aren't made any easier when the one man who may know anything about exactly what's going on is murdered.

The action decamps to Milan, where Bill displays an unseemly interest in the activities of Monks' girlfriend, Karen Foster. It seems his suspicions are well founded; the agent is not really dead. The murdered man was someone whose face had been made to resemble that of Monks through the judicious use of plastic surgery, a fact that was given away by an unaccounted-for tattoo on the cadaver in question. But just what is the "dead man" up to?

Well, hanging around in questionable nightclubs, mostly, although he does manage to lure our hero into a particularly lame ambush. It appears that he is receiving orders from a mysterious Mr. Fargo, who is paying him handsomely for his underhand services. Fargo is the head of a criminal organization and, apart from trying to make a dishonest buck out of the aforementioned stolen documents, is also having a bit of trouble with the local Mafia.

*Siete minutos* is a respectable genre entry, no better and no worse than many others of its type. There's plenty of decent location work, especially that filmed in Hong Kong—which was a popular destination for sixties exploitation films. Deservedly so, given its winding alleys and bobbing junkets, not to mention the inevitable temples and palaces that cinematographers were so keen to capture on celluloid.

Direction is adequate, if hardly memorable. Things are kept moving with a bare minimum of extravagance or elaboration (as reflected by the sparse running time of just under 80 minutes). Every 10 minutes or so, you have the obligatory fight or chase scene, and the plot barely even registers. By way of gadgets, you get a nasty guillotine-protected safe (which takes the hand off a minor villain in a well-edited, squirm-inducing sequence) and the age-old room-with-closing-walls routine.

Fortunately, all this is elevated substantially by a good cast. Rosalba Neri plays her token brunette bitch, Ruben Rojo makes an innocuously slimy villain and Betsy Bell is suitably wide-eyed. George Hilton has a secondary role (this was before he became a serious Euro-star) and acts louche, hops about in a helicopter (looking relaxed to the point of slumber) and is—unsurprisingly for giallo fans—revealed to be the villain of the piece. He would partner up with the excellent Paolo Gozlino (a busy character actor of the time) for the pleasing spaghetti western *One More in Hell*, although by that time their position in the credits had neatly reversed.—MB

CREDITS: Production: Urfesa, S. Caruso; Director: Ray Feder [Ramon Fernandez]; Story and Screenplay: A. Di Risso, Gianni Scolaro, Ramon Fernamdez, E. Urrutia; Cinematography: Aldo Di Robertis {Eastmancolor}; Music: Jose Torregrosa; Original running length: 78 mins; Filming locations: Hong Kong, Milan, Genoa; Country: Italy/Spain; Year: 1968

CAST: Paul Stevens [Paolo Gozlino] (*Bill Howard*), George Hilton (*Agent Mike Russo*), Betsy Bell (*Virna*), Ruben Rojo (*Ray Monks*), Jose Marco, Mario Donen (*mafia head*), Marisol Ajuso, Julio P. Tabernero, Francisco Sanchez, Fajda Nicol, Emilio Rodriguez (*the consul's assistant*), Rufino Ingles (*the American consul*), Margaret Lhy, Mary Leyva, Nieves Navarro (*nightclub singer*). Uncredited: Elizabeth Wu, George Wang (*Mafia representative*)

## SLALOM

Lucio (Vittorio Gassman) is on his way to a holiday at the ski resort of Sestriere with his wife, Ilde (Emma Danieli), and a couple of friends. Bored during the journey—and rather harried by his over-attentive wife—he stops off for a walk at a station and bumps into a mysterious blonde, Helen (Bebe Loncar). She immediately catches his fancy, and he is both pleasantly and disconcertingly surprised when she also turns out to be staying in Sestriere.

He soon becomes embroiled in mystery when an English friend of Helen's is murdered in an isolated country cottage. When he returns to the scene of the crime, he finds it has turned into a mountain tavern and is full of Austrian country dancers. More peculiar things happen: He's shot at by a sinister chap while on a chair lift; nearly crushed by tumbling logs; and, just to take the biscuit, kidnapped and chloroformed by a gaggle of young lassies dressed in Santa Claus costumes.

When he comes to he's shocked to discover that a) he's on a plane to Cairo, b) he's apparently a British citizen called Charles Irving and c) he's married to a new wife! Understandably, he finds this rather perturbing. Even more so because the strange killers are still on his trail.

Nonetheless, he soon discovers that his new identity has its advantages. He spends a lot of time in shady nightclubs, starts wearing sharp suits and discovers belly dancers throwing themselves at him. Yes, it seems that everyone

**Soundtrack for *Slalom***

is mistaking him for the FBI agent Charles Irving—who was supposed to meet Helen at the aforementioned train station, hence the mix-up.

The only way out of the situation is for Lucio to complete Irving's mission by smashing an international counterfeiting operation that threatens to destabilize the economies of the Western world. Can he do it?

Director Luciano Salce specialized in making light-hearted, extremely competent films. This is no exception, with an amiable (and good-looking) cast, an entertaining story, a jolly Morricone soundtrack and some classy cinematography. All in all, a perfect slice of Euro-fluff, the ideal accompaniment to a dry martini and the reckless wearing of a smoking jacket. Honestly, this is just the type of thing that you can't imagine being made any more (although maybe the Coen brothers could have a shot at it), and current cinema is all the poorer for it.

As well as making great use of locations, *Slalom* also satirizes the conventions of the spy film genre relentlessly. Lucio is the complete antithesis of the average celluloid secret agent, a hapless, ineffectual everyman who's slightly out of touch with the world (let alone the world of espionage). He can't ski, he can't swim and he certainly can't fight people five times his size. Yet somehow he muddles his way through things, often by complete mistake, and even gets to canoodle ineffectually with a couple of gorgeous babes.

Make no mistake, this is no Franco and Ciccio-style parody. It's a gentler, less desperate entertainment. Although that doesn't mean it's not above including a couple of pratfalls and comedy chase scenes. One running joke is to make completely innocuous people look sinister through the way that they're photographed. In one sequence an Arab sidles toward the hero and draws a knife (he's trying to sell it as a souvenir). In another a man appears in the foreground holding a pistol (he's a swimming instructor about to start a race). The film also has a few things to say about the ridiculousness of the whole macho posturing of the genre, and how people often dream of leading lives of adventure to which they'd be hopelessly ill suited.

Bravo. Another one that should be chalked up as a potential DVD release.—MB

CREDITS: Production: Fair Film, Les Films Cocinor, Copro Film; Director: Luciano Salce; Story and Screenplay: [Franco] Castellano, Pipolo [Giuseppe Moccia]; Cinematography: Alfio Contini {Techniscope - Technicolor}; Music: Ennio Morricone; Original running length: 108 mins; Filming locations: Turin, Cairo; Country: Italy/France/Egypt; Year: 1965

CAST: Vittorio Gassman (*Lucio Ridolfi*), Adolfo Celi (*Riccardo*), Daniela Bianchi (*Nadia*), Beba Loncar (*Helen, the FBI agent*), Loubna A. Aziz (*the air hostess*), Emma Danieli (*Ilde, Lucio's wife*), Adolfo Celi (*Riccardo*), Robert Oliver (*George*), Isabelle Biagini (*Simonetta, Riccardo's wife*), Corrado Olmi (*the Italian embassy official*), Nagua Fuad, Piero Vida (*the assassin*)

SO DARLING, SO DEADLY

aka Agent Joe Walker: Operation Far East (US, unconfirmed), Agente Jo Walker: operazione estremo Oriente (It), Commissaire X dans les griffes du dragon d'or (Fr), Kommissar X—In den Klauen des Goldenen Drachen (WG), Operazione tre gatti gialli (It)

High Priests of Hokedom Brad Harris and Tony Kendall are off to Singapore in this sequel to *Hunting the Unknown.* Sensing the impeding avalanche of typical sixties smoothie behavior and dodgy chat-up lines, the local arbiters of taste attempt to have them shot. No luck. Before you can say "Brylcreem" they're eyeing up the "lay-dies" and frolicking by the pool with a couple of martinis. The assassination attempts continue, but are all foiled by the fact that the respective libidos of our dynamic duo ensure that they always seem to be in exactly the right place at exactly the right time.

When they're not too busy indulging in the art of girl-watching, they do actually have a mission. They must protect a local Professor (Ernst Fritz), who has invented a super strong laser that could be used to blow planes out of the sky. A group of nasties, The Golden Dragon (who are led by some bloke with a red cloth on his head), are looking to get their hands on it.

Being one of the more deranged of the series, there's plenty of fun to be had with

**German lobby card features Tony Kendall in pulp-style danger in *So Darling So Deadly***

this enjoyable affair. The action is well choreographed (by star Brad Harris), the fascinating locations are well shot and the music is an enjoyable cocktail of easy-listening tunes.

Parolini's direction is as accomplished as ever, with plenty of silly gadgets and devious torture devices to keep the audience entertained. Of course, his stars must have been so used to working with each other by this stage that they probably didn't need much guidance. Kendall could copyright the smirk as his trademark facial expression, while Harris is perpetually bemused and/or pounding the crap out of someone. In one particularly endearing moment, they both have a boogie in a local bar, and while the latter jitters around like an epileptic, the former clicks his fingers while displaying his slinky moves!

Interestingly, this film also features another bunch of women who spend a substantial amount of their time in typical fetish gear (including whips) and beating up men, which seems to have been something of a genre obsession.—MB

CREDITS: Production: Danny Film, Filmidis, Les Films Jacques Willemetz, Parnass Film,

Ceylon Tours; Director: John Eastwood, Cehett Grooper [Gianfranco Parolini]; Story and Screenplay: Mike Ashley [Mino Roli], Rudolf Zehetgruber; Cinematography: Francesco Izzarelli {Eastmancolor – Ultrascope}; Music: Gino Marinuzzi, Jr.; Original running length: 100 mins; Country: Italy/Austria/France/Columbia; Year: 1966

**Belgian poster for the Roger Hanin vehicle *The Solitaire Attacks***

CAST: Tony Kendall [Luciano Stella] (*Kommissar X, Joe Walker*), Brad Harris (*Captain Tom Rowland*), Ernst Fritz Furbringer (*Professor Akron*), Barbara Frey (*Sybille*), Gisella Hahn (*Stella*), Rose Margaret Keil (*Selena*), Jacques Bezard (*Charly*), Joseph Matthews [Giuseppe Mattei] (*Benny*), Charles Tamblyn [Carlo Tamberlani] (*Taylor*), Nicola Popovic (*Lihuwang*), Zorica Gajdas, H. Amin (*Takato*), John F. Littlewords [Gianfranco Parolini] (*Rex*), M. Ojatirato (*Lapore*), Ursua Parker [Luisa Rivelli] (*Shabana*), Sarah Abdullah (*Exotin*), Pixie Montero (*the telephone operator*)

THE SOLITAIRE ATTACKS
aka Le Solitaire passe à l'attaque (Fr),
El Solitario pasa al ataque (Sp)

Roger Hanin was in a long string of spy flicks in the sixties, including but not limited to the Agent Tiger films. They are not the best of the genre, but they are certainly not the worst. That said, this particular film is one of his lesser efforts. Director Ralph Habib doesn't have a lot to work with here—the story is dull and predictable—but this feels like a phoned-in job on top of it all.

This is one of those race-against-the-clock stories that should move and generate some tension, but it was not to be. Frank Norman (Hanin) is after a case that was stolen from a courier. This case is rigged to blow up if it is opened unless a special tape recording is played into its little microphone. In fact, it's going to blow up in a few days anyway. Norman's search takes up the entire length of the film. He has plenty of time to woo the women and such, and disarms the case within moments of its destruction, of course. In situations like this, we know from the start that he will not fail because the whatsit in the case must be retrieved. The fun is supposed to be in the chase. But it ain't fun, it's boring.

Not much really happens and what does is cliché and poorly staged. There are a couple of car chases and some stuff blows up, but the action lacks punch. The few fistfights—a Hanin specialty—are lackadaisical. One of these fights, such as it is, takes place in Park Guell in Barcelona, an amazing city park designed by the incomparable Antonio Gaudi. Unfortunately, the park does not get its due, with little of its unique charm present on film. We do get to see the lovely Sophie Agacinski bound and gagged on a conveyer belt, for what that's worth. Norman gets to drive around a of couple pieces of heavy equipment, but I find scenes like these almost sleep inducing.

Bernard Gerard's score is occasionally interesting, but more often inconsequential. Hanin is a likeable actor; it's too bad he wasn't in better movies. He just doesn't have enough of that certain something that would let him carry a bad movie, and this is a bad movie.—DD

CREDITS: Production: Pro Artis Ibérica, Consortium Financier de Production de Films, Sorefici; Director: Ralph Habib; Story: Andre Haguet; Screenplay: Michel Lebrun; Cinematography: Miguel F Mila {Eastmancolor - Techniscope}; Music: Bernard Gerard; Original running length: 92 mins; Country: Spain/France; Year: 1966

CAST: Roger Hanin (*Frank Norman*), Jean Lefebvre (*Robert Le Goff*), Teresa Gimpera (*Machka*), Milo Quesada (*Bernsen*), Gerard Tichy (*Friedman*), Sofia Agacisky (*Sylvie*), Gisèle Grandpré, Charles Millot (*Varescas*), Georges Riquier, France Rumilly

It can in no way be considered a classic of the cinema, but it does highlight the way in which these productions were less tailored to audience demographics—thus allowing individuals with slightly odd (or some might say warped) sensibilities to make popular entertainment. One of my favorites.—MB

SOME GIRLS DO
aka Mas peligrosas todavia (Sp)

This is just the tonic! It seems slightly worthless to attempt a semiotic breakdown of the deep-narrative subtext of this particular title for, as Michel Foucault (should have) said, "Heck, when there's cool threads, cheesy humor and robotized babes—who gives a damn!"

A sequel to the marginally successful *Deadlier Than the Male*, this is another outing of semi-parody Bondage. Richard Johnson plays Bulldog Drummond, suave insurance investigator and general all 'round hero. While attempting to unwrap himself from assorted females, he becomes involved in a plot to destroy a new experimental airplane but, of course, things are a lot more complicated than that.

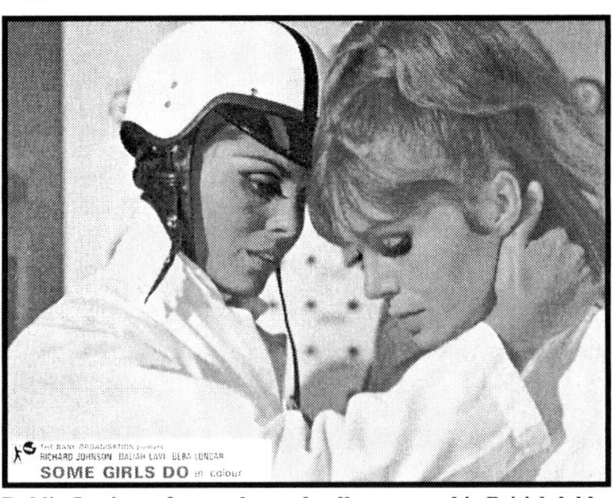

**Dahlia Lavi comforts a doomed colleague on this British lobby card for *Some Girls Do***

It turns out that a vile Swede (c'mon, that's stretching things a bit far!) named Thorenson is behind everything. Staked out on a handy-dandy desert island with his army of mechanized madams, he is using lethal soundwaves to provide a means to extort money from just about everyone. Of course, it all ends in a nice big shootout and a nice big explosion.

Okay okay, so it's nothing special, but... well, I suppose what it boils down to is that for all its faults, this film enjoys a certain level of vivacity that it is increasingly hard to find in contemporary works. Everyone concerned seems to be having fun, and this transmits itself to the audience. From the absurd gadgetry to the sight of lovely Robert Morley teaching a roomful of diplomats to whisk eggs, this captures a feeling of surreal liberation that can also be seen in popular television series such as *The Avengers* and *Department S*.

CREDITS: Production: Ashdown Film Productions, Rank Film Organisation; Director: Ralph Thomas; Story and Screenplay: Liz Charles-Williams, David D. Osborn; Cinematography: Ernest Steward; Music: Don Black, Charles Blackwell; Original running length: 88 mins; Filming location: Spain; Country: UK; Year: 1967

Cast: Richard Johnson (*Hugh Drummond*), Daliah Lavi (*Baroness Helga Hagen*), Beba Loncar (*Pandora*), James Villiers (*Carl Petersen*), Vanessa Howard (*robot number seven*), Maurice Denham (*Mr. Mortimer*), Robert Morley (*Miss Mary*), Sydne Rome (*Flicky*), Adrienne Posta (*Angela, Drummond's daily*), Florence Desmond (*Lady Manderley*), Ronnie Stevens (*Peregrine Carruthers*), Virginia North (*robot number nine*), Nicholas Phipps (*Lord Dunnberry, Air Minister*), George Belbin (*Major Newman*), Yutte Stensgaard (*robot number one*), Richard Hurndall (*president of aircraft company*), Marga Roche (*Birgit*), Douglas Sheldon (*Kruger*). Uncredited: Joanna Lumley

SOMEBODY'S STOLEN
OUR RUSSIAN SPY
aka O.K. Stuchensko (Sp),
O.K. Yevtushenko (Int)

Here we have a workman-like bit of Bondage with one notable point of recommendation, a cast list at the end that allows us to put names to some of those faces that regularly crop up in the European exploitation film field. *Somebody's Stolen Our Russian Spy* was in fact the third of a series, the first two of which were the far more effective *Licensed to Kill*, aka *The Second Best Secret Agent in the Whole Wide World*, and *Where the Bullets Fly* (directed by Lindsay Shonteff and John Gilling, respectively). Bizarrely, while both of these were solid UK productions, this is a resolutely Spanish film—despite the presence of a smattering of Brits among the cast.

Charles Vine is an ultra-suave secret agent. Charles Vine is also played by Tom Adams, an actor with all the charm of a boiled chicken. His latest job is to relocate a Russian spy, Yevtushenko (Barta Barry), who has gone missing. It is soon discovered that he has been kidnapped by a certain Major Kovacs (Tim Barrett) on behalf of the Albanian government. Our styleless hero is soon captured, and everyone relocates to a dusty studio in Spain, which they all appear to believe is Albania. From here on, nothing much happens. Everyone escapes, everyone gets recaptured, an antagonistic babe (Diana Lorys) appears, a fat baddie appears, the babe falls in love with the hero, everyone escapes again, etc.

When the end comes, you suddenly realize that you have just been kidnapped by aliens and have spent one-and-a-half hours being prodded by disproportionate green people who have subsequently wiped your memory of all that has happened.

I really can't think of much else to say about this film. It's not bad, but not good. It's watchable, but forgettable. One spark of originality is provided by the fact that the villain for once does not die by falling off a ledge. All in all though, it would be safe to say that there is nothing in this production that is going to make you have a mystical experience or develop stigmata in unusual places.—MB

CREDITS: Production: Puck Films, Andorra Films; Director: Jose Luis Madrid; Story: Jose Luis Madrid; Screenplay: Michael Pittock; Cinematography: Raul Artigot {Eastmancolor - Panoramico}; Music: Angel Arteaga; Original running length: 108 mins; Filming locations: Spain, Portugal; Country: Spain; Year: 1968

CAST: Tom Adams (*Charles Vine*), Tim Barrett (*Major Kovacs*), Diana Lorys (*Galina Samarav*), Maria Silva (*Pandora Lee*), Mari Paz Pondal (*Sara*), Jose Riesgo (*Colonel Stubov*), Barta Barry (*Colonel Yevtushenko*), Gene Reyes (*Ly Chee*), Antonio Molino Rojo (*Colonel Borodin*), Eric Chapman (*Potts*), Tito Garcia (*Captain Milovitch*), Jose M. Lavernier (*Walls*), Antonio G. Escribano (*Rockwell*), Angel Menendez (*Major Torrens*), Victor Israel (*Trilby*), Ingrid Thucin (*the blonde girl*), Spencer Teakle (*Dr. Howard*), Victor Iregua (*Philipo*), Jose Bermudez (*the shoe boy*)

SPECIAL CYPHER
aka Cifrado especial (Sp),
Cifrato speciale (It), Message chiffre (Fr),
Der schwarze skorpion (WG)

1945. The war is about to end with victory for the Allies. A German plane is ordered to drop two armored cases into the ocean just off the Turkish coast. After the mission has been carried out, the boobytrapped plane crashes into a mountain, leaving the only surviving pilot a raving madman. He is committed to a lunatic asylum, where he stays for 20 years before escaping, *Halloween*-style.

American Intelligence is concerned. They have reason to believe that the armored cases contain an anti-gravity device invented by Nazi scientists. They're anxious to retrieve it for themselves, but have no idea where it was actually dumped, so they send tip-top agent Curd Muller (Lang Jeffries) to try to recover it.

He heads off to Istanbul, where he immediately becomes the focus of attention for assorted hoodlums and spies. Matters are complicated even further by the activities of loony Andrea Scotti, who wants to recover the device for himself, thereby enabling him to sell it to the highest bidder. He is willing to go to any lengths to fulfill this ambition, including dastardly crimes against fashion such as wearing V-neck jumpers over his shirt or forcing his men to wear loose-fitting PVC suits.

Eventually, Muller hooks up with an extremely untrustworthy millionaire called Hoover (Jorge Rigaud), who believes him to be the missing pilot. Hoover wants to claim a reward by salvaging the device, and has hired a diving expert named Professor Richard (Philippe Hersent)—who has his own bathysphere—to assist in locating it. Unfortunately, a number of the people in his employ have the habit of turning up murdered, and Muller is the prime suspect.

**Lang Jeffries, Jorge Rigaud and Jose Greci in a curious situation on this German lobby card for *Special Cypher***

This is a prime slice of spy hokum. There's a great soundtrack (more understated than could have been expected), it all looks fantastic and there are some wacky directorial touches. Hardly five minutes goes by without a fistfight of some form or other (heck, even gorgeous Jose Greci gets to beat the crap out of several extras). This—along with the relatively well-constructed story—keeps things moving, but it can get a tad tiresome at times. Let's not get carried away, *Special Cypher* is not a great film, but it's definitely one of the better examples of its kind. Mercanti's direction is entirely competent, the actors do their job (although Scotti does personify the mundane aspects of corruption rather too much), and there are more babes than you could shake your hat at.

There's also a clutch of really effective sequences: an assassination attempt involving a truly scary-looking ski lift; the initial pop-arty asylum escape and some entertaining ghost train shenanigans. This is yet another film to feature a masked ball. This one boasts a duplicitous character in a comedy duck mask, and ends when an unfortunate waiter receives a dart in the neck. No, not a poison dart; an actual, bulls-eye, 180-type dart (which could easily have been thrown by a particularly clumsy drunkard from a neighboring pub, for all the explanation we're given).

So, what else do you get for your money? Well, watching Lang Jeffries accosting stuntman/genre regular Claudio Ruffini with a stuffed antelope scores some points, as does the wealth of gadgets on display. I was particularly taken with the flamenco guitar that kills. Mention must also be made of the totally preposterous bathysphere, which, equipped with a large pair of spindly claws, looks like nothing so much as a giant scampi.

My favorite moment, however, is when Jeffries and the cravat-sporting Jorge Rigaud force a female spy to strip down to her panties (and don't ask me why). Rigaud's smarmy expression is frankly priceless.—MB

CREDITS: Production: Daiano Film, Athena Film, Atlantida Film, France Cinema; Director: Herbert J. Sherman [Pino Mercanti]; Story and Screenplay: Ernesto Gastaldi, Ugo Guerra; Cinematography: Angelo Filippini, Masino Manunza {Technicolor}; Music: Riz Ortolani; Original running length: 95 mins; Filming locations: Costa Brava, Istanbul, Rome; Country: Italy/Spain/France; Year: 1966

CAST: Lang Jeffries (*Curd*), Jose Greci (*Lynn*), Georges Rigaud (*Hoover*), Philippe Hersent (*Professor Richard*), Helga Line (*Mrs. Richard*), Andrea Scotti, Jeanine Reynaud (*Sheena*), Umberto Raho (*Vasili*), Jacques Stany, Peter Ceccar [Pietro Ceccarelli] (*Jan, thug with knuckledusters*), Thomas Pico, Anna Maria Conte, Giorgio Cerioni, Ignazio Leone, Claudio Ruffini (*Hoover's henchman*), Gianluigi Crescenzi, Marcello [Max] Turilli

SPECIAL MISSION LADY CHAPLIN
aka 077 Special Mission Lady Chaplin (Int), L'Affaire Lady Chaplin (Fr), Mission Speciale, Lady Chaplin (Fr), Missione speciale Lady Chaplin (It), Operación Lady Chaplin (Sp)

This is Ken Clark's most Bondian adventure and it is a hoot. Ken is CIA agent Dick Malloy (the numbers "077" are prominently featured on the door of a taxi taken by Malloy) and although he looks slightly uncomfortable in his designer duds, he's still mighty dapper. *SMLC* was Ken's fourth spy flick, and it's one of the most enjoyable, especially for those who want to come down easy from Bond. It's full of gadgetry and has a Fleming feel to the plot.

Jacques Bergerac is the main villain: the man who not only steals a sunken nuclear submarine but puts it back in its original resting place once he's lifted its cache of Polaris missiles—talk about a neatnik. Bergerac plays Kobra Zoltan (what a great name) who, because he was born under the sign of Scorpio, keeps pet scorpions. Not only that, but he stages scorpion fights on his coffee table at parties. How this villain can be boring is the big question, but Bergerac just doesn't generate much excitement here. If we ever needed Adolfo Celi, it is in the role of Kobra Zoltan.

Probably the main reason that Bergerac is so forgettable in this movie is because he's competing with Daniela Bianchi. They didn't name the movie after her for nothing. Bianchi takes charge as Lady Arabella Chaplin, Zoltan's cohort in crime. This is the woman you want working for you when you have big criminal aspirations. She can do it all, like separate train cars and wield a machine gun while dressed as a nun. Not only is she in charge of a fashion house that features many bad designs, she can blend missile propellant in with dress fabric to smuggle it out of the country. Just don't get shot while wearing it though. One gal makes the mistake of trying to steal one and when she's hit with a bullet, she explodes!

Lady Chaplin's a master of disguise too. At one point she pretends to be an old lady who uses a wheelchair with guns in the arms to snuff a traitor to her evil cause. She uses all sorts of gadgets to accomplish her deeds, like a mini blowtorch and a compact case that displays televised images from a camera embedded in the belly of a Buddha. The best part is when Zoltan throws her out of his plane and she uses her skirt as a parachute! Not only that, but when she finally hits the ground she's wearing a snazzy custom camouflage jumpsuit and sporting that nifty girl-sized machine gun again. Yes, Lady Chaplin is a criminal, but she's a heck of a dame and gorgeous too.

Other good things about this movie include a gun battle in a bullfight ring, a henchman with a hook for a hand, and lots of good fights with the energetic Malloy. The score by Bruno Nicolai is, sadly, unremarkable. Ken drives a big old Cadillac convertible for a while, until he's trapped by heavy equipment and must abandon the vehicle by ejecting himself out through the trunk. The ironic ending isn't lost on Zoltan, as he is bitten by his own scorpions. Why they are on the ship with the Polaris missiles is a question we shouldn't ask. Don't miss this fun adventure. It's easily as entertaining as any Bond flick despite the absence of a charismatic villain.—DD

**Rare Romanian poster for *Special Mission Lady Chaplin* starring Ken Clark**

CREDITS: Production: Fida Cin.ca, Les Productions Jacques Roitfeld, Sincronia Film; Director: Alberto De Martino; Story: Sandro Continenza, Marcello Coscia, Hipolito De Diego Lopez; Screenplay: Sandro Continenza, Marcello Coscia, Giovanni Simonelli, Hipolito De Diego Lopez; Cinematography: Alejandro Ulloa {Techniscope – Technicolor}; Music: Bruno Nicolai; Original running length: 99 mins; Filming locations: Cinecitta Studios, Rome, Madrid, Paris, London, New York; Country: France/Italy/Spain; Year: 1966

CAST: Ken Clark (*Dick Malloy*), Daniela Bianchi (*Lady Chaplin*), Jacques Bergerac (*Kobra Zoltan*), Evelyn Stewart [Ida Galli] (*Constance*), Philippe Hersent (*Heston*), Mabel Karr (*Jacqueline*), Alfredo Mayo, Peter Blades, Tomas Blanco, Raymond Jourdan, Rafael Albaicin, Alberto Cevenini. Not on print: Jose Panizo, Helga Line (*the client*)

LA SPIA CHE VIENE DAL MARE
"the spy who comes from the sea"
aka K. 17 attaque à l'aube (Fr)

It's amazing how the way that you watch films alters your view of their particular qualities (or lack thereof). *La Spia* reminded me very much of a late-fifties noir, but I have no doubt that this was partly—if not mainly—due to the fact the copy under review was French-language and in black and white. That said, it keeps rigidly within the realm of the thriller, eschewing the more spectacular or fantastical elements of the genre (until the last 10 minutes at least). That it was obviously made on a limited budget helps ensure plenty of (cheap to film) scenes set in hotel rooms and lots of running through poorly lit streets.

After a frantic—speeded up—car chase through the streets of Geneva, special agent K17, John Prentis (John Elliot), takes refuge in a church. All of the guests look exceptionally suspicious, and Luciano Pigozzi is playing the organ (never a good sign). After meeting an attractive blonde, Prentis' luck runs out when he's captured by the two hoods who were originally pursuing him. One of them even kills a pussycat to prove his dastardliness. They work for Albert (Freddy Unger), who runs a criminal organization behind the cover of a fashion house.

Prentis is, of course, on a mission. There is an international conference being held in the town, and American Intelligence has reason to

**More dramatic action from the Italians on this poster for *Spia che viene dal mare***

believe that one of their representatives, atomic scientist Professor Lindstrom, is in danger. More specifically, they think that someone is planning to destroy a plane on which he is likely to be traveling. It is the agent's job to find out exactly who is behind the plot, and to ensure that any attempt upon the professor's life is foiled. Albert is the prime suspect.

Despite keeping himself busy by wooing a moody French tourist, Simona (Simone Mitchell), K17's investigations do progress—and lead in the direction of San Marino. They also lead toward the aforementioned Pigozzi, who seems to be skulking about in the background wherever they happen to be, and who has a giant rocket—particularly useful for shooting down planes—kept in a rickety shack on the beach!

Despite being undeniably small-scale, *La Spia* is not unenjoyable. The script, direction and photography are all adequate. As well as plenty of fistfights and chases, there's a particularly effective sequence in which the villain's army emerges from the sea in scuba gear. You also get yet more cable car action and a smattering of gadgets (a buzz saw contained within a watch and a ray gun stored in the false heel of a shoe).

Interestingly, heroine Simona Mitchell spends most of the running time trying to avoid being groped by John Elliot, which makes a refreshing change from the usual sexual irresistibility that's displayed by the heroes of these films. Unfortunately, this unique point is somewhat diminished by the familiar problem of having two actresses who look extremely similar. As one's the heroine and the other a femme fatale, this leads to some confusion.

Lamberto Benvenuti was better known as a scriptwriter (as on Giuliano Carmineo's excellent western *Find a Place to Die*). As well as this, he made three other films in the late sixties: *La morte nella valiglia* (a thriller made back to back with *La Spia*, and also featuring cast members Elliot, Reynaud, Pigozzi and Unger); the Mark Damon melodrama *Temptation*; and *Damnation*, aka *La Stirpe di cano*. As with this film, they all remain willfully obscure.—MB

CREDITS: Production: Spectra Film; Director: John O'Burghess [Lamberto Benvenuti]; Story and Screenplay: John O'Burghess [Lamberto Benvenuti]; Cinematography: Angelo Filippini {Eastmancolor}; Music: Berto Pisano; Original running length: 85 mins; Filming locations: Instituto Luce, Rome, Venice, San Marino; Country: Italy; Year: 1966

CAST: John Elliot (*John Prentis, aka K17*), Simone Mitchell (*Simone*), Hector Ribot [Ettore Ribotta] (*Mario*), Jeanine Reynaud (*Mme. Lina*), Cynthia Pace (*Cinzia*), Giampiero Littera (*Ercole*), Rita Klein (*Laura*), Goffredo Unger (*Albert*), Mario Siletti (*the general*), Hildegard Golez, Giuliano M Anellucci (*the stuttering man*), Gary Gold, with Alan Collins [Luciano Pigozzi] (*Dr. Benitez*). Uncredited: Jo Atlanta, Vincent Cousey, Giovanni Carigi, Maria Grof, Giorgio Grilli, Giuliano Isidori, Diana Stewart

### SPIA, SPIONE
"spy, spying"
aka Una Ladrona para una espia (Sp)

Buffoonish waiter Carlo Barazzetti (Lando Buzzanca) spends most of his time goofing around, believing he's some kind of secret agent (e.g., making faces in the mirror, throwing darts at a superman poster, etc.). Unbeknown to him, he is being watched, or, to be more accurate, his apartment is being watched. It is situated above a bank, which makes it a perfect base for a bunch of crooks—led by "the Professor" (Guy Deghy)—to carry out a daring robbery (their target being a ring made of a secret, precious alloy). In order to gain access to the apartment, the beautiful Ursula (Teresa Gimpera) is sent to seduce him. It doesn't prove too difficult.

Their plan goes swimmingly; apart from the fact that poor Carlo walks in on them (conveniently falling through the hole they've drilled in the floor in order to access the bank). Rather than having to resort to murder, they decide to take him along—as a captive—while they hide out in Spain. Carlo tries his best to escape from them. His best, however, proves sadly inadequate when an attempt to sabotage their car ends with his accidentally ruining the brakes (causing the disruption of an unfortunate funeral). Complicating matters further is the fact that another band of villains is on their trail and after the ring.

The Professor decides that he needs Carlo's help to keep it safe, and to win him over he pretends to be a spy. This, of course, makes Carlo extremely excited—not least because he thinks he's going to be equipped with all kinds of outlandish gadgetry.

*Spia, spione* followed a couple of years behind the successful Bruno Corbucci/Lando Buzzanca comedies, *James Tont Operazione UNO* and *James Tont Operazione DUE*. Like them, it uses the spy film genre to showcase the "talents" of the star. Unlike them, it only really belongs within the spy film genre by default; there are no spies, just an idiot duped into thinking that he's working for the Secret Service. In fact, the target of parody in this case is the caper film, most particularly Jules Dassin's classic *Rififi*, which is pilloried most in the heist sequence.

It's not a bad film. Corbucci's direction is adequate, there's an okay-ish soundtrack, and the supporting cast does their stuff. It's great to see Teresa Gimpera in a large role, and it's even better to see her dressed up to the nines in leather. Cristina Gajoni makes a (frankly minuscule) cameo, yet receives prominent billing—which probably reflects the bigness of her hair rather than the quality of her performance. Guy Deghy, a chubby Hungarian actor who spent most of his career in English films playing Russians or Germans, has one of his largest roles as the scheming if hapless Professor. He can also be seen in *The One-Eyed Soldiers*, as well as nongenre productions such as *Where Eagles Dare*, *The Mouse That Roared* and *Cry of the Banshee*.

Unfortunately, as the whole thing is designed as a vehicle for its star, the extent to which you'll enjoy it is ultimately determined by the amount you can take of Buzzanca's somewhat tiresome comic antics. With his substantial chin, love of pratfalling and complete lack of sex appeal, Lando Buzzanco reminds me of a Mediterranean version of dear old Bruce ("Brucie") Forsythe, and *Spia, spione* is about as enjoyable—and as substantial—as an episode of *The Generation Game*.—MB

CREDITS: Production: Colt Prod. Cin.che, Mega Film, Prod Cin.cas Balcazar; Director: Bruno Corbucci; Story: Jaime Jesus Balcazar; Screenplay: Mario Guerra, Vittorio Vighi, Bruno Corbucci; Cinematography: Juan Gelpi {Eastmancolor}; Music: Federico Martinez Tudo; Original running length: 94 mins; Country: Italy/Spain; Year: 1967

CAST: Lando Buzzanca (*Carlo Barazetti*), Teresa Gimpera (*Ursula*), Guy Deghy (*the Professor*), Linda Sini (*Ascha*), Cristina Gajoni (*the actress in the advert*), Paco Sanz (*Paco*), Mario Pisu (*member of the Professor's gang*), Marisa Traverso [Traversi] (*Maria*), Tito Garcia (*the Spanish gangster*), Tomas Torres, Fernando Rubio, Carmen Giraldes, Franco Morici, Pippo Starnazza, Fred Coplan (*member of the Professor's gang*), Aldo Sala

SPIES AGAINST THE WORLD
aka Le Carnaval Des Barbouzes (Fr), Gern hab' ich die Frauen gekillt (WG), Killer's Carnival (Int), Los matones (Sp), Spie contro il mondo (It)

So here's a lackluster anthology made on the cheap with a good cast, but the lack of money and effort put into the production doom this one from the start. The framing story this time features Richard Munch, who played Jerry Cotton's boss in that series of German

**Striking Italian poster for the anthology film *Spies Against the World***

films. Munch is a professor of sorts, whose home is invaded by an alleged murder who wants a free ride out of the country. Munch tells him three stories while they wait for the morning flight.

First up is the disagreeable Stewart Granger as an adventurer much in The Saint mold, who goes after the drug smugglers who murdered his client's brother. The story takes place in Vienna and features a car chase and an unbilled Herbert Fuchs getting a gun shot out of his hand. Unfortunately that's about it. Granger was slumming in Europe at the time making spy flicks and this movie probably paid for his whisky for a month.

The next story takes place in Rome and is the only true spy tale of the bunch. Pierre Brice, using his own name, is a Secret Service agent assigned to deliver some documents. These, of course, are intercepted by silly Russian agents and "comedy" ensues. It must be funny because zany sound effects tell us so. Many tired gags are on display here, such as Brice getting his orders from a phonograph record that he must eat afterwards. Luciano Pigozzi plays a confused thug and Margaret Lee gets tied up as an enemy agent. There's a decent soundtrack for this segment by Claudius

Alzner and the most notable action is when an old Chevy Belair is run off a cliff.

Last, Lex Barker is a private detective in what is supposed to be San Francisco (not even close) investigating the murder of two barmaids. He knows they're barmaids because he "knows every barmaid in town if they're worth knowing." Somehow these murders lead to an assassination attempt in Rio during Carnival, of course. This segment features Agnes Spaak, Karin Dor and Klaus Kinski as a greasy thug who gets killed. Big surprise. There's a fight in a slaughterhouse and Barker says things like, "No one ever died young from drinking whisky." Where has he been?

Back to the framing story where Munch has finished boring his guest with these exciting tales. It is soon revealed that the murderer who broke in on him is really a cop and Munch is really the murderer! Unfortunately, the viewer has lost interest by this time so the revelation lacks some punch. This one's for diehard fans of the genre only. I warned you.—DD

CREDITS: Production: Intercontinental Film, Metheus Film, Interproduction; Director: Albert Cardiff [Alberto Cardone], Robert Lynn, Sheldon Reynolds; Story and Screenplay: Ernesto Gastaldi, Rolf Olsen, Vittorio Salerno, Marlon Sirko [Mario Siciliano], Sheldon Reynolds; Cinematography: Gino Santini, Siegfried Hold {Eastmancolor}; Music: Claudius Alzmer; Original running length: 104 mins; Country: Italy/France/Austria; Year: 1966

CAST: Stewart Granger, Pierre Brice, Lex Barker, Margaret Lee, Jerry Wilson, Alan Collins [Luciano Pigozzi], Pascale Petit, Agnes Spaak, Klaus Kinski, Karin Dor, Carrol Brown, Walter Giller, Spean Convery [Spartaco Conversi], Richard Munk, Peter Vogel, Tita Barker, Johanna Matz, Alan Pinson, Robert Favart

## SPIES STRIKE SILENTLY

aka Los espías matan en silencio (Sp), Leise töten die Spione (WG), Ombres sur le Liban (Fr), Le spie uccidono in silenzio (It)

This half-baked spy thriller starts out promisingly enough with a cool title sequence fueled by the sounds of Francesco De Masi. If only the rest of the film measured up to this auspicious beginning. Unfortunately we end up in tepid water rather quickly and never find our way out.

Lang Jeffries does his best as Mike Drum, who's assigned to find out just what the heck is happening when several of the world's great scientists are killed off. Well, we never figure out exactly why either, but it doesn't matter much. What the villain, Dr. Rashid (Andrea Bosic), really wants at the moment is to rule a world of zombies via a drug that eliminates the will of those to whom it is administered. That is, until near the end of the film, when a new weapon is unveiled by our ambitious evil thinker: a ray that will enable him to transmit his thought waves to anyone on earth. It definitely feels like this stuff was being made up as they went along.

The movie is as scatterbrained as the villain and the promising characters are never given the chance to develop. To begin with, the mad doctor has a couple of potentials in his employ. His secretary, Pamela Kohler (Erika Blanc), is a knockout with plenty of evilness to spread around—not to mention that she's a drug addict—but she's hardly given enough to do here. The other character is Henry Brook, a Secret Service agent who is, unbeknown to anyone else, under the drugged influence of Rashid. He wears sunglasses all the time because the drug does funny things to one's eyes. He has a mean streak, but we never get to see him do any dirty work. He gets his just desserts however, when Drum sets him on fire with the thought ray thing that the doc developed. Rashid clued us in on the potentiality of the ray earlier in the film and Drum made careful mental notes.

The top-billed female is Emma Bianchi, who plays Grace, but she doesn't even show up until almost an hour has gone by. She spends most of her time in the film at the mercy of Rashid, and her only purpose is to be rescued. But then that's par for the course.

However, there are some decent things about the film to mention. Jeffries is a good fighter and gets plenty of chances to show it because there's a fight every 10 minutes or so. That part's okay. There are also a couple of gadgets on display, one of which is the old receiver-in-the-compact-case trick. Part of

**A classic Eurospy image from the Spanish poster for *Spies Strike Silently***

Drum's standard equipment is a Detect-A-Bug in his cigarette pack, and then there's the exploding tape recorder. And don't forget the excellent score by De Masi. It's the one asset to the film that never lets up as Drum jets from Beirut to London to Madrid to Beirut and back to London, before returning to Beirut for the finale.

At one point Drum is strapped to a chair in a room with op art on the walls. Rashid promises that when he injects Drum with the zombie drug he will experience hallucinations. No such luck. But that's a typical nonhappening in director Mario Caiano's only discernible spy flick. So unless you're a Lang Jeffries completionist or just like to hear a good score, stay away from this slapdash effort.—DD

CREDITS: Production: Terra Film, Filmes Cin. ca, Estela Film; Director: Mario Caiano; Story: David Moreno Mingote; Screenplay: Guido Malatesta, Mario Caiano; Cinematography: Julio Ortas {Techniscope - Technicolor}; Music: Francesco De Masi; Original running length: 86 mins; Country: Italy/Spain; Year: 1966

CAST: Lang Jeffries (*Michael Drum*), Emma Danieli (*Grace*), Andrea Bosic (*Rachid*), Erika Blanc (*Pamela Kohler*), Jose Bodalo (*Craig*), Mario Lanfranchi, Jose Marco, Gaetano Quartararo, Enzo Consoli (*Edward*), Mary Badmajew

SPY CATCHER

aka Suspense au deuxième bureau (Fr)

Spy films are typically known for their exotic locations, but the bulk of this film's short running time is spent inside a house—a cramped house. This (obviously) low- budget entry does have a couple of things going for it, however, that we'll talk about later. Gil Delamare is Col. Bordy, an agent assigned to impersonate a professor Sellier by temporarily living with the professor's wife and her sister in their home. The plan is to discover who wants the papers stashed in a safe in the house. Delamare was a stuntman, and he looks it with his bodybuilder physique. He was in a few other spy flicks but didn't play the lead in any of them.

Forty-five minutes into the film, Bordy discovers that the hired help are really enemy agents. The valet, Lucien (Frederic O'Brady), and the maid, Vera (Gisele Robert), make an interesting pair of spies. O'Brady is short and bald-headed and reminds one of Erich von Stroheim. He plays the valet with typical long-suffering patience, putting up with Bordy's antics with dry sarcasm. It's Vera, however, who remains the film's most enigmatic character. To our eyes, the full-figured Vera seems rather plain, even masculine, but she is supposed to be the femme fatale, tempting Bordy with her sex kitten attitude. Her attempts at seduction seem ridiculous and when Bordy woos her near the end of the film, it's downright laughable. What a strange role for the top-billed Robert. Oddly enough, this was apparently the last film for both O'Brady and Robert.

Colette Duval is the professor's ice queen wife, Claire, who suspiciously listens to German radio broadcasts, and Catherie Candida plays her sister, Denise, who acts like a star-struck schoolgirl over Bordy. Neither would go on to stardom in films. Needless to say, the acting vies with the claustrophobic atmosphere for the film's weakest element. The lone bright spot in the acting department is this early role for Michel Lemoine—he of the glowing eyes—who had a long career in genre cinema ahead of him.

Here he plays Hans, the determined leader of the gang of spies desperate for the mysterious invention of the professor's.

Other than Lemoine's limited role, there are two main reasons for sticking with the film. One is the score: a mixture of experimental free jazz and traditional jazz that is fun and interesting entertainment for the ears when there isn't much for the eyes to feast upon. The other is the last 15 minutes, which contain a car chase through the Parisian night and subway fisticuffs by Bordy and Hans. Photographed in film noir tradition, these sequences take on an almost expressionistic look, while the free jazz adds another level of tension to the goings-on. Delamare also does an impressive stunt of lying beneath a subway train; it's a wonder the barrel-chested actor lives through it.

There are a couple laugh lines along the way as well. When Lucien is falsely accused by Hans of stealing the papers they are looking for, he gets "the treatment...without anesthetic!" This means they pour acid on his hands (offscreen) and his weak heart gives out, the poor fellow. When Vera's true vocation of spy is revealed to Denise, she remarks, "I hope you're better at spying than you are as a maid." Other than these few bright spots, this obscure entry in the genre doesn't have a lot going for it.—DD

CREDITS: Production: Sigmadis; Director: Christian de Saint-Maurice; Story and Screenplay: Christian de Saint-Maurice; Cinematography: Pierre Levent; Original running length: 82 mins; Country: France; Year: 1960

CAST: Catherine Candida (*Denise*), Gil Delamare (*Colonel Bordy*), Colette Duval (*Claire Sellier*), Michel Lemoine (*Hans*), André Luguet (*the intelligence chief*), Frédéric O'Brady (*Lucien*), Gisèle Robert (*Vera*)

SPY HUNT IN VIENNA

aka Operazione terzo uomo (It), Der Professionelle (WG, alt), Schüsse im 3/4 Takt (WG, alt), Schüsse im Dreivierteltakt (WG), Shots in 3/4 Time (Int)

There's not much to recommend here, really. A good cast does not a good spy movie make. Rather, this plays like a late-cycle Edgar

**The identity of the bad guy is given away on the Belgian poster for the krimi-inspired *Spy Hunt in Vienna***

Wallace krimi with the Scotland Yard detective as a secret agent and a murderer who happens to have stolen a top-secret invention. The circus milieu (the Palladium in Vienna) is quite tedious, but other Vienna locations are nice to look at—like the empty amusement park where the villain hides out.

Pierre Brice is Philippe Taylor (changed from "Tissot" for the English dub, apparently), an agent on the trail of the device. Brice was a looker who made a lot of westerns in the sixties, but most may recognize him from *Mill of the Stone Women*. He's very bland here, but that suits the rest of the film.

Heinz Drache gets to play the villain for a change. He's Gilbert Demarez, a trapeze artist (yeah, right), who's selling the invention he stole to the highest bidder. It just so happens the Red Chinese are interested enough to pay a million bucks for it. Drache spent most of the sixties sleuthing in the Edgar Wallace mysteries that Germany cranked out by the dozens.

Also involved is Dahlia Lavi, playing Irina Broder, in a terrible blonde wig. She is merely a pawn in the action and is a far cry from her career-defining role in Mario Bava's *Whip and the Body*.

A couple of minor parts are played by Anton Diffring and Terence Hill. Diffring plays a good guy—believe it or not—but he seems bad for most of the movie, naturally. Hill went on to stardom in westerns, most notably the Trinity series, but never so much as glanced at another spy film. Senta Berger also has a tiny part. Don't we wish we could see more of her!

The score by Charly Niessen (arrangements by Gert Wilden), is okay, but is occasionally inappropriate for the action on the screen. Director Alfred Weidenmann can't do much with this material either—the script is just plain weak. For instance, when Taylor goes to a meeting with a clown from the Palladium show who is going to give him information, Taylor finds him poisoned. His response is, "Too bad. He should've stuck to clowning."

There's a bad gag later in the film when Taylor is cornered by enemy agents in the subway. He buys several cans of aerosol and throws them in a chestnut seller's fire. Naturally (but too quickly) they blow up. The gag here is that it not only allows our hero to escape, but gives him a black face and he doesn't know it. Ha ha.

There are plenty of other tired and predictable antics along the way. At one point, Taylor and company follow a Red Chinese agent to the amusement park hideout of Demarez. Wouldn't you know it, there happen to be air ducts the size of small apartments for them crawl around in and listen from the grates. There are not one but two "lights out" moments, and a wax museum where Demarez stands holding his gun like a wax figure.

Even the climax is a letdown: Demarez makes his getaway in a helicopter, which Taylor shoots down resulting in an extremely cheesy explosion. I had high hopes for this one, but you can skip it knowing you haven't missed a darn thing.—DD

**Turkish poster for the early Coplan adventure *The Spy I Love***

CREDITS: Production: Bavaria Film, Cinegai, Nora Film, Wiener Stadthalle; Director: Alfred Weidenmann; Story: Herbert Reinecker; Screenplay: Franco Prosperi, Ludmilla Kirsch; Cinematography: Karl Lob; Music: Charly Niessen; Filming locations: Paris, Vienna; Country: Germany/Austria/Italy; Year: 1965

CAST: Pierre Brice (*Philippe Taylor/Tissot*), Heinz Drache (*Gilbert Demarez*), Daliah Lavi (*Irina Broder*), Jana Brejchova (*Violetta*), Charles Regnier (*Henry*), Walter Giller (*Renato Balli*), Terence Hill (*Enrico*), Gustav Knuth (*Igor*), Anton Diffring (*Burger*), Senta Berger (*Captain Jenny*), Daniel Sola (*Joscha*), Walter Regelsberger (*Gorba*), Hans Unterkircher (*Bernard*), Karl Zarda (*Ledin*), Erica Vaal (*Jeanette*)

## THE SPY I LOVE

aka Agente Coplan: missione spionaggio (It), Coplan agent-005 (UK), Coplan agente secreto (Sp), Coplan prend des risques (Fr), FBI Agent Cooper—Der Fall Tex (WG)

This is a low-to-the-ground espionage story shot in the style before James Bond made the splash heard around the world in *Dr. No*, even though it was released two years later. The simple story, about a stolen nuclear rocket propellant called the SR 712, is told in a nuts-and-bolts manner and the low-key hero will barely register on those brought up on the larger-than-life Bond.

Dominique Paturel is Francis Coplan, the spy protaganist of Paul Kenny's novels in this early adventure. The Coplan character was taken over by several leading men during the spy boom, in more Bondian fashion than displayed here, but this black and white wonder hearkens back to the dark ages of spy cinema with its post-war echoes. It probably seemed old fashioned upon release and was Paturel's only foray in the genre.

Top-billed Virna Lisi is Ingrid Carlson, the reluctant spy blackmailed into helping the bad guys. She's not given much to do here except watch the boys do their work and take her portion of punishment: She's nearly drowned in the bathtub, shot and then slapped around by Coplan for no good reason. Lisi had a long career but alas, not within the spy genre, and maybe her experience here was part of the reason. Not even Tommy Duggan, our main villain Stratton, made another mark in the spy genre. It's pretty bland going for spotters of familiar faces but you may recognize a thug or two.

The story unfolds like a police procedural with only a few of the elements of exploitation now considered a must for spy flicks. The torture and shooting death of Coplan's old friend and ex-agent Legay (Andre Weber) would be among them, although it's not dwelled on for any length of time. There's a pretty good little piece of practical suspense when Coplan and company become trapped in a darkroom hidden in a cellar. They bust through an interior wall, following a drainpipe to put a small explosive in the pipe that blows a hole in the exterior wall.

The most exciting sequence happens aboard a moving train as Coplan chases down some escaping thugs. They even use the old "bad guy who doesn't duck when the train goes into a tunnel" gag. The train bit climaxes with a fight between Coplan and Bianco (Roger Dutoit) that has the two fall under the train and keep fighting as the cars pass over the top of them—talk about unlikely events.

There are some pretty fair judo fights and a few humorous lines. One of these occurs after the SR 712 is recovered by Coplan before Stratton can sell it to the Chinese. The Chinese guy shrugs his shoulders after the deal falls through and actually says, "That is way fortune cookie crumble."

The door is left (very conspicuously) open for another Coplan adventure, even positing the title "The Calcutta Affair," but it was not to be. Let's just say that skipping *The Spy I Love* will not cause you too much remorse.—DD

CREDITS: Production: Cinephonic, Da-Ma Cinematografic, Cibelux; Director: Maurice Labro; Story based on the story by Paul Kelly; Screenplay: Pascal Jardin; Cinematography: Pierre Petit {B&W}; Music: Georges Van Parys; Original running length: 105 mins; Country: France/Italy/Belgium; Year: 1964

CAST: Dominique Paturel (*Coplan*), Virna Lisi (*Ingrid*), Jacques Bautin (*Fondane*), Jacques Monod (*the old man*), Yvonne Clech (*Mme Rochon*), Henri Lambert (*Scarpelli*), Roger Dutoit (*Bianco*), Margo Lion (*Mme. Slasinska*), Andre Valmy (*Pelletier*), Guy Kernier (*Ronchon*), Tommy Dugan (*Stratton*), Andre Weber (*Legay*), Anne Vallon, Monique Morisi, Eugene Deckers, Francis Lax, Henri Desagneaux, Charles Bouillard

## SPY IN YOUR EYE

aka Berlino, appuntamento per le spie (It),
Berlin cita con los espias (Sp),
Berlin, operation «Laser» (Fr),
Das Verräterische Auge (WG)

Paula Kraus (Anna Maria Pierangeli), the daughter of a prominent atomic scientist, is kidnapped by the Russians. They hope to blackmail her father into revealing a top-secret formula on which he had been working. Secret agent Bert Morris (Brett Halsey) is sent to rescue her, a task he succeeds in accomplishing without too much trouble (and with the assistance of a chum wearing a booby-trapped false hunchback).

However, their troubles are far from over. While Bert was away, his boss, Colonel Lancaster (Dana Andrews) had an operation in which his glass eye has been replaced by a new-fangled "seeing" upgrade. Unfortunately, it's not only the Colonel who's pleased as punch with this. The Russians have also tapped into this vision and are using him as an unconscious, walking video camera.

As well as all the invaluable intelligence information that this brings, their primary aim is still to wrestle the secret formula from Paula. This task is further complicated because the Chinese, who already have the formula, are concurrently trying to murder her. Fortunately, Bert is on hand to protect her—and it doesn't take him too long to figure out that something weird is going on.

Despite its unusual premise of the "spying eye," this really boils down to a fairly standard, above-average espionage thriller. Secret formulas, the exact composition of which are only known by the inventor's daughter/secretary/assistant/dog, are dime-a-dozen in these films. In fact, the Colonel Lancaster thread of the storyline never really makes it past the periphery, despite the weight given it by the English-language title.

That said, although *Spy in Your Eye* may be formulaic, it is also well made and, best of all, distinctly odd. As well as the aforementioned killer hunch, you get tons of gadgets including deadly cameras, radio umbrellas, rope-cutting watches and—heck—even a lethal waxwork statue of Napoleon! The Chinese agents all walk around in suits and bowler hats which, although it may have helped them fit in at the London stock market at the time, is distinctly less effective when applied to the beach. This is also possibly the only film imaginable in which kidnap victims are hidden in giant tubes of toothpaste.

Beyond that, this film features possibly the strangest sets to be found in the genre. There's a chase in a warehouse that appears to be full of rejected special effects from either a ghost train or a Z-grade monster movie. There's also a subclimax, which takes place in a "self-disguising" room. The walls reverse to make the villains' hideout appear to be a harmless…well, it looks like a kitchen accessory showroom, but I couldn't swear to that. Of course, this all goes dreadfully wrong and leads to a confused fight while everything goes haywire, with people getting crushed left, right and center (not to mention old Napoleon making a reappearance).

If this all sounds like a light-hearted romp, it's not. It's actually handled with an admirable level-headedness, if not to say undeserved seriousness. Vittorio Sala's direction keeps things moving in an idiosyncratic fashion and Riz Ortolani's score is surprisingly unobtrusive. Brett Halsey contributes a good, nonflashy performance, and Gaston Moschin makes a good, hefty villain. Unfortunately, Pier Angeli (it's customary to say the phrase "porcelain beauty" at this point) is rather insipid as the female lead. There's also Dana Andrews, who gives his customary terrible performance (and looks seriously blotto in some scenes).

The other major downside of *Spy in Your Eye* is that, despite having quite a wide (and in-

**Brett Halsey emerges from the shadows on the French poster for *Spy In Your Eye***

ternational) cinema release, it is dreadfully hard to track down nowadays. The only copy we were able to find was a dupe of an old German VHS, and it's a crying shame that this doesn't seem to exist anywhere in an English-language version. I also have the feeling that the stylistic touches would become more apparent if treated to the deluxe, letterboxed treatment. Nonetheless, one of the best.—MB

CREDITS: Production: Publi Italia, Italian International Film; Director: Vittorio Sala; Story and Screenplay: Adriano Bolzoni, Adriano Baraco, Romano Ferrara; Cinematography: Fausto Zuccoli {Eastmancolor – Widescreen}; Music: Riz Ortolani; Original running length: 90 mins; Filming locations: Portofino, Viareggio, Paris; Country: Italy; Year: 1965

CAST: Annamaria Pierangeli (*Paula Krauss*), Brett Halsey (*Bert Morris*), Dana Andrews (*Colonel Lancaster*), Gastone Moschin (*Boris*), Tanya Beryll, Mario Valdemarin (*Willie*), Tino Bianchi (*Doctor Von Donghen*), Marco Guglielmi (*Kurt Weiss*), George Wang (*Ming, a Chinese agent*), Renato Baldini (*Belkeir*), Alessandro Sperli (*Karalis*), Luciana Angiolillo (*Miss Hopkins*), Luciano Pigozzi (*Leonida*), Massimo Righi (*Johnny Davis*), Franco Baltimor [Franco Beltramme] (*Sergei*), Aldo De Franceschi, Giulio Mecale [Giuliano Maculani] (*Stanko*), Aghul Rain Bozan, Pio Tou (*Pio*)

SPY KILLER

Produced in Britain for ABC television, this talky drama then qualifies as Eurospy by the skin of its teeth. The screenplay was written by Jimmy Sangster from his novel, and it is a chess game between two old rivals who once worked together. Robert Horton (television's *Wagon Train*) is ex-agent John Smith, who was a killer for the government in the old days when he worked for Max (Sebastian Cabot, television's *Family Affair*). Smith is now a private detective and he's set up to deliver suspect information to the opposition resulting in—Max hopes—the elimination of Russian agents in China.

The set-up begins when Smith is hired by his ex-wife, Barbara Shelley—looking quite fetching here—to spy on her current husband. Smith happens onto the fellow's murder and it's here that Sangster stumbles a bit before regaining his footing. Smith is supposed to be an experienced spy, but what he does at the scene of the murder is strictly amateur: He gets blood all over himself and then picks up the murder weapon just as the police walk in. The foolishness of it all nearly teeters Sangster's house of cards from the beginning.

Luckily the twists and turns of the plot are of a high-enough grade to keep the viewer interested. A lot depends on Horton and Cabot—their characters' exposition and verbal sparring are the central concerns—and fortunately they have the chemistry and talent to pull it off.

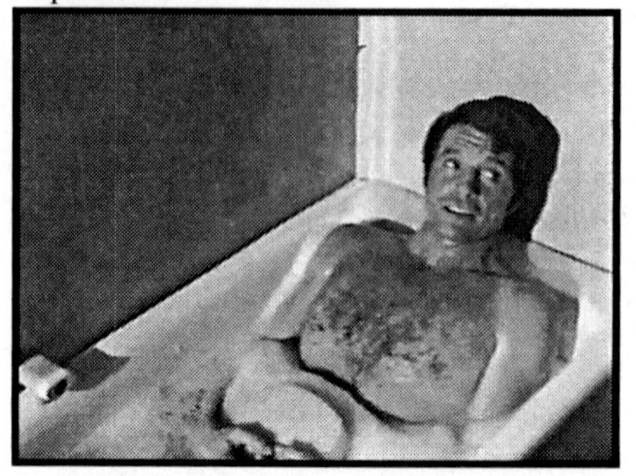

**Robert Horton as John Smith in *Spy Killer***

Smith's love interest is played by Jill St. John. She's there just to take a shower, sleep with Smith and cook his breakfast. Not much of a role, but if she was any more conspicuous she'd be getting in the way of the sly games the boys are playing.

There's very little action per se, but at least we can enjoy the post-industrial setting used for the all-important information-for-money exchange and following gun battle. The soundtrack by Johnny Pearson is occasionally near-hip in an easy-listening, jazzy kind of way, but most of the time it has the bland and innocuous manner of television. The film, meant to fit into a 90-minute time slot, barely runs 80 minutes, but it is an engaging match of wits for fans who can enjoy the machinations of plot for its own sake.—DD

CREDITS: Production: American Broadcasting Company, Halsan Productions; Director: Roy Ward Baker; Story and Screenplay: Jimmy Sangster; Cinematography: Arthur Grant; Music: Philip Martell, Johnny Pearson; Original running length: 75 mins; Filming location: London; Country: UK/US; Year: 1969

CAST: Robert Horton (*John Smith*), Sebastian Cabot (*Max*), Jill St. John (*Mary Harper*), Eleanor Summerfield (*Mrs. Roberts*), Lee Montague (*Igor*), Douglas Sheldon (*Alworthy*), Robert Russell (*police sergeant*), Barbara Shelley (*Danielle*), Harvey Hall, Donald Morley (*Dunning*), Kenneth J. Warren (*Diaman*), Philip Madoc (*Gar*), Michael Segal, Timothy Bateson, Douglas Blackwell, Sonny Caldinez, John Slavid, Anthony Stamboulieh

SPY TODAY, DIE TOMORROW
aka Die Slowly, You'll Enjoy It More (UK, unconfirmed), Mister Dinamita, mañana os besará la muerte (Sp), Mister Dynamit—morgen Küsst Euch der Tod (WG), Muori lentamente...te la godi di più (It)

The UK title of this movie is "Die Slowly, You'll Enjoy It More," a phrase uttered several times during the course of this run-of-the-mill adventure. It's not a very comforting notion and the weak sentiment reflects the bland happenings on display. What saves this film from being a complete waste of time is a cast of recognizable faces and a nice easy-listening score by Gianni Marchetti.

Lex "Tarzan" Barker is Bob Urban, aka Mr. Dynamite, a German BND agent. Self-assured to the point of parody, Urban has the capacity to escape from even the most unlikely scenarios. No matter how many armed men may surround him, Urban can fight his way to freedom. Either he's some sort of superman or henchman help has reached absurdly low levels. Barker is a likeable leading man, however, and a big plus here.

This film opens with a very poor approximation of a ship being torpedoed but thankfully it's the worst of the not-so-special effects we're supposed to accept. No attempt at convincing us of the appropriate scale of the ship is made and it looks like a toy in a bathtub as a result. Hilarious. Toys do play an important part in the film though. The villain of the piece, Bardo Baretti (Amedeo Nazzari), is obsessed with model trains. His train set-up at home doubles as his command center, with rotating panels and monitors that pop up from the towns and mountains on the table. He even has a train set in his car for those long, villainous drives! Baretti is in constant contact with his operatives, who report to him like television newscasters over the many monitors at his disposal. You have to wonder about all those television cameras his henchmen have to carry around with them. Nazzari is one of the recognizable faces I mentioned earlier. He was in a lot of sword and sandal flicks, but no other spy flicks that I could find.

Others in the cast familiar to lovers of Eurocinema are Dieter Eppler, who plays a pilot forced to go along with Baretti's mad scheme and Wolgang Priess, who plays Urban's boss. Eddie Arent gets his comic punch in as the wacky scientist who invents the gadgets that secret agents use in their fight against evil. Even Joachim Fuchsberger has an unbilled cameo as an American MP who reads *Playboy* and makes embarrassing remarks to women. Brad Harris is here too as a fellow agent of Urban's. The interesting thing about his role is that he dies with a knife in the neck.

Maria Perschy is Lu Forrester, the female who sleeps with generals and villains in the line of duty. She doesn't sleep with Urban though, who's too busy beating up 20 armed men at a time and bedding floozies on the beach. The

**The sparse Belgian poster reflects the budget limitations of *Spy Today, Die Tomorrow***

most amusing floozy scene is one in which the babe in a bikini wants Urban to have sex with her where the rubber meets the beach when she demurely purrs, "I always wanted to see a Mercedes from underneath." Perschy, meanwhile, drops out of the action near the end of this movie, so we don't know if she made her escape from Baretti or not. Baretti does manage to get away however, setting things up for a sequel that never happened. *STDT* isn't very accomplished but is reasonably enjoyable in a pinch. You could do worse.—DD

CREDITS: Production: Discobolo Film, Parnass Film, Teide P.C.; Director: Franz J. Gottlieb; Story: C.H. Guenther; Screenplay: Franz J. Gottlieb; Cinematography: Juan Gelpi {Eastmancolor - Panoramica}; Music: Gianni Marchetti; Original running length: 108 mins; Filming locations: Spain, Germany, US; Country: West Germany/Spain/Italy; Year: 1966

CAST: Lex Barker (*Bob Urban*), Maria Perschy (*Lu Forrester*), Amadeo Nazzari (*Bardo Baretti*), Jose Suarez (*General Burch*), Ulrich Haupt (*General Forman*), Wolfgang Priess (*BND Chief Sebastien*), Ralf Wolter (*Spiegel*), Siegfried Rauch (*Tazzio*), Dieter Eppler (*Captain Reichel*), Eddie Arent (*Professor Strahlmann*),

Gustavo Rojo (*Peppino*), Brad Harris (*Cliff*), Carl Rapp (*CIA Director*), Werner Fuetterer (*General Probst*), Hannes Schmidhauser (*the Captain*), Antonio Pica (*Flynn*), Gerard Landry (*General Johnson*), Werner Hauff (*Von Tiefenbach*), Charles Fawcett (*General Stikker*), Gustavo Re (*Morgan*), Miguel de la Riva (*Alf Rogerson*), Luis Induni (*U-Boat Captain*), Pino [Giuseppe] Mattei (*Balbo*), Carmen G. Cervera (*Michelle*), Gisela Hahn (*Meisje*), Silvia Solar (*Natascha*), Raoul Retzer (*the masseur*), Birgit Adenau (*Gina*), Damaso Muni (*Corsar*), Giancarlo Bastianoni (*Carlos*), Joachim Fuchsberger (*military captain*), Uta Levka, Jorge Rigaud, Howard Hagan, Wilhelm Cervera, Hercules Cortes [Cortez], Francisco Cebrian, Joachim Teege

SUBTERFUGE
aka Subterfugio (Sp)

Here's one that tries to be cynical and hip but fails on both accounts. Director Peter Graham Scott was involved with both the *Danger Man* and *The Avengers* television series, but drops the ball here, churning out a staid but not altogether lifeless espionage nonthriller.

Gene Barry is Michael Angelo Donovan, an agent "attached to the Pentagon" who is in London to track down a double agent. Barry is an old-style Roger Moore-type actor who doesn't really pull off the secret agent bit very well. Donovan is given the unsavory duty of cuddling up to Anne Langley (Joan Collins) to find out if her husband Peter (Tom Adams) is the guilty one. Adams obviously relishes his role as the cold-hearted villain, tossing aside his comic image as Charles Vine from that series of films.

**Video cover art for *Subterfuge***

The film does have its bright spots. Langley's bosses Redmayne and Kitteridge (Richard Todd and Colin Gordon, respectively) snipe at each other as if they'd had some sort of lover's quarrel before we met them. At one point, Langley meets Redmayne at Redmayne's favorite club and discovers his boss drawing pictures of female nudes with Kitteridge's head on them! Redmayne tries to explain this away by saying, "I was never quite sure about Kitteridge." Perhaps Redmayne is the guy to be worried about.

It's at this same club where we are treated to a lame song by The Marmalade, a painfully hip, third-tier musical group. I guess this was supposed to draw the kids into the theaters, but I'm sure they stayed away in droves anyway. The whole thing is embarrassing and just shows that the filmmakers were out of it, man.

For the first half-hour Donovan does nothing but get beat up and tortured, some of it at the hands of Donetta (Suzanna Leigh), a nasty, sadistic, but underused villainess. After giving Donovan some treatment with her electrical devices, she gives him a big kiss while he's unconscious. His resistance under torture must have given her immense pleasure. Donetta enjoys slapping Anne around too—and who wouldn't. Too bad Donetta's not more of a presence in the film.

This is a cynical story, but the dialogue is weak and old-fashioned. Take this exchange between Donovan and Anne, for example. She: "I always thought that America was a matriarchal society." He: "I wouldn't know, I always voted Democrat." What does that mean?

Sure, spies have marital problems and scary kids, but the kitchen-sink approach to making espionage films doesn't cut it. It all adds up to bad wigs on Joan and worse fashions. When Donovan is in the same room with his boss (Michael Rennie) and Redmayne, it's a contest as to who has the worst toupee.

The action sequences sound better than they really are. For instance,

Donovan and Anne split up while checking out a lead concerning her missing hubby. While Donovan is being shot at with a high-powered rifle and buzzed by a plane, she is being attacked by bums and accidentally sets fire to the abandoned building she's in—and it's still boring.

The coolest scene in the movie occurs when Kitteridge is being menaced in the subway by Langley. A car backs Kitteridge up against a wall and suddenly…! Oh, I don't want to spoil it for the few of you who decide to dig this one up.

There isn't much else to say about this largely old-fashioned entry from the tail-end of the sixties cycle except you might try to avoid it if possible.—DD

CREDITS: Production: Intervel VTR, Rank Film Distributors; Director: Peter Graham Scott; Story: David Whittaker; Cinematography: Horst Werzel {Eastmancolor}; Music: Cyril Ornadeli; Original running length: 89 mins; Country: UK; Year: 1968

CAST: Gene Barry (*Donovan*), Joan Collins (*Anne Langley*), Richard Todd (*Col. Victor Redmayne*), Tom Adams (*Peter Langley*), Suzanna Leigh (*Donetta*), Michael Rennie (*Goldsmith*), Marius Goring (*Shevik*), Scott Forbes (*Pannell*), Colin Gordon (*Kitteridge*), Guy Deghy (*Dr. Lundgren*), Dermot Kelly (*the van driver*), Stuart Cooper (*Dubrossman*), John Welsh (*Heiner*), Clifford Earl (*the policeman*), Ron Pember (*the photographer*)

SUPER SEVEN CALLING CAIRO
aka Super Sept Appelle Le Sphinx (Fr),
Superseven chiama Cairo (It)

This is director Umberto Lenzi's second spy flick and it is the first of his three starring Roger Browne. While a major improvement over his first effort, *A 008 Operation Exterminate*, this isn't quite as entertaining as those that followed. Strong-jawed Roger Browne makes for a good secret agent; he dresses up well and fights even better. But despite having an excellent villain in Massimo Serato and a decent (but minor) role for Rosalba Neri, this is only a modest success because of a lack of action and a plot that—surprisingly—is not complex enough.

**Despite the claims made by the Turkish poster, *Superseven Calling Cairo* is not part of the Agent Z-55 series**

This time Browne plays a pipe-smoking Canadian, Martin Stevens, who works for the British Secret Service. A sample of a new metallic, radioactive element, baltonium—that is 100 times more radioactive than uranium—is stolen and fashioned into a movie camera lens, which is then inadvertently sold to a tourist. Ex-Nazi Alex (Serato), who let this slip through his evil fingers, and Stevens, chase the globe-trotting tourist around trying to get their hands on this camera. There are scenes (supposedly) in London, Cairo, Switzerland, Rome, and the Italian countryside, so we spend a lot of time in travel.

The level of violence promised by the opening scenes (Stevens kills a gun-toting lover before the credits roll) is unfortunately not sustained throughout the film. Sure, one woman is slapped around and forced to overdose on heroin and one guy is crushed to death with a car, but there are only a couple of fights and gun battles.

As mentioned earlier, one big plus is a small but significant role for Rosalba Neri. Here she plays an innocent used by enemy agents to get the best of Stevens and she doesn't get killed. She introduces herself with the old "I borrowed your shower" gambit when he checks into his hotel room. She falls for him of course and makes several short appearances in the film until the end, when she gets promoted to Love Interest because Stevens' main squeeze is revealed as being in cahoots with Alex the whole time. This femme fatale is played by Fabienne Dali and Stevens makes the mistake of dragging her around with him because she supposedly knows what the tourist with that special camera looks like. She'd have fooled me too.

Lenzi's not above reusing footage here and there to pad things out and recasting the same actors to fill out the usual roles. Speaking of footage, there's an interesting shot of a fellow climbing on one of the pyramids at Giza that really gives you an idea of just how enormous these man-made wonders really are.

Other cool things would be a razor that shaves on 110 volts and transmits on 220, a strip act in a groovy club, a kind of psychedelic sequence, an ill-defined torture device, a pen gun, some go-kart action and a micro-bomb hidden in our hero's shoe heel. But the topper is the fact that the same song sung by Ingrid Schoeller in *A 008*, and sung by another nightclub singer in *Last Man to Kill* (another Lenzi flick), is heard here over a loudspeaker system in an Italian campground! Angelo Francesco Lavagnino's soundtrack has its moments, but he did better work elsewhere.—DD

CREDITS: Production: Romana Film, Prodex; Director: Umberto Lenzi; Story based on the novel "S7 Calling Cairo" by Humphrey Humbert [Umberto Lenzi]; Screenplay: Umberto Lenzi, Piero Pierotti; Cinematography: Augusto Tiezzi; Music: Angelo Francesco Lavagnino; Original running length: 95 mins; Country: Italy/France; Year: 1966

CAST: Roger Browne (*Super Seven*), Fabienne Dali (*Denise*), Massimo Serato (*Alex*), Anthony Gradwell [Antonio Gradoli] (*Jussef*), Andrew Ray [Andrea Aureli] (*the Easterner*), Dina Di Santis (*Tania*), Rosalba Neri (*Faddja*), Stella Monclar (*Nietta*), Mino Doro (*the Professor*), Franco Castellani (*Inspector Stugel*), Nando Angelini (the *radioactivity technician*), Emilio Messina (*Nickols*), Paolo Bonacelli (*Captain Hume*), Francesco De Leone (*Professor Gabin*), Claudio Biava (*Hans*), Wilbert Bradley, Vincenzo Maggio, Sandro Pellegrini, Gaetano Quartararo, Piera Clerici, Dominico Calderone

## THE SURVIVAL FACTOR

aka Escape from Taiga (unconfirmed),
Escape from the KGB (Int),
Liebesnächte in der taiga (WG)

The US suspects that the Russian government is building a large base, for the purpose of space exploration, in the wilds of Siberia. Desperate to know more, they send CIA agent Heller (Thomas Hunter)—a Latvian with an expertise in Russian customs—to infiltrate a local village and weed out any information possible. Unfortunately, his mission is made more difficult when the KGB becomes aware that something of the kind is going on. It's also made more difficult by the appearance of a pea-brained model and ex-lover (Magda Konopka), who immediately blows his cover.

Nevertheless, he soon manages to shake off his pursuers and makes his way to the village, where he poses as an engineer at a local lumber works. He becomes pals with Soviet babe Ludmilla (Maria Versini), whose status as local Communist representative means that he can get access to all kinds of information through (and unbeknown to) her. Before long he has managed to appropriate some microfilm that confirms American suspicions, and plans to make an escape.

Before he can do so, however, Ludmilla—with whom he has fallen in love—finds out his true identity, so he is forced (not unwillingly) to take her along with him. Knowing that all the roads and railway stations are being watched, they must head out into the desolate, snowbound countryside in hopes of reaching the border. Their adventures have only just begun.

*Survival Factor* is a reasonably effective little production, especially in the second half when it becomes more of an out-and-out action movie. It's not as light-hearted as the majority of spy films, reflecting the fact that it came at the very end of the cycle, when filmmakers were trying to push the genre into different directions. It's much more of a "Cold War" than a "secret agent" film; it has a similar atmosphere (and music) to the war films that were being produced in the late sixties. There's also lots of "Sunday afternoon" melodrama involving the two central characters (accompanied by soaring string music), which unfortunately slows everything down a bit too much. There's only so much "If you love me, leave me here"-type histrionics you can take.

The Russian setting means there are lots of downtrodden peasants, plenty of vodka drinking and copious amounts of fur hat-wearing (Marie Versini certainly looks far better in her Soviet uniform and comfy headpiece than out of it). The film's most unique point is a rather nasty sequence in which people are tortured by being tied to the trunks of cliff-side trees. These are then chopped down so they—and the attached unfortunates—tumble over the precipice.

**Romance behind the Iron Curtain between Thomas Hunter and Maria Versini in *The Survival Factor***

The cinematography does look a bit flat, but it's not really helped by the slightly gloomy concentration camp-style sets. Harald Philip is hardly the most imaginative of filmmakers, and although he knows how to point a camera in the right direction (which is more than can be said about some of the directors whose work features in this work), he doesn't have the talent to make anything particularly memorable. That said, there are some decent stunts and explosions. The climax, as the central characters attempt to escape across a dangerous looking waterfall, is also relatively powerful.

Thomas Hunter spends a lot of time running around being chased, not unlike his performance in *The Magnificent Tony Carrera.* Ex-American footballer and popular Euro-performer Walter Barnes (*The Big Gundown*) puts in a characteristically ursine performance as the leader of a gang of *Big Silence*-style outlaws hiding out in the Siberian wilderness. Hellmut Lange (*FBI operazione vipera gialla*) is an all-drinking, all-womanizing agent sent in to help. In all, a far better film than I've probably made it sound.—MB

CREDITS: Production: Franz Seitz Filmproduktion; Director: Harald Philip; Story based on the novel by Heinz G. Konsalik; Screenplay: Werner P. Zibaso; Cinematography: Helmut Meewes {Eastmancolor}; Music: Manfred Hubler; Original running length: 105 mins; Country: West Germany; Year: 1967

CAST: Thomas Hunter (*Heller*), Marie Versini (*Ludmilla*), Ivan Desny (*Colonel Kirk*), Walter Barnes (*Yuri*), Christiane Nielsen (*Tanja, a doctor*), Rolf Boysen (*Colonel Karpuchin*), Biggi Freyer (*Marta, Karpuchin's aide*), Hellmut Lange (*Jimmy Braddock*), Magda Konopka (*Bibi Randall*), Kurd Pieritz (*Kusnezoff*), Stanislav Ledinek

UN TANGO DALLA RUSSIA
"a tango from Russia"aka Agente segreto 070: un tango dalla Russia (It, alt)

Making a film is a tricky business. It requires a group of specialists, working together to mold their individual contributions into a worthwhile whole. Some of these contributors are respected and honored: the actor, the director, the composer. Some are not. It is all too easy to forget the craftsmen who put their little touch of magic into a production. Easy, that is, until you are confronted by an instance in which one element is so goddamned awful that it makes you sit up and appreciate the sheer bloody quality that must exist under normal circumstances. *Un Tango dalla Russia* is, quite frankly, the most poorly edited film I have ever seen—scenes are cut together with all the care of a kick in the mouth—and it really makes you understand just how much value good editing brings to a film.

It all starts off with a particularly silly title sequence in which the eyes of a cartoon mouse roll around insanely while the credits run. This segues into compiled footage of natural disasters, which is then replaced by the shot of a group of teens doing the twist intercut with a series of newspaper headlines (about 30 of the darned things). Meanwhile, some people ride go-karts.

Don't worry, this all makes perfect sense compared to that which follows; a bunch of nutters gather in an underground cavern adorned with pseudo-swastikas. They all wear pig (or clown) masks. Who can make sense of all this absurdity? Well, maybe agent 070, Charles Duff (Dan Christian).

After a three-minute bout of flamenco dancing (which keeps being interrupted by other scenes as though something's about to happen [nothing does]), we finally meet a short villain in sunglasses. He disappears five minutes later without explanation. There's some more dancing (to an orchestral tango being played—impressively—by a traditional four-piece pop band). The bar is decorated with china hands stuck to the wall. Duff finds the body of a friend in his hotel room. The camera pans round to watch a hamster (I think it's supposed to be a mouse) running around the baseboard.

He tries to search the house of a suspect, but is knocked unconscious by Asian babe Katya (Seyna Seyn)—only to wake up in his hotel room. A mysterious old man, Fred (Attilio Dottesio), congratulates the hamster on a job well done (?). Just when you think things can't get any more demented, a couple of other spies turn up dressed in scout uniforms. This admittedly looks quite fetching on the female agent, but doesn't make anything even approaching sense (which in the context of the film so far seems absolutely reasonable). They are murdered.

Somewhere amidst all of this, there is the skeleton of a plotline. A mad professor has devised a disease that will wipe out all of humanity, apart from those of a specific (master) race—hence the Nazi-style regalia. He has disappeared, and only his daughter (Britt Semand) knows anything about where he may have hidden the virus.

Director Cesare Canevari, hiding behind the unbelievable "Berwang Ross" pseudonym, is generally thought to have made possibly the strangest spaghetti western ever: *Matalo*, a psychedelic concoction involving sagebrush hippies and boomerang- throwing cowboys. With *Tango*, he can also lay claim to directing a truly astonishing spy film. It's awful, true, but it's certainly not easily forgotten.

As well as the aforementioned incompetent editing, this features some truly terrible choreography, all of the production values of a sixties porn loop and a dreadful soundtrack. As zany as this all sounds, Canevari hadn't yet perfected his later, demented style—and it's all very low- (as well as undoubtedly off-) key. The general weirdness of it all is actually quite disconcerting. Sometimes it's undoubtedly due to general incompetence, but sometimes there does seem to be a level of surrealism at work. This is perhaps most evident during the scenes set in the underground dungeon (straight out of a Parisian Grand-Guignol stage show) equipped with pig mask-wearing torturer. And no, the hamster is never explained.

Terrible, but at the same time one of the most entertaining films to have been spawned by the genre, it was obviously thought that this merited a sequel, *Agente segreto 070 Thunderbay—missione Grasshopper*. Neither of them were shown anywhere much, the distributors obviously realizing that even drugged-out beatniks wouldn't be able to make any sense of this utter balderdash.—MB

CREDITS: Production: Isabella Paolucci; Director: Berwang Ross [Cesare Canevari]; Story based on a story by Cornelius Monk; Screenplay: Cornelius Monk, Henry Gozzo; Cinematography: Maurice Moschion {B&W}; Music: M. Necopi; Original running length: 80 mins; Country: Italy; Year: 1965

CAST: Dan Christian (*Charles Duff/Agent 070*), Britt Semand (*Evelyn*), Seyna Seyn (*Katya*), Liv Ferrer, Gara Grand, Attilio Dottesio (*Fred*), Don Tesdal, Mark Tessier

### TARGET FOR KILLING

aka Geheimnis der gelben monche (WG),
How to Kill A Lady (US, unconfirmed),
Operacion gigante (Sp), The Secret of the
Yellow Monks (Int, unconfirmed),
Tiro a segno per uccidere (It)

Stewart Granger is again an FBI agent and indeed, is even supposedly the same man who thwarted the smuggling racket in *Red Dragon*, but he has a different name: James Vine. Luckily, this time the results for viewers are much improved as the groovy credit sequence will attest: hip graphics and a cool rock song kick things off nicely. Here, Granger isn't quite the smarmy character he was in *Red Dragon*, but he is still the unlikely beneficiary of a relationship with a pretty young thing—even pledging to marry her in the end.

Vine is after an evil organization run by The Giant (Curd Jurgens), operating out of a monastery in Montenegro. The Giant's activities involve gunrunning and developing a telepathic technique of brainwashing—but it's all rather vague. As The Giant puts it, his profession is "too complicated for a young lady to understand." Or anyone else for that matter. For Vine, bringing this organization down is secondary to protecting Sandra Perkins (Karin Dor). The attempts on her life, not fully explained until the end of the film, involve someone wanting to get their hands on money she'll inherit on her next birthday. I must say that The Giant should pay better for his henchman help, as their murderous activities are exceedingly weak. They don't follow orders and manage to botch numerous opportunities to put Perkins away for good.

At the beginning of the film, when Vine and Perkins "meet cute" on an airplane, the astute viewer will notice that Vine uses the same lame fortune-telling gag on Perkins as Granger did on Janet Leigh in *Scaramouche*. This is just before the flight crew abandons the plane in mid-air in order to kill Perkins (and everyone else on board), but Vine manages to land the plane—he was in the Air Force, you know.

There is a woman of power in the film but it isn't Sandra Perkins, whose deer-in-the-headlight look was Karin Dor's stock in trade. No, it's Scilla Gabel as Tiger, The Giant's right-hand woman. Clad in black leather pants, Tiger really shines when she's terrorizing a cohort with a machine gun. There's a funny moment in the film when Tiger is kissing Klaus Kinski, another would-be assassin. As they kiss the camera moves down and we see Klaus put his hand between her legs, but his motive turns out to be to steal her cigarettes. Tiger is a strong presence in the film—smart and ruthless—but because she is evil she must eventually die for her sins.

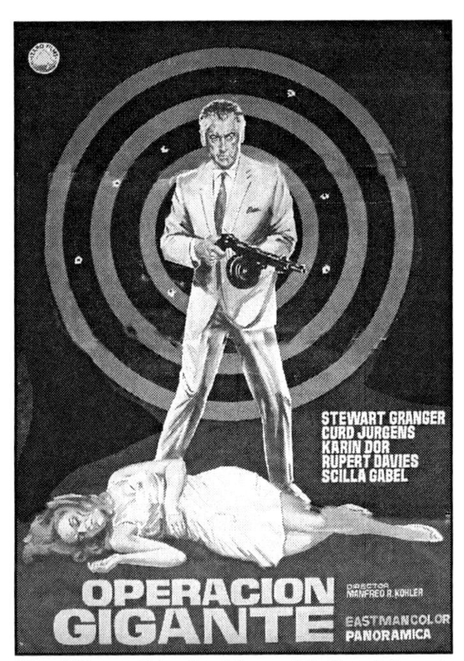


**The "Gigante" in the title on this Spanish poster for *Target For Killing* refers to villain Curd Jurgens**

Unfortunately, the Perkins character is a weak and gullible sort of female, just the type to turn on the macho James Vine, who says "I like a girl to be dependent on me." Vine treats her like a child, which becomes painfully apparent when the various attempts on her life are made. You know the routine: Girl narrowly escapes being murdered, girl tells man, man thinks she's imagining things. This happens not once but several times in the course of the film and it does get tiring.

Perkins is menaced several times in the film, even to the point of absurdity. Once, running out of her hotel room in just her slip, she's pursued down the road by a "runaway" truck. Go figure. After she is finally captured by The Giant's sub-par thugs, he submits her to an "electro-psychic massage" which turns out to be Perkins chained to a cell door and shocked by manta rays while the evil Dr. Young brainwashes her with his mind from across the room.

So it turns out that Perkins' uncle (Adolfo Celi) wants her killed so he'll get the money she would otherwise inherit. When The Giant learns how much Perkins will be worth, he wants the dough for himself and subjects Celi to a horrible death by rats. What's interesting about this is that The Giant wants the money so he can escape the evilness biz altogether. His motives aren't the usual world domination theme, but instead to escape his life of crime and make a new start. He is so notorious that he is literally a prisoner in his monastery. He doesn't want to rule the earth, he just wants to go down to the waterfront and visit the shops!

The villain of the piece may have his evil priorities mixed up, but the gadgets used by both sides in this war of dollars are right up spy alley. We have an egg that conceals not only a recorder but a little speaker for playback too. There's the old needle-in-the-Winston-pack trick, the cylindrical metal listening device thrown into a room for eavesdropping purposes, the tiny camera in the electrical socket, and last but not least, the old "bomb in the hotel key ignited by the pipe stem" trick. There's even a funky graphic of a gun barrel superimposed on one scene when a sniper intends to shoot someone—a "killer cam" so to speak.

I have to mention a bit more about this telepathic technique that The Giant is working on with Dr. Young. Apparently Young can not only hypnotize people into losing all will of their own, he can send his thoughts into other people's heads at random. Near the end of the film, the talented doctor tries to do just that to The Giant, sending the command for The Giant to kill himself. The Giant is too smart for the old man however, because he simply holds up a mirror to the doctor's face to divert the telepathic thoughts. And we thought that only worked with lasers.

Aside from my earlier complaints, director Manfred Kohler has made a vast improvement on Granger's previous spy outing and the talented cast is a real asset to the film's modest successes.—DD

CREDITS: Production: Intercontinental Film Produktion, P.E.A.; Director: Manfred R. Kohler; Story and Screenplay: Anatol Bratt; Cinematography: Siegeried Hald {Eastmancolor}; Music: Marcello Giombini (Eureka); Original running length: 92 mins; Country: Austria/Italy; Year: 1966

CAST: Stewart Granger (*James Terrence Vine*), Karin Dor (*Sandra Perkins*), Rupert Davies (*Police Commissioner Saadi*), Scilla Gabel (*Tigre*), Klaus Kinski (*Caporetti*), Molli Peters (*Vera*), Curd Jurgens (*The Giant*), Adolfo Celi (*Uncle Henry Perkins*), Erika Remberg (*the stewardess*), Luis Induni (*Dr. Young*), Jose Marco Rosello (*Cloyd*), Allen Pinson (*the co-pilot*), Demeter Bitenc (*a killer*), Wilbert Gurley, Slobodan Dimitrijevic (*a killer*)

TARGET GOLDSEVEN

aka Danger a Tanger (Fr), Operazione Goldseven (It), Técnica de un espía (Sp), Tecnica di un spia (It)

One of the many spy films released in 1966, this never saw much in the way of distribution, and only received so-so box office receipts. It's also sometimes miscredited to hack director supreme Alfonso Brescia. Although certainly poor enough to qualify as his work, it unfortunately has nothing whatsoever to do with him.

A ship called The Trinidad is ambushed, the crew murdered and its cargo—50 barrels of uranium—stolen. The immediate suspect is a character known as The Snake, head of a powerful criminal organization committed to some nonsense or other. Secret agent Alan Milner (Tony Russel), who is already familiar with The Snake's nefarious activities, is assigned to the case.

His investigations promptly lead him to Lisbon, where he attracts the attention of a suspicious blonde, Erika (Erika Blanc), whom he discovers searching his room. After giving her a bit of a slap, they proceed to share a bottle of Dom Perignon and a quick canoodle (an unsophisticated piece of plotting, even for the genre). It's all a trap, of course, but he manages to escape thanks to his prowess at fisticuffs.

After much minor intrigue, he fixes his attention upon Otis (Conrado Sanmartin), the owner of a shipping company who lives on an isolated desert island. His suspicions are correct. Otis had stolen the uranium to carry out some experiments into an "immunizing vaccination" against radiation, for which he is to be paid by the mysterious Snake. Milner infiltrates the island by disguising himself as one of the villain's henchman (who sports a patently false beard, thus making the impersonation that much easier), and sets about foiling the evil plan.

*Target Goldseven* has a mediocre script that uses the familiar "anti-radiation serum" MacGuffin (from *Crime Story* and others), and suffers from some serious oversights (just who exactly is The Snake, and just why does he want the serum?). This is all made even more sluggish by the nailed-down camerawork and complete inadequacy of the director. Somehow everything manages to look even cheaper than it actually must have been, with lots of tedious driving about and model boats in a bathtub masquerading as ships. Probably the "high point" of the action is a protracted drag-bike race, which lasts a good couple of minutes (despite the film being partially speeded up). Even Piero Umiliani's score is rather subdued (apart from the great torch song, "Play to Win").

It's a shame, as there's a reasonable cast lurking about in there somewhere. Conrado Sanmartin makes a smarmy, handsome villain, and Tony Russel a serviceable lead. Both Erika Blanc and Dianik Zurakowska, however, are entirely wasted (although it is quite fun watching the latter prance around the villain's lair in great mod threads). There's also a typically sturdy performance from the spectacular island retreat, which must have been used in at least 10 films contained within this book. Unsurprisingly, the rather less effective cinematic qualities of Alberto Leonardi marked his only outing in the director's chair.

Watch out for the particularly amusing crap stopwatch (counting down toward an explosion in which the hero will die, natch), which is clearly being operated by a set designer with a dodgy sense of rhythm.—MB

**French poster for *Target Goldseven***

CREDITS: Production: Duca Compagnia Cin. Ca, Prod Cin.Cas Santos Alcocer; Director: Albert B. Leonard [Alberto Leonardi]; Story and Screenplay: M.C. Martinez Roman; Cinematography: Alfonso Nieva {Eastmancolor - Widescreen}; Music: Piero Umiliani; Original running length: 90 mins; Filming location: Lisbon; Country: Italy/Spain; Year: 1967

CAST: Tony Russel (*Alan Milner*), Erika Blanc (*Erika Brown*), Conrado Sanmartin (*Otis*), Diannyk [Dianik] Zurakowska (*Mitzi*), Fernando Cebrian (*Kare*), Peter White [Adriano Micantoni] (*Louis Kerez Fischer, a Portuguese agent*), Wilbert Bradley (*Steiner*), Joseph Giuseppe Fortis, Alberto [Adalberto] Rossetti, Pica Serrano, Evar(isto) Maran. Uncredited: Antonio Pica (*Alex, Erika's friend*)

THAT MAN IN ISTANBUL
aka Colpo grosso a Galata Bridge (It),
Estambul 65 (Sp), L'homme d'Istambul (Fr),
Operacion Estambul (Fr),
Unser Mann aus Istanbul (WG)

Sylva Koscina is the CIA agent, Kenny, but Horst Buchholz, as Tony Maecenas, gets most of the action in this middle-of-the-pack spy adventure. Kenny drops out of the picture for long periods of time because she's a girl, I guess. Maecenas sure treats her like a second-class citizen, calling her "baby fat" and even going so far as to lock her in a closet so she won't get mixed up in the "one man job" of ferreting out the kidnapped scientist. When Kenny goes to Maecenas looking for a job, he forces her to her strip in front of his boys and then ignores her. What a guy. He makes amends later however, advising Kenny to "tighten your judo belt around that 21-inch waist. Round one is about to begin." Mr. Suave.

Maecenas really gets around too, if you know what I mean. Everywhere he goes, pretty girls say "Ciao, Tony!" and the gag gets a bit stale by the end of this overlong picture. At one point, Maecenas is in drag and some guy calls out "Ciao, Tony!" in a reversal of that funny business. Buchholz is not a very likeable actor in general and the character he plays, scrawny adventurer Maecenas, is really no exception. His asides to the camera—"What? Me worry?"—wear thin too. Sure, he drives a red Jaguar and dresses up nicely, but he's not the kind of guy you'd want to hang out with.

You know things aren't going to go too well when early in the film there's one of those silly bar fight-type scenes. Luckily it's the worst of those sorts of antics, and it's out of the way before we hit the 15-minute mark. The film does boast a cool credit sequence with hip sixties graphics and a swinging musical number though. The locations around Istanbul are used to pretty good effect too, with lots of action occurring in ancient places.

The gang Kenny and Maecenas are up against is fairly high-tech. They keep in constant radio contact with little radio transmitters and car phones. Klaus Kinski, pretty high up on the henchman pecking order, talks to the head honcho on a portable radio that must be a Russian model based on its size. At one point the gang is talking to the boss using a pair of sunglasses. Nice gadget, but visually speaking what you see is a bunch of thugs sitting around a table talking to a pair of glasses. Could've been snazzier. They also have one of those omniscient surveillance cameras, the kind that move around with whoever they're spying on and manages all sorts of complex angles. The only gadget the good guys have is a tie-clip camera.

**The Spanish poster for *That Man in Istanbul* features an extremely busy Horst Buccholz**

Not that Maecenas needs gadgets. He can jump out of his Jag onto the moving truck he just crashed into as the car goes over a cliff. Later, Maecenas finds himself at a construction site late at night (a good nighttime location) with four cars coming toward him from different directions. What does he do? He shoots out their headlights so they all run into each other. He can even shoot out four headlights with one bullet. When a hitman tries his luck shooting at him from a hotel swimming pool (I'm sure no one would notice), Maecenas jumps in for an underwater knife fight (yawn), after which he escapes through a giant drain hole in the pool and emerges into a shallow fountain in the front of the hotel.

We do get a knock-down, drag-out fight between Maecenas and Kinski, which is fun. Unfortunately, Klaus loses. Earlier while Klaus had the drop on Maecenas, Klaus gets to say the line, "I'm considered a good shot by those I've killed." We are also treated to a couple of really cheesy explosions, the kind that are superimposed on the object supposedly blowing up. The end of the film is stretched out so we can have a final helicopter stunt and the Kenny/Maecenas reunion, with the million dollars, of course.—DD

CREDITS: Production: Isasi P.C., EDIC, CCM; Director: Antonio Isasi; Story: Giorgio Simonelli, Nat Wachsberger; Screenplay: Luis Jose Comeron, Antonio Isasi, Jorge Illa; Cinematography: Juan Gelpi {Technicolor – Techniscope}; Music: Georges Garvarentz; Filming locations: Istanbul, Barcelona, Costa Brava, Garraf; Country: Italy/France/Spain; Year: 1965

CAST: Horst Buchholz (*Tony Maecenas*), Sylva Koscina (*Kenny*), Mario Adorf (*Bill*), Perrette

Pradier (*Elisabeth*), Klaus Kinski (*Schenk*), Alvaro De Luna (*Bogo*), Gustavo Re (*"brain"*), Jorge Rigaud (*the CIA chief*), Christine Maybach (*Josette*), Gerard Tichy (*Hansi*), Agustin Gonzales (*Gunther*), Rocha [Jacques Rocha] (*the Chinaman*), Angel Picazo (*Inspector Mallouk*), Umberto Raho (*Professor Pendergast*), Barta Barri, Alberto Dalbes, Manuel Bronchud, Luis Induni, Christine Mercier, Henry Cogan, Nadia Brivio, Marta Flores

**Eddie Constantine is everywhere on the Belgian poster for the Eurospy classic *There's Going To Be a Party***

THERE'S GOING TO BE A PARTY
aka Ça va être ta fête (Fr),
Passaporto falso (It), Wer zuerst schiesst,
hat mehr vom Leben (WG)

One of the best of Eddie Constantine's spy films, this relatively low-key adventure is filled with genuine humor, surreal imagery and has an intriguing mystery at its core. This time, Eddie is John Jarvis, agent KS21, and his mission is to ferret out a mysterious double agent known as Marc Lemoine—and kill him. The whole thing turns out to be a ploy to expose a leak in the spy network, a photographer named Bragarian (Claude Cerval).

Constantine was already a big star in Europe by this time. His string of adventures vary in quality, naturally, but Eddie's charm is what kept drawing the crowds into the cinemas. Here he has a great foil in the lovely Barbara Lange, who plays journalist Michèle Laurent, an innocent swept up by circumstance into this spy game. The sarcastic interplay and natural chemistry between the two leads is a refreshing change from the usual innuendo-laden dialogue between ladies' man and conquest.

Director Pierre Montazel was a cinematographer for a large portion of his career. Here he captures a film noir look for the many night scenes, but even more notable are the audacious camera tricks and New Wave allusions sprinkled throughout. This is a fun movie to watch not just for the cast and the clever script but also for the great care taken with many of the visuals. Another first-rate aspect is the free jazz score by the Jazz Group of Paris and Martial Solal that manages to highlight and accent without overwhelming the proceedings.

Jarvis breaks the "fourth wall" once, making a remark to the camera, but this never becomes a tongue-in-cheek spoof. It's played straight for the most part. Don't get me wrong, there's plenty of intentional humor. When a fellow traveler tries to sell him life insurance, Jarvis remarks, "No one wants to sell me insurance. I'm a toreador." And when Jarvis and Michele steal a bus to escape from the bad guys, Jarvis calms the shaken passengers by telling them "It's okay, I'm the brother-in-law of the driver." When a cop pulls the bus over shortly thereafter, the two fugitives steal his motorcycle.

One of the best sequences is when Jarvis is knocked unconscious upon boarding a small plane; when he awakens there's no one flying the damn thing—it's on autopilot and running out of fuel. Jarvis doesn't know how to fly a plane, of course, and we hear his thoughts as he tries to figure his way out of the predicament, pushing all the buttons and twisting all the knobs. At one point he says to himself, "I've only one chance left. If I miss, they'll have to get another guy to shoot this kind of movie." It becomes surreal when the fuel runs out and the only noise is the wind whistling through the plane. How does he escape? You'll have to watch to find out.

There are odd bits, like a pair of lesbian killers, but the coup de grace is the fabulous shot of Bragarian's death. Trying to escape by jumping onto a milk truck, Bragarian is shot down, sprawled out in a spreading stain of milk in the street. Be sure to catch this recommended film; you won't be disappointed.—DD

CREDITS: Production: Belmont Films, Chaillot Films, Cinerad-Cinematografica Radici, Federal International Films, Société Générale Européenne de Films, Unidex; Director: Pierre Montazel; Story and Screenplay: Norman Krasna, Pierre Montazel, Clarence Weff; Cinematography: Michel Kelber {B&W}; Music: Jazz Group of Paris, Martial Solal; Original running length: 80 mins; Filming location: Lisbon; Country: France/Italy; Year: 1960

CAST: Eddie Constantine (*John Jarvis*), Barbara Lange (*Michèle Laurent*), Stefan Schnabel, Claude Cerval (*Bragarian*), Saro Urzì, Norma Burgo, Clarence Weff (*the killer*), Lucien Callamand, Albert Médina, Anny Nelsen, Jean-Pierre Zola

THREE GOLDEN DRAGONS
aka Island of Lost Girls (US), Kommissar X—Drei goldene Schlangen (WG)

The first thing that you notice about the sixth installment of the Kommissar X series is the fantastic soundtrack by the underrated Roberto Pregadio. That this is accompanied by the blandest of travel footage is of no concern, just sink into those groovy vibes. Aaah, pure heaven.

There is only one word to describe this extraordinarary concoction of a film: hokey. Whereas previous entries trod a fine line between the ridiculous and the sublime, *Three Golden Dragons* launches itself unashamedly into the stratosphere. Embarrassing as it is to admit, this is a personal favorite of mine. So sue me.

Tony Kendall and Brad Harris are reunited as Joe Walker and Captain Tom Rowland, here pursuing a kidnap ring in Bangkok. Pitted against a gamut of Asian would-be assassins, all of whom wear a tattoo of three intertwined snakes upon their wrists, they discover that a variety of young western women are being introduced to the ways of prostitution. Imprisoned on a tropical island, this brigade of "beauties" is force fed opium and subjected to the Chinese water torture. This, of course, turns them into sexual playthings. Hmm, never thought of trying that one myself...

Behind all this rampant idiocy is a Chinese dame with a dislike of white males, and a patently distrustful "expert on Oriental culture," Walter Brandi, who also happens to know more about poisons than is really healthy. Their henchmen wear loud shirts and are repeatedly beaten up, but do manage to assassinate a few disposable characters with blow darts.

After several chases, fistfights and examples of bad acting, everyone ends up having a mud fight! Tony and Brad share a laugh, give each other a cigar and walk off into the realms of another adventure. They don't make them like that anymore, and I'm sure that any sane person would express sincere gratitude. However, as a sucker for any film that features gratuitous midget abuse, this to me is simply ambrosia.

**A rare Herbert Fuchs (left) lobby card with Tony Kendall in *Three Golden Dragons***

Roberto Mauri is an interesting director in that while his films are all remarkably cheap and devestatingly derivative, they are all great fun. Further attrocities in his filmography include *The King of Kong Island* and *Sartana in the Valley of Death*, but he unfortunately never made another spy film. Walter Brandi was a regular accomplice and former heartthrob, and it's nice to see him here a good few years past his prime.

A great politically incorrect way to waste 90 minutes of your life.—MB

CREDITS: Production: Hampton International, International Artists; Director: Roberto Mauri; Story based on the novels by Bert Island; Screenplay: Robert F. Atkinson, James Brewer, Manfred R. Köhler; Cinematography: Francesco Izzarelli {Eastmancolor}; Music: Roberto Pregadio; Filming location: Bangkok; Country: West Germany/Italy; Year: 1968

CAST: Tony Kendall (*Joe Walker*), Brad Harris (*Tom Rowland*), Monica Prado (*Kathin Russel*), Loni Heuser (*Maud Leighton*), Hansi Linder (*Phyllis Leighton*), Vilaiwan, Vatanapanich, Herbert Fuchs, Pino Mattei, Walter Brandi, Rotraut De Neve, Carlos De Castro

## TICKET TO DIE
aka Agente segreto 777:
invito ad uccidere (It)

John Gordon is an embittered ex-spy, kicked out of the Secret Service for undisclosed reasons (it is later revealed that he is suffering from cancer, and only has a year to live). Knowing that "…a spy's pension stretches about as far as a cop's salary," he decides to use his inside knowledge to appropriate a formula. Devised by a missing Professor Krueger, this is much desired by assorted governments—despite it never becoming clear exactly what it does.

The only problem is that it is in three parts, and although he recovers two of them without much difficulty, the final fragment is more problematic. He knows that it's in the hands of an underworld character called Velasquez, but no one actually knows who this is—and there isn't even a description. The only clue is that one of his henchmen (conveniently killed in a car crash) used to frequent The Casino Club. While investigating, he meets up with an old associate from the Intelligence Services, Clyde (Umberto Raho), who offers him $200,000 to help recover the formula.

After nearly being killed in a plane crash *and* an ambush on his car, Gordon manages to carve his way through several other cast members. Finally he discovers that a friend of his, Houseman, is the mysterious Velasquez, and after disposing of him manages to salvage the final fragment. However, Clyde has received orders from his superiors that he must kill his erstwhile partner, who is now seen as a huge security risk.

*Ticket to Die* is an absolutely infuriating film. In theory, it is an interestingly different take on the spy film genre: slow moving, downbeat, noir-ish and completely lacking in fripperies. In reality, unfortunately, it is a dull, plodding mess—and the fact that you can see what the filmmakers were trying to achieve only makes it more irksome.

Take, for instance, the fact that a large amount of the narrative is revealed through the use of a voiceover. Now there's nothing wrong with this at all, it can be well used to highlight mood and the thought processes of the main protagonists. And although effective at first, partly because of its unfamiliarity in films of this type, it soon becomes blatantly clear that it is really being used because otherwise the plot would make absolutely no sense. Until the point at which the entire formula is recovered, the audience is in a total state of bewilderment as to who all of these characters—most of whom only appear for a minute or two of screen time—actually are. Could it possibly have been that the production ran out of finances before completion? It sure looks like it.

Beyond that, it is all seriously dour. The direction is subdued, the cinematography dingy and there's an extraordinary amount of walking around. The dialogue is stilted, performances generally wooden and there's some deeply appalling choreography (which almost looks like some kind of performance art). As is regularly the case with dull Euro-productions, the main saving grace is a good score by Marcello De Martino—and a typically capable contribution from ubiquitous character actor Umberto Raho.

This must have been made just after the obscure Mark Damon-starring *Agente segreto 777: operazione Mistero*, but if the intention was to start a series it floundered badly. Lewis Jordan, whoever he may be, appeared as a secondary character in *Mistero* and is an unusual hero, older than usual and totally lacking in humor. Enrico Bomba, who worked regularly as a producer (*Last Plane to Baalbeck* amongst others), directed a few films before this: *Prigioneri delle tenebre*, (parts of) *The Rape of the Sabines* (starring future Bond Roger Moore!) and *La Spada dell'Islam*. He wouldn't helm another until 1972, when he made the decidedly minor *L'aretino nei suoi ragionamenti...sulle cortigiane, La Maritate e il cornuti contenti* and *Le Mille e una notte...e un altra ancora.*—MB

CREDITS: Production: Protor Film; Director: Henry Bay [Enrico Bomba]; Story: Tiziano Contini; Screenplay: Tiziano Contini, Vittorio Orano; Cinematography: Vitaliano Natalucci, Enrico Betti Berutto {Eastmancolor}; Music: Marcello De Martino; Original running length: 90 mins; Country: Italy; Year: 1966

CAST: Lewis Jordan (*John Gordon, Agent 777*), Helene Chanel (*Jean Cartier*), Claudie Lange (*Elsie*), Umi [Umberto] Raho (*Clyde/Linus Jericho*), Cina Doren (*Gloria*), Halina Zaleska [Zalewska] (*Frida*), Daniel Turk (*the inspector*), Anita Todesco, Giorgio Valletta, Simeon Ross (*Tukir*), Alida Ricci, Guido Sartori

TIFFANY MEMORANDUM
aka Charada internacional (Sp),
Coup de force a Berlin (Fr),
Sciarada internazionale (production title)

**Ken Clark leaps into the audience on the French poster for *Tiffany Memorandum***

While not the best of Ken Clark's spy adventures, *Tiffany Memorandum* is by no means the bottom of the lot. It has a great score by Riz Ortolani, some good locations in Paris and Berlin, lots of exciting fisticuffs and death by clock. *TM*'s main failing is the overly complicated and not very exciting plot. There are so many twists and false identities that it is sometimes hard to tell who is doing what and to whom.

This time, according to the English-dubbed print anyway, Ken is Dick Hallan, a journalist for the Herald-Tribune. He gets mixed up in international politics through a series of incredible coincidences and is finally coerced by the CIA (not really) to follow the intrigue to its unremarkable end. You won't believe what befalls Hallan in this film. For instance, he just happens to be gambling in an illicit casino in Paris where he chums up with a fellow who turns out to be none other than a candidate for the presidency of El Salvador. When they leave the building, Hallan is jumped by several men—for causing the gambling house some bad luck—while a few feet away his new friend is assassinated. Talk about being in the wrong place at the wrong time.

And it doesn't stop there. Later Hallan follows the late candidate's chauffeur aboard a train. While rummaging through the chauffeur's compartment, Hallan finds a watch, and just when he puts it in his pocket the train collides head on with another train. Because Hallan had the watch in his coat after the crash, the bad guys think he's the chauffeur and is thrown into the whole nasty business. Then things get really complicated.

There's a guy named Shadow who wants the damning evidence of the assassination that the chauffeur had, because it will determine the oil rights in El Salvador or something like that. There are fake CIA guys, fake fake CIA guys and real CIA guys that we think are bad guys. There's even a fake Checkpoint Willie in Berlin.

Hallan teams up with a female, naturally, during the course of the adventure. Irina Demick plays Sylvie Maynard, who was with the chauffeur on the train and, it turns out, is a rival journalist who scoops Hallan on the whole El Salvador story. Ken and Irina have a nice chemistry together, and watching the two of them having fun helps get us through the machinations of the plot. Hallan calls Sylvie his secretary and at one point explains; "The secretaries I have don't know shorthand, they just know how to take their clothes off." And she does.

I mentioned the fellow named Shadow. It's a nice mysterious part for Gregoire Aslan, though he doesn't last nearly long enough in the film. Shadow has a major clock fetish. This is where the clock death comes in. Hallan gets into it with a bad guy at Shadow's place, which is filled to the brim with clocks. Eventually, the thug meets his timely end by having his neck sliced by the pendulum of a very large grandfather clock. There's a strange bit just before this too: As the fight starts to heat up, Hallan throws a chair, which hits a television set. This turns on the television, which begins blaring the soundtrack music, but the image on the tube is of a band that is obviously not playing this music.

By the way, it won't spoil the fun to know that the Tiffany Memorandum is a videotape of the presidential candidate's killer—none other than his rival for the office (Luigi Vannucchi). Clearly, politics draws the finest and most concerned individuals. Speaking of fun, other things to keep the viewer amused are the toy train wreck that Hallan has the misfortune of being in, a guy who gets to watch himself die on an X-ray device and a magician who is easily the best dressed in Berlin.—DD

CREDITS: Production: Fida Cinca, Les Productions Jacques Roitfeld; Director: Terence Hatahaway [Sergio Grieco]; Story and Screenplay: Sandro Continenza, Roberto Gianviti; Cinematography: Stelvio Massi {Technicolor - Techniscope}; Music: Riz Ortolani; Original running length: 95 mins; Filming locations: Cinecitta Studios, Rome, Paris, Ancy Le Fran, Berlin; Country: Italy/France; Year: 1967

CAST: Ken Clark (*Dick Hallan*), Irina Demick (*Sylvie*), Luigi Vannucchi (*Inspector Brooke*), Loredana Nusciak (*Mme. Tiffany*), Gregoire Aslan (*The Shadow*), Jacques Berthier (*Colonel Callaghan*), Carlo Hintermann (*the kidnapper*), Michel Bardinet (*Francisco Aguirre*), Giampiero Albertini, Franco Giornelli, Valentino Macchi, Andrea Scotti (*Callaghan's agent*), Angelo Infanti (*Pablo*), Solvi Stubing, Piero Palermini, Tom Felleghi, Adriano Urriani, Peter Blade, Mirella Pompili, Dario De Grassi, Antonio Marsina

THE TIGER LIKES FRESH MEAT

aka Der Tiger liebt nur frisches Fleisch (WG), The Tiger Likes Fresh Blood (US, unconfirmed), El Tigre (Sp), Le tigre aime la chair fraîche (Fr), La tigre ama la carne fresca (It)

Nowadays Claude Chabrol is best known as the purveyor of delectably polished little mysteries such as *La Ceremonie* and *The Color of Lies*. As regular as clockwork they come, one per year, with a small but loyal following. Afforded a level of critical respectability (mainly due to arthouse favorites *Le Boucher* and *Les Biches*) he is, in many ways, the Woody Allen of the Gallic thriller—albeit without the questionable sexual hang-ups and irritating love of jazz. In the sixties, however, he was one of the more prolific adventurers in the realm of the spy film.

Louis Rapiere (Roger Hanin, who also scripted), aka The Tiger, is depressed because his friend—also a secret agent—has been killed in the line of duty. It's a good thing, therefore, when a nice, juicy case comes along. A Turkish

**Roger Hanin smooches with Daniela Bianchi in this British lobby card for *The Tiger Likes Fresh Meat***

diplomat, Baskine (Sauveur Sasporte), is taking part in an important arms deal with the French government, and a terrorist group—called the The Masai—has given warning that they plan to murder him before it can be completed.

Almost immediately he manages to foil one assassination attempt. Seeing that he's a good man, Baskine's garrulous wife (Maria Mauban) and daughter, Mehlica (Daniele Bianchi), decide to put him to good use. They take him on a shopping trip (these women just never change). That evening the villains strike. They create a diversion at the opera by murdering a singer (not just as a critical statement about her voice) and kidnap Mehlica. It appears as though there are actually two different bunches of bad guys, each of whom is acting independently of the other.

Unfortunately, *The Tiger Likes Fresh Meat* (great title) counts as a huge disappointment. Chabrol, capable though he was to become at handling slow-building tension, proves severely lacking in the art of crafting a decent action film. The choreography—including a big bust-up at a wrestling rink—is frankly terrible, real bargain-bucket stuff. You'll see more realistic fight scenes at the pantomime. The pacing is dreadfully haphazard too. In mitigation, this undoubtedly has something to do with the fact that the only commonly available English-language print has been shortened from 100 to a shocking 65 minutes! That alone, though, can't explain its deficiencies—which also include a lack of a suitably hissable antagonist for the hero and a sprawling, unfocused storyline. It also criminally wastes the talents of the second most gorgeous gal to appear in Eurospy films, Daniela Bianchi, who hardly even gets to say a line of dialogue.

On the positive side, there are plentiful Bond references (such as Ian Fleming books at airport bookstands) and an entertainingly dastardly (proto Nik Nak) midget villain, who at one point even dresses up in a child's cowboy costume, but with—heh, heh—real guns. Apart from being called "Jean Luc" (in possible homage to Chabrol's New Wave chum, the venerable Monsieur Godard), he also—in a particularly amusing sequence—gets to deliver himself to a potential victim in a birdcage (with real parrot still inside). There's also possibly the most pointless gadget to be featured in this book, a gun that shoots backwards. Of course, as soon as it's mentioned, you just know that someone is going to aim it at the hero and pull the trigger.

I'm reluctant, given the shoddiness of the prints under review, to come down too hardly upon this film. It has an amiable, light-hearted feel—but it certainly didn't leave me with much of an urge to track it down further.—MB

CREDITS: Production: Pro-Ge-Fi; Director: Claude Chabrol; Story: Antonie Flachot [Roger Hanin]; Adaptation: Jean Halain; Cinematography: Jean Rabier; Music: Pierre Jansen; Original running length: 100 mins; Country: France; Year: 1964

CAST: Roger Hanin (*Louis Rapiere*), Daniela Bianchi (*Mehlica*), Maria Mauban (*Mme. Baskine*), Roger Dumas (*Duvet*), Mario David (*Dobrovsky*), Pierre-Francois Moro (*Ghislain*), Roger Rudel (*Benito*), Jimmy Karoubi (*Jean-Luc*), Sauveur Sasporte (*Baskine*), Antonio Passalia (*Koubarsi*), Carlo Nell (*the assassin in the theatre*), Henri Attal (*the false reporter*), Crista Lang (*Dobrovsky's daughter*), Stephane Audran (*the singer*), Dominique Zardi (*2nd false reporter*), Guy Davout (*the French minister*), Charles Audisio (*the tenor*), Mick Besson, Michel Charrel, Francis Terzian, Marcel Gassouk, Claude Salez (*the men from DST*), Albert Dagnan (*General Conde*), Serge Bento (*Dobrovsky's man*), Jacques Vandooren (*the wrestler*), Mariana

LE TIGRE SORT SANS SA MERE
"the Tiger leaves without his mother"
aka Da Berlino l'apocalisse (It),
Heisses pflaster für spione (WG),
Spy Pit (unconfirmed)

In France this was marketed as a successor to the Claude Chabrol Tiger films, which was a trifle misleading, as star Roger Hanin does not play Louis Rapiere—the hero of that particular series. Instead, he stars as Julien Saint Dominique, another high-living secret agent as handy with his wisecracks as with his fists.

This particular mission starts when Saint Dominique meets up with another agent, Felix (Edy Biagetti), on a barge in Berlin (such glamorous settings these masters of intrigue frequent). While talking, Felix is shot and falls dead into the water (although it could just be that he's leaping away from his chum's particularly lurid, bright red jacket). It appears that Felix had found something out about a large criminal undertaking that is about to take place, and Dominique is charged with finding out what this could be.

While strolling through the city after a hard day's paddling on the lake, he meets Olivia (Margaret Lee), saving her from some thugs who are attempting to bundle her into a car. Things get a bit peculiar when, the next day, he comes across the same bunch of thugs attempting to bundle a completely different girl—Ingrid (Helga Sommerfield)—into their car. She explains that she is the daughter of an eminent scientist who has been kidnapped by agents from East Germany.

Believing this has something to do with the case, he doesn't take too long to locate the Professor, tied to a billiard table in the house of dodgy Gunther (Peter Carsten). Unfortunately, he dies before revealing anything of value. Things become increasingly more complex: Olivia is revealed to be an enemy agent; Ingrid is killed during another kidnap attempt; Julien heads of to Mexico for some reason or other and drives around in a cool sports car.

Of course, the real trouble lies closer to home. Felix, far from being dead, is the mastermind behind a plot to cause the outbreak of a new war in Europe. Before doing this, the villains get down to the more important business of pumping Julien full of mescaline (which unfortunately doesn't give rise to lava lamp-style visual effects).

In many ways, I actually preferred this film to its ostensible predecessors, *Our Agent Tiger* and *The Tiger Likes Fresh Meat*. It's trashier, certainly, but it also doesn't have the stilted quality that Chabrol brought to his films. There's a deft comic touch (that most definitely doesn't become overbearing) and the action sequences are handled with some aplomb. The climax, set in the sewers connecting East and West Berlin, is particularly effective. This is even more surprising when contrasted with director Mario Maffei's best-known film, the deadly dull spaghetti western *Ringo's Big Night*. OK, the villains don't really get what they deserve, Ivan Desny isn't used as much as

**Margaret Lee dominates the Belgian poster for *Le Tigre sort sans le mere***

could be and the plot tends to meander, but such lapses are tolerable.

It also benefits from having a superb Bruno Nicolai soundtrack, with blaring horns and jazz funk beats that accentuate the many Bond-ish aspects of the film. With winning performances from Hanin (more at ease than ever) and Lee (with more to do than usual), this little-known production stands as a truly solid genre entry.

As a trivia point, the Mexican sequences appear to have been shot on location with local actors. Jorge Rado, who appears briefly as a devious agent, also appeared in a number of Santo movies, including *Santo contra Blue Demon en la Atlantida* and *Santo en Anonimo Mortal*. He also pops up *way* down the credits in Sam Peckinpah's *The Wild Bunch*.—MB

CREDITS: Production: European Incorporation, Transister Film, Ufa International; Director: Mario Maffei; Story based on the novel "Caline Olivia" by Jean Laborde; Screenplay: Vincenzo Flamini, Carlo Gaultieri, Albert Kantoff, Mario Maffei; Cinematography: Mario Fioretti {Techniscope – Technicolor}; Music: Bruno Nicolai; Original running length: 100 mins; Country: Italy/France; Year: 1967

CAST: Roger Hanin (*Julien Saint Dominique*), Margaret Lee (*Olivia*), Peter Carsten (*Gunther*),

Claude Dauphin (*Colonel Lasalle, head of Secret Service*), Helga Sommerfeld (*Ingrid, daughter of Raichsau*), Ivan Desny (*Steve McCrane, an American agent*), Brigitte Wentzel (*Frida, assistant to Papillon*), Jane Massey (*Lord Kinsey's assistant*), Giovanna Lenzi (*Saint Dominique's girlfriend*), Ennio Balbo (*Hans, aka Papillon*), Edy Biagetti (*Felix, a secret agent*), Ugo Pagliai (*an assassin*), Waldemar Frahm (*Raischau*), Yves Brainville (*General Piquet*), Jorge Rado (*Lord Kinsey*), Enio Girolami (*Albert*)

### TIP NOT INCLUDED
aka Un cerceuil de diamants (Fr),
Die Rechnung—Eiskalt Serviert! (WG)

*TNI*, the fourth Jerry Cotton film, is probably the funniest of the series, though we're laughing more at it than with it. Director Helmuth Ashley (*Secret of the Red Orchid*) handles the action sequences well, but it seems he gave up and left details like special effects to his kids.

When the chief controller at the US Treasury is mugged on the day of a large money shipment, the FBI is called in to investigate. Jerry (George Nader) convinces the bank president to delay the shipment, but regulations require the money to be moved soon. The next day the shipment is stolen in an elaborate robbery, putting the bank president on the brink of suicide. Jerry assumes full responsibility for the shipment and is promptly fired for doing so. Can Jerry track down the thieves and earn back his badge?

To those of us who are sticklers for details, the heist sequence holds the best and worst of what this film has to offer. Keeping in mind that the action is supposed to be happening in America, notice when the money is being loaded into the armored car for shipping that the name on the truck is "Mells Fabo" rather than the "Wells Fargo" one would expect. As the various players converge on the site of the robbery, we witness some of the sloppiest blue screen work ever recorded. Riders in cars appear to be moving in a different direction from the scenery whizzing by. The plan is to drop a gas bomb from an overpass onto the road below, and when the Mells Fabo truck drives over it, the bomb will mysteriously attach itself to the underside of the vehicle. The fact that the entire robbery hinges on this most unlikely event gives one pause as to the level of optimism within the gang.

The robbery itself is a thing of short-lived beauty. The bomb explodes, disabling the truck, and the section of highway becomes enshrouded in a dense and poisonous fog. The gang, wearing gas masks, swiftly transfers the money to an ambulance and makes their getaway. The eerie scene echoes the robbery in the film noir *Criss Cross*. There's even a point-of-view shot from inside a gas mask.

The film kicks off with a minor revelation for fans of Peter Thomas. Yvonne Monlaur, playing the nightclub singer girlfriend of one of the gang members, sings a sultry jazz rendition of the Thomas tune "Love is Swinging in the Air." This version of the song is not one of the three versions included on the "100% Cotton" CD, nor is it on "Filmmusik," the other Thomas compilation containing Cotton tunes.

Shortly after this, Jerry is involved in a fun fracas in the Wilhem Parklift (so much for the Manhattan milieu). He tackles two thugs on one of the parking platforms as it moves around inside the building, and when he's done mopping the floor with them he hands them over to a waiting cop, saying, "That makes five for today. Too bad you guys don't give green stamps for them." Jerry is a nonstop crime-fighting god.

Jerry gets fired from the FBI during this adventure, and for good reason. After the robbery, the bank president contemplates suicide. Because he feels sorry for the guy, Jerry announces to the press that he himself takes full responsibility for the stolen money. The bank president dies of a heart attack moments later anyway, and now the public wants Jerry's head. His bone-headed move puts Jerry on the outs with his boss, Mr. High (Richard Munch), and he's subsequently canned. Since Jerry's whole life is the FBI, this moment is played for all it's worth, with Nader reaching deep for the hurt.

The bank president is played by Walter Rilla, who will be familiar to fans of the Dr. Mabuse films since he was in half of them. The gang leader this time is played by Horst Tappert, who was in a couple of the late-cycle Edgar Wallace thrillers, not to mention Jess

**Another nice Belgian poster, this time for a surreal Jerry Cotton entry *Tip Not Included***

Franco's *She Killed in Ecstasy*. Rainer Brandt (*Horrors of Spider Island*) also has a bad guy part.

This time the gang hides out in a wrestling arena, which affords us the treat of watching several minutes of mid-sixties German wrestling footage, not that this is particularly interesting. But the grand finale will hold one's attention, as not only unbelievable but ineptly executed by the filmmakers. Jerry performs the Jackie Chan-style stunt of leaping from a rooftop onto the helicopter of the escaping villain. The sequence provides a laughable ending to a rather silly and slapdash entry in the Cotton canon.—DD

CREDITS: Production: Allianz Filmproduktion, Constantin Film Produktion GmbH, Prodex; Director: Helmuth [Helmut] Ashley; Story and Screenplay: Georg[e] Hurdalek; Cinematography: Franz X. Lederle; Music: Peter Thomas; Editor: Alfred Srp; Original running length: 98 mins; Filming location: New York; Country: West Germany/France; Year: 1966

CAST: George Nader (*Jerry Cotton*), Yvonne Monlaur (*Violet*), Horst Tappert (*Charles Anderson*), Heinz Weiss (*Phil Decker*), Ullrich Haupt (*George Davis*), Walter Rilla (*John M. Clark*), Helga Schlack (*Helen*), Christian Doermer (*Tommy Wheeler*), Birke Bruck (*Mary*), Art [Arthur] Brauss (*Billiboy*), Axel Scholz [Scholtz] (*Happy*), Ilija Ivezic (*Caruso*), Rainer Brandt (*Stanley*), Richard Munch (*Mr. High*)

## TO CHASE A MILLION

Culled from the UK television series *Man in a Suitcase*, *To Chase A Million* retains the look and feel of its origins: There's lots of talk on cheesy sets instead of action and plenty of stock footage and rear projection substituting for exotic locations.

Richard Bradford is McGill, an American ex-intelligence agent whose friendship with Max (Anton Rodgers), a Russian agent, engulfs him in a cat and mouse game worth a cool million. Max stole money and put it in a bank in Lisbon, so the movie spends its time with McGill's journey of retrieval and the efforts of various factions to spoil his plans. Yoko Tani fills the bill as Taiko, the love interest that McGill would like to secure with the cash. She plays the long-suffering lady with lots of sad stories about being abandoned by McGill years ago. It's all rather a yawn. Naturally, McGill doesn't get to keep the money, this being a morality play for all the punters sitting in front of their tellies. Sorry to spoil the ending for you.

Max gets all the best lines, and there are lots of lines. When attempting to woo a "gear fab" teen at the coffee shop, Max waxes philosophical: "Only great cultures can afford

**Richard Bradford as McGill in *To Chase a Million***

to be decadent. So be proud of your mini-skirt, brag about your Beatles, they are your modern equivalent of the Parthenon." The air-headed chick doesn't get it, another comment on our decadent culture. Max is shot down in a dark alley for his dastardly deed but manages to spill the beans to McGill about the money. He then expires, but not before spouting the immortal line, "I'm losing a lot of alcohol." Aubrey Morris plays his small role as a dealer in documents with relish. Between the two of them, they steal the show from Bradford, he of the Brando mumbling school and Tani, the watery-eyed wonder.

Unless you have a sentimental attachment to the *Man in a Suitcase* (something to which I will admit) or just like talky drama, skip this low-rent feature and watch one of Yoko Tani's other espionage thrillers.—DD

CREDITS: Director: Pat Jackson; Original running length: 97 mins; Country: UK; Year: 1967

CAST: Richard Bradford (*McGill*), Ron Randell, Anton Rodgers (*Max*), Norman Rossington, Yoko Tani (*Taiko*), Aubrey Morris

TOM DOLLAR

An Iranian prince is murdered while on his way to sign a vital trade treaty with the US government. His successor, Princess Samia (Giorgia Moll), is happy to initiate the treaty—but the CIA is justifiably worried that a similar fate will await her before she can set foot upon American soil. As a safeguard, they arrange for a shop assistant, Louise, to have plastic surgery that will transform her into the double of the Princess—which she has agreed to do for the huge sum of $20,000. They also arrange for special agent Tom Dollar (Maurizio Poli) to journey to Tehran and discover just who has it in for their Iranian friends.

As soon as he arrives, a gang of thugs set upon him, but he manages to overcome them thanks to his fantastic prowess at martial arts. Unfortunately, they are all killed before he is able to find out any information from them. The one clue is they have an "S"-shaped serpent branded on their chest. Despite this discovery, Dollar's investigations are hindered by continually having to save the life of Samia/Louise and the sudden appearance of an old flame, Lady Crane (Erika Blanc), with whom he feels obliged to take in the sights.

He eventually discovers that the significance of the brand is that anyone who sports it is a member of a secret society called The Sings. They manage to take Dollar prisoner during a well-handled sequence set in a waxwork museum (they conveniently wear alabaster masks, allowing them to blend in nicely). However, it appears as though the true conspirators lie closer to home, and perhaps it isn't wise to trust someone who is willing to undergo surgery for money…

*Tom Dollar* is an adequate addition to the genre, but suffers from a serious inconsistency of approach. The first 20 minutes or so are great, the middle is poor and then after the hour mark has passed it picks up, drifting effectively toward the underwhelming climax. While certain sequences are very good (particularly a chase across a dusty hillside covered with Persian rugs), others are thoroughly inept. This incongruity makes it difficult to settle down into enjoying the film, and certainly from enjoying it as much as certain aspects of it make you feel as though you should.

There are other problems. The hero has an assistant modeled on Kato from *The Pink Panther* films, who seems hell-bent on thrashing the bejesus out of him at every opportunity. Although this is initially amusing, he crops up rather too repeatedly throughout the film, karate chopping everyone in his immediate vicinity. Well-choreographed though this all may be, it doesn't half play havoc with the continuity. It seems as though director Marcello Ciorciolini was so enamored with this chap's chop-socky skills (or else faced with such a diminutive running time) that he simply let him carry on as he pleased.

However, this probably gives too negative an impression. It's by no means the worst of its type, just one of the more frustrating. The camerawork is good, and the soundtrack—despite veering a bit too far into the principality of cheese at times—has some fine cues. The locations are also very well employed (despite looking suspiciously like Istanbul masquerading as Tehran). And let's be honest, is there a cooler character name in the genre than "Tom Dollar?"

It's also good to see regular Italian support actor Maurizio Poli in the lead role. He didn't get the chance that often, and makes full use of the opportunity to wear a variety of particularly fine sports jackets (as well as the obligatory ice-cream tuxedo). As a performer, he was more suited to ambivalent roles, and this definitely works in the film's favor by bringing a cruel edge to the character. Jacques Herlin also contributes an effective cameo as a camp, twitchy plastic surgeon.—MB

CREDITS: Production: Tigielle 33, Les Films Jacques Leitienne, Imp.Ex.Ci; Director: Frank Red [Marcello Ciorciolini]; Story based on fotoromanza by Al Petrie; Screenplay: John Connery, Pierre De Vreis; Cinematography: Rino Filippini {Eastmancolor}; Music: Giosafat, Mario Capuano; Original running length: 90 mins; Country: Italy/France; Year: 1967

CAST: Maurice Poli [Maurizio Poli] (*Tom Dollar*), Giorgia Moll (*Princess Samia*), Franco Ressel (*Mr Gaber*), Jacques Herlin (*Mr Osborne*), Erika Blanc (*Lady Barbara Crane*), Sojiro Kikukawa (*Tom's assistant*), Mirko Ellis, Jean Rougel (*"Chrysanthemum"*), Alberto Plebani (*Sonia's uncle*), Calisto Calisti (*police administrator*), Peter Luc (*the ambassador*)

TOP SECRET
aka Le Requin est au parfum (Fr),
Segretissimo (It)

The American Intelligence Services are suspicious. A man named Von Klausen (Antonio Gradoli) has managed to escape from a Soviet prison, and has access to some extremely valuable information. However, they are far from sure that he can be trusted, since certain circumstances about his escape have aroused their suspicions. Before they can find out anything more, he disappears—along with some top-secret documents that originate from Hitler's personal files. Agent John Sutton (Gordon Scott) is put on the case, and his mission commences with the investigation of a plane crash in which several of Von Klausen's associates appear to have died.

**Belgian poster for *Top Secret***

As is often the case with these things, Sutton's first clue comes when he's approached by a mysterious Arab, who claims to know something of what's going on. As is also often the case with these things, this mysterious Arab soon turns up decidedly dead. Scott discovers a letter to this unfortunate fellow from Zaira (Aurora De Alba), so he jets off to Naples in search of her. He also keeps on bumping into Sandra Dubois (Magda Konopka)—who unsurprisingly turns out to be a Russian spy. This, of course, doesn't prevent them from hastily getting down to some serious rumpy-pumpy.

Despite these distractions, Sutton soon succeeds in tracking down Zaira (she performs at an ornate nightclub). She reveals that the Arab had stumbled upon a bunch of German documents while smuggling contraband. After many more adventures, it becomes clear that Van Klausen is an imposter. He is playing the Russians (who had let him escape in the rather dimwitted expectation of his returning to them after his mission had been completed) and Americans against each other to raise the value of the documents. And just what are these documents? Well, that's top secret.

*Top Secret* starts as it means to go on, with a cheesy voiceover—that takes the bite out of the Bond phenomenon—followed by a hyper-groovy title tune (lots of ba-da-ba-da's and blaring trumpets). We then get about five minutes of rudimentary plot development—which is as fast-paced as it is confusing—before getting down to the meat of the business, Magda Konopka and Gordon Scott mucking about in a variety of jet-set locales. After about 45 minutes of this, you suddenly realize that you have absolutely no idea what's going on, but—hang it!—it's all delirious fun, so who cares anyway.

The cornerstone of the narrative revolves less around the activities of the villainous Van Klausen (who proves to be a pretty shoddy miscreant), than the relationship between the two agents, both of whom insist upon pretending that they don't know exactly who the other really is. Fortunately, Scott and Konopka make a winning pair, and it's hardly an endurance to watch them do their thing. There are also some neat reversals of expectation. The male agent is beaten up by his female counterpart, and she also finishes by—quite justifiably—wrapping up the mission and gaining all of the kudos. Any lads out there may also be interested to note that Ms. Konopka's breasts also make a brief cameo, a rare appearance of the unclothed bosom in a sixties spy film.

But the show really does belong to Gordon Scott, who's much better here than in his other genre outing, *Danger!! Death Ray*. Armed with some choice dialogue (looking in the mirror, he proclaims, "Ah, what a man!"), he makes a most amiable hero, even stopping to help a small child playing with a garbage lid in the street. Hold up—playing with a garbage lid? Did children ever do this? Thank the Lord for the wonder of Playstation.

He also gets involved in a number of increasingly mind-boggling scrapes: interrupting a film shoot (for something called "Agent Segretto," natch), getting attacked by a bunch of villainous nuns, and being kidnapped in a cage dangling from a helicopter (on waving to some caravanners for help, they just wave back like you see this type of thing every day). Above all, however, is the totally outrageous sequence in which he manages to escape from a Fiat Uno, stalled in front of an approaching train, by removing its roof with a can opener! They sure don't make cars like that any more—and the can opener isn't even electric.

In all, then, *Top Secret* is a jolly entertaining genre entry, which keeps its tongue firmly in its cheek and passes as easily as a fine bottle of wine and a plate of tasty antipasto. There's a good soundtrack (apart, maybe, from the strange twanging noise that pops up for no good reason every five minutes) and Fernando Cerchio's direction is more than adequate. Unfortunately—considering this has the potential to be a prime late-night cult favorite—it is surprisingly difficult to track down. If you get the chance, nab a copy.—MB

CREDITS: Production: Filmes Cin.ca, Tulio Demicheli; Director: Fernando Cerchio; Story and Screenplay: Nino Stresa; Cinematography: Emilio Foriscot {Techniscope - Technicolor}; Music: Piero Umiliani; Original running length: 94 mins; Filming locations: Incir-De Paolis Studios, Madrid, Morocco; Country: Italy/Spain; Year: 1966

CAST: Gordon Scott (*John Sutton*), Magda Konopka (*Sandra Dubois*), Aurora De Alba (*Zaira*), Antonio Gradoli (*Von Klausen*), Paco [Francsico] Moran (*Miguel*), Mirko Ellis (*Hardy*), Pietro Marescalchi (*Hans*), Umberto Raho (*Giorgio, the hotel manager*), Dali Bresciani (*the cameraman*), Santiago Rivero (*Colonel Zikowsky*), Brizio Montinaro, Norma Dugo, Pedro Rodriguez de Quevedo, Emilio Arnaiz, Hector Quiroga

## UPPERSEVEN, THE MAN TO KILL

aka Espionnage a Capetown (Fr),
The Man of a Thousand Masks (Int),
Der mann mit den 1,000 masken (WG),
Upperseven mision insolita (Sp),
Upperseven l'uomo da uccidere (It)

The original German title for this film translates to "the man of a thousand masks that all look like Paul Hubschmid unless another actor is in his place." Hubschmid is no Lon Chaney. The device of a spy who is a master of disguise is a good idea, but it isn't carried off very well here. The few masks that Hubschmid actually don are ridiculously ineffective, and the one successful instance is when he is impersonating a character actually played by himself in a dual role. At one point in the film, Hubschmid, when queried as to why he isn't wearing a disguise, says that he was afraid he would have been recognized if he was wearing one of his uncanny masks! When another actor is playing the part of Hubschmid in disguise, he's really good, even good enough to fool the villain's woman in bed.

But enough on that. Paul Hubschmid is Paul Finney, Upperseven, master of disguise. Hubschmid is so cocky in the role that he becomes annoying. He is a good-looking actor, but his demeanor is so disingenuous that he's better suited to playing rogues and unsavory types, such as his role of Johnny Vulcan in *Funeral in Berlin*. I wouldn't trust the guy.

**A classic Belgian poster for the not-so-classic Paul Hubschmid vehicle *Upperseven, The Man to Kill***

Finney's love interest is fellow spy, CIA agent Helen (Karin Dor). Dor has a better character here than her "frightened innocent" roles in the Edgar Wallace flicks. She actually gets in on the action and is much more interesting to watch than usual. Our villain is Kobras, played by Nando Gazzolo, who is a competent foe for a change. Calm and quick thinking, Kobras enjoys the details of his work much more than the typical evil megalomaniac. His partner in crime is played by Vivi Bach, who is a complement to the organization as well. She's a blonde beauty but she's no airhead. You may recognize Kobras' top henchman, played by Guido Lollobrigida; he had many such roles throughout the sixties and seventies. We can't forget the presence of the delectable Rosalba Neri, a genre favorite. She's here mainly to seduce Finney, sing a bad song and get smacked around before being killed off. Neri was queen of the cameo in spy films, rarely having enough to do.

This is one of those spy flicks that trots the globe just because it can. We visit Copenhagen, London, Basil (Switzerland), Johannesburg, Cape Town, and Rome in the course of the adventure. The plot has diamonds from South Africa being traded for American dollars in order to help finance a new "Pan-African" alliance, and the whole enterprise is under threat of sabotage so the Chinese can build a missile base without being bothered by the political maneuvering of the Africans.

This isn't very exciting stuff, we'll admit, but there is some fun to be had here. Aside from his disguises, Finney sports some nifty gadgets: a lighter that squirts knockout gas, a can that shoots spikes among other things, an exploding belt, and a spear gun that shoots tear gas bombs. Director Alberto De Martino, who was capable of better things, pulls a couple of humorous sub-standard tricks. One has Finney displaying his amazing workshop, where he designs those famous masks, to Helen, his "first" visitor. Underneath a cover is his latest set of creations, the heads of Kobras and his henchman, but it's really just the two actors with their heads through the table. The other kicker is the old favorite of using red yarn as infrared beams.

There are lots of judo-type fights, and Bruno Nicolai turns in a very good soundtrack, but ultimately this film won't hold up past an initial viewing.—DD

CREDITS: Production: European Incorporation, Roxy International Film; Director: Alberto De Martino; Story and Screenplay: Alberto De Martino; Cinematography: Mario Fioretti {Technicolor}; Music: Bruno Nicolai; Original running length: 104 mins; Filming locations: Titanus Studios, Copenhagen, London, Madrid, Switzerland, Cape Town, Madrid; Country: West Germany/Italy; Year: 1965

CAST: Paul Hubschmid (*Paul Finney/Upperseven*), Karin Dor (*Helen Farheit*), Nando Gazzolo (*Kobras*), Vivi Bach (*Birgit*), Guido Lollobrigida (*Santos*), Rosalba Neri (*Corinne*), Tom Felleghy (*Gibbons*), Bruno Smith (*M*), Mario Maffei (*Duke Robin*), Evi Rigano, Tullio Altamura

**Belgian poster for *The Versailles Affair* touts the film's literary source in the lower right corner**

THE VERSAILLES AFFAIR
aka Monsieur Suzuki (Fr)

This is one of those movies where a Caucasian actor plays an Asian character. In this case, Jean Thielment is Monsieur Suzuki, a special agent called in to help find documents relating to oil prospects in time for a conference being held in Versailles.

It's easy to get past the impersonation however, because Thielment and the movie in general are so good. It's a first-rate, albeit low-budget, production. The script is sharp and witty, with good characters, and the actors have the ability to bring them to life. Suzuki has a very short deadline in which to find the documents, and this picture moves quickly as he provokes and eliminates his suspects. The score, by Louiguy, is spare and has occasional Asian flavor, but sticks mostly with conventional and classical motifs.

Ivan Desny is Stankovitch, the double dealer who stole the documents and plans to sell them to the highest bidder. Desny is excellent as the cocksure thief—suave and disarming but with a frightening temper. At one point, he's called an "ignoble adventurer," an insult only the French would invent, and his response is, "There's no nobler profession in the world than adventurer."

Jean Tissier gets top billing as Ulrich, the middleman who is going to sell the documents for Stankovitch. Another actor worth mentioning is Don Ziegler as Axelrod, one of Suzuki's cohorts. At one point, he's assigned to keep an eye on Ulrich. The two spend the day in the bar drinking (eight double whiskys in four hours), after which Axelrod returns to Suzuki just the other side of tipsy. It's a great comic turn that could easily have been overplayed, but Ziegler has just the right touch so it doesn't get sloppy and irritating.

All of the humor in the film is genuine and intentional. For instance, Suzuki, in attempting to provoke one of his suspects, matter-of-factly says to her, "I have sad news for you. Your husband's a spy." When one of the surveillance guys working with Suzuki is caught reading a comic book, he says, "Well, you can't always read Karl Marx." Suzuki, in hot pursuit of a suspect, borrows the bike of pastry delivery man and then gives away his cakes to a bunch of kids. It turns out that Stankovitch and Suzuki are old, friendly rivals. At one point they chat about having dinner together that evening and Stankovitch asks his girl if she thinks she can find a partner for Suzuki. She quips, "Marilyn would love to come. I know she just adores Japs!"

There's a fun cameo in the film by Robert Dalban as the captain of a barge where Suzuki is held for a short time. He brings food to Suzuki and then proceeds to describe the colorful ways he could kill him and dispose of his body.

The climax of this recommended film boasts a car chase through the twilight of the foggy French winter and a train yard denouement, both handled expertly by director Robert Vernay.—DD

CREDITS: Production: Élysée Films; Director: Robert Vernay; Story based on the novel "Monsieur Suzuki prends la mouche" by Jean-Pierre Conty; Screenplay: Roger Saltel, Robert Vernay; Cinematography: Jacques Mercanton {B&W}; Music: Luiguy; Original running length: 98 mins; Country: France; Year: 1960

CAST: Jean Thielment (*Suzuki*), Danielle Godet (*Gina*), Ivan Desny (*Stankovitch*), Jean Tissier (*Ulrich*), Pierre Dudan (*Commissioner Laurent*), Claude Farell (*Françoise Girène*), Maurice Teynac (*the virtuoso*), Don Ziegler (*Inspector Axelrod*), Célina Cély (*the chaimbermaid*), Robert Dalban (*barge captain*)

IL VOSTRO SUPERAGENTE FLIT
"your super agent Flit"

A series of bizarre incidents (e.g., unknown people blowing raspberries at Russian diplomats) causes a state of international tension, and with it the growing threat of nuclear war. There's only one man who can possibly find out what's going on, agent Flit (Raimondo Vianello). Flit is reluctant at first, enjoying his relaxed life—surrounded by harp-playing babes—in Paris. After a quick spot of levitation to get his head together, he agrees to help out. As this seems to involve him sticking a piece of rolled-up paper in his ear, it's quite possibly help that could be done without!

Anyway, Flit heads merrily off to Berlin where, despite his apparently superhuman powers, he is immediately hypnotized by an unseen, unearthly being, and insults the Russian intelligence chief (Fernando Sancho). Condemned to death, he manages to escape thanks to his miraculous burrowing electric razor. After disguising himself as a (really crap) Arab, he heads back to Paris, where he suspects some shenanigans may be about to take place.

**Martini in one hand, gun in the other on the Turkish poster for *Il Vostro superagente Flit***

He is correct. An official causes a ruckus at a conference while under the hypnotic influence of a mysterious, beautiful woman, Aura (Raffaella Carra)—the same woman who had also been present when Flit had his problems in Berlin. It seems that Aura is from another planet, a planet whose inhabitants look exactly like human beings. They have one weakness, a mortal fear of the common goldfish. And, of course, Aura is a female, so she has an additional Achilles heel, the fact that Flit is irresistible to the opposite sex.

Following the popularity of the James Bond films, a number of high-profile parodies were released in America. The most popular—and by far the best—of these was *Our Man Flint*, which starred James Coburn as a languid secret agent with a harem of babes stashed in his apartment. As well as making a star of Coburn and spawning a sequel, *In Like Flint*, it also inspired this, a spoof, so to speak, of a spoof.

Despite this worrying background, *Flit* turns out to be a surprisingly amiable production. It wears its influences on its sleeve, in fact it highlights and makes a feature of them. This Flit is, like his inspiration, a karate-kicking babe magnet. He is introduced to us fencing, playing chess and having a kung fu fight—all at the same time. And that's before scampering off to carry out a life-saving operation. The main differing point is that, despite having almost superhuman powers, he tends to screw up with disturbing regularity. His disguises are immediately seen through, he repeatedly beats up the wrong people and—worst of all—he insists on jumping out of a window that happens to be just above a bloody great big precipice.

Fortunately, Raimondo Vianello is actually very good in the role. He plays it all in a more straightlaced fashion than most of the other staples of Italian comedy—Lando Buzzanca, for instance, or Franco and Ciccio—and only resorts to relentless mugging as a very last resort. The fact that he's actually quite masculine looking, as well as quite mature, helps him carry things off with a touch of authority.

The film also looks very nice. The cinematography is extremely competent, and the alpine locations have a definite touch of *The Sound of Music* about them. Considering that director Mario Laurenti drifted into the realm of the pedestrian sex comedy in the seventies, he holds things together extremely well. Of course, he's helped by the enjoyable soundtrack, some amusing title animations and, not least, having the excellent Fernando Sancho on hand (and in a pleasingly substantial role).

The major singularity about *Flit* is that the villains are, rather than power-crazed megalomaniacs, pure and simple extraterrestrials. Quite what their motivation for causing all this political upset could be is beyond my ken. Maybe it has something to do with the fact that, dressed up in their silver suits and peroxide hair, they look like a really terrible eighties electro-pop band. It would be enough to cause palpitations in the best of people, whichever planet they may happen to come from.—MB

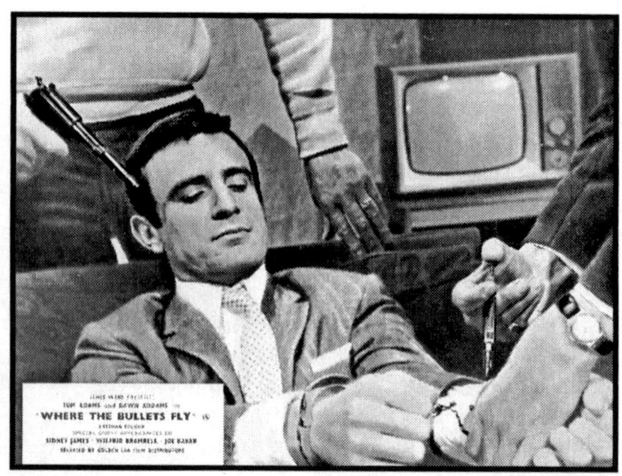

**Time for more interrogation for Tom Adams in *Where the Bullets Fly***

CREDITS: Production: Ima Film; Director: Mariano Laurenti; Story: Framco Siniscalchi; Screenplay: Bruno Corbucci; Cinematography: Tino Santoni {Eastmancolor – Widescreen}; Music: Bruno Canfora; Original running length: 95 mins; Country: Italy; Year: 1966

CAST: Raimondo Vianello (*Agent Flit*), Raffaella Carra (*Aura*), Pamela Tudor (*Mrs. Smirnoff*), Alfredo Marchetti (*Hayes*), Giorgio Bonora, Kitty Swan (*Flit concubine*), Lilia Neyung, Ursula Janis, Anna Creedon, Faida Nicol, Franco Morici (*the head of the aliens*), Alfred Thomas (*Flit's butler*), Doro [Teodoro] Corra, with Fernando Sancho (*Smirnoff*). Uncredited: Giuseppe Castellano (*stunt double for Raimondo Vianello*)

## WHERE THE BULLETS FLY

*Where the Bullets Fly* has a cracker of an opening. A bunch of no-goods park at the opposite bank of the Thames to the Houses of Parliament, aim a dirty great rocket at it and start the countdown to shoot. Only for a group of female American tourists, in reality Secret Service agent Charles Vine (Tom Adams) and his men, to shoot them all down. And then the fabulous soundtrack starts.

Anyway, on to the plot. British scientists have come up with a fantastic new invention called "Spurium," which can act as a protective shield for any military equipment. Unfortunately, the first test run goes dreadfully wrong when the plane carrying it is hijacked, although the RAF are able to shoot it down before it falls into enemy hands. Worried that something of the kind may happen again, the Intelligence Services assign Vine to ensure that nothing does. He doesn't do very well, being kidnapped before he even makes it to the scene of the crime.

His captor is a certain Mr. Angel (Michael Ripper), who wants to get his hands on a sample of the Spurium, which he will then be able to sell to the Russians. His sidekick, Seraph (Tim Barrett), impersonates the secret agent to gain access to the factory at which the metal is made and, once there, steal a sample. Despite Vine's best efforts—he has managed to escape—they are successful. Successful, that is, until Seraph (as well as the sample) is blown up by the Russians, who mistakenly believe him to have double-crossed them.

Angel determines to have another go, and decides to attack the airfield at which another Spurium-enabled plane is kept. Will Vine be able to frustrate their plans? Well, what do you think?

This was the second of the Charles Vine trilogy of films, following Lindsay Shonteff's *The Second Best Secret Agent in the Whole Wide World* and prefacing Jose Luis Madrid's inferior *Somebody's Stolen Our Russian Spy*. It's a likeable slice of humbug, which emphasizes the humorous aspects of the plot, and features a number of turns from popular comedians such as Wilfred Brambell, Joe Baker and—most particularly—Sid James. All of which means that things are kept lighthearted and easygoing, if distinctly rickety when it comes to narrative and pacing.

In truth, *Bullets* never really manages to reach the eminence of the Bulldog Drummond films *Some Girls Do* and *Deadlier Than the Male*, to which it obviously aspires. This is partly due to the performance of Tom Adams, who is less deadpan than frankly dead. It is also because none of the female performers are given the chance to be glamorous, let alone significant to the plot. Whereas the Drummond films couldn't have come from any other time than the sixties, the Vine series seems less bound up with the cultural explosion that was happening at the time.

That said, there is a lot to enjoy. There are plenty of bowler-hatted gents, old-school buffoons and bewhiskered Wing Commanders. Michael Ripper, taking a break from appearing as "Landlord" in assorted Hammer horror films, makes an amusing—if rather unthreatening—villain. Tim Barrett gives a very effective performance as a dodgy geezer with a deadly umbrella, and it's only a shame that he is disposed of two-thirds of the way through the running time.

There are also a couple of bizarre directorial touches, presumably thrown in by Gilling to play up to the genre. A tedious debriefing session is filmed from the point of view of a cat (for no reason whatsoever), there's a great chase through sewers filled with laughing gas and, just to keep the boys happy, there's a delirious striptease performance from a girl with a giant ice cream cone on her head.—MB

CREDITS: Production: Embassy; Director: John Gilling; Story and Screenplay: Michael Pittock; Cinematography: David Holmes {Eastmancolor}; Music: Philip Martell; Original running length: 90 mins; Country: UK; Year: 1966

*CAST:* Tom Adams (*Charles Vine*), Sidney James (*mortuary attendant*), Dawn Addams (*"Fiz," flight officer Moonlight*), Wilfred Brambell (*train guard*), Joe Baker (*Minister*), Tim Barrett (*Seraph*), Michael Ripper (*Mr. Angel)*, John Arnott (*Rockwell*), Ronald Leigh-Hunt (*Thursby*), Marcus Hammond (*Group Captain O'Neil),* Maurice Browning (*Cherub*), Michael Ward (*Michael*), Bryan Mosley (*Connolly*), Terence Sewards (*Bertie, the minister's P.A.*), Heide Erich (*Carruthers*), Suzan Farmer (*Caron*), Maggie Kimberley (*Jacqueline*), Julie Martin (*Verity*), Sue Donovan (*Celia*), Tom Bowman (*Russian colonel*), Patrick Jordan (*a Russian*), Gerard Heinz (*Venstram*), James Ellis (*flight lieutentant Fotheringham*), Charles Houston (*co-pilot*), Tony Alpino (*butler*), Michael Balfour (*band leader*), Garry Marsh (*major*), Michael Cox (*lieutenant Guyfawkes*), Peter Ducrow (*professor Harding*), Barbara French (*Harding's secretary*), John Horsley (*air marshall*), Michael Goldie (*laborer*), Joe Ritchie (*truck driver*), John Watson (*controller*), David Gregory (*R.A.F. sergeant*), Roy Stephens (*staff officer*)

WHERE THE SPIES ARE
aka Donde Estan Los Espias (Sp)

Oh brother. The English are certainly capable of making good spy films, whether they be comedic or serious, but this is not only a poor example of that country's talents, it also manages to be a sorry excuse for a spy movie in general. David Niven, well past his athletic prime (if he ever had one), is Dr. Jason Love, who is recruited by a desperate MI5 to make contact with a missing agent in Beirut. Of course he gets tangled up with all sorts of trouble—political assassinations, sexy spies, not so sexy spies, murder, torture and other adventures—all of which are exceedingly rote, boring, or just plain embarrassing.

Love is bribed with the offer of a Le Baron automobile to undertake these shenanigans, but I doubt it was worth it. He's outfitted with an assortment of gadgets to get the job done—a pen that shoots two different kinds of needles, a spy-kit briefcase, a transmitter watch, a camera ring that emits a blinding flash—and some of these toys actually come in handy since he's given the perfect situations to use them.

**Beautiful Belgian poster for the tepid *Where the Spies Are***

Love meets up with fellow spy Vikki (Françoise Dorléac) and has one of those vaguely revolting relationships between an over-the-hill star and a pretty young thing who could be his granddaughter. She turns out to be a double agent with a heart of gold who must die in the end for her sins against the free world. Dorleac is a transparent actress who may be better known as Catherine Deneuve's older sister.

Very little of interest happens in the film. It's typical old-fashioned cloak and dagger stuff and Niven spends much of the time with a puzzled look on his face, tugging at his ear, like the out-of-place dinosaur that he was. Director Val Guest leaves no imprint on this bland, overlong popcorn movie that probably bored even the staid older set in Britain upon its release. Even with somewhat of a budget, Niven spends too much time feigning danger in front of a blue screen and there are too many scenes of a cheesy model airplane supposedly carrying Russian spies. These spies are dishing out mild tortures to Love, since a spy of his age can't take too much. As if you couldn't tell by now, you may skip this powder puff of a star vehicle and you'll be none the worse for it.

A minor note would be the small role of Noel Harrison, who played Mark Slate in the ill-fated *Girl from UNCLE* television show.—DD

CREDITS: Production: Metro-Goldwyn-Mayer; Director: Val Guest; Story based on the novel "Passport to Oblivion" by James Leasor; Screenplay: Val Guest, Wolf Mankowitz; Cinematography: Arthur Grant {Metrocolor}; Music: Mario Nascimbene; Original running length: 110 mins; Country: UK; Year: 1966

CAST: David Niven (*Dr. Jason Love*), Françoise Dorléac (*Vikki*), John Le Mesurier (*MacGillivray*), Cyril Cusack (*Rosser*), Eric Pohlmann (*Farouk*), Richard Marner (*Josef*), Paul Stassino (*Simmias*), George Pravda (*1st agent*), Noel Harrison (*Jackson*), Ronald Radd (*Stanilaus*), Alan Gifford (*Security*), Bill Nagy (*Aeradio*), George Mikell (*the assassin*), Nigel Davenport (*Parkington*), Gábor Baraker (*2nd agent*), Geoffrey Bayldon (*the lecturer*), Derek Partridge (*the duty officer*), Robert Raglan (*Sir Robert*), Riyad Gholmieh (*1st taxi driver*), Muhsen Samrani (*2nd taxi driver*), Basil Dignam (*Major Harding*), Gordon Tanner (*a police inspector*)

WHO'S GOT THE BLACK BOX?
aka Criminal Story (It), The Road to Corinth (UK), La Route de Corinth (Fr), La ruta de Corinto (Sp), Die Strasse von Korinth (WG)

If the prospect of watching Jean Seberg dangle from a crane is appealing to you, then perhaps you may get something out of this pointless exercise. As it stands, there is really very little to recommend here other than the luminous beauty of the star.

The story—the smuggling of little black boxes that jam Greek radar stations—is nothing to get excited about, and director Claude Chabrol refuses to inject much in the way of action or suspense to offset it. Chabrol made a few spy flicks early in his career, but this one must be considered the weakest.

Things start out promisingly as a magician is stopped prior to boarding a ship and a search of his critter-infested car reveals a small black box of unknown capability. The third degree results in little except the man's suicide, but the sequence has its comic moments as the magician makes fools of his captors. Robert Ford (Christian Marquand) is assigned the task of tracing the devices and follows a lead from an informer (Chabrol himself). Ford is killed before 20 minutes have gone by, and his widow,

**Belgian poster for Claude Chabrol's lighter-than-air spy mystery *Who's Got the Black Box?***

Shanny (Seberg), takes over. By the way, Chabrol's character is later slain by knife-wielding priests in a cemetery. Perhaps they were the film's producers.

Of the cast members, only Michel Bouquet (other than Seberg) registers, and that is only because his character, Sharps, is such a creep. He has one good line when he's outfoxed yet again by Seberg: "When things get too mysterious, you have to pretend that you arranged them."

The villain, Kalhides (Sandro Urzi), is a plain businessman with a fairly clever plan to smuggle the black boxes in statues, but when it comes to hiring killers, he could use some advice. One hit man is a dandy who wears a straw hat and white gloves, and another is a pasty-faced Oliver Hardy-type in a tight suit. They don't exactly put the fear of God into anyone.

There's one cool gadget in the film: a pair of binocular sunglasses. The soundtrack by Pierre Janssen, however, is a collection of southern Mediterranean noodlings that sound like standard television fare.

The film opens with an anonymous quotation: "I don't ask you to believe it but I suggest that you dream about it." There is a certain dream-like quality to the proceedings, but this lackadaisical film is nearly anti-spy cinema. If the question is, "Who has the black box?" the reply simply has to be: "Who cares?"—DD

CREDITS: Production: Films Le Boetie, Andre Girones, Compania Generale Finanzaria Cinematografica, Orion Films; Director: Claude Chabrol; Story based on a story by Claude Rank; Screenplay: Claude Brule, Daniel Boulanger; Cinematography: Jean Rabier; Music: Pierre Jansen; Original running length: 90 mins; Filming locations: Greece, France; Country: France; Year: 1967

CAST: Maurice Ronet (*Dex*), Jean Seberg (*Shanny*), Michel Bouquet (*Sharps*), Christian Marquand (*Robert Ford*), Sandro Urzi (*Khalides*), Antonio Passalia (*the killer*), Paolo Giusti (*Josio*), Claude Chabrol (*Alicbiade*), Romain Gary (*the man on the plane*), Steve Eckart (*Socrates*), Zaninos (*a killer*), Max Roman, Vassili Diamantopoulosh

WOMEN ARE LIKE THAT
aka Comment quel'est! (Fr),
FBI y las damas (Sp)

Eddie Constantine stars yet again as the super secret agent Lemmy Caution in another whisky-soaked adventure. This time his prey is the head of an international spy ring, and the twists and turns of the plot call for much alcohol consumption and fistfighting—and that's just in the audience! But seriously folks, this is one of Eddie's more entertaining escapades and not only for the clever story. This has plenty of snappy dialogue and, typical of the cycle, some of the genre's most beautiful and capable actresses in the two female leads.

Things kick off with Caution in the middle of a bar fight, of course, and it hardly slows down from there. He's loaned to the French Secret Service to work with one of their agents, Demur (Renaud Mary), who is the only one who could recognize the mysterious Varley, the villain they're all after. Caution gets mixed up with a femme fatale gallery owner (Francoise Prevost), goes revenging after an agent friend (Billy Kearns) is killed, enlists the help of an old pal (Robert Berri), suspects a mobster (Alfred Adam) and uses a general's beautiful daughter (Francoise Brion) as bait. The twist ending is fairly well concealed, but the hunt is the fun of it.

In between the fisticuffs, the witty banter is nonstop. Caution intones another of his mottos early on: "I drink my whisky straight

**Unusual, strong graphic style of the Belgian poster for *Women Are Like That***

and when I see a girl, I chase 'er." An attractive female is described thusly: "Dark eyes and everything pointing the right way." The ladies also have their fair share of good lines: "You know when it comes to the truth a woman has several versions." When Caution's agent friend is discovered with a book of Rimbaud's poems in his dead hands, Caution has another pal start reading the book aloud in hopes of finding a clue. After several hours of this, the pal says, "It's a stroke of luck your friend wasn't reading the Encyclopedia Britannica." When Caution wakes up his boss with a late-night phone call, his wife says, "If someday we have a little coronary, let's call it Lemmy."

The two lead actresses, Brion and Prevost, have both shared others of Eddie's adventures, and here third-billed Prevost gets all the screen time while second-billed Brion only comes on for a small but pivotal role near the end. We get a good look at the collection of modern art in Prevost's gallery, and it turns out the abstract paintings are being used as color-coded messages. On the other hand, Paul Misraki's score, whether posed as bouncy dance-hall fare or dressed up as a classical quartet, is hopelessly lightweight and not even close to his trademark superior jazz.—DD

CREDITS: Production: C.I.C.C.R. Borderie, Prodis; Director: Bernard Borderie; Story: Peter Cheney; Screenplay: Bernard Borderie, Marc-Gilbert Sauvageon; Cinematography: Robert Juillard {B&W}; Music: Paul Misraki; Original running length: 90 mins; Country: France; Year: 1960

CAST: Eddie Constantine (*Lemmy Caution*), André Luguet (*General Rupert*), Françoise Brion (*Martine*), Françoise Prévost (*Isabelle*), Alfred Adam (*Girotti*), Colin Drake, Renaud Mary (*Demur*), Robert Berri (*Dombie*), Charles Bouillaud, Henri Cogan (*Zucco*), Fabienne Dali (*Danielle*), Nicole Darc, Gérard Darrieu (*Paulo*), Georges Demas, Elisabeth Fanty, Emile Genevois (*the second agent cyclist*), Ingrid Harrisson, Guy Henry (*an agent at the cabaret*), Billy Kearns (*Charlie*), Henri Lambert (*the porter*), Jean Landier, Darling Légitimus (*Palmyre*), Albert Michel (*an agent at the cabaret*), Charles Morosi, Marcel Pérès (*the first agent cyclist*), Jacques Seiler (*the commissioner*), Nicolas Vogel (*Mayne*), Dominique Zardi

YOUR TURN DARLING
aka A toi de faire, mignonne (Fr),
Agente federale Lemmy Caution (It),
FBI frente a Scotland Yard (Sp),
Zum Nachtisch: Blaue Bohnen (WG)

Of the Eddie Constantine films, this is only a fair example. It's still fun however, and you could do a lot worse than this tongue-in-cheek adventure. Eddie reprises his role as Lemmy Caution, the hero of Peter Cheyney's novels, this time in search of a scientist supposedly kidnapped for his formula for a new lightweight solid fuel. The formula turns out to be a bust, and the scientist, Elmer Whittaker (Guy Delorme), arranged his own kidnapping simply to get his hands on a million dollars.

This particular film boasts a good cast, which is where the most fun is derived, but the whole thing is rather silly. I expect that by this time it was just a matter of giving the audience what they wanted without making things too complicated or heavy.

Philippe Lemaire plays the egomaniacal Henri Pronzetti, who claims to be running the show but is really just a less-than-equal partner in the plot. Lemaire has good comic timing and is really quite funny as the hapless villain. Remarking about the prospect of negotiating with Lemmy Caution for the "return" of the scientist, Pronzetti says, "If I'd known he'd get into this business, I'd have called off the deal, stayed at home, watched TV and not thought of anything!"

There are also three lovely ladies to behold here: Gaia Germani is Geraldine, Whittaker's fiancee, who turns out to be a British Intelligence agent; Christiane Minazzoli is Carletta, whose jealousy leads to her death; and Elga Andersen is Montana, whose brains really hold the strings of the gang together. There are not one but two girl fights in the film, if that's your cup of tea. It's Carletta who takes the brunt of the violence, however: First, she's the victim of an (offscreen) belt beating, and then a bullet in the back prevents her from revealing the truth to Caution.

**Eddie Constantine as Lemmy Caution with his trademark glass of whiskey on the Italian poster for *Your Turn Darling***

Director Bernard Boderie had previous experience working with Constantine. Here he keeps the show moving, but lets things slide uncomfortably into farce toward the end with a silly, slapstick fight scene used to finish off the gang. While the film is not an outright spoof, the comedy comes often enough that no one would dare take it seriously, especially with Lemmy winking or chatting into the camera several times.

We mentioned earlier about Caution being obsessed with whisky. This character trait reaches a zenith of sorts when Geraldine volunteers to deliver the ransom money for her fiancee to the gang. Caution and his boss take to a helicopter to follow her, hoping to track the whereabouts of the gang, all the while drinking whisky out the bottle. It's funny that no one ever seems to get drunk. Based on the amount of alcohol consumed in this movie, the entire cast should've been blotto before we reach the halfway mark.

The Paul Misraki score is fun and jazzy, as one would expect, although it's not as prevalent as one would hope. If you're in the mood for light fare, this film will probably do but don't blame me if you're still hungry for a juicy spy flick afterwards.—DD

CREDITS: Production: C.I.C.C., Films Borderie, Euro International Cine; Director: Bernard Borderie; Story based on a book by Peter Cheyney; Screenplay: Marc-Gilbert Sauvajon, Bernard Borderie; Cinematography: Henri Person {Francscope}; Music: Paul Misraki; Original running length: 93 mins; Country: France/Italy; Year: 1963

CAST: Eddie Constantine (*Lemmy Caution*), Christiane Minazzoli (*Carletta Strasser*), Elga Andersen (*Montana*), Philippe Lemaire (*Henri Pronzetti*), Gaia Germani (*Geraldine*), Noel Roquevert (*General Walker*), Guy Delorme (*Elmer Whittaker*), Henri Cogan (*Pierrot*), Robert Berri (*Kriss*), Colin Drake (*Colonel Willis*), Hubert Deschamps

**One of the wildest Eurospy posters of the 1960's is this German poster for *Ypotron***

YPOTRON

aka Agente Logan missione Ypotron (It),
Mission secrete pour Lemmy Logan (Fr)

*Ypotron* boasts a colorful, sci-fi, pop art pre-credit sequence. A sliding door opens to reveal our hero, dressed in a tuxedo, who puts on a pair of night-vision glasses. He enters the room and while trying to figure out a strange design on the wall, is shot in the back with a machine gun. It turns out he was testing his bulletproof vest, but it was a fun introduction to world of Lemmy Logan. The credit sequence itself is also worthy of note. It has Logan cavorting with several bikini babes on a boat, but the film is shown in negative! Kind of creepy actually. We are treated to a terrific score by Nico Fidenco throughout the film, and the swinging theme song is performed by The Sorrows.

Luis Davila is Lemmy Logan, aka Cosmos 1, a NASA security agent. Davila is billed as Luis Devil, an interesting pseudonym, and Lemmy is called Robbie in the English-dubbed print. This is only the beginning of the confusion. Argentinean-born actor Luis Davila is recognizable mostly for his spaghetti westerns, but you can also catch him in the weak Italian sci-fi flick *Mission Stardust* and in *Paranoia* with Carroll Baker.

This film has enough bad guys for three movies and the confusing plot doesn't help any. We have the supposed good guy, "kidnapped" scientist Professor Morrow (Alfred Mayo) who is really Eichmann, a brilliant but twisted war criminal with a mad scheme to control space. Then there's corporate industrialist Revel (Alberto Dalbes), who is funding Eichmann, and last but certainly not least, there is Streich (Luciano Pigozzi), who is after the plans for the project. It's hard to tell who is in charge here.

The ladies are easier to keep straight. Jean Morrow (Gaia Germani) is the professor's daughter; Carrol (Janine Reynaud as a bad bleached blonde) is in cahoots with Revel. Both are crazy about Logan, of course. Logan has a sidekick too, Wilson (Jesus Puente, a regular in westerns at the time), who calls himself "the spy who's always left out in the cold," because Logan gets the babe duty while Wilson does the boring stuff like order the missile strike on the villain's compound.

Our heroes get to use all manner of fancy gadgets in their pursuit of evil. Lighter communicators get a workout, and there's an instant oil slick capsule to derail those bad guys chasing you. They use a briefcase movie camera (which not only develops the film automatically but will also project it onto a tiny screen), a receiver in a Norelco shaver, a nifty gadget that makes phones ring, and a radar-tracking device in a Bible. Not to leave the bad guys out, even Revel has a tape recorder in a cigar box.

Things to look forward to are scenes with wind tunnel peril, a strange stripper act and dialogue that loses something in the translation. At one point, thinking that Logan is dead, Streich says to Jean, "I must congratulate you because your friend has been killed." Once Streich infiltrates the villain's lair, he gives the signal to his goons to take over. His biggest gorilla then screams, "Now I kill!"—and he does.

Streich has a great scene explaining to Carrol the slow miserable death she's about to endure after she pricks her finger on a poisoned briefcase latch. It's a terrific speech that Pigozzi delivers with relish. Not to be completely outdone, Carrol manages to give a short message in Morse code to Logan with her eyelids just before she expires. Now that is excellent training.

Note: The bloodthirsty among you will enjoy the bullfight scenes, where you witness the actual killing of a bull.

So what is Ypotron? It is "the first space weapon," and with it you can rule the world!—DD

CREDITS: Production: Dorica Film, Euro International Film, Atlantida Film; Director: George Finley [Giorgio Stegani]; Story: Jose Luiz Martinez Molla; Screenplay: Jose Luis Martinez Molla, Remigio Del Grosso, George Finley [Giorgio Stegani]; Cinematography: Raphael Pacheco; Music: Nico Fidenco; Original running length: 95 mins; Country: Italy/Spain; Year: 1965

CAST: Luis Devil [Luis Davila] (*Lemmy Logan*), Gaia Germani (*Jeanne Morrow*), Alfredo Mayo (*Morrow/Eichmann*), Jesus Puente (*Wilson*), Jeanine Reynaud (*Carrol*), Albert Dalbes (*Revel*), Nando Angelini (*the video technician*), Alan Collins [Luciano Pigozzi] (*Striech*), Benny Reeves [Benito Stefanelli] (*Dwan*), Dina Loy (*the secretary*), Fernando Bilbao (*Goro*), Xan Dan Bolas (*the hotel porter*), Maria Paz Pondal

# BIBLIOGRAPHY


### BOOKS

99 Donne. Manlio Gomarasca, Davide Pulici. 1999, Media Word S.a.s. (Milan)
The Bond Affair. Umberto Eco. 1966, MacDonald (London)
Dizionario del cinema Italiano: i film vol. 3. Roberto Poppi, Mario Pecorari. 1992, Gremese editore. (Rome)
The Espionage Filmography. Paul Mavis. 2001, McFarland and Co., Inc. (US)
Film Fatales: Women in Espionage Films and Television, 1962-73. Tom Lisanti, Louis Paul. 2002, McFarland and Co., Inc. (US)
The Great Spy Films. Leonard Rubinstein. 1979, Citadel (US)
The Great Spy Pictures I/II. James Robert Parish, Michael R. Pitts. 1974/1986, The Scarecrow Press, Inc. (US)
Histoire du Cinema Francais: encyclopedie des films 1961-65, 1966-70. Maurice Bessy, Raymond Chirat, Andre Bernard. 1996, Editions Pygmalion/Gerard Watelat (Paris)
Spies and Sleuths. James J. Mulay, Daniel Curran, Jeffrey H. Wallenfeldt. 1988, Cinebooks (US)

### OTHER PUBLICATIONS

Amarcord. Editor: Igor Molino Padovan. Via de'Tornabuoni, 4 - 50123 - Firenze - Italy. utenti.lycos.it/amarcord_cinema
European Trash Cinema. Editor: Craig Ledbetter. ETC Video - P.O. Box 12161 - Spring - TX 77391-2161. www.eurotrashcinema.com
Monster Bis: Espions a l'Italienne. Joel Cabanes. www.macabre.net/monsterbis
Spaghetti Cinema. Editor: William T. Connolly. 6635 DeLongpre #4 - Hollywood - CA 90028 - USA. home.earthlink.net/~scinema

### WEBSITES

Banca Dati del Cinema Mondiale. www.cinematografo.it/bdcm/bancadati.asp
The Eurospy Guide. www.eurospyguide.com
Latarnia. www.latarnia.com
The Spaghetti Western Web Board. disc.server.com/Indices/160642.html
Mobius European Cult Cinema Discussion. www.mhvf.net/forum/euro

### VIDEO SOURCES

European Trash Cinema. www.eurotrashcinema.com
Sinister Cinema. www.sinistercinema.com
Something Weird Video. www.somethingweird.com
Video Search of Miami. www.vsom.com

# APPENDIX A: SERIES FILMS

Several Eurospy characters had the distinction of appearing in multiple films regardless of whether it was intentional or not. Some spies had been literary creations prior to being reinvented as movie heroes, while others were created whole out of celluloid, spawned simply by the popularity the genre enjoyed during 1960s. Most featured the same lead actor in the recurring role but of course, some spy shoes were too big for one actor alone. As was common with European co-productions, a film could be marketed as one of a popular series in one country when in fact it had nothing to do with the actual series character in other markets. We try to cover the official, the curious, and the exploited in our look at the spy franchises.

AGENT 3S3

George Ardisson played Walter Ross, agent 3S3, in two films—officially that is—but we'll get to that in a moment. 3S3 is a designation meaning secret agent number 3 of the 3rd Special Division, and Ardisson was clearly up to the task. He had a feline athletic quality and roguish good looks that stood him well in these and other spy films. The Ardisson film *Date For A Murder* was reportedly marketed in Germany as a 3S3 adventure, but it is a murder mystery, not a spy film. Amusingly, a completely unrelated film, *13 Days to Die*, starring Thomas Alder, was marketed as *Agente S3S Operazione Uranio*, which could be construed as a clever attempt to pass for one of Ardisson's films by reversing the letters and numbers.

FILMS: Passport to Hell (65); Hunter of the Unknown (66)

BOB FLEMING

Another miniseries featured Bob Fleming, mild-mannered secret agent. Richard Harrison took the role in two films and Stephen Forsyth stepped in for a third. Neither of Harrison's two adventures represent anything more than mediocre examples of the genre helmed by directors with less-than-sterling reputations. The Forsyth film, however, is a cut above. It is curious to note that the two Harrison/Fleming films were sold in various markets as part of the ambiguous 077 series (see separate entry).

FILMS: Secret Agent Fireball (65); Killers Are Challenged (66)—both Richard Harrison; Furia a Marrakesh (66)—Stephen Forsyth

BULLDOG DRUMMOND

The character of Bulldog Drummond was created by "Sapper" (Herman Cyril McNeile) way back in 1919. He had first appeared onscreen in 1929, as portrayed by the Oscar-nominated Ronald Coleman in *Bulldog Drummond*. Over the years, actors ranging from Ralph Richardson to Ray Milland had filled the role, although the last thespian to step into his shoes before the sixties was Walter Pidgeon in Victor Saville's *Calling Bulldog Drummond*. Despite the character being almost as old as the cinema itself, the sixties version shows distinct differences from his earlier incarnations: There's a libertarian amount of swinging skin on show, the violence goes way beyond simple fisticuffs, and it's all treated with the spoofy air that it frankly deserves.

These films, both starring Richard Johnson, were extremely popular, featured on the

front pages of several British film magazines, and were staples on UK television throughout the seventies and early eighties. *Deadlier Than the Male* has recently enjoyed a classy DVD release.
FILMS: Deadlier Than the Male (66); Some Girls Do (69)

CHARLES VINE

There were three Charles Vine films, all starring Tom Adams (later on UK television favorites *The Onedin Line* and *Emmerdale Farm*) as a rather charmless secret agent. The first two were made in Britain under the auspices of Alistair (aka Alastair) films. The third was a Spanish offshoot. They're lighthearted productions, and tend to divide critics, but the second was probably our favorite of the bunch.
FILMS: The Second Best Secret Agent in the Whole Wide World (65); Where the Bullets Fly (66); Somebody's Stolen Our Russian Spy (68)

FRANCIS COPLAN

No fewer than five actors played the role of Paul Kenny's literary spy hero Francis Coplan. Kenny was actually a pseudonym for two Belgian writers, Gaston Van den Panhuyse and Jean Libert, and their novels inspired each of the films. Coplan hit the screens from 1964 to 1967, and horror specialist Riccardo Freda had the distinction of being the only director to helm two adventures, which, by the way, were his only films in the genre. All of the Coplan films are available in English on the gray market, but one should note that Freda's *Entre las redes*, known in the US as *Mexican Slay Ride*, is missing half an hour from the middle of the film. Reportedly the French version is complete.
FILMS: The Spy I Love (64)—Dominique Paturel; FX-18 (64)—Ken Clark; FX 18 Superspy (65)—Richard Wyler; Mexican Slay Ride (66)—Lang Jeffries; Coplan sauve sa peau (Coplan Saves His Skin) (67, not reviewed)—Claudio Brook

JAMES TONT

Warning: Comedy spy alert! James Tont was a popular Italian character played by comedian Lando Buzzanca. Broad spoofs of the 007 films, the two productions feature idiot secret agent Tont solving cases by accident as much as skill (along the same lines as Peter Sellers in the *Pink Panther* films). Although not likely to appeal to everybody's palate, they were big grossers in Italy, and have their low-brow moments.
FILMS: James Tont operazione UNO (65); James Tont operazione DUE (65)

JEFF GORDON

Jeff Gordon is another of Eddie Constantine's secret agent characters, and like Lemmy Caution and Nick Carter, Gordon seemed simply an alter ego for the bigger-than-life Eddie in a run of three films.
FILMS: Jeff Gordon, Secret Agent (63); Laissez tirer les tireurs (64, not reviewed): Ces dames s'en melent (64, not reviewed)

JERRY COTTON

Jerry Cotton was a hugely popular character, played by George Nader, in a series of eight films produced by longstanding German company Allianz Filmproduktion. A number of different directors worked, with varied results, on the Cotton productions including genre favorite Harald Reinl, who took the helm for the last three entries.

Perhaps the series' greatest asset, however, is the music of jazz stylist Peter Thomas. A natural innovator, the Thomas scores integrate so carefully with the visuals that we can't imagine one without the other. Simply crimes films to some, the Cottons are slices of skinny-tie pie, Euro-modern jazz capsules deserving of a greater appreciation.
FILMS: Operation Hurricane: Friday Noon (65); Manhattan Night of Murder (65); 3-2-1 Countdown for Manhattan (65); Tip Not Included (66); Body in Central Park (66); Death and Diamonds (67); Death in a Red Jaguar (68); Dead Body on Broadway (68)

JUDOKA

Judoka was a minor figure in the spy film hall of fame. As the name would indicate, the character was a judo expert with a sideline as a secret agent. He featured in two films, albeit played by two different actors. Neither film seems to be available in English language, nor are they particularly worth seeking out for any apart from the most rabid of genre fanatics.

FILMS: Judoka Secret Agent (66)—Jean-Claude Bercq; Le Judoka dans l'enfer (68)—Marc Briand

KOMMISSAR X

One of the most popular and entertaining of sixties spy series, the Kommissar X films were based upon the novels of Bert F. Island (in reality a pseudonym for prolific German pulp-author Paul Alfred Muller). The central company involved in their production was Parnass Films, a German organization who also put money into *Spy Today, Die Tomorrow*, *Date For A Murder* and *Judoka dans l'enfer*. Fully-fledged international co-productions, they also received backing from a variety of other groups around the world, from Italy (Mario Siciliano's Metheus Films) to Columbia (Ceylon Tours).

The main reason for their success was undoubtedly the inspired paring of actors Tony Kendall and Brad Harris as Joe Walker and Captain Tom Rowland, respectively. Kendall has the flashy role, chatting up the babes, acting the charmer and generally being an all-round smarmy hero. Harris is even more effective as the straight man, upright (and often uptight), earnest and the butt of continual jokes. Both display an admirable sense of humor, and seriousness is never of the utmost import here. A major plus was Bobby Gutesha's exasperatingly catchy, "I Love You, Joe Walker" title tune, used throughout the series.

FILMS: Hunting the Unknown (65); So Darling So Deadly (66); Death is Nimble, Death is Quick (66); Death Trip (67); Kill Panther Kill (68); Three Golden Dragons (68); The Tiger Gang (71)

LEMMY CAUTION

The most famous Lemmy Caution film is, of course, Jean Luc Goddard's *Alphaville*, but there are another 10 adventures, all starring Eddie Constantine as the hard-drinking agent (the earliest Caution mention is a segment in an anthology from 1952 that starred John Van Dreelen). It's a role that Eddie made his own from 1953 until 1991; always thirsty for whisky, game for the ladies and ready for a fight.

We should note here for the curious among you that you will not find a review of *Alphaville* within these pages, because we do not consider it a spy film; we consider it art.

FILMS (1960s): Women Are Like That (60); Ladies Man (61); Your Turn Darling (63); Alphaville (65, not reviewed)

THE MONOCLE

There were three Monocle films, all starring Paul Meurisse as Theobald Dromar, aka The Monocle. As embodied by Meurisse, The Monocle is a fey secret agent who cultivates a wide array of eccentricities while being exceptionally successful at outwitting the opposition. Only the third film, which also stars Barbara Steele, is available in the US, but if the other two are anything like it, these comedies are among the oddest the genre has to offer.

FILMS: Le Monocle noir (The Black Monocle, 61, not reviewed); L'Oeil du Monocle (The Eye of the Monocle, 62, not reviewed); The Monocle (64)

NICK CARTER

Eddie Constantine twice took the role of famed pulp detective Nick Carter. The character appeared in films as far back as 1908, but Eddie took him in a new direction in the sixties: Nick became…well, Eddie, of course. And that's okay. The one Nick Carter film reviewed here not only has pulp adventure written all over it, but it has spies!

FILMS: License to Kill (64); Nick Carter et le trefle rouge (Nick Carter and the Red Club, 65, not reviewed)

OSS 117

One of the most popular series featured Hubert Bonnisseur de la Bath, otherwise known as OSS 117. More than half a dozen films spanning the entire decade of the 1960s were based on the spy novels of Jean Bruce. The suave and deadly OSS 117 began screen life in 1956 with Ivan Desny—who made a career of playing oily villains—taking the unlikely lead. Much better suited to the role were Kerwin Mathews, who starred in the next two films, and Frederick Stafford, who played Hubert in the following two films. The series took a permanent vacation after 1969, but not before contributing a couple of genuine classics to the genre.

FILMS: OSS 117 n'est pas mort (OSS 117 Is Not Dead, [56], not reviewed)—Ivan Desny; OSS 117 se dechaine (63)—Kerwin Mathews; Shadow of Evil (64)—Kerwin Mathews; OSS 117 Mission for a Killer (65)—Frederick Stafford; OSS 117 From Tokyo with Love (66)—Frederick Stafford; OSS 117 Double Agent (68)—John Gavin; OSS 117 prend des vacances (69)—Luc Merenda

THE TIGER

Respected director Claude Chabrol helmed two Tiger films, which proved extremely popular and cemented the perception of Roger Hanin as the primary French spy-film star. His character, Louis Rapiere, is a somewhat dour secret agent, and the films don't stand up as well as some today—despite showing some admirably left-field humor—partly because they're only available in abridged or poor-quality versions.

There were a further two films that cashed in on the Tiger character, through their French titles, and both of these confusingly starred Hanin, although *not* as Louis Rapiere.

FILMS: The Tiger Likes Fresh Meat (64); Passeport diplomatique agent K8 (Operation Diplomatic Passport, [65], unofficial, not reviewed); Our Agent Tiger (66); Le Tigre sort sans se mere (67, unofficial)

077

The 077 films are the perfect illustration of international marketing exploitation technique. Ken Clark starred in three films as Dick Malloy that are considered the official entries in this confusing and amusing series. The other films listed below are included for reasons as subtle as having the numbers 077 make their way unexplained up on the screen or because they were marketed as 077 entries in one country or another.

FILMS: Operation Hong Kong (64, marketed in Italy as 077); Mission Bloody Mary (65, official entry); Ypotron (65, marketed in Germany as 077); FX 18 Superspy (65, reportedly marketed as 077); Secret agent Fireball (65, marketed as 077 in the US); Espionage in Tangiers (65, unofficial entry); Espionage in Lisbon (65, the subtlest mention of the series when someone writes "0-7-7" on a casino napkin); Piege pour un espions (65, marketed as an OSS 77 film to confuse fans of both the 077 films and the OSS 117 films); Killers Are Challenged (66, unofficial entry); Fury On the Bosphorus (66, official entry); Special Mission Lady Chaplin (66, official entry); Golden Eyes Secret Agent 077 (68, unofficial entry from India!)

# APPENDIX B: SPY BIOGRAPHIES

ARDISSON, George [Giorgio] (b. Turin [Italy], 12/31/31)

An athletic blond, Ardisson was the actor who became most associated with the genre in Italy, even known for a period as "the Italian James Bond." In fact, his career had been been quite succesful before his first spy role. After debuting in Mauro Bolognini's *You're On Your Own*, he appeared as a secondary player in a number of peplums, most particularly *Last of the Vikings*, *Hercules in the Haunted World* and *Erik the Conqueror*—all of which were directed by Mario Bava.

His spy film credentials were firmly sealed by his appearance in the two Sergio Sollima 3S3 movies. Relatively young to portray a secret agent, his characters tended to make up in physical agility what they lacked in gravitas. And of course, they never failed to prove popular with the ladies. In the fringe genre entry *Date For a Murder*, he played an ex-spy who becomes mixed up in a crime scenario, a role that neatly played on his previous secret agent performances (he is first introduced training himself to dodge bullets).

Never short of work, Ardisson also spent time as a leading man in spaghetti westerns (Guido Zurli's *A Man Called Amen*, Pasquale Squitieri's *Django Against Sartana*) and giallos (Alfonso Brescia's obscure *Il Tuo dolce corpo da uccidere*, Bitto Albertini's *Human Cobras*). As the seventies went on, he was driven—like so many leading men—to find unsatisfactory roles in a variety of sex comedies, a genre to which he seemed decidedly unsuited.

FILMS: Hunter of the Unknown; Inferno a Caracas; Operation Counterspy; Passport to Hell
SPECIAL SKILLS: Youthful, handsome, teeth like marble tombstones
ONE TO WATCH: Passport to Hell

BARKER, Lex (b. New York, 05/08/19 – d. New York, 05/11/73)

Barker, also known as "Sexy Lexy," began his career as a bit player in many US films before landing the titular role in *Tarzan's Magic Fountain*, the first of six times he played the jungle hero. His first films in Europe were historical adventures, such as Carlo Campogalliani's *Captain Falcon* and Giorgio Simonelli's *Robin Hood and the Pirates*, and he also took time out to appear in Fellini's *La dolce vita*. But, then again, who didn't?

His initial genre roles were as FBI foils for the omniscient Dr. Mabuse, but he also appeared in English and German spy films. It would seem that *Spy Today, Die Tomorrow* was planned as the first of a series, based on the character of "Mr. Dynamite," but this was never to be. Ultimately, he remains best remembered among Eurotrash fans as "Old Shatterhand" in the long-running Winnetou series, filmed in Yugoslavia and based on the novels of Karl May.

FILMS: Spies Against the World; Spy Today, Die Tomorrow
SPECIAL SKILLS: Upright and straightlaced. He may have a thing for the ladies, but it would never interfere with duty. No Sir!
ONE TO WATCH: Spy Today, Die Tomorrow

**Roger Browne cuts a dash in leisure wear. (*Assalto a tesoro di stato*)**

BROWNE, Roger (b. ? – d. ?)

Roger Browne has proved to be an elusive fellow. One of the most prolific—and most effective—of Eurospy stars, very little is known of him beyond the facts that a) he is an American, b) he worked for many years as a dubber in Rome and c) he returned to the US in the early 1980s.

His first film credit was as a supporting performer in Emimmo Salvi's *Vulcan, Son of Jupiter*, although he soon graduated to leading roles. He tended to work for the same directors repeatedly, most particularly Michele Lupo (*The Revenge of Spartacus*, *Seven Slaves Against Rome*). In the spy genre, he forged effective partnerships with both Sergio Grieco and Umberto Lenzi.

In the seventies he popped up in a number of eccentric films, such as the jaw-dropping *The Jungle Master* and *Emmanuelle in America*. He could always be relied on to bring a good mixture of humor, physicality and charm to his roles.

FILMS: Assalto al tesoro di stato; Last Man to Kill; Operation Poker; Password: Kill Agent Gordon; Rififi in Amsterdam; Superseven Calling Cairo

SPECIAL SKILL: Impersonating jewel thieves

ONE TO WATCH: Password: Kill Agent Gordon

CHRISTIAN, Dan (b. ? – d. ?)

Dan Christian appeared in two of the most obscure—not to say strangest—spy films made, which qualifies him for some kind of recognition. Unfortunately, nothing much is known about him beyond that. He had a small role in the US/Italian television movie *Hercules and the Princess of Troy*, but whether he is American or an Italian working under a pseudonym is unknown.

FILMS: Agente segreto 070 Thunderbay—missione Grasshopper; Un Tango dalla Russia

SPECIAL SKILLS: Anonymity. Who is this guy?

ONE TO WATCH: Agente segreto 070 Thunderbay—missione Grasshopper is just a tiny bit weirder, so it wins on points.

CLARK, Ken (b. Neffs [USA], 06/04/27)

Before his European work, Ken Clark had experienced modest success in American productions such as *Love Me Tender*, *South Pacific* and *Attack of the Giant Leeches*. The money that was being made in Europe by muscle beach regulars proved tempting, and he soon found roles in a handful of peplums and adventure films, none of which exactly set the box-office alight. Westerns, too, proved a hard nut to crack, and despite working with Mario Bava on *Arizona Bill* , the results were mostly forgettable.

His spy films, on the other hand, are among the best of the genre. Not the most natural of secret agents—there's something of the hayseed about his big, blond looks—he partnered with Sergio Grieco to play Dick Malloy (or varients thereof) in a series of above-average productions.

FILMS: Fuller Report; Fury On the Bosphorus; FX-18; Mission Bloody Mary; Special Mission Lady Chaplin; Tiffany Memorandum

SPECIAL SKILLS: Could have stepped out of *The Waltons*

ONE TO WATCH: Fuller Report

COBOS, German (German Sanchez Hernandez Cobos, b. Seville, 07/07/27)

It's probably not too harsh to say that one of the reasons for German Cobos becoming a lead man in Eurospy films was his marked similarity to Sean Connery. In all fairness, though, he's pretty decent in the roles, and certainly has nothing to be ashamed of. He has also had a substantial career in Spanish cinema, stretching from the early fifties with *The Lioness of Castille* to Bernard Rapp's *No Big Deal*, which co-starred Alejandro (*El Topo*) Jodorowsky!

The peak of his work as an actor was undoubtedly in the boomtime of the late fifties and sixties, where he found regular work in adventure films (*The Castillian*), westerns (*Lola Colt*) and capers (*A Fistful of Gold*). His spy films are sturdy fillers rather than exceptional, but he made use of the rare opportunity for a lead role with some aplomb.

FILMS: Blueprint for A Massacre; Desperate Mission

SPECIAL SKILL: Resembling Sean Connery

ONE TO WATCH: Blueprint for a Massacre

CONSTANTINE, Eddie (Edward Constantinowsky, b. Los Angeles, 10/29/17 – d. Wiesbaden, 02/25/93)

As demonstrated by his casting in Jean-Luc Godard's *Alphaville*, Eddie Constantine was less an actor than an icon. His face became as much part of French cinema as those of Jean Seberg, Alain Delon and Jean Paul Belmondo, even if his renown didn't filter out to the same extent.

He started work as a singer, a trade he learned in Vienna under the auspices of Edith Piaf, before drifting into acting. His first major role was as Lemmy Caution in *Poison Ivy*, a role he repeated many times throughout the following decades. The films were noirish, low-budgeted affairs that found a significant audience, and Eddie never really changed his act. Even in his spy films, he's still Lemmy Caution (or, some would say, Eddie Constantine) in all but name. Nonetheless, it's a charming persona, equally happy with fists as with a quick aside. He seems to be one of us. Whereas the secret agents tended to be a cut above the characters around them (and therefore the audience), Eddie was just a wily old goat, nothing more special than that.

Apart from Lemmy Caution, his most notable characters, spy-wise, were Nick Carter and Jeff Gordon. There is some debate as to whether these really are spy films or a logical extension of his fifties ouevre, and the answer is probably a little bit of both. Certainly, his casting in Jesus Franco pictures *Residence for Spies* and *Attack of the Robots* indicates that he was firmly established in the espionage tradition.

Astonishingly, he continued making Lemmy Caution films virtually until his death in 1993. He interspersed these with an occassional art movie (Lars Von Trier's *Zentropa*) or more culty fare such as *It Lives Again* and *The Long Good Friday*.

FILMS: Attack of the Robots; It Means That to Me; Jeff Gordon, Secret Agent; Ladies' Man; License to Kill; Make Your Bets, Ladies; Residence for Spies; There's Going To Be a Party; Women Are Like That; Your Turn Darling

SPECIAL SKILLS: Being Eddie, what more could you need?

ONE TO WATCH: There's Going To Be a Party

DANTON, Ray (Raymond Kaplan, b. New York, 09/19/31 – d. Los Angeles, 02/11/92)

As with Guy Madison, Ray Danton had experienced a degree of success before his European work. He'd won a Golden Globe as the most promising newcomer in 1956, and his portrayal of the title character in Budd Boetticher's Oscar-nominated *The Rise and Fall of Legs Diamond* won plaudits around the

**Ray Danton in *Code Name: Jaguar***

world. He also had a decent role in *The Longest Day*, and appeared in the early American spy flick *FBI Code 98*.

He started appearing in specifically Europroductions with a couple of adaptations of Emilio Salgari's Sandokan novels: *Sandokan Against the Leopard of Sarawak* and *Sandokan Fights Back*, both of which were directed by Luigi Capuano and co-starred Guy Madison.

He made several spy films, and is among the most effective of performers found in the genre. As well as being capable in action sequences, he also developed an impressive talent for humorous straight-to-camera asides in both *Lucky the Inscrutable* and *Flatfoot*.

In the seventies he acted in a few US productions, including a late attempt to resurrect the Derek Flint franchise with the 1976 television movie *Our Man Flint: Dead on Target* (in which he played the hero). He also directed a couple of cult horror films: *Deathmaster* and *Psychic Killer*, as well as some extra footage for his ostensible *Flatfoot* director Julio Slavador's *Crypt of the Living Dead*, before settling into the television treadmill as a journeyman director.

FILMS: Code Name: Jaguar; Flatfoot; Lucky the Inscrutable; Secret Agent Superdragon

SPECIAL SKILLS: Witty asides

ONE TO WATCH: Secret Agent Superdragon

DAVILA, Luis (Hector Gonzales Ferrantino, b. Buenos Aires, 07/15/27 – d. Buenos Aires, 08/21/98)

It wasn't just Americans who flocked to the booming film industry in mainland Europe during the mid-sixties. Like Jorge Rigaud and Alberto de Mendoza, Luis Davila was born in Argentina (albeit to a Spanish mother), and was a familiar face in films of that country through the late fifties. His first brush with Euro-cinema was through acting opposite the singer Carmen Sevilla (who filmed some of her works in Argentina), and the Italian co-production *Vacanze in Argentina.* This obviously created a favorable impression, and he moved abroad to seek work.

Through the sixties and early seventies, he appeared in many spaghetti westerns (*Death on the High Mountain*, *Matalo*), war films (*Eagles Over London*) and giallos (*The Two Faces of Fear*). In most of these he was in secondary supporting roles, often playing an authority figure, but he did play the lead in a couple of spy films. He proved to be an effective performer, and more than up to task of filling a heroic role. In the seventies he returned to Argentina, where he found regular work in various television series.

FILMS: Espionage in Tangiers; Make Your Bets, Ladies; Ypotron

SPECIAL SKILLS: Authoritative, handsome in an old-school fashion

ONE TO WATCH: Ypotron

FRANCHI, Franco (Francesco Benenato, b. Palermo, 09/28/22 – d. Rome, 12/09/92) and INGRASSIA, Ciccio (Francesco Ingrassia, b. Carini [Palermo], 10/05/22 – d. Rome, 04/28/03)

Rather atypical secret agents, Franco and Ciccio were Italy's top comedy double act of the post-war era. They spoofed every film, as well as every genre, to achieve a degree of success, and the Bond series inevitably came within their sights. Whatever you think of their work, there's no denying its popularity, and it's also interesting to note that their 100-plus films proved a useful training ground for filmmakers who were later to find success in other genres (Sergio Corbucci, Lucio Fulci and others).

They began their career by performing sketches in the streets of Palermo, graduating to the theater before making the step up into cinema. At first they had cameo parts in productions such as the peplum *Hercules In the Valley of Woe*, but soon they became the main selling point of the films. Like Eddie Constantine in France, they became iconic figures, and their partnership—despite fading in the mid-seventies—continued until Paolo and Vittorio Taviani's *Kaos*.

It was Franco who got most of the laughs in their films, but Ciccio managed to accumulate an interesting resume as an actor in his own right: Florestano Vanzina's *Violenza: quinto potere*, Fellini's *Amarcord* and Elio Petri's *Todo modo* amongst others.

FILMS: 002 agenti segretissimi; 002 operazione Luna; Dr. Goldfoot and the Girl Bombs; Due mafioso contro Goldginger

SPECIAL SKILLS: Pratfalling, mugging, humiliating each other

ONE TO WATCH: Due mafioso contro Goldginger

HALSEY, Brett (b. Santa Ana [USA], 06/20/33)

Brett Halsey's career kicked off with a series of appearences in 1950s B movies, including *Hot Rod Rumble*, *High School Hellcats* and *Return of the Fly*. Attracted by the cinematic riches of Italy, he relocated to Europe and found work in historical adventures (most notably Riccardo Freda's *The Magnificent Adventurer*), before landing his two spy film roles. Rangy and with a somewhat languid aura, he was perhaps more suited to spaghetti westerns, where he scored notable success with the excellent *Today It's Me, Tomorrow You.*

After a fallow period in the seventies, during which his activities were mainly restricted to television soaps and guest appearences, he suddenly started reappearing in many films through the mid-eighties and nineties, from Lucio Fulci productions to Coppola's *The Godfather: Part III.* Other notable appearances included Aldo Florio's caper film *All on the Red* and a very strange giallo, *Perversion Story*.

FILMS: Espionage in Lisbon; Spy in Your Eye

SPECIAL SKILL: Languor

ONE TO WATCH: Spy in Your Eye

HANIN, Roger (Roger Levy, b. Algiers, 10/20/25)

Algerian actor Roger Hanin was the pre-eminent star of French spy films. Many others, such as Jean Marais and Gerard Barray, proved adept at playing secret agents, but it was Hanin who became most associated with the genre. This was partly because of his casting as Louis Rapiere, aka The Tiger, in two films for Claude Chabrol. These proved so popular that both *Operation Diplomatic Passport* and *Da Berlino l'apocalisse* were marketed as Tiger sequels. Also, however, he was happy acting in similar international co-productions, such as the sadly elusive *Our Men in Baghdad*, either as the lead or in supporting roles.

**Dietmar Schonher (left), Brad Harris and a flask of high quality LSD spell rouble in *Death Trip*.**

He had started of his career as a stage actor in the late forties, before picking up the occassional bit part in films (such as the early Eddie Constantine picture, *Poison Ivy*). His roles increased in size throughout the fifties, but his sturdy looks often led to his being cast as heavies or henchman. It was in the early sixties, and with the increasing popularity of the espionage theme, that he really came into his own. He was maybe a slightly unusual spy: Heavyset and lacking the lithe nimbleness of some of his American counterparts, he brought a certain depth to his characters. Not that they were afraid of getting involved in some heavy-duty fisticuffs, of course. He also proved adept at comedy, and many of his performances are laced with light-hearted humor.

After the genre burst, he appeared in a number of French and Italian thrillers (such as Duccio Tessari's *Big Guns*) and even popped up in *The Revengers*, a US western featuring William Holden. He also worked with some success as a writer-director (he had scripted the original Tiger films), and won a number of plaudits for his 1984 production, *Hell Train*.

FILMS: A Touch of Treason; Carre de dames pour un as; Code Name: Jaguar; Marie-Chantal vs. Dr. Kha; Our Agent Tiger; The Solitaire Attacks; The Tiger Likes Fresh Meat; Le Tigre sort sans se mere

SPECIAL SKILLS: Philosophical but with a keen sense of the ridiculous

ONE TO WATCH: Our Agent Tiger

HARRIS, Brad (b. St. Anthony [USA], 07/16/33)

Brad Harris, along with Gordon Mitchell, had the longest career of all the people to make their way from muscle beach to Rome, and was also one of the most prolific stars of the Eurospy genre.

After a couple of tiny roles in US productions and work as a stuntman on *Spartacus*, his big break came with the epic *Samson*. This was directed by Gianfranco Parolini, a filmmaker with whom he went on to forge a fruitful partnership. Their films together included several more peplums (*The Fury of Hercules*, *The Old Testament*) as well as the long-running Kommissar X and Three Fantastic Supermen series.

One of the reasons that he was able to continue with some success after the decline of the Hercules craze was that he was always more of an athlete than a bodybuilder. This is reflected by his credit as stunt co-ordinator on several films, most notably *Death is Nimble, Death is Quick*, where his work in that capacity counts as among the best in the genre. He's also interesting in that his performances range through the entire gamut of the genre, from early German productions (*Hong Kong Hot Harbor*) to the very dregs in the early seventies (*The Tiger Gang*).

Into the seventies, Harris continued working in a number of cheapjack westerns, war films and horror oddities (*The Mutations*, *The Mad Butcher*). He also had a part when Luigi

Cozzi attempted to resurrect the peplum genre in the early eighties with *Hercules*, albeit in a mature role and leaving much of the bicep flexing to Lou Ferringo.
FILMS: Cave of Diamonds; Death is Nimble, Death is Quick; Death Trip; Hong Kong Hot Harbor; Hunting the Unknown; Kill Panther Kill; Operation Hong Kong; Our Man in Jamaica; So Darling So Deadly; Spy Today, Die Tomorrow; Three Golden Dragons
SPECIAL SKILLS: Straight man par excellance
ONE TO WATCH: Death is Nimble, Death is Quick

HARRISON, Richard (b. Salt Lake City [USA], 05/26/35)

Richard Harrison was one of the most familiar of sixties Euro-stars, appearing in a huge range of productions. Strangely, he was never really in any standout films. It could be uncharitably argued that his recognizablitiy stems more from the volume than the quality of his work.

As with many American actors, he sought work in Europe when it looked like his career was going nowhere. He had tiny roles in films like *Kronos*, *South Pacific* (also starring Ken Clark) and *Master of the World*. Having left the States, he soon found work in adventure films like Pedro Lazaga's *Gladiators 7* and Antonio Margheriti's entertaining *Giants of Rome*. Athletic rather than musclebound, his homespun American looks made him a natural choice when Spanish and Italian filmmakers began making westerns, and he was summarily cast in the early *Gunfight at Red Sands*. He continued making westerns, which tended to decrease in quality, well into the seventies.

His spy films were less numerous, but perhaps more consistent. He scored a hit as agent Bob Fleming in two films produced by Luciano Martino and Mino Loy, and was in the excellent *Master Stroke*, which parodied his western identity. He was a regular in caper films as well, appearing in Aldo Florio's *Hot Diamonds in Cold Blood*.

After appearing in a variety of low-budgeted films throughout the seventies—and directing his own western, *Jesse and Lester*—he moved sideways and appeared in a number of Hong Kong Ninja movies that also have their followers.
FILMS: Fantabulous Inc.; Killers Are Challenged; Master Stroke; Ring Around the World; Secret Agent Fireball
SPECIAL SKILLS: Pearly white teeth, and looks good in a suit
ONE TO WATCH: Master Stroke

HOVEN, Adrian (Wilhelm Arpad Peter Hofkirchner, b. Wollersdorf [Austria], 05/18/22 – d. Tegernsee [Germany] 04/28/81)

Austrian actor Adrian Hoven appeared in a number of spy films, both as hero and villain. He's probably best known in the Eurotrash field for his work with Jesus Franco in the late sixties, particularly *Necronomicon* (68), but in fact he had a long acting career that began in the 1940s.

Starting off in second-string roles, his first appearances of particular note came during the krimi craze. He played a police inspector in Helmut Ashley's *Secret of the Red Orchid*, and also featured in the likes of *The White Horse Inn* and *The Black Cobra*. He popped up in a couple of early westerns: Joaquin Romero Marchent's *Seven Hours of Gunfire* and *The Son of Jesse James*.

After his brush with Franco, Hoven turned his hand to directing, and gave the world trash favorites *The Long, Swift Sword of Sigfried* and *Mark of the Devil II*. He continued acting until his death from a heart attack in 1981.
FILMS: Death On a Rainy Day; Kiss Me Monster; Sadisterotica
SPECIAL SKILLS: His cameleon-like acting abilities
ONE TO WATCH: Death On a Rainy Day

HUBSCHMID, Paul (Paul Hugo Hubschmid, b. Schonenwerd [Switzerland] 07/20/17 – d. Berlin, 12/31/01)

Paul Hubschmid only appeared in three spy films, but made his most favorable impression as the dubious agent Johnny Vulkan in *Funeral in Berlin*. In fact, he was better known out of the genre; first for being one of the first major Swiss films stars and second for appearing—under the pseudonym Paul Christian—in the classic monster movie *Beast From 20,000 Fathoms*.

**Paul Hubschmid strikes a pose with Vivi Bach (left) and Karin Dor (right) in Upperseven, The Man to Kill.**

After making a name for himself as a stage actor, he appeared as the romantic lead in a huge number of films from the thirties through the sixties. Most of these were made in Germany, and not many of them received much international distribution. Nonetheless, he became extremely popular and even won an award for his contribution to German Cinema in 1980.
FILMS: Cave of Diamonds; Upperseven, The Man to Kill
SPECIAL SKILLS: Upright, mature
ONE TO WATCH: Upperseven, The Man to Kill

JEFFRIES, Lang (b. Ontario, 06/07/30 – d. Huntingdon Beach [USA], 02/12/87)

American actor Lang Jeffries had served in the US army during the Korean War before drifting into the acting profession. He appeared in a short-lived US television series, *Rescue 8*, before heading for Rome. He quickly found work in epics such as *Revolt of the Slaves* and *Alone Against Rome*, but it was in spy films that he truly flourished.

One of the most prolific of genre stars, his films aren't as famous as some, but among afficionados they form a remarkably well-respected collection. A rather dour presence, he tended to appear more comfortable with action scenes than when required to be a lothario, and his characters often have a no-nonsense attitude that sets them apart from the flippant playboys who characterized the Eurospy genre.

During this period he delved into other types of film, making the entertaining sci-fi flick *Mission Stardust* and an effective spaghetti western, *Duel in the Eclipse*. In the seventies, however, the roles dried up and he moved back to the US, where he worked in real estate.
FILMS: Agent X-17; The Beckett Affair; Mark Donen agente Z7; Mexican Slay Ride; Our Man in Casablanca; Special Cypher; Spies Strike Silently
SPECIAL SKILLS: Serious, cool, actually looked like he knew what he was doing
ONE TO WATCH: Special Cypher

JOHNSON, Richard (b. Upminster [UK], 07/30/27)

Many British actors made spy films: Tom Courtenay, Dirk Bogarde, Laurence Harvey and more. The only one who really became associated with the genre, however—apart from the assorted Bonds, of course—was Richard Johnson. A "proper" actor, Johnson's most famous role is that of Bulldog Drummond in two very popular films. Curiously enough, at the very beginning of his film career Johnson had an uncredited role in *Calling Bulldog Drummond*, with Walter Pidgeon playing the titular insurance investigator.

A noted stage performer, Johnson started out as a member of John Gielgud's repertory company before joining the Navy in World War II. After appearing in a number of small-scale UK productions, he started popping up in a number of interesting European productions (Terence Young's *The Rover*, Damiano Damiani's *The Witch*). This was a pattern he was to continue, mixing high-ish brow British films with an eclectic mixture of international pictures. His filmography includes acclaimed historical titles such as *Julius Caesar* and *Lady Jane*, adventure films (*The Four Feathers*) and cult Italian B-movies like *Zombie* and *Beyond the Door*.
FILMS: Danger Route; Deadlier Than the Male; Some Girls Do
SPECIAL SKILLS: Good sense of humor
ONE TO WATCH: Deadlier Than the Male

KENDALL, Tony (Luciano Stella, b. Rome, 08/22/36)

With his classic good looks, Luciano Stella moved into acting after appearing in a number of "fotoromanzi" (Italian comic strips using models photographed to portray a story). His first film performance was in Steno's *Female Three Times*, but it wasn't until after 1962's *Brennus, Enemy of Rome* that he started winning lead roles. At this time he adopted the pseudonym Tony Kendall—suggested by Vittorio De Sica—and starred in Mario Bava's *Whip and the Body*.

Many of his sixties films were German co-productions, including early spaghetti westerns such as Jurgen Roland's *Pirates of the Mississippi* and Ernst Hofbauer's *The Black Eagle of Santa Fe*. It was in the Kommissar X series, however, that he found fame (allegedly his offscreen behavior wasn't too far removed from that of his onscreen character at this time). He also appeared in the obscure spy film *Serenade for Two Spies* and cult favorite *The Three Fantastic Supermen*.

As the seventies arrived, he continued working in a variety of genres: spaghetti westerns (*Brother Outlaw*), giallos (*In the Eye of the Hurricane*) and horror films (*Return of the Blind Dead*). One of the few spy film stars to have continued working to the present day, he also appeared in a couple of successful television series: Nino Salerno's *Aquile* and Giorgio Capitani's *Un Prete da strada*.

FILMS: Death is Nimble, Death is Quick; Death Trip; Hunting the Unknown; Kill Panther Kill; So Darling, So Deadly; Three Golden Dragons

SPECIAL SKILL: The lay-dies simply can't resist him

ONE TO WATCH: Death Trip

MADISON, Guy (b. Bakersfield [USA], 01/19/22 – d. Palm Springs [USA], 02/06/96)

Guy Madison was a huge star even before moving to Italy. While working in the Coast Guard during World War II, he was cast in a small role as a sailor in *Since You Went Away*, despite having no acting experience whatsoever. His brief appearence, filmed during a weekend shore leave, proved to be extremely popular, and he returned from his tour of duty on the cusp of fame.

His status grew during the fifties, as he appeared in a well-received television series *The Adventures of Wild Bill Hickok*, as well as a couple of interesting, small-budget films (such as *The Beast of Hollow Mountain*). Like so many others, he emigrated to find work in Europe, and appeared in a number of adventure films and westerns.

Although he only made two spy films (as well as the Paolo Bianchini superhero movie *Superargo and the Faceless Giants*), they can be counted among the weirdest examples of the genre—which stands as a pretty impressive record. More mature than some of his rivals, he exuded a dapper charm that worked well within the genre. As the seventies approached, he became a firm favorite in low-budget war films such as Giuseppe Vari's *A Place in Hell* and Jose Luis Merino's *Hell Commandos*.

FILMS: The Devil's Man; LSD: Hell For a Few Dollars More

SPECIAL SKILLS: Choosing very strange films to appear in

ONE TO WATCH: LSD: Hell For a Few Dollars More

MARAIS, Jean (Jean Villain Marais, b. Cherbourg, 12/11/13 – d. Cannes, 11/08/98)

Jean Marais was one of the staples of French cinema from the 1940s until his death in 1998. He appeared in a handful of spy films, as well as related productions such as the three Andre Hunebelle Fantomas films (*Fantomas*, *Fantomas Strikes Back* and *Fantomas Against Scotland Yard*) and as Simon Templar, aka The Saint, in Christian-Jaque's *The Saint Lies in Wait*.

After drama school and a brief spell as a male model, he started finding jobs in the theater and in small film roles. His first experience of stardom, however, came with Jean Delannoy's *Love Eternal*. After this, his reputation was cemented by appearences in several films by his friend, Jean Cocteau (*Beauty and the Beast*, *Orpheus*). He interspersed these, however, with roles in more populist fare (*The Count of Monte Cristo*, *The King's Avenger*, etc.).

His brush with stardom came mainly from the two "Stanislas" films he made with Jean-Charles Dudrumet (*The Reluctant Spy*, *Killer Spy*), and toward the end of the sixties his work rate began to slow slightly. This didn't stop him

appearing in a number of television series (such as *Joseph Balsamo*) and high-profile cinema productions (Bertolucci's *Stealing Beauty*). He was awarded an honorary Cesar award 1993.
FILMS: The Reluctant Spy
SPECIAL SKILLS: Mature, suave, French icon
ONE TO WATCH: The Reluctant Spy (the only one we've seen so far!)

MARK, Robert (b. ?)

Former medical student Robert Mark—who often used the name Rod Dana—started out acting in US commercials and television shows during the late 1950s. After becoming frustrated with Hollywood, he returned to his studies and decided to do part of his course in Rome. Once there, he started acting in small roles as a way of making some extra cash, and caught the bug again while filming *Cleopatra*.

He made three spy films, which, it would be fair to say, came from the lower end of the budgetary spectrum (with the possible exception of the excellent *Sicaro 77*). He proved to be an impressive hero, bringing a raw physicality to the roles, and looks as though he was having a ball. As well as starring in a couple of spaghetti westerns, he also found work in the dubbing trade, recording English-language dialogue that could be used for export versions of Italian films (other dubbers included Tony Russel and Roger Browne, not to mention character actors John Karlsen and Geoffrey Coppleston).

In the seventies he left Rome to pursue other interests, and apart from small roles in a couple of productions (most notably Richard Donner's *Ladyhawke*), he retired from acting.
FILMS: Handle With Care; Operation White Shark; Siccario 77—vivo o morto
SPECIAL SKILLS: Looks damn good in a fight
ONE TO WATCH: Sicario 77 vivo o morto

MATHEWS, Kerwin (b. Washington [USA], 01/08/26)

Kerwin Mathews was another actor to play agent OSS 117, Hubert Bonnisseur de la Bath, in the popular series of Eurospy films that ran through the 1960s. In fact, the character had first been portrayed—in *OSS 117 Is Not Dead*—by Ivan Desny in 1956, but it was with *OSS 117 se dechaine*, wherein Mathews assumed the role, that things really got going.

A former teacher, he gained his first acting experience working on US television series such as *The Ford Television Theater*. He soon started finding lesser film roles (including *Five Against the House* with future Eurospy Guy Madison), before hitting gold dust with *The 7th Voyage of Sinbad*. After appearing in the similarly themed *The Three Worlds of Gulliver* and *Jack the Giant Killer*, he made a couple of second-string Hammer movies (*The Pirates of Blood River* and *Maniac*), before appearing in several spy films.

In the seventies his acting career seemed to dry up, and after turning up in a couple of eccentric productions (*Octaman*, *The Boy Who Cried Werewolf*), he retired to pursue other interests.
FILMS: The Killer Likes Candy; OSS 117 se dechaine; Shadow of Evil
SPECIAL SKILLS: Slaying giants...oops, wrong genre!
ONE TO WATCH: Shadow of Evil

NADER, George (b. Pasadena, 10/19/21 – d. Woodland Hills [USA] 02/04/02)

George Nader's first starring role was in the cult classic *Robot Monster*, a camp favorite in which he played one of the final surviving humans, battling a deadly "Ro-man" menace: an unfortunate stuntman disguised in a gorilla costume and with a fishbowl on his head. Despite being frankly terrible, it proved a huge success and led to a contract with Universal. He soon won a Golden Globe award for being the "Most Promising Newcomer" in 1955.

Other appearences during the fifties included *Lady Godiva* and *The Female Animal*, but he never managed to break out of second-string features. After severing his ties with Universal, he starred in a number of television series (*The Further Adventures of Ellery Queen*, *The Man and the Challange* and *Shannon*). His first European production was Siro Marcellini's *The Secret Mark of D'Artagnan*, but it was as Jerry Cotton in the mid-sixties that he found stardom, in Germany at least.

After this period of intense activity, his output declined during the seventies, con-

**George Nader in *Death and Diamonds***

fined to a secondary role in Eddie Romero's *Beyond Atlantis* and the odd guest star role on television. He retired from acting after suffering an eye injury in a car accident, and went on to become a writer, claiming the honor of penning the first gay science fiction novel, "Chrome."

One of the more curious aspects about Nader's career was that, despite his featuring as a subject of beefcake photos in the fifties, he was one of the very few actors at the time who—if not openly gay—made no attempt to camouflage their sexuality (most commonly by having a "beard," ostensible female partners, allowing the maintainance of a facade of machismo). He also lived with his partner for many years, and was a close friend of Rock Hudson (who made him a beneficiary of his will). There is also some suggestion that his career was never allowed to flourish as much as it could have, in order to protect Hudson's reputation.

FILMS: 3-2-1 Countdown for Manhattan; Body in Central Park; Dead Body on Broadway; Death and Diamonds; Death In a Red Jaguar; Manhattan Night of Murder; The Million Eyes of Sumuru; Operation Hurricane: Friday Noon; Tip Not Included

SPECIAL SKILL: Capable, light-hearted heroism

ONE TO WATCH: 3-2-1 Countdown for Manhattan

RUSSEL, Tony (Tony Russo, b. ? – d. ?)

Like Roger Browne, Tony Russel interspersed his acting career with moonlighting work as a dubber. Unlike Roger Browne, something is known of his origins: He had acted in American productions such as *The Sign of Zorro* before moving to Italy in the hope of kickstarting his career.

Once in Europe he dabbled in many genres, including a couple of spy films in which he proved an effective lead. He remains best remembered for his heroic performances in a couple of cult Antonio Margheriti sci-fi films: *Wild, Wild Planet* and *War of the Planets*. He returned to the US in 1967 and acted sporadically in films and television shows.

FILMS: The Secret of the Sphinx; Target Goldseven

SPECIAL SKILL: As American as apple pie

ONE TO WATCH: The Secret of the Sphinx

SCOTT, Gordon (b. Portland [USA], 09/03/27)

Very few of the musclemen who found popularity in the pelpums of the early sixties managed to extend their career throughout the decade. Gordon Scott—like Brad Harris—was one of them...for a time at least. Discovered by Hollywood agents while working as a lifeguard, his first taste of fame came with six Tarzan films from 1955-60 (including the excellent *Tarzan's Greatest Adventure*, which also featured a young Sean Connery).

Some of these were made in Britain, so it wasn't unnatural for him to relocate to Europe when the Steve Reeves Hercules films proved huge box-office successes. Appearing in titles such as Riccardo Freda's *Samson and the Seven Miracles of the World*, Giorgio Ferroni's *Hercules Against the Moloch* and Sergio Corbucci's *Duel of the Titans* (also co-starring Reeves), he laid some claim to the title of being the second biggest star of the genre.

After appearing in a couple of westerns, not unsuccesfully, he made two spy films. As with all of the body-builder actors, he looked rather more uncomfortable in a suit than a loincloth, but managed to overcome this and give charming performances. After *Danger!!*

*Death Ray*, though, he brought a timely end to his career, and hasn't acted in anything since.
FILMS: Danger!! Death Ray; Top Secret
SPECIAL SKILL: Big, handsome guy
ONE TO WATCH: Top Secret

STAFFORD, Frederick (Friedrich Strobel von Stein, b. 03/11/28 – d. 07/28/79)

Czech-born Austrian Frederick Stafford was one of the most effective of spy film performers. Charming, handsome and with a light touch, he made a likeable Hubert Bonnisseur de la Bath in two of the OSS 117 films. The son of a Slovak factory owner, he was a chemistry graduate, had represented his country as a swimmer in the Olympic Games and been the director of an international hotel chain before being "discovered" by Andre Hunebelle.

He certainly made the most of the opportunities that the espionage genre afforded him, using it as a springboard toward appearing in decently budgeted crime films *The Gold Robbers* and a trio of above-average war films (*Dirty Heroes*, *The Battle of El Alamein* and *Eagles Over London*). His big break came when Alfred Hitchcock gave him the lead role in the US spy film *Topaz*, but this proved to be less succesful than was anticipated, and his career didn't take off as hoped.

The seventies brought roles in a number of eccentric productions, of which the giallo *Shadows Unseen* and Rino di Silvestro's wild *Werewolf Woman* are probably best known. His last credit, before prematurely dying in a small plane collision, was as the star of German Lorente's French/Spanish crime film *Hold Up*.
FILMS: Formula C-12 Beirut; Million Dollar Man; OSS 117 From Tokyo with Love; OSS 117 Mission for a Killer
SPECIAL SKILL: Charming and sophisticated
ONE TO WATCH: OSS 117 Mission for a Killer

WYLER, Richard (Richard Stapley, b. Westcliff [UK], 06/20/23)

British actor Richard Wyler appeared in a number of US productions from the late 1940s onward, generally using the name Richard Stapley. He seemed to favor adventure films, appearing down the credits in titles such as *King of the Khyber Rifles* and *Jungle Man Eaters*. After returning to the UK in search of better roles, he landed the lead in a spy-related television series *The Man From Interpol*.

His first taste of filmmaking in mainland Europe came with Rudolph Mate's *The Barbarians*, which starred Jack Palance. He went on to appear in a number of westerns (including the excellent *The Bounty Killer*) and the Jesus Franco extravaganza *Rio 70*. After this burst, though, his film career fizzled out in the early seventies with a tiny, uncredited role in Alfred Hitchcock's *Frenzy*.
FILMS: Dick Smart 2.007; FX 18 Superspy
SPECIAL SKILL: Deadly serious…but seeing the funny side
ONE TO WATCH: FX 18 Superspy

# APPENDIX C: AUTHORS' LISTS

**TOP TEN FILMS—DD**

The Beckett Affair
Danger Route
Dead Run
Fuller Report
Moving Target
Only the Cool
Passport to Hell
The Quiller Memorandum
Special Mission Lady Chaplin
There's Going To Be A Party

**TOP TEN FILMS—MB**

Dealier Than the Male
Due mafioso contro Goldginger
Fuller Report
Marie-Chantal vs. Dr. Kha
Operation Atlantis
The Secret of the Sphinx
Sicario 77—vivo o morto
Slalom
Spies Strike Silently
Spy in Your Eye

**SEVEN FAVE SPIES—DD**

George Ardisson
Roger Browne
Ken Clark
Lang Jeffries
Kerwin Mathews
George Nader
Frederick Stafford

**TOP TEN VILLAINS—MB**

Dirk Bogarde
Adolfo Celi
Alberto Dalbas
Eduardo Fajardo
Horst Frank
Carlo Hintermann
Umberto Raho
Franco Ressel
Gianni Rizzo
Daniele Vargas

**FOUR FUNNY FILMS—DD**

Italian Secret Service
Otley
Our Man in Marrakesh
The Reluctant Spy

**TOP TEN HENCHMEN—MB**

Claudio Biava
Sal Borgese
Pietro Ceccarelli
Daniel Emilfork
Klaus Kinski
Giuseppe Mattei
Luciano Pigozzi
Claudio Ruffini
Andrea Scotti
Gerard Tichy

**SEVEN STRANGE FILMS—DD**

The Big Blackout
The Devil's Man
Espionage in Tangiers
From Istanbul—Orders to Kill
LSD: Hell For A Few Dollars More
Lucky the Inscrutable
The Monocle

**TOP FIVE DODGY ORIENTALS—MB**

Mitsouko
Seyna Seyn
Moha Tahi
Yoko Tani
George Wang

**TOP FIVE LOCATIONS—MB**

Egypt
(A 008 Operation Exterminate, Slalom)
Hong Kong
(Desperate Mission, Siete minutos paramorir)
Istanbul
(Fury on the Bosphorus, Intrigue at Suez)
Beirut
(Formula C-12 Beirut, Secret Agent Fireball)
Lisbon
(High Season for Spies, Target Goldseven)

# APPENDIX D: ACTOR/DIRECTOR/ COMPOSER CROSS-REFERENCES

## ACTORS

ADAMS, Tom: License to Kill; Someone's Stolen Our Russian Spy; Subterfuge; Where the Bullets Fly
ADORF, Mario: The Dirty Game; That Man in Istanbul
ALDER, Thomas: 13 Days to Die
ALTAMURA, Tulio: Assalto al tesoro di stato; Danger!! Death Ray; Dick Smart 2.007; Last Man to Kill; One-Eyed Soldiers; Operation Atlantis; Operation White Shark; Rififi in Amsterdam; Secret of the Sphinx; Upperseven, The Man to Kill
ALTMAYER, Tor, see Tulio Altamura
AMBESI, Adriana: Cave of Diamonds; Secret Agent Superdragon
ANDREI, Franco: Passport to Hell; Requiem for a Secret Agent
ANDREW, Frank, see Franco Andrei
ANDREWS, Dana: The Cobra; Spy in Your Eye
ANDREWS, Harry: A Dandy in Aspic; Danger Route; The Deadly Affair; Modesty Blaise
ANDRONICO, Enzo: 002 agenti segretissimi; Due mafioso contro Goldginger; Italian Secret Service; Password Kill Agent Gordon
ANGELI, Pier: M.M.M. 83; Shadow of Evil; Spy in your Eye
ANGELINI, Nando: 002 agenti segretissimi; A 008 Operation Exterminate; Agent X-17; Operation Double 007; Our Man in Jamaica; Superseven Calling Cairo; Ypotron
ANTHONY, Robert, see Espartaco Santoni
ARBESSIER, Louis: The Dirty Game; The Great Spy Chase; The Reluctant Spy
ARDEN, Mary: 002 agenti segretissimi; Master Stroke
ARDISSON, George [Giorgio]: Hunter of the Unknown; Inferno a Caracas; Operation Counterspy; Passport to Hell
ARENA, Fortunato: A 008 Operation Exterminate; Madigon's Millions
ASLAN, Gregoire: A Man Could Get Killed; Our Man in Marrakesh; Ravishing Idiot; Tiffany Memorandum
ATTAL, Henri: Marie-Chantal vs. Dr. Kha; OSS 117 Mission for A Killer; OSS 117 se dechaine; The Tiger Likes Fresh Meat
AUDRAN, Stephane: Marie-Chantal vs. Dr. Kha; Only the Cool; The Tiger Likes Fresh Meat
AUDRET, Pascale: A Touch of Treason; Inferno a Caracas
AURELI, Andrea: Death Trip; Superseven Calling Cairo
AVALON, Frankie: The Million Eyes of Sumuru
BAAL, Karin: Mission to Venice
BACH, Vivi: Elektra 1; Upperseven, The Man to Kill
BADMAJEW, Maria, see Maria Badmyev
BADMYEV, Maria: Agente segreto 777: operazione Mistero; Elektra 1; Our Agent In Casablanca; Sicario 77—vivo o morto; Spies Strike Silently
BAGOLINI, Silvio: Fantabulous Inc.; Furia a Marrakesh; Ring Around the World
BALBO, Ennio: Fury on the Bosphorus; Master Stroke; Le Tigre sort sans se mere
BALDASSARRE, Raffaele: OSS 117 Double Agent; Our Man in Jamaica
BALDWIN, Ralph, see Raffaele Baldassarre
BARATTO, Luisa: The Devil's Man; The Last Chance
BARCLAY, Peter, see Pietro Ceccarelli
BARDOT, Brigitte: The Ravishing Idiot
BARKER, Lex: Spies Against the World; Spy Today, Die Tomorrow
BARRAY, Gerard: Baraka X 77
BARRETT, Liz, see Luisa Baratto
BARRETT, Tim: Someone's Stolen Our Russian Spy; Where the Bullets Fly
BARTHA, Janos [John]: Our Man in Jamaica
BARRI, Barta: Espionage in Tangiers; Kiss Me Monster; Someone's Stolen Our Russian Spy; That Man in Istanbul
BARRY, Barta, see Barta Barri
BARRY, Gene: Subterfuge
Beir, Fred: Assassination; M.M.M. 83
BERCQ, Jean-Claude: Judoka Secret Agent
BERGAMONTI, Rosella: Danger!! Death Ray; Death Trip; Password: Kill Agent Gordon; 7 Golden Women Against Two 07 (Treasure Hunt); Si muore solo una volta
BERGER, Senta: Our Man in Marrakesh; The Quiller Memorandum; Spy Hunt in Vienna
BERRI, Robert: Ladies' Man; Women Are Like

Kill; OSS 117 Mission For a Killer; OSS 117 se dechaine
CHRISTIAN, Dan: Agente segreto 070 Thunderbay—missione Grasshopper; Un Tango dalla Russia
CIANFRIGLIA, Giovanni: Desperate Misson; The Devil's Man; Hypnos—follia di un massacro
CLAIR, Jany: FX-18; FX 18 Superspy; Mission to Caracas
CLARK, Ken: Fuller Report; Fury On the Bosphorus; FX-18; Mission Bloody Mary; Special Mission Lady Chaplin; Tiffany Memorandum
CLAY, James [Jim], see Aldo Cecconi
CLIFT, Montgomery: The Defector
COBOS, German: Blueprint For a Massacre; Desperate Mission
COGAN, Henri: It Means That to Me; Passport to Hell; Women Are Like That; Your Turn, Darling
COLLINS, Alan, see Luciano Pigozzi
CONNERS, Mike: Kiss the Girls and Make them Die
CONNERY, Neil: Operation Double 007
CONSOLI, Enzo: James Tont operazione DUE; Operation Double 007; Spies Strike Silently
CONSTANTINE, Eddie: Attack of the Robots; It Means That to Me; Jeff Gordon, Secret Agent; Ladies' Man; License to Kill; Make Your Bets, Ladies; Residence for Spies; There's Going To Be a Party; Women Are Like That; Your Turn, Darling
COPPLESTON, Geoffrey: 7 Golden Women Against Two 07 (Treasure Hunt); James Tont operazione DUE; Matchless
CORTES, Juan: Goldsnake; High Season for Spies; Operation Poker
COSTER, Claudine: Ladies' Man; Only the Cool
COURTENAY, Tom: A Dandy in Aspic; Otley
DAKAR: Due mafioso contro Goldginger; Last Man to Kill; Passport to Hell
DALBAN, Robert: The Great Spy Chase; The Monocle; The Versailles Affair
DALBAS, Alberto: Danger!! Death Ray; Espionage in Tangiers; Intrigue At Suez; M.M.M. 83; That Man in Istanbul; Ypotron
DALI, Fabienne: Fury on the Bosphorus; The Killer Likes Candy; Superseven Calling Cairo; Women Are Like That
DAMON, Mark: Agente segreto 777: operazione Mistero
DANA, Rod [Rodd], see Robert Mark
DANIELI, Emma: Slalom; Spies Strike Silently
DANTON, Ray: Code Name: Jaguar; Flatfoot; Lucky the Inscrutable; Secret Agent Superdragon
DARC, Mirielle: The Balearic Caper; The Great Spy Chase
DAVILA, Luis: Espionage in Tangiers; Make Your Bets, Ladies; Ypotron
DAYLE, Daphne: Jeff Gordon, Secret Agent; License to Kill
DE ALBA, Aurora: Agent X-17; Crime Story; Top Secret
DE BENEDETTIS, Giovanni, see Giovanni Di Benedetto
DE GRASSI, Dario [Dean]: Fury on the Bosphorus; Operation Atlantis; Password: Kill Agent Gordon; Tiffany Memorandum
DE LA RIVA, Miguel: Password: Kill Agent Gordon; Rififi in Amsterdam; Spy Today, Die Tomorrow
DE LUNA, Alvaro: Mark Donen agente Z7; That Man in Istanbul
DE SANTAS, Dina: A 008 Operation Exterminate; Last Man to Kill
DEAN, Max, see Massimo Righi
DEGHY, Guy: One-Eyed Soldiers; Spia, spione; Subterfuge
DELAMAIRE, Gil see Gil Delamare
DELAMARE, Gil: FX 18 Superspy; License to Kill; Spy Catcher
DELORME, Guy: Carre de dames pour un as; Dead Run; FX-18; Ladies' Man; OSS 117 Mission for a Killer; Your Turn Darling
DEMICK, Irina: OSS 117 se dechaine; Tiffany Memorandum
DESNY, Ivan: The Becket Affair; Daniella by Night; Secret of the Sphinx; The Survival Factor; Le Tigre sort sans se mere; The Versailles Affair
DEUS, Beni: FX-18; Hunter of the Unknown; Operation Atlantis; Password: Kill Agent Gordon; Requiem for a Secret Agent
DI BENEDETTO, Giovanni: 7 Golden Women Against Two 07 (Treasure Hunt); Furia a Marrakesh; Killers are Challenged
DIFFRING, Anton: The Double Man; Spy Hunt in Vienna
DOR, Karin: Spies Against the World; Target

KENT, Stanley, see Stelio Candelli

KINSKI, Klaus: The Dirty Game; Million Eyes of Sumuru; Only the Cool; Our Man in Marrakesh; Spies Against the World; Target For Killing; That Man in Istanbul

KNEFF, Hildegarde: None But the Lonely Spy

KOCH, Marianne: The Devil's Agent; Hong Kong Hot Harbor

KONOPKA, Magda: The Survival Factor; Top Secret

KOSCINA, Sylva: Baraka X 77; Carre de dames pour un as; Deadlier than the Male; That Man in Istanbul

LAMBERT, Herni: Jeff Gordon, Secret Agent; Million Dollar Man; Mission to Caracas; The Spy I Love; Women Are Like That

LANDRY, Gerard: Death on a Rainy Day; Elektra 1; FBI operazione vipera gialla; Spy Today, Die Tomorrow

LANFRANCHI, Mario: Agente Sigma 3—missione Goldwather; The Big Blackout; M.M.M. 83; One-Eyed Soldiers; Operation Hong Kong; Spies Strike Silently

LANGE, Claudie: James Tont operazione DUE; Ticket to Die

LANGE, Helmut: FBI operazione vipera gialla

LAVI, Daliah: Nobody Runs Forever; Some Girls Do; Spy Hunt in Vienna

LAWFORD, Peter: Dead Run

LEE, Bernard: Operation Double 007; Ring of Spies

LEE, Margaret: Dick Smart 2.007; Fury on the Bosphorus; Kiss the Girls and Make Them Die; Master Stroke; Our Agent Tiger; Our Man in Marrakesh; Secret Agent Superdragon; Spies Against the World; Le Tigre sort sans se mere

LEIGH, Wandisa, see Wandisa Guida

LEIPNITZ, Harald: Formula C-12 Beirut; Inferno a Caracas

LEMAIRE, Philippe: Cave of Diamonds; Death is Nimble, Death is Quick; Operation Hong Kong; Your Turn, Darling

LEMOINE, Michel: Hunter of the Unknown; Kiss Me Monster; Mission to Caracas; Sadisterotica; Spy Catcher

LE MESURIER, John: Our Man in Marrakesh; Where the Spies Are

LENZI, Giovanna: Agente Sigma 3—missione Goldwather; Le Tigre sort sans se mere

LEONE, Ignazio: 002 operazione Luna; Elektra 1; Mission Bloody Mary; Special Cypher

LINDER, Christa: Death Trip; Hunting the Unknown; Inferno a Caracas

LINE, Helga: Crime Story; Mission Bloody Mary; Operation Poker; Password: Kill Agent Gordon; Special Cypher; Special Mission Lady Chaplin

LISI, Virna: The Spy I Love

LOGAN, Christopher, see Mauro Parenti

LOLLOBRIGIDA, Guido: The Cobra; Mexican Slay Ride; Operation Double 007; Upperseven, The Man to Kill

LONCAR, Bebe: Fuller Report; Slalom; Some Girls Do

LORENZON, Livio: Crime Story; Master Stroke

LORYS, Diana: The Devil's Man; Lightning Bolt; Residence for Spies; Someone's Stolen Our Russian Spy

LOVE, Lucretia: From Istanbul, Orders to Kill

LOY, Dina: Attack of the Robots; Hunter of the Unknown; Residence for Spies; Ypotron

LUGUET, Andre: Ravishing Idiot; Spy Catcher; Women Are Like That

LULLI, Folco: Last Plane to Baalbeck; Lightning Bolt

LULLI, Piero: OSS 117 Double Agent

LUPO, Alberto: A 008 Operation Exterminate

MACCHI, Velentino: Assalto al tesoro di stato; Assassination; The Big Blackout; Danger!! Death Ray; Dick Smart 2.007; The Killer Likes Candy; Last Man to Kill; Moving Target; Tiffany Memorandum

MACULANI, Giulio: A Man Could Get Killed; Danger!! Death Ray; Fantabulous Inc.; Spy in Your Eye

MADISON, Guy: The Devil's Man; LSD: Hell For a Few Dollars More

MANFREDI, Nino: Italian Secret Service

MARAIS, Jean: The Reluctant Spy

MARANDI, Evi: Fury on the Bosphorus; Hunter of the Unknown; James Tont operazione UNO

MARCO, Jose: Passport to Hell; Siete minutos para morir; Spies Strike Silently; Target for Killing

MARIOTTA, Leontina: Desperate Mission; Hunter of the Unknown; Operation Counterspy; Passport to Hell

MARK, Robert: Handle With Care; Operation White Shark; Siccario 77—vivo o morto
MARTELL, Peter: The Cobra
MARTIN, George: Elektra 1; Kiss Kiss Bang Bang
MARTINELLI, Elsa: Madigan's Millions; OSS 177 prend des vacances
MASON, James: The Deadly Affair
MATHEWS, Kerwin: The Killer Likes Candy; OSS 117 se dechaine; Shadow of Evil
MATTEI, Giuseppe [Pino]: Hunting the Unknown; Kill Panther Kill; Mark Donen agente Z7; So Darling, So Deadly; Spy Today, Die Tomorrow; Three Golden Dragons
MATTHEWS, Joseph, see Giuseppe Mattei
MAY, Leontine, see Leontina Mariotta
MAYO, Alfredo: Attack of the Robots; Due mafioso contro Goldginger; Espionage in Lisbon; Make Your Bets, Ladies; Mission Bloody Mary; Special Mission Lady Chaplin; Ypotron
MCFEE, Juri see Nino Fuscagni
MCGOOHAN, Patrick: Koroshi
MECALE, Giulio, see Giulio Maculani
MELL, Marisa: Secret Agent Superdragon
MENENDEZ, Angel: Attack of the Robots; Password: Kill Agent Gordon; Someone's Stolen Our Russian Spy
MERENDA, Luc: OSS 177 prend des vacances
MESSENGER, Bob see Roberto Messina
MESSINA, Emilio: The Big Blackout; Operation Counterspy; Operation Poker; OSS 117 Double Agent; Superseven Calling Cairo
MESSINA, Roberto: Agente segreto 070 Thunderbay—missione Grasshopper; The Becket Affair; Operation Poker; OSS 117 Double Agent; Superseven Calling Cairo
MEURISSE, Paul: The Monocle
MICANTONI, Adriano: LSD: Hell For a Few Dollars More; Nazi SS; Target Goldseven
MIKEL, Adrian, see Adriano Micantoni
MILLOT, Charles: A Touch of Treason; The Great Spy Chase; Ravishing Idiot; The Solitaire Attacks
MINAZZOLI, Christiane: Your Turn, Darling
MITCHELL, Gordon: The Killer Likes Candy; Moving Target
MITSOUKO: Furia a Marrakesh; Killers Are Challenged; License to Kill; Mark Donen agente Z7; Mission Bloody Mary
MOLL, Giorgia: Italian Secret Service; Requiem for a Secret Agent; Tom Dollar
MONLAUR, Yvonne: Ladies' Man; License to Kill; Mission to Caracas; Tip Not Included
MONOD, Jacques: A Touch of Treason; Mission to Venice; Ravishing Idiot; The Spy I Love
MONTALBANO, Renato: Assalto al tesoro di stato; James Tont operazione DUE; Last Man to Kill; Lightning Bolt; Ring Around the World; Sfida nel citta d'oro
MONTEFIORI, Luigi: The Cobra; Master Stroke; OSS 117 Double Agent
MONTES, Elisa: The Cobra; Due mafioso contro Goldginger
MORETTI, Sandro: Fantabulous Inc.; Nazi SS; Piege pour un espions
MORGAN, Sheryll, see Helen Chanel
MORGIA, Piero: 002 agente segretissimo; 002 operazione Luna; Sicario 77—vivo o morto
MORICI, Franco: 002 operazione Luna; Kiss Kiss Bang Bang; Spia, Spione; Il Vostro superagente Flit
MOSCHIN, Gaston: Italian Secret Service; Spy in Your Eye
MULLER, Paul: From Istanbul, Orders to Kill; Handle with Care; Nazi SS; Manhattan Night of Murder
MUNCH, Richard: 3-2-1 Countdown for Manhattan; Body in Central Park; Dead Body on Broadway; Death and Diamonds; Death In a Red Jaguar; Manhattan Night of Murder; Operation Hurricane: Friday Noon; Spies Against the World; Tip Not Included
MUNK, Richard, see Richard Munch
MURGIA, Antonella: The Big Blackout; Furia a Marrakesh; James Tont operazione DUE
NADER, George: 3-2-1 Countdown for Manhattan; Body in Central Park; Dead Body on Broadway; Death and Diamonds; Death In a Red Jaguar; Manhattan Night of Murder; The Million Eyes of Sumuru; Operation Hurricane: Friday Noon; Tip Not Included
NAVARRO, Nieves: Kiss Kiss Bang Bang; Siete minutos para morir
NELLI, Barbara: Due mafioso contro Goldginger; Espionage in Lisbon; Our Agent In Casablanca
NENG, Walter: Agente segreto 777: operazione Mistero; Agente Sigma 3—missione Goldwather; Ring Around the World
NERI, Rosalba: Due mafioso contro Goldginger; Elektra 1; Lucky the Inscrutable;

RANDALL, Monica: 002 operazione Luna; Occhio per occhio, dente per dente; Sicario 77—vivo o morto
RANDALL, Tony: Our Man in Marrakesh
RANK, Ursula: Agente segreto 070 Thunderbay—missione Grasshopper; Hunter of the Unknown; The Million Eyes of Sumuru
RAUCH, Siegfried: Death is Nimble, Death is Quick; Kill Panther Kill; Spy Today, Die Tomorrow
RAVAIOLI, Isarco: Agente segreto 777: operazione Mistero; Crime Story; Last Plane to Baalbeck; LSD: Hell For a Few Dollars More
RAY, Andrew, see Andrea Aureli
RE, Gustavo: Cero siete con el dos delante (Agente Jamie Bonet); The Day the Hotline Got Hot; Spy Today, Die Tomorrow; That Man in Istanbul
REGNIER, Charles: Code Name: Jaguar; Mistress of the World; Spy Hunt in Vienna
REID, Milton: Deadlier Than the Male; Desperate Misson
RENNIE, Michael: The Last Chance; Moving Target; Subterfuge
RESSEL, Franco [Frank]: Assalto al tesoro di stato; Blueprint for a Massacre; Fury on the Bosphorus; James Tont operazione DUE; James Tont operazione UNO; The Last Chance; The Magnificent Tony Carerra; Operation Atlantis; Password: Kill Agent Gordon; Rififi in Amsterdam; The Secret of the Sphinx; Superseven Calling Cairo; Tom Dollar
REVILL, Clive: The Double Man; Italian Secret Service; Modesty Blaise; Nobody Runs Forever
REY, Fernando: Attack of the Robots; Due mafioso contro Goldginger; Espionage in Lisbon
REYNAUD, Janine: Killers Are Challenged; Kiss Me Monster; Operation White Shark; Sadisterotica; Special Cypher; La spia che viene dal mere; Ypotron
RICHARD, Pierre: Formula C-12 Beirut; The Monocle
RIGANO, Evi: James Tont operazione UNO; Upperseven, The Man to Kill
RIGAUD, Jorge [George/Georges]: The Black Box Affair; Kiss Kiss Bang Bang; Make Your Bets, Ladies; Our Agent Tiger; Special Cypher; Spy Today, Die Tomorrow; That Man in Istanbul
RIGHI, Massimo: The Becket Affair; Crime Story; Danger!! Death Ray; Spy in Your Eye
RIVELLI, Luisa: Handle with Care; Lightning Bolt; So Darling, So Deadly
RIVERS, Michael see Miguel De La Riva
RIZZO, Gianni: Cave of Diamonds; Desperate Mission; Man on the Spying Trapeze; Requiem for a Secret Agent
ROBLEDO, Lorenzo: Attack of the Robots; Code Name: Jaguar; Elektra 1; Fury on the Bosphorus; FX-18; Mark Donen agente Z7
ROCA, Vicente: Attack of the Robots; Espionage in Lisbon; Sadisterotica
ROCHA, Augustin Moises: Danger!! Death Ray; The Day the Hotline Got Hot; Occhio per occhio, dente per dente; Sicario 77—vivo o morto
RODRIGUEZ, Emilio: 002 operazione Luna; Siete minutos para morir
ROJAS, Alfonso: A Ghentar si muore facile; Code Name: Jaguar; Espionage in Tangiers; Password: Kill Agent Gordon
ROJO, Gustavo: Madigan's Millions; Spy Today, Die Tomorrow
RONET, Maurice: Who's Got the Black Box?
ROQUEVERT, Noel: The Great Spy Chase; The Reluctant Spy; Your Turn Darling
ROSANO, Francesca: Espionage in Lisbon; Password: Kill Agent Gordon; Si muore solo una volta
ROSSI, Luciano: The Last Chance; LSD: Hell For a Few Dollars More; Sicario—vivo o morto
ROSSI STUART, Giacomo: The Big Blackout; Occhio per occhio, dente per dente; Ring Around the World
RUBIO, Fernando: Cero siete con el dos delante (Agente Jaime Bonet); Danger!! Death Ray; Spia, spione
RUFFINI, Claudio: Fantabulous Inc.; Fury on the Bosphorus; Hunter of the Unknown; Last Man to Kill; Mark Donen agente Z7; Requiem For a Secret Agent; Special Cypher
RUPP, Sieghardt: The Killer Likes Candy; Red Dragon
RUSSEL, Tony: The Secret of the Sphinx; Target Goldseven
SANCHO, Fernando: Fury on the Bosphorus; Hunter of the Unknown; Hypos—follia di un massacro; The Magnificent Tony Carrera; Passport to Hell; Il Vostro superagente Flit
SANDERS, George: Last Plane to Baalbeck; The Quiller Memorandum

SANMARTIN, Conrado: The Cobra; Code Name: Jaguar; Target Goldseven
SANTONI, Espartaco: Il Coraggioso, lo spietato, il traditore
SANZ, Paco: Crime Story; Desperate Mission; Lightning Bolt; Passport to Hell; Spia, spione
SCHIPPERS, Erik: Blueprint for a Massacre; Moving Target; Occhio per occhio, dente per dente
SCHOELLER, Ingrid: 002 agenti segretissimi; A 008 Operation Exterminate
SCHONHERR, Dietmar: Death Trip; Operation Hong Kong
SCOTT, Andrew, see Andrea Scotti
SCOTT, Gordon: Danger!! Death Ray; Top Secret
SCOTTI, Andrea: The Becket Affair; Furia a Marrakesh; Mission Bloody Mary; Operation Poker; Password: Kill Agent Gordon; Special Cypher; Tiffany Memorandum
SCRAT, Ivan G,. see Ivan G. Scratuglia
SCRATUGLIA, Ivan G.: The Becket Affair; Crime Story; Rififi in Amsterdam; Sicario 77—vivo o morto
SEBERG, Jean: Who's Got the Black Box?
SEDLAK, Helene, see Helen Chanel
SEGAL, George: The Quiller Memorandum
SERATO, Massimo: FBI operazione vipera gialla; Superseven Calling Cairo
SERNAS, Jacques: The Balearic Caper; The Dirty Game; Last Plane to Baalbeck
SEYN, Seyna: 002 agenti segretissimi; 7 cinesi d'oro; Agente segreto 777: operazione Mistero; The Big Blackout; Kiss the Girls and Make Them Die; OSS 117 Double Agent; Passport to Hell; Un Tango dalla Russia
Shippers, Erik, see Erik Schippers
SILVA, Henry: Assassination; Matchless
SINI, Linda: 002 operazione Luna; Our Man in Jamaica; Spia, spione
SMYRNER, Ann: Death is Nimble, Death is Quick; The Killer Likes Candy
SOLAR, Sylvia: Agente Sigma 3—missione Goldwather; Danger!! Death Ray; Death and Diamonds; Manhattan Night of Murder; Mexican Slay Ride; M.M.M. 83; Si muore solo una volta; Spy Today, Die Tomorrow
SOMMER, Elke: Daniella by Night; Deadlier than the Male
SOMMERFELD, Helga: Code Name: Jaguar; Man on the Spying Trapeze; Red Dragon; Le Tigre sort sans se mere
SPAAK, Agnes: Baraka X 77; Spies Against the World
STACCIOLI, Ivano: A 008 Operation Exterminate
STAFFORD, Frederick: Formula C-12 Beirut; Million Dollar Man; OSS 117 From Tokyo With Love; OSS 117 Mission For a Killer
STANY, Jacques: The Cobra; Intrigue at Suez; Special Cypher
STEVENS, Craig: The Limbo Line
STEWART, Evelyn, see Ida Galli
STUART, Jack, see Giacomo Rossi Stuart
SUAREZ, Jose: Baraka X 77; Spy Today, Die Tomorrow
SUN, Sabine: Death Trip; FX-18; Mexican Slay Ride
SWAN, Kitty: Deadlier Than the Male; Hunter of the Unknown; Nazi SS; Il Vostro superagente Flit
TABERNERO, Julio Perez: Rififi in Amsterdam; Sadisterotica; Siete minutos para morir
TAHI, Moha [Moana]: 7 cinesi d'oro; Agent X-17; The Black Box Affair; Dr. Goldfoot and the Girl Bombs; Nazi SS
TAMBERLANI, Carlo: 13 Days to Die; Death Trip; Hong Kong Hot Harbor; So Darling, So Deadly
TAMBLYN, Charles, see Carlo Tamberlani
TANI, Yoko: 7 cinesi d'oro; Desperate Mission; Goldsnake; Last Plane to Baalbeck; Piege pour un espions; To Chase a Million
TAYLOR, Jack: Agente Sigma 3—missione Goldwather
TAYLOR, Rod: The Liquidator; Nobody Runs Forever
TERZIEFF, Laurent: None But the Lonely Spy
TERZO, Nino: 002 agenti segretissimi; Due mafioso contro Goldginger
TEYNAC, Maurice: The Reluctant Spy; The Versailles Affair
THAI, Moa, see Moha Tahi
THOMPSON, Carlos: Mistress of the World
TICHY, Gerard: Baraka X 77; The Day the Hotline Got Hot; Madigan's Millions; The Magnificent Tony Carrera; Marie-Chantal vs. Dr Kha; Master Stroke; The Solitaire Attacks; That Man in Istanbul
TOLO, Marilu: The Balearic Caper; The Big Blackout; Espionage in Lisbon; Intrigue at Suez; Judoka Secret Agent; The Killer Likes Candy; Kiss the Girls and Make Them Die

**DIRECTORS**

AINSWORTH, John: One-Eyed Soldiers
ANDERSON, Michael: The Quiller Memorandum
ANDRE, Raoul: Jeff Gordon, Secret Agent; Mission to Caracas
ANTON, Amerigo see Tanio Boccia
ASH, Dan, see Giorgio Gentili
ASHLEY, Helmut: Operation Hong Kong; Tip Not Included
BAKER, Roy Ward: Spy Killer
BALCAZAR, Alfonso: Elektra 1
BALDANELLO, Gianfranco: Danger!! Death Ray
BALDI, Ferdinando: Goldsnake
BALDI, Marcello: Inferno a Caracas
BAVA, Mario: Dr. Goldfoot and The Girl Bombs
BAY, Henry, see Enrico Bomba
BENVENUTI, Lamberto: La spia che viene dal mare
BERGONZELLI, Sergio: M.M.M. 83
BIANCHINI, Paolo: The Devil's Man; Hypnos—follia di un massacro
BOCCIA, Tanio: Agent X-17
BOISROND, Michel:Million Dollar Man; OSS 117 From Tokyo With Love
BOMBA, Enrico: Agente segreto 777: operazione Mistero; Ticket to Die
BONNARDOT, Claude-Jean: None But the Lonely Spy
BORDERIE, Bernard: Ladies' Man; Women Are Like That; Your Turn, Darling
BRADY, Hal, see Emilio Miraglia
BUTLER, Alex, see Carlo Ferrero
CAIANO, Mario: Spies Strike Silently
CALLEGARI, Giampaolo: Agente Sigma 3—missione Goldwather
CANEVARI, Cesare: Agente segreto 070 Thunderbay—missione Grasshopper; Un Tango dalla Russia
CAPUANO, Luigi: The Big Blackout
CARROL, Frank G., see Gianfranco Baldanello
CARDIFF, Albert, see Alberto Cardone
CARDIFF, Jack: The Liquidator
CARDONE, Alberto: 13 Days to Die (credited on Italian version); Spies Against the World, with Robert Lynn and Sheldon Reynolds
CARSTAIRS, John Paddy: The Devil's Agent
CASCINO, Vincenzo: 7 cinesi d'oro (not credited on Italian print); 7 Golden Women Against Two 07 (Treasure Hunt)
CASHINO, Vincen,t see Vincenzo Cascino
CERCHIO, Fernando: Top Secret
CERRATO, Renzo: OSS 117 Double Agent w/Jean-Pierre Desagnat and Andre Hunebelle
CHABROL, Claude: Marie-Chantal vs. Dr. Kha; Our Agent Tiger; The Tiger Likes Fresh Meat; Who's Got the Black Box?
CHENTRENS, Frederico: The Killer Likes Candy
CHRISTIAN-JACQUE: Dead Run; The Dirty Game, with Terence Young and Carlo Lizzani
CIORCIOLINI, Marcello: The Black Box Affair; Tom Dollar
CIVRIANI, Osvaldo: The Beckett Affair; Operation Poker
CLEMENT, Dick: Otley
CLOCHE, Maurice: Baraka X 77 (French version); FX-18
COLL, Julio: High Season For Spies
COMAS, Ramon: Death on a Rainy Day
COMENCINI, Luigi: Italian Secret Service
CORBUCCI, Bruno: James Tont operazione DUE; James Tont operazione UNO; Spia, spione
CORBUCCI, Sergio: Moving Target
DAWSON, Anthony, see Antonio Margheriti
DE LA LOMA, Jose Antonio: The Magnificient Tony Carrera
DE MARTINO, Alberto: Operation Double 007; Special Mission Lady Chaplin; Upperseven, the Man to Kill
DE ORDUNA, Juan: Man on the Spying Trapeze
DE SAINT-MAURICE, Christian: Spy Catcher
DECOIN, Henri: License To Kill
DELANNOY, Jean: Only the Cool
DEMICELI, Tulio: Espionage in Lisbon; Our Agent in Casablanca
DESAGNAT, Jean-Pierre: OSS 117 Double Agent w/Renzo Cerrato and Andre Hunebelle
DIETERLE, William: Mistress of the World
DONEN, J. Lee (or Martini), see Mino Loy and Luciano Martino
DUDRUMET, Jean-Claude: The Reluctant Spy
EASTWOOD, John, see Gianfranco Parolini

FEDER, Ray, see Ramon Fernandez

FERNANDEZ, Ramon: Siete minutos para morir

FERRARA, Romano: Intrigo a Los Angeles

FERRERO, Carlo: From Istanbul, Orders to Kill

FERRONI, Giorgio: Secret Agent Superdragon

FINLEY, George, see Giorgio Stegani

FLEMING, Paul, see Domenico Paolella

FORQUE, Jose Maria: The Balearic Caper

FRANCO, Jesus [Jess]: Attack of the Robots; Kiss Me Monster; Lucky the Inscrutable; Residence For Spies; Sadisterotica

FREDA, Riccardo: FX 18 Superspy; Mexican Slay Ride

FREEMOUNT, Roy, see Romano Ferrara

FULCI, Lucio: 002 agenti segretissimi; 002 operazione Luna

GALLU, Samuel: The Limbo Line; The Man Outside

GENTILI, Giorgio: Madigan's Millions

GIANNINI, Marcello: Last Plane to Baalbeck

GILLING, John: Where the Bullets Fly

GOTTLIEB, Franz J.: Spy Today, Die Tomorrow

GRIECO, Sergio: Fuller Report; Fury on the Bosphorus; Mission Bloody Mary; Password: Kill Agent Gordon; Rififi in Amsterdam; Tiffany Memorandum

GRIMBLAT, Pierre: It Means That to Me

GROOPER, Cehett see Gianfranco Parolini

GUERRINI, Mino: Sicario 77—vivo o morto

GUEST, Val: Where the Spies Are

HABIB, Ralph: The Solitaire Attacks

HARRIS, James, see Marcello Ciorciolini

HARVEY, Laurence: A Dandy in Aspic (took over for Anthony Mann)

HATHAWAY, Terence, see Sergio Grieco

HEUSCH, Paolo: Intrigue at Suez

HOFBAUER, Ernst: Red Dragon

HOLT, Seth: Danger Route

HUNEBELLE, Andre: OSS 117 Double Agent, with Jean-Pierre Desagnat and Renzo Cerrato; OSS 117 Mission For a Killer; OSS 117 se dechaine; Shadow of Evil

HUXLEY, John, see Bruno Paolinelli

IGLESIAS, Miguel: Occhio per occhio, dente per dente

IQUINO, Ignacio: Cero siete con el dos delante (Agente Jaime Bonet)

ISASI, Antonio: That Man in Istanbul

JACKSON, Pat: To Chase a Million

JACKSON, Richard, see Ernest Von Theumer

JACOBS, Werner: Body in Central Park

JEAN-CHRISTOPHE, see John Ainsworth

KALFON, Pierre: OSS 117 prend des vacances

KING, Lewis, see Luigi Capuano

KLIMOVSKY, Leon: A Ghentar si muore facile

KOHLER, Manfred: 13 Days to Die; Formula C-12 Beirut; Target for Killing

KRAMER, Frank, see Gianfranco Parolini

KUGELSTADT, Hermann: Sfida nella citta d'oro (German version)

LABRO, Maurice: Code Name: Jaguar; Le Judoka dans l'enfer; The Spy I Love

LATTUADA, Alberto: Matchless

LAURENTI, Mariano: Il Vostro superagente Flit

LAUTNER, Georges: The Great Spy Chase; The Monocle

LAWSON, Edgar, see Silvio Siano

LENZI, Umberto: A 008 Operation Exterminate; Last Man to Kill; Superseven Calling Cairo

LEONARD, Albert B., see Alberto Leonardi

LEONARDI, Alberto: Target Goldseven

LEVIN, Henry: Kiss the Girls and Make Them Die, with Dino Maiuri

LEVY, Raoul: The Defector

LEWIS, Stanley, see Walter F. Ratti

LIZZANI, Carlo: The Dirty Game, with Terence Young and Christian-Jacques

LOSEY, Joseph: Modesty Blaise

LOY, Mino: Furia a Marrakesh, with Luciano Martino; Secret Agent Fireball, with Luciano Martino

LUMET, Sidney: The Deadly Affair

LUPO, Michele: Master Stroke

LYNN, Robert: Spies Against the World, with Alberto Cardone and Sheldon Reynolds

MADRID, Jose Luis: Somebody's Stolen Our Russian Spy

MAFFEI, Mario: Le Tigre sort sans sa mere

MAIURI, Dino: Kiss the Girls and Make Them Die, with Henry Levin

MANN, Anthony: A Dandy in Aspic (died before completion, see Laurence Harvey)

MARCHAL, Juan Xiol: Il Coraggioso, lo spietato, il traditore

MARGHERITI, Antonio: Killers Are Challenged; Lightning Bolt

MARSHALL, Billy, see Marcello Baldi
MARTINO, Luciano: Furia a Marrakesh, with Mino Loy; Secret Agent Firebal, with Mino Loy
MAURI, Roberto: Three Golden Dragons
MAXWELL, Paul, see Paolo Bianchini
MEDORI, Alfredo: FBI Operazione Vipera Gialla; Sfida nella citta d'oro
MERCANTI, Pino: Special Cypher
MERINO, Jose Luis: Crime Story
MIDA, Massimo: LSD: Hell For a Few Dollars More
MIDDLETON, Mike, see Massimo Mida
MILLER, David: Hammerhead
MIRAGLIA, Emilio: Assassination
MOLINARO, Edoardo: A Touch of Treason; Ravishing Idiot
MONTAZEL, Pierre: There's Going To Be a Party
MONTERO, Roberto Bianchi: Blueprin for a Massacre; Desperate Mission
NEAME, Ronald: A Man Could Get Killed
NOSTRO, Nick: Operation Counterspy
O'BURGHESS, John, see Lamberto Benvenuti
OPHULS, Marcel: Make Your Bets, Ladies
OWENS, Richard, see Frederico Chentrens
PADGET, Calvin Jackson, see Giorgio Ferroni
PAOLELLA, Domenico: Operation Atlantis
PAOLINELLI, Bruno: Nazi SS; Piege pour un espions
PAROLINI, Gianfranco: Cave of Diamonds; Hunting the Unknown; Kill Panther Kill; So Darling, So Deadly
PECAS, Max: Daniella by Night
PERIER, Etienne: The Day the Hot Line Got Hot
PHILIPP, Harald: 3-2-1 Countdown ,for Manhattan; Manhattan Night of Murder;
The Survival Factor
PIEROTTI, Piero: Assalto al tesoro di stato
POITRENAUD, Jacques: Carre de dames pour un as
POLAK, Jindrich (Henrik): Agent for Panic
PRAGER, Stanley, see Giorgio Gentili
PROSPERI, Franco: Dick Smart 2.007
RATTI, Walter F.: Operation White Shark
RED, Frank see Marcello Ciorciolini
REINL, Harald: Dead Body on Broadway; Death and Diamonds; Death in a Red Jaguar
REYNOLDS, Don see Giancarlo Romitelli
REYNOLDS, Sheldon: Spies Against the World, with Alberto Cardone and Robert Lynn
ROLAND, Jurgen: Hong Kong Hot Harbor
ROMITELLI, Giancarlo: Mark Donen agente Z7; Si muore solo una volta
ROSATI, Niny [Giuseppe]: The Last Chance
ROSS, Berwang see Cesare Canevari
SALA, Vittorio: Spy in Your Eye
SALCE, Luciano: Slalom
SCATTINI, Luigi: Ring Around the World
SCHAFFNER, Franklin J.: The Double Man
SCOTT, Peter Graham: Subterfuge
SEQUI, Mario: The Cobra
SHANNON, Frank, see Franco Prosperi
SHARP, Don: Our Man in Marrakesh
SHERMAN, Herbert J., see Pino Mercanti
SHONTEFF, Lindsay: The Million Eyes of Sumuru; The Second Best Secret Agent in the Whole Wide World
SIANO, Silvio: Baraka X 77
SIMONELLI, Giorgio: Due mafioso contro Goldginger
SOLLIMA, Sergio: Hunter of the Unknown; Passport to Hell; Requiem for a Secret Agent
SPINA, Sergio: Fantabulous Inc.
STEGANI, Giorgio: Operation Hong Kong (Italian version); Ypotron
STERLING, Simon, see Sergio Sollima
SUTER, Karl: Bonditis
TALLAS, Gregg: Assignment Skybolt; Espionage in Tangiers
TESSARI, Duccio: Kiss Kiss Bang Bang; The Secret of the Sphinx
THOMAS, Ralph: Deadlier Than the Male; Hot Enough For June; Nobody Runs Forever; Some Girls Do
TRONSON, Robert: Ring of Spies
TRUMAN, Michael: Koroshi (Koroshi episode), also see Peter Yates
UMGELTER, Fritz: Operation Hurricane: Friday Noon
VAN HOOVEN, Burton, see Cesare Canevari
VERNAY, Robert: The Versailles Affair
VERSINI, Andre: Mission to Venice
VON THEUMER, Ernest: Our Man in Jamaica
WEIDENMANN, Alfred: Spy Hunt in Vienna
WHITE, Robert, see Roberto Bianchi Montero
WHITEMAN, Albert L., see Giampaolo Callegari
YATES, Peter: Koroshi (Shinda Shima episode),

also see Michael Truman
YOUNG, Terence: The Dirty Game, with Christian-Jacques and Carlo Lizzani
ZEHETGRUBER, Rudolf: Death is Nimble, Death is Quick; Death Trip
ZIMMER, Pierre: Judoka Secret Agent
ZURLI, Guido: Handle With Care

## COMPOSERS

ABRIL, Anton Garcia: The Cobra
ALONSO, Odon: Residence For Spies, with Adolfo Waitzman
ALZMER, Claudius: Spies Against the World
ANDERSON, James, see Gianni Ferrio
ARNELL, Richard: The Man Outside
ARTEAGA, Angel: Somebody's Stolen Our Russian Spy
AZNAVOUR, Charles: Daniella by Night, with Georges Garvarentz
BACALOV, Luis Enrique: Piege pour un espions
BARCLAY, Eddie: FX-18 w/Michel Colombier
BARLY, Andre: OSS 117 prend des vacances
BARRY, John: The Quiller Memorandum
BAXTER, Les: Dr. Goldfoot and The Girl Bombs (US version)
BLACK, Don: Some Girls Do, with Charles Blackwell
BLACKWELL, Charles: Some Girls Do, with Don Black
BOLLING, Klaus [Claude]: Elektra 1
BOTTCHER, Martin: Cave of Diamonds
BRUGNOLINI, Sandro: Fantabulous Inc.; From Istanbul, Orders to Kill
CALVI, Gerard: Dead Run
CANFORA, Bruno: James Tont operazione DUE; Il Vostro superagente Flit
CAPUANO, Giosafat and Mario: Tom Dollar
CARPI, Fiorenza: Italian Secret Service
CHAPPELL, Bertram: The Second Best Secret Agent in the Whole Wide World
COLOMBIER, Michel: FX-18, with Eddie Barclay
DANKWORTH, John: Modesty Blaise
DE MARTINO, Marcello: Agente segreto 777: operazione Mistero; Last Plane to Baalbeck; Ticket to Die
DE MASI, Francesco: Death Trip; Desperate Mission; FBI Operazione Vipera Gialla; Master Stroke; Sfida nella citta d'oro, with Hugo Strasser; Spies Strike Silently
DE ROUBAIX, Francois: Only the Cool
DE STEFANO, Felice: 7 Golden Women Against Two 07 (Treasure Hunt), with Italo Fischetti
DELERUE, Georges: Nobody Runs Forever; The Reluctant Spy
DI STEFANO, Felice: Il Coraggioso, lo spietato, il traditore
DUHAMEL, Antoine: Le Judoka dans l'enfer, with Van Tyenen
ESCOBAR, Enrique: Cero siete con el dos delante (Agente Jaime Bonet)
FERRIO, Gianni: 7 cinesi d'oro; The Black Box Affair; Danger!! Death Ray
FIDENCO, Nico: Ypotron
FISCHETTI, Italo: 7 Golden Women Against Two 07 (Treasure Hunt), with Felice De Stefano; Agente segreto 070 Thunderbay—missione Grasshopper
FRANCOIS, Samson: None But the Lonely Spy
FREEMAN, Ernest: The Double Man
FUSCO, Giovanni: Our Agent in Casablanca
GAINSBOURG, Serge: Carre de dames pour un as; The Defector
GARVARENTZ, Georges: Daniella by Night, with Charles Aznavour; Million Dollar Man; That Man in Istanbul; Baraka X 77
GERARD, Bernard: The Solitaire Attacks
GHIGLIA, Benedetto: The Balearic Caper; Espionage in Tangiers; Secret Agent Superdragon
GIOMBINI, Marcello: James Tont operazione UNO; Kill Panther Kill; Our Man in Jamaica; Target For Killing
GORAGUER, Alain: Mission to Venice
GORI, Carlo [Coriolano]: 002 operazione Luna; Dr. Goldfoot and The Girl Bombs (Italian version)
GREEN, Philip: The Devil's Agent
GUTESHA, Bobby: Hunting the Unknown
HADJIDAKIS, Manos: Assignment Skybolt
HOUDY, Pierick: License To Kill
HUBLER, Manfred: The Survival Factor
ILLIN, Evzen: Agent For Panic
JANSEN, Pierre: Marie-Chantal vs. Dr. Kha, with Gregorio Garcia Segura; The Tiger Likes Fresh Meat; Who's Got the Black Box?
JAZZ GROUP OF PARIS: There's Going To Be a Party, with Martial Solal
JONES, Quincy: A Dandy in Aspic; The Deadly Affair
KAEMPFERT, Bert: A Man Could Get Killed
KRUSE, Werner: Bonditis
LACOME, Jacques: Mexican Slay Ride
LAVAGNINO, Angelo Francisco: A 008 Operation Exterminate; Assalto al tesoro di stato; Hot Enough For June; Last Man to Kill; Mission

Bloody Mary; Superseven Calling Cairo
LEGRAND, Michel: Code Name: Jaguar; It Means That to Me; Ravishing Idiot
LEGUY, Patrick: The Devil's Man
LOCKYER, Malcolm: Deadlier Than the Male; Our Man in Marrakesh
LUIGUY: The Versaille Affair
MACCHI, Egisto: LSD: Hell For a Few Dollars More
MAGNE, Michel: FX 18 Superspy; The Great Spy Chase; Mission to Caracas; The Monocle; OSS 117 From Tokyo With Love; OSS 117 Mission For a Killer; OSS 117 se dechaine; Shadow of Evil
MARCHETTI, Gianni: The Killer Likes Candy; The Magnificient Tony Carrera; Spy Today, Die Tomorrow
MARINUZZI, Gino, Jr.: Death is Nimble, Death is Quick; Matchless, with Ennio Morricone and Pierro Piccioni; So Darling, So Deadly
MARTELL, Philip: Spy Killer, with Johnny Pearson; Where the Bullets Fly
MATTHES, Willy: Operation Hong Kong
MAYER, John: Danger Route
MELLIN, Robert: The Dirty Game, with Gian Piero Reverberi
MIGLIARDI, Mario: The Secret of the Sphinx
MISRAKI, Paul: Attack of the Robots; The Day the Hot Line Got Hot; Ladies' Man; Women Are Like That; Your Turn, Darling
MORCILLO, Fernando Garcia: Kiss Me Monster, with Jerry van Rooyen and Daniel White; Sadisterotica
MORRICONE, Ennio: Formula C-12 Beirut; Matchless, with Gino Marinuzzi and Pierro Piccioni; Operation Double 007, with Bruno Nicolai; Slalom
MYERS, Stanley: Otley
NASCIMBENE, Mario: Dick Smart 2.007; Kiss the Girls and Make Them Die; Where the Spies Are
NAVARRO, Jose Luis: High Season For Spies
NECOPI, M.: Un Tango dalla Russia
NIESSEN, Charly: Spy Hunt in Vienna
NICOLAI, Bruno: Kiss Kiss Bang Bang; Lucky the Inscrutable; Operation Double 007, with Ennio Morricone; Le Tigre sort sans sa mere; Special Mission Lady Chaplin; Upperseven, The Man to Kill
OLEA, Antonio Perez: Requiem for a Secret Agent
ORLANDI, Nora: The Beckett Affair
ORNADELI, Cyril: Subterfuge
ORTOLANI, Riz: Lightning Bolt; Red Dragon; Special Cypher; Spy in Your Eye; Tiffany Memorandum
PARRA, Manuel: Agente Sigma 3—missione Goldwather
PEARSON, Johnny: Spy Killer, with Philip Martell
PEGURI, Gino: Handle With Care
PERSIN, Henri: Jeff Gordon, Secret Agent
PICCIONI, Piero: Fury on the Bosphorus; Matchless, with Gino Marinuzzi and Ennio Morricone; M.M.M. 83; OSS 117 Double Agent
PIGA, Aldo: Mark Donen agente Z7
PISANO, Berto: The Big Blackout; La spia che viene dal mare
PISANO, Franco: Occhio per occhio, dente per dente; Operation Counterspy
POITEVIN, Robby: Assassination; Operation White Shark
PREGADIO, Roberto: Three Golden Dragons
REVERBERI, Gian Piero: The Dirty Game, with Robert Mellin
RICCIO, Marcello: Sicario 77—vivo o morto, with Giorgio Zinzi
RUSTICHELLI, Carlo: The Last Chance
SAVINA, Carlo: A Ghentar si muore facile; Furia a Marrakesh; Goldsnake; Hypnos—follia di un massacre; Killers Are Challenged; Secret Agent Fireball; Si muore solo una volta
SCHIFRIN, Lalo: The Liquidator
SCOTT, John: The Million Eyes of Sumuru
SEGURA, Garcia [Gregorio]: Madigan's Millions; Marie-Chantal vs. Dr. Kha, with Pierre Jansen
SOLAL, Martial: A Touch of Treason; There's Going To Be a Party, with Jazz Group of Paris
SPENCE, Johnnie: The Limbo Line
STRASSER, Hugo: Sfida nella citta d'oro, with Francesco De Masi
SWINGLE, Ward: Make Your Bets, Ladies
THOMAS, Peter: 3-2-1 Countdown For Manhattan; Body in Central Park; Dead Body on Broadway; Death and Diamonds; Death in a Red Jaguar; Manhattan Night of Murder; Operation Hurricane: Friday Noon; Tip Not Included

TORREGROSA, Jose: Siete minutos para morir
TROVAJOLI, Armando: Fuller Report
TUDO, Frederico Martinez: Spia, spione
TYENEN, Van: Le Judoka dans l'enfer, with Antoine Duhamel
UMILIANI, Piero: 002 agenti segretissimi; Agent X-17; Blueprint For a Massacre; Death on a Rainy Day; Due mafioso contro Goldginger; Hunter of the Unknown; Inferno a Caracas; Intrigo a Los Angeles; Intrigue at Suez; Man on the Spying Trapeze; Operation Poker; Passport to Hell; Password: Kill Agent Gordon; Rififi in Amsterdam; Ring Around the World; Target Goldseven; Top Secret
USUELLI, Teo: Nazi SS; Operation Atlantis
VAN PARYS, Georges: The Spy I Love
VAN ROOYEN, Jerry: Death on a Rainy Day (German version); Kiss Me Monster, with Fernando Garcia Morcillo and Daniel White
VANDOR, Ivan: Moving Target
VINCENT, Roland: Judoka Secret Agent, with Armand Zeggian
VLAD, Roman: Mistress of the World
WAITZMAN, Adolfo: Residence for Spies, with Odon Alonso
WHITAKER, David: Hammerhead
WHITE, Daniel: Espionage in Lisbon; Kiss Me Monster, with Fernando Garcia Morcillo and Jerry van Rooyen
WIENER, Jean: Our Agent Tiger
WILDEN, Gert: 13 Days to Die; Hong Kong Hot Harbor
ZEGGIAN, Armand: Judoka Secret Agent, with Roland Vincent
ZINZI, Giorgio: Sicario 77—vivo o morto, with Marcello Riccio

# APPENDIX E: ORIGINAL TITLE INDEX